International Trust and Divorce Litigation

International Trust and Divorce Litigation

Editors

Mark Harper
Withers LLP, London

Dawn Goodman
Withers LLP, London

Patrick Hamlin
Withers LLP, London

Paul Matthews
Withers LLP, London; Visiting Professor, King's College London

Published by Family Law
A publishing imprint of Jordan Publishing Limited
21 St Thomas Street
Bristol BS1 6JS

Whilst the publishers and the author have taken every care in preparing the material included in this work, any statements made as to the legal or other implications of particular transactions are made in good faith purely for general guidance and cannot be regarded as a substitute for professional advice. Consequently, no liability can be accepted for loss or expense incurred as a result of relying in particular circumstances on statements made in this work.

British Library Cataloguing-in-Publication Data

A catalogue record for this book is available from the British Library.

ISBN 978 1 84661 018 9

Typeset by Letterpart Ltd, Reigate, Surrey

Printed in Great Britain by Antony Rowe Limited, Chippenham, Wiltshire

FOREWORD

This is a much needed book. It will be much used due to its practical advice and insights, soundly based on clear legal analysis.

There is an increasing number of spouses invoking the English courts' divorce jurisdiction against spouses who almost inevitably will have set up offshore trusts to cover most of the wealth that they have generated. To what extent can such trusts be attacked using divorce law and procedure or trust law principles – and to what extent can such attacks be prevented or minimised? These are the key issues that the book deals with.

It highlights the impact of English courts now focusing upon the resources, rather than the needs, of the spouses (or civil partners). The economically weaker spouse (or civil partner), 'W', seeks to have trust property, in respect of which the economically stronger partner, 'S', is a beneficiary, treated as an available resource of S to justify a very substantial judgment against S. The pragmatically robust attitude of the English courts to treating trust property as an available resource obviates any need to allege that the trust for a range of beneficiaries was a sham, because really a bare trust for S, or that the trust was an ante or post-nuptial settlement (as very broadly defined) that should be varied under the Matrimonial Causes Act in favour of W.

This available resource approach bypasses the safeguards for the protection of other beneficiaries since they and the offshore trustee do not need to be joined as parties. Moreover, it also bypasses offshore legislation that refuses recognition of foreign court orders relating to offshore trusts.

However, if the substantial judgment against S, taking account of the trust property as an available resource of S, is not fully satisfied, W could fall back on a claim that the English court should vary the offshore trust as a nuptial settlement. Other beneficiaries then become involved, while the offshore trustees will for their own protection not do anything without an order from the offshore court. Indeed, when S applies to the trustees for financial assistance in respect of satisfying a judgment in W's favour, the trustees may well need to seek the court's protection before making a payment that could well be regarded as improperly detrimental to other beneficiaries. Thus, the English court order does significantly interfere with the offshore trustees' discretionary duties, especially if the offshore court does not consider the trust property to be an available resource of S.

Family Division judges need to be more aware of the problems caused by too robust an approach to trust property as an available resource, while dealing appropriately with those for whom all or part of trust property is genuinely an available resource. Significantly, the Court of Appeal in *Charman (No 4)* [2007] EWCA Civ 503 at [58] has accepted that for a Family Division judge to take jurisdiction to declare an offshore trust to be a sham would 'generally be exorbitant', and that when a party applies for a variation of an offshore trust under the MCA such a judge should 'give serious consideration to declining to exercise' the MCA jurisdiction and inviting the offshore court to exercise its own jurisdiction along suggested lines. In the case of alleged available resource cases, perhaps the judge could give serious consideration to making conditional orders, e g that S is to pay W or transfer to W assets of £30m aggregate value, but that £20m thereof (or any lesser amount) is only to be paid if the offshore trustees are authorised by the offshore court to make such payment.

Striking the right balance between the integrity of trust law and the scope of divorce law measures for the proper protection of W is very difficult indeed in the international context, especially when fearful offshore courts are ready to direct trustees not to participate in English proceedings and are prepared to find that the alleged comity is not enough to justify giving effect to English judgments that are too robust. Indeed, fearful offshore legislatures (as in Guernsey) are ready to enact legislation prohibiting recognition of variations of local trusts by foreign courts, while some may be contemplating if there is some way in which they can try to counter what they consider to be the iniquitous results of an overly robust available resources approach by foreign courts. Is the only satisfactory way forward an attempt to obtain some international agreement, e g with Commonwealth countries or at least with British Overseas Territories and Crown Dependencies?

Meanwhile, the very best that can be done is to learn from this book how best to preserve the integrity of a trust and how to appreciate what are the risks run if a major beneficiary (especially if also the real settlor) becomes a party to divorce proceedings.

The Honourable Mr Justice David Hayton
Caribbean Court of Justice, Trinidad
1 October 2007

PREFACE

We hope that this book will help both those in the wealth planning and trust world to understand better the approach of the English Courts on divorce to trusts, and divorce lawyers and the Family Division judiciary to understand trusts better.

As we go to press, *A v A and St George Trustees Ltd (No 2)* [2007] EWHC 1810 (Fam) is a warning from Munby J to those who run hopeless cases on sham and trust issues. The total costs in that case were £950,000, the majority of which the wife was ordered to pay, therefore spending over half of her final award of £1.3m on costs.

Our thanks go to everyone at Withers who has helped us with this book, in particular Katy Richards, Peter Burgess, Sue Medder, Oliver Church and Colin Shaper. We also thank Mr Justice Hayton for writing the Foreword, and the many foreign lawyers who have helped us to try to understand their law on this subject.

Mark Harper
Dawn Goodman
Patrick Hamlin
Paul Matthews

London
October 2007

CONTENTS

TABLE OF CASES

References are to paragraph numbers.

TABLE OF STATUTES

References are to paragraph numbers.

TABLE OF STATUTORY INSTRUMENTS

References are to paragraph numbers.

CHAPTER 1

OVERVIEW AND CONTEXT

1.1 INTERNATIONAL TRUSTS AND DIVORCE LITIGATION: OVERVIEW AND CONTEXT

In recent years there has been significant growth in both divorce rates and the use of offshore trusts. While these phenomena are generally unrelated, they are the seeds of much high value matrimonial litigation in the Family Division of the English High Court.

1.1.1 Growth in offshore trust services

In Britain, the post-war years saw steadily rising estate duty rates which were nevertheless relatively easily avoided by structures such as discretionary trusts. The unusual and unique English law rule regarding domicile has played a key role in the growth of the use of offshore trusts.

For non-UK citizens, they can retain their non-UK domicile of origin whilst being resident for the foreseeable future in the UK. With proper advice, and often by setting up an offshore trust, they can live off capital and avoid remitting to the UK foreign income or capital gains, thereby avoiding UK tax. This makes the UK one of the best tax havens in the world, especially for non-US citizens. This in turn partly explains the very high London property prices, boosted by wealthy foreigners wanting to be UK tax resident and to enjoy the benefits of the non-domicile rule.

For high net worth families, the emergence of Jersey and Guernsey as offshore centres offered sophisticated, confidential, financial services coupled with an entirely legitimate means of avoiding estate duty (at least until legislation from the late-1960s onwards began to curtail tax planning opportunities for UK domiciliaries). The attractiveness of these arrangements has been compounded by the fact that all assets held offshore remain beyond the grasp of British death duties provided the relevant parties are domiciled outside the UK. Even English real estate can be held offshore by the simple device of holding the property through an offshore company whose shares are then themselves held in an offshore trust. From the late 1960s, the newly independent Caribbean states such as the Bahamas, joined the offshore club while Cayman, Bermuda and the

British Virgin Islands chose to remain British overseas territories. Offshore trusts remain attractive to settlors who while resident in England, have been able to retain their non-domiciliary status. Arguably, the possibility of these fiscal advantages being removed by legislation has increased their attractiveness to such taxpayers. These jurisdictions have begun to produce legislation designed to attract the offshore investor. The Cayman Islands, for example, have produced 'Star Trusts' (The Special Trust Alternative Regime Law 1997) while the BVI are vigorously promoting Vista Trusts, principally as vehicles for family companies.

Against this background all the major financial institutions now offer bespoke private banking services for high net worth individuals. Offshore tax and trust services are marketed hand-in-hand with upmarket banking services.

1.1.2 Growth and globalisation of wealth

London has become arguably the leading financial centre of the world, recently overtaking New York. Wealth has increased dramatically; now assets of £70m are required to make it into the *Sunday Times* 'Rich List 2007'. In their first list in 1989, a £70m fortune meant a position of 92, whereas in 2007 it takes £770m to reach the same position.

Much of the wealth is new rather than inherited; in 1989 75% of those on the Rich List had inherited their wealth, whereas now 78% have made the money themselves.

A significant proportion is international too; mostly thanks to the non-domicile tax regime. Boston Consulting Group has estimated that there are 1,500 non-domiciliaries living in the UK, worth £28bn; some would say the number is an under-estimate. Since 1995, the number of work permits for financial services in the City has doubled.[1] In the prime central London property market, foreign buyers account for one-third of all buyers, which rises to 75% for properties worth more than £5m.[2]

1.1.3 Recent developments in divorce

Whatever the reason, there is no doubt that divorce is on the increase. In 1961 there were 27,224 divorces in Great Britain. By 2004 the figure for the UK as a whole had risen to 167,116.[3] There is no reason to suspect that high net worth individuals are as a group under represented in this explosion of matrimonial litigation, indeed anecdotal evidence would suggest quite the contrary.

---

[1] (2006) *The Economist*, 21 October.
[2] Knight Frank Survey 2007.
[3] Source: Office for National Statistics.

In terms of financial provision on divorce, the watershed occurred in October 2000 when the House of Lords gave judgment in *White v White*.[4] Prior to that case, the court's approach to financial provision had focused almost exclusively on meeting the recipient spouse's 'reasonable requirements'. In principle, this meant identifying capital needs such as a home (or two or three), a car and so on. The court would then go on to fix an appropriate annual budget and calculate a suitable capital sum to finance that budget using a 'Duxbury' calculation based on expected investment return, life expectancy and taxation. All this inevitably meant a glass ceiling for the claims of wealthy husbands' wives. Such a wife might very well end up with a fairly small percentage of the family wealth.

Lord Nicholls giving the lead judgment in *White v White* said that there should be no bias in favour of the money creator as against the homemaker and the child carer. The yardstick of equality was to be an important safeguard against discrimination. As a general guide, equality was to be departed from only if, and to the extent that, there was good reason for doing so. The focus therefore has shifted from the needs of the recipient spouse to whether there is any valid reason to depart from a 50/50 split of the couple's assets.

1.1.4 Trends in matrimonial litigation

The increase in the divorce rate, growing prosperity serviced by a sophisticated private wealth industry and latterly the aftermath of a seismic shift in the law on ancillary relief have all combined to produce an increase in litigation involving trusts and divorce. This change in the law will apply to any forthcoming dissolution of civil partnerships between same sex couples, in effect same sex marriage. Since the law on financial claims on dissolution is virtually the same as on divorce, all references to ancillary relief in this book include financial claims on civil partnership dissolution. Empirical evidence is hard to collate but an examination of the Law Reports indicates that the courts appear to be spending more time on trust and divorce issues.

1.1.4.1 *Minwalla v Minwalla*[5]

The Royal Court in Jersey enforced 'as a matter of comity' an order of the English court effectively requiring the Trustees of a Jersey Trust to transfer significant assets to the wife in satisfaction of an ancillary relief order.

---

4   [2000] 2 FLR 981, HL.
5   [2005] 1 FLR 771, FD.

1.1.4.2   *Re B Trust*[6]

More recently in this case, the Royal Court, while giving substantive effect to a judgment of the English Family Division, went on to express the view that the English courts could follow a more restrained approach towards Jersey trusts:

> 'It would in our view, avoid sterile argument, and expense to the parties, if the English Courts were, in cases involving a Jersey Trust, having calculated their award on the basis of the totality of the assets available to the parties, to exercise judicial restraint and to refrain from invoking their jurisdiction under the Matrimonial Causes Act to vary the trust. Instead they could request this Court to be auxiliary to them.'

1.1.4.3   *Charman v Charman*[7]

The English Court of Appeal upheld a letter of request directed to the Bermudian court seeking information from the trustees of a Bermudian Trust as to assets settled into trust by the husband. The Supreme Court of Bermuda however rejected the request as a 'fishing expedition' and contrary to the established authorities such as *Re Westinghouse*. Coleridge J went on to make an order for £48m in favour of the wife. That order looks through the trust assets and treats them as if all available to the husband. On appeal, the Court of Appeal upheld the judgment at first instance, considering the trustees likely to advance all the capital of the trust to the husband (who was the settlor and a beneficiary) in the event of need, concluding:

> 'It is essential for the Court to bring to it [an enquiry as to the attributability of the assets in a trust] a judicious mixture of worldly realism and of respect for the legal effects of trusts, the legal duties of trustees and, in the case of offshore trusts the jurisdictions of offshore Courts. In the circumstances of the present case it would have been a shameful emasculation of the Court's duty to be fair if the assets which the husband had built up in [the trust] during the marriage had not been attributed to him.'

The flurry of judicial activity in the offshore world resulting from orders of the English Family Division is being matched on the legislative front. Jersey has recently enacted a new Art 9 of the Trust (Jersey) Law 1984 which brings Jersey into line with many of its offshore competitors in terms of providing a defence against attacks by other jurisdictions. It is interesting to speculate whether any of the recently decided cases in Jersey would have been decided differently had that legislation been in force earlier: *Re B Trust* was decided just after the legislation came into force. Guernsey is set to introduce similar legislation this year.

---

[6]   2006 JLR 562.
[7]   [2006] 1 WLR 1053, CA.

Meanwhile in Guernsey, the final report of the revision of Trust Law Committee has recommended that Foundations be introduced in Guernsey law. These would be corporate entities with a Founder and a Council but no beneficiaries in the conventional trust sense. Foundations have already been introduced in the Bahamas and are being considered elsewhere in the trust world, having been available in Liechtenstein for nearly 80 years and more recently in Panama. It will be interesting to see if such structures became popular in the wealth management industry as a potential shield against spouses seeking to enforce ancillary relief orders against such entities.

Difficult issues arise for trustees facing an attack on their trust, mounted by a spouse seeking to enforce an ancillary relief order against the trust. The settlor, frequently the other spouse or partner, will expect the trustee to defend the trust with all the resources of the trust assets. However, trustees who enter into the fray would do well to bear in mind the cautionary note struck by Lightman J in *Alsop Wilkinson (a firm) v Neary*[8] where he held that generally if the validity of a settlement needs to be defended it should be left to beneficiaries under the settlement to do so, protecting their interests under the settlement at their own risk as to costs. If the trustees assume the burden of defending the trust from an onslaught by one of the parties to matrimonial proceedings, then they may well also assume the risk of becoming personally liable as to costs. The role of a trustee has seldom been more difficult.

1.1.4.3.1 Charman v Charman (No 4):[9] The widening gap between the divorce and trust worlds

The Court of Appeal judgment in *Charman (No 4)*, delivered in May 2007[10], may be seen as the apogee of the English divorce jurisdiction's robust attitude towards offshore trusts, and as widening the gap which has developed over the past few years between the Family Division on the one hand and the trust industry on the other as to the respect to be accorded to trusts.

With the noteable exception of the reasoning of Munby J in *A v A*[11] the Family Division judiciary have viewed trusts, and self-settled offshore discretionary trusts in particular, with a high decree of scepticism. As Coleridge J stated in *J v V (disclosure: offshore corporations)*:[12]

> 'These sophisticated offshore structures are very familiar nowadays to the judiciary who have to try them. They neither impress, intimidate, nor fool anyone. The Courts have lived with them for years.'

---

[8]   [1995] 1 All ER 431, ChD.
[9]   [2007] EWCA Civ 503, CA.
[10]   See Appendix 2.
[11]   [2007] EWHC 99 (Fam).
[12]   [2003] EWHC 3110 (Fam), FD.

And as Munby J himself referred to in *Re W (Ex Parte Orders)*:[13]

> 'the robustness with which the Family Division ought to deal in appropriate
> cases with husbands who seek to obfuscate or to hide or mask the reality
> behind shams, artificial devices and similar contrivances. Nor do I doubt for
> a moment the propriety and utility of treating as one and the same a
> husband and some corporate or trust structure which it is apparent is simply
> the alter ego or creature of the husband.'

This is all well and good in an appropriate case. But where the same
attitude is evinced towards a trust where rights and expectations genuinely
have been created in favour of third parties, tension will necessarily occur
if the Family Division treats the trust as a creature of one of the spouses
or (which amounts to much the same thing) that the assets in the trust are
a resource of that spouse. The problem in the latter respect is particularly
acute, given that the claim that the assets/source of the assets in trust are
to be treated as a resource of one of the spouses bypasses the safeguards
intended by the rules – the joinder of the trustee and minor children to an
application to vary a trust or treat it as a sham.

It also bypasses an important safety valve introduced by most offshore
jurisdictions to protect trusts and those interested in them: the
non-recognition of foreign orders affecting the validity of a trust or giving
directions as to its administration including variation. While the Royal
Court of Jersey (which has had to deal with the largest number of English
ancillary relief orders affecting trusts to date) has afforded a high degree
of comity to such decisions, it has made it clear that it does not expect the
Family Division to exercise exorbitant jurisdiction by varying or declaring
sham Jersey law trusts.[14] Ironically, the Court of Appeal in *Charman*
agreed[15] and acknowledged as important the suggestion made by the
Royal Court of Jersey in *Re B Trust*[16] – that the Family Division should
decline to vary a Jersey trust but instead invite the offshore court to act as
an auxiliary to it in regard to any proposed variation.

But the Court of Appeal went on to decline to do so in *Charman*,
expressing the view that Mrs Charman was fortunate in neither having to
ask for a variation nor to allege sham because she 'had the evidence with
which to identify the assets of Dragon [the offshore trust] as part of the
husband's resources'.

To a trust lawyer, this assertion is startling. Dragon was a properly
constituted discretionary trust established by the husband some 20 years
previously which was, by the time of the trial, governed by the law of
Bermuda. A highly reputable professional trust company was trustee.
There had been no capital distributions out of the trust. The husband's

---

13   [2000] 2 FLR 927, FD.
14   *Re Fountain Trust* 2005 JLR 339.
15   At para 58: see Appendix 2 below.
16   2006 JLR 562.

letters of wishes, in conventional precatory terms, described him as wishing to be treated as 'primary beneficiary' while at the same time making it clear that he expected other members of his family to receive benefit from the trust. No evidence was adduced of the trustee's intention as to distributions to the husband. Notwithstanding, the Court of Appeal approved the decision of Coleridge J at first instance[17] taking the whole of the assets of the trust into account as a resource of the husband, on the basis that if asked, the trustee would be likely to advance the entire capital of the trust to him.

This decision is likely to put pressure on any discretionary trust in conventional form created by one of the parties to the marriage. It takes to new lengths the 'robust' attitude of the court towards trusts, effectively treating assets which are acknowledged to be in third party ownership and control as no more than an extension of a spouse's bank account: it does not treat assets in trust in the same way as the Chancery Division would, as Munby J urged in *A v A*.[18]

The Court of Appeal in *Charman*, while noting with some surprise that the court in Bermuda had not agreed with its decision on the Letter of Request in *Charman*,[19] rejected the suggestion that it was sending out a message to the offshore world that in family cases trusts do not matter, while expressing the anticipation that the courts of Bermuda 'will be disposed to help to ensure, within the parameters of its laws, that whatever may ultimately be awarded to the wife in these proceedings will clearly be paid'. The House of Lords has now refused Mr Charman leave to appeal against the Court of Appeal's decision.

The offshore courts will undoubtedly be placed in a difficult position as the result of orders such as this which, while not directly affecting the validity of trusts governed by their laws or purporting to vary them seek to put pressure on trustees to advance substantial sums to one of their beneficiaries to avoid enforcement proceedings and possibly bankruptcy of the beneficiary. Trustees placed in such a position will undoubtedly want to seek the directions of their own court as to whether to comply with a request made by the affected beneficiary in such circumstances because among other concerns, they will be concerned that:

(a) they may be making a payment to a beneficiary for an ulterior purpose – to pay to another who may not be a beneficiary. Accordingly, the question arises as to whether that is a proper application of trust funds (which can only be applied for the benefit of a beneficiary);

---

[17] [2006] EWHC 1879 (Fam), [2007] 1 FLR 593, FD.
[18] [2007] EWHC 99 (Fam).
[19] [2006] 1 WLR 1053, CA, at para 25.

(b)   whether any request emanating from a beneficiary in such circumstances is a genuine request or whether it is vitiated by duress;

(c)   whether the interests of other beneficiaries (who will be represented in those proceedings) would be adversely affected by such a payment and the extent to which any such detriment should be taken into account;

(d)   whether the interests of the requesting beneficiary would be better secured by funds remaining in trust for potential future benefit than by assisting with the payment to the beneficiary's spouse.

In an acute case it may be that trustees will surrender their discretion to the court.

To what extent the offshore courts will be prepared to assist, as envisaged by the Court of Appeal, or whether for policy reasons or otherwise they will politely resist the pressure exerted on trusts imposed by such orders, remains to be seen.

Settlors and the trust industry will undoubtedly take note of this trend in the Family Division's decisions and adjust practices and procedures to address concerns that conventional discretionary trusts may be treated without more as an extension of the settlor.

Fixed interest or hybrid trusts may become more fashionable. Trusts may be made purely in favour of children where the reality is that only they are intended to benefit. Appointments may be made where otherwise assets would remain in a general discretionary pot. Undoubtedly, great care will be taken as to the location of trust assets and the wording of letters of wishes.

CHAPTER 2

OVERVIEW AND EXPLANATION OF TRUSTS

2.1 WHAT IS A TRUST?

A trust is a fiduciary relationship in which the trustee holds assets given to him by the settlor for the benefit of beneficiaries in accordance with the duties imposed on the trustee by the terms of the trust and the law by which it is governed. The control and management of the assets is with the trustee or trustees: the enjoyment or benefit of them with the beneficiaries.

A trust does not have an independent legal personality (unlike a company or a foundation): the trustee has possession and control of the assets and the business of the trust is effected in the name of the trustee.

Although a trust may be characterised in some civil code and US jurisdictions as a contractual arrangement between the settlor and the trustee, under the English/offshore development of the trust it is not a contract between the settlor and the trustee for the benefit of third persons capable of being enforced by the settlor (save in Guernsey): it is not subject to the law of contract and neither can it be enforced by the settlor. As the imposition of a series of fiduciary obligations upon the trustees, the trust is subject to rules of equity and the supervision of the court. In England and Wales, this supervisory function is exercised by the Chancery (not the Family) Division.

Beneficiaries under trusts have rights to enable them to enforce the due administration of the trust, their ultimate right being to bring any matters of concern to the court so that the court can exercise its supervisory function over the trustee.

A trust must be contrasted with a nomineeship, mandate or agency agreement. In these arrangements the mandatee, agent or nominee acts in accordance with the instructions of the mandator/principal and owes contractual and/or fiduciary obligations to that person. Title to the asset may have passed to the nominee/mandatee/agent but control has not passed from the principal or mandator. Such arrangements are sometimes referred to as bare or simple trusts.

Where, as sometimes happens, an allegation is made in divorce (or other) proceedings to the effect that a trust is a sham, it is usually a claim to the effect that in spite of documentation indicating the contrary, the trustee is effectively the nominee or mandatee of the settlor.

The three certainties to create a valid trust must be satisfied: the settlor must intend to create a trust on the terms specified, there must be certainty of subject matter and certainty of objects. If any of these crucial features is absent – the settlor had no intention to part with his assets, there is a lack of clarity over what assets are subject to the trust or who is to benefit under the trust – it will fail.

2.2 TYPES OF TRUST

2.2.1 Revocable or irrevocable trusts

Trusts can be revocable or irrevocable. In the former, the settlor can decide to revoke the trust whereupon the assets will be returned to him. Unless and until the settlor revokes the trust, it is valid and enforceable on its terms. It will become irrevocable on the settlor's death or incapacity to revoke. Most settlements in England and the offshore world are irrevocable. In the US, it is common for trusts to be revocable, where they are often used as will substitutes to avoid probate and to enable the effective management of the settlor's estate if he becomes unable to manage his own affairs. Revocable trusts may not be recognised in all jurisdictions: for example, the patrimony (in the sense of a person's assets past, present and future together with their liabilities) available to satisfy the succession regime of a civil law settlor may well be regarded by the law of his nationality/habitual residence as including the assets of a revocable trust.

2.2.2 Fixed interest trusts and their variation

Traditionally trusts were intended to provide for the family of the settlor in a defined way: the enjoyment of the assets was intended to pass from father to son, to cater for a widow for the remainder of her lifetime and then to the children of the settlor, to provide for a disabled child, or to assist with the education and other expenses of grandchildren. Such trusts were explicit as to who was to benefit and in what way: who was to take income/be the life tenant (which is an interest in possession trust), at what age beneficiaries were to be able to receive capital and so on. Effectively, they fixed the interests of the beneficiaries at the outset and those arrangements could not be changed without variation agreed by all those beneficially entitled or by order of the court.

It is possible in Anglo-Saxon trusts not following the US model for beneficiaries absolutely entitled between themselves to agree to bring a trust to an end. Such beneficiaries can also rearrange the beneficial interest as they wish. So, for example, in the case of an interest in possession trust with the settlor's widow having a life interest and her two sons the capital equally on her death, they can agree to partition the capital (usually on the basis of an actuarial valuation of their respective interests) or rearrange the trust interests between them. But if one or more beneficiaries are not competent or, as is commonly the case, the class of beneficiaries includes minor beneficiaries and/or beneficiaries not yet born ('unborns') or beneficiaries who cannot yet be identified save as a class ('unascertaineds'), the competent beneficiaries cannot vary the trust by agreement between them. The only way in which this can be achieved is by order of the court on a variation application, where the court has to conclude that the variation is for the benefit of those who cannot speak for themselves or, in some jurisdictions, be satisfied that it is not detrimental to their interests. The court's function in such applications is to provide agreement on behalf of those who cannot agree: it cannot consent on behalf of those who are competent, however misguided the court may consider their objection to be.

Accordingly, the jurisdiction of the Chancery Division of the High Court under the Variation of Trusts Act 1958 in England and Wales (and similar legislative provisions across the offshore world) is fundamentally different from that exercised in the Family Division under s 24 of the Matrimonial Causes Act 1973 ('MCA 1973'): in Chancery proceedings the application is consensual and great care is taken not to damage (and in most jurisdictions, care is taken to enhance) the position of minors, unborns and unascertaineds; in the Family Division the court is predominantly interested in the position of the nuclear family before it and can – and sometimes does – cut severely across the interests and expectations of others under the trust.

A method of mitigating such potential damage to those not directly affected by the divorce but who otherwise may be perceived to get short shrift in the Family Division is for the Family Division to make its variation order conditional upon an order to like effect being made in the home court of the trust, failing which the ancillary relief application returns to the Family Division for further consideration. This method also avoids the risk that the final order will prove not to be enforceable in the trust jurisdiction, most of the offshore jurisdictions having passed legislation directed to preventing the enforcement of such an order arising from foreign divorce proceedings.

2.2.3   Discretionary trusts and letters of wishes

Over the past 40 years or so it has become more common for trusts to be discretionary, or hybrid – an interest in possession trust (eg for the settlor, widow of settlor or child) followed by the exercise of the trustees' discretion as to who should benefit and in what proportions as between a class of discretionary beneficiaries or objects.

The distinction between discretionary beneficiaries and objects of a power is that with discretionary beneficiaries the trustees are obliged to consider how to exercise their power to distribute as between them; with a power, trustees are authorised but not obligated to distribute. The discretionary beneficiaries or objects of a power have a hope of benefit but no defined expectation.

Discretionary trusts may have a narrow class of beneficiaries: for example, the settlor, his wife or widow, their children and issue. Alternatively the class may be wide – any person living in Cheltenham on a specific date – or the members of the class may be unknown at the outset, but must be capable of being ascertained by reference to specific criteria.

The form of discretionary trust known as the 'black hole' or 'Red Cross' trust became very common in the 1970s–1990s: a well-known charity was named as default beneficiary with the trustee (sometimes with the consent of the settlor or protector) or settlor/protector having power to add beneficiaries. This was often done to preserve confidentiality as to the real beneficial interest. Settlors and their spouses were often excluded from benefit for tax reasons.

Because the choice of beneficiary(ies) and the manner in which they are to benefit as to capital, income, or both is at the discretion of the trustee (who must use his discretion appropriately, taking into account all relevant factors and no irrelevant ones) the practice has developed in the Anglo-Saxon trust world (but not in the US), of the settlor giving a letter of wishes to the trustee to guide the trustee in this choice.

A properly drawn letter of wishes will make it clear that the wishes of the settlor are not intended to be binding but simply to aid the trustee in the exercise of his discretion. As a matter of law such letters do not bind the trustee unless, exceptionally, they are clearly intended to constitute the real terms of the trust and so override the terms of the trust instrument. The trustee should take the letter of wishes (or other expression of the settlor's aspirations) into account as one of the relevant factors but should not adhere slavishly to the settlor's wishes, particularly where there have been material changes in circumstances since the wishes were expressed.

Too often the tendency in the Family Division is to regard the letter of wishes (or the latest such letter) on its own as setting out the terms of the trust or being such that the trustee will inevitably put the settlor's wishes into effect. But that is neither to understand the true nature of the normal letter of wishes nor the duties of the trustees when exercising their discretionary duties or powers, which duties and powers are subject to the supervision of the court if exercised improperly.

A variation on the discretionary trust is the accumulation and maintenance settlement, a form of settlement made popular in England and Wales with the advent of Capital Transfer Tax in the mid-1970s but now likely to be less common following the Finance Act 2006. The purpose of the accumulation and maintenance trust was to provide for minors and young people – typically grandchildren – until the age of 25.

A further variation is a disabled trust for the benefit of a disabled person. Such a trust can confer a life interest (and accordingly entitlement to income) on the disabled person but because this would frequently interfere with state benefits to which the disabled person would otherwise be entitled it is more common for the trust to be discretionary in form so that the disabled person has no right to any particular benefit. The trustees can then decide to assist the disabled person on an occasional basis, such as by providing funds for a holiday or to buy a piece of equipment.

Protective or spendthrift trusts are commonly used where there is a concern about the financial maturity of the person proposed to benefit. The beneficiary has a life interest but this automatically terminates in the event that he/she becomes bankrupt or takes any steps to alienate his/her interest under the trust. On such an occurrence the trust immediately becomes discretionary, enabling the trustee to provide for the beneficiary (if appropriate) in a less structured manner and to provide for the other members of the discretionary class, often members of his/her family.

Trusts common in the US include asset protection trusts which are trusts created with the expectation that the trust assets will be shielded from the claims of the settlors' creditors. This is in contrast to the position in England and Wales and the offshore world although a number of jurisdictions (most notably the Cook Islands) have enacted legislation which severely limits the time within which a claim can be made by a creditor.

US trusts are often designed to take advantage of specific provisions of the Internal Revenue Code to achieve a tax advantage. Examples are bypass trusts (designed to take advantage of spouse's tax exemptions), QTIPS or marital trusts (to qualify for the marital deduction) and generation-skipping trusts (to enable advantage to be taken of the generation-skipping transfer tax legislation).

Incentive trusts take discretionary trusts to a further level: they contain powers that reward (with distributions) behaviour considered to be desirable and punish (by withholding distributions) behaviour regarded as unsatisfactory such as drug abuse or indolence. Such trusts are becoming popular in the United States.

2.2.4   Charitable or purpose trusts

In England and Wales trusts must (with a few limited exceptions) be for the benefit of one or more individuals who are capable of being ascertained or be for exclusively charitable purposes. A charitable trust has impersonal objects, such as for education, the care of the elderly or medical research.

In a number of offshore jurisdictions, purpose trusts are possible: the trust is set up to fulfil or provide a specific purpose (eg to manage a company or fulfil a non-charitable object) or, with the STAR Trust regime in the Cayman Islands, for mixed purposes: for individuals and charity/other impersonal purposes.

2.3   THE POSITION OF THE SETTLOR

Unless the settlor has some other role in relation to the trust, the role of the settlor (otherwise known as 'grantor' or 'trustor' in the US) is simply that of the transferor of assets to the trustees and the creator of the trust document. Once that has taken place the settlor has no continuing role to play as settlor, except to provide expressions of his wishes to guide (but not bind) trustees and any protector as to the exercise of their discretion in the case of a discretionary trust. Trustees will usually accord due deference to the wishes of the settlor without accepting that they must accede to them. Guernsey is unique in conferring ongoing rights to the settlor to receive trust information and to have the standing, without permission of the court, to bring proceedings with regard to the administration of the trust.

The role of the settlor who merely created the settlement is often exaggerated in proceedings in the Family Division. The settlor may continue to wield influence in another capacity (eg as trustee), because he has retained powers or as beneficiary, but purely as settlor:

(a)   he has no ability to retrieve the assets of the trust unless (atypically in trust jurisdictions except in the US) the trust is revocable;

(b)   he cannot amend the terms of the trust, change the trustees, prevent distributions and so on unless he has retained specific powers to do so;

(c)   he has no standing to receive accounts of the trust or trust information (save under a Guernsey law trust);

(d)   he has no standing on account of being a settlor to apply to the court for directions to be made to the trustee. (The only jurisdiction which caters for the settlor to make such an application without leave of the court is Guernsey.)

The settlor may, of course, have another role to play in the trust administration in consequence of being also a trustee, beneficiary or of having retained certain powers. If the settlor is also a trustee, he is subject to the same fiduciary obligations as any other trustee and he must fulfil his duties as trustee in accordance with the terms of the trust and any obligations laid on him by the law of the jurisdiction which governs the trust: it will provide no defence in a breach of trust action to protest that he is the settlor. (Note that the position may be different in the US in relation to will substitute trusts where the settlor may be able to override the terms of the settlement during his lifetime and the trustees are relieved of liability for breach if they act in accordance with his directions. Such a 'trust' may not be recognised as a trust in other jurisdictions, including England and most offshore trust jurisdictions.)

If the settlor is also a beneficiary, he has the same rights and expectations as any other beneficiary with that beneficial interest. He may be able to exert a degree of influence over the trustee through expression of his wishes as settlor, but his rights to information and to enforce the terms of the trust remain that of a beneficiary.

The settlor may, without being a trustee or a beneficiary have reserved powers to himself in order to retain some control or influence over the trust. This does not invalidate the trust unless the reserved powers are so wide that on a true construction of the settlement the trustee cannot exercise any significant powers without the settlor's consent.

In order to avoid an allegation that the trust is thereby rendered invalid, some jurisdictions have enacted legislation to confirm that where the settlor has reserved certain powers this does not render the trust a nomineeship or sham. Such powers may be positive powers – to add beneficiaries or to remove a trustee – or veto powers, enabling the settlor to prevent certain steps by the trustee. Depending on the nature of those powers, the settlor may have fiduciary duties to exercise in their performance and as such is entitled to such information about the trust as he needs properly to exercise that function. If the powers are fiduciary, he cannot exercise them selfishly but must do so in the interests of the beneficial class as a whole. So, for example, if a settlor has the power to remove trustees, this is a fiduciary power. Accordingly, he cannot ask the trustee to benefit him and if the trustee refuses, simply remove the trustee because the trustee is not acceding to his wish. Such action would be susceptible to the supervision of the court.

2.4   TRUSTEES AND PROTECTORS

It is beyond the scope of this book to provide more than an introduction to the role of trustees and protectors: for further details please refer to a major work on trusts such as *Lewin on Trusts* (17th edn) or *Underhill & Hayton on the Law relating to Trusts and Trustees* (17th edn).

Trustees hold title to and control and manage the trust assets for the benefit of the class of beneficiaries set out in the trust instrument or added to the class in accordance with powers to add conferred by the trust instrument.

Trustees are chosen by the settlor in the first instance and may be lay people, professionals or a trust company. Trust companies in some of the major offshore trust centres are heavily regulated to promote acceptable standards of trusteeship. In general, the understanding of the duties entailed in the office of trustee or protector is much better now than in the 1970s and 1980s.

Trustees have onerous duties laid upon them by the trust instrument itself, by the law of equity as developed in case law and by statute. A breach of these duties can result in personal liability for breach of trust, from which the trustee may be able to claim the protection of an exoneration clause in the settlement or, infrequently, the relief of the court.

Trustees, in common with others performing fiduciary roles such as protectors, also have an obligation not to act in breach of fiduciary duty. Unless this duty is a qualified one (such as where the trustee or protector is also a beneficiary and can make a decision to benefit himself or herself without it being impugned merely on that account) the fiduciary duty is a duty of loyalty to the beneficial class as a whole.

The duty of loyalty has two main strands:

(a)   not to profit from the fiduciary position (this is the origin of the rule that a trustee or protector cannot be remunerated unless the trust deed or the court specifically authorises remuneration); and

(b)   not to put themselves in a position where their duty and interest conflict. If a trustee/protector acts in a situation of conflict, the resulting transaction can be set aside as of right by the beneficiaries.

The performance of the trustee's duties is subject to the supervision of the court. A trustee or a beneficiary can ask the court to give directions to the trustee as to the administration of the trust and can hold the trustee to account for a breach of trust or fiduciary duty.

Protectors are commonly appointed where the assets are held on discretionary trusts and the settlor has no particularly close connection with the trustee. Accordingly, the appointment of protectors has become very common in the offshore world where corporate trustees are often appointed.

The protector is usually a close friend or confidant of the settlor or a trusted professional advisor. Less often, the protector is a professional corporate which specialises in the provision of protectorship services.

In most jurisdictions the role of protector is not defined by statute and their powers derive purely from the trust deed. Unless the protector's powers are specifically described in the trust instrument as personal, they will almost always be considered fiduciary, particularly if the powers are quite extensive. This means that they must be exercised in the interests of the beneficial class as a whole and the exercise of their powers is subject to the supervision of the court.

The protector's powers may be positive or veto powers. At minimum, they entail a power to remove (and usually replace) trustees but their powers may be more extensive, covering addition and exclusion of beneficiaries, approval/veto of distributions and sometimes approval of certain administrative steps.

Unless the settlement so provides, a protector is not entitled to be paid remuneration for his time and effort but is entitled to be paid out of pocket expenses.

2.5 RIGHTS OF BENEFICIARIES

If beneficiaries have fixed interests or interests contingent upon a specific event (such as attaining a particular age) they are entitled to receive the benefits which are appurtenant to that interest upon it falling in. So life tenants can call the trustees to account for the income due to them and capital beneficiaries can generally require the trustees to account for the capital.

By contrast, a discretionary beneficiary or object of a power has only a hope of benefit: he or she cannot claim specific benefit unless the trustees have exercised their powers in his/her favour.

It has been said that if the trustee could not be held to account for the trusteeship, there is no trust. Beneficiaries need to have access to accounts and information to enable them to review the administration of the trust and if need be, call the trustees to account. Until recently, it had been thought that this right entailed a proprietary right to access trust documents but following *Schmidt v Rosewood Trust Ltd*[1] it is now clear that the right is a right to apply to the court to exercise its discretion to order disclosure rather than an absolute right to receive trust documents upon request to the trustees. The attitude of the trustee to a request for trust documents will depend in large measure on whether there are any counter indications (such as loss of confidentiality, a threatened attack on the trust itself or commercial reasons for secrecy) and on the proximity of the requesting beneficiary to benefit. If the beneficiary has a fixed interest or is anticipated to benefit significantly he or she is likely to be given trust documentation, but one with a remote interest or expectation of benefit may be declined.

Trustees have important obligations of confidentiality towards their beneficiaries and so should not be expected to respond to a request for information or documentation from the spouse of a beneficiary unless the spouse is also a beneficiary.

The important topic of accessing trust documentation is addressed in more detail in Chapter 7. However, it should be noted that it cannot be assumed without more, that all the information typically sought by the beneficiary's spouse in divorce proceedings will necessarily be made available by a trustee to a beneficiary.

---

[1]   [2003] 2 AC 709.

CHAPTER 3

JURISDICTION FOR DIVORCE AND TRUST MATTERS AND APPLICABLE LAW

3.1 INTRODUCTION

When contemplating a divorce involving trusts, or becoming involved in such litigation, a key issue to consider is the jurisdiction for the relevant court not only to grant a divorce but also to make orders which may be binding both on the spouses and on third parties such as trustees. From a trust law or conflicts law perspective, this is a complex issue. However, from the perspective of the English Family Division of the High Court, it is a straightforward matter since once the court has jurisdiction to grant a divorce, it also has jurisdiction to make all forms of financial orders on divorce, including orders varying ante or post-nuptial settlements under s 24(1)(c) of the MCA 1973.[1] Furthermore, the matter for the English Family Division of the High Court is also straightforward when it comes to considering what is the relevant applicable law to the dispute, since only English law is applied to financial matters on divorce. In contrast, in continental Europe, it is commonplace for courts in those countries to apply a foreign law. This approach is almost entirely unique to the English Family Division, since other Divisions of the High Court are well used to applying foreign law. It may be in the light of proposals by the European Union,[2] even the English Family Division will have to begin to apply foreign law.

In the context of trusts in divorce, these issues can be fundamental in determining whether or not orders made by the English court directly or indirectly against trustees will be enforceable in their home jurisdiction. This chapter will consider the English court's jurisdiction for divorce, and touch on jurisdiction regarding trust issues. Conflicts of law and applicable law will be referred to in more detail in Chapter 8. In a divorce context these issues are highly relevant to 'forum shopping'; finding the best jurisdiction in terms of a financial outcome for the individual spouse. The same issues arise in the context of trusts being attacked or defended in divorce, in that different jurisdictions may have different powers to treat

---

[1] See Chapter 5 for more discussion about this point.
[2] The draft Regulation known as 'Rome III' – the latest draft being 5274/07 – 'Jurisdiction and applicable law in matrimonial matters' and the Green Paper on 'Conflict of Laws in Matters Concerning Matrimonial Property Regimes' COM (2006) 400 final.

trust assets as available or vary the terms of a trust, and some jurisdictions may not recognise trusts at all.

3.2 ENGLISH DIVORCE JURISDICTION

The English court's jurisdiction to entertain a petition for divorce, judicial separation or nullity is based almost entirely on the European Union Regulation known as 'Brussels II'.[3]

Although Brussels II deals with divorce jurisdiction within the European Union (except Denmark) the alternative grounds for jurisdiction set out in Brussels II also apply to cases involving countries outside the European Union.

Article 3 of Brussels II states:

'1. In matters relating to divorce, legal separation or marriage annulment, jurisdiction shall lie with the courts of the Member State—

    (a)   in whose territory:
- the spouses are habitually resident, or
- the spouses were last habitually resident, insofar as one of them still resides there, or
- the respondent is habitually resident, or
- in the event of a joint application, either of the spouses is habitually resident, or
- the applicant is habitually resident if he or she resided there for at least a year immediately before the application was made, or
- the applicant is habitually resident if he or she resided there for at least 6 months immediately before the application was made and is either a national of the Member State in question or, in the case of the United Kingdom and Ireland, has his or her "domicile" there;

    (b)   of the nationality of both spouses or, in the case of the United Kingdom and Ireland, of the "domicile" of both spouses.

2. For the purpose of this Regulation, "domicile" shall have the same meaning as it has under the legal systems of the United Kingdom and Ireland.'

Where no court of a Member State, except Denmark, has jurisdiction under Brussels II and either of the parties to the marriage is domiciled in England and Wales on the date when the proceedings are begun, then the English court has that as an additional ground for jurisdiction.[4]

---

[3] Council Regulation (EC) No 2201/2003 of 27 November 2003, sometimes known as 'Brussels II' bis., which repealed Regulation (EC) No 1347/2000.

[4] Domicile and Matrimonial Proceedings Act 1973, s 5.

A detailed analysis of Brussels II is outside the scope of this book. However, jurisprudence is only beginning to develop as to the meaning of some of the terms set out in the Regulation, in particular habitual residence. There has been litigation which reached the French Cour de Cassation, the highest court in France, as to whether an American wife was habitually resident in France. The French court held that there had to be one definition of habitual residence throughout the European Union under Brussels II.[5] In a case decided before Brussels II came into force,[6] involving a forum dispute between England and Nigeria, it was held that a spouse could have two habitual residences, and the wife was habitually resident in England even though she had only spent 161 days of the year prior to presenting her divorce petition in England. It is unclear whether such a concept is valid as a matter of European Union law.

The key fact to appreciate regarding competing divorces within the European Union (except Denmark) under Brussels II is that pursuant to Art 19, the court second seised must, of its own motion, stay its proceedings until such time as the jurisdiction of the court first seised is established. In a nutshell, first in time wins.

Under Art 16, a court shall be deemed to be seised:

> 'at the time when the document instituting the proceedings or an equivalent document is lodged with the court, provided that the applicant does not subsequently fail to take the steps he was required to take to have service effected on the respondent'.

There are no exceptions whatsoever to the first in time wins rule.

If the draft EU regulation known as 'Rome III'[7] passes into law, then it will be possible for spouses to choose in advance not only which court will deal with any divorce, but also which law is to be applied in respect of the divorce, as opposed to division of property and maintenance issues. When dealing with an international couple, it is perfectly possible for a continental European court to apply one foreign law in respect of the divorce, a different foreign law regarding division of property and a third foreign law regarding maintenance claims. The EU's Green Paper on Matrimonial Property Regimes[8] seeks to simplify these matters.

Although Brussels II does not apply to financial matters on divorce, in practice in most cases a divorce in England will lead to financial matters also being resolved in England.

---

5   *Moore v Moore* [2006] IL Pr 29.
6   *Ikimi v Ikimi* [2001] 2 FLR 1288, CA.
7   The latest draft of the Regulation being 5274/07 – 'Jurisdiction and applicable law in matrimonial matters'.
8   The Green Paper on 'Conflict of Laws in Matters Concerning Matrimonial Property Regimes' COM (2006) 400 final.

Brussels I[9] and the Lugano Convention[10] may be relevant and mean that issues to do with spousal maintenance may have to be dealt with in another Member or Contracting State, again depending upon which State was first seised with the maintenance issue. In practice in the context of Brussels II and an EU case, except Denmark, if the English court is first seised with the divorce proceedings, it is likely to be first seised for maintenance issues, assuming there have been no prior proceedings in another Member State. This is because all divorce petitions in England, the documents used to start a divorce, tend to include a 'prayer' for ancillary relief and will include a claim for maintenance.

Such a claim for maintenance is as a matter of practice included in all divorce petitions, even if the economically stronger spouse starts the divorce. There is authority for the court having power to make an order for maintenance against an applicant and this is useful to ensure that the issue of maintenance is before the English court first of all.[11]

The word 'maintenance' has been given a wide definition by the European Court of Justice under Brussels I – *Van den Boogaard v Laumen*.[12] In that case, the European Court of Justice held that an English ancillary relief order, which included provision by way of capitalised maintenance, fell within the definition of maintenance, as did any provision for capital such as for housing.

This reflects the significant difference between the approach of the English court to financial matters on divorce and that of the courts of continental Europe. The English court deals with division of property and payment of maintenance, pension sharing and the like, all as one matter. In contrast, in continental Europe the question of the 'liquidation of the matrimonial property regime' and payment of maintenance is usually separate and distinct. The liquidation of the matrimonial property regime, usually separate property, deferred acquisition of gains or full community property, is dealt with on an administrative basis by a notary. Such 'property rights' are excluded from the scope of Brussels I since they form 'rights in property arising out of a matrimonial relationship'.[13] In contrast, maintenance does fall within the scope of Brussels I. The Lugano Convention has identical provisions.

This is different from the position in most US states since there has to be 'sufficient minimum contact' between the respondent to a divorce and the state in question for the courts of that state to have jurisdiction to deal with financial matters.

---

9   Council Regulation (EC) 44/2001 on jurisdiction and the recognition and enforcement of judgments in civil and commercial matters.
10   The Convention of 16 September 1988 on jurisdiction and the enforcement of judgments in civil and commercial matters.
11   *Dart v Dart* [1996] 2 FLR 286, CA.
12   [1997] 2 FLR 399, ECJ.
13   Art 1(2)(a).

3.3   DIVORCES IN RELATED JURISDICTIONS

In some cases not involving countries or territories within the European Union (except Denmark), there are obligatory rules to determine in which country competing divorces are to take place. This is not a first in time wins rule. Those cases are where a divorce is filed in England or a competing jurisdiction defined as a 'related jurisdiction'.[14]

Where the divorce is in a related jurisdiction an obligatory stay may apply.[15] This is only if:

> 'It appears to the court on the application of a party to the marriage—
>
> (a)   that in respect of the same marriage proceedings for divorce or nullity of marriage are continuing in a related jurisdiction; and
>
> (b)   that the parties to the marriage have resided together after its celebration; and
>
> (c)   that the place where they resided together when the proceedings in the court were begun or, if they did not then reside together, where they last resided together before those proceedings were begun, is in that jurisdiction; and
>
> (d)   that either of the said parties was habitually resident in that jurisdiction throughout the year ending with the date on which they last resided together before the date on which the proceedings in the court were begun,
>
> it shall be the duty of the court ... to order that the proceedings in the court be stayed.'

Since many offshore trusts may be administered from or have trustees situated in, or proper laws of Jersey, Guernsey and the Isle of Man, this little known provision can be extremely helpful.

3.4   NON-BRUSSELS II CASES

Where the dispute is between the English court and a court outside the scope of Brussels II, the English court has a discretionary power to stay the divorce on the grounds of *forum non conveniens*. This 'inconvenient forum' test is an alien concept to almost all of continental Europe, and to many American states.

In continental European countries such as Switzerland, to which Brussels II does not apply, once the court has jurisdiction either to grant a divorce, or to deal with financial matters, the court is competent to do so and only if a foreign court grants a divorce or possibly a final financial order beforehand will jurisdiction be lost.

---

[14]   Domicile and Matrimonial Proceedings Act 1973, Sch 1, para 3(2) which means Scotland, Northern Ireland, Jersey, Guernsey (including Alderney and Sark) and the Isle of Man.

[15]   Domicile and Matrimonial Proceedings Act 1973, Sch 1, para 8.

In England it is essential to appreciate that once jurisdiction for a divorce has been established, that enables the court to deal with all financial matters, and, in theory make orders against trusts, trustees and trust assets situated or based outside England. Whether such an order will be enforceable is dealt with in more detail in Chapter 8 but many of the issues dealt with in this chapter impact on and are relevant to the question of enforceability.

A detailed consideration of the test to obtain a discretionary stay is outside the scope of this book. However, the relevant provision[16] states:

'(1) Where before the beginning of the trial or first trial in any matrimonial proceedings, other than proceedings governed by [Brussels II] which are continuing in the court it appears to the court—

(a)   that any proceedings in respect of the marriage in question, or capable of effecting its validity or subsistence, are continuing in another jurisdiction; and

(b)   that the balance of fairness (including convenience) as between the parties to the marriage is such that it is appropriate for the proceedings in that jurisdiction to be disposed of before further steps are taken in the proceedings in the court or in those proceedings insofar as they consist of a particular kind of matrimonial proceedings,

the court may then, if it thinks fit, order that the proceedings in the court be stayed or, as the case may be, that those proceedings be stayed insofar as they consist of proceedings of that kind.

(2) In considering the balance of fairness and convenience for the purposes of sub-paragraph (1)(b) above, the court shall have regard to all factors appearing to be relevant, including the convenience of witnesses and any delay or expense which may result from the proceedings being stayed, or not being stayed.'

In a nutshell, the test is to see which jurisdiction is most closely connected to the marriage and the parties. However, this is a complex and developing area of the law and reference should be made to other textbooks on the subject.

3.5   JURISDICTION IN TRUST MATTERS

If the Family Division has made an ancillary relief order which relates to a trust governed by English law, enforcement is unlikely to be a problem. In most high value cases however, it is likely that any relevant trust assets will be held by an offshore trust. The UK along with many other trust jurisdictions is a party to the Hague Convention on Trusts. The international obligations enshrined in the convention were given effect in English domestic law by the Recognition of Trusts Act 1987.

---

[16]   Domicile and Matrimonial Proceedings Act 1973, Sch 1, para 9.

The 1987 Act provides (inter alia) that the validity, construction, effects and administration of a trust are governed by the law chosen by the settlor or, in the absence of any such choice, by the law with which the trust is most closely connected. Assuming therefore that the law of the trust is not English law, the question becomes whether the law of the trust will permit the offshore trustees to comply with the order of the English court. If it does not, the trustees will not be in a position to comply with the order of the English court for if they do, they will inevitably face a claim by the beneficiaries for paying away trust assets without lawful authority. This subject is dealt with more fully in Chapter 8.

CHAPTER 4

ENGLISH ASSET DIVISION ON DIVORCE

4.1 INTRODUCTION

This chapter is a broad overview of English asset division on divorce. It is only an overview and the current state of flux in this area of the law means that an entire book could be written on this subject.

4.2 THE POWERS OF THE ENGLISH COURT

The English courts have a very broad discretion when making financial orders on divorce. Unlike other jurisdictions, there is no simple arithmetical division of assets – instead each case is considered on its own facts as applied to the statutory framework.

The court has the power, upon a divorce, to make a variety of orders – with a view to creating a bespoke solution to each set of circumstances. Its powers derive primarily from the Matrimonial Causes Act 1973 ('MCA 1973') – in particular ss 23 and 24.

Section 23 states that upon a divorce the court can order any one or all of the following:

(1)   that one party pays to the other periodical payments (ie regular ongoing maintenance payments) either for a fixed period or until either party dies or remarries;

(2)   that such periodical payments are 'secured' (ie that the recipient can have automatic recourse to a fund in the event that the payer defaults);

(3)   that one party pays to the other a lump sum, or sums;

(4)   that one party pays to the other periodical payments for the benefit of a child;

(5)   that such payments for the child are secured; and

(6) that one party pays to the other a lump sum for the benefit of a child.

Section 24 states that upon a divorce the court can order that:

(1) one party transfers to the other (or to a child of the family or to any other specified person for the benefit of a child) specified property to which the first party is entitled;

(2) one party settles property to which he is entitled on the other party or upon a child of the family or for their benefit;

(3) any ante-nuptial or post-nuptial settlement (including any such settlement made by will or codicil) made on either of the parties to the marriage be varied so as to benefit the other party and/or any child of the family; and

(4) that any interest held by either of the parties in such a settlement be extinguished or reduced.

The powers set out in the latter two subsections are dealt with in more detail in the following chapter, dealing with variation of settlements, which includes an analysis of what comprises a 'nuptial' settlement.

In addition, s 24A of the MCA 1973 gives the court power to order the sale of any property in which a party to a marriage has a beneficial interest.

The Welfare Reform and Pensions Act 1999 inserted a further section – s 24B – into the MCA 1973. This makes a further order available to the court – the pension-sharing order (whereby the administrator of one party's pension is ordered to transfer a specified percentage of it to a pension to which the other party is entitled).

All of these orders can also be made by the court upon a decree of nullity – which is where a marriage is considered to be voidable due to reasons such as, for example, the incapacity or refusal of one of the parties to consummate it, or to lack of valid consent to the marriage, mental disorder or venereal disease. All, save for a pension-sharing order, can also be made on a judicial separation – which is where parties are able to demonstrate that one of the facts required for a petition for divorce exists (ie adultery, unreasonable behaviour, separation or desertion) but that the marriage has not irretrievably broken down.

4.3 FACTORS THE COURT MUST CONSIDER

When deciding which orders to make in any one case the English court is obliged to consider s 25 of the MCA 1973. This sets out in detail the matters to which the court must have regard.

Section 25(1) states that the court's first (although not paramount) consideration is to the welfare of any child of the family under the age of 18. The definition of 'child of the family' is to be found at s 52(1) of the MCA 1973. It makes clear that a 'child of the family' is any child who has been treated by both parties as a child of the family. He or she does not have to be the biological or legal child of either party.

Section 25(2) then sets out a list of factors which a court must then consider in each case before deciding what orders are appropriate. These factors are as follows:

(a)   the income, earning capacity, property and other financial resources which each of the parties to the marriage has or is likely to have in the foreseeable future including in the case of earning capacity any increase in that capacity which it would in the opinion of the court be reasonable to expect a party to the marriage to take steps to acquire;

(b)   the financial needs, obligations and responsibilities which each of the parties to the marriage has or is likely to have in the foreseeable future;

(c)   the standard of living enjoyed by the family before the breakdown of the marriage;

(d)   the age of each party to the marriage and the duration of the marriage;

(e)   any physical or mental disability of either of the parties to the marriage;

(f)   the contributions which each of the parties has made or is likely in the foreseeable future to make to the welfare of the family, including any contribution by looking after the home and caring for the family;

(g)   the conduct of each of the parties, if that conduct is such that it would in the opinion of the court be inequitable to disregard it;

(h) in the case of proceedings for divorce or nullity of marriage, the value to each of the parties to the marriage of any benefit which by reason of the dissolution or annulment of the marriage, that party will lose the chance of acquiring.

It is worth noting that this list is not exhaustive. The courts are obliged to consider all the circumstances of the case when exercising their powers. There is no hierarchy amongst the various factors – all must be considered and given appropriate weight.

The courts are also obliged, due to the direction at s 25A(1) of the MCA 1973, to consider, in every case, whether a 'clean break' can be achieved. A 'clean break' is what it says – a termination of each party's financial obligations towards each other as soon after the decree of divorce as is practicable. In practice, this generally means that instead of one party paying ongoing maintenance to the other, there will be a lump sum payment or transfer of assets in an amount sufficient to meet the capital equivalent of that ongoing maintenance need, in addition to whatever other capital orders are considered to be appropriate.

4.4 APPLICATION OF THE COURT'S POWERS – THE CASE OF *WHITE*

Inevitably, case-law has provided guidance as to how the various s 25 factors are likely to be interpreted. One case in particular has dramatically altered the way in which the s 25 factors are considered and applied by the courts.

The House of Lords' decision in the case of *White v White*[1] was groundbreaking. The courts' focus, prior to this decision in October 2000, was upon ensuring that the 'reasonable requirements' of the applicant were met. There was no statutory basis for this focus, which tended to prioritise consideration of one party's needs over all the other s 25 factors. It resulted in orders (in cases where resources outstripped the parties' basic needs) where the homemaker (as opposed to the spouse who had worked outside the home to build up the assets) would be awarded a home (or homes) and sufficient income (often capitalised) to meet his or her stated domestic budget. The breadwinner then kept the balance, irrespective of the fact that this may provide him with a significant surplus over and above his or her needs or reasonable requirements. Whilst this approach had the benefit of being predictable, it meant that there was an inevitable ceiling to claims, and the wives of very wealthy men were often left with a very modest proportion of the family wealth.

In *White*, the House of Lords held that this approach was wrong. It held that the courts' analysis of the facts by reference to each of the factors in

---

[1]   [2000] 2 FLR 981, HL.

s 25 of the MCA 1973 should result in an outcome that was 'fair'. Furthermore, there should be no discrimination between the homemaker and the breadwinner when considering the contributions which each had made to the marriage. Although it was explicitly stated that there should be no presumption or starting-point of equal division, as 'a presumption of equal division would go beyond the permissible bounds of interpretation of s 25', Lord Nicholls said that:

> 'a judge would always be well advised to check his tentative views against the yardstick of equality of division. As a general guide, equality should only be departed from if there is a good reason for doing so.'

Obviously, in the vast majority of cases, the parties' needs will not outstrip their resources, and the court's role will be focused more upon achieving a division of the resources in a way which meets as many of those needs as is possible. However, in the 'bigger money' cases, the effect of *White* was to unshackle the homemaker from being limited to receiving his or her 'reasonable requirements' and to force the courts to look at a 'fair' and non-discriminatory division of the assets which were surplus to the parties' needs. The focus now is upon whether there is any valid reason to depart from a 50/50 split of assets.

The check against the 'yardstick of equality' has been said to apply to any case where all or the bulk of the wealth has been built up during the marriage, irrespective of the length of that marriage. In the Court of Appeal case of *Foster v Foster*,[2] for example, the marriage subsisted for only four years, and the parties were in their mid-thirties. They had amassed modest wealth by property-dealing and developing during the marriage. It was held that where substantial assets had been generated by the joint efforts of the spouses, the fact that the marriage had been a short one was irrelevant for the purposes of deciding how those assets should be distributed. Hale LJ (as she then was) stated that:

> 'where a substantial surplus had been generated by their joint efforts, it could not matter whether they had taken a short or a long time to do so'

and

> 'each should be regarded as having made an equal contribution to the assets accumulated in a joint enterprise which should then be shared equally unless there are other considerations telling against this'.

---

[2] [2003] EWCA Civ 565, [2003] 2 FLR 299, CA.

4.5   INTERPRETATION OF THE LAW POST-*WHITE*

Following *White*, in cases which are not 'needs' driven, legal practitioners, driven on by their clients, have made (and continue to make) repeated attempts to find valid reasons to depart from equality. These have included:

4.5.1   Separate or inherited property/pre-marital property

Of particular relevance (particularly when, as here, one is considering the impact of divorce upon trusts) is the argument that if assets have not been built up during the course of the marriage (such as inherited wealth – an interest in a family trust for example) they should be treated differently.

Unlike most of our European neighbours, there is no concept in English law of community of property and no declaration made by way of marriage contract at the point of entry into marriage as to whether the matrimonial 'regime' will be to pool all assets or to differentiate between what belongs to each party from the outset.

Instead, at the point of divorce, all assets – whenever and however acquired – are considered to fall within the marital 'pot' available to be distributed. That said, the courts have recognised that if an asset was acquired prior to the marriage, or was inherited by (or gifted to) one of the spouses during the marriage, this represents a contribution by that spouse to the marriage. The weight to be accorded to such a contribution will depend upon the circumstances.

This distinction was drawn in the case of *White* itself by Lord Nicholls, who said:

> 'property owned by one spouse before the marriage and inherited property whenever acquired, stand on a different footing from what may be loosely called matrimonial property. According to this view, on a breakdown of the marriage these two classes of property should not necessarily be treated in the same way. Property acquired before marriage and inherited property acquired during marriage come from a source wholly external to the marriage. In fairness, where this property exists, the spouse to whom it was given should be allowed to keep it. Conversely, the other spouse has a weaker claim to such property than he or she may have regarding matrimonial property.
>
> Plainly, when present, this factor is one of the circumstances of the case. It represents a contribution made to the welfare of the family by one of the parties to the marriage. The judge should take it into account ... However, in the ordinary course, this factor can be expected to carry little weight, if any, in a case where the claimant's financial needs cannot be met without recourse to this property.'

There has not been a great amount of case law on the point. However, the question of inherited wealth was considered in the case of *Norris v Norris*.[3] In that case Mrs Norris argued that significant funds which she had in part inherited, and in part received from family trusts, should be left out of account altogether when considering the overall assets to be divided. The judge held that it was not appropriate to leave those assets out of the equation altogether. Bennett J stated (at para 64) that:

> 'the Court is required to take into account all property of each party. That must include property acquired during the marriage by gift or succession or as a beneficiary under a trust. Thus, what comes in by statute through the front door ought not, in my judgment, be put out of the back door and thus not remain within the Court's discretionary exercise, without very good reason. In my judgment, merely because inherited property has not been touched or does not become part of the matrimonial pot is not necessarily, without more, a reason for excluding it from the Court's discretionary exercise.'

In *H v H (Financial Provision: Special Contribution)*,[4] there was further consideration of how various inheritances received by the husband and wife should be treated. There, the husband had a cash reserve of almost £400,000 which was kept in the US and which he had inherited some years prior to the divorce from his grandmother and a great aunt. The wife had inherited shares in a family business on the death of her father. These were gradually realised over the years and used either to renovate one of their homes or invested by the husband on the wife's behalf. The husband also inherited around £80,000 on the death of his father, and this money went into the purchase of their London property. The judge decided that the wife's inheritance formed part of the parties' resources, the husband having played an instrumental role in its realisation and investment. Furthermore, one of the husband's inheritances (the amount coming from his father) had similarly been put into the family pot and should be taken into account when considering how to split the parties' resources. The inheritance which had always been kept separate and apart by the husband in America should not be taken into account, given that without it a fair balance could be struck.

This approach was confirmed in *S v S (divorce: distribution of assets)*[5] in which a number of properties owned by the husband were held to be 'non-matrimonial assets' because they had been acquired by him prior to the marriage and he had done 'nothing to increase their value other than to generate passive economic growth or natural capital growth'. Burton J held in that case that the yardstick of equality should be applied to matrimonial property, with non-matrimonial property only brought into consideration if needs dictate.

---

[3] [2002] EWHC 2996, [2003] 2 FLR 1124, FD.
[4] [2002] 2 FLR 1021, FD.
[5] [2006] EWHC 2793 (Fam), [2007] 1 FLR 1496, FD.

4.5.2 Post-separation accrual

There has also been debate about how assets, which were acquired post-separation but prior to a final court hearing, should be treated. Nicholas Mostyn QC, sitting as a High Court Judge in the case of *Rossi v Rossi*[6] has held that in all ancillary relief cases a primary function of the court is to identify the matrimonial and non-matrimonial property. In order to establish within which category a particular asset falls he applies a number of dicta which include, for example:

(1)	'assets acquired or created by one party after (or during a period of) separation may qualify as non-matrimonial property if it can be said that the property in question was acquired or created by a party by virtue of his personal industry and not by use (other than incidental use) of an asset which has been created during the marriage and in respect of which the other party can validly assert an unascertained share. Passive economic growth on matrimonial property that arises after separation will not qualify as non–matrimonial property;' and

(2)	'where the post-separation asset is a bonus or other earned income, if it relates to a period when the parties were cohabiting, or to a period immediately following separation, it cannot be claimed as non-matrimonial. Indeed, a post-separation bonus should not be classed as non-matrimonial unless it related to a period which commenced at least 12 months after separation.'

In *S v S*[7] the financial proceedings were drawn out over 10 years during the course of which the husband had developed his business into a successful enterprise without any support or contribution from the wife. Singer J held that the length of the separation and the current state of company made it unfair for the wife to ask for a share in the potential of the husband's company. Although assets were to be valued as at the date of hearing rather than at the date of separation, what happened in the intervening years could be very significant. In this case the value of the husband's shares were more akin to non-matrimonial property. Singer J approved the approach in *Rossi*.

In the most recent decision of *H v H*,[8] Charles J took a different view on post-separation accrual from *Rossi v Rossi* and *S v S*. The case involved a 20-year marriage with four children. The husband worked for a major bank and his remuneration consisted of substantial bonuses and stock options. The couple separated in early January 2005. The husband received bonuses and stock options later in January 2005 and in the next two following years.

---

[6]	[2006] EWHC 1482 (Fam), [2007] 1 FLR 790, FD.
[7]	[2006] EWHC 2339 (Fam).
[8]	[2007] EWHC 459 (Fam).

The question was to what extent the bonuses and stock options formed part of the marital acquest. The total assets excluding the 2007 bonus amounted to £27m and an equal division of the assets excluding the three bonuses was agreed.

Charles J took the view that the wife was entitled to one third of the 2005 bonus, one sixth of the 2006 bonus and one twelfth of the 2007 bonus. Charles J looked at the significance of the husband's enhanced earning capacity, but stated that only a small part of the future income comprised an enhanced earning capacity to which the wife had contributed and which could be said to be a fruit or product of the marital partnership.

If there is to be a clear rule then perhaps the more arbitrary 12 month rule in *Rossi* is preferable.

Ultimately, each case will turn on its own facts, but it seems clear that inherited, pre-acquired and post-acquired wealth cannot be simply ring-fenced against claims by spouses, particularly in long marriages.

4.5.3   Exceptional/'stellar' contributions

One argument which was popular for the period immediately following the judgment in *White*, and which appears to have again returned to favour with the courts, is that if a party made an exceptional, or 'stellar', contribution to the marriage, this was a reason to move away from strict equality of division.

This argument was first considered by the Court of Appeal in the case of *Cowan v Cowan*.[9] Mr and Mrs Cowan had been married for 35 years and had accumulated assets totalling £11.5m (all of which had been built up during the marriage). Mr and Mrs Cowan had adopted traditional roles during the marriage – in that he had run the family business (developing polythene and plastic products – in particular bin-liners) while she was the homemaker. Mr Cowan argued that there should be a departure from equality of division of the assets because his particular business flair and acumen led directly to the spectacular success of the company and the family's wealth. At first instance the judge held that:

> 'the initial steps which she took, although by no means insignificant, weigh light in the balance by contrast to the contribution made by the husband's entrepreneurial flair and drive and his technical knowledge and inventiveness'.

The Court of Appeal agreed – and upheld the award to Mrs Cowan of only 38% of the total assets.

---

9   [2001] EWCA Civ 679, [2001] 2 FLR 192, CA.

Coleridge J in *G v G (financial provision: equal division)*[10] expressed his concern that assessing contribution carried with it the same disadvantages as assessing conduct (an approach which was approved more recently by Burton J in the case of *S v S* (see above)):

> 'Both concepts are compendious descriptions of the way in which one party conducted him/herself towards the other and/or the family during the marriage. And both carry with them precisely the same undesirable consequences. First, they call for a detailed retrospective at the end of a broken marriage just at a time when parties should be looking forward not back. In part that involves a determination of factual issues (and obviously the court is equipped to undertake that). But then, the facts having been established, they each call for a value judgment of the worth of each side's behaviour and translation of that worth into actual money. But by what measure and using what criteria? Negative "conduct" is one thing (particularly where it is recognisably "obvious and gross") but the valuing of positive "contribution" varies from time to time. Should a wealth creator receive more because, eg, his talents are very unusual or merely conventional but well-employed? Should a housewife receive less because part of her daily work over many years was mitigated by the employment of staff? Is there such a concept as an exceptional/special domestic contribution or can only the wealth creator earn the bonus? These are some of the arguments now regularly being deployed. It is much the same as comparing apples with pears and the debate is about as sterile or useful ...
>
> the parties are not assisted to achieve compromise when they are encouraged by the law to indulge in a detailed and lengthy retrospective involving a general rummage through the attic of their marriage to discover relics from the past to enhance their role or diminish their spouse's. Perhaps "obvious and gross" has a renewed role here. "Obvious" because it imports the concept of being very easily discernible and "gross" in the sense of it being quite abnormally large. Unless this or something similar is soon introduced to curb these debates, I fear there is a real danger that the forward-looking *White v White* innovations will be lost in a sea of post-break-up, backward-looking mutual recrimination and the court's task and role in this already uncertain area will thereby be set back at least a generation.'

Lord Nicholls in *Miller* approved that latter paragraph.

The argument was further discredited in the case of *Lambert v Lambert*.[11] In that case Mr and Mrs Lambert had been married for 23 years, and held assets totalling some £20m. The assets were in large part the proceeds of sale of a company which the husband had developed during the marriage. At first instance he had some success with his argument of 'special contribution', and Mrs Lambert was awarded 37%. However, on appeal to the Court of Appeal, this decision was overturned and the award was increased to 50%. Thorpe LJ said:

---

[10]   [2002] EWHC 1339 (Fam); [2002] 2 FLR 1143, FD.
[11]   [2002] EWCA Civ 1685, [2003] 1 FLR 139, CA.

'There must be an end to the sterile assertion that the breadwinner's contribution weighs heavier than the homemaker's ...'

and in relation to the duty of the court to assess each party's contribution:

'I do not accept that the duty requires a detailed critical appraisal of the performance of each of the parties during the marriage'.

In *H v H (Financial Provision: Special Contribution)*,[12] Peter Hughes QC (sitting as a Deputy High Court Judge) held that the contribution of the husband – a senior partner in a large City law firm – was not stellar. He said that:

'It is not easy to define what may amount to a "stellar" or really special contribution, but rather like the elephant, it is not difficult to spot when you come across it.'

The number of such 'elephants' found in reported family law cases subsequently declined until, in 2005/2006, two further cases seemed to re-establish the validity of 'stellar contribution' as an argument for moving away from the yardstick of equality. These two cases were *Sorrell v Sorrell*[13] and *Charman v Charman (No 2)*.[14]

In the former, the husband was the founder of and driving force behind the advertising agency, WPP. The family's net assets amounted to some £73m. It was a long marriage, in excess of 30 years, in the course of which they had had three children.

Despite the judge finding that Lady Sorrell had done all that could be expected of her in her role as housewife and mother, he nevertheless, decided that the assets should be divided unequally – giving 40% to her (£29m) and 60% to him (£44m), the division suggested by the husband. The judge explained that the departure from equality was due to the husband's stellar contribution. Bennett J said:

'In my judgment, the evidence establishes that the true explanation for this extraordinary success story is that the husband does possess the "spark" or "force" or "seed" of genius, call it what one will. It was by his talents as I have set out above that he generated the fortune for the family. One only has to glance at the schedule to see that the overwhelming preponderance of the fortune is derived from shares in WPP. His genius was the generator of that fortune.

The next issue, therefore, is does his "special" contribution in exceptional circumstances (for so I find) deserve recognition ... I have no difficultly in

---

[12] [2002] 2 FLR 1021, FD.
[13] [2005] EWHC 1717 (Fam), [2006] 1 FLR 497, FD.
[14] [2006] EWHC 1879 (Fam), [2007] 1 FLR 593, FD.

reaching the conclusion that it does, in the circumstances of this case. It simply would be unfair not to recognise it. If it was ignored it would in my judgment create an unfair outcome.

I do not base my decision upon the factor that the size of the family fortune "... alone justifies a conclusion of special contribution" but I do find, as I hope I have made clear, that there is within the husband "exceptional and individual" qualities as the generator of the fortune.'

In the case of *Charman*, which is discussed in detail later in this chapter the family's assets, which were found to be in the order of £131m, and which were built up entirely during the marriage, were split 37% to the wife, and 63% to the husband. Again this was largely due to the judge's finding that:

'Whether the husband's remarkable abilities in the insurance world, his energy and wealth creation (as I have summarised above and as fully described in his affidavits, those of his witnesses and in argument) are "conduct" or "a contribution to the welfare of the family" in the broadest sense their product is wholly exceptional, "gross and obvious" ...

I consider that one way or another this factor weighs and departure from equality is fair. So far so good.'

The difficulty Coleridge J found was in quantifying the departure from equality. He stated that he 'can find little hard ground once the self-justifying fairness of 50/50 is departed from'. He did not identify how he reached his conclusion that 37% was the correct departure from equality, save to say:

'If adjustment is appropriate, especially in these huge money cases, I think, it should be meaningful and significant and not a token one.'

4.5.4   Sheer scale of wealth

In *Charman*, Coleridge J was alive to the fact that in cases where significant sums were involved (he referred to cases of £30m or more):

'the sums involved and at stake make the cost of the litigation although very high, relatively proportionate, so full contests result. The parties need all the help they can get from previous authority to assist in negotiation. In a field as discretionary as this one it is often hard to provide real guidance which limits rather than promotes debate.'

His suggestion, although he was careful to say that he had not applied this methodology to his judgment in *Charman*, was that a tariff 'of percentage bands which decreased as the size of these extraordinary fortunes increased might prove to be helpful guidance and, ultimately no less fair than the current expensive uncertainty'. It remains to be seen whether this is taken up. Any such tariff would (unless there were further legislation not envisaged at present) always remain subject to the s 25 factors.

On Appeal to the Court of Appeal, Coleridge J's decision was upheld.[15]

The Court of Appeal confirmed that the notion of a special contribution 'survived' the decision in *Miller*. The judgment confirmed that special contribution could be non-financial as well as financial and that in some cases the amount of the wealth generated will be so extraordinary that that will be sufficient to demonstrate an exceptional and individual quality which deserves special treatment.[16]

In other cases the Court of Appeal held that it would be necessary for the spouse to independently establish an exceptional and individual quality, whether by genius in business or in some other field.

The Court of Appeal declined to identify any figure as a guideline threshold for special contribution.[17]

However, the suggested threshold from Counsel for both parties, namely £30m to £50m seems to be in the right area, even though not expressly approved. The Court of Appeal went on to make clear that where special contribution is established that would lead to at least a 55%–45% division but that even in an extreme case it 'would be most unlikely to give rise to percentages of division of matrimonial property further from equality than 66.6%–33.3%'.[18]

4.6 REFINEMENT OF CASE LAW IN *MILLER* AND *MCFARLANE*

On 24 May 2006, the House of Lords handed down their judgment in the cases of *Miller and McFarlane*.[19] This was the first family law judgment handed down by the House since *White* in 2000. It was eagerly anticipated. The hope was that it would clarify the issues raised in the earlier case law and allow practitioners to advise with rather more certainty about the outcome of financial claims made on divorce. However, to date the judgment appears to have created more debate than it has resolved.

The facts of each case were unusual.

In *Miller*, the parties were married for less than three years. Mr Miller was worth about £17.5m, plus shares in a company which he had bought

---

[15] *Charman v Charman (No 4)* [2007] EWCA Civ 503, CA.
[16] At para 80.
[17] At para 88.
[18] At para 90.
[19] [2006] UKHL 24, [2006] 1 FLR 1186, HL.

during the marriage and which were estimated to be worth somewhere between £12m and £18m. This latter represented the only significant amount which was acquired during their relationship. Mrs Miller was awarded £5m at first instance, which award was upheld in the Court of Appeal and by the House of Lords.

In *McFarlane*, the parties had been married for 16 years. They had three children, aged 16, 15 and 9 at the time of the House of Lords' judgment. Mr McFarlane was a partner in Deloitte & Touche, the leading firm of accountants. Mrs McFarlane gave up her career as a solicitor when she was pregnant with their second child. Their combined capital assets were in the region of £3m. Mr McFarlane's net annual income was in the order of £750,000. They agreed to split the capital equally, but this was insufficient in itself to meet Mrs McFarlane's income and capital needs. She estimated that her income needs were £128,000 per annum. As the husband estimated his own income needs at only £60,000 to £80,000 per annum there was a significant surplus of income. The district judge awarded her £250,000 per annum during their joint lives. On the husband's appeal this amount was reduced to £180,000, but then reinstated to £250,000 by the Court of Appeal. The Court of Appeal's judgment was upheld by the House of Lords on this point.

In the judgment, both Lord Nicholls and Baroness Hale identify three strands to be considered in every case when looking at the s 25 factors – namely needs, compensation and sharing.

As Lord Nicholls puts it, in considering needs 'in most cases the search for fairness largely begins and ends at this stage'. Baroness Hale makes it clear that needs are to be generously interpreted.

The concept of 'sharing' is also familiar to practitioners since the judgment in *White* in 2000. Lord Nicholls confirms that this principle is as applicable to short marriages as to long marriages, and that to confine the application of *White* to long marriages would 're-introduce precisely the sort of discrimination the *White* case was intended to negate'. He draws a distinction between 'matrimonial' assets (which he defines as the financial product of the parties' common endeavour) and 'non-matrimonial' assets (being property which the parties bring with them into the marriage or acquire by inheritance or gift). As to the first, he says that 'in principle the entitlement of each party to a share of the matrimonial property is the same however long or short the marriage is'. However, when considering 'non-matrimonial property' the duration of the marriage becomes:

> 'highly relevant ... With longer marriages, the position is not ... straightforward. Non-matrimonial property represents a contribution made to the marriage by one of the parties. Sometimes, as the years pass, the weight fairly to be attributed to this contribution will diminish, sometimes it will not.'

So far, the post-*White* case-law is endorsed. However, Baroness Hale goes further by suggesting that non-matrimonial, or 'non-family assets' include business or investment assets which have been generated solely or mainly by the efforts of one party.

The concept of 'compensation' is entirely new, and is not prefigured anywhere within the legislation. It is defined by Lord Nicholls as 'aimed at redressing any significant prospective economic disparity between the parties arising from the way they conducted their marriage' and by Baroness Hale as being for 'relationship-generated disadvantage'. In *McFarlane* the relationship-generated disadvantage is clear. Mrs McFarlane had foregone a professional career as successful and highly paid as that of Mr McFarlane, in order to devote herself to acting as the primary carer of the children. The award of periodical payments over and above her simple needs was said to be, in part, a recognition of this relationship-generated disadvantage. How this might be applied other than in relation to this very specific set of facts remains to be seen.

The procedure to be adopted when considering these three principles was suggested by Lord Nicholls to be 'to consider first the requirements of compensation and then to give effect to the sharing entitlement'. Baroness Hale however, suggests that there:

> 'cannot be a hard and fast rule about whether one starts with equal sharing and departs if need or compensation supply a reason to do so, or whether one starts with need and compensation and shares the balance'.

As to the question of special contribution, both Lord Nicholls and Baroness Hale are united in their suggestion that any such contribution (like any form of conduct) should be considered only if it is so marked that it would be inequitable to disregard it.

4.7 FURTHER DEVELOPMENT BY THE COURT OF APPEAL IN *CHARMAN*

The Court of Appeal in *Charman* endeavoured to reconcile some of the differences in the House of Lords' judgments in *Miller*. However, the most surprising statement by the Court of Appeal, at least in theoretical terms, was that there is no longer a yardstick against which provisional awards are to be measured, but rather a presumption of equal sharing, which is no longer required to be postponed until the end of the statutory exercise.[20]

The Court of Appeal went on to say that apart from in short marriage cases, the principle of equal sharing 'applies to all the parties' property but, to the extent that their property is non-matrimonial, there is likely to

---

[20] At para 65.

be better reason for departure from equality'.[21] This presumption of equal sharing reflects the reality of the approach of many practitioners and the judiciary and therefore to some extent it justifies and codifies the reality of what has been happening in the courts since *White*.

The Court of Appeal further stated that the enquiry in an application of ancillary relief is always in two stages, namely computation and distribution. Likely future income always has to be considered, even if the assets are substantial, although the Court of Appeal declined to indicate whether it thought that a party's earning capacity was in itself an asset which should, to some extent, be subject to the sharing principle.

Counsel for the husband had suggested that Coleridge J should have undertaken an 'incremental' approach in going through the MCA 1973, s 25 factors. That criticism was not accepted and it was stated that there are cases in which the result of applying the sharing principle will subsume the result of applying the principles of need and (if engaged) of compensation. This was particularly so in cases of very substantial assets. The Court of Appeal concluded[22] that 'it seemed pointless to undertake an elaborate process of provisional quantification if such then had to be abandoned by reference to percentages. But, to the extent that the yardstick constrained it to approach the matter in that way, *Miller* has released the court from that constraint'.[23]

4.8   PRE-NUPTIAL AGREEMENTS

Unlike many other jurisdictions in England and Wales, it is not possible to agree, in any binding way, what the financial outcome should be on any subsequent divorce/dissolution of civil partnership. Attempts to do so, by entering into pre-nuptial agreements, have been said to be contrary to public policy (see *Hyman v Hyman*[24]).

The current legislation does not deal specifically with pre-nuptial agreements (or their civil partnership equivalent) and there is no requirement that a court should either ignore, or follow, their terms. To date, entry into such agreements has tended to be considered by the courts as part of all the circumstances of the case (s 25(1) of the MCA 1973), and as conduct which it would be inequitable to ignore (s 25(2)(g)).

That there can be no absolute guarantee of any particular outcome on the dissolution of a marriage or civil partnership because of the discretionary nature of English divorce law, is both its strength and its weakness. It

---

[21]   At para 66.
[22]   At para 76(b).
[23]   At para 76(b).
[24]   [1929] AC 601, HL.

allows for bespoke solutions to any individual set of facts, but also means that there is a significant range of possible outcomes in any particular case.

The UK Government has, in the past, identified the discretionary system as a problem. At para 4.46 of the 1998 Consultation Paper *Supporting Families* it said:

> 'The court's discretion to allocate property means that the outcome of the case is hard to forecast, even with the advice of experienced lawyers. It is not possible, from the existing legislation, for the lay person to get a clear view of what they can expect to receive on divorce.'

To remedy this it suggested that pre-nuptial agreements should be binding. Supporting Families suggested an over-arching objective ('that the court should exercise its powers so as to endeavour to do that which is fair and reasonable between the parties and any child of the family') together with a framework, which the court should follow when reaching a decision on financial settlement on divorce. It proposed (at para 4.49) that, subject to meeting the housing needs of the family, the next step would be to consider and apply the terms of any pre-nuptial agreement provided that:

(1) there are no children of the family;

(2) the agreement is not unenforceable under the general law of contract;

(3) both parties had independent legal advice;

(4) implementation of its terms would not, in the view of the court, cause significant injustice;

(5) both parties gave full disclosure of assets and property; and

(6) the agreement was made at least 21 days prior to the marriage.

Case-law, and opinion within the legal profession, demonstrates a definite shift towards recognition and support for pre-nuptial agreements. In *S v S (divorce: staying proceedings)*[25] Wilson J, in a much quoted paragraph, said that:

> 'Where other jurisdictions ... have been persuaded that there are cases where justice can only be served by confining the parties to their rights under prenuptial agreements, we should be cautious about too categorically asserting the contrary. I can find nothing in section 25 to compel a conclusion, so much at odds with personal freedoms to make arrangements

---

[25] [1997] 2 FLR 100, FD.

for ourselves, that escape from solemn bargains, carefully struck by informed adults, is readily available here. It all depends.'

In 2003, in *K v K (Ancillary Relief: Prenuptial Agreement)*,[26] Rodger Hayward-Smith QC, sitting as a Deputy High Court Judge, held a wife to the capital sum (£120,000) to which she had agreed in the pre-nuptial agreement, notwithstanding that the husband was worth £25m.

In that case the husband and wife, who had one child, separated after a marriage of only 14 months. Prior to the marriage the wife, who had a trust fund of £1m from which she drew income, discovered she was pregnant and her mother exerted pressure on the husband to marry her. The husband had wanted a long engagement, but the couple agreed to marry and signed a prenuptial agreement at the instigation of the wife's father. The couple received independent financial advice and the solicitors were informed of the pregnancy.

The judge held that there was no injustice to the wife in holding her to the terms of the agreement insofar as capital was concerned – particularly as the marriage was so short and the wife had contributed nothing to the husband's wealth. He took into account also the fact that the husband had married under pressure from the wife's family and on the understanding that capital provision on divorce (if the marriage was a short one) would be governed by the agreement.

He did, however, accept that the wife would (as the primary carer of their child) have a housing need and made provision for the husband to acquire an appropriate property for the wife and child – to be held in trust on the basis that the capital would eventually revert to the husband. He also awarded the wife a modest amount of maintenance for herself given that she would be making an ongoing contribution to the family by way of caring for the child.

In *C v C (Divorce: Stay of English Proceedings)*,[27] Johnson J gave considerable weight to the fact that the French husband and wife in that case had both entered into a prenuptial agreement drawn up under French law and subsequently executed mutual wills in accordance with French law under which they reaffirmed that their financial relationship both during life and after death should be regulated by the French Civil Code. In those circumstances, where there was a dispute about the appropriate forum for the dissolution of their marriage, he held that it would be contrary to fairness to allow the wife's English proceedings to continue, and they should be stayed whilst the French proceedings initiated by the husband should continue.

---

[26]   [2003] 1 FLR 120, FD.
[27]   [2001] 1 FLR 624, FD.

There have been two recent cases on pre-nuptial agreements. The first is *Ella v Ella*.[28] In that case the Court of Appeal considered the terms of a 'pre-nuptial contract' under Israeli law. Although it is not clear from the judgment, it seems as if the agreement was in fact a marriage contract similar to the continental European model, electing separate property with future assets belonging exclusively to the spouse creating them. It also made clear provision that the law of Israel should apply on any questions affecting property as between the spouses.

The existence of the marriage contract stating that all matters arising from the marriage should be dealt with in the Israeli courts was one of the decisive factors in the English divorce being stayed in favour of the Israeli divorce. The Court of Appeal stated (at para 26) that the judge 'was perfectly right ... to regard the pre-nuptial agreement as a major factor'. This was despite the fact that the couple had lived primarily in London, rather than Israel, throughout the marriage.

The other recent case concerning pre-nuptial agreements is that of *Bentinck v Bentinck*.[29] That was an Anglo-Swiss forum dispute in which the existence of a Swiss marriage contract was a key element in the English court's decision to stay the English divorce in favour of the Swiss divorce which was commenced first of all.

Another main aspect leading to the stay of the English divorce was the fact that the husband's claim for maintenance against himself in the Swiss court rendered the Swiss court first seised under the purposes of Art 21 of the Lugano Convention.

Both of these cases are examples of how the existence of a pre-nuptial agreement or marriage contract, given the right circumstances, electing that the divorce takes place in a country outside England, can carry significant weight with the English court.

Despite the growing strength of opinion in support of the validity of pre-nuptial agreements, there has been no change to UK legislation, nor does it seem likely in the current political climate that there will be any in the immediate future, although there is currently[30] a move to bring a private member's Bill before Parliament to enable their enforceability. To date, there has been no reported case in which a pre-nuptial agreement has been upheld in its entirety. Some members of the judiciary have hinted that, in the right case, the Court of Appeal could and would make clear that pre-nuptial agreements should carry more weight in the construction of s 25, but at present the, rather uncertain, position remains.

---

[28]   [2007] EWCA Civ 99.
[29]   [2007] EWCA Civ 157.
[30]   July 2007.

The Court of Appeal in *Charman v Charman (No 4)*,[31] in particular in the postscript from para 106, and earlier at the end of para 86, implied a willingess to give greater weight to pre-nuptial agreements.

4.9   FINANCIAL DIVISION UPON DIVORCE IN OTHER JURISDICTIONS

It is beyond the scope of this book to comment in any real detail upon the way in which finances are dealt with on divorce in other jurisdictions. However, it is a truism that the English court's discretion in deciding the outcome of financial applications on divorce is very broad. Commonwealth jurisdictions such as Australia and New Zealand have legislation for asset division on divorce similar to the English system, and many offshore jurisdictions have legislation and thus an approach which is virtually identical to the English system. However, in almost every country in Europe (and indeed in most states in America) the outcome is much more circumscribed by legislation, or capable of being much more circumscribed in that pre-nuptial agreements or marriage contracts are upheld.

In most countries in continental Europe, for example, couples are obliged to elect a matrimonial regime upon marriage to provide either for community of property (where all assets acquired during a marriage are considered to be held equally by the spouses) or for a regime where each party's assets are considered to be absolutely separate. In the absence of an election generally a particular form of community of property regime will be said to apply.

In many states in America a similar concept of community of property or equitable distribution applies to assets or wealth built up during a marriage.

The difference lies in the application of pre-nuptial agreements in these jurisdictions. Whilst a clearer (and perhaps stricter) mathematical division of assets tends to apply upon divorce, parties are at least able to specify at the outset of a marriage whether or not they wish that regime to apply or how they wish to vary it.

It is notable that, at present, as a result of the broad discretion and the recent case-law outlined above, where there is a choice of jurisdiction, the economically weaker spouse will regularly be advised to begin divorce proceedings in England, in preference to other jurisdictions.

---

[31]   [2007] EWCA Civ 503, [2007] 1 FLR 1246, CA.

CHAPTER 5

DIVORCE LINES OF ATTACK ON TRUSTS

5.1 INTRODUCTION

There are two ways in which a trust may be attacked in the context of ancillary relief proceedings. Where the trust is categorised by the family court as a 'nuptial settlement', the court has the power to make an order against the trustee to vary the settlement. In the alternative, the court could choose to take the trust assets into account as a resource of one or both of the parties to the marriage and make an order against the beneficiary spouse taking account that resource who is a party to the marriage where the court considers that that party will have funds made available to him or her by the trustee. In this chapter, these lines of attack will be considered in detail, together with the likely circumstances in which the court would use each of them. Settlors and beneficiaries of trusts often assume that since the trust assets are not in their name, they will not be taken into account on divorce and so safe from attack.

The impact of the House of Lords decision in *White v White* in October 2000 is only beginning to feed through into reported decisions as to the treatment of trusts on divorce. Since ancillary relief is now concerned with percentage division of assets on divorce, rather than on a pre-*White* needs based approach, trusts are increasingly considered as part of the asset pool to be divided. This is particularly so after the Court of Appeal decision in *Charman v Charman (No 4)*,[1] in which it was held that an equal division of assets from all sources, not just generated during the marriage, is a presumption, no longer a starting point or yardstick against which to measure provisional awards; this presumption is rebuttable in appropriate cases based on the source of the assets.

Charman v Charman has in effect affirmed a view of some commentators that England now has a form of community property and so assets generated during the marriage and settled by one spouse on trust are perceived to be part of the other spouse's 'unascertained share'. This has blurred the trusts as a resource approach to such an extent that trust assets in some cases can be treated as if those assets were in the settlor's bank account, which is clearly wrong as a matter of family and trust law.

---

[1]   [2007] EWCA Civ 503, [2007] 1 FLR 1246, CA. See further Appendix 2.

Post-*White* the starting point has to be to work out what assets are to be shared. The question is, how should trust assets be regarded?

Trust assets are not the same as the personal assets of a spouse. In the same way, as explained by the Court of Appeal in *Martin-Dye v Martin-Dye*[2] pensions are treated differently, and different types of assets should be shared; one spouse should not end up with either all cash or all pensions.

In this section two ways in which a court can take into account trust assets on divorce will be analysed and explained. Although reference is made to spouses throughout the chapter, the law is identical on dissolution of a civil partnership. Therefore, reference to spouses should include civil partners unless otherwise stated.

5.2   VARIATION OF NUPTIAL SETTLEMENTS

The most significant and direct power the court has regarding trusts is to vary the terms so as to provide a non-beneficiary spouse with money from the trust. This power exists for foreign trusts with foreign assets too, subject to issues of enforcement dealt with in Chapter 8.

The statutory authority for the court's power to vary a nuptial settlement is set out in the MCA 1973, s 24(1)(c), which states:

'On granting a Decree of [divorce, nullity or judicial separation] or at any time thereafter the court may make ... an order varying for the parties of the marriage and of the children of the family or either or any of them any ante-nuptial or post-nuptial settlement (including such a settlement made by will or codicil) made on the parties to the marriage, other than one in the form of a pension arrangement (within the meaning of s 25D below)'.

There are parallel provisions in the Civil Partnership Act 2004 which allow a variation upon dissolution or nullity proceedings or separation order following a civil partnership:[3]

'6(1) The court may make one or more property adjustment orders—

(a)   on making a dissolution, nullity or separation order, or
(b)   at any time afterwards ...

7(1) The property adjustment orders are— ...

(c)   an order varying for the benefit of—
        (i)   the civil partners and the children of the family, or
        (ii)   either or any of them,

a relevant settlement; ...

---

[2]   [2006] EWCA Civ 681, [2006] 2 FLR 901, CA.
[3]   CPA 2004, Sch 5, paras 6 and 7.

(3) In this paragraph— ...

> "relevant settlement" means, in relation to a civil partnership, a settlement made, during its subsistence or in anticipation of its formation, on the civil partners including one made by will or codicil, but not including one in the form of a pension arrangement (within the meaning of Part 4).'

No doubt in drafting this definition the Parliamentary draftsperson intended to encapsulate the current law on divorce. The reference to 'anticipation of its formation' may be more restrictive than on divorce.

The English court also has powers to award financial relief following an overseas divorce under Pt III of the Matrimonial and Family Proceedings Act 1984. These powers are subject to certain jurisdictional requirements as follows:

An applicant can apply for relief and the court will have in mind a checklist of factors including:[4]

(a) the connection which the parties to the marriage have with England and Wales;

(b) the connection which those parties have with the country in which the marriage was dissolved or annulled or in which they were legally separated;

(c) the connection which those parties have with any other country outside England and Wales;

(d) any financial benefit which the applicant or a child of the family has received, or is likely to receive, in consequence of the divorce, annulment or legal separation, by virtue of any agreement or the operation of the law of a country outside England and Wales;

(e) in a case where an order has been made by a court in a country outside England and Wales requiring the other party to the marriage to make any payment or transfer any property for the benefit of the applicant or a child of the family, the financial relief given by the order and the extent to which the order has been complied with or is likely to be complied with;

(f) any right which the applicant has, or has had, to apply for financial relief from the other party to the marriage under the law of any country outside England and Wales and if the applicant has omitted to exercise that right the reason for that omission;

---

[4]   Matrimonial and Family Proceedings Act 1984, Pt III, s 16(2).

(g) the availability in England and Wales of any property in respect of which an order under this Part of this Act in favour of the applicant could be made;

(h) the extent to which any order made under this Part of this Act is likely to be enforceable;

(i) the length of time which has elapsed since the date of the divorce, annulment or legal separation.

The powers of the court are identical to those on divorce with one qualification in s 20, the relevant parts of which are as follows:

> **'20 Restriction of powers of court where jurisdiction depends on matrimonial home in England or Wales**
>
> (1) Where the court has jurisdiction to entertain an application for an order for financial relief by reason only of the situation in England and Wales of a dwelling-house which was a matrimonial home of the parties, the court may make under section 17 above any one or more of the following orders (but no other)—...
>
> (e) an order varying for the benefit of the parties to the marriage and of the children of the family or either or any of them any ante-nuptial or post-nuptial settlement (including such a settlement made by will or codicil) made on the parties to the marriage so far as that settlement relates to an interest in the dwelling-house; or
>
> (f) an order extinguishing or reducing the interest of either of the parties to the marriage under any such settlement so far as that interest is an interest in the dwelling-house ...'

As explained below, in many circumstances the purchase of a property by a trust, which may not be a nuptial settlement, for spouses to live in, will constitute itself the creation of a nuptial settlement. The power to vary a nuptial settlement after a foreign divorce may come as a surprise to settlors and trustees.

5.2.1 History

The power of the court to vary settlements on divorce dates back to the Matrimonial Causes Act 1859, although the power to settle property following divorce (in very limited circumstances) dates back two years earlier to the Matrimonial Causes Act 1857. It was commonplace in the nineteenth century for wealthy families to establish settlements upon marriage for the benefit of the wife in order to preserve for her an interest in her own property (which would have otherwise belonged to her husband at least prior to 1882). On divorce it was considered appropriate that the court should be able to make an award in the husband's favour, varying that trust especially if the wife had caused the breakdown of the marriage. Although the practice of marriage settlements has become almost non-existent, the importance of this statutory power should not be understated. Over time, its application has broadened to include other settlements and other arrangements which include a 'nuptial element' although the introduction of property adjustment orders and lump sum orders has made this power of the court somewhat specialised. As far as the interpretation of the section is concerned, the court has traditionally applied the same commonsense and 'broad brush' approach which applies elsewhere in ancillary relief proceedings.

5.2.2 The breadth of the court's power

Indeed, the court has made use of the power to vary settlements not only where a formal trust exists but also in circumstances where there is no formal arrangement. In such instances, the court has construed the existence of a trust arrangement or settlement so that it could be varied for the benefit of the applicant. Not only does the power extend to informal arrangements, but it even extends beyond the court's jurisdiction in England. Even where the proper law of the trust is not the law of England and Wales, the trustee is not resident in England and the trust assets are held outside of the court's jurisdiction, the court has the power to vary a nuptial settlement.[5] In the 1934 case of *Goff v Goff*[6] Sir Boyd Merriman P was concerned with a New York trust. He said:

> 'It is clear from the decisions in *Nunneley* and *Forsyth* that this court has the power to vary a settlement inter partes even though it comprises property out of the jurisdiction and the trusts are administered by trustees out of the jurisdiction and the settlement is governed by foreign law.'

The issue in such circumstances then becomes one of whether an order of the English court for variation of a foreign settlement is enforceable against assets in England and/or in that jurisdiction. For more detail on this question, see Chapter 8.

5.2.3 What is an 'ante or post-nuptial settlement'?

In order to determine whether a settlement is one capable of variation by a court, it must first be identified as being an 'ante or post-nuptial settlement'.

There are two limbs to this question:

(1)   What is a 'settlement'? and

(2)   What constitutes the 'ante/post-nuptial' element?

---

[5]   *Nunneley v Nunneley and Marrian* (1890) 15 PD 186.
[6]   [1934] P 107.

The present power derives from the Matrimonial Causes Act 1973 (as set out above). An extract from the 1969 Law Commission Report No 25 'Family Law: Report on Financial Provision in Matrimonial Proceedings'[7] reveals more about the thinking behind the section:

> '[66] The next problem is to define the powers of the court on such an application. In our view the court should have power:
>
> (a) to order settlements or transfers of any property to which either or both spouses are entitled, whether in possession or reversion, for the benefit of the spouses and children or any of them; and
>
> (b) to vary, for the benefit of the spouses, the children or any of them any ante- or post-nuptial settlements.
>
> Proposal (a) widens the existing law in section 17(2) of the Matrimonial Causes Act 1965 by enabling the court to order the husband to settle or transfer property (at present he can only be ordered to pay cash under s 16) and by generalising its application so that it applies to nullity as well as to divorce and judicial separation, and irrespective of the grounds upon which any of these decrees are based. Proposal (b) merely extends the existing section 17(1) of that Act so that it applies to judicial separation as well as to divorce and nullity. Its scope of operation would, however, be somewhat diminished in practice. As we have pointed out, because of the present restricted scope of section 17(2) the courts have given an exceptionally wide construction to "settlements" it will be necessary to invoke section 17(1) only where there is a settlement in the true sense; where there is joint property it will no longer be necessary to treat this as settled property since the same result will be achieved more rationally by ordering a settlement or transfer of the interest of one or other spouse under the amended section 17(2). We think, too, that the power to vary should continue to be limited to ante- or post-nuptial settlements (ie those made on the parties qua husband and wife) and not to all settlements; only if the settlement is a "marriage" settlement in this broad sense is it appropriate that the court should have power to vary it in exercise of its matrimonial jurisdiction. We have considered whether some clearer expression could be substituted for "ante- or post-nuptial" but are unable to suggest anything better. The existing expression is familiar to lawyers and the courts, hallowed by long usage and, in meaning, now reasonably definite; to change it would be likely to do more harm than good. It should, however, be made clear that the expression "ante- or post-nuptial settlements" includes one made by will as well inter vivos settlements; it has been held that disposition by will is not at present included even though this directs the property concerned to be held on the same trusts as a marriage settlement which can be varied.'

5.2.3.1 'Settlement'

As explained above, 'settlement' has a broad meaning in this context. In *Lort-Williams v Lort-Williams*[8] a life policy which was taken out during the marriage was varied under the equivalent power to s 24(1)(c). It was held that the object of taking out the policy was that the wife would

---

7   HC 448.

8   [1951] 2 All ER 241, CA.

benefit from it, provided the power of appointment was exercised in her favour. In that case, the judgment of Denning LJ (as he then was) included the following clarification:

> 'The word "settlement" in s 25 of the Matrimonial Causes Act 1950, is not used in the conveyancing sense; it includes any provision by a husband for the future benefit of his wife if it proceeds on the footing of the then existing marriage. It does not cease to be a settlement on her because the provision is not absolute but only contingent; nor does it cease to be a settlement on her because it may in its terms also be applicable for the benefit of a second wife by a subsequent marriage.'

The House of Lords considered the point in the 1995 case of *Brooks v Brooks*.[9] In that case, Mr Brooks' retirement benefit scheme (which was set up after the marriage) was held to be a nuptial settlement as the scheme rules provided for payment of pension to Mr Brooks on his retirement with a provision that he could elect a portion of his pension to provide, from the date of his death, a deferred pension for life for his spouse. In addition, these death benefits were payable at the discretion of the company to the members of the class comprising Mr Brooks' spouse, children, parents and grandchildren and the issue of any of them, and any persons nominated by Mr Brooks in his life, with a longstop provision in favour of Mr Brooks' executors.

In his judgment, Lord Nicholls said:

> 'The section is concerned with a settlement "made on the parties to the marriage". So, broadly stated, the disposition must be one which makes some form of continuing provision for both or either of the parties to a marriage, with or without provision for their children.
>
> Applying this approach, there is no difficulty with a disposition which creates interests in succession in specified property. Nor is there difficulty where the interests are concurrent but discretionary. Concurrent joint interests are nearer the borderline, such as a case where parties to a marriage hold the matrimonial home as beneficial joint tenants or tenants in common. Even in such a case, however, given the restrictions which will impede any sale of the house while the marriage subsists, this type of case has rightly been held to fall within the scope of the section [s 24(1)(c) of the Matrimonial Causes Act 1973]. Periodical payment provisions have also been controversial. But income provision from settled property would readily qualify, and it is only a short step from this to include income provision which takes the form of an obligation by one party to the marriage to make periodical payments to the other. This was held to be so from the earliest days of this statutory provision whose ancestry stretches back to the Matrimonial Causes Act 1859.'

---

[9]   [1995] 3 ALL ER 257, HL.

Reliance on Lord Nicholls' comments has recently been criticised by Thorpe LJ in the 2004 case of *Charalambous v Charalambous*[10] in which he said, with reference to Leading Counsel for the husband's reliance upon Lord Nicholls' definition:

> 'That is, of course, an unimpeachable generalisation that was perfectly sufficient for the needs of the case then before the House. It is, in my judgment, unrealistic to suggest that it is conclusive of a point that was not before the House and one that is not covered by any existing authority. The words taken out of context provide an insubstantial foundation for Mr Francis's submission, particularly since it is at odds with the facts and circumstances surrounding The Hickory Trust.'

It is not clear precisely what Thorpe LJ meant by this statement. In *Brooks*, the issue before the House was as to whether s 24(1)(c) of the MCA 1973 was broad enough to encompass the Husband's pension scheme. The House of Lords was not asked to define the meaning of a 'nuptial settlement', and therefore Lord Nicholls' comment above must be obiter.

Notwithstanding Thorpe LJ's analysis, the jurisprudence all tends to suggest that the court has been anxious to preserve the breadth of the definition. In the 1902 case of *Blood v Blood*,[11] Gorell Barnes J commented on the equivalent section at that time as follows:

> 'I have considered the words of s 5 of the Act with great care and it appears to me that they do confer such a power as is contended for by the Petitioner. Those words are extremely wide, and I am anxious that they should not, by any construction the court may put upon them, be narrowed in any way. To narrow them would be undesirable for this reason: the various circumstances which come before the court, and for which this section is brought into operation, are so diverse that it is to my mind extremely important that, so far as possible, the court should have power to deal with all the cases that come before it, and in dealing with them, to meet the justice of the case. I, therefore, do not desire to see any narrow interpretation placed upon the words of the section.'

In the recent case of *N v N*,[12] Coleridge J referred to this quotation, and quoted Pearce J in the 1951 case of *Parrington v Parrington*:[13]

> 'In my opinion, I am entitled, as Henn Collins J did in *Joss v Joss*, to put myself in the position of the settlor and take the relevant facts as being recited in the deed, not for the purpose of inquiring into the motive of either party or of contradicting the deed by consideration of some motive that I might infer from such facts, but merely to find out what was the substance of the transaction.'

[10] [2004] EWCA Civ 1030, [2004] 2 FLR 1093, CA.
[11] [1902] P 190, CA.
[12] [2005] EWHC 2908 (Fam), [2006] 1 FLR 856, FD.
[13] [1951] 2 All ER 916.

Coleridge J considered the facts. The trust had been set up for the benefit of the husband's grandmother. After the death of the husband's mother and her sister, the continuation of the trust conveyed no benefit for the husband's cousins, who were also beneficiaries, because they were not resident in the UK for tax purposes, and the offshore status of the trust did not materially affect them. Once funds had been distributed to them, the fund continued for the benefit of the husband as the sole discretionary beneficiary. The parties were married in 2000 and shortly before, at the husband's request, the trustee purchased a property called 'Woodlands' via a Bahamian corporation. They also made a distribution so that the wife could run an equestrian centre at the property. A few months prior to her claim for ancillary relief being filed by the wife in Form A, a tenancy agreement was signed to give comfort to the mortgagees of the property that the parties' occupation of Woodlands was a proper commercial arrangement between the trustee as landlord and the parties as tenants and that interest on a loan would be paid.

Coleridge J had no hesitation in classifying this tenancy arrangement (as opposed to the trust itself) an ante-nuptial settlement. In doing so, he identified (at para 33) the approach to be taken:

> 'My task is to consider what the real substance of the arrangement was which governed this property. The authorities make it clear that I should consider the question broadly and ask myself whether or not it was an arrangement which made ongoing provision for the husband, wife and/or child in those capacities. Motive is irrelevant.'

He had this to say on the substance of the arrangement:

> 'This property was bought by the trust during the parties' engagement and prior to their marriage. I think there can be no doubt that it was nuptial. In terms of the question of ongoing provision for them during their marriage, it is hard to think of any arrangement that is more ongoing than the provision of a matrimonial home.'

Nor did the existence of the tenancy provide any shield for the husband in resisting the wife's application to vary the settlement:

> 'If the court examines the true character of the arrangement, the husband and the trustees always remained in the relationship of trustee and beneficiary and the tenancy did not affect that fundamental position. In my judgment that was a subordinate and intermediate legal arrangement which did not undermine the fundamental relationship of trustee and beneficiary which pre-existed its creation and has carried on since its expiry. As I see it, the settlement stood behind that tenancy which, in a sense, was only a part of the terms of the settlement.'

On the facts, Coleridge J held that there was power to vary the settlement of the property, as opposed to the original trust purchasing the property through the offshore company. Therefore the wife was entitled to a share of the sale proceeds.

Assuming that this decision is correct and not successfully appealed in another case, it has wide ranging consequences for the past or future purchase of properties by offshore trusts in England. All such property purchases, assuming the properties are to be used by both spouses, are assets of nuptial settlements capable of variation on divorce in England.

If such a nuptial element unusually cannot be inferred, then if there is evidence that the underlying company has been controlled by the husband, the corporate veil may be lifted; see *Nicholas v Nicholas*,[14] and *Green v Green*,[15] more recently considered and explained by Bodey J in *Mubarak v Mubarak*.[16]

The following arrangements, in the past, also have been held to constitute settlements capable of variation:

- a disposition creating interests in succession in specified property;

- income provision from settled property;

- income provision taking the form of an obligation by one party to the marriage to make periodical payments to the other (*Worsley v Worsley and Wignall*[17]);

- a Separation Deed (*Worsley v Worsley and Wignall*); and

- the outright transfer of half of a house (Denning J in *Smith v Smith*[18]) (although this decision was subsequently challenged in *Prescott (formerly Fellowes) v Fellowes*[19]).

While it is possible to classify a life assurance policy as a nuptial settlement capable of variation, the power to vary a pension scheme in the same way has now been removed following the coming into force of the Welfare Reform and Pensions Act 1999 and the introduction of specific powers in relation to pension sharing. After the coming into force of this Act, s 24(1)(c) of the MCA 1973 was amended specifically to exclude pension arrangements which could be shared using the new powers under

---

[14]   [1984] FLR 285, CA.
[15]   [1993] 1 FLR 326, FD.
[16]   [2001] 1 FLR 673, FD.
[17]   (1869) LR 1 P & D 648.
[18]   [1945] 1 All ER 584.
[19]   [1958] P 260, CA.

s 24B of the MCA 1973. Section 24(1)(c) has now been adjusted and includes a reference to pension arrangement as defined in s 25D.

In essence, the family court is more than happy to construe an arrangement not traditionally considered a settlement as such for the purposes of variation under the statutory provision.

5.2.3.2 'Ante- / post-nuptial'

For a settlement to be considered a 'nuptial settlement' there has to be a connection between the settlement and the marriage – ie the settlement has to be upon the husband or wife or both in the character of spouses, with reference to their present or future married state. The case-law suggests that it is significantly easier to determine the existence of this element if the settlement was made after the date of the marriage (a 'post-nuptial settlement'). Having said that, it should be perfectly possible (though more difficult to prove), where a settlement has been made after the marriage with only one party as a beneficiary, for that settlement not to be nuptial. This is especially so where the settlor is not one of the spouses.

In the case of *Compton (Marquis of Northampton) v Compton (Marchioness of Northampton) and Hussey*[20] the husband settled his money during the marriage for the benefit of the parties' two daughters and two sons. The wife was a trustee of all four settlements and had a contingent life interest in the settlements for the daughters and a power of appointment under those in favour of the sons. The husband subsequently executed a deed of gift such that property and other investments were transferred to the wife. Following the divorce, the husband applied for an order that the wife's powers and interests under the four settlements be extinguished as from the date of the final decree as if she had died on that date. In respect of the contingent life interest, this was not resisted. The husband also applied for an order on the wife that she execute a settlement in favour of the children out of the funds he had gifted to her.

The wife's argument that this was not a post-nuptial settlement was rejected. The court held that a post-nuptial settlement can settle on the parties to the marriage power over the disposal of property (such as with the trusts for the sons here) as well as over the property itself. The court also ruled that it did not have power to remove the wife as a trustee and that the proper place for that application to be heard was in the Chancery Division.[21] The husband's application that the wife's power of appointment be extinguished was dismissed. The court saw no reason to think that she would abuse the power of appointment if she remained a

---

[20] [1960] P 201, [1960] 3 WLR 476.
[21] This aspect was later distinguished/held to be incorrect in *E v E (Financial Provision)* [1990] 2 FLR 233, FD.

trustee and continued to act in good faith. The court allowed the husband's application for an order on the wife for her to settle property on the children out of the funds gifted to her.

The significance of *Compton* is the fact that the wife was not a beneficiary of the trusts for the sons – the mere power for the wife to appoint made it a nuptial settlement given that the children were also beneficiaries.

If the settlement is made before the date of the marriage and is to be classified as an 'ante-nuptial settlement', it must have been made with an intention to make provision for one or other spouse in their character as a party to the marriage. It follows then that if property is settled in advance of a marriage and before the parties even met and the other spouse is not included in the class of beneficiaries, it would subsequently be difficult for one spouse to make an application under s 24(1)(c) to vary the trust since there can have been no intention to make provision for that spouse specifically in their character as a party to the marriage.

Likewise, it may be difficult for a spouse to show that a settlement made after the date of the marriage had a nuptial element where no express provision had been made to benefit that spouse. However, as referred to above, Lord Nicholls in *Brooks v Brooks* said:

> 'The section is concerned with a settlement "made on the parties to the marriage". So, broadly stated, the disposition must be one which makes some sort of continuing provision for both or either of the parties to a marriage, with or without provision for their children.'

This may be taken to mean that a trust of which only one spouse is a beneficiary could be nuptial. It may be that Thorpe LJ in *Charalambous v Charalambous*[22] was placing a marker to indicate that this may not be correct.

Other factors indicative of a settlement with a nuptial element (none of which are determinative) include:

- the identity of the settlor as a party to the marriage or a close relative;

- the absence of other beneficiaries;

- the identity of any other beneficiaries;

- the content of any letter of wishes;

- the time at which the settlement was made; and

---

[22]   [2004] EWCA Civ 1030.

- the terms of the settlement itself, including the existence of a specific power to add a spouse as a beneficiary.

The 1926 case of *Hargreaves v Hargreaves*[23] is an example of how a trust set up shortly prior to a marriage may not necessarily be a nuptial settlement. The trust was only set up six weeks before the marriage in 1914. It was not expressed to be in contemplation of marriage. The future wife was not referred to at all in the trust document, although it was drafted so as to contemplate a future marriage and it included powers to take effect if the settlor married. Just over two weeks prior to the wedding, the settlor exercised his power of appointment in favour of his future wife to grant her an annual allowance. It was held the trust was not made in contemplation of any particular marriage but simply gave the husband power to appoint an interest to any future wife. Hill J held that a nuptial settlement was one that was 'made in contemplation of, or because of marriage, and with reference to the interests of married people or their children'.

This test was expanded in the 1930 case of *Prinsep v Prinsep*.[24] In that case, certain trust funds were settled by the husband's mother on trust to pay the income to the husband for life or until he became bankrupt and after his death to pay the income to the wife until she remarried. There were provisions for resettlement of trust funds on a potential different wife of the husband. In 1920, eight years after the original trust was made, the husband's mother settled further funds to apply the income at the discretion of the trustee for the benefit of the husband and his issue by any marriage and any wife of his. On divorce eight years later, the trustee argued that the 1920 settlement had nothing to do with this marriage and was not a settlement in consequence of the marriage and was therefore not a post-nuptial settlement capable of variation. Hill J decided that the August 1920 settlement was a post-nuptial settlement because it was a settlement providing for the husband or his wife in their character as husband and wife.

Even a settlement made after the signing of a Petition is capable of variation. In *Melvill v Melvill and Woodward*,[25] the wife settled property on herself for life, together with a power to appoint the income to any surviving husband. The husband's attempt to vary the settlement was at first instance unsuccessful but Bates J's decision was overturned because the marriage was still in existence and a potential benefit had been conferred on the husband. It appears from the speech of Greer LJ that a settlement settled during the marriage which gives some interest to either spouse or their offspring will be regarded as nuptial:

---

23   [1926] P 42.
24   [1930] P 35, CA.
25   [1930] P 159, CA.

'But you cannot have a settlement after a marriage which has not some relation to marriage if it settles property on one of the parties to the marriage, and still more if it settles property on the children of the marriage, one of the main objects of marriage being, according to the words in the Prayer Book, the procreation of children.'

Where the beneficiaries of a trust are expressed to be a class or several classes and the exercise of powers of appointment or income and capital are at the discretion of the trustee, and the relevant trust was set up prior to the marriage in question, it will be far more difficult to show that a settlement was made in contemplation of a *specific* marriage.

As elsewhere in matrimonial proceedings though, each case will turn on its own facts and it will be for the court to decide whether the requisite intention to provide for the benefit of one or other or both of the spouses in the context of their marriage date exists. Of course post-*White*, now all assets may go into the pot for division on divorce, courts will inevitably take trust assets into account, especially where post nuptial and settled with matrimonial assets – quite different to the legal circumstances that existed at the time of the older cases.

5.2.4   The powers of the court

The English court can vary the terms of a nuptial settlement in any way it deems appropriate. Variation might include the distribution of capital for the benefit of a spouse, the creation of an income provision for a spouse or the creation of an entirely new trust for one spouse out of the capital of the trust, and the removal of trustees or a protector.

The 1990 case of *E v E*[26] is a good example of a situation in which a variation of settlement order was appropriate. The husband's father was paymaster throughout the marriage and provided funds to set up an offshore discretionary trust to hold shares in a Panamanian company which in turn held the title to the matrimonial home in London. The property was worth £1.25m at the date of the hearing. The husband, wife and the children were members of the class of beneficiaries and the husband's father was the protector of the trust. The powers of the trustee were only exercisable with the consent of the protector. The husband was also employed by his father. He argued at the trial that his salary had been discontinued because of his father's unwillingness to countenance a capital settlement to the wife. The wife claimed that this discontinuance was a device designed to defeat her claims. There were also disputes concerning the value of the assets in the offshore trust, which the wife claimed was far greater than the husband stated.

Ewbank J varied the settlement by removing the husband's father as protector, removing the trust company acting as trustee and granting the

---

[26]   [1990] 2 FLR 233, FD.

wife £50,000 outright from the settlement with a life interest in £200,000 from it and the remainder to the children. This was in contrast to the approach of the court in *Compton* (above) in which it was said that the proper place for an application for a change of trustee was the Chancery Division. The fact that the property was onshore was key, and the fact that once joined as parties, the trustee participated in the proceedings and so submitted to the English court's jurisdiction.

It is not always the case, of course, that property is settled only or mainly for the benefit of one spouse or other or both. In practice, this tends to be the exception rather than the rule. It is more than likely, that there will be some third party interest (for example minor beneficiaries) which may well be prejudiced by any variation of the settlement. Those third parties would need to be represented. The court may need to have regard to the rights of that most curious of interested parties – the 'unborn'. In such circumstances, as elsewhere, the court will have to take account of all the circumstances of the case.

There may be instances where one spouse is applying for a variation of settlement to provide her with sufficient capital to purchase suitable accommodation to house her and her children. If the children were also beneficiaries, there would clearly be a unity of interest in having a parent properly housed. The detriment to minor third party beneficiaries who are children of the family might also be outweighed if a capitalisation of maintenance and 'clean break' could be achieved by variation of the trust fund. As Lord Nicholls in *Brooks v Brooks* said (at p 263):

> 'In order to promote the best interests of the parties and their children in a fundamentally changed situation, it is desirable that the court should have power to alter the terms of the settlement.'

In *Prinsep* it was held that a contingent interest of one party's siblings as third party beneficiaries was too remote an interest to be taken into account by the court. In that case, the husband's brothers would have benefited from the trust if the protective trust for the husband was triggered. The brothers intervened in the proceedings, but it was held that their interests were too remote and contingent upon there being no child of the husband who retained a vested interest and the husband not making an appointment.

In Chapter 7 of this book, we will consider the practice and procedure of joinder of third parties, but it is worth noting at this point that the Official Solicitor may intervene on behalf of minor beneficiaries in order to make their position known. In fact, such intervention is cited as one of the more common examples of where the Official Solicitor might intervene on behalf of a child whose own welfare is not the subject of family proceedings.[27] The intervention of the Official Solicitor may be requested by the court or a party, if there is no other suitable guardian ad litem to represent them in the proceedings. Acquiescence by a third party who is aware that proceedings are on foot may be grounds for the court to disregard the interests of that person.

Rule 2.57 of the Family Proceedings Rules 1991, requires the court to direct that children are to be separately represented on an application for variation of a settlement where their rights may be prejudiced:

> '(1) Where an application is made to the High Court or a designated county court for an order for a variation of settlement, the court shall, unless it is satisfied that the proposed variation does not adversely affect the rights or interests of any children concerned, direct that the children be separately represented on the application, either by a solicitor or by a solicitor and counsel, and may appoint the Official Solicitor or other fit person to be guardian ad litem of the children for the purpose of the application.
>
> (2) On any other application for ancillary relief the court may give such a direction or make such appointment as it is empowered to give or make by paragraph (1).
>
> (3) Before a person other than the Official Solicitor is appointed guardian ad litem under this rule there shall be filed a certificate by the solicitor acting for the children that the person proposed as guardian has no interest in the matter adverse to that of the children and that he is a proper person to be such guardian.'

Subparagraph 2 gives the court discretion to make the direction on any application for ancillary relief even if it does not include an application for variation of settlement. A spouse claiming that trust assets are a resource available to the other spouse might be a relevant situation in which to invoke this rule.

This rule is often overlooked by practitioners and the court despite it being an important safeguard for third party interests.

5.2.5   The international element

The advent of complicated offshore structures in wealth planning has added a new and more complex dimension to the question of variation of settlements under the Matrimonial Causes Act 1973. As was made clear in the case of *Nunneley*[28] (see above), the trust need not have a direct connection with England to be the subject of an order varying its terms. The facts of *C v C (variation of post nuptial settlement: company shares)*[29] are a good example of this.

---

[27]   Practice Note *Official Solicitor: Appointment in Family Proceedings* (2 April 2001) [2001] 2 FLR 155.

[28]   (1890) 15 PD 186.

[29]   [2003] EWHC 1222 (Fam), [2003] 2 FLR 493, FD.

The parties married in 1984, separating in 2000 when they were both in their fifties. They had one child. The wife was found to have made a full contribution to the marriage in both financial and non-financial terms. The husband had settled shares in his UK business, worth £3.5m at the time, in a trust established in the Cayman Islands in early 1998. The financial proceedings were launched in late 2001. Shortly before the trial the shares were valued at around £300,000 making the total net assets £600,000. The husband was not domiciled in the UK, not in receipt of fixed income nor in possession of any substantial liquid capital.

The Cayman trustee was advised that the Cayman court would almost certainly not enforce any order of the English court varying a Cayman trust expressly stated to be subject to Cayman law and the exclusive jurisdiction of the Cayman court. Nonetheless, the English court considered whether it had jurisdiction to vary an offshore trust. Coleridge J satisfied himself that:

> 'there are adequate powers in this court to deal with the question of implementation of a variation of trust order if I deem it appropriate, and this is particularly so where the underlying assets are onshore, that is to say the shareholding is in an English Company.'

Accordingly, the court's jurisdiction to vary the foreign settlement was not seriously challenged. The case proceeded to be fought over the issue of whether the trust should be varied so that the wife received some of the shares (rather than cash) and free from the trust, or whether she should simply be awarded monetary compensation in lieu of transfer.

Ultimately, the wife satisfied the court that she wished to play an active role in the business as a shareholder, and she received a little over 30% of the shares held in the trust (15% of the shares in the company overall), free from the trust. The likely future increase in the value of the company was a key factor.

The wording of the variation order was as follows:

> 'The post nuptial settlement represented by the DMRC 1998 Trust with B Private Bank and Trust (Cayman) Limited dated 10th February 1998 be and is hereby varied so far as is necessary to give effect to the following rulings of the court:
> (a) to transfer or cause to be transferred to the Petitioner in specie and free from the aforementioned trust (or her nominee under such trusts as shall be directed by her) 236,750 Ordinary Shares of 1p each in the company X Limited, it being recorded that the aforementioned number of shares equates to 15% of the total number of ordinary shares issued in X Ltd;
> (b) to transfer or cause to be transferred to the Petitioner in specie and free from the aforementioned trust (or her nominee under such trusts as shall be directed by her) 3 Ordinary "B" Shares in the aforementioned company, it being recorded that the aforementioned

number of shares equates to 30% of the shareholding of 10 Ordinary "B" Shares otherwise held by the Trust,
AND the trustees of the DMRC 1998 Trust are hereby directed to exercise their powers and duties in such a way as to give effect to the above provisions.'

The English court has even seen fit to vary nuptial settlements where they contain an 'exclusive jurisdiction clause' for another jurisdiction. This is a clause in the trust document which states that any dispute about the trust should be resolved in the court of a specified jurisdiction, in most cases mirroring the jurisdiction of the trust's proper law. In *C v C (Ancillary Relief: Nuptial Settlement)*[30] (later *Charalambous v Charalambous*), Wilson J (as he then was) conceded that there would be cases where the exclusive jurisdiction clause might apply but in the light of the trustee not being Jersey resident and the situs of the trust assets being within the English court's jurisdiction, he held that there was no need to defer to the Jersey court.

In *C v C (Variation of Post-nuptial Settlement)*, the parties had married on 17 June 1984. Before the birth of their second child the husband's mother created the Jersey settlement known as the Hickory Trust. On 1 October 2000 Bankruptcy Petitions were issued against H. The marriage broke down in 2002. The husband denied that the Hickory Trust was a nuptial settlement and alternatively he relied upon the provision of the settlement conferring exclusive jurisdiction on the Jersey court and the provision in the settlement establishing Jersey law as the proper law. He further argued that at the date of formation the Trust constituted a post-nuptial settlement. However, he suggested that by removing himself and his wife as beneficiaries in 2001 the settlement became non-nuptial.

However, the parties had remained joint protectors. Their children remained in the beneficial class and the court found that the parties' removal was motivated by the desire to preserve the assets against claims that might have been brought by the husband's creditors. Both spouses could also be reinstated to the beneficial class. In any event, as joint protectors, any decision of the trustees to distribute or accumulate required their consent. Subsequent to the removal of the parties there was clear evidence that the husband was in fact benefiting substantially from the trust. As such, the court found that the trust was to be considered nuptial.

Wilson J considered whether or not a settlement could lose its nuptial status and whether or not that prevented the court from varying it in accordance with the statute. He held that:

'provided that it [the settlement] exists at the date of the order, the court has jurisdiction to vary a settlement which, when made, was ante-nuptial or

---

[30]   [2004] EWHC 742 (Fam), [2004] 2 WLR 1467.

post-nuptial, notwithstanding that prior to the date of the order the features which made it nuptial have been removed from it.'

Interestingly, Arden LJ in the Court of Appeal, when *C v C (Ancillary Relief: Nuptial Settlement)* was appealed as *Charalambous v Charalambous*,[31] seemed to throw doubt on Wilson J's approach at first instance, by saying that it is possible for a post-nuptial settlement to lose its status as such:

'To fall within the type of order which can be made under s 24(1)(c) of the Matrimonial Causes Act 1973, the settlement must be an "ante-nuptial or post-nuptial settlement ... made on the parties to the marriage". The words "made on the parties to the marriage" constitute a condition for the application of s 24(1)(c) which is separate from, and additional to, the requirement for the settlement to be an ante-nuptial or post-nuptial settlement. The word "made" relates back to the moment of creation of the settlement. At that point in time, it must be within the description "made on the parties to the marriage". It probably must also have been an ante-nuptial or post-nuptial settlement at the date of creation though it is not necessary to decide at that point. However, it is clear that the settlement must be an ante-nuptial or post-nuptial settlement at the time when the order is made: otherwise the section would have referred to former ante-nuptial or post-nuptial settlements as well.'

However, she held that the fact that the parties remained protectors was enough for the trust to retain its status as a post-nuptial settlement.

Despite this, Thorpe LJ stated that there may be circumstances in which a settlement, previously nuptial, could be de-nuptialised in legitimate circumstances. At para 45 he said:

'however, I cannot agree that a settlement which was nuptial when made retained that essential character come what may. It is easy to instance the head of a family who has created a number of settlements to preserve the family's fortune through two or more generations. His scheme may at one stage include nuptial settlements for his sons, their wives and issue. However, at a later stage, to reflect events in the family or changes in the Taxing Act, he might well radically revise the scheme and in so doing remove from one particular settlement a son, his wife and issue, compensating them with some advance of other security. So whether the removal of the spouses from the beneficial class does or does not erase the nuptial element must, in my judgment, depend on the facts and circumstances of the individual case.'

In his judgment at first instance, Wilson J also considered the Hague Convention on the Recognition of Trusts and on their Enforcement (given effect in England under the Recognition of Trusts Act 1987) which provides that the law chosen by the settlor should govern a trust including, among other things the variation or termination of the trust. His analysis was that:

---

[31] [2004] EWCA Civ 1030.

'English law chooses no substantive law other than its own for the dispatch of applications for ancillary relief for divorce even though belatedly it is beginning to recognise the need, in a case with foreign connections, for a sideways look at foreign law as part of the discretionary analysis required by its substantive law ...'

He continued and concluded by saying that:

'[An exclusive jurisdiction clause] cannot derogate from the jurisdiction of [an English divorce court] under s 24(1)(c) of the 1973 Act'.

On appeal, in confirming that the English court had jurisdiction, Thorpe LJ said (at para 30):

'This power to vary is derived not from the settlement but from the matrimonial regime of the state. Equally the right to seek variation derives not from the settlement but from the matrimonial regime of the jurisdiction that dissolves the marriage. So clause 3(2) of the settlement [the exclusive jurisdiction clause] cannot oust or defeat the wife's exercise of her statutory right to apply under s 24 of the Matrimonial Causes Act 1973 for a variation of settlement order. The clause is of no avail to the husband.'

Arden LJ further observed that:

'If Mrs Charalambous obtains an order under s 24(1)(c) of the Matrimonial Causes Act 1973 varying the terms of The Hickory Trust, she will have to take separate proceedings against the trustees, probably in Jersey, in order that they too should be bound by the order. I note that in *Compass Trustees Ltd v McBarnett*[32] the Royal Court of Jersey (Le Cras, Commissioner) was prepared as a matter of comity to recognise an order made in England under s 24(1)(c) of the Matrimonial Causes Act 1973 as the English court had considered the matter fully and concluded that the need to provide capital to the wife outweighed the disadvantage caused to the other beneficiaries.'

As discussed above, the issue then becomes one of enforcement (see Chapter 8).

At present, there is only one reported English case where the English courts have purported to vary a trust based in an offshore jurisdiction that has 'exclusion of foreign law' legislation, e g Cayman, Bahamas, Bermuda, BVI, Isle of Man and more recently Jersey, and where the underlying trust assets are offshore. In the most recent decision in the saga of *Mubarak v Mubarak*,[33] Holman J varied the Jersey Trust where the principal asset was shares in a Bermudian holding company. The variation was ordered by the court as a last resort, the husband having refused to pay the lump

---

[32] 2002 JLR 321.
[33] [2007] EWHC 220 (Fam).

sum of £4.6m and having amassed arrears of maintenance of approximately a further £500,000, not to mention the wife's costs from previous hearings.

It should be noted also that *Re B Trust*[34] concerned an application for directions by the trustees of a Jersey trust that had been varied by the English court using its power under the Matrimonial Causes Act 1973. By a quirk of law, the English order and the hearing of the application were either side of the Trusts (Amendment No 4) Jersey Law 2006 which brought in the protective legislation. The Trust assets in that case comprised a Jersey company holding, inter alia, real property situated in the UK.

5.3   TRUSTS AS A RESOURCE

Where a spouse wishes to make a claim over trust assets, and she either cannot show that the trust amounts to a settlement capable of variation by the court, or she chooses not to make such a variation application, the spouse can still allege that the trust assets are a resource available to the other spouse. For those in the trust industry and private client/trust lawyers, this aspect of the treatment of trusts on divorce is the most frustrating and incomprehensible. Advisers may spend a great deal of time and energy in creating trust structures for perfectly valid tax planning and succession purposes, distancing the settlor from the assets settled in trust, only to find that the Family Division can be willing to look through those structures.

Given the international nature of wealth in London, the judiciary have become well accustomed to dealing with complex trust and corporate structures.

The key question is to what extent are all, or more likely part, of the trust assets available to the other spouse. It will be easier to show that the trust assets are a resource available to the other spouse if that spouse was the settlor of the trust, but it may also be possible to prove that the trust assets are a resource available in other cases too. The drafting and terms of the Deed of Settlement, any Letters of Wishes and the pattern of distributions by the trustee over the years is the key.

In the case of *J v V (Disclosure: Offshore Corporations)*,[35] a case involving complex corporate structures, Coleridge J stated (at para 17):

> 'Respondents to such applications are required to be from the outset perhaps even fuller and franker in the exposure and explanation of their assets than in conventional onshore cases. Otherwise skulduggery is

---

[34]   2006 JLR 562.
[35]   [2003] EWHC 3110 (Fam), [2004] 1 FLR 1042, FD.

instantly presumed. Applicants justifiably believe that advantage is being taken to hide assets from view amongst complex corporate undergrowth.'

He concluded his judgment by adding (at para 130):

> 'Clients whose cases fall into this category do need to be reminded by their advisers that these sophisticated offshore structures are very familiar nowadays to the judiciary who have to try them. They neither impress, intimidate, nor fool anyone. The courts have lived with them for years. If clients "duck and weave" over months or years to avoid coming clean they cannot expect much sympathy when it comes to the question of paying the costs of the enquiry which inevitably follows.'

In numerous judgments, it has been stated that the approach is to look at *'the reality of the situation'*. That approach seems to have a long history. In *N v N*,[36] Lord Merrivale P of the Family Division referred to the practice of the Ecclesiastical Courts before the Matrimonial Causes Act 1857. He stated (at p 327) that the Ecclesiastical Courts 'were not misled by appearances ... they looked at the realities' and referred to looking at what monies a husband could have 'if he liked'.

In *Howard v Howard*,[37] the husband applied to vary so as to reduce maintenance for his former wife. The original order made on divorce had varied a trust set up by the husband's great-aunt so that the wife received maintenance out of that trust.

The husband's application had been triggered in part by his illness and inability to work but also because the trustee of the same trust which was paying maintenance to the wife, had informed him that he would receive no payment from the trust for a considerable time.

Lord Greene MR said:

> 'Trustees who have a discretion are bound to exercise it, and if they do so nobody can interfere with it. In my opinion there is no jurisdiction in the Divorce court to make an order that will leave the husband in a state of starvation (to use rather picturesque language) with a view to putting pressure on trustees to exercise their discretion in any way in which they would not have exercised it but for that pressure. Under discretionary trusts (as, indeed, under this trust) other persons are potential beneficiaries. In many such trusts the range of potential beneficiaries is a very wide one ... on what grounds should pressure be put upon the trustees to exercise their discretion in such a way as to pay to the husband, in order that he may pay maintenance to his wife, sums which in their discretion they would not otherwise have paid to him? It seems to me that such an order is as bad as an order on a man to pay a sum far in excess of what he could be ordered to pay out of his own means merely to put pressure on a rich relation to support him ... what has to be looked at is the means of the husband, and

---

[36] [1928] All ER Rep 462, (1928) 44 TLR 324.
[37] [1945] P 1, CA.

by "means" is meant what he is in fact getting or can fairly be assumed to be likely to get ... similarly in a case of a discretionary trust, if the court finds that the husband is in fact receiving regular payments under such a trust it is perfectly entitled to make an order on the footing that those payments will in all probability continue, leaving it to the husband to come back to the court if at some future date they are stopped. But in this case the trustees have exercised their discretion so that the husband will, as frequently happens under these discretionary trusts, get nothing ...

In my opinion the practice, if it be a practice, indirectly to put pressure on trustees in this sort of way to commit a breach of their duty and to exercise their discretion in a way contrary to what they desire, is wrong ... the result is that they are bound by law to exercise their discretion properly, and it is not right that the court, by making so stringent an order against the husband ..., should endeavour to put pressure on them.'

The views in the Court of Appeal in *Howard v Howard* were considered again in 1982 in *B v B (financial provision)*.[38]

The parties were married for over 20 years and although the husband had a good salary, he had no assets. The wife was from a wealthy family and was a beneficiary under two settlements. Under the first, made by her father eight years before the marriage, the trustee had power in their absolute discretion to vest the whole or any part of the trust capital in the wife absolutely. Under the second, made after the marriage the wife as settlor and beneficiary was permitted to withdraw all or any part of the trust assets with the consent of the trustee. The trustee gave evidence that it was their policy not to consent to the withdrawal of the funds from the settlement but the trustee was also the wife's solicitor in the divorce. The settlements had assets at the date of a trial in October 1980 worth £78,000 and £212,000 respectively. The wife had substantial free assets consisting of her home and other assets, in total worth about £120,000.

The judge at first instance ordered the wife to pay the husband's £50,000 in full and final settlement of his claim. That was upheld on appeal.

Ormrod LJ stated:

'Both settlements are potential sources of capital for the wife and are, therefore, 'other financial resources', though not under her absolute control ... It is not to be supposed that the trustees would withhold their consent if the wife wished to free capital for any reason or purpose, more especially when the other beneficiaries are already amply provided for.'

Ormrod LJ also stated at the end of the judgment:

'We do not think that the Judge was putting or attempting to put pressure on the trustees; on the contrary it could be said that the trustees were

---

[38]   (1982) 3 FLR 298, CA.

attempting to put pressure on the court. She was dealing in practical terms with the realities of the case and refusing to be misled by appearance.'

The 1988 Court of Appeal decision in *Browne v Browne*[39] was the key decision in which the ratio was on the question of trust assets as a resource, prior to the House of Lords' decision in *White v White* in October 2000.

In *Browne* after a long marriage, the husband, a Conservative MP, had no substantial means whereas the wife had substantial assets most of which were in offshore trusts. Both trusts were set up with assets from the wife's mother. The Jersey trust had assets of £430,000 and the wife was in effect the sole beneficiary. There was a further trust in Liechtenstein which was worth in excess of £100,000, although it was not clear whether the wife was the sole beneficiary of that trust.

The wife was ordered to pay to the husband a lump sum of £175,000 and costs. The wife's assets outside the trust were such that she was able to pay the lump sum and the husband's costs save for about £60,000.

Initially the wife did not pay the lump sum and therefore the husband applied for the wife's committal. By the time of the appeal hearing the lump sum of £175,000 had been paid.

Butler-Sloss LJ stated:

> 'In considering whether or not, as the Judge found, she had effective control over these trusts, it is of some relevance to note that, prior to the divorce and parting of the husband and wife, every application by the wife for funds for herself and for her husband for any of the pursuits that they wished to engage in, pleasure as well as the buying of property, was met and the sums asked for were advanced at the request of the wife. Although, perhaps, the phrase "effective control" might more appropriately be expressed as "immediate access to the funds", in my judgment, the Judge was entirely justified in coming to the conclusion as at 6 February that every request had been granted and that she was in a position to ask for money and to have it paid, and there was nothing to show that the trustees would not do so.'

Butler-Sloss LJ also quoted from the unreported Court of Appeal decision of *Milburn v Milburn* (3 October 1979) in which, looking at the position of trusts, Roskill LJ said:

> 'The whole purpose of this modern legislation is to enable a court to look at the reality of a particular situation. The reality at present is that there are these vast capital assets in Switzerland and Liechtenstein to which the husband has no legal or equitable title, but from time to time money can be, and on a balance of probabilities, will be, made available if the necessity

---

[39] [1989] 1 FLR 291, CA.

arises for purposes discharging such obligations as making periodical payments under an order of this court.

So far from *Howard v Howard* being authority against the appellant I think it is authority for the proposition that, though the court must not make orders designed to put pressure on discretionary trustees, nonetheless, the court should look at the reality of the situation, at what is, or is likely to be in all probability, the totality of the resources of a particular party to the marriage. I can see nothing wrong in principle in taking into account the fact that there are these large sums from which requests for payments can be made.'

The Court of Appeal case of *Thomas v Thomas*,[40] involved a husband who jointly owned a majority share in the family company, although his shareholding was not held in a trust. However Glidewell LJ took the view that the situation was similar as to the treatment of trust interests. He stated (at p 678):

'Those which are the most helpful in this case are, in my view, the decisions of this court in *O'D v O'D* [1976] Fam 83, *B v B* (1982) 3 FLR 298 and *Browne v Browne* [1989] 1 FLR 291. From these authorities I derive the following principles:
(a)   Where a husband can only raise further capital, or additional income, as the result of a decision made at the discretion of trustees, the court should not put improper pressure on the trustees to exercise that discretion for the benefit of the wife.
(b)   The court should not, however, be 'misled by appearances'; it should 'look at the reality of the situation'.
(c)   If on the balance of probability the evidence shows that, if trustees exercised their discretion to release more capital or income to a husband, the interests of the trust or of other beneficiaries would not be appreciably damaged, the court can assume that a genuine request for the exercise of such discretion would probably be met by a favourable response. In that situation if the court decides that it would be reasonable for a husband to seek to persuade trustees to release more capital or income to him to enable him to make proper financial provision for his children and his former wife, the court would not in so deciding be putting improper pressure on the trustees.
In relation to the facts of the present case, I would apply these principles to the family company as if it were a trust, and the shareholders (the husband, his mother and brother) the trustees.'

The sad, long-running case of *Mubarak v Mubarak*[41] involves a wife's attempt to enforce an order made in her favour against a recalcitrant husband and his trust interests.

---

[40]   [1995] 2 FLR 668, CA.
[41]   [2001] 1 FLR 673, FD; [2001] 1 FLR 698, CA; [2003] 2 FLR 553, FD; [2004] 2 FLR 932, FD. See further Appendix 2.

It is a salutary tale as to the problems and traps in dealing with trust interests in divorce. Final judgment was given by Bodey J in December 1999 and the wife is still attempting to enforce the judgment.

The husband was a highly successful international jeweller and in 1997 placed the assets of his businesses into a discretionary Jersey trust of which he, the wife and the four children of the family were original beneficiaries. The following year, when the marriage was in difficulties, the husband exercised his power under the settlement to remove the wife as a beneficiary of the trust. The trust owned shares in a series of offshore companies through which the businesses themselves were owned. The husband disappeared from the middle of the final hearing which led to the husband being ordered to pay the wife a lump sum of £4,875,000.

Even though the Jersey trust appears to have been a post nuptial settlement capable of variation by the court on divorce, it seems as if the wife did not initially make such an application. That was no doubt in part because at the outset of the case, the husband's first solicitors were instructed to make the following statement in correspondence:

> 'For the purposes of these proceedings the husband accepts that the assets of the trust will be treated as being his.'

That statement was made without the approval of the trustee. Although it is common to ask for similar concessions to be made and such concessions are sometimes still made, only such a concession with the consent of the trustee can be binding upon them.

In one of the many reported judgments in the case,[42] Jacob J stated that:

> 'There is no reason, as far as I can see, why some sort of remedy against the husband's interest in that trust is not directly obtainable. The fact the trust is abroad, the fact that many of the assets of the trust are also abroad, is neither here nor there. He is here and any order made will be in personam and enforceable against him.'

In 2005, the wife launched an application to vary the trust in England as a nuptial settlement. In proceedings in Jersey in which the trustee sought directions as to what stance it should take in the English variation proceedings, the Royal Court held that it was appropriate for the trustee to withdraw its application to set aside the order made in the English proceedings for its joinder and for specific discovery. In the judgment given on 8 December 2005 the Bailiff stated that in acceding to the application of the trustee to withdraw its application to set aside the joinder order:

---

[42] [2001] 1 FLR 698, CA.

'The court in the exercise of its equitable jurisdiction in relation to trusts, does not smile upon those who flout the orders of other courts in matrimonial proceedings to the detriment of a wife and children. We understand the desire of [the adult children] to have all these matters resolved in the interests of their mother as quickly as possible ... without in any way prejudging the issues, it seems clear that the timing and manner of the exclusion of the wife as a beneficiary give rise to arguable considerations as to whether the exclusion was a lawful and proper exercise of power.'

On the wife's application to debar the husband from participating in the wife's applications made in 2005 in England to vary the trust it was held by Bodey J[43] that the husband should be placed on certain terms namely (1) that the husband write to the trustee informing them that he was bound by the court orders already made, and those which might yet be made in the proceedings, (2) he wished the trustee to assist him in meeting his obligations under those orders, and (3) that for each £1 he paid his own lawyers for preparation, representation and advice in respect of the forthcoming hearing, he would pay £1 into a joint account in the name of the parties' respective solicitors. The money was to be held to the order of the court, to be paid to the wife's solicitors at the conclusion of the forthcoming hearing, unless, when dealing with costs at the conclusion of that hearing, the court should positively rule otherwise in its overall discretion.

In January 2007 Holman J gave judgment on the wife's variation application.[44] He described the letter written by the husband's first solicitors at the start of the case, that the trust assets 'will be treated as his' as a 'fatalistic acceptance rather than an unequivocal concession'.[45] He went on to grant the wife's variation application, in place of the original lump sum order. His main reason for doing so was the husband's non payment of the lump sum and his conduct of the litigation since the final hearing in 1999, although he also confused the test for determining whether trust assets are available as a resource with the approach to variation. He said:[46]

'In reality, it always has been, and remains, the alter ego of the husband himself, interposed only (on his own evidence and case) as a means of avoiding tax and ultimately enabling orderly succession. I see no reason at all why I should not treat the assets of the trust as being those of the husband himself, as every single one of the other beneficiaries so strongly urged me to do.'

---

[43]   [2006] EWHC 1260 (Fam), [2007] 1 FLR 722, FD.
[44]   [2007] EWHC 220 (Fam).
[45]   At para 28.
[46]   At para 161.

With respect, there is no such concept of a trust being an alter ego of a beneficiary. It remains to be seen what attitude the Jersey court takes to this decision; the Jersey court is bound to be sympathetic to the wife's plight.

In 2005, in the Court of Appeal decision of *Charman v Charman*,[47] Wilson LJ considered the issue of trust assets as a resource in obiter comments. The judgment concerned an order made by Coleridge J for Letters of Request to be sent to the Bermudian Court to obtain information from the trustee of a Bermudian trust.

Wilson LJ said (at paras 12 and 13):

> 'Superficially the question is easily framed as being whether the trust is a financial "resource" of the husband for the purpose of s 25(2)(a) of the Matrimonial Causes Act 1973, "the Act of 1973". But what does the word "resource" mean in this context? In my view, when properly focused, that central question is simply whether, if the husband were to request it to advance the whole (or part) of the capital of the trust to him, the trustee would be likely to do so. In other cases the question has been formulated in terms of whether the husband has real or effective control over the trust. At times I have myself formulated it in that way. But, unless the situation is one in which there is ground for doubting whether the trustee is properly discharging its duties or would be likely to do so, it seems to me on reflection that such a formulation is not entirely apposite ... A trustee – in proper "control" of the trust – will usually be acting entirely properly if, after careful consideration of all relevant circumstances, he resolves in good faith to accede to a request by the settlor for the exercise of his power of advancement of capital, whether back to the settlor or to any other beneficiary ...
>
> Thus in effect, albeit with one small qualification, I agree with the suggestion of Butler-Sloss LJ in this court in *Browne v Browne*[48] at 239d–e that, in this context, the question is more appropriately expressed as whether the spouse has "immediate access to the funds" of the trust than "effective control" over it. The qualification relates to the word "immediate". In that case the Trial Judge knew that, if he was to proceed also to order the wife to pay the husband's costs, she would be unable to comply with his order for her swift payment of a lump sum and costs without recourse to the offshore trusts over which he found her to have "effective control": see 295b–c. So the question in that case was whether her access to their funds was immediate. In principle, however, in the light of s 25(2)(a) of the Act of 1973, the question is surely whether the trustee would be likely to advance the capital immediately or in the foreseeable future.'

Butler-Sloss LJ in *Browne* was right to state that the phrase 'effective control' was incorrect. That phrase implies that the trustee may not be fulfilling its duties properly. The test as to whether trust assets are a

---

47 [2005] EWCA Civ 1606, [2006] 2 FLR 422, CA.
48 [1989] 1 FLR 291, CA.

resource available to the spouse is often confused with a spouse having control over the trust assets which implies allegations of sham. Wilson LJ in *Charman* recorded that although Counsel for the wife had referred to the possible 'unity of interest' between the trustee and the husband and had referred to the trustee as the 'quasi-agent' of the husband, it was wise that Counsel withdrew those statements in oral argument.

In Coleridge J's judgment of the wife's application for ancillary relief in *Charman v Charman (No 2)*,[49] he did not address this issue in this way. The case involved a long marriage, approaching 30 years, in which Coleridge J held that the assets of trial amounted to £131m. Of those assets £68m were offshore in a Bermudian law trust with Bermudian trustees settled by the husband during the marriage.

It was the husband's case that the trust was a dynastic trust for future generations, not even the adult children who were the sole beneficiaries of a separate very substantial trust. However, the two main letters of wishes prepared by the husband as settlor of the trust, set up during the marriage, referred to the husband as being the main beneficiary. Although the trust initially was in standard discretionary form, largely for tax reasons the husband was given a life interest later. Over a period of some 13 years there were only four years in which any income was distributed to the husband. No distributions of capital were ever made and the last income distribution was in 1997.

Coleridge J found that there was no such dynastic intention and accordingly held that the entirety of the trust assets should remain on the asset schedule as available to the husband. At no time did he explicitly address the legal test for deciding whether the trusts assets or part of them were to be regarded as a resource available to the husband.

Coleridge J also discussed in his judgment as to whether it was possible in principle for a spouse to settle trust assets built up during the marriage thereby alienating them from division by the court on divorce. He stated (at para 79 of his judgment):

> '[79] The test is whether the assets in the trust should be regarded by the court as a "resource". That is a very broad definition. These assets are held in a discretionary trust in conventional form. I will not repeat the very helpful descriptive analysis of such a trust in the Jersey High Court adopted by Potter P in his judgment dismissing the husband's appeal against my order relating to letters of request. [See *Re Esteem Settlement* [2004] WTLR 1.] It is a very useful description of general application in cases like this. And as Lloyd LJ on the same occasion pointed out the assets in the trust "could be available to him on demand without being his money", as [Counsel for the husband] was constrained to agree.

---

[49] [2006] EWHC 1879 (Fam), [2007] 1 FLR 593, FD. See further Appendix 2.

[80] So even if the husband had got home on the facts, for the court simply to have ignored the assets would have been, I consider, wrong and, in my experience, entirely novel.

[81] Can a spouse remove from consideration under S 25, at the stroke of eg a letter of wishes, half the assets accumulated during a marriage without the consent of the other spouse? At the end of a marriage of this length for a spouse to be excluded from benefit by such an informal arrangement even if consensual and created at the time when the marriage was sound would be grotesquely unfair. He or she must be able to say, surely, in such circumstances "whatever may have been your/our intentions then, now that the marriage is over I have changed my mind and these assets must be on the table for consideration like all the others. I will decide following receipt of my portion what I want to do with them and whom I want to benefit now and in the future."

[82] So in the end I am persuaded by [counsel for the wife's] ... arguments and all the assets in the trust remain well and truly on the main schedule.'

Here Coleridge J is referring to the debate as to whether one spouse has an entitlement to a share in the other spouse's assets built up during the marriage. Some commentators have referred to this as the non-owning spouse's 'inchoate' or 'unascertained' share of the resources.

The recent decision of the House of Lords in *Miller v Miller* and *McFarlane v McFarlane*[50] has not clarified the matter. On the one hand Baroness Hale stated on several occasions about the fact that England has a system of separate property. However, Lord Nicholls (at para 9) referred to financial provision on divorce not being in the nature of 'largesse' or taking away from the one spouse and giving to the other, property which belongs to the former. Rather, each party is entitled to a fair share of the available property.

Since in family law so much turns on the individual circumstances of the case, it is submitted that Coleridge J's comments are not correct. Trusts assets should be treated like other assets which are not in a party's name, such as pensions.

The Court of Appeal upheld Coleridge J's judgment.[51] The Court of Appeal accepted that before the judge attributed all of the assets of the trust to the husband, the judge had to be satisfied that, if so requested by the husband, the trustee would be likely to advance them to him. At para 53 the Court of Appeal stated:

---

50   [2004] UKHL 24, [2006] 1 FLR 1186, HL.
51   [2007] EWCA Civ 503, [2007] 1 FLR 1246, CA. See further Appendix 2.

'it is in law a perfectly adequate foundation for the aggregation of trust assets with a party's personal assets for the purpose of s 25 (2)(a) of the Act that they should be likely to be advanced to him or her in the event only of "need".'

The Court of Appeal went on to say (at para 57):

'For reasons of policy we are pleased to find ourselves able to uphold the judge's attribution to the husband of all the assets in Dragon. Although the list of matters to which, upon an application for ancillary relief, the court must have regard pursuant to s 25(2) of the Act presently remains unchanged, the decision in *White* alters the necessary extent of the focus upon some of those matters in cases of substantial wealth. The needs of the parties remain to be considered, but in many cases focus upon them has waned as a result of an early conclusion that they will on any view be met as part of the outcome of other aspects of the requisite exercise. As a result of the advent of reference to proportions, the focus has largely shifted to computation of resources. Prior to the decision in *White v White*[52] the elaborate inquiry in the present case as to the attributability of the assets in a trust to a party as part of his or her resources would probably have been unnecessary. But, whenever it is necessary to conduct such an inquiry, it is essential for the court to bring to it a judicious mixture of worldly realism and of respect for the legal effects of trusts, the legal duties of trustees and, in the case of off-shore trusts, the jurisdictions of off-shore courts. In the circumstances of the present case it would have been a shameful emasculation of the court's duty to be fair if the assets which the husband built up in Dragon during the marriage had not been attributed to him.'

It is clear that the Court of Appeal has gone much further than *Browne v Browne*. It is no longer a question of only looking at the pattern of distributions. The question is whether such an approach to attribution of trust assets to one spouse is appropriate at all, and in particularly so if the settlor is not one of the spouses and/or the assets settled on trust are not assets generated during the marriage.

Since Mr Charman's application for permission to appeal to the House of Lords was refused, the Court of Appeal's decision remains binding.

The trustees' attitude towards a divorcing spouse's request to assist in meeting an award is addressed in Chapter 7.

5.3.1 Divorce lines of attack in other jurisdictions

It is clear that the importance of the forum of the proceedings cannot be overstated from the point of view of trustees' involvement and the issue of enforcement. In many offshore jurisdictions, however, the court has similar powers to the court in England and Wales, but the trustees do not have the shield of protective exclusion of foreign law legislation.

---

[52] [2001] 1 AC 596, [2000] 2 FLR 981, HL.

5.3.1.1   Jersey

The power to vary a settlement is contained in Art 27 of the Matrimonial Causes (Jersey) Law 1949:

> **'27   Power of court to vary settlements, etc**
>
> (1) Where a decree of divorce or of nullity of marriage has been made, the court may, upon the application of either party to the marriage which is the subject of such decree, or upon the application of any person beneficially interested, cancel, vary or modify, or terminate the trusts of, any marriage contract, marriage settlement, post-nuptial settlement, or terms of separation subsisting, between the parties to the marriage, in any manner which, having regard to the means of the parties, the conduct of either of them insofar as it may be inequitable to disregard it or the interests of any children of the family, appears to the court to be just.
>
> (2) The court may exercise the powers conferred by this Article notwithstanding that the marriage was contracted, or the marriage contract, marriage settlement, post-nuptial settlement or terms of separation was made or entered into, in an extraneous jurisdiction.'

The leading case in Jersey is *J v M*.[53] The parties married in 1986. In 1995, the husband's father settled a discretionary trust with assets worth £32.7m at the time of the trial. The terms of the trust were that the beneficiaries were the husband, the husband's issue and any charity. The wife was not named as a beneficiary. The parties were finally divorced in 2000.

The court held that it had no power to vary the settlement as a post-nuptial settlement because it was not a settlement 'between the parties to the marriage'. (This wording is almost identical to the Guernsey legislation and so the same point will almost certainly apply there.) The settlor was aware of the marriage and yet the trust did not purport to confer benefits directly upon its beneficiaries as husband or wife. It was not a settlement between the parties to the marriage because the wife was in no way connected with the settlement, either at its execution or as a beneficiary, and it could be inferred that the husband's father had intentionally excluded the wife from being a beneficiary. It was appropriate, however, that the assets in the trust be taken into account as a resource (see below). Finally, it is worth noting that the court held that while a fair division was usually appropriate in such cases, without discriminating as to the parties' respective roles in the marriage, because the assets had been built up by the husband's father, the appropriate yardstick was the wife's 'reasonable requirements'. This is at odds with the position in English law (see Chapter 4).

---

[53]   2002 JLR 330.

The more recent case of *Re B Trust*[54] shows the attitude of the Jersey court towards variation orders made by the English court and in particular its desire that the English courts should refrain from varying Jersey trusts directly:

> 'It would, in our view avoid sterile argument, and expense to the parties, if the English courts were, in cases involving a Jersey Trust, having calculated their award on the basis of the totality of the assets available to the parties, to exercise judicial restraint and refrain from invoking their jurisdiction under the Matrimonial Causes Act to vary the trust. Instead they could request this court to be auxiliary to them. Such an approach is adopted by courts exercising jurisdiction in relation to insolvency and in other areas of law too. It is true that such jurisdiction to seek assistance from a foreign court may usually have its basis in statute. Nonetheless, we can see no reason why the trustee or one or more of the parties before the English court as the case might be, should not be directed to make the appropriate application to this court for assistance in the implementation of the English court's order. It appears to us that this would be a more seemly and appropriate approach to matters where the courts of two friendly and civilised countries have concurrent interests. It would furthermore be likely to avoid the risk of the delivery of inconsistent judgments.'

Such observations represent the culmination of the Jersey court's views on this matter commencing with the observations made in *Re Fountain Trust*[55] (referred to in *Re B*), where it was stated that:

> '... as a general rule ... it would be an exorbitant exercise of jurisdiction for a foreign court to purport to vary the terms of a Jersey settlement ...'

5.3.1.2 *Guernsey*

The Guernsey court has jurisdiction to dissolve a marriage where the parties are sufficiently connected with Guernsey in that at least one of them is domiciled there on the date on which the Petition was filed or was habitually resident there for a period of one year ending on the date of the Petition. Like the English court, it has power to vary a settlement contained within Art 45 of the Matrimonial Causes Law (Guernsey) 1939 (as amended), which reads as follows:

> '(1) The court, after the making in the Island of Guernsey of a decree of divorce or nullity of marriage may, upon the application of either party to a marriage which is the subject of such decree, or upon the application of any person beneficially interested;
>
> (a) cancel, vary or modify, or
> (b) terminate the trusts of any marriage contract, marriage settlement, post-nuptial settlement, or terms of separation subsisting between the parties to such a marriage in any manner

---

[54] 2006 JLR 562.
[55] 2005 JLR 359.

which, having regard to the means of the parties, the conduct of either of them appear or the interests of any children of such a marriage appears to the court to be just.'

Subsection (2) of the provision extends to settlements or arrangements entered into outside Guernsey.

5.3.1.3 Isle of Man

In the Isle of Man, in the context of matrimonial proceedings, the Manx court has substantially the same powers to vary as under English law.[56] The court also has an inherent jurisdiction to vary trusts in the same way the English court does. Of course, there are also specific trust provisions that allow for variation.[57]

5.3.1.4 Bermuda

The relevant statutory authority for a variation of settlement in Bermuda is s 28(1)(c) of the Bermuda Matrimonial Causes Act 1974. This section is almost identical to its English counterpart.

The Bermuda court also has jurisdiction to vary a settlement under s 48 of the Trustee Act 1975. This is the section which would be employed if the Bermuda court were asked to make a mirror order for variation subsequent to an English variation order under s 24(1)(c) of the Matrimonial Causes Act 1973. However, the powers of the court under this section are far more limited than under the Bermuda Matrimonial Causes Act 1974 because the court cannot make such a variation order if an adult beneficiary objects to the variation, no matter how spurious the dissent from that beneficiary or how beneficial the potential variation would be for the Trust. The court is limited under this section to considering variations for the benefit of minors and the unborn. 'Benefit' is construed widely as being 'not confined to financial benefit but may extend to moral and social benefit'.[58]

5.3.1.5 Hong Kong

In Hong Kong, the relevant provision is s 6 of the Matrimonial Proceedings and Property Ordinance (Cap. 192), which is an exact copy of the English provision.

The question of when trust resources can be taken into account has also been the subject of case law. This was the question which arose in *Baroness Baillieu v Baron Baillieu*.[59] The husband was the head of the

---

[56] Matrimonial Proceedings Act 1986, ss 24 and 25.
[57] Variation of Trusts Act 1961 and Trustee Act 1961.
[58] *Re Holt's Settlement* [1969] 1 CH 100, [1968] 1 All ER 470, ChD.
[59] [1996] 1 HKC 32551.

Australian branch of the family, and as such was entitled to income or capital as the remainderman for six of the eight trusts that had a total worth of AU$5.9m. The wife was seeking a lump sum which could only be satisfied by borrowing or by having recourse to these funds. The trust document contained a power to advance funds in 'untoward or special circumstances'.

The judge at first instance felt that ordering the husband to pay a sum which required the advance funds in this way was prejudicial to other beneficiaries and outside the ambit of 'untoward or special circumstances'. He therefore made a small award to the wife of AU$350,000.

However, the Court of Appeal disagreed and increased the award to AU$550,000, saying that the balance required (a further AU$155,000) from the trustee was not disproportionate to the remainder of the trust assets.

5.3.1.6   Singapore

In Singapore, under the Women's Charter there is no power to vary an existing Singaporean settlement made for genuine reasons.

If, however, a sham trust were settled by or for the benefit of one spouse specifically for the purpose of defeating the other spouse's claims to a fair entitlement on divorce, the court has the power to draw adverse inferences against the settlor/beneficiary spouse and can attribute the value of the trust assets to the available pool for division.

Under the Women's Charter, an application can also be made pursuant to s 132 to set aside any disposition of property if the disposition is intended to reduce the paying spouse's means to pay maintenance to the recipient spouse. It is arguable that under this section it is possible for the court to set aside any trust created by the paying spouse for a third party assuming that trust is intended to defeat the purposes envisaged by the Women's Charter.

The powers of the court to order division of capital do include a power to settle assets on trust:

> '(3) The court may make all such other orders and give such directions as may be necessary or expedient to give effect to any order made under this section.
>
> (4) The court may, at any time it thinks fit, extend, vary, revoke or discharge any order made under this section, and may vary any term or condition upon or subject to which any such order has been made.
>
> (5) In particular, but without limiting the generality of subsections (3) and (4), the court may make any one or more of the following orders—

    (a)   an order for the sale of any matrimonial asset or any part thereof, and for the division, vesting or settlement of the proceeds …

    (d)   an order for any matrimonial asset, or the sale proceeds thereof, to be vested in any person (including either party) to be held on trust for such period and on such terms as may be specified in the order;

     …

(10) In this section, "matrimonial asset" means—

    (a)   any asset acquired before the marriage by one party or both parties to the marriage

        (i)   ordinarily used or enjoyed by both parties or one or more of their children while the parties are residing together for shelter or transportation or for household, education, recreational, social or aesthetic purposes; or

        (ii)   which has been substantially improved during the marriage by the other party or by both parties to the marriage; and

    (b)   any other asset of any nature acquired during the marriage by one party or both parties to the marriage,

but does not include any asset (not being a matrimonial home) that has been acquired by one party at any time by gift or inheritance and that has not been substantially improved during the marriage by the other party or by both parties to the marriage.'

5.3.1.7 New York

In New York there is no express power in the matrimonial regime to vary a settlement, but assets held in trust can be subject to equitable distribution where they comprise marital property owned in the name of one or both spouses. An irrevocable trust constitutes property held by a third party which cannot be redistributed. Property held on revocable trusts is often regarded as belonging to the grantor or subject to the direction of a trustee.

The exception to this basic principle is where property has been transferred by one spouse into trust with the intention of defeating the other's claims.

The leading case is *Riechers v Riechers*,[60] in which the court ruled it did not have jurisdiction over assets held offshore in the Cook Islands, nor had the wife proven to the court's satisfaction that those entities were created with the intention of defeating her claims. The approach taken, however, was that the property in the trust should be included as marital property and taken into consideration as to do otherwise would be inequitable.

Similarly, in *Alvares Correa v Correa*,[61] while there could be no equitable distribution of property under the terms of a pre-nuptial agreement, it

60   178 Misc 2d 170 (Sup Ct Westchester Co 1998).
61   285 A D 2dm123, 726 N Y S 2d 668 (2d Dept 2001).

was held that the husband had control over the income from offshore trusts and that was taken into account in calculating spousal and child maintenance.

In *Surasi v Surasi*,[62] a husband placed all his assets into a trust. That trust was later held to be revocable and created with the specific intention of defeating the wife's claims. Allegations of sham were upheld and the court ruled that the trust either be set aside or property be transferred directly to the wife.

In *Spector v Spector*[63] the court determined that it need not have jurisdiction over the trustee to make an order for equitable distribution as the order can be made directing one or other spouse to co-operate in the dissolution of the trust or transfer of trust assets. However, if the situs of the trust is outside New York, the court will either direct the party-grantor or a third party trustee to co-operate or will simply take the trust assets into account when determining an appropriate award to the recipient spouse.

5.3.1.8 Connecticut

In Connecticut, the relevant provision is as follows:

> **'Sec. 46b-81 (Formerly Sec. 46-51)** **Assignment of property and transfer of title**
>
> (a) At the time of entering a decree annulling or dissolving a marriage or for legal separation pursuant to a complaint under section 46b-45, the Superior Court may assign to either the husband or wife all or any part of the estate of the other. The court may pass title to real property to either party or to a third person or may order the sale of such real property, without any act by either the husband or the wife, when in the judgment of the court it is the proper mode to carry the decree into effect.
>
> (b) A conveyance made pursuant to the decree shall vest title in the purchaser, and shall bind all persons entitled to life estates and remainder interests in the same manner as a sale ordered by the court pursuant to the provisions of section 52-500. When the decree is recorded on the land records in the town where the real property is situated, it shall effect the transfer of the title of such real property as if it were a deed of the party or parties.
>
> (c) In fixing the nature and value of the property, if any, to be assigned, the court, after hearing the witnesses, if any, of each party, except as provided in subsection (a) of section 46b-51, shall consider the length of the marriage, the causes for the annulment, dissolution of the marriage or legal separation, the age, health, station, occupation, amount and sources of income, vocational skills, employability, estate, liabilities and needs of each of the

---

[62] 2001, WL 1607927, 2001 Slip Op 40408 (U) (Sup Ct Richmond Co 2001).
[63] 18 A D 3d 380, 797 N Y S 2d 437 (1st Dept 2005).

parties and the opportunity of each for future acquisition of
capital assets and income. The court shall also consider the
contribution of each of the parties in the acquisition, preservation
or appreciation in value of their respective estates.'

In *Dryfoos v Dryfoos*,[64] the husband's mother had set up a charitable trust
in 1996 that gave the principal to charity in June 2000 or on the earlier
death of all of her children. She had also set up another trust with
charitable remainder trusts but which provided a monthly income of
$5,000 to the husband. The question before the court was whether these
trusts were property that could be distributed equitably by the court in the
wake of the breakdown of the marriage.

It was held that where an interest in a trust was a 'mere expectancy' or 'the
bare hope of succession to the property of another' it was not property
for the purposes of equitable distribution, as in the case of a discretionary
trust. However, where an interest was contingent only on reaching a
certain age, it was analogous to a pension plan as a 'presently existing
enforceable right to receive the benefit from the trust subject only to the
contingency of surviving to a certain date.'

In such circumstances, the trust was property which could be the subject
of an equitable distribution.

5.3.1.9   *Australia*

The statutory provision to vary a post or ante-nuptial settlement is
contained in the Family Law Act 1975, s 85a:

'Ante-nuptial and post-nuptial settlements

(1) The court may, in proceedings under this Act, make such order as the
court considers just and equitable with respect to the application, for the
benefit of all or any of the parties to, and the children of, the marriage, of
the whole or part of property dealt with by ante-nuptial or post-nuptial
settlements made in relation to the marriage.

(2) In considering what order (if any) should be made under subsection (1),
the court shall take into account the matters referred to in subsection 79(4)
so far as they are relevant.

(3) A court cannot make an order under this section in respect of matters
that are included in a financial agreement.'

In *BP v KS*,[65] the Family Court of Australia considered arguments of
sham and the circumstances in which a husband might be found to be the
alter ego of the trust. This was a case in which the wife was seeking a
lump sum provision, the transfer of the husband's shares in the trustee
company, NTE, to be added as a beneficiary of the trust and to be

---

[64]   2000 Conn Super LEXIS 2004.
[65]   [2002] Fam CA 1454 (Aust).

appointed as a trustee herself. She was also alleging that the trust was a sham and that it was in fact the alter ego of the husband. The court rejected her application to be made a trustee:

'[81] There are a number of Family court cases in which findings were made that the capital of discretionary trusts was either "property" of a person who could control the trust or the "de facto property" of such a person. While such findings might impliedly leave the court at liberty to deal with that property as the court sees fit, this is not necessarily so.

[82] The significance of such a finding may initially be that the assets of the trust can properly be included in a "pool" of assets for division between the parties. To do so is a notional step in a process of reasoning, as distinct from the executive nature of a court order dealing with trust assets.

[83] Even when such a finding underpins a court order, there is a difference between firstly, an order requiring a payment from, for example, husband to wife, (albeit the only source of funds is the capital of a discretionary trust of which the husband is trustee or appointor or otherwise in control), leaving it to the husband to act, presumably according to law, and secondly an order requiring a trustee to pay funds from a trust to satisfy an order for property settlement.

[85] While the distinction between orders *designed to facilitate* satisfaction of other orders for property settlement by distribution from a trust and orders that *direct* that result may seem fine, it is nonetheless real.

[86] In the instant case, the wife seeks a transfer to her of the husband's shares in the trustee company NTE. In other words, the wife is not even yet a trustee. She does not seek an order (as she originally did) requiring the husband as trustee to take particular steps (which no doubt she would argue were lawful) in relation to the trust, for example, to distribute money to himself, albeit perhaps by indirect means through a nominated beneficiary. Nor does she seek an order which in practical terms might only be met by the husband 'accessing' trust funds. She seeks that she become the trustee solely for the purpose of making amendments to the trust to obtain for herself the trust assets.

[87] I find that the wife has pre-determined that if she is placed in a position of control of NTE she intends to distribute all (or alternatively some) of its capital to herself.

[88] In my view, this goes a step beyond the position under consideration in Davidson, and the orders sought, on the evidence, cross the line between facilitation and even expectation, to pre-determination. Therefore, they should not be made.'

In the unreported case of *Toohey v Toohey*,[66] the court was asked to consider an application in relation to a discretionary trust of which the husband was a beneficiary and one of three trustees. The husband's father

---

[66]   No PA3239 of 1988 Family Law.

was the appointor. The court considered the application under s 85. The court held that the trust deed was intended to benefit the husband's blood relatives first to the exclusion of the spouses. The existence of many other potential beneficiaries whose interests were substantial made it less easy to characterise the trust as a nuptial settlement capable of variation.

In the Australian case of *Webster v Webster*[67] the wife came from a wealthy family. One of the trusts involved, known as the Q Trust, had assets of AU$5m. The judge was asked to consider whether the assets in the trust should be treated as a resource or as an asset available to the wife. The wife was the appointor of the trust and the beneficiaries were the wife, her children and remoter issue.

The court accepted the wife's undertaking only to exercise any power under the trust in favour of the children of the family.

The judge's decision was upheld on appeal although the significant contribution of the husband to the financial resources of the wife represented by the Q Trust and the value of that resource was taken into account.

5.3.2　Freezing injunctions

In the course of highly contentious ancillary relief proceedings where there are offshore trusts – often (and erroneously) regarded as of themselves an indication of skulduggery – it is not uncommon for a freezing order to be obtained which not only purports to prohibit the respondent from dealing with assets but also the foreign trustee from disposing of or otherwise dealing with trust assets.

The court has broad powers to prevent future dispositions or set aside historic transactions designed to defeat an applicant's claims. This power comes from s 37(2) of the MCA 1973:

'(2) Where proceedings for financial relief are brought by one person against another, the court may, on the application of the first-mentioned person—

(a)　if it is satisfied that the other party to the proceedings is, with the intention of defeating the claim for financial relief, about to make any disposition or to transfer out of the jurisdiction or otherwise deal with any property, make such order as it thinks fit for restraining the other party from so doing or otherwise for protecting the claim;

(b)　if it is satisfied that the other party has, with that intention, made a reviewable disposition and that if the disposition were set aside financial relief or different financial relief would be granted to the applicant, make an order setting aside the disposition;

---

[67]　[1998] Fam CA 1517 (Aust).

(c)   if it is satisfied, in a case where an order has been obtained under any of the provisions mentioned in subsection (1) above by the applicant against the other party, that the other party has, with that intention, made a reviewable disposition, make an order setting aside the disposition;

and an application for the purposes of paragraph (b) above shall be made in the proceedings for the financial relief in question.'

The court therefore has powers, where it is satisfied that the respondent is acting with the requisite *intention*:

- to grant an injunction preventing a disposal about to be made with that intention;

- to set aside a disposition already made with that intention; or

- to set aside a disposition already made with that intention where financial relief has already been granted.

There is an exception if the disposition was made for valuable consideration to a person acting in good faith and without notice of any intention on the part of the respondent to defeat the applicant's claim (s 37(4) of the MCA 1973).

There is a rebuttable presumption, if the disposition took place less than three years before the application, that the respondent is making the disposition with the intention of defeating the applicant's claims (s 37(5) of the MCA 1973). Applications may still be made outside of this timeframe, but the benefit of the presumption is lost.

A rare example of an application to set aside a transfer of assets in trust is *Mubarak*.[68] As explained above, the husband and wife set up a Jersey trust and transferred their respective 90% and 10% interests in a company into that trust in 1997. In 2005 the wife applied to set aside that transfer of shares under s 37 of the MCA 1973. Holman J held[69] that the requisite intention had not been proven:

'The fact is that the husband plainly did have legitimate and appropriate intentions, namely orderly succession and, very critically, avoidance of tax, which are capable of fully and wholly explaining and justifying the setting up of the trust and the transfer of the shares. All the available documentary evidence supports those intentions and gives no hint of any other.'

In *Ghoth v Ghoth*[70] the Court of Appeal held that a *Mareva*[71] injunction in family proceedings should be limited to the extent of the applicant's

---

68   [2007] EWHC 220 (Fam).
69   At para 65.
70   [1992] 2 FLR 300, CA.

potential claims. The court also noted the importance of inserting provisions to protect bona fide third parties from being in contempt of court for assisting a party in breach of the injunction (*Babanaft International Co SA v Bassatne*[72] and *Derby & Co Ltd v Weldon (Nos 3 and 4)*[73] applied).

The application under the MCA falls under the Family Proceedings Rules 1991, r 2.68 which reads as follows:

'2.68 Application for order under section 37(2)(a) of Act of 1973 or paragraph 74(2) of Schedule 5 to the Act of 2004

(1) An application under section 37(2)(a) of the Act of 1973 paragraph 74(2) of Schedule 5 of the Act of 2004 for an order restraining any person from attempting to defeat a claim for financial provision or otherwise for protecting the claim may be made to the district judge.

(2) Rules 2.65 and 2.66 shall apply, with the necessary modifications to the application as if it were an application for ancillary relief.'

In the alternative, the court can grant a freezing injunction as in non-family law civil proceedings. In these circumstances, the court could use either:

(i)   its inherent jurisdiction to grant a freezing injunction where the balance of convenience favours such a course (per *Roche v Roche*[74] and *Shipman v Shipman*[75]); or

(ii)   s 37(1) of the Supreme Court Act 1981, fortified by s 7 of the Civil Procedure Act 1997.

Under current rules, this would fall still within RSC, as the matter almost always would be within family proceedings. Part 25 of the Civil Procedure Rules gives guidance as to how a freezing order should be drafted. That provision reads as follows:

'25.1 The court may grant the following interim remedies—

(f)   an order (referred to as a "freezing injunction")—
(i)   restraining a party from removing from the jurisdiction assets located there; or
(ii)   restraining a party from dealing with any assets whether located within the jurisdiction or not;

---

[71]   *Mareva Cia Compania Naviera SA v International Bulkcarriers SA* [1975] 2 Lloyd's Rep 509.
[72]   [1990] Ch 13, CA.
[73]   [1990] Ch 65, CA.
[74]   (1981) 11 Fam Law 243, CA.
[75]   [1991] 1 FLR 250, FD.

    (g)   an order directing a party to provide information about the location of relevant property or assets or to provide information about relevant property or assets which are or may be the subject of an application for a freezing injunction'.

An example of a freezing injunction is appended to the Practice Direction to Pt 25 of the CPR and is copied below:

'FREEZING INJUNCTION

    5.   Until the return date or further order of the court, the Respondent must not remove from England and Wales or in any way dispose of, deal with or diminish the value of any of his assets which are in England and Wales up to the value of £...

[For worldwide injunction]

    5.   Until the return date or further order of the court, the Respondent must not—
        (1)   remove from England and Wales any of his assets which are in England and Wales up to the value of £...; or
        (2)   in any way dispose of, deal with or diminish the value of any of his assets whether they are in or outside England and Wales up to the same value.

[For either form of injunction]

    6.   Paragraph 5 applies to all the Respondent's assets whether or not they are in his own name and whether they are solely or jointly owned. For the purpose of this order the Respondent's assets include any asset which he has the power, directly or indirectly, to dispose of or deal with as if it were his own. The Respondent is to be regarded as having such power if a third party holds or controls the asset in accordance with his direct or indirect instructions.
    7.   This prohibition includes the following assets in particular—
        (a)   the property known as [title/address] or the net sale money after payment of any mortgages if it has been sold;
        (b)   the property and assets of the Respondent's business [known as [name]] [carried on at [address]] or the sale money if any of them have been sold; and
        (c)   any money standing to the credit of any bank account including the amount of any cheque drawn on such account which has not been cleared.

[For injunction limited to assets in England and Wales]

    8.   If the total value free of charges or other securities ("unencumbered value") of the Respondent's assets in England and Wales exceeds £..., the Respondent may remove any of those assets from England and Wales or may dispose of or deal with them so long as the total unencumbered value of his assets still in England and Wales remains above £...

[For worldwide injunction]

    8.

(1)   If the total value free of charges or other securities ("unencumbered value") of the Respondent's assets in England and Wales exceeds £..., the Respondent may remove any of those assets from England and Wales or may dispose of or deal with them so long as the total unencumbered value of the Respondent's assets still in England and Wales remains above £...

(2)   If the total unencumbered value of the Respondent's assets in England and Wales does not exceed £..., the Respondent must not remove any of those assets from England and Wales and must not dispose of or deal with any of them. If the Respondent has other assets outside England and Wales, he may dispose of or deal with those assets outside England and Wales so long as the total unencumbered value of all his assets whether in or outside England and Wales remains above £...'

The application for a freezing injunction available in civil proceedings can, if appropriate, be made in the county court under reg 3(3) of the County Court Remedies Regulations 1991, as well as the High Court. The application is governed by the old Rules of the Supreme Court and County Court Rules in force in 1999, except to the limited extent (in the context of costs and expert evidence) they have been superseded by the CPR 1998.

Applications can be made without notice where there is good cause for doing so, but an applicant for a without notice injunction is under a strict obligation at a without notice hearing to give full disclosure of facts which suggest an order should not be made[76] and to provide to the absent respondent copies of any papers given to the judge and a full note of the hearing.

5.3.2.1   Forum disputes and freezing injunctions

In *Owners of Cargo Lately Laden on Board the Siskina v Distos Compania Naviera SA*,[77] known as 'The Siskina', the House of Lords held that the court did not have power to grant a freestanding freezing injunction where there was no cause of action in the relevant jurisdiction. This authority is still followed in many offshore jurisdictions even though, as explained below, thanks to Brussels I the rule no longer applies in England.

Freestanding freezing injunctions are possible in the context of proceedings covered by EC Council Regulation (EC) No 44/2001, also known as 'Brussels I', or under the Lugano Convention (in non-EU Contracting States to the Convention).[78] Article 24 (which mirrors the equivalent provision in the Lugano Convention) reads as follows:

---

[76]   *Re W (Ex Parte Orders)* [2000] 2 FLR 927, FD.

[77]   [1979] AC 210, HL.

[78]   See Chapter 3, regarding maintenance claims falling under this Regulation Convention.

'Application may be made to the courts of a Contracting State for such provisional, including protective measures as may be available under the laws of that State, even if, under this Convention, the courts of another Contracting state have jurisdiction as to the substance of this matter.'

In other words, the courts of one jurisdiction will support those of another Contracting jurisdiction, provided the second jurisdiction is seized of proceedings including a claim for maintenance in the context of family cases.

The original Brussels I Convention which became the Brussels I Regulation was brought into force by the Civil Jurisdiction and Judgments Act 1982. Section 25 states:

'**25   Interim relief in England and Wales and Northern Ireland in the absence of substantive proceedings**

(1) The High Court in England and Wales or Northern Ireland shall have power to grant interim relief where—

   (a)   proceedings have been or are to be commenced in a Brussels or Lugano Contracting State or a Regulation State other than the United Kingdom or in a part of the United Kingdom other than that in which the High Court in question exercises jurisdiction; and

   (b)   they are or will be proceedings whose subject-matter is within the scope of the Regulation as determined by Article 1 of the Regulation (whether or not the Regulation has effect in relation to the proceedings).

(2) On an application for any interim relief under subsection (1) the court may refuse to grant that relief if, in the opinion of the court, the fact that the court has no jurisdiction apart from this section in relation to the subject-matter of the proceedings in question makes it inexpedient for the court to grant it.'

Subparagraph 7 of this section provides that the English court has power to make any order in these circumstances as it could if the proceedings were within its own jurisdiction, save for a warrant for the arrest of property or an order making provision for obtaining evidence. This therefore includes a *Mareva* type injunction.

As can be seen from the wording of s 25(1), it is possible to apply using this power for a freestanding freezing injunction without the need for proceedings to be already on foot, provided they are to be commenced and will fall within the type of proceedings covered by the Convention. The Convention will apply in any family proceedings where one party is suing another for maintenance in another signatory state.

In the very recent case of *Rhode v Rhode and Pembroke Square Ltd*,[79] Baron J determined that the proper procedure in matrimonial proceedings was by way of originating summons, together with an affidavit in support confirming that the applicant has a good claim for interim relief. Although the Family Proceedings Rules 1991 are in the process of being revised to bring them in line with the Civil Proceedings Rules 1998, this procedure remains governed by RSC Ord 29, r 8A and RSC Ord 11, r 8A and not (as the husband's Counsel argued) under Pt 8 of the CPR. No leave to serve out of the jurisdiction is required.

On the facts of the case, the interim injunction was not continued by the judge for a number of reasons. First, because the potential amount caught was so small as to make little difference to the eventual award to be determined by the French court in the context of financial proceedings there. Secondly, because the husband was neither resident nor domiciled in England (although his children from a previous marriage were at school in England). Thirdly, and most importantly, the French judge had declined to grant an injunction. The court considered the checklist of considerations in *Motorola Credit Corp v Uzan*[80] as follows:

(i)   whether the making of an order would interfere with the management of the case in the primary court;

(ii)   whether the policy in the primary jurisdiction in relation to the order sought affects the court's decision;

(iii)   whether there is a danger that the order made would give rise to disharmony or confusion, a risk of inconsistent or overlapping orders;

(iv)   whether at the time the order was sought there was likely to be a potential conflict as to jurisdiction, rendering it inappropriate to make the order; and

(v)   where jurisdiction is resisted or disobedience is expected, whether this court would be making an order that it could not enforce.

The court also has power to grant a freestanding freezing order when the other proceedings are not in a Brussels I or Lugano State. This is thanks to s 25(3) of the 1982 Act set, which was brought into force by a 1997 Order.[81]

---

[79]   [2007] EWHC 496 (Fam).
[80]   [2003] EWCA Civ 752, [2004] 1 WLR 113, CA.
[81]   The Civil Jurisdiction and Judgments Act 1982 (Interim Relief) Order 1997, SI 1997/302.

5.3.2.2   What should the attitude of a trustee be on receipt of a freezing order?

A trustee may be affected by a freezing order (in England) or a *Mareva* order (offshore) in a number of ways, usually the following:

(a)   A freezing order may be made ancillary to the English divorce proceedings restraining the respondent from taking certain steps, which may include dealing with assets of an offshore trust. Notice of such an order will commonly be given to the trustee to improve the chances of compliance with the injunction. In most circumstances it will not be difficult for the trustee to avoid assisting the respondent to breach the order if the trustee has the trust assets properly under its control.

(b)   An order may be made freezing third party assets, ie the assets of the trustee. This is not usual but can occur–
   (i)   when there is good reason for supposing that the assets are in truth the assets of the respondent (as in *Dadourian Group International Inc v Simms*[82]). This may occur with a trust or a company where it is suggested that either is the alter ego of the respondent;
   (ii)   when the respondent has a remedy against a third party which will be rendered worthless unless the third party assets are frozen (as in *C Inc v L*[83]);
   (iii)   where the injunction against a third party is ancillary and incidental to the injunction against the respondent, even if the petitioner and has no direct cause of action against the respondent (*Mubarak v Mubarak*[84]); or
   (iv)   to assist the enforcement of an order, such as in *Mubarak* where an English lump sum order was registered in Bermuda and an injunction granted against the respondent and others to assist enforcement.

Such orders may be made in the jurisdiction where the divorce is taking place or if there is jurisdiction to do so, where the third party is resident. If the order is made in the jurisdiction in which the trustee is resident, the trustee can apply at the on notice appointment (such orders usually being made without notice in the first instance) for the order to be discharged on the basis that it is unfounded, was procured by inadequate disclosure of the facts or that a satisfactory undertaking is offered in its place. An application may be made to vary the injunction on the basis that it is oppressive, eg because it prevents normal trust business or distributions. Clearly, the trustee will need advice on how to respond to such a situation,

---

[82]   [2006] EWCA Civ 399.
[83]   [2001] 2 All ER 446 (Comm).
[84]   5 ITELR 345.

but should be cautious not to breach the order, however oppressive, before the return day for the on notice application.

Where the freezing order is obtained in England, where possible the applicant will obtain a 'mirror' freezing order in the offshore jurisdiction where the trustees are based. In some offshore countries, such as Jersey, this is possible. In others, such as Bermuda, where the House of Lords authority of *The Siskina*[85] is followed, the local court has no jurisdiction to grant a freestanding freezing order without a separate cause of action.

The most acute problems arise when the injunction is made in England against the trustee and the trustee is situated elsewhere and does not wish to submit to the jurisdiction. The trustee should take advice in England as to the possibility of challenging jurisdiction to make the order against it without submitting to the jurisdiction; consideration of the issues entailed in such an application is beyond the scope of this book but in general entering an appearance in matrimonial proceedings is regarded as risky and unless there is very strong advice and directions from the trustee's local court to support, unwise.

This may leave the trustee in the unhappy position that it would not wish to breach the terms of an English injunction made against it but that its terms may seriously impede trust business and or cause hardship to beneficiaries who rely on distributions from the trust such that compliance with the English order may be perceived to be at variance with its duty as trustee.

Accordingly, the choices would appear to lie between the beneficiary spouse seeking the variation of the injunction – drawing to the attention of the court the issues the trustee would raise were it in a position to do so – the trustee complying with the injunction or seeking the directions of the trustee's home court as to the extent to which the trustee should be relieved from any obligation to comply with the injunction. This is not a wholly satisfactory situation with the potential for the foreign court's order to be at variance with that of the English divorce court and the trustee perceived in England to be acting in contempt of an English order of which it has notice. Clearly, the trustee will need to take appropriate advice.

---

[85]   [1979] AC 210, HL.

CHAPTER 6

NON-DIVORCE LINES OF ATTACK ON TRUSTS

6.1 INTRODUCTION

When a substantial proportion of the family wealth is held in trust, attention will be focused on whether the assets in the trust should be viewed as a resource available to one spouse or civil partner (see Chapter 5) or, possibly whether the assets are actually held for one of the spouses/civil partners because the trust is invalid. One method of attacking trusts on divorce is to consider the origin of a trust and to question whether it has been validly constituted: if it has not, the assets held by the trustees are held on bare trust for the settlor.

This involves looking at trust law rather than family law issues and applying the appropriate trust law concepts to determine the validity of the structure.

Throughout this chapter, references to 'spouses' should be regarded as including references to 'civil partners'.

6.2 FORMALITIES

6.2.1 Valid constitution and compliance with formalities

Before a party to a failing marriage considers whether a trust in which the other spouse has an interest might be attacked as being invalid on the basis of some technical flaw, the potential attacker should consider whether to do so will achieve an advantage for him or her. It will only serve, if successful, to restore assets to the estate of the other spouse (and so make the assets readily available for redistribution between the spouses by the court) if the other spouse was the settlor. In the 1970s and 1980s it was quite common for trusts, particularly offshore, to be created with a corporate or a dummy settlor to keep the identity of the real settlor confidential. In such a case the fact that another is named as the settlor is not fatal to the restoration to the true settlor's estate of the trust assets should the trust be found to be invalid, but it would be necessary to satisfy the court that the other spouse was the real economic settlor. An attack on the validity of a trust will be a futile exercise if it would result in the restoration of the assets, for example, to the estate of the other spouse's parent, unless that parent is dead and the spouse the sole or a significant beneficiary of his or her parent's estate. In that case the possible benefit to be derived from the exercise may be significantly eroded by death and other taxes.

But in a limited number of cases (such as where variation of the trust is unlikely to be put into effect in the trust jurisdiction or where the trust creates fixed interests in favour of third parties and there is limited scope to suggest that the assets of the trust are a resource of the settlor spouse) an attack on the validity of a trust may be an appropriate alternative to an application to vary the terms of a settlement or an allegation that the reality of the situation is that the trust assets are a resource of the other spouse and so can be taken into account in the division of assets.

The majority of trusts are constituted by a settlor transferring the legal title to property to a trustee or trustees and declaring in writing (in the form of a trust deed) the terms upon which that property is to be held. Alternatively, the settlor may hand the trust property to the trustee and the trustee executes a declaration of trust over the assets. Sometimes the declaration of trust is purely verbal: this method typically leads to difficulties evidencing the declaration and uncertainty as to its terms.

As far as English law trusts of land are concerned the Law of Property Act 1925, s 53(1)(b) provides:

> 'A declaration of trust respecting any land or any interest therein must be manifested and proved by some writing signed by some person who is able to declare such trust or by his will.'

Although the declaration itself need not be in writing, writing is required to evidence the intention of the settlor to make a trust of land. There is no obligation to evidence the creation of a trust in writing where the assets settled are personalty.[1] Under English law dispositions of equitable interests must be in writing or they will be void (s 53(1)(c) of the Law of Property Act 1925). Under s 9 of the Wills Act 1837, all testamentary trusts must also be in writing, signed by the testator and by two witnesses.

Under the Hague Convention on the Law Applicable to Trusts and on Their Recognition, trusts may be made orally but must be evidenced in writing. The Convention was given effect in the United Kingdom by the Recognition of Trusts Act 1987.

In the United States, unless statute otherwise requires, trusts can be oral but such a trust will need clear and convincing evidence to establish it. The Uniform Trust Code, adopted (with variations) in numerous states, follows the general law in this respect (s 407 of the Uniform Trust Code).

---

[1]　*M'Fadden v Jenkyns* (1842) 1 Ph 153; *Paul v Constance* [1977] 1 WLR 527, CA.

It is important to check that the trust complies with the formal requirements of the law to which it is expressed to be subject. This is particularly important when considering 'designer' trusts such as purpose trusts in those jurisdictions which have introduced legislation to permit such trusts (which are otherwise invalid in common law jurisdictions unless the trusts are exclusively charitable – *A-G of Cayman Islands v Wahr-Hansen*[2]) and STAR trusts under the Cayman Islands The Special Trusts (Alternative Regime) Law 1997.

Similar considerations apply to the transfer of assets to a Foundation, an entity which unlike a trust but similar to a company, has its own legal identity. Foundations are predominantly creations of civil law jurisdictions (although the Bahamas has recently introduced Foundations) and accordingly particular importance is attached to form and other requirements such as registration, failure to comply with which may render the entity invalid.

Trusts created during a settlor's lifetime are commonly used to ameliorate tax, and in order to be tax effective there must be clear documentary evidence of the date of creation of the settlement, the transfer of assets into it and of its terms.

The general rule is that a settlor may create a trust by manifesting an intention to create it although a general intention to benefit someone will not suffice.[3] Accordingly, the words and/or actions of a settlor must be sufficient to establish his intention to part with legal title over an asset and for it to be held by trustees for the benefit of others. In a divorce context, as with trusts designed to reduce tax burdens, trusts which are inadequately documented will give rise to difficulty and a party to a divorce seeking to rely on a trust created by him or her which is inadequately supported by contemporaneous documentation may not be able to establish to the satisfaction of the court that title to the assets purportedly settled has left his or her estate.

The trust deed or declaration of trust may detail the assets settled but it is very common for the deed or declaration to refer to an initial settled sum (typically £100 or US $1,000) and the substantive assets to be settled later in one or more tranches. Additions to the settlement are often poorly documented and difficulties may arise establishing the extent of the assets added, their provenance and the date of the addition. The latter point may be of great importance if it is suggested that the addition was before the marriage or within the three-year period during which there will be a presumption in favour of clawback under s 37 of the MCA 1973 (see Chapter 5). (Note that a clawback claim may be subject to enforcement issues if the trustees are offshore.)

---

[2]   [2000] 3 All ER 642, PC.
[3]   *Jones v Lock* (1865) 1 Ch App 25; *Paul v Constance* [1977] 1 WLR 527, CA.

Each addition to a settlement may be treated as a new settlement on the same terms as the previous settlement so all the criteria which require to be fulfilled for a valid settlement to be created apply also to additions to the settlement. This is particularly important where it appears that the settlement was validly created with only nominal assets, with the substantial assets being settled after some time when the settlor's circumstances had altered.

Where detailed tax planning is the driving force behind the creation of a lifetime trust, it is likely that there will have been a complicated series of transactions, often using corporate vehicles, in order to effect the maximum tax saving. Holding companies may be established, the shares of which are held by offshore trusts. Compliance with the formalities of establishing those companies and their administration must be as rigorous as that of any company. Particular attention should be paid to the appointment of directors, share transfers and company constitution. If inadequate care is taken the vehicle may simply be looked through, as in *Trustor v Smallbone*.[4] Courts in the US are particularly apt to look through corporate vehicles or trusts which they consider lack economic substance, as in *Lund v Commissioner of Internal Revenue*.[5] If the company underlying the trust has not been properly constituted or the shares improperly issued or transferred it may be that the corporate assets do not in fact constitute assets of the trust.

6.2.2　Invalid gifts

Gifts into a trust may also be found to be ineffective if improperly constituted. The equitable maxim 'equity will not aid a volunteer' has been interpreted by the courts to mean that equity will not perfect imperfect gifts. In *Milroy v Lord*,[6] a gift was found to be imperfect because the donor had signed the wrong kind of document – one that was not appropriate to effect a transfer of the legal title to a subject matter of the intended gift. However, it was established that if the donor of a gift had done everything in his power to effect that gift then accordingly it was valid, regardless of the actions of third parties. This line of reasoning was followed in *Re Rose*[7] 'everything in the donor's power necessary' and *Re Rose*[8] 'everything necessary to be done by the donor'.

However, the recent decision in *Pennington v Waine*[9] has moved the law on. What is now required for a valid gift is determination of: firstly, whether the intending donor has executed a document in the right form, or done in the right manner any other act necessary to pass legal title to

---

4　　[2001] 1 WLR 1177, ChD.
5　　[2000] 3 ITELR 343.
6　　(1862) 4 De GF & J 264.
7　　[1949] Ch 78.
8　　[1952] Ch 499 at 511.
9　　[2002] 1 WLR 2075, CA.

the donee and secondly, whether it would be conscionable to allow the donor to withdraw from the gift. Whether it is conscionable or not depends on an evaluation of the facts by a judge in each case.

Where there had been a string of trusts and transfers of assets, it is important to trace back to the original trust and to ensure that the powers of appointment in all trust deeds have been properly effected and perpetuity periods not exceeded. It is not uncommon to find that conditions attached to the exercise of powers have not been fulfilled: a common example being that the Protector's consent has not been secured or the advance or appointment is other than by deed, if that was specified. An appointee on advance from one trust to another which has been imperfectly constituted or where the advance was invalid is at risk of a claim that those assets remain held on the original trusts: this may make the assets available for division on divorce.

6.2.3   The three certainties

Lord Langdale MR declared the three essentials for the creation of a valid trust in *Knight v Knight*.[10] These are certainty of words, certainty of subject matter and certainty of objects:

6.2.3.1   *Certainty of words / intention*

As touched on briefly above, express lifetime trusts are often created by duly executed deeds, even though the strict requirement under English law that they be in writing is only applied to dispositions of an interest in land. Certainty of words, whether written or spoken, is necessary to show an intention on the part of the settlor that a trust should be created. In most cases there is no difficulty in discovering such an intention because the settlor directs that the trust property is to be held 'in trust' or 'upon trust'. However, beyond the formality of whether the correct intention is displayed in words the following issues need to be explored:

6.2.3.1.1   *Competence*

A settlor must be competent to declare a trust. The basic test for capacity to give away substantial assets is set out in the case of *Re Beaney*.[11] This case is authority for the proposition that the level of competence required is relative to the size of the gift and if a very substantial proportion of the settlor's assets have been given away, the test for competence is as stringent as that for making a will (the highest level of competence required under English law). In *Re Morris*,[12] the court decided that if the

---

[10]   (1840) 3 Beav 148.
[11]   (1978) 1 WLR 770, ChD.
[12]   [2001] WTLR 1137.

settlor/donor suffered from any mental disorder it was up to the trustees/beneficiaries to prove that the settlor was none the less competent.

6.2.3.1.2   Absence of undue influence

Where a donor has trust and confidence in a donee (either because this is actual or presumed by law) the donee is obliged to establish that the donor acted of his own free will: if he cannot, the gift or transfer into trust is set aside. This was the basis of the allegations in the extremely expensive *Thyssen–Bornemeisza* litigation in Bermuda. In the case of *Hammond v Osborn*,[13] the donee could not rebut the presumption of undue influence which arose when an elderly gentleman left all his free capital to a woman who befriended him in the year or so before his death. A presumption of undue influence cannot be rebutted merely by proof that the conduct of the donee has been unimpeachable (*Padgham v Rochelle*[14]). In *Jennings v Cairns*[15] the defendant failed to show that the disposition into trust had been of the settlor's own free and informed will, the settlor having been mistaken as to the nature of the trust she was establishing and not having received quality independent advice.

6.2.3.1.3   Absence of intention

Intention to create a valid trust requires an intention at that time to part with possession and control of the trust assets on the terms of the settlement (*Re Kayford Ltd*[16] and *Re Pfrimmer*[17]). Accordingly, there is real difficulty as to the validity of trusts which in reality are will substitutes. (These appear to be acceptable in most US states, the Uniform Trust Code adopted (with variations) in a number of states, envisaging a hybrid between a trust and a will which ensures that the assets so settled do not need to be subjected to probate upon the settlor's death but form part of the settlor's estate for insolvency purposes.)

In England and those jurisdictions whose law is based on English law, a trust which endeavours to give effective control to the settlor during his lifetime and where the powers and discretions of the trustees do not really commence until the settlor's death is unlikely to be upheld: in the old English case *Cock v Cooke*[18] it was emphasised that irrespective of whether the disposition was in the form of a trust, if it was intended to take effect on death, it is in effect testamentary.

---

[13] [2002] EWCA Civ 885.
[14] [2002] WTRLR 1403.
[15] [2003] EWCA Civ 1935.
[16] [1975] 1 WLR 279, ChD.
[17] [1936] DLR 577 (Manitoba Court of Appeal).
[18] (1866) 15 WR 89.

It is common for settlors to wish to retain rights and this is permissible provided that the trustees have genuine powers and discretions to exercise and are not mere nominees. Settlors commonly retain consent or veto powers over various dispositive matters such as additions to the beneficial class and distributions to beneficiaries. The settlor may have the power to remove and or appoint trustees. (If the settlor retains such a power it cannot be exercised selfishly: it is a fiduciary power (*Re Skeats Settlement*[19]). So it is not possible to submit, in cases where it is alleged that trust assets are a resource of one spouse, that if the trustees do not comply with a request by the settlor for a distribution he can simply remove them if he has retained the power to do so. This issue was described as 'peripheral' by the Court of Appeal in *Charman* but will doubtless require to be addressed more fully in due course.)

If the settlor wishes to remain involved in the investment of the trust assets, the settlor may be named as the investment adviser. There is no reason why a settlor should not be involved in making recommendations to the trustee on investments or in managing investments provided that the ultimate decision is that of the trustee (except in those cases where the trust deed removes the trustees' obligations in that respect). The settlor's involvement in assisting in the selection of investments or in managing them is often regarded by the Family Division as an indication of control by the settlor of all aspects of the trusteeship. This is unfortunate, since the trustee may be uninfluenced by the settlor (save by perfectly properly taking his wishes into consideration but not adhering to them slavishly) in relation to dispositive decisions – which beneficiaries receive what benefits. It is very common for the settlor who has built up significant wealth to have particular skills in managing/selecting investments in a particular asset class and the trustee may be perfectly happy (and may properly) consider it appropriate that the settlor applies that skill to the assets of the settlement. This does not mean that the trust is a sham or that the settlor controls the destination of the benefits to be conferred by the trustees.

The Virgin Islands Special Trusts Act 2003 ('VISTA') sets out the powers which may be reserved by the settlor under BVI law without rendering the settlement invalid (on the basis that it might otherwise be regarded as a nomineeship). Apart from BVI law governed trusts and even with a VISTA trust which has assets in or substantial connections with another jurisdiction such that the court of a jurisdiction other than BVI may be considering the validity of the trust, it is dangerous for a settlor to reserve too many powers: to do so may give rise to allegations of invalidity or at the least, allegations of effective control or that the trust assets are a resource of the settlor in the context of divorce proceedings.

There may be genuine concerns as to whether the settlor did intend to create a trust rather than a nomineeship or mandate arrangement,

---

[19]   [1889] 42 Ch D 522.

particularly if the settlor's first language is not English and/or he or she comes from a culture where the trust concept is not widely understood. In such a case, unless there is evidence that the settlor received advice (preferably in a language with which he or she was familiar) as to the nature and consequences of transferring assets into the settlement the trust may fail for lack of intention.

Problems also arise where it is suggested that the settlement did not have the effect that the settlor intended. In *Jennings v Cairns*[20] the settlor, also found to have been labouring under undue influence, had not intended to create an irrevocable settlement. However, other recent attempts by settlors to claw back into their estates assets now in settlements which they were finding inconvenient have failed, primarily because contemporaneous evidence has demonstrated that later allegations to the effect that the settlements did not provide what they intended did not accord with reality at the time of creation of the settlements. (See, for example, *The Holmaengen Trust*[21] and *Hotung v Ho Yuen Ki*[22] .)

6.2.3.1.4   Mistake

The settlor may be able to establish that he did not intend the settlement to have the effect that it did and that he was operating under a mistake in law or in fact as to the effect of the settlement. If this can be established without relying on self serving statements the settlement may be set aside as a mistake (*Gibbon v Mitchell*[23]). The court has a wide equitable jurisdiction to relieve from the consequences of mistake. It may be that a settlement will be set aside on the basis that its terms exceeded instructions given by the settlor or that he did not have a fair opportunity of understanding its nature and operation before he executed it (*Meadows v Meadows*[24]). The burden on such a claimant is a heavy one and it is not sufficient to say that the settlor was mistaken as to the advantages – whether fiscal or otherwise – to be afforded by the settlement rather than its legal consequences.

6.2.3.1.5   Sham

6.2.3.1.5.1   INTRODUCTION

In *A v A and St George Trustees Ltd*[25] (the latest case on shams in the Family Division) Munby J deprecated ill-founded and ill-thought through allegations of sham. He pointed out that, as Neubeger J had found in *National Westminster Bank plc v Jones*[26] there is a strong and natural

---

[20]   [2003] EWCA Civ 1935.
[21]   (1998–1999) 1 ITELR 901.
[22]   7 ITELR 795.
[23]   [1990] 3 All ER 338.
[24]   (1853) 16 Beav 401.
[25]   [2007] EWHC 99 (Fam).
[26]   [2001] BCLC 98, ChD.

presumption against holding a provision or document a sham and that it is a very serious allegation, because a degree of dishonesty is involved. He emphasised that:

> '... even in the Family Division, a spouse who seeks to extend her claim for ancillary relief to assets which appear to be in the hands of someone other than her husband must identify and by reference to established principle, some proper basis for doing so. The Court cannot grant relief merely because the husband's arrangements appear to be artificial or even "dodgy"'

and he went on:

> '... what it is important to appreciate (and too often, I fear, is not appreciated at least in this Division) is that the relevant legal principles which have to be applied are precisely the same in this Division as in the other two Divisions. There is not one law of "sham" in the Chancery Division and another law of "sham" in the Family Division. There is only one law of "sham", to be applied equally in all three Divisions of the High Court ....'

6.2.3.1.5.2 THE ESSENCE OF SHAM

An allegation of a sham trust is an allegation that the settlor lacked the intention to create a valid trust and moreover that the trustee was party to that intention, joining in with the creation of a misleading document intended to mask the true relationship: that of principal and agent/nominee under a bare trust rather than settlor and trustee of the complex trust arrangements the documents describe.

The word 'sham' is overrated, overused and tends to be too freely applied in divorce proceedings. A trust itself is not a sham; it is the document which creates or purports to create a trust which might be a sham document because it was intended, quite deliberately, to give the appearance of creating different rights and obligations from those which the parties actually intended. It is, 'a cloak, a device or a mask' – effectively an allegation of deceit on the part of the settlor and trustees, causing any respectable trustee much concern. The trustee should however, think very carefully before joining in proceedings other than in its home jurisdiction to defend this allegation, if it has the choice of staying out.

In the case *Snook v London and West Riding Investment Ltd*[27] Lord Diplock identified the elements in a sham transaction as:

> 'acts done or documents executed by the parties to the "sham" which are intended by them to give to third parties or to the court the appearance of creating between the parties legal rights and obligations different from the actual rights and obligations (if any) which the parties intend to create ... for

---

[27] [1967] 2 QB 786, CA.

acts or documents to be a sham, with whatever legal consequences follow
from this, all the parties thereto must have a common intention that the acts
or documents are not to create the legal rights and obligations which they
give the appearance of creating. No unexpressed intentions of a "shammer"
affect the rights of a party whom he deceived.'

The 'common intention' test has been recently affirmed in the Court of
Appeal's decision in *Hitch v Stone (Inspector of Taxes)*,[28] by the Royal
Court of Jersey in *Re The Esteem Settlement*,[29] and in *MacKinnon v
Regent Trust Co Ltd*,[30] and in *Shalson v Russo*[31] (all cited with approval by
Munby J in *A v A and St George Trustees Ltd*[32]). As the law stands it is
clear that it is not sufficient to show that the settlor alone had the
'shamming' intention, although in cases where it could be established that
he/she had no intention to create a trust at all or not on those terms, it
could be alleged that one of the three certainties was lacking.

In *Hitch v Stone (Inspector of Taxes)*[33] Arden LJ considered that there
were five issues to be addressed when considering whether a document
was a sham or a genuine reflection of parties' instructions:

(1)   the court can examine external evidence such as the parties'
       explanations and circumstantial evidence, including evidence of the
       subsequent conduct of the parties;

(2)   the parties must have intended to create different rights and
       obligations from those appearing in the relevant document, and have
       intended to give a false impression of those rights and obligations to
       third parties;

(3)   uncommerciality, or even artificiality, does not by itself indicate that
       the document is a sham;

(4)   the fact that parties subsequently depart from an agreement does not
       necessarily mean that they never intended the agreement to be
       effective and binding;

(5)   the intention must be a common intention to mislead or give a false
       impression.

The Court of Appeal also decided that the fact that certain parts of the
agreement had been implemented was not a bar to finding that other
parts which did not affect third parties were a sham.

---

28   [2001] EWCA Civ 63, [2001] STC 214, CA.
29   2003 JLR 188.
30   [2004] JRC 211.
31   [2003] EWHC 1637 (Ch).
32   [2007] EWHC 99 (Fam).
33   [2001] STC 214.

In *Re The Esteem Settlement*,[34] a case which has been described as defining the law of Jersey on shams, a victim of fraud alleged that a trust established by the fraudster but which contained some clean assets was a sham. The Royal Court confirmed that both parties to the 'sham' document must have an intention to mislead or give a false impression, and that it was unlikely that a professional trustee intended to act otherwise than in accordance with the trust deed. It was also noted that the trustee had not given assurances that it would comply with the settlor's wishes and that the trustees' files demonstrated that they had independently considered each request made by the settlor.

In declaration of trust cases where the settlor is also the trustee it will only be necessary to establish the deceitful intention on the part of the settlor/trustee. Such a situation nearly arose in *Midland Bank Plc v Wyatt*[35] where a husband purported to settle his assets on trust by executing a declaration of trust to which his wife was also a party. The question arose as to whether a shamming intention on her part had to be proved. The judge held:

> 'A sham transaction will still remain a sham transaction even if one of the parties to it merely went along with the "shammer" not either knowing or caring about what he or she was signing. Such a person would still be a party to the sham.'

Munby J agreed with this analysis in *A v A and St George Trustees Ltd*,[36] confirming that while a common intention is required 'reckless indifference will be taken to constitute the necessary intention'.

The approach of the Royal Court in *Esteem* to 'sham' trusts was subsequently followed by the English High Court in *Shalson v Russo*[37] and by the Royal Court in *MacKinnon v Regent Trust Co Ltd*.[38]

6.2.3.1.5.3   SHAM IN DIVORCE PROCEEDINGS

The concept of sham is relevant to divorce proceedings because it had become popular in divorce proceedings to allege that a trust in which the spouse is involved is a sham, rather than simply alleging that it is within the effective control of the spouse, or that it can be taken into account as a resource and an order made against the spouse accordingly (as in *Browne v Browne*[39]).

Before making such an allegation, the question must be asked whether an allegation of sham is going to achieve any benefit for the attacking

---

[34]   2003 JLR 188.
[35]   [1995] 1 FLR 696, ChD.
[36]   [2007] EWHC 99 (Fam).
[37]   [2003] WTLR 1165.
[38]   [2004] JRC 211.
[39]   [1989] 1 FLR 291, CA.

spouse? Unless a spouse settled the assets (or most of them), an allegation that the trust deed is a sham is not capable of resulting in the restoration of assets into that spouse's estate. (The wife in *A v A and St George Trustees Ltd*[40] made this fundamental mistake in alleging sham in respect of trusts settled with assets of her husband's father and brother. If her allegation had succeeded, the trust assets would have been held for the husband's brother and the father's estate, not for the husband.)

The spouse contemplating such an attack should also give careful consideration to whether an attack is capable of damaging their position as a beneficiary of the settlement. Clearly this is not an issue if the attacking spouse is not a beneficiary but an attacker who is also a beneficiary should be aware that equitable principles prevent an attacker from claiming benefits (whether distributions or information) as a beneficiary at the same time as attacking the settlement: in effect the beneficiary has to choose between claiming rights under the settlement or against it.

Such a situation arose in *Re M Trust*[41] in which a wife was claiming that the trust was a sham in the course of divorce proceedings in Illinois and at the same time asking for copies of trust documents in a beneficiary capacity (ie on behalf of her children who were beneficiaries). On the trustees seeking directions from the Royal Court of Jersey, the court declined to permit the disclosure of documents to the wife all the time she was alleging that the settlement was invalid.

The Family Division of the High Court in England is well known for its broad brush approach and emphasis on looking at the reality of the situation rather than the strict legal position, such as the appropriate legal principles to establish whether or not the settlement is valid according to the law which governs it. This is unfortunate because it may result in valid structures being affected by a judgment of sham, honest trustees' probity maligned and other beneficiaries' interests inappropriately damaged, all without hearing the benefit of submissions addressing the appropriate legal issues and often without being referred to the law of the jurisdiction which governs the trust. The problem of inadequate submissions being made to the family judge is all the more acute if, as is common, trustees offshore do not submit to the jurisdiction and so are unable to make submissions as to the validity of the settlement. Accordingly, the spouse potentially detrimentally affected should be prepared to marshal proper trust based arguments as to why the trust should not be set aside as a sham.

---

[40]   [2007] EWHC 99 (Fam).
[41]   [2003] WTLR 491.

In the recent English divorce case of *Minwalla v Minwalla*[42] the judge was asked to declare that Jersey trusts of which it was alleged the husband retained dominion and control were shams.

The judge considered the test in *Snook* and reviewed recent English decisions with regard to 'sham' trusts and (having reviewed the conduct of the husband and the trustees) had no hesitation declaring the trusts to be a sham, with the consequence that the assets of the two trusts vested in the husband absolutely. This was a very obvious case, the husband doing his cause no good by his obstructive conduct. The judge did not, however, apply Jersey law (as established in *Re The Esteem Settlement*[43] and *MacKinnon v The Regent Trust Co Ltd*[44]) to this issue, notwithstanding that this was a trust governed by Jersey law and that the Recognition of Trusts Act 1987 provides (at Art 8) that the law specified by Arts 6 and 7 (choice of governing law by the settlor or the law with which the settlement is most closely connected) governs the validity of the trust, its constructions and effects. Although the facts in this case were unfortunate, the husband and the trustee behaving badly, it is unfortunate that in this first English case in which the family court pronounced on an issue of trust law, the analysis of general trust law principles was so poor and the applicable law which had been so amply expounded in *Esteem*, wholly ignored.

When the matter came to be considered in the Royal Court of Jersey when the wife endeavoured to enforce the order (in *CI Law Trustees Ltd v Minwalla* the '*Fountain Trust*' case[45]), the Royal Court, not surprisingly, considered that Jersey law should have been applied to determine whether or not this Jersey law trust was a sham. The Royal Court was critical of the English family court for involving itself in the determination of sham, stating:

> 'as a matter of generality, we would regard an assumption of jurisdiction by a foreign court to declare a Jersey trust sham to be exorbitant and we would be reluctant to enforce any judgment based on such an assumption'.

However, on the facts of this particular case the Royal Court was willing to enforce the English order transferring the trust assets to the wife because it considered that the family court had sought to do justice between the parties where the husband had flouted his obligations to his wife. The trustee had also submitted to the jurisdiction.

(The postscript to this case is that the criminal authorities then sought a Confiscation Order in respect of the trust assets on the basis that they

---

[42]   [2005] 1 FLR 771, FD.
[43]   2003 JLR 188.
[44]   [2004] JRC 211.
[45]   [2005] JRC 099.

were probably the proceeds of criminal conduct. That application was dismissed[46] but payment has not been made to the wife because there is a third party claim to the trust assets.)

In the most recent divorce case in which an allegation of a sham trust was made (*A v A and St George Trustees Ltd*[47]), the Jersey trustee of an English law trust participated and satisfied the court that the allegation of sham lacked foundation.

While Munby J accepted that where a spouse sought to obfuscate, hide or mask the reality behind shams the Family Division should deal with the case robustly, treating 'as one and the same a husband and some corporate or trust structure which it is apparent is simply the alter ego or creature of the husband' the court should not 'simply ride roughshod over established principle, least of all where there are, or appear to be, third party interests involved'.

Munby J emphasised that in approaching an allegation of sham in respect of assets to which a third party (the trustees) had title, the court must determine the issue 'on exactly the same legal basis as if it were being determined in the Chancery Division' and that the law of sham had to be applied on precisely the same principles in the Family Division.

While dismissing the wife's allegations of sham as ill-founded, and not conforming to established law (such as *Snook*, *Esteem* and *Hitch v Stone*) Munby J addressed two further interesting issues:

(a)   can a valid trust become a sham, and vice versa?

(b)   can a document be a sham for one purpose and valid for another?

As to whether a valid trust can become a sham, drawing heavily on a dicta by Rimer J in *Shalson v Russo*,[48] Munby J concluded as a matter of principle that 'a trust which is not initially a sham cannot subsequently become a sham'.

The trust property cannot lose its charter as trust property by the settlor subsequently deciding to deal with it as his own: if the trustee accedes to the settlor's pressure to that effect and behaves as though the trust property belongs to the settlor (rather than giving due consideration to the settlor's wishes) the trustee will simply be committing a breach of trust:

> 'A trustee who has bona fide accepted office as such cannot divest himself of his fiduciary obligations by his own improper acts. If, therefore, a trustee

---

[46]   *Chief Officer of The States of Jersey Police v Minwalla* [2007] JRC 137.
[47]   [2007] EWHC 99 (Fam).
[48]   [2003] EWHC 1637 (Ch), [2005] Ch 281, ChD.

who has entered into his responsibilities, and without having any intention of being party to a sham, subsequently purports, perhaps in agreement with the settlor, to treat the trust as a sham, the effect is not to create a sham where previously there was a valid trust. The only effect, even if the agreement is actually carried into execution, is to expose the trustee to a claim for breach of trust and, it may well be, to expose a settlor to a claim for knowing assistance in that breach of trust.'

(Munby J did not touch on this possibility but it may be that if there is an addition to the settlement, it could none the less be argued that the addition was, in reality, on the basis of a nomineeship and not on the terms of the express trust.)

Conversely, Munby J thought it possible that a trust document which might have masked the shamming intention of the settlor and original trustee might spring into reality upon a new trustee, without knowledge of the shamming intention, taking on the trusteeship. At that point the settlor may intend a sham (as to which his evidence contrary to the deed may not count as being self-serving) and the new trustee intend properly to fulfil his duties as trustee of the trusts expressed in the trust deed. He concluded:

'whatever the settlor or anyone else may have intended, and whatever may have happened since it was first created, a trust will not be a sham – in my judgment cannot as a matter of law be a sham – if either:
(i)   the original trustee(s); or
(ii)   the current trustee(s)
were not, because they lacked the relevant knowledge and intention, party to the sham at the time of their appointment. In the first case, the trust will never have been a sham. In the second case, the trust, even if it was previously a sham, will have become a genuine – a valid and enforceable trust as from the date of appointment of the current trustee(s).'

A point which arises in the context of attempts to deceive fiscal authorities is the validity of documentation intended to mask the true position from the revenue authorities. It may be that such documentation is maintained to be valid in a tax investigation but in a divorce, sought to be described as a sham. Munby J concluded that he could not see how:

'a transaction can be a sham for one purpose but not for another. A transaction is either genuine or it is a sham. If it is genuine, then in principle the function of the Court is simply to ascertain its legal nature and effect and enforce it accordingly. If it is a sham, then it is in principle ineffective, indeed void ... So, for example, a transaction cannot be genuine between a husband and the Revenue whilst being at the same a sham as between him and his wife.'

Munby J then referred to the analogous position which arises when property is put in a wife's name to avoid the claims of creditors: the husband cannot subsequently say it was his and not his wife's in the context of a divorce (*Tinker v Tinker*[49]).

6.2.3.1.5.4   THE OFFSHORE COURT'S ATTITUDE TOWARDS FINDINGS OF SHAM
              IN THE FAMILY DIVISION

As described earlier in this chapter, the Royal Court of Jersey was willing to enforce the English judgment based on a finding of sham in *Minwalla v Minwalla*,[50] the case being a very obvious one. Nonetheless, the Royal Court expressed its unhappiness at the Family Division of the High Court exercising its powers so as to declare a Jersey trust a sham (particularly without receiving evidence as to Jersey law on sham) and in general expressed the view that a foreign court declaring a Jersey trust a sham was an exercise of 'exorbitant' jurisdiction noting its reluctance to enforce such a judgment.[51]

In *Charman v Charman (No 4)*[52] the Court of Appeal agreed with the Royal Court of Jersey – that the assumption of jurisdiction to declare a foreign law trust a sham would generally be exorbitant.

The Court of Appeal signalled that the way ahead may well be for non-trust spouses, as with Mrs Charman, to allege instead that the trust assets are a resource of the other spouse, so side-stepping the more stringent requirements of proving sham or those associated with variation. How the onshore and offshore trust profession will respond – whether it will be '*disposed to help, within the parameters of its laws*' (as the Court of Appeal suggested) or whether it will consider such improper pressure on trustees and damaging the interests of other beneficiaries who have had no opportunity to be heard in the matter, remains to be seen.

If the trust is governed by English law, the trustee has little choice but to participate and bring to the judge's attention the test for establishing whether a trust deed is a sham and the impact of such a decision on other beneficiaries. If the trustee is offshore the trustee will want to consider very carefully whether or not to submit to the jurisdiction, making enforcement in their home jurisdiction easier. The question of how the trustees should react to ancillary relief proceedings is addressed in more detail in Chapter 7.

6.2.3.2   Certainty of subject matter

As to certainty of subject matter, the property comprising the trust estate must be identified with sufficient certainty. There have been a number of cases in which considerable doubt has been cast as to just what property

---

[49]   [1970] P 136, CA.
[50]   [2005] 1 FLR 771, FD.
[51]   *CI Law Trustees Ltd v Minwalla* 2005 JLR 359, [2005] JRC 099, [2006] WTLR 807.
[52]   [2007] EWCA Civ 503. See further Appendix 2.

was subject to the trust, for example, in *Hunter v Moss*[53] the court held that a declaration of trust over 50 out of 950 shares in a company was sufficiently certain, it not being necessary to identify any particular shares in the total holding. However, this may not work in relation to all types of property such as a trust over wine which to be effective has to identify specific or ascertained bottles (*Re London Wine Co (Shippers) Ltd*[54]).

6.2.3.3 Certainty of objects

The beneficiaries of the trust must be clearly identifiable so, for example, precatory trusts are not considered to be valid trusts, purpose trusts will fail for lack of certainty (unless established in accordance with the law of a jurisdiction which caters specifically for purpose trusts and the trust in question is in conformity with the relevant legislation) unless the purposes are exclusively charitable. In *Steele v Paz*,[55] a Red Cross or Black Hole trust nearly failed. It was suggested that because the only named beneficiary – a charity – was never intended to benefit and the real beneficiaries were intended to be added by a Protector, but no protector had been appointed, the trust must fail. The Court of Appeal decided that the trust should not fail for want of a fiduciary, that it could appoint a Protector and so enable genuine beneficiaries to be added.

The issue of certainty of objects is closely linked to the accountability of trustees. In the early nineteenth century case *Morice v The Bishop of Durham*,[56] Lord Eldon said:

> 'if a trustee could not be nor was intended to be compelled to carry out the obligations imposed on him by the trust, the question arose as to whether or not the trust had failed'.

Settlors often attempt to cut down the trustees' accountability to their beneficiaries, sometimes by restricting the provision of information to them. The Bahamas statute provides that the beneficiaries' access to information may be limited. In the revocable trust profiled in the US Uniform Trust Code (adopted with some variations in a number of US states) the settlor can override the ostensible powers and duties imposed by the trust instrument by direct instruction to the trustees, and beneficiaries whose interests follow that of the settlor cannot complain of breach of trust. While it is generally thought that provided someone can enforce the trust the trustees will be considered accountable, questions might arise outside the US as to whether it is adequate in this type of 'trust' that the settlor should be able to enforce, given that the relationship between the settlor and trustee in such an arrangement is more in the nature of a nomineeship than a trust.

---

[53] [1993] 1 WLR 934, ChD.
[54] [1986] PCC 121.
[55] [1993-1995] Manx LR 102.
[56] (1804) 9 Ves 399.

6.2.4   Invalid exercise of powers of appointment/advancement

If the aim is to attack the distributions or advancements made from a trust, probably to maintain that those assets are retained within a nuptial settlement, the ruling in *Re Hastings-Bass*,[57] recently revisited in *Re Barr's Settlement Trusts*[58] and *Sieff v Fox*[59] may be useful. In *Hastings-Bass*, the Court of Appeal stated that if a trustee is given discretion to make a decision and it is clear that he would not have acted as he did:

> '(a)   had he not taken into account considerations which he should not have taken into account; or
> (b)   had he not failed to take into account considerations which he ought to have taken into account'

then a court may declare that decision void (or possibly voidable). An application under this principle is usually made by the trustee but it could be made by a beneficiary in the hope of overturning a disposition unfavourable to the beneficiary. Unless the application is supported by the trustee (in which case they will probably make it themselves) it will be a hostile and high risk strategy for a spouse, carrying with it all the usual difficulties of attacking the propriety of the exercise of the trustees' dispositive powers. HMRC may participate in the proceedings if the application might have fiscal consequences.

6.3   OWNERSHIP OF ASSETS

The settlor of a trust must have the right to dispose of the assets which he puts into trust. When a trust is being attacked during divorce proceedings the issue of whether or not the settlor had a right to settle the assets in the trust in the first place may be an avenue to explore.

6.3.1   Flawed assets

Where assets that either did not belong to a settlor or to which a settlor only had defective title are placed into trust, the trust may not hold the assets. If assets procured as the result of fraud are purportedly settled by the fraudster, they are liable to be held by the trustee for the defrauded party. This is not only because the fraudster may not have title to the assets but also because the real settlor – the victim of the fraud – will not have had any intention to settle the assets on the terms of this trust, typically for the benefit of the fraudster's family.

Where a fraudster mixes his own assets with fraudulently-obtained property it will be possible for the defrauded victim to pursue his assets by

---

[57]   [1975] Ch 25, CA.
[58]   [2003] 1 All ER 763, ChD.
[59]   [2005] 1 WLR 3811, ChD.

means of tracing into the trust fund (see *Re Hallett's Estate*[60] and *Foskett v McKeown*[61]). As a general rule an innocent trustee caught up in such a situation should take an entirely neutral stance. Lightman J in *Alsop Wilkinson (a firm) v Neary*,[62] in which a settlor had established a trust for the purpose of defrauding his clients, held that the trustee should not take an active part in such proceedings since the trustee's job was to hold the trust assets for whoever owned the beneficial interest and not decide who those beneficiaries were to be. If the assets have clearly been settled with the intention of defrauding creditors or have been settled within the period of reviewable dispositions they are likely to be clawed back for the benefit of creditors.

Similarly, where the assets of the settlement are the proceeds of crime they will be liable to confiscation by the relevant authorities. The risk of a claim by a spouse involving trust assets which turn out to be subject to a claim for confiscation as the probable proceeds of criminal conduct was highlighted in the latest case in the *Minwalla* saga[63] although in that case the claim did not succeed.

In such cases there is little point in the divorcing spouses spending time disputing the destination of the trust assets as between themselves, since they are likely to be restored to the victims of fraud, criminal authorities or creditors of the settlor.

6.3.2   Constructive trusts and proprietary estoppel claims

Spouses may both have an interest in assets whether by virtue of holding the assets as joint tenants or tenants in common or because the spouse who holds title to all the assets is considered to hold part of his or her interest on constructive trust for the other pursuant to an express or implied agreement between them.

If a spouse who holds assets impressed with a trust in favour of the other or to which the other has joint title which is not considered to have been severed by the act of settlement purports to transfer that interest into trust, the spouse whose interest is adversely affected may allege that title to the affected part of the property or the property as a whole did not pass to the trustee. The argument is similar to that which arises in community property cases (see **6.3.3** below). The result will be that the trust terms will not bite on the other spouse's wrongly-settled interest; the trustees will have to return that property to the other spouse.

---

[60]   (1880) 13 Ch D 696, CA.
[61]   [2001] 1 AC 102, HL.
[62]   [1995] 1 All ER 341, ChD.
[63]   *Chief Officer of The States of Jersey Police v Minwalla* [2007] JRC 137.

6.3.3   Community property claims

A spouse who maintains that he or she married in a jurisdiction which provided for their assets or a portion of them (such as assets acquired during the marriage) to be subject to a form of community property regime may claim that the whole or a proportion of the assets settled by his or her spouse was not validly settled in the absence of their consent. In effect the non consenting spouse is making a proprietary claim to the assets or a proportion of the assets in trust on the basis that they were his or hers and the settlor lacked title/the unfettered title to deal with them. Such a dispute will typically give rise to complex issues such as which law applied to the parties' marriage and which matrimonial regime was applicable, whether the parties opted out of the default regime, whether the assets in question were or were not part of the community and whether the affected spouse consented to the transfer into trust.

Such a situation arose after the death of both spouses in the Jersey case, *Representation of I.*[64] The settlor had settled assets merged under a community property regime into a Jersey trust following the death of his spouse. However, he was only in a position to settle his half of the matrimonial assets as he only had a life interest in his deceased's wife's share. After his death, and upon the determination of his life interest in the community property which he thought he had settled, his deceased spouse's position was claimed by and duly reverted to his children.

In an unreported Isle of Man case in 2006 (ultimately resolved by consent), a wife commenced divorce proceedings in California where she lived. She obtained a freezing order in both California and the Isle of Man in respect of a Manx trust settled by her husband during the marriage. The freezing order was based on her community property claim over the assets settled by the husband on trust.

In some cases the unilateral transfer of joint or merged property without consent will make the transfer of the entirety of assets into trust voidable. In other cases it will only vitiate the transfer of one half (or other appropriate portion) of the assets or mean that the settlor was only able to transfer a lesser interest in them, such as a usufruct.

A useful overview of specific countries' community property regimes can be found in David Hayton (ed) *European Succession Law* (2nd edn).

6.3.4   Empty shell trusts

The ostensible assets in the settlement may turn out to be worth little. Title to a valuable property may be held by the trust but if the property is heavily mortgaged, the value of the trust's interest may be small. Similarly,

---

[64]   4 ITELR 446.

the value of company shares may be severely depressed by commercial arrangements entered into by the company which may reduce its capital value and income.

The assets ostensibly settled may be subject to a claim of transactional sham: that although the trust deed itself created a valid settlement the documentation purporting to demonstrate that valuable assets had been settled was a device intended to deceive third parties (commonly fiscal authorities) as to the ownership of the assets. In such a case it is likely that the title to the assets will remain with the ostensible settlor and so be available for redistribution on divorce to his or her spouse.

CHAPTER 7

PRACTICE AND PROCEDURE FOR DIVORCING SPOUSES AND TRUSTEES

7.1 OUTLINE OF PROCEDURE FOR FINANCIAL CLAIMS ON DIVORCE

The procedure for financial claims on divorce is distinct from, but linked to procedure for the divorce itself.

A divorce in England is started by filing a petition and other accompanying documents. Once service has been acknowledged, the applicant ('petitioner') can apply for directions for trial so that decree nisi is listed. Six weeks after decree nisi, decree absolute can be applied for, as that application is purely administrative. Only the pronouncement of decree nisi is in open court, when in practice simply a list of surnames is read out.

An application for financial claims, which is known as 'ancillary relief', is started by filing at court Form A.[1] The same form is used whether the claim for financial relief is being made by the petitioner or respondent to the divorce. There is authority for the application to be commenced by the party with greater financial resources, in effect, for an order against himself.[2]

On the filing of Form A, the court automatically lists the first hearing, known as the First Appointment. That hearing has to take place 12 to 16 weeks after the filing of Form A. Attendance at the First Appointment by both parties is compulsory and permission from the court has to be obtained if one party has a good reason for non-attendance.

Five weeks prior to the First Appointment, both parties must file and serve by way of exchange their Forms E. This is a comprehensive and detailed financial statement, refined over the years to elicit the information from the most recalcitrant spouse. Two weeks prior to the First Appointment, both parties must file and serve draft questionnaires, a request for information and documents. Those questionnaires will be approved by the District Judge at the First Appointment, setting out what

---

[1]   See, generally, rr 2.51D–2.71 of the FPR 1991, known as 'the Ancillary Relief Rules'.
[2]   *Dart v Dart* [1996] 2 FLR 286, CA.

relevant information and documents have to be provided, so as to further clarify and understand the other spouse's finances.

At the First Appointment, the district judge will also consider what other directions should be made for the future conduct of the case. This will include orders for a single joint expert to be appointed to value any properties, if a value is disputed, and possibly to value businesses.

Where one spouse knows of the existence of a trust interest of the other spouse and wishes to apply for variation of settlement, the relevant box will be ticked on the Form A. A copy of the Form A and Form E will then have to be served on the trustees of the settlement and the settlor. Either person has the right to file a statement in answer, sworn to be true.[3]

Where one spouse knows nothing about the identity of the other spouse's trust interest, and information is disclosed in Form E, it is likely that an application for leave to amend the Form A will be made at the First Appointment. Otherwise, it may be that an application will be made to join the trustees, but that may depend upon the extent of the other spouse's disclosure given regarding the trust interest in the Form E, or in the replies to questionnaire.

The district judge at the First Appointment will also list the matter for the next hearing, the Financial Dispute Resolution appointment. If the case is complex or involves substantial assets, then the matter is likely to be transferred to the High Court and heard by a High Court judge.

The FDR appointment[4] is usually an effective means of achieving a settlement although that can be more difficult in substantial or complex cases involving trusts. All offers, proposals or responses made wholly or partly without prejudice have to be placed before the judge hearing the FDR. That judge can have no further involvement in the case after the FDR. The role of the judge is to indicate what likely order would be made at the final hearing and so broker a settlement.

In cases when the FDR is not successful in reaching a settlement, the matter will then be listed for final hearing or trial. In substantial or complex matters, it is likely that a 'Section 25 affidavit' will have been prepared after the First Appointment and prior to the FDR. Otherwise, such affidavits will certainly be ordered after the FDR. Those affidavits can be limited to relevant factors in dispute or more extensive dealing with all of the relevant MCA 1973, s 25 factors.

At any time prior to the filing of Form A, or after, the court has the power to grant a financial consent order. This is only once decree nisi has been reached. The order is only effective in all respects on decree absolute.

---

3   FPR 1991, r 2.59(3), (5).
4   FPR 1991, r 2.61E.

It is a fundamental principle of family law that only a formal court order is absolutely binding since an agreement between spouses cannot oust the jurisdiction of the court.

7.2 WHAT SHOULD THE ATTITUDE OF TRUSTEES BE WHEN A BENEFICIARY/BENEFICIARIES ARE GETTING DIVORCED?

Trustees are placed in a difficult situation whenever a beneficiary is in the process of getting divorced, particularly where both divorcing parties are beneficiaries. In the lead up to the divorce one of the parties to the marriage or someone close to them may ask the trustee to take radical steps such as excluding a spouse from benefit, settling the assets on new trusts or moving the trust assets to an obscure jurisdiction. Once the divorce proceedings commence the trustee may be asked searching questions by the spouse of a beneficiary or by the beneficiary himself or herself which the trustee believes the beneficiary is asking under compulsion of the divorce proceedings and would not choose to be answered.

The trustee may be faced with an order that the trustee be joined to the proceedings for the purposes of securing more detailed information from the trustee, because a spouse is asking the court to vary the trust as an ante or post nuptial settlement under s 24 of the MCA 1973 or to review a disposition to the trust under s 37 of the MCA 1973. Alternatively, a spouse may be alleging that the trust is a sham and that the beneficial interest in the trust assets should be determined to be that of the other spouse so that the trust assets should be regarded as entirely free for the court to divide between the spouses as it thinks fit. The trustee may also find that a freezing order has been made by the family court directing the trustee to take no steps to move or distribute the trust assets.

The first consideration for any trustee in this difficult position is what is proper for the trustee to do in fulfilment of its fiduciary obligations to the beneficial class as a whole? Although at first sight this may appear to indicate that the trustee should act to preserve the confidentiality of the trust from strangers and to protect it from onslaught, the position is not so straightforward. Much depends on whether the trustee is subject to the jurisdiction of the family court in any event, what is the private international law position on enforcement of a judgment delivered in another state, where the trust assets are situated and whether the action which the trustee could take to assist the beneficiary subject to the divorce proceedings would, in fact result in making matters worse for the trustee, the trust as a whole and the divorcing beneficiary in particular.

If a trustee knowing of impending divorce proceedings is asked to move assets to an inaccessible jurisdiction or exclude the other spouse from benefit, as in *Charalambous v Charalambous*[5] the trustee should consider very carefully whether or not to comply with such a request, particularly if it emanates from the divorcing beneficiary. If the trustee makes a momentous decision based on a request from a beneficiary who is likely to be undergoing divorce proceedings in the English court, not only will the court think poorly of the trustee for behaving in a partisan fashion but will also be more likely to regard the trustee as acting as the nominee of the beneficiary or as demonstrating that the trust assets, while not in his name, are in effect a resource of that beneficiary. Further, if the decision has been taken for inappropriate reasons it may be challenged on trust grounds as not being a valid decision in any event, with the result that the trustee may be left with significant costs exposure, not only in defending its decision but also in meeting the costs of the former beneficiary who has challenged the decision.

This does not mean that it could never be appropriate to take such steps, and it may be that in an exceptional case it would be a proper trustee decision to do so, but such a decision will inevitably be controversial and should not be taken without careful consideration of all relevant factors and appropriate advice and directions.

7.2.1 Avoiding partisanship

The need to avoid partisanship arises principally in the situation envisaged above – when a beneficiary (usually the settlor or descendant of the settlor) asks the trustee to take steps to make assets less accessible to another beneficiary (the intended divorcing spouse) or to exclude that person from benefit/transfer assets to another trust of which that spouse is not a beneficiary. The need to avoid partiality may also arise in connection with the provision of information in the course of the divorce proceedings.

If the trustee favours one beneficiary over another or appears too protective of the position of a divorcing beneficiary, it is likely to make the position materially worse. If the trustee favours one beneficiary over another, the trustee may be subjected to criticism and possibly adverse costs orders in the divorce proceedings and this may heighten the risks of a heavy award against the beneficiary so favoured or an unpalatable decision on a variation of settlement application. If the trustee is considered to be in breach of its duty of impartiality and fairness as between beneficiaries, the trustee may also expose itself to breach of trust proceedings. In *E v E (Financial Provision)*[6] the trustee and protector, both regarded as having behaved in a partisan manner in seeking to protect the interests of the husband in the trust, were removed by order of the English divorce court notwithstanding that the trust was not governed

---

5   In which the spouses were removed as beneficiaries: [2004] EWCA Civ 1030.
6   [1990] 2 FLR 233, FD.

by English law. In *Minwalla v Minwalla*[7] the Jersey trustee came under severe criticism for appearing to support the husband to the detriment of the wife and children and of acting as a cipher of the husband. The English family court, in the first reported decision of its kind, decided that the trust governed by Jersey law was a sham (failing to apply the law of Jersey in so doing) but notwithstanding its concern at the lack of comity displayed by the English family court, the Royal Court of Jersey decided that the judgment in England sought to do justice between the parties where the husband had flouted his obligations to his wife. The trustee had also submitted to the English jurisdiction. Accordingly, the Royal Court was willing to permit the enforcement of the English divorce award. The decision left the trustee in the unenviable position of exposure to possible breach of trust claims (if, contrary to the English decision, the Royal Court considered the trust valid) and to regulatory enquiry as to the manner in which it had conducted trust business. In the Jersey case *In the matter of A and B Trusts*[8] the Royal Court of Jersey was critical of a trustee which had submitted to the jurisdiction of the divorce and declined to give retrospective approval to the trustee so doing.

7.2.2   Acting in the interests of the beneficial class as a whole

Although the guideline for any trustee decision is to act in the interests of the beneficial class, the guideline is not easy to apply in divorce situations. Much depends on the particular circumstances of the case. So, for example, while it is generally considered not to be in the interests of a foreign trust for the trustee to submit to the English jurisdiction (see below) if there are significant trust assets in England (whether held directly by the trust or through underlying entities) such that there is a risk that an English award could be enforced directly against those assets without the home court of the trust taking into account the interests of beneficiaries other than those who are parties to the marriage, the trustee may consider that it is right to intervene or submit to being joined in the proceedings in order to make appropriate submissions to the family court. However, such a decision may well increase the risk of enforcement against assets outside England and Wales and so should not be taken without very careful consideration and the directions of the trust's home court.

It is usually in the interests of the beneficiaries as a whole that the duty of trustee to preserve the confidentiality of the trust's affairs (and the individual beneficiaries' affairs) is maintained, but there may be circumstances in which disclosure of information or documents which would not normally be disclosed is the best course. This should not be done without the sanction of the trustee's home court unless the trustee is acting under compulsion of an order of a court to which the trustee is

---

[7]   [2005] 1 FLR 771, FD.
[8]   [2007] JRC 138.

subject. Such a situation arose in *Re Rabaiotti 1989 Settlement*[9] where, with the support of the beneficiaries, the Royal Court of Jersey directed the trustee to disclose letters of wishes in each of four settlements which it would normally have regarded as documents confidential to the trustee: it did so because it was perceived that the family court in England was under a misapprehension as to the wishes of the settlor and that if this were not corrected, the result would be unfortunate for the divorcing beneficiary and the beneficial class as a whole.

7.2.3 Seeking the court's guidance – *Beddoe* and other directions applications

In all trust jurisdictions the trustee has the facility to apply to its home court for guidance in difficult situations such as whether to participate in proceedings on behalf of the trust. Often the divorce proceedings will place the trustee in a position of difficulty or potential controversy such that the trustee will feel the need of the court's assistance. Provided that the trustee brings the full relevant facts to the attention of the court, the trustee will not be at risk of breach of trust proceedings if the trustee acts in accordance with the court's direction.

The trustee may wish to have the benefit of the directions of the court in connection with a request for disclosure of trust information, particularly information not usually discloseable (as in *Re Rabaiotti*), where the information is sought on behalf of beneficiaries while at the same time an attack is being launched on the integrity of the trust (as in *Re M*[10]) or where the information is sought by or on behalf of a non-beneficiary or by a beneficiary under circumstances of compulsion. The trustee may have been subjected to proceedings for disclosure of information by an inspection appointment or Letters of Request and seek guidance as to whether to make objections as to the ambit of the disclosure sought or apply to challenge the scope of the disclosure sought, as is clear from *Charman v Charman (No 2)*[11] which occurred following the Court of Appeal decision regarding Letters of Request in *Charman v Charman*.[12]

Seeking and acting in accordance with the directions of its home court should also assist in dispelling suggestions of partisanship or unco-operativeness on behalf of the trustee.

If the trustee is contemplating taking an unusual step – such as submitting to a jurisdiction where the trustee, the trust and the trust assets are outside that jurisdiction – it is important for the trustee's own protection from criticism or claims and to ensure that it is able to take its costs incurred in connection with those proceedings from the trust fund

---

9   2000 JLR 173.
10   [2003] W1LR 491.
11   [2006] EWHC 1879 (Fam), [2007] 1 FLR 593, FD.
12   [2005] EWCA Civ 1606, [2006] 2 FLR 422, CA.

that it seeks the court's authority to do so in the form of a *Beddoe* order (after *Re Beddoe*[13]). If the trustee does not secure the court's authority to participate in the proceedings (assuming that the trustee has any choice as to whether to do so) and as to the extent and manner of its participation the trustee may not be able to access the trust fund to indemnify itself in respect of its own costs and any costs awarded against it in favour of another party (typically the spouse seeking the participation of the trustee in the divorce proceedings.)

In short, a directions application in its home jurisdiction is most important in difficult situations to protect the trustee from criticism, allegations of breach of trust and adverse costs orders and to endeavour to demonstrate to the family court in this jurisdiction that the trustee is behaving responsibly.

7.3   THE TRUSTEES' RESPONSE TO REQUESTS FOR INFORMATION AS TO PROPOSED EXERCISE OF DIRECTION

If a spouse claims that assets in trust are a resource of the other spouse which should be taken into account when considering an award the trustee may be asked how it proposes to exercise its discretion or whether it will be prepared to assist in meeting an award.

Such a request is appropriate only to a trust where the other spouse is a beneficiary and where the trustees have a discretion to benefit that person: it would be inapposite in respect of a fixed interest trust where there is no scope for the exercise of the trustees' dispositive powers. If in doubt as to the nature of a spouse's interest, clarification can be sought from the trustee. As with any request for information the trustee should be careful not to disclose confidential information to a stranger to the trust and accordingly responses to requests for such information should be directed to the beneficiary spouse/his or her lawyer. Assuming that the trust is wholly discretionary or that it is in part, discretionary trustees have generally been unwilling in the past to indicate how they might exercise their powers not only because at an early stage in proceedings the facts may not be clear for them to form a view but also because they will not wish to fetter their discretion. Further, they may wish to seek the court's guidance on any provisional decision they might make in that respect.

However, the decision in *Charman (No 2)*[14] upheld by the Court of Appeal in *Charman (No 4)*[15] demonstrates that no indication by the trustees as to how they might exercise their dispositive powers may risk the court concluding that if asked, they would be prepared to apply all or

---

[13]   [1893] 1 Ch 547, CA.
[14]   [2006] EWHC 1879 (Fam), [2007] 1 FLR 593, FD.
[15]   [2007] EWCA Civ 503, [2007] 1 FLR 1246, CA.

a substantial part of the assets to the requesting spouse, particularly if the requesting spouse were making the request under pressure of an order providing heavy 'judicious encouragement' to the trustee.

Accordingly, careful consideration now needs to be given by trustees as to how to address such a request in the interests of the beneficiaries as a whole, particularly since the other beneficiaries (including minors) will not be convened to the proceedings at which the question whether the trust assets should be treated as a resource of another beneficiary will be determined.

The response of the trustee will need to be tailored to the individual circumstances of the case and made having taken appropriate advice but may in future provide some indication, as to assets it would not consider available for distribution or as to its attitude towards preservation of assets for other beneficiaries. The trustee will doubtless wish to make it clear that it is not fettering its discretion in any way and, (if this is the case) that any provisional decision it makes will be submitted to the trust's home court for approval.

Factors the trustees may wish to take into consideration in their response include existing commitments to beneficiaries, availability of assets, administrative earmarking for classes of beneficiaries and balancing the expectations and needs of all the beneficiaries. So if, for example, the assets are illiquid and/or the diminution of the trust's shareholding in a company would be severely detrimental to the beneficial class as a whole the trustees might indicate unwillingness on that account to make any distribution for the foreseeable future. If the trust fund has been informally divided into subfunds for different family branches or members it may be appropriate to indicate that realistically the spouse's expectation of benefit relates only to the subfund for his branch, and so on.

Great care must be taken in respect of any such response to avoid creating unrealistic expectations either on the part of the spouse involved in the divorce or on the part of other beneficiaries. *In the matter of the A & B Trusts*[16] is a salutory example of a situation where difficulty was occasioned in the divorce proceedings by the trustee creating unattainable expectations on the part of the English court by providing an indication of willingness to make available funds which in that event could not be produced. Equally care will need to be taken by parties to proceedings and the court not to rely too much on heavily-caveated indications by the trustees.

---

[16]		[2007] JRC 138.

7.4 COMPLYING WITH THE BENEFICIARY SPOUSE'S REQUEST TO ASSIST HIM/HER TO MEET AN AWARD

7.4.1 The possibility of committing a fraud on a power

A trustee may be asked to assist a beneficiary to meet a judgment awarded in favour of his or her spouse, sometimes under threat of bankruptcy if the trustee were to decline. This situation may arise if the settlement is not a nuptial settlement but the family court has taken the availability of trust assets into account as a resource and so made an award in favour of the other spouse which the beneficiary cannot meet or has difficulty meeting from his or her other resources. The trustee has, in effect, received 'judicious encouragement' to assist in meeting the award.

Where the spouse with the benefit of the judgment is a beneficiary, the trustee may be asked to consider whether to exercise its discretionary power to make a distribution to him or her (taking into account the availability of assets of the other spouse to meet the judgment and the needs and resources of other beneficiaries who can expect to benefit from the trust). In contrast, a request to distribute to a beneficiary knowing that the funds are going to be passed on to a non-beneficiary places the trustee in particular difficulty.

Trustees are authorised to use their powers only for the benefit of their beneficiaries. They are not at liberty to distribute to a beneficiary in the knowledge that the funds are going to be given to a non-beneficiary because they would then be exercising their powers for a purpose foreign to the trust – to benefit a non-beneficiary. This would be a fraud on a power and the trustee's decision would be void as well as leaving the trustee open to a claim for breach of trust.

7.4.2 Meeting a beneficiary's legal or moral obligations

So are there any circumstances in which a trustee can decide to distribute funds to a beneficiary to help him or her to meet an award in favour of their non-beneficiary spouse? This is a difficult area but it seems clear that, with the blessing of the court, the trustee may be able to do so in certain cases such as:

(a) where the beneficiary has already met the judgment out of his own resources and the trustee's decision is to make good the loss he has sustained, so that the payment is definitely for his benefit (*Netherton v Netherton*[17]);

---

[17]   [2000] WTLR 1171.

(b) where the beneficiary would otherwise be at jeopardy of imprisonment (as in *Browne v Browne*[18]), bankruptcy or grave financial difficulty by reason of enforcement proceedings;

(c) where the court considers that it would be in the interests of the beneficiary spouse and children to avoid continued hostile litigation, relieve the beneficiary spouse of the risk of a worsening financial position and provide security for the children (*Re X Trust*[19]);

(d) where the trustee considers that the beneficiary has a legal and or moral obligation to provide for his/her spouse (and children) and that the trustee is benefiting the beneficiary by enabling him/her to discharge that obligation, as in *Compass Trustees Ltd v McBarnett*.[20] Such a payment can be made directly to the other spouse on the beneficiary's behalf and even without the beneficiary's agreement, although it will be rare for the court to authorise a payment in the face of opposition from the beneficiary on whose behalf the payment is to be made (as in *Re The Esteem Settlement*[21]).

In any such case the trustee would be unwise to make a distribution to the beneficiary to discharge his/her obligations or, even more controversially, to the non-beneficiary spouse directly without the benefit of a direction from the court authorising the trustee to do so, after all relevant factors have been considered and the views of the other beneficiaries have been canvassed. It may be that a distribution of the magnitude required to discharge the indebtedness would deplete the trust such that it would not be able to provide for other beneficiaries who are being supported or could legitimately expect to receive benefit from the trust, or that the beneficiary on whose behalf it is contemplated that payment might be made would be left in difficult financial circumstances without resort to the trust assets. In a hard case it may be that bankruptcy of the beneficiary, with the trustee having the ability for the future to exercise its discretion in favour of the beneficiary and his or her family, is the better option.

If the trustee considers that, whatever the 'encouragement' to which it is being subjected, the right course is not to accede to the pressure of the judgment but to preserve the trust assets for the benefit of the beneficial class that decision itself may be sufficiently momentous that the trustee will feel the need of the protection of the direction of the home court to that effect.

---

[18]   [1989] 1 FLR 291, CA.
[19]   [2002–03] 5 ITELR 119, 2002 JLR 321.
[20]   [2002] 5 ITELR 119.
[21]   2003 JLR 188.

7.5   JOINDER OF TRUSTEES

As with all ancillary relief applications, an application to the English court to vary an ante or post-nuptial settlement can be made at any point after a petition is issued. If the trust interest was only discovered by the applicant after Form A (the form of application for ancillary relief) had already been filed, then leave would be required to amend the Form A to include a variation application.

The English ancillary relief procedure requires each spouse to complete a Financial Statement in Form E. The relevant part of Box 2.14 of the Form E is reproduced below:

'2.14 **Give details of any other assets not listed in Parts 1 to 4 above. INCLUDE** (the following list is not exhaustive):
- **Trust interests** (including interests under a discretionary trust), stating your estimate of the value of the interest and when it is likely to become realisable. If you say it will never be realisable, or has no value, give your reasons.
- Any asset that is likely to be received in the foreseeable future
- Any asset held on your behalf by a third party
- Any asset not disclosed elsewhere on this form even if held outside England and Wales

You are reminded of your obligation to disclose all your financial assets and interests of ANY nature.

Type of Asset	Value	Total NET value of your interest
TOTAL value of ALL your other assets: **TOTAL G**	**£...'**	

If this box is completed in such a way that it gives little or no clue about the assets in the trust, it is likely to give rise to suspicion and following exchange of Forms E and in advance of the First Appointment, a lengthy Questionnaire from a spouse who feels that he/she is being kept in the dark about their spouse's interests. Typical examples of questionnaire questions might be:

'1. Trust Interests

1.1   Is the Respondent the Settlor or a beneficiary, in possession or in reversion, discretionary or otherwise, of any trust(s)? If so, please provide:

(a) copy(ies) of the Trust Deed(s) and any amendments, supplemental deeds, trustee resolutions, documents executed by Trustees, memoranda of wishes and Deed(s) of Appointment;

(b) copies of the last 10 years' audited accounts of the trust(s);

(c) copies of any Letter(s) of Wishes;

(d) if it is not clear from the accounts, particulars of all income and capital distributions and loans received by the Respondent during the last 10 years, together with supporting documentation;

(e) if it is not clear from the accounts, particulars of all income and capital distributions and loans received by the siblings/children of the Respondent, together with supporting documentation;

(f) copy(ies) of (an) up to date portfolio valuation(s) of the assets of the trust(s);

(g) particulars of any trusts of which the child(ren) of the family is/are (a) beneficiary(ies) and the information and copy documentation requested above.'

In the absence of evidence to the contrary, that is a view that is likely to be shared by the English court. Adverse inferences may be drawn about resources the extent of which is being withheld from the court.

The general rule is that it is almost always better *for the parties* to co-operate. *Trustees* will inevitably find themselves in a difficult position potentially balancing the interests of at least one of the two spouses against their duties to other beneficiaries. If the trustees are offshore, it is sensible for them to apply to their local court for directions as to how to proceed. Inevitably, taking steps of this sort is likely to incur legal costs, but will almost certainly lead to savings in the longer term when compared with the alternative of taking no action and becoming embroiled in enforcement proceedings after the court of whatever jurisdiction dealing with the divorce has made an order.

Where a spouse applies for a variation of settlement order, r 2.59(3) of the Family Proceedings Rules 1991 ('FPR 1991') provides that a copy of the application in Form A and Financial Statement in Form E must be served on the trustee. Under r 2.59(5) of the FPR 1991, the trustee may, within 14 days from the date of service, file a sworn statement in response.

Service of the application in Form A and Financial Statement in Form E does not of itself make the trustee a party to the proceedings (*T v T (Joinder of Third Parties)*[22]). Trustees should therefore not make the mistake of regarding themselves as thereby joined to the proceedings, although it is common for trustees to be joined to assist with enforcement against them. Even so, trustees are not bound by the decision or regarded as having submitted unless they are under the jurisdiction of the court or submit to it, such as by participating in the proceedings or confirming that they will be bound by the decision of the court.

---

[22]　[1996] 2 FLR 357, FD.

The Rules of the Supreme Court apply in family proceedings in the form existing prior to the introduction of the Civil Procedure Rules by reason of r 1.3 of the Family Proceedings Rules 1991. The court has the power to order trustees to be parties to proceedings (RSC Ord 15, r 6(2)(b)). Wilson J (as he then was) said in *T v T (Joinder of Third Parties)* that this was a power to join any other party:

> 'whose presence before the court was necessary, or where it was just and convenient to determine an issue arising between either party to the proceedings and the third party'.

T v T (Joinder of Third Parties) involved a Jersey law trust, which the spouses conceded was a nuptial settlement capable of variation. The trustee was joined as a party since the husband asserted that he did not have effective control over the trust assets. The trustee applied, unsuccessfully, to discharge the joinder order and was ordered to pay the costs of the wife of that application. Wilson J also said:

> 'a crucial matter for my determination will be to evaluate the real control over the assets of this trust (by the husband) ... I have come to the view that the enforcement of any orders (for variation) that I might make is likely to be facilitated by the trustees remaining as parties to the proceedings ...

> I have already said that I would consider it far easier for the wife to enforce against the trust assets in England if the trustees remained a party. I would also expect and believe that, notwithstanding that there might be difficulties about the automatic enforcement in Jersey of any order that I made in the event that following this afternoon the trustees failed to take an active part in these proceedings, nevertheless their having been made parties to the proceedings would be likely to assist the wife in, if not direct enforcement, the obtaining of an analogous or supplementary judgment in Jersey; and, indeed, might assist her in putting before the Jersey court, as facts which have been found and from which there should be no escape, facts found by me at a hearing in which, whether they actively participated or not, the trustees were parties.'

The general unhelpfulness and lack of co-operation by the trustee was a contributory factor to the judge's decision.

Re T (Divorce: Interim Maintenance: Discovery)[23] a decision of Ward J (as he then was), is an example (albeit not in the context of trustees) of an application for joinder failing. In that case the wife sought joinder in effect solely for the purpose of seeking discovery from her father-in-law, rather than by way of declaration of ownership of certain property.

This power to join is independent of any application to vary a nuptial settlement. Of course the mere making of an order for joinder does not

---

[23]   [1990] 1 FLR 1, FD.

bind a foreign trustee unless that trustee submits to the English jurisdiction, or the English court has jurisdiction over the trustee.

7.5.1   Submission to the jurisdiction

The danger is that a trustee may unwittingly 'submit' to the English jurisdiction. Almost any involvement in the case can be viewed as submission and could be fatal to a trustee's attempts to remain unaffected by the divorce proceedings. Even an application for an extension of time could be considered submission to the jurisdiction.

The matter is complicated by the fact that the relevant rules do not fit easily with divorce and ancillary relief procedure. The originating process is the divorce petition, to which the respondent spouse can file an Answer by way of defence. There is no defence filed in answer to an ancillary relief application as such.

Under the old Rules of the Supreme Court (replaced in 1999 for the purpose of civil proceedings by the Civil Procedure Rules but still applicable in certain Family Division High Court applications), Ord 12, r 8(3), where the trustee wished to dispute jurisdiction, he had to give notice to the court of an intention to defend the proceedings. Not doing so when served would be considered a submission to the jurisdiction.

However, since divorce petitions are all issued out of the County Court (including the Principal Registry in London) and then transferred up to the High Court when necessary, the Rules of the Supreme Court do not apply. The County Court Rules which would apply have no provision parallel to RSC Ord 12, r 8. Under Ord 9, r 12 of the County Court Rules filing a defence does not constitute a submission to the jurisdiction. This assumes that by the time there is any question of joinder or submission, the matter has not already been transferred to the High Court, as happens in substantial or complex cases.

Article 18 of the Lugano Convention states that a court may be given jurisdiction by a defendant (respondent) entering a defence. Case-law suggests, however, that it is possible to enter a defence while challenging jurisdiction without this constituting a submission to the jurisdiction.[24]

7.5.2   What should trustees do when joined?

Trustees not in the jurisdiction who are advised that they have been joined to English divorce proceedings have to consider very carefully indeed before submitting to the jurisdiction or even applying to set aside the

---

[24]   See *Elefanten Schuh GmbH v Pierre Jacqmain* [1981] ECR 1671 (relating to the same provision in the Brussels Convention); *Etablissements Röhr SA v Ossberger* [1981] ECR 2431; and *CHW v GJH* [1982] ECR 1189.

joinder order. The trustee in *Minwalla*[25] made the error of submitting to the jurisdiction by agreeing to be bound by the court's decision – thus rendering any judgment by the court easier to enforce against the trust assets – but took no steps to make submissions which might have assisted in preserving the trust assets or drawing the position of other beneficiaries to the attention of the court. The trustee was criticised for taking this step and some suggestion made that it might have acted in breach of trust in so doing (*CI Law Trustees Ltd v Minwalla*[26]).

The Royal Court of Jersey has had considerable experience of giving directions to trustees faced with a joinder order as the result of which the following guidelines can be drawn:

(a) It is generally inappropriate to attempt to argue against the joinder. Jersey trustees did so in *T v T (Joinder of Third Parties)*[27] unsuccessfully and in addition to being found to have submitted were ordered to pay the wife's costs of opposing their application. In *The Craven Trust Co Ltd v SM*[28] the trustee applied to the court for directions as to whether to make an application for non joinder but thought better of it and was directed not to do so. (It should be noted that this is not necessarily the position in divorce proceedings in other jurisdictions, and in the Ohio case *James v James*[29] although the court was clearly disturbed about certain features of the trust it granted the trustee's application for non joinder on the basis that it should not exercise long arm jurisdiction against the trustee.)

(b) There may be an advantage in the trustee bringing to the attention of the family court considering its variation jurisdiction, the interests of beneficiaries to the trust. Otherwise the family court is focused on the nuclear family before it, and will not have had the benefit of submissions on behalf of other beneficiaries (apart from representatives for children of the marriage who will have been joined pursuant to FPR 1991, r 2.57). However, this advantage is likely to be outweighed by the greater ease of enforcement, without due consideration by the home court of the trust, which would be afforded by the trustee's submission to the jurisdiction.

(c) An exception might be where the assets or substantially all the trust assets are vulnerable to enforcement in any event because they are situated in England and Wales.

---

[25] [2005] 1 FLR 771, FD.
[26] 2005 JLR 359 ('The Fountain Trust' case).
[27] [1996] 2 FLR 357, FD.
[28] Jersey (unreported (2005) 8 December).
[29] 8 ITELR 845.

These guidelines were most cogently set out in *Re H Trust*[30] where the Royal Court concluded that it was unlikely to be in the interests of a Jersey trust for the trustee to submit to the jurisdiction of an overseas court, because to do so would be to confer an enforceable power on the overseas court to act to the detriment of the beneficiaries of the trust when the primary focus of that court is the interests of the two spouses before it. This follows *Re Rabaiotti*[31] and *The Craven Trust*,[32] in both of which the Royal Court expressed the clear view that trustees should keep all options open by not submitting. The Royal Court may however have directed disclosure to enable the family court to have the appropriate information before it when considering how to exercise its powers.

It is appreciated that a trustee is in a very difficult professional position when an allegation of sham is made in English divorce proceedings, because that allegation imports a degree of dishonesty – at the least deceit – on the part of the trustee which could seriously impact upon the trustee's reputation and occasion severe regulatory difficulties for the trustee. Nonetheless, it is usually unwise for the trustee to submit to the jurisdiction in order to try to argue to the contrary because by doing so any judgment of the court will be more readily enforceable against the trust assets. This was the scenario envisaged by the Jersey court in *Re B Trust*,[33] a case in which the Jersey Trustees did cooperate and submit to the English jurisdiction. Contrast *A v A and St George Trustees Ltd*[34] in which the Jersey trustee of an English law trust submitted to defend (successfully) a poorly formed allegation of sham.

Given the succession of cases in which the issue has been addressed in Jersey and the consistency of the decisions not to submit, in most cases a foreign trustee should not submit unless it has secured a direction of its home court to do so, failing which it may come under very considerable criticism for exposing the trust to the cost of unnecessary proceedings and more importantly, having facilitated the enforcement of a foreign judgment. This applies even in the difficult situation where an injunction is made against the trustees (as to which see Chapter 5). The case of *In the matter of A & B Trusts*[35] emphasises the dangers of an ancillary relief award being enforceable against trustees who have submitted for the purposes of arguing against an injunction.

7.6   DISCLOSURE BY TRUSTEES

The disadvantage of being joined as a party is that the court has wider powers to order disclosure by a party than of a non-party. The advantage

---

[30]   2006 JLR 280.
[31]   2000 JLR 173.
[32]   Jersey (unreported (2005) 8 December).
[33]   2006 JLR 562.
[34]   [2007] EWHC 99 (Fam).
[35]   [2007] JRC 138.

is that, especially where there is an application for variation of settlement, the trustees may be better able to have their views heard if they are parties and separately represented.

In *Re Rabaiotti 1989 Settlement*[36] concerned an application by Jersey trustees of four trusts for directions, after they had been given leave to intervene in English financial proceedings, as to whether they should intervene in the proceedings and what disclosure should be given to the wife of a beneficiary. The English court had ordered the husband to disclose copies of trust and ancillary documents of four settlements of which he was a beneficiary. Of the four settlements, two were based in the BVI and two in Jersey. No application to vary the settlements as nuptial settlements had been made in the English proceedings. The Jersey court was asked to consider how to balance the husband's right to the information against the other beneficiaries. Deputy Bailiff Birt stated:

> 'The main concern of the trustees is that if they were to submit to the jurisdiction of the English court and if that court were to purport to vary any of the settlements under its statutory power, the trustees would find it more difficult to contest any subsequent proceedings in Jersey brought to enforce the order of the English court for variation. Conversely, if the trustees had not submitted to the jurisdiction, they would be able to argue strongly that this court should not enforce an order of an English court in respect of a settlement governed by Jersey law or BVI law and administered in Jersey. The trustees argue that it is in the best interests of the beneficiaries as a whole that they should preserve their freedom of action in this respect.
>
> The court regards it as unlikely that an English court would so exceed the normal bounds of comity as to purport to vary a settlement governed by Jersey or BVI law, administered in Jersey by Jersey trustees, and which had no connection with England save that some of the beneficiaries resided there. However, they accept that the trustees are right to take a cautious approach. Furthermore, it is hard to see any specific advantage for the settlements in the trustees' submitting to the jurisdiction. By reason of the orders we have made in respect of disclosure, the English court will be aware of the position in relation to the settlements without the need for the trustees to appear. In any event, as a matter of general principle, it seems inappropriate for trustees to become involved in litigation between a particular beneficiary and a third party to the settlement (in this case, the spouse of a beneficiary).
>
> Accordingly, the court was of the clear view that the trustees should not intervene in the English matrimonial proceedings between Mr Rabaiotti and his wife.'

Another case on this point is *Re M Trust*.[37] The facts of the case were that there were two Jersey discretionary settlements, the wife being a beneficiary of one of those settlements. The wife claimed the trusts were

---

[36] 2000 JLR 173.
[37] [2003] WTLR 491.

intended to shield the husband's true net worth in the context of child support proceedings before the Illinois court and that they were shams.

The trustee sought directions from the court in Jersey as to what part, if any, it should play in the Illinois proceedings. Deputy Bailiff Birt stated (at para 18):

> 'The difficulty with the Illinois proceedings at present is that, having started out as a conventional dispute between a mother and father as to the level and enforcement of a child maintenance order, the proceedings have now changed their character so that the validity of the trusts will be adjudicated upon. These are trusts governed exclusively by Jersey law and administered in Jersey by a Jersey based trustee. On the face of it, this court is the most appropriate forum to adjudicate upon whether the trusts are valid or whether, for the reasons put forward by the mother, they should be regarded as shams so that the assets belong in law to the settler.'

This case also dealt with the issue of disclosure and at para 21 Deputy Bailiff Birt stated:

> 'The difficulty at present is that the mother alleges in the Illinois proceedings that the trusts are invalid. If she is right, the beneficiaries under the trusts will be entitled to nothing. On the face of it, we think that any beneficiary would have a difficult task in suggesting on the one hand that she wishes to invalidate a trust but, on the other hand, asks the Court to order disclosure of documents to her in her capacity as a beneficiary so that she might use them in her action to invalidate the trust. It is hard to see that the making of such an order would often be in the interest of the beneficial class as a whole.'

The Jersey court ruled that while the wife was attacking the validity of the trusts, she was not entitled to any information. If the allegation were discontinued, the Jersey court would order the requisite disclosure such that the Illinois court would have a clearer picture of the settlor's financial position and the trustees could comply with the order of the Illinois court.

One of the lessons to be drawn from this case, however, is that the issue of disclosure is fact-specific; the question is always what will best protect the beneficiaries in an individual case.

7.7 MINOR BENEFICIARIES

FPR 1991, r 2.57 requires that minor beneficiaries be separately represented where a variation of settlement application is on foot and the proposed variation might adversely affect them:

> '(1) Where an application is made to the High Court or a divorce county court for an order for variation of settlement, the court shall, unless it is satisfied that the proposed variation does not adversely affect the rights or

interests of any children concerned, direct that the children be separately represented on the application, either by a solicitor or by a solicitor and counsel, and may appoint the Official Solicitor or other fit person to be guardian ad litem of the children for the purpose of the application.

(2) On any other application for ancillary relief the court may give such direction or make such appointment as it is empowered to give or make by paragraph (1).

(3) Before a person other than the Official Solicitor is appointed guardian ad litem under this rule there shall be filed a certificate by the solicitor acting for the children that the person proposed as guardian has no interest in the matter adverse to that of the children and that he is a proper person to be such guardian.'

7.8 CHANNEL ISLANDS LAW ON DISCLOSURE BY TRUSTEES

Jersey and Guernsey both have statutory provisions which provide for disclosure by trustees of information relating to a trust. The Guernsey provisions come from the Trusts (Guernsey) Law 1989, s 22 which reads as follows:

'(1) Subject to the terms of the trust, a trustee shall, at all reasonable times, at the written request of any beneficiary (including any charity named in the trust) or of the settlor, provide full and accurate information as to the state and amount of the trust property.

(2) In its application to a trust arising from a document or disposition executed or taking effect before the commencement of this Law, subsection (1) shall only operate for the benefit of a beneficiary whose interest in the trust property becomes vested before the commencement of this Law, but this subsection shall not prejudice any rights the beneficiary may have under the terms of the trust.'

It goes on (at s 33) to provide details of documentation which a trustee is not obliged to disclose:

'A trustee is not (subject to the terms of the trust and to any order of the court) obliged to disclose documents which reveal:

(a)   his deliberations as to how he should exercise his functions as trustee;

(b)   the reasons for any decision made in exercise of those functions; and

(c)   any material upon which his decision might or might have been based.'

The Jersey statutory provision mirrors that in Guernsey (it should be noted that, atypically, this provides for disclosure to the settlor) and (as to beneficiaries, not as to settlor) comes from the Trusts (Jersey) Law, 1984, Art 29:

'Subject to the terms of the trust and subject to any order of a court, a trustee shall not be required to disclose to any person any document which:

(a)   discloses the trustee's deliberations as to the manner in which the trustee has exercised a power or discretion or performed a duty conferred or imposed upon him or her;

(b)   discloses the reason for any particular exercise of such power or discretion or performance of duty or the material upon which such reason shall or might have been based;

(c)   relates to the exercise or proposed exercise of such power or discretion or the performance or proposed performance of such duty; or

(d)   relates to or forms part of the accounts of the trust,

unless, in a case to which sub-paragraph (d) applies, that person is a beneficiary under the trust not being a charity, or a charity which is referred to by name in the terms of the trust as a beneficiary under the trust or the enforcer in relation to any non-charitable purposes of the trust.'

One of the court's considerations in not ordering the disclosure of the information might be that it could prejudice other, third party beneficiaries. If one party to matrimonial proceedings were attacking the validity of a trust, the offshore court may be less likely to provide assistance in the form of disclosure.

These were exactly the circumstances which were under scrutiny in the *Rabaiotti* case (see above). Although the court was of the clear view that the trustees should not intervene in the proceedings, they did, however provide copies of Letters of Wishes such that the English court had the fullest possible picture of the trusts and because some had previously been disclosed.

A similar approach was taken in the Jersey case of *Re M Trust* as outlined above. Whilst there has not been any Guernsey jurisprudence on this point in the context of matrimonial or children proceedings, there has been a significant amount of litigation in other contexts.

7.9   HOW SHOULD THE TRUSTEE DEAL WITH THE ISSUE OF DISCLOSURE?

7.9.1   The trustee's obligation of confidentiality

This duty is often misinterpreted as being a duty of confidentiality to keep the affairs of the trust secret for the benefit of the settlor. This is not the correct analysis of the duty, which is owed to the beneficiaries as a whole, although it would be a breach of the trustee's duty of confidentiality to the settlor to disclose a document delivered to the trustee by the settlor in circumstances where it is intended to be kept confidential. This is typically the situation which arises in connection with the settlor's Letter of Wishes which is commonly not disclosed to the beneficiaries.

The duty of confidentiality is a duty, not without just cause (such as in response to money laundering requirements or an order of a court of competent jurisdiction) not to disclose matters relating to the trust to a stranger to the trust (*Heerema v Heerema*[38]). So compliance with a request by lawyers for a non beneficiary spouse for detailed disclosure of the trust's affairs and those of its beneficiaries would be unwise as being in breach of this duty. The safer course is for the trustee to advise the lawyers for the non-beneficiary spouse that the trustee is not in a position to breach its duty of confidentiality, and then provide such information as it is appropriate to provide to the beneficiary spouse who can in turn pass it to the other spouse's lawyers.

7.9.2   Dealing with disclosure requests by a beneficiary/a beneficiary's spouse

This begs the question as to what information it is appropriate to provide to the beneficiary spouse. It used to be the case that the beneficiary was regarded as entitled to receive trust documents and the nature of the documents to be disclosed was, subject to any restrictions imposed by the trust or local statute (such as the Trustee Act 1998 in the Bahamas) fairly well established by case-law. In general fixed interest or discretionary beneficiaries were entitled to access trust documents but objects of a power of appointment were not. The documents to be disclosed included the formal trust documents (including deeds of retirement and of appointment), accounts and supporting vouchers and documents showing how the trust assets were invested. Documents regarded as confidential to a third party – such as the settlor's letter of wishes or letters from a beneficiary asking for funds – were not discloseable, and neither were documents evidencing the reasons for the trustee's dispositive decisions (whether to benefit one beneficiary rather than another).

Since the Privy Council decision in *Schmidt v Rosewood Trust Ltd*[39] the position is less clear cut. The decision whether or not to provide disclosure rests with the court as part of its function to supervise the administration of trusts. It is no longer the invariable rule that objects of a discretion cannot access trust documents nor that discretionary beneficiaries can do so: much will turn on the proximity of the beneficiary to benefit. Fundamentally, no beneficiary is to be regarded as having a right to access trust documents. So, if a spouse is a discretionary beneficiary of a trust with other discretionary beneficiaries and his or her prospects of receiving

---

[38]   1985–86 JLR 293.
[39]   [2003] UKPC 26.

any benefit are very remote, the trustee may be justified in declining to provide any documentation or information to the beneficiary.

The extent of the documentation to be disclosed in appropriate cases is also less well defined, although it is generally thought that for the most part the long established guidelines in place before *Schmidt* will apply.

From a divorce perspective all this means that it can no longer be assumed that the trustee will be bound to disclose trust documents to a beneficiary such that he or she would be failing in making the requisite efforts if they cannot produce them. However, the changes brought about by the decision in *Schmidt v Rosewood* may be poorly understood by the parties, their divorce lawyers and by the family judge, who may perceive the trustee's refusal to provide documentation to a beneficiary as obstruction or evidence of trying to protect the beneficiary spouses' position with the possibility of adverse inferences being drawn. Accordingly, the trustee making what it considers to be a wholly appropriate decision not to make disclosure to a remote beneficiary needs to consider carefully how to phrase its response and, if there is real concern that the situation will be misconstrued, seek directions as to whether or not to disclose. The beneficiary seeking disclosure will in all probability be a party to that application and can then disclose the judgment to his/her spouse and the family court.

The breadth of information sought commonly poses problems for the trustee. Form E obliges a party to the divorce proceedings to include details of trust interests, including interests under a discretionary trust, stating an estimate of value of the interest and when it is likely to become realisable. If the spouse completing the form maintains that his or her trust interest is of no value, he or she has to give reasons.

If the spouse's response is that his or her interest is as a discretionary beneficiary and that his or her interest has no value or is impossible to possible to quantify this is likely to provoke a series of further enquiries, such as for the formal trust deeds and copies of the last two to three years' accounts, a portfolio valuation and details of all distributions to the beneficiary spouse. More controversially, it is common for any letters or memoranda of wishes of the settlor to be requested together with details of distributions to other beneficiaries, such as the divorcing spouse's children or siblings. The former request is problematic because it seeks disclosure of a document which is not normally made available to beneficiaries because it is confidential and the latter, because it seriously impinges on the expectations of confidentiality of other beneficiaries. Accordingly, a trustee faced with a request by a beneficiary for disclosure of such information to enable him or her to comply with such a request should first consider whether any disclosure should be made or whether the beneficiary's interest is too remote or there are other good reasons why disclosure should not be made and then consider the extent to which to comply with the request. The trustee may consider it appropriate to provide copies of the formal settlement instruments and the accounts (redacted to blank out the identity of any recipient of discretionary distributions other than to the beneficiary requesting the information) and explain, by reference to the proper duties of a trustee, why the remaining information requested is not being produced or that the court's direction are being sought as to whether it should be produced.

Other reasons why disclosure may be declined in the interests of the beneficial class as a whole include where there is a concern that the information so obtained will be used to further a competing interest, such as where the divorcing spouse is in competition with the business underlying the trust and the information disclosed could be used to damage the interests of the trust's companies. The trustee needs to take great care in such a situation, and may well need the assistance of the court as to whether to give disclosure and if so, subject to what safeguards.

Another problem is where information is being sought on the basis that the person requesting the information is a beneficiary, but at the same time he or she is alleging that the trust is a sham. This is contrary to the doctrine of election – a beneficiary must elect whether he or she is claiming rights under a settlement or seeking to attack it. Such a situation arose in the case of *Re M Trust*[40] where a wife involved in divorce proceedings in Illinois in which she was alleging that a Jersey trust was a sham sought disclosure of trust documents on behalf of her children who were beneficiaries. On application by the trustee to the Royal Court of Jersey for directions, the court declined to direct disclosure, but indicated that it would look with sympathy on such a request once the wife had dropped her allegation of sham.

The Royal Court of Jersey has had considerable experience of giving directions to trustees in connection with disclosure of trust documents in the context of divorce proceedings. In *Re H Trust*,[41] where both husband and wife were beneficiaries, the Royal Court decided that in that case it was important that the husband and wife should have the 'fullest information concerning the financial affairs of the Trust so that any compromise which they reach, failing which any decision of the Family Division, is based on the true financial position'.

This attitude is likely to prevail unless there are countervailing factors, such as those described above.

---

[40]   [2003] WTLR 491.
[41]   2006 JLR 280.

7.10 INSPECTION APPOINTMENTS AND LETTERS OF REQUEST

It is not uncommon for a spouse to find themselves embroiled in divorce and financial proceedings but to have no idea of the extent of their spouse's resources. Beyond Forms E and Questionnaires, a spouse may find themselves with more questions remaining than answers. The court therefore retains a very broad power to compel disclosure by a third party where appropriate. It can order the examination of witnesses either in England and Wales or abroad or require the production of documents necessary for the examination. There are various means by which this end can be achieved.

- Broadly speaking in family proceedings where documents are to be produced by a person in England and Wales, an **inspection appointment** should be ordered under FPR 1991, r 2.62(7). The practice, however, is that the person attending the inspection appointment should provide answers to any questions necessary to enable the inspection to proceed effectively.

- Where oral testimony is to be given by a person in England and Wales, a **subpoena** can be issued under FPR 1991, r 2.62(4), or a **deposition** can be made before an examiner under RSC Ord 39, r 1.

- Where documents are to be produced by a person abroad or oral evidence is to be taken from a person abroad, a Letter of Request should be issued.

7.10.1 Inspection Appointment

The power to order an Inspection Appointment is contained within FPR 1991, r 2.62:

'(4) At the hearing of an application for ancillary relief the District Judge shall, subject to rules 2.64, 2.65 and 10.10 investigate the allegations made in support of and in answer to the application, and may take evidence orally and may at any stage of the proceedings, whether before or during the hearing, order the attendance of any person for the purpose of being examined or cross-examined and order the disclosure and inspection of any document or require further statements.

(4A) A statement filed under paragraph (4) shall be sworn to be true ...

(7) Any party may apply to the court for an order that any person do attend an appointment (an "Inspection Appointment") before the court and produce any documents to be specified or described in the order, the inspection of which appears to the court to be necessary for disposing fairly of the application for ancillary relief or for saving costs.

(8) No persons shall be compelled by an order under paragraph (7) to produce any document at an Inspection Appointment which he could not be compelled to produce at the hearing of the application for ancillary relief.

(9) The court shall permit any person attending an Inspection Appointment pursuant to an order under paragraph (7) above to be represented at the appointment.'

The notes to this section set out in the *Family Court Practice 2007* explain that, on the premise that the third party is entitled to respect for the privacy of his documents, the application is normally a two-stage process. The first stage is on notice to the other party with supporting sworn statement.[42] The sworn statement should set out:

(1)   the nature of the proceedings;

(2)   the necessity for the production of the documents;

(3)   the precise document(s) sought; and

(4)   whether the applicant intends to call the witness at the hearing.

At the first application stage, the district judge will weed out any unnecessary or oppressive applications. If the application is successful at the first stage, it proceeds to the second stage at which the third party has the right to be represented and to object to the production of the documents. The court has to strike a balance between the interests of the parties against those of a third party. As elsewhere in family proceedings, the exercise in the court's discretion should be based on the facts of each case.

The threshold for a successful application is high and many applicants have failed. In *Morgan v Morgan*,[43] a wife was unsuccessful in her application for the husband's father to reveal his testamentary intentions. In *Frary v Frary*,[44] an application that a cohabitant's financial records be disclosed was refused. However, in *H v H (disclosure by third party)*,[45] in the course of valuing the wife's shareholding in a company, the company's chairman was ordered to produce documents showing the rent payable to the company. Other successful applications for Inspection Appointments include an application for production of documents by HM Revenue and Customs[46] and for an accountant to produce documents.[47]

---

[42]   *B v B (No 2)* [1995] 1 FLR 913, FD.
[43]   [1977] 2 All ER 515.
[44]   [1993] 2 FLR 696, CA.
[45]   (1981) 2 FLR 303, FD.
[46]   *R v R (Disclosure to Revenue)* [1998] 1 FLR 922, FD.
[47]   *D v D (Production Appointment)* [1995] 2 FLR 497, FD.

7.10.2   Witness Summons or Subpoena

Subparagraph 4 of r 2.62 of the FPR 1991 also empowers the court to order the attendance of an individual to give evidence, irrespective of whether they are a party or have filed a sworn statement. The same effect can be achieved using a subpoena ad testificandum (for oral evidence) or a subpoena duces tecum (to produce documents) via an application in the High Court. In the County Court, a witness summons to procure evidence or documents can be issued without leave being required. The same principles run through CPR 1998, rr 34.2–34.7. Any such witness may apply to set side on the same ground he would use to object to the inspection of the documents.

7.10.3   Letters of Request

Even where the third party whose testimony or documents are requested is based abroad, the court still has powers to require that individual to give evidence or produce documents. This is known as 'Letters of Request' or a 'Request for International Judicial Assistance'. The jurisdiction to do so comes from the Rules of the Supreme Court ('RSC') Ord 39, r 1(i) and (ii) which provide that:

> '1.
>
> (i)   The court may, in any cause or matter where it appears necessary for the purposes of justice, make an order ... for the examination on oath before a judge, an officer or examiner of the court or some other person at any place, of any person.
>
> (ii)   An order under paragraph (i) may be made on such terms (including in particular, terms as to the giving of discovery before the examination takes place) as the court thinks fit and may contain an order for the production of any document which appears to the court to be necessary for the purposes of the examination.'

RSC Ord 39, r 2 provides that where a deposition cannot be taken because the individual is out of the jurisdiction, an application can be made for an order that a Letter of Request be issued to the judicial authorities of the relevant country so that that person's evidence can be taken. In the alternative, the evidence can be taken by a special examiner. In countries which are signatories to conventions on the taking of evidence, the British Consul in the country in question can be appointed as special examiner.

If written questions are to be put to the individual then, together with the Letter of Request, a copy of the interrogatories and cross-interrogatories should be lodged. Where applicable, a certified translation should accompany the written questions. It should also be accompanied by an undertaking by the person obtaining the order that he will be personally responsible for all expenses incurred in the issuing of the Letter of Request.

Bilateral conventions have been made with the following countries: Austria, Belgium, Croatia, Czech Republic, Denmark, Estonia, Finland, France, Germany, Greece, Hungary, Iraq, Israel, Italy, Latvia, Lithuania, Netherlands, Norway, Poland, Portugal, Serbia, Slovakia, Slovenia, Spain, Sweden and Turkey.

In these countries, the taking of evidence under r 2 before the British Consular authority is permitted, albeit that in most of these jurisdictions, it is only permitted in respect of willing witnesses, and in Hungary and Turkey only willing witnesses of British nationality. By contrast, the Hague Convention on the Taking of Evidence Abroad in Civil or Commercial Matters (the 'Hague Convention')[48] allows evidence to be taken between any of the Signatory States: Australia, Barbados, Belgium, Cyprus, Czech Republic, Denmark, Germany, Finland, France, Israel, Italy, Luxembourg, Monaco, Netherlands, Norway, Portugal, Singapore, Slovakia, Spain, Sweden, UK, UK territories (Gibraltar and Hong Kong), USA and US possessions.

Countries that are signatories to the Hague Convention and have brought its terms into force in their domestic law appear to be making increasing use of it.

7.10.3.1 Case-law on Letters of Request

The application of the principles of RSC Ord 39 have been the subject of much judicial comment in commercial matters.

7.10.3.1.1 Outgoing / Incoming

There is a distinction to be drawn between outgoing Letters of Request and incoming Letters of Request. An outgoing Letter of Request is one which emanates from the English court to another jurisdiction. An incoming Letter of Request is one which is received from another jurisdiction.

The jurisdiction of the court to make an outgoing Request arises from the court's jurisdiction under RSC Ord 39. The principles to be applied for incoming Letters of Request are those enshrined in the Hague Convention, which came into force in September 1976. This was given force in English law by the Evidence (Proceedings in Other Jurisdictions) Act 1975. Section 2(1) of that Act says that the English court has power to 'make such provision for obtaining evidence as may appear appropriate

---

[48]   18 March 1970.

for the purposes of giving effect to the Request'. In particular, an order which requires a person to take appropriate steps may make provision for the examination of witnesses either orally or in writing (s 2(ii)(a)) and for the production of documents (s 6(ii)(b)).

Although the basis for outgoing Letters of Request differs from incoming Letters of Request, similar principles should apply. As Nicholls VC in *Panayiotou v Sony Music Entertainment (UK) Ltd* (the 'George Michael case'):[49]

> 'The Act is concerned with incoming Letters of Request. It is not confined to a request from the courts of countries which are signatories of the Hague Convention. Nevertheless it would be surprising if the English courts were not at liberty to request, even from Hague Convention countries, assistance corresponding to the assistance United Kingdom courts may now give to the courts of countries outside the United Kingdom. Indeed, in *MacKinnon v Donaldson, Lufkin and Genrette Securities Corporation* [1986] CH 482, 491, Hoffmann J took it for granted that the English court could issue a Letter of Request to the New York courts seeking the production of documents.'

When ratifying the Convention, the UK did so subject to certain conditions. The government declared at the time that it would not 'execute Letters of Request issued for the purpose of obtaining pre-trial discovery of documents' and letters which required a person:

'(a) to state that documents relating to the proceedings to which the Letter of Request relates are or have been in his possession, custody or power; or

(b) to produce any documents other than particular documents specified in the Letter of Request as being documents appearing to the requested court to be, or like to be, in his possession, custody or power.'

In other words, when considering an incoming Letter of Request, the UK said it would not execute a Letter of Request where that Letter either:

(a) sought knowledge about which documents were in a party's possession; and/or

(b) sought the production of documents that were conjectural.

Helpful guidance is given by Nicholls VC in the George Michael case:

> 'Where an applicant has not seen the document sought and does not know what they contain, the application can more readily be characterised as a discovery exercise. Further, to be the subject of a Letter of Request, a document must be admissible in evidence; it must be directly material to an issue in the action; and the court must be satisfied the document does exist

---

[49] [1994] Ch 142.

or did exist, and it is likely to be in the possession of the person from whom production is being sought. Actual documents are to be contrasted with conjectural documents, which may or may not exist ...'

7.10.3.1.2   Direct / Indirect material

The authorities draw a distinction between 'direct material immediately relevant to the issue in dispute' and 'indirect material obtained by way of discovery'. The principles state that the production of direct material is permissible whilst mere discovery is not. Lord Fraser in *Re Westinghouse Electric Corporation Uranium Contract Litigation MDL Docket 235 (No 2)*[50] said that:

> 'The first question in instant appeals is whether the court should be satisfied, as required by paragraph (b) of Section 1, that the requests made in the letters rogatory are for "evidence" in the sense in which the word is used in the paragraph or whether they are truly for a wider discovery. Unless the application passes through this filter, no order can be made to give effect to it ...
>
> The distinction between evidence and discovery is recognised in Article 23 of the Hague Convention, and in Section 2(4) of the Act of 1975, and is fully accepted by counsel for Westinghouse who do not dispute that, if the letters rogatory were *merely* seeking discovery, they ought not to receive effect.'

It is possible to specify a *class* of documents rather than *individual* documents. In *Jim Beam Brands Co v Kentucky Importers Pty Ltd*[51] Jones J said that:

> 'the words "particular documents" must be given a strict construction and the request must not amount to a fishing expedition. However, a compendious description is acceptable provided that all the documents can be clearly identified.'

7.10.3.1.3   Part permissible / part impermissible

It is also accepted that where a Letter of Request could fall between the permissible and the impermissible; for example where some questions have the purpose of seeking pre-trial discovery and some are legitimately seeking evidence which the applicant knows to be in existence and which may lawfully be used at trial, the court may accede to part of the letter.

In contrast to the approach outlined above, in the Bermudian case of *Netbank v Commercial Money Center*,[52] Kawaley J said that:

---

[50]   [1978] AC 547, HL.
[51]   [1992] 2 HKC 581 (High Court of Hong Kong).
[52]   [2004] Bda LR 46, Berm SC.

'So, in a case as here where it is admitted that the relevant request contains improper documentary discovery requests combined with proper oral examination requests, the court has a discretion to exercise in regard to whether the admitted defect should be regarded as invalidating the otherwise lawful oral examination request.'

Although Bermuda is not a signatory to the Hague Convention, the statute is couched in identical terms to the English statute, and so in effect the same test as under the Hague Convention is applied.

In summary, the existing authorities established that:

(a) the court will not give effect to an incoming Letter of Request or issue an outgoing Letter of Request if that letter is aimed at pre-trial discovery as opposed to obtaining evidence which may be admissible and is necessary for the purposes for which it is requested;

(b) for a Letter to be given effect, it must be aimed at obtaining direct evidence as set out by Lord Fraser in *Re Westinghouse Electric Corporation Uranium Contract Litigation MDL Docket 235 (No 2)*; and

(c) whilst the court has the power to order the production of documents alone, it cannot order the production of documents either in an outgoing or incoming application unless they are individually described, although a compendious description where all documents falling within that group is clearly indicated is permissible.

7.10.3.1.4   Use in family proceedings

This method of eliciting information from trustees was expressly approved of by Singer J in *Minwalla v Minwalla*.[53] The trial judge noted that the requests had been dealt with 'with the utmost courtesy, speed and efficiency'. He also noted that the wrong procedure had been used – there is a statutory procedure in Jersey by which, if there is an oral hearing on the Letters of Request, English Counsel have a right of audience, 'so that they may investigate the matters arising on the Letters of Request with the Respondent to the hearing' and that no order for costs is subsequently made.

In the unreported case of *C v C*, Baron J criticised the wife for failing to use Letters of Request as a means of eliciting information regarding the husband's Manx trust.

However, a recent Court of Appeal decision, if upheld on any later challenge in the House of Lords in another case, has broadened the

---

[53] [2005] 1 FLR 771, FD.

potential scope of both incoming and outgoing Letters of Request in financial proceedings ancillary to a divorce.

7.11 CASE STUDY: *CHARMAN V CHARMAN* [2005] EWCA CIV 1606

This was an appeal by the husband in financial proceedings ancillary to a divorce against an order made by Coleridge J on 20 October 2005, that a Letter of Request be issued to the authorities in Bermuda requiring production of documents and examination of a director of the corporate trustee; and an order that the family accountant should attend an inspection appointment and produce documents.

7.11.1 Facts

The central issue between the parties in the financial proceedings was whether or not the resources contained within a Bermuda trust called The Dragon Holdings Trust ('Dragon') should be taken into account. The husband maintained that Dragon was not a resource which the court should consider in its assessment of the parties' resources because his intention had always been that the trust was 'dynastic'.

As acknowledged by Wilson LJ, irrespective of a percentage swing in favour of the husband on the basis of his special contribution, the difference between inclusion and exclusion of Dragon was likely to make a substantial difference to the award to the wife.

The order sought by the wife, therefore, would be a lump sum order which would in effect require the husband to ask the trustees of Dragon to distribute a lump sum to him out of the capital of the trust, in accordance with the principles set out in *Browne v Browne*[54] and *Thomas v Thomas*.[55] It was therefore central to the wife's case at the final hearing that she have sufficient evidence to demonstrate that this trust was a resource which the court should consider, and, more specifically, that the husband had 'immediate access to the funds'. An allegation that the trustees were quasi-agents of the husband was withdrawn by the wife's counsel in oral argument before the Court of Appeal.

7.11.2 The Trust

Dragon itself was set up in Jersey in 1987. The husband's case was that he was strongly influenced by members of a Chinese family with whom he worked in the mid-1980s. The beneficiaries of the trust were the husband, the wife, their two children, any future child or remoter issue of the husband, charities and such other persons as the trustees might add. The

---

[54] [1989] 1 FLR 291, CA.
[55] [1995] 2 FLR 668, CA.

trustees had power to distribute capital as well as income to any beneficiary. The first Letter of Wishes is set out at para 6 of Wilson LJ's judgment.

The trust began as a conventional discretionary trust. However, because of mismanagement by a Jersey trust company, it was treated as an interest in possession trust with the capital and income in segregated accounts. The husband did not receive any distributions out of the accumulated income account from 1997 onwards.

The husband then moved to Bermuda and in April 2003 he changed the trustee to a Bermudian trust company, Codan, and the proper law of the trust was changed to Bermuda. Codan formally confirmed the previous trustee's decision to treat Dragon as 'an interest in possession trust'. In May 2004, the husband drafted a further letter of wishes in which he said that he would like the trustee to treat him as the primary beneficiary. In June 2004, the husband asked Codan, subject to one specific disbursement, to reappoint all the accumulated income into the capital fund of the trust. The husband stated that Codan did not appear to have acted upon this instruction.

Wilson LJ said that the central issue in the case was whether 'if the husband were to request it to advance the whole (or part) of the capital of the trust to him, the trustee would be likely to do so.' There was also a subsidiary question as to whether the income of the trust was being made available and whether it would be likely to continue to be made available in the foreseeable future 'for deployment at the husband's direction'.

7.11.3   The first instance decision

The husband's arguments were summarised at para 18 of Wilson LJ's judgment:

'(a)   The applications are in aid of a *"fishing"* expedition and thus impermissible;

(b)   In so far as the applications are for *the production of documents the very existence of which the wife cannot prove*, they are impermissible;

(c)   The orders are *unnecessary* and thus impermissible;

(d)   The orders are *disproportionate* and so should in the exercise of discretion be refused;

(e)   The orders are *oppressive*, and particularly in relation to Mr Anderson [the director of the trust company], and so should in the exercise of discretion be refused; and

(f)   At least in part the orders go *too wide* and should be cut down.'

At first instance, the judge said that under normal circumstances, he would consider that the issue of Letters of Request would be a 'disproportionate procedural step'. However, it was the vast sums of money and the centrality of this issue to the case that persuaded him to make an order that the Letters of Request be issued:

> 'The court should make a decision that is determinative of an issue of that gravity on the basis of the best possible evidence ... It may be that there is nothing else. If so, that too may be relevant. It may be that there are documents and communications between the husband and the trustees that deal with his intentions, past, present or future. If so, I need to see them.'

The orders were made by Coleridge J that, a director of Codan, be orally examined and required to:

(a)   produce trust accounts for the two most recent completed years;

(b)   produce any trust deeds, written resolutions and Letters of Request, other than identified documents of each class already disclosed by the husband;

(c)   state whether it was the practice of the trustee to consult the husband, and/or to be guided by him about prospective policy decisions, whether as to investment, distribution or otherwise, and, if so, give full details and produce all relevant documents;

(d)   state whether the trustee and the husband had discussed the possible collapse of the trust or change in the expression of his wishes and, if so, give full details and produce all relevant documents; and

(e)   state whether there had been any communications between the husband's accountant and the trustee 'regarding the trusts' and, if so, give full details and produce all relevant documents.

The Letter of Request also requested that the wife's representative be allowed to ask follow up questions.

The order for the inspection appointment obliged the husband's long-standing accountant in the UK to produce:

> 'any documents ... containing evidence of any advice given to, discussions with, or communications from, [the husband] relating to the past, present and future treatment of the trust funds or which bear upon the conception, creation and possible ultimate dissolution of [Dragon] ....'

7.11.4   Outgoing v Incoming

Paragraph 29 of the Court of Appeal's judgment in *Charman v Charman* endorses Nicholls VC's approach in the George Michael case. Wilson LJ says:

'It would be unconscionable for the English court to make an outgoing request in circumstances in which, had it been incoming, it would not give effect to it; nor could the foreign court reasonably be expected to give effect to the English court's request in such circumstances.'

Wilson LJ agreed that the principles for either incoming or outgoing requests should be derived from the statute which governs incoming requests; the Evidence (Proceedings in Other Jurisdictions) Act 1975 (the '1975 Act').

Wilson LJ went on to consider the various arguments raised by the husband.

7.11.4.1 *'Fishing'*

At para 32 of his judgment, Wilson LJ endorsed the approach of Kerr LJ in *Re State of Norway's Application*[56] that:

'It is perhaps best described as a roving enquiry, by means of the examination and cross-examination of witnesses, which is not designed to establish by means of their evidence allegations of fact which have been raised bona fide with adequate particulars, but to obtain information which may lead to obtaining evidence in general support of a party's case.'

In the second *Norway* case,[57] Woolf LJ in the Court of Appeal cast doubt on whether the concept of fishing was applicable to a request that a witness should be required to give oral evidence. However, in a further appeal, the House of Lords declined to comment on this issue.

The relationship between oral testimony and the production of documents was considered by the Court of Appeal. Wilson LJ considered the decision of the Supreme Court of Bermuda in *Netbank v Commercial Money Center*,[58] in which it was noted that since oral examination normally relates to the documents requested, if those documents are improperly sought, the oral examination will also fall away. Wilson LJ noted that on the instant facts, the oral testimony was free-standing as it related to the relationship between the trustee and the husband as settlor.

Wilson LJ summarised that:

'(a)   In so far as I see production of documents, the orders for the letter of request and for the inspection appointment could not lawfully have been made if they represent an attempt to go "fishing"; and

(b)   In so far as the letter of request seeks the taking of oral evidence, it may be preferable to conduct its initial appraisal not by reference to "fishing" but by asking, perhaps in effect only slightly differently,

---

[56]   [1987] 1 QB 433, CA.
[57]   *Re State of Norway's Application (No 2)* [1990] 1 AC 723 at 781G.
[58]   [2004] Bda LR 46, Berm SC.

whether the intention is to obtain Mr Anderson's evidence for use of trial and there is reason to believe that he has knowledge of the matters relevant to issues at trial.'

Wilson LJ went on to consider whether or not the approach should be different in financial proceedings following divorce. His view was that (referring to the decisions of Dunn J in *B v B (Matrimonial Proceedings: Discovery)* [59] and the Gibraltar case of *Zakay v Zakay* [60]), a wife in ancillary relief proceedings is likely to have a general overview of the husband's financial position, but she is unlikely to know the details of the sources of his wealth or the precise figures. In this case, the wife raised an allegation, and she was seeking to elicit evidence in support of the allegation for use at the forthcoming hearing. Since the request in the case was not part of 'a search for material which might enable the wife to raise an allegation', it was not to be considered 'fishing'.

7.11.4.2   *Documents not proved to exist*

Wilson LJ considered the examples given from commercial litigation such as *Re Westinghouse* [61] and the Asbestos Insurance case in which, respectively, Lords Diplock and Fraser considered the construction of s 2(4)(b) of the 1975 Act. Whilst Lord Diplock construed the phrase as meaning 'individual documents separately described', Lord Fraser considered that the phrase meant that the request could seek production only of actual documents rather than conjectural documents. In the George Michael case, Nicholls VC said that the request had to be confined to particular documents but these could be 'compendiously described'.

In Wilson LJ's view, in ancillary relief proceedings, the wife would very seldom have the knowledge with which to prove the existence of a document which, if it existed, could have a crucial bearing on the outcome of her application. There was therefore no 'room' for such limitation in deciding whether to order a non-party to produce documents. Wilson LJ pointed to the 'quasi-inquisitorial role of the judge in ancillary relief proceedings' as set out in *Parra v Parra*,[62] which derived its statutory authority from s 25 of the MCA 1973. A parallel could be drawn with inspection appointments, where if the limitations were too strict, necessary information could be lost.

---

[59]   [1978] Fam 181.
[60]   [1998] 3 FCR 35.
[61]   [1978] AC 547, HL.
[62]   [2003] 1 FLR 942, CA.

7.11.4.3   Necessity

Wilson LJ rejected this argument out of hand, stating that if the wife already had enough information with which to put her arguments, he could not see how the husband could continue to reject her arguments so stoutly.

7.11.4.4   Proportionality

Wilson LJ pointed to the overriding objective contained in r 2.51(b)(3) of the FPR 1991 and accepted the wife's submission that 'any question of proportionality is overcome by the magnitude of the trust assets in question'. This would not apply in cases involving trusts with much smaller assets.

7.11.4.5   Oppression

The question was as to whether the order made by Coleridge J at first instance was so oppressive upon the trustee and the family accountant as to outweigh the likely value of the material in the determination of the case. Wilson LJ rejected this argument on the basis that first and foremost, both individuals were professionals. Wilson LJ felt that where the beneficiaries were the husband and wife (and also children and issue) it seemed obvious that the trustee should impart such knowledge as was relevant to the debate in court as to the fair outcome of the dispute between two beneficiaries.

7.11.4.6   Excessive width

Whilst Wilson LJ doubted that communications between the husband and the trustee relating to prospective investment decisions would assist the court in answering the central question, he was persuaded by the wife's submission that the way in which such questions were answered might throw light on the relationship between the husband and trustee.

Sir Mark Potter, the President of the Family Division, added his own gloss to the judgment of Wilson LJ. At para 75, he rejected the husband's reliance on Nicholls VC's comments in the George Michael case in which he said 'actual documents are to be contrasted with conjectural documents, which may or may not exist':

> 'It is these words which ..., Leading Counsel for the husband] submits ... govern this case, and as such are fatal to the wife's application. If he is right, that seems to me a most unsatisfactory situation. It means that, although it would be legitimate as a matter of practice and procedure in this country to call Mr Anderson and ask him in the course of his evidence whether a certain document or class of documents exists and, if so, to produce them (they being material and admissible evidence), there is no power by means of

letters of request to ask a foreign court to assist in that respect, if willing under its own rules of practice or procedure, to do so. Whilst there may be good reason in practice why that should be the position in inter parties litigation elsewhere than in the Family Division, it does not seem to me appropriate, unless it is unavoidable, to adopt the same approach in relation to financial proceedings following divorce, both for the reasons given by Wilson LJ ... and because of the overriding need to do justice between parties in an unequal position to which I have referred at the beginning of this Judgment. None of the authorities to which we have been referred involved, or focused upon, the position in relation to ancillary relief claims in family cases.'

Lloyd LJ considered the position that the Bermudian court might take to a request phrased in the form annexed to the wife's application:

'If objection is taken by the trustee, it will be for the court in Bermuda to rule on it, by reference to the particular points taken as regards the particular obligations sought to be imposed as regards the production of documents and the giving of oral evidence. Nothing that this court says can, or should be taken as intended to, pre-empt or anticipate the decision of that court on whatever points are taken before it. Nevertheless, if the Bermudian court would be bound to recognise the validity of that objection on the part of the trustee it could be futile to issue the letters of request. It seems to me proper, therefore, to give some thought as to whether such an objection would be bound to succeed.'

Lloyd LJ did not see that there could be any conflict to prevent the trustee disclosing the trust accounts. He also pointed to the decision of the Privy Council in *Schmidt v Rosewood Trust Ltd*[63] in saying that he could not see that even as mere discretionary beneficiaries, the husband and wife did not have a sufficient interest to be entitled to disclosure.

He also pointed out that the trustee had a duty to act in the best interests of the beneficiaries. If the wife's allegations were not true, it would be positively in the interests of the beneficiaries that the trustee produce the evidence sought so as to set the record straight.

The Appeal was therefore unanimously dismissed.

7.11.5   Postscript to the Court of Appeal judgment

- Pending the husband's appeal, the trustee had applied to set aside the order obtained in Bermuda requiring the trustee to comply with the Letter of Request. This was relisted after judgment was given in the Court of Appeal.

- Once the Court of Appeal had dismissed the appeal, the hearing to set aside proceeded in Bermuda.

---

[63]   [2003] UKPC 26.

- The trustee's application to set aside the order obtained by the wife in Bermuda was successful. The judge did not give a formal judgment, but the transcript shows that he was persuaded that on the authorities, this was an impermissible 'fishing' expedition by the wife. He stated that he preferred to follow the decisions of the House of Lords on this issue, and held that the documents she was seeking were conjectural. He therefore cut down the scope of the order such that only six questions had to be answered by the trustee and the wife did not have the opportunity to ask follow-up questions. Moreover, he held that no documents had to be produced by the trustee.

- The wife did not appeal the decision in Bermuda, on the basis that that appeal would hold up the final hearing listed for seven days in two months' time.

7.11.6   Comment

Despite Coleridge J subsequently describing Bell J's decision as 'churlish and parochial', the Bermudian judge was applying the Hague Convention which was expressly intended to cover divorce and family matters. It is not permissible to read into an international convention a special test in family cases, although it may lead to a harsh and unsatisfactory result in some family cases where it cannot be shown what documents are in existence. The law should be changed by statutory amendment rather than by impermissible judicial interpretation. The author's view is that the decision of the Court of Appeal is unlikely to survive an appeal to the House of Lords in another case, and that practitioners should not assume that outgoing requests following *Charman* will be upheld in offshore jurisdictions. The outcome will depend on what the local law is, whether the Hague Convention is followed and whether the House of Lords approach is preferred to that of the Court of Appeal in *Charman*.

7.11.6.1   Summary of current state of law

In practice, for the time being at least in England, the ambit of a Letter of Request appears to be broadly similar whether incoming or outgoing in this jurisdiction, despite the fact that the two types have a different basis in statute and procedure.

In family proceedings, it is not limited to actual documents which can be proven to exist by the party making the request. This is because of the 'quasi inquisitorial' nature of family proceedings and the overriding objective as set out in FPR 1991, r 2.51(b)(3), the court is prepared to make an order for a Letter of Request to be issued where the oral testimony or documents requested are:

(1)   relevant for the purposes of proving or disproving a particular allegation raised by a party; and

(2)   admissible in court.

The wife's ability to elicit information through an inspection appointment against an intermediary should serve as a lesson that communications with intermediaries can be as discoverable as those between trustee and beneficiary/settlor.

7.11.6.2   *What should the trustee's attitude be?*

If the trustee is situated in England and Wales the trustee can be ordered to attend an inspection appointment and can be subpoenaed or a deposition taken by an examiner (FPR 1991, r 2.62 and RSC Ord 39, r 1). The trustee has the right to attend and object to the disclosure sought, e g that it is oppressive and inappropriately breaches the duty of confidentiality to the beneficial class or other beneficiaries in particular. Where the trust is discretionary it is common for a trustee to be asked as to its dispositive intentions. This places the trustee in particular difficulty, given that the trustee's duty is to consider exercising its powers in light of the circumstances pertaining at the time, and not to speculate or enter into any commitments as to how it might exercise its discretion in the future. In such a situation the trustee's best course may be to respond by describing the nature of its duty and hence its inability to give any firm indication as to the future exercise of its powers, while indicating assets which are charged or otherwise not available to be distributed and commitments made or expectations raised as to other beneficiaries' support.

An inspection appointment may also be used to try to ascertain whether the trustee has been acting substantially in accordance with the wishes of the beneficiary spouse in order to support an allegation that the trust should be viewed as a resource of a spouse or, possibly, that the trust is a sham.

The trustee may wish to seek directions in trust proceedings in the Chancery Division as to how to respond to such a request and in particular, whether to object to the appointment and what documents, if any, to withhold.

Finally, the trustee should consider whether on the particular facts of the case, providing the English court with the information or documents requested may in fact be of positive benefit to the beneficiaries or may prevent the court drawing inferences adverse to the interests of one or other of the beneficiaries.

CHAPTER 8

INTERNATIONAL ENFORCEMENT ISSUES RELATING TO TRUSTS

8.1 INTRODUCTION

The attitude of the Family Division of the High Court towards trusts is well known. Many a judicial pronouncement, uttered by family judges as a statement of the obvious, raises nothing but groans from chancery lawyers.[1] Take this recent example:[2]

> 'Almost uniquely our jurisdiction does not have a marital property regime and it is scarcely appropriate to classify our jurisdiction as having a marital regime of separation of property. More correctly we have no regime, simply accepting that each spouse owns his or her own separate property during the marriage but subject to the court's wide distributive powers in prospect upon a decree of judicial separation, nullity or divorce. The difficulty of harmonising our law concerning the property consequences of marriage and divorce and the law of the Civilian Member States is exacerbated by the fact that our law has so far given little status to pre-nuptial contracts. If, unlike the rest of Europe, the property consequences of divorce are to be regulated by the principles of needs, compensation and sharing, should not the parties to the marriage, or the projected marriage, have at the least the opportunity to order their own affairs otherwise by a nuptial contract?'

But, with respect, it is simply not right to say that we in England have no marital property regime.[3] However, instead of having supinely to choose one of several pre-digested regimes ordained by the legislator, as they have to do in civil law countries, in this country individual autonomy rules. Everyone can make their own regime, to fit their own individual circumstances. And, in the past, the monied classes did. Even middle class people had marriage settlements – *trusts*.[4] Today the mechanism remains

---

[1]   It is only right to say that this is not always the case. The decision and reasoning in *A v A* [2007] EWHC 99 (Fam) is a recent and an honourable exception.

[2]   *Charman v Charman (No 4)* [2007] EWCA Civ 503, para 124 (the court in this occasion comprised the President of the Family Division, the Vice-President of the Family Division and one former Family Division judge). See further Appendix 2 below.

[3]   Nor, indeed, that the English position (whatever it is) is almost unique: it is the position in nearly all common law countries.

[4]   See e g Holdsworth *A History of English Law* (2nd edn, 1937) vol 7, pp 376–381 and 547–559; *Williams on Settlements* (1879) especially Lecture XV; Cheshire *The Modern*

there, albeit modified for settlements of land in 1996.[5] Precedents are still to be had.[6] There is a thriving community of lawyers who know all about them, and who regularly advise their clients on them.[7] The reason that new ones are not created so frequently today is simply the impact of capital taxation. Paradoxically, the harsher that that becomes (and fiscal drag by itself is doing that for the Chancellor of the Exchequer, even without the need to introduce more unpleasant anti-trust regimes), the less likely it is that anyone will use the institution. On the other hand, for those who are not subject to the crushing burden of UK capital taxation,[8] the marriage settlement can be an attractive way of ordering the devolution of family property, presenting significant advantages[9] over, say, pre-nuptial contracts, which are after all, well, just *contracts*. But what is really depressing is that three senior English judges apparently have no idea of the history of marital property in this country, and give no thought to calling for more attractive tax regimes to be introduced for marriage settlements.

This chapter is about one aspect of English family litigation, and that is its impact on trustees (and assets) of foreign trusts. Suppose that an English court in matrimonial litigation has made an order affecting foreign trustees, not within the jurisdiction of the court. Probably the foreign trustees will not comply with that order unless and until the *foreign* court directs or permits them to do so, because otherwise they think they will be at risk of action by their beneficiaries for doing something without legal sanction.[10] The question whether and to what extent the foreign court will in effect enforce the English order is a complex one, and is the subject of this chapter.

However, logically the first point to be addressed is whether the English court has jurisdiction to make that order. This has two aspects. The first is whether the English court asserts jurisdiction. The second is whether the *foreign* court considers that the English court has jurisdiction. The latter, however, will only arise with practical significance after the English court has first asserted jurisdiction and made the order. For that reason this

---

Law of Real Property (1st edn, 1925), 367–72; Megarry & Wade *The Law of Real Property* (2nd edn, 1959), 381–89; Stebbings *The Private Trustee in Victorian England* (2003), especially at 10–11.

5	By the Trusts of Land and Appointment of Trustees Act 1996.

6	See *The Encyclopedia of Forms and Precedents* (5th edn, 2005 reissue) vol 40(1), paras 2690–2800.

7	See eg *X v A* [2005] EWHC 2706 (Ch) for a recent case concerning a marriage settlement made in 1964.

8	Eg those not domiciled (or deemed for inheritance tax purposes to be domiciled) in the UK, or those whose assets are subject to 100% relief (eg agricultural or business property).

9	Including protection from bankruptcy and the ability to trace into the products of wrongfully alienated assets, to mention but two.

10	For recent examples, see *Re Rabaiotti 1989 Settlement* 2000 JLR 173; *FM v ASL Trustee Company Ltd* [2006] JRC 020A, para 11; *Re H Trust* [2006] JRC 057.

aspect is discussed later, in the section that discusses recognition and enforcement of English judgments in foreign jurisdictions.

8.2 ENGLISH JURISDICTION

The word 'jurisdiction', when used in the context of the jurisdiction of the English court, is used in at least two different senses in English law. First, there is 'territorial' jurisdiction, ie answering the international question *which* persons are (or are claimed by English law to be) within the reach of the English court. In English law this extends not only to persons actually within the physical territory of England and Wales, but also to include some cases where the potential defendant is elsewhere (what the Americans call 'long arm' jurisdiction). The second sense of jurisdiction is 'power' jurisdiction, ie the circumstances in which the English court will *in fact* deal with a particular matter, in relation to a defendant who is undoubtedly within the jurisdiction of the court in the first ('territorial') sense.[11]

In this section we are examining purely the issue of jurisdiction arising from divorce[12] and ancillary relief.[13] We are not therefore discussing jurisdiction over trustees per se but rather jurisdiction relating to matrimonial assets including trust assets (and hence the trustees) in matrimonial proceedings.

The power of a court making a decree of divorce to vary a nuptial settlement, under the MCA 1973, s 24,[14] has already been discussed.[15] The jurisdiction of the English court to make an ancillary relief order in general is summarised in *Dicey, Morris & Collins on the Conflict of Laws*.[16] Rule 91 (1) states that:

> 'English courts have jurisdiction to make an ancillary order for financial provision on or after granting a decree of divorce, nullity of marriage or judicial separation whenever they have jurisdiction in the main suit'.

In other words, if the English court has jurisdiction to grant a divorce, then it has jurisdiction to deal with all financial matters arising out of the divorce.

---

[11] On these two kinds of jurisdiction, see *Mercedes-Benz AG v Leiduck* [1996] AC 284, PC.

[12] The reference to divorce in this chapter includes for this purpose a reference to similar decrees such as nullity, judicial separation, and dissolution or annulment of a civil partnership.

[13] As to the English Court's approach to ancillary relief, see Chapter 7.

[14] Or the Matrimonial and Family Proceedings Act 1984, s 17, in the case of a foreign decree.

[15] See Chapter 5.

[16] (14th edn, 2006).

The English court also has jurisdiction even if the divorce did not take place in England.[17] According to para 2 of r 91:

> 'English courts have jurisdiction to make an order for financial provision after the grant in a country outside the United Kingdom, the Channel Islands and the Isle of Man of a divorce, annulment of marriage or legal separation which is entitled to be valid in England if—
>
> (a) the applicant or respondent is domiciled in England either on the date of the application for leave to proceed or on the date on which the divorce, annulment or legal separation took effect in the foreign country; or
>
> (b) the applicant or the respondent was habitually resident in England throughout the period of one year ending with either of those dates; or
>
> (c) the applicant or respondent has (or both of them have) at the date of the application for leave to proceed a beneficial interest in possession in a dwelling house situated in England which was at some time during the marriage a matrimonial home of the parties.
>
> Provided that if the respondent is domiciled in a State (other than the United Kingdom) to which Council Regulation (EC) 44/2001 or the 1968 Convention[18] or the Lugano Convention[19] applies, the English courts have jurisdiction to make such orders if and only if the jurisdictional requirements of the Judgments Regulation or the relevant Convention are satisfied.'

This means that English courts can exercise the full range of powers to make financial provision or property adjustment orders after proceedings have taken place in an overseas country – provided that the decree is entitled to be recognised in England. It should be noted, however, that the applicant must first obtain the leave of the court and the parties must have a genuine connection with England. There are additional rules on jurisdiction, in particular in relation to failure to provide reasonable maintenance, and to varying or revoking financial arrangements.[20]

Dicey, Morris & Collins also note[21] that once an English court has jurisdiction to make any ancillary orders it can 'make an order for periodical payments by a husband even though he is domiciled and resident abroad and has no assets in England', and that it can 'vary a settlement which comprises property situated abroad and is governed by foreign law and the trustees of which reside abroad'.[22] In the older cases where the court did so vary a foreign law trust, the foreign trustees

---

[17] Matrimonial and Family Proceedings Act 1984, s 17(a)(ii).

[18] In practice, since March 2002 the 2001 Regulation has completely replaced the Brussels Convention as between EU States.

[19] This Convention applies as between the EU States and certain other European countries, now just Iceland, Norway and Switzerland.

[20] See paras 1–8 of r 91.

[21] See para 18-171.

[22] *Nunneley Nunneley v Nunneley and Marrian* (1890) 15 PD 186; *Forsyth v Forsyth* [1891] P 363; *Goff v Goff* [1934] P 107, 111.

submitted to the jurisdiction.[23] Whether it can or should do so, in a case where the foreign trustees do not submit to the English jurisdiction, is perhaps more difficult.

Importantly, however, it will 'decline to exercise its powers in cases where any order that it might make would be wholly ineffective'.[24] The issue of asserting jurisdiction is therefore tied up with enforceability.

8.2.1 Jurisdiction over the trustees

The question of jurisdiction to grant a decree of divorce has been dealt with elsewhere.[25] But that does not concern the trustees of any trust in that capacity. And there are no rules in England and Wales concerned *specifically* with jurisdiction in relation to trusts and ancillary relief on divorce. There are, however, *general* jurisdictional rules covering trusts and trustees.

Before we consider those general rules, we can summarise the English court's possible approaches to the question of jurisdiction in family proceedings as follows:

(1) the court may decide that it has jurisdiction, and go on to deal with the substance of the case; or

(2) the court may declare that it has no jurisdiction in the matter; or

(3) the court, even though it has jurisdiction, may declare that it is forum non conveniens, on the basis that there is another court with jurisdiction which is clearly more appropriate, and that it is not unjust to deprive the claimant of the right to trial in England.[26]

Provided that the court has established that it has jurisdiction, the court may go on to decide the matter even if the trustee does not appear before the court. However, it must be borne in mind that in some cases the jurisdiction (either 'territorial' or 'power') of the court will actually depend on the trustee's submission to and appearance before the court. Ordinarily in such cases the court is not able to decide the matter if the trustee does not submit, because the court will have no jurisdiction. But, as we shall see, in modern English family cases this does not apply. It should also be noted that the court may grant an anti-suit injunction against the party who is litigating elsewhere, where the appropriate conditions are satisfied.[27]

---

[23] *Nunneley v Nunneley and Marrian* (1890) 15 PD 186; *Forsyth v Forsyth* [1891] P 363.
[24] *Tallack v Tallack and Broekema* [1927] P 211; *Goff v Goff* [1934] P 107; *Wyler v Lyons* [1963] P 274.
[25] See Chapter 3.
[26] See *Dicey, Morris & Collins*, r 31(2).
[27] See *Dicey, Morris & Collins*, r 32.

Let us now turn to the general jurisdictional rules relating to trustees. As a general principle, the English court has jurisdiction over the trustees of a trust if originating process can properly be served on them, except that, if they are outside England and Wales, the court has jurisdiction only when such process has actually been served (or is deemed to have been served) in accordance with English rules.[28] Formerly, it was clear that the rules did not permit such service on persons outside the jurisdiction in respect of property outside the jurisdiction.[29]

The position appears now to be otherwise. The procedure in ancillary claims cases is described in detail elsewhere,[30] but the principal rules of procedure currently applying to family proceedings are the Family Proceedings Rules 1991 ('FPR 1991').[31] However, even when first introduced, these were never a complete procedural code, and it was expressly provided that the Rules of the Supreme Court 1965 ('RSC') and the County Court Rules 1981 ('CCR 1981') should apply to the proceedings ('with the necessary modifications') wherever the FPR did not provide for the situation concerned.[32] In 1999 almost all the rest of the English civil justice system migrated from the RSC and the CCR 1981 to a single unified set of rules, the Civil Procedure Rules 1998 ('CPR 1998'). But most family proceedings, including ancillary relief claims, continue to be governed by the FPR, supplemented by the RSC and the CCR in their final form (ie before replacement by the CPR). Despite the general proposition in the FPR that the RSC and the CCR 'should continue to apply' to family proceedings,[33] many of the FPR 1991 also make reference to particular rules of the RSC or CCR 1981 for specific purposes.[34]

The originating process for a decree of divorce is called the petition. For the purpose of family proceedings, a petition is 'served personally or by post on every respondent or co-respondent'.[35] This provision appears to apply to service out of the jurisdiction as to service within it. The original parties to the petition are of course the spouses in the marriage, and the co-respondent (in rare cases where the co-respondent is named), ie a person with whom the respondent spouse is alleged to have committed adultery or had an improper association.[36] However, there is no provision

---

28 *Altertext Inc v Advanced Data Communications Ltd* [1985] 1 WLR 457.
29 See *Tallack v Tallack and Broekema* [1927] P 211; *Goff v Goff* [1934] P 107; *Wyler v Lyons* [1963] P 274.
30 See Chapter 7.
31 See FPR 1991, r.1(2)(1), defining 'family proceedings' by reference to s 32 of the Matrimonial and Family Proceedings Act 1984.
32 FPR 1991, r 1.3.
33 FPR 1991, r 1.3.
34 Eg discovery (disclosure), service out of England and Wales.
35 FPR 1991, r 2.9(1).
36 FPR 1991, r 2.7.

for other third parties, such as trustees, to be made original parties to the petition, and this is never done, though as we shall see they can be joined to the proceedings later.

In consequence, it seems that any ancillary relief application and any order for joinder in family proceedings fall within the category of documents which under the rules may be served on the respondent to the application and the trustees:

(a)   within the jurisdiction, by sending it (by post, DX or fax) to their solicitors,[37] by posting it to their address for service, or their last known address, or by serving personally upon them or leaving it at such address;[38] the court has power in limited cases to dispense with service,[39] but care must be taken to exercise that power compatibly with (inter alia) Art 6 of the European Convention on Human Rights;[40]

(b)   outside the jurisdiction, by serving it on them in accordance with the law of the country in which service is effected, either by the applicant or his agent (if this is allowed under the local law)[41] or through the relevant foreign government or judicial authority;[42] it should be noted that no leave of the court is required to do this: it is a strong form of 'long-arm' jurisdiction. However, where service is to be effected on a person resident in another Member State of the European Union, these provisions are subject to the Service Regulation.[43]

The original petition should include any claim for ancillary relief that the petitioner intends to make.[44] However, it does so only in the most general terms, not identifying any trusts or trustees who may be involved. If the *respondent* is not so well off, he or she may make such an application. In the latter case the application should be made in the answer (the rarely used formal defence to the petition).[45] But the court may give leave later on for the application to be made if not in the petition, or the parties may agree.[46] In any event, whether the application was included in the petition or not, notice of intention to proceed with the ancillary relief application

---

[37]   FPR 1991, r 10.2.
[38]   FPR 1991, r 10.3.
[39]   FPR 1991, r 10.3(3).
[40]   Human Rights Act 1998, s 6(1). For the position before the HRA 1998, see *Purse v Purse* [1981] Fam 143, CA.
[41]   In some it is a criminal offence, so great care must be taken.
[42]   FPR 1991, r 10.6, referring to RSC Ord 11, rr 5 and 6 in the High Court, and CCR Ord 8, rr 8–10 in the county court.
[43]   Council Regulation (EC) No 1342 of 2000.
[44]   FPR 1991, r 2.53(1).
[45]   FPR 1991, r 2.53(1).
[46]   FPR 1991, r 2.53(2).

must first be given (the so-called 'Form A').[47] Where the application is for a variation of a nuptial settlement, a copy of the notice must also be served on the trustees (and on the settlor, if living).[48] The fact that a copy Form A has been served on the trustees in accordance with the rules does not make them parties already.[49]

But trustees and others may then be *joined* to the proceedings where this is appropriate. The joinder provisions of the old RSC, ie Ord 15, r 6(2), probably still apply to family proceedings, and hence the trustees of a trust may be added as parties subsequently, even before the hearing of the application for ancillary relief.[50] If the trustees have been joined to the proceedings by an order made without notice to them (formerly called 'ex parte'), the trustees may of course apply to the judge to set it aside.[51] Joinder as a party to proceedings has the effect in English law that the party so joined is bound by the result.[52]

In ordinary civil proceedings there are additional, discretionary bases on which the court will accept jurisdiction over a defendant outside the jurisdiction. They were formerly in RSC Ord 11 and CCR Ord 8, and have been taken over – with amendments – into CPR 1998, Pt 6. So far as trustees are concerned, they include the cases where the trust property is in England and Wales,[53] and where the trust is in writing and governed by English law.[54] It is to be noted that the FPR 1991 do not *specifically* incorporate into family proceedings any such methods of conferring jurisdiction over foreign trustees on the English court. However, they may nonetheless be applicable to family proceedings by virtue of the general provision that the RSC and CCR 1981 'should continue to apply' to family proceedings, even after their replacement by the CPR 1998.[55] The argument against this result is that FPR 1991, r 10.6(1) expressly refers to RSC Ord 11, but only applies rr 5 and 6 in terms, thereby excluding the operation of the other rules in Ord 11 ('expressio unius, exclusio alterius'); otherwise, it can be said, the reference to rr 5 and 6 would be otiose. Such arguments have found favour with divorce judges in the past.[56] But it is conceived that a Family Division judge today would find this argument excessively technical, and possibly leading to injustice, and would wish to reject it.

---

[47] FPR 1991, r 2.61A.
[48] FPR 1991, r 2.59(3)(a).
[49] *T v T (Joinder of Third Parties)* [1996] 2 FLR 357, 363–364.
[50] *T v T (Joinder of Third Parties)* [1996] 2 FLR 357, relying on FPR 1991, r 1.3. The word 'probably' is used because this case was decided before the replacement of the RSC by the CPR. See also *Re Representation Lincoln Trust Company (Jersey) Ltd* [2007] JRC 138.
[51] *T v T (Joinder of Third Parties)* [1996] 2 FLR 357.
[52] *Vandervell Trustees Ltd v White* [1971] AC 912, HL.
[53] Cf RSC Ord 11, r 1(1)(g),(i), CPR, r 6.20(10).
[54] Cf RSC Ord 11, r 1(1)(j), CPR, r 6.20(11).
[55] FPR 1991, r 1.3.
[56] *Goff v Goff* [1934] P 107, 112-113; *Wyler v Lyons* [1963] P 274, 281.

It is accordingly desirable to say something about these two other heads of jurisdiction. But it must be noted that they are in terms *discretionary* (ie the court's leave is needed) rather than as of right.

To understand them, two concepts need to be explored further:

(1)   when is trust property located in England; and

(2)   what is meant by the proper law of a trust (and how it is to be ascertained).

8.2.2   Location of property

Here we are concerned with the concept of situs, ie the place where a thing is or an action takes place. For tangible things, whether land or chattels, the question of situs is unlikely to give rise to difficulty. Land is where it is.[57] Tangible movables are where they are,[58] though ships and aircraft, as 'flag carriers', are sometimes subject to special rules.[59] But intangible property – movable and immovable – is more problematic. Choses in action are normally situated where they are recoverable or can be enforced.[60] Registered company shares are situated where they can be dealt with, ie where the register is.[61] But bearer securities[62] and deeds[63] are situated where they actually are from time-to-time. A mortgage of or other security interest in land is presumably situated where the land is.[64] And intellectual property rights are situated in the territory whose legal system has created them.[65] The situation of a beneficiary's interest under a trust depends on the proper law of the trust, and in particular whether it regards the beneficiary as having a proprietary interest in the trust assets or merely a personal right against the trustee to compel due administration of the trust. In the former case (true for most trust law systems), it is situated where the trust assets are, but in the latter case (as in Scotland, India, and some of the USA, for example) it is situated where the trustee is.[66]

An example of the problem is the decision in *N v N and F Trust*,[67] where the main question was whether the former matrimonial home was held

---

[57]   *Dicey, Morris and Collins*, op cit, r 120(2).

[58]   *Dicey, Morris and Collins*, op cit, r 120(3).

[59]   See *Dicey, Morris and Collins*, op cit, paras 22E-057, 22E-060.

[60]   *Alloway v Phillips (Inspector of Taxes)* [1980] 1 WLR 888, 893–894, CA; *Kwok Chi Leung Karl v Comr of Estate Duty* [1988] 1 WLR 1035, 1040, PC; *Dicey, Morris and Collins*, op cit, paras 22-025–22-051.

[61]   *Erie Beach Co Ltd v AG for Ontario* [1930] AC 161, PC.

[62]   *Winans v A-G* [1910] AC 27, HL.

[63]   *Comr of Stamps v Hope* [1891] AC 476, PC; *Royal Trust Co v A-G for Alberta* [1930] AC 144, PC.

[64]   Cf *Re Hoyles* [1911] 1 Ch 179, CA.

[65]   See *Dicey, Morris & Collins*, op cit, para 22-051 and cases there cited.

[66]   See *Dicey, Morris & Collins*, op cit, para 22-048 and cases there cited.

[67]   [2006] 1 FLR 856, FD. See text at **5.2.3.1** above.

under a trust which was capable of variation or whether the husband who was a beneficiary of that trust was merely a tenant of the trustees pursuant to a tenancy agreement. It was held that the purchase of property in England as a matrimonial home, which was owned by a Bahamian company all the shares of which were owned by a trust of which the husband was a beneficiary, was in fact a nuptial settlement capable of variation pursuant to s 24 of the MCA 1973. Thus (although this was not the main finding in that case), even though onshore property is held by an offshore company whose shares are owned by an offshore trust, ultimately that property was situated in England. Similarly, in *C v C (variation of post-nuptial settlement: company shares)*,[68] a Cayman trust was varied to enable the wife to receive shares owned by the trust in a UK registered company in specie. Coleridge J found no 'impediment to the court dealing with this trust, either because it is foreign or discretionary' and presumably would have had no problem in dealing with the shares regardless of where they were situated.

8.3   THE PROPER LAW OF A TRUST

The proper law of a trust is that system of law by reference to which the trust in question is to be governed. 'Proper law' for this purpose usually means *municipal* law, ie not including the conflict of laws rules and therefore relates to wholly domestic cases. The proper law will have an impact on many different aspects of the trust, including its form, essential validity, interpretation and the substantive rights and obligations of the parties to it.

How is the proper law of a trust chosen? At common law, this was not at all clear. One English case held that the proper law was 'the law by reference to which the settlement was made and which was intended by the parties to govern their rights and liabilities'.[69] This was interpreted in an earlier edition of *Dicey and Morris on the Conflict of Laws* as meaning 'in the absence of any express or implied selection of the proper law by the settlor, the system of law with which the trust has its closest and most real connection'.[70] Offshore authority was even more meagre than English. In one Jersey case,[71] there was a suggestion, but no more, that the proper law of the settlement might even be the law of the *domicile* of the settlor at the time of creating it.

Subsequently, the Hague Convention on the Law Applicable to Trusts and on their Recognition put forward appropriate rules as a kind of international model. The UK incorporated the Hague Convention into

---

[68]   [2003] 2 FLR 493, FD.
[69]   *Marlborough (Duke) v A-G* [1945] Ch 78, 83, CA.
[70]   (11th edn, 1987), 1072, cf (13th edn, 2000), (14th edn, 2006), para 29R-001: 'in the absence of any such choice, by the law with which the trust is most closely connected'.
[71]   *Rahman v Chase Bank (CI) Trust Company Ltd* (1983) JJ 1.

UK law in the Recognition of Trusts Act 1987[72] (extended by Order in Council to a number of British territories,[73] though not all of them). It is important to note that editions of *Dicey and Morris*[74] after the 11th (1987) concentrate on the rules to be found in the 1987 Act, rather than the common law position (which is dealt with in outline only).

Some British offshore jurisdictions were not content with the Hague Convention to introduce conflicts rules for them, but enacted their own rules on the subject. Jersey and Guernsey, for example, acquired comprehensive rules on choice of law in trusts on the enactment of the Trusts (Jersey) Law 1984 and the Trusts (Guernsey) Law 1989 respectively. They therefore had no need to incorporate the rules of the Convention into their law, although as a matter of international law it was extended to those jurisdictions – and others[75] – by subsequent UK declarations under Art 29, lodged with the Hague Secretariat.[76] Thus, in Jersey, Art 4(1) of the 1984 Law (as amended in 1991) provides that, subject to changes in the proper law pursuant to the terms of the settlement,[77] the proper law is in substance the law of the jurisdiction:

(a)   *expressed* by the trust as the proper law; or, failing that;

(b)   to be *implied* from the terms of the trust; or, failing either;

(c)   with which the trust had the *closest connection* on creation [emphasis supplied].

A problem arises where a particular law is expressed or implied, but either it does not provide for trusts at all, or it does not provide for the category of trust concerned. In such a case the proper law so expressed or implied is simply ignored.[78] Another problem arises where the law chosen does not provide for trusts, in which case it is simply ignored. A further difficulty is if the trust provides that the proper law is to be 'that selected by the trustees' and the trustees have as yet made no selection. It cannot be said that a proper law has been *expressed* or *implied*. In such cases it would be necessary to resort to the third limb of Art 4(1), in para (c).

---

[72]   Section 1 and Schedule; however, some provisions of the Convention (in particular, Art 13) were not incorporated into English law by this means.

[73]   By the Recognition of Trusts Act 1987 (Overseas Territories) Order 1989, SI 1989/673, applying to Bermuda, British Antarctic Territory, Falkland Islands, St Helena and Dependencies, South Georgia and the South Sandwich Islands, the Sovereign Base Areas of Cyprus and the British Virgin Islands.

[74]   Now Dicey, Morris & Collins.

[75]   Hong Kong, Montserrat and the Turks and Caicos Islands. The extension to Hong Kong was officially confirmed by the Chinese Government after the cession of that territory in 1997. The Convention has never applied to the Cayman Islands.

[76]   *Cf Charalambous v Charalambous* [2005] Fam 250, para 54, per Arden LJ, and see Matthews (2005) 9 JL Rev 1, para 3.

[77]   See Art 37.

[78]   Art 4(2)(b).

Paragraph (c) is similar to the test in the 11th edition of *Dicey and Morris* quoted above, with the omission of the words 'and most real' before 'connection'.[79] Article 4(3) sets out four facts to which reference should *in particular* be made in ascertaining the law with which a trust is most closely connected. These are: the place of administration, the place where the trust property is, the residence of the trustees and the objects and place of performance of the trust. But it is clear that these are not the only factors involved. Suppose a settlor domiciled in jurisdiction A settles property situate in jurisdiction B on trustees in jurisdiction C for the benefit of beneficiaries in jurisdiction D. Once the trust is 'up and running', the factor of the settlor's domicile at the time of the creation is of little importance: what matters then is the administration of the trust and (perhaps) the flowing of benefits to the beneficiaries. But *at the time of creation* there is no administration going on, and no benefits are likely to be flowing to the beneficiaries. The domicile of the settlor is clearly a factor at that stage.[80]

The relative weight given to the place of residence of the trustees and the place where property is situate is plainly dependent on whether one sees the trust as essentially constituting personal obligations of the trustees (which may be best enforceable in the place of the trustees' residence) or property rights of the beneficiaries (probably best enforceable where the property is). The traditional common law view is that trusts cannot be regarded as purely *personal* obligations of the trustees, and that they are better regarded as sounding *in property*. It is true that in one English case[81] the High Court took the view (on the *Dicey, Morris & Collins* test) that the most important factor was the place where *administration* of the trust was to take place (ie normally the trustee's place of residence). But that was a case where it was not necessary to come to any decision as to the proper law, and the court expressly refrained from doing so. It was also a case where the question, if it arose at all, arose after the trust had been in existence for some years.

8.3.1   Impact of proper law

In English matrimonial courts, the lex causae is almost always the lex fori, ie English. It is as true for applications for ancillary relief[82] as it is for a decree of divorce. This chauvinistic approach is not followed in other English courts, in relation to, say, ordinary trust disputes. Nor indeed is it followed in family disputes in other countries.

In trust disputes the lex causae is usually the proper law of the trust. This is because, broadly speaking, at common law the proper law of a trust governs its essential validity, its interpretation and its effect, including

---

[79]   See the 12th edn (1993) at 1090-1, and now the 14th edn (2006) at para 29R-001.
[80]   Cf *Iveagh v IRC* [1954] Ch 364.
[81]   *Chellaram v Chellaram* [1985] Ch 409.
[82]   *Sealey v Callan* [1953] P 135; *Cammell v Cammell* [1965] P 467.

ascertainment of the rights of the beneficiaries and the duties of the trustees,[83] though *not* the capacity of the settlor to dispose of the property needed to create it.[84] Thus, if a trust (or a part of a trust) is by its proper law invalid (eg by infringing the rules against perpetuities existing under that law) it will not matter that by another law which *might* have been the proper law it would have been valid.

If the proper law of a trust is a foreign law, then, depending on the terms of the local statute law, the foreign court may have jurisdiction in relation to it. But foreign trust statutes typically do not form a complete code, and sometimes important matters (eg the question of capacity) are not dealt with by them.

Where the proper law of the trust is the law of a foreign jurisdiction then an important question arises as to how far the English courts otherwise having jurisdiction may vary the trust under *English*, as opposed to the *proper*, law. As already mentioned, the Recognition of Trusts Act 1987 gives legislative force in English law to Art 8(2)(h) of the Hague Trusts Convention, which provides that, if a foreign law governs the trust, then it is that foreign law's substantive provisions on variation of trusts which should be applied, and not those of English law. However, it has been held by the Court of Appeal that the power of a divorce court to vary a settlement should be exercised in accordance with the English lex fori as part of the whole range of powers exercisable in those contexts and that 'the Recognition of Trusts Act 1987 does not affect that position'.[85] This is 'on the basis that although Art 8(2)(h) of the Convention subjects the question of variation to the law applicable to the trust, this is subject to the mandatory rules identified in Art 15,' and s 24 of the MCA 1973 is one of those rules. This view has been criticised by Harris.[86] He argues that before the Recognition of Trusts Act the English courts simply applied English law as the lex fori. But Art 8(2)(h) now makes it clear, subject to (inter alia) Art 15, that the law applicable to variation is to be the law governing the trust rather than the lex fori. He also argues that there is no reason to treat s 24 of the MCA 1973 as containing mandatory rules within Art 15 and that the rules on the law applicable to the variation of the trust should be disapplied if and only if they are incompatible with English public policy. It has also been said that the 'mandatory rules' within Art 15 are those *other* than for trusts.[87] These arguments may be thought to have much force, at any rate outside the cocoon of the Family Division. But the Court of Appeal's view must prevail unless and until the House of Lords says that it is wrong.

---

[83]   See *Dicey and Morris* (12th edn, 1993) at 1092; cf 13th edn (2000), para 29-011 (dealing with position under Recognition of Trusts Act 1987). See also *Augustus v Permanent Trustee Co (Canberra) Ltd* (1971) 124 CLR 245, HCtAus.

[84]   As to which see Matthews (2002) 6 Edin LR 176.

[85]   *Charalambous v Charalambous* [2005] Fam 250. The Royal Court of Jersey, perhaps surprisingly, appears to have taken the same view: *Re B Trust* 2006 JLR 562, para 15.

[86]   (2005) 120 LQR 16.

[87]   *Re Barton* (2002) 4 ITELR 715, para 42, per Lawrence Collins J.

If the trustees are in another jurisdiction, then there is an additional aspect to the matter, and that is whether the trustees having been joined to the litigation should actually take any part in it. This has been discussed at length in Chapter 7 at **7.5**. Suffice to say here that in general terms, if the trustees having been joined by order of the English court decide to take part in the proceedings then they will not normally thereafter be able to argue that the English court did not have jurisdiction over them.[88] This may mean that an important ground of defence against the enforcement in their own jurisdiction of the order made by the court is no longer available to them.

Clearly, if the trustees are joined to the proceedings by the English court, but they take no part in those proceedings, and remain outside the jurisdiction,[89] then it will be much more difficult to enforce that order against the trustee in the offshore jurisdiction. The whole question may therefore turn on whether or not the trustees are either present or have assets within the jurisdiction of the English court or the forum. If they do then, having been joined as parties to the proceedings it may not matter to the non beneficiary spouse whether the trustee takes part or not. The order can be enforced against the assets within the jurisdiction.[90] Alternatively, as provided for in the s 4(3) of the Debtors Act 1869, the person of a trustee who is present in the jurisdiction can be attached and committed to prison. But if there are no trust assets and no trustee presence within the jurisdiction (or trustee intention to travel there), then the trustee may consider it more appropriate not to take part in the proceedings, on the basis that the order will have to be enforced if at all outside the jurisdiction of the English court, in particular, in the jurisdiction where the trustees are. But without their active participation, they have not submitted to the jurisdiction of the English court, and consequently the order cannot be enforced against them in that jurisdiction without at least some difficulty.

8.4   ENFORCEMENT ABROAD

It needs to be borne in mind that there are effectively two totally separate (and different) ways that one spouse can get at assets held in a genuine trust created by the other or by a third party:

(1)   First, the settlement can be varied by the order of a court of competent jurisdiction possessing the appropriate power to make such a variation. Not all courts have jurisdiction. Not all courts with jurisdiction possess power to vary. But the order if made has – or at

---

[88]   *Cf T v T (Joinder of Third Parties)* [1996] 2 FLR 357.

[89]   As in *Re L & M Trusts* 2003 JLR N-6; see also *Re H Trust* 2006 JLR 280, paras 11–17 and *FM v ASL Trust Company Ltd* [2006] JRC 020A, para 10

[90]   A consideration which may have influenced the Jersey trustees in *T v T (Joinder of Third Parties)* [1996] 2 FLR 357.

least purports to have – direct effect on the trust assets and hence (in theory at least) the trustees are bound to give effect to it.

(2)   Alternatively, the order can be that one spouse pays or transfers to the other a sum of money or certain assets. The size of this obligation may be such that in practice it can only be performed if the trustee will advance sufficient funds. Thus, the latter is enforceable against the other spouse and therefore only indirectly involves the trustee.

The enforceability of the court order in another jurisdiction may well depend upon which one of these options the attacking spouse chooses.

According to English notions of private international law, there are two kinds of recognition and enforcement. The first is at common law. The second is pursuant to an international agreement (whether bilateral or multilateral). Although historically the former preceded the latter, in practice today the common law approach is resorted to only when there is no appropriate international agreement. It is therefore sensible to begin with the latter.

Systems of mutual recognition and enforcement of judgments between various states or groups of states come about typically as a result of either (a) bilateral agreements between individual pairs of states,[91] negotiated one by one, or (b) multilateral agreements between groups of states,[92] to which further states may in time accede if they (and the original members) wish.[93] Moreover, multinational systems usually supersede the bilateral agreements to the extent of overlap (but leave them in force to the extent of any gaps left).[94] However, agreements in category (a) may be facilitated by the fact that the states concerned have the same sovereign (eg within the then British Empire), and indeed may be implemented by imperial legislation.[95] And agreements in category (b) can be implemented by supra-national legislation (eg by means of an EU Regulation).[96]

---

[91]   In England and Wales these are implemented by means of orders under the Foreign Judgments (Enforcement) Act 1933 (covering Australia, Austria, Belgium, Canada, France, Germany, Guernsey, India, Israel, Italy, Jersey, Isle of Man, Netherlands, Norway, Pakistan, Suriname, Tonga); in the other contracting states there will be parallel implementing legislation.

[92]   Eg the Brussels Convention 1968, now Council Regulation (EC) No 44 of 2001 (EU States); the Lugano Convention 1988 (EU and EFTA States, including Switzerland, Iceland, Norway).

[93]   As happened to the United Kingdom in acceding to the Brussels Convention in 1986 (under the Civil Jurisdiction and Judgments Act 1982) and the Lugano Convention in 1992 (under the Civil Jurisdiction and Judgments Act 1991).

[94]   See the Brussels and Lugano Conventions, Titles VII.

[95]   Eg the Administration of Justice Act 1920, Pt II; see SI 1984/129, as amended by SI 1985/1994 and SI 1997/2602 for the complete list of Commonwealth states and territories concerned under that Act (but Hong Kong is no longer included).

[96]   Eg the EU Council Regulation No 44 of 2001, replacing the Brussels Convention as between EU States (except Denmark, until 2007).

These systems are not all the same. Some (especially the earlier, bilateral ones) provide only for the enforcement of simple money judgments. Others extend more widely, and may cover trust matters, but still exclude matrimonial property, wills and succession, and insolvency.[97] So the text of the particular system must be carefully considered to be sure that the judgment sought to be enforced falls within it. Usually they only apply to judgments of the High Court (and above), and not those of the county court. Although it is possible to transfer judgments of the county court to the High Court for the purposes of execution, it should be noted that the local law may[98] or may not[99] treat a judgment of the county court transferred to the High Court as a judgment of the High Court for enforcement purposes.

Normally these systems operate by way of registration of the English judgment in the foreign court. There is usually only limited opportunity to challenge the registration on (eg) public policy grounds,[100] but no opportunity to review the judgment either to see whether the originating court actually had jurisdiction, or to consider the soundness of the substantive judgment. Once registered, the judgment is enforced in the same way as any local judgment.

A similar system operates as between the constituent legal systems of the United Kingdom, ie England and Wales, Scotland, and Northern Ireland.[101] Once the proceedings are over and any appeal has been finally disposed of, or the time for appealing has expired without any appeal having been launched, the successful party can obtain a certificate which may be registered in the superior court of the jurisdiction where enforcement is to take place, and thereafter the original judgment may be enforced as if it were a judgment of the registration jurisdiction. It is moreover no objection to enforcement that the originating legal system lacked jurisdiction by the rules of the enforcing system.[102] The rules are slightly different, depending on whether the original judgment is a money[103] or a non-money[104] judgment but there are no special rules for trusts.

Within the European Union there is now an additional Regulation, due to come into force on 12 December 2008, providing for the *direct*

---

[97] See eg the Brussels and Lugano Conventions, Art 1.
[98] As in the Isle of Man: *Video Vision Broadcast v Stapleford Flying Club* [1990-93] MLR 236; see (2000) 4 JL Rev 2.
[99] As in Jersey: *Re Hardwick* 1995 JLR 245; see Matthews (1996) 112 LQR 221.
[100] See eg *Cass 1er Civ. 16 mars 1999, No 92, Pordéa c/ Société Times Newspapers* (English costs order consequent on judgment obtained in default of security being provided by French plaintiff held unenforceable in France under the public policy exception in Art 27(1) of the Brussels Convention, on the basis that the order infringed Art 6(1) of the European Convention on Human Rights).
[101] Civil Jurisdiction and Judgments Act 1982, s 18.
[102] Civil Jurisdiction and Judgments Act 1982, s 19.
[103] Civil Jurisdiction and Judgments Act 1982, Sch 6.
[104] Civil Jurisdiction and Judgments Act 1982, Sch 7.

enforcement in all other Member States of a judgment obtained in one of them in respect of an unopposed claim.[105] So in this limited class of case there is no need for registration before enforcement can take place. However, as long as the provisions in the Regulation intended to safeguard the rights of defendants who have not been given due notice of the proceedings are complied with, it is unlikely that this Regulation will have much effect on cases where trusts are affected by matrimonial proceedings.

Of course, even if there is a reciprocal enforcement arrangement (and supporting legislation) it may not assist the applicant for a variation of a trust. For example, although both Jersey and Guernsey have laws allowing for the registration and enforcement of foreign judgments of reciprocating countries in certain circumstances, and the UK is a reciprocating country, the laws generally require that the judgment to be enforced must be of a Superior Court, must be final and conclusive, and must be for *payment of a sum of money*. Therefore, if an order for the variation of a trust were not made in terms of a specified amount of money, this route to enforcement would not be available to the applicant for variation.

It is true that some reciprocal enforcement legislation contains wording extending *recognition* to at least some foreign judgments not for a sum of money.[106] But the meaning and effect of this obscure wording has never been properly tested,[107] and it is in any event limited by express provision in the case of actions in rem[108] to cases where the property is within the country of the foreign court.[109]

8.4.1 Recognition and enforcement of any court order in a common law system

Recognition does not necessarily imply enforcement. The judgment of a court in one state may be *recognised* by the court of another state as having effect, without necessarily *enforcing* it. For example, the judgment may give rise to an issue estoppel,[110] or it may alter a person's status. But other judgments need both recognition and enforcement, for instance a judgment for a money sum in one state against a defendant who has assets only in another state. Typically, in the majority of modern legal systems, there are two kinds of rules for the recognition and enforcement of foreign trust judgments: the local rules of a particular jurisdiction, and

---

[105] Regulation (EC) No 1896/2006.
[106] Eg Foreign Judgments (Reciprocal Enforcement) Act 1933, s 8(1), and Commonwealth legislation based on it.
[107] See *Black-Clawson International Ltd v Papierwerke AG* [1975] AC 591, 617; *Verwaerke v Smith* [1981] Fam 77; *Maples (formerly Melamud) v Maples* [1988] Fam 14.
[108] See below for discussion of this concept.
[109] 1933 Act, s 8(2)(b), referring to s 4(2)(b).
[110] See e g *Showlag v Mansour* 1994 JLR 113, PC.

the international rules agreed to by two or more states in a treaty or convention. The former will obviously vary from place to place. The latter have already been discussed.

In common law jurisdictions a foreign judgment will normally be recognised, subject to public policy constraints,[111] where the recognising court accepts that the foreign court possessed jurisdiction by common law notions.[112] This may be a judgment affecting legal status (eg adoption[113]), or power over assets of a person subject to the court's jurisdiction. Or a judgment giving rise to an issue estoppel may be recognised as a defence to a claim in the local court.[114] More importantly for our purposes, a foreign judgment *for a money sum* will be recognised as giving rise to a debt under the same conditions. This can be enforced by bringing a fresh action on the foreign judgment in the local court,[115] which action can usually be short-circuited by applying for summary judgment under the relevant procedural rules.[116]

There are cases in Jersey however which go further, where the court has enforced a foreign judgment for *the transfer of particular property*. In one case[117] the Jersey court ordered the transfer by the husband's representative to the wife following a divorce and ancillary relief order of the English court to that effect. In another case the same court ordered the Jersey trustee of a discretionary trust to make a distribution of assets to the plaintiff (who had obtained an order of a foreign court that the assets in question should belong to him).[118] These are plainly not cases of a court of competent jurisdiction imposing a money obligation on the defendant, which is then enforced by action elsewhere. If the assets concerned were in Jersey (and in at least one of them this was so), then these judgments could be justified as judgments in rem.[119] But the courts did not say that. Instead these cases have been put on the rather vague basis of 'comity', and the mechanism of 'enforcement' of the foreign judgment is *to give directions* to the trustees of the trust which, if followed, remove the risk of being sued for failing to follow the terms of the trust.[120] The doctrine of comity is discussed further below. In

---

[111] Eg fraud, denial of natural justice, foreign revenue or penal liability.
[112] *Poingdestre v Stephen* (1825) 6 CR 47; *Re Dagless* (1972) 260 Ex 401.
[113] *Lee v Lee* (1965) JJ 505; *Re Gutwirth* 1985-86 JLR 233.
[114] *Lane v Lane* 1985-86 JLR 48.
[115] *Dodds v Westle* (1968) 257 Ex 60; *Showlag v Mansour* 1994 JLR 113, 118.
[116] Eg CPR 1998, Pt 24; (Jersey) Royal Court Rules 1992, Pt VII.
[117] Eg *Lane v Lane* 1985-86 JLR 48.
[118] *Cadwell v Cadwell* (1989) 1 / TLI 132, RCt.
[119] See below for discussion of this concept.
[120] See eg *Re B Trust* 2006 JLR 562, para 15.

insolvency cases, the courts usually have power to act in aid of certain foreign courts, including making orders which enforce the foreign court's order.[121]

8.4.2   Recognition requirements: common law

8.4.2.1   *The jurisdiction of the English court from the point of view of the foreign court*

It is necessary to distinguish two quite different cases:

(a)   First, a foreign judgment in personam may be enforced in a common law jurisdiction by a claim made in a fresh action there, if the judgment is for a debt or definite sum of money, is final and conclusive, *and the foreign court had jurisdiction according to the common law conflicts rules.*[122]

(b)   The second situation is that the court in a common law jurisdiction will recognise (or, in some cases, enforce) the effect of a judgment in rem if the subject matter of the proceedings in relation to which the foreign judgment was given was property (moveable or immoveable) which at the time of the proceedings was in that foreign country. In this second case, common law does not require the foreign court to pass any jurisdiction test according to *common law* conflicts rules.[123]

Thus the key distinction is between judgments in personam and in rem. Dicey, Morris & Collins state that:

'A claim in personam may be defined positively as a claim brought against a person to compel him to do a particular thing, eg the payment of a debt or of damages for a breach of contract or for tort, or the specific performance of a contract, or to compel him not to do something, *eg* when an injunction is sought.'[124]

They also say:

'A judgment in rem is a judgment whereunder either (1) possession or property in a thing is adjudged to a person, or (2) the sale of a thing is decreed in satisfaction of a claim against the thing itself. The term is used also to describe (3) an adjudication as to status such as a decree of nullity or dissolution of marriage, and (4) a judgment ordering property to be sold by way of administration in bankruptcy or on death ... The question whether a foreign judgment is in personam or in rem is sometimes a difficult one on

---

[121]   Eg UK: Cross-Border Insolvency Rules 2006; Jersey: Bankruptcy (Désastre) (Jersey) Law 1990, Art 48; see Dessain & Wilkins *Jersey Insolvency Law in Practice* (3rd edn, 2006).

[122]   *Dicey, Morris & Collins*, r 35.

[123]   *Dicey, Morris & Collins*, r 40.

[124]   In para 11-002 in the text to r 22.

which English judges have been divided in opinion. But unless the foreign judgment claims to operate in rem, it cannot be recognised in England as a judgment in rem.'[125]

A recent decision of the Privy Council[126] has clarified the position. In it, Lord Mance laid down that:

'Although its application in the light of evidence of foreign law may sometimes be difficult, the relevant principle distinguishing between judgments in personam and in rem in the sense of rule 40 appears clearly enough, particularly in the House of Lords in [*Castrique v Imrie* (1870) L.R. 7 H.L. 414]. The joint opinion of five of the six judges advising the House was given by Blackburn J [...] [He] described a decision in rem as one by a tribunal with "jurisdiction to determine not merely on the rights of the parties, but also on the disposition of the thing".'

And later:

'a judgment in rem in the sense of rule 40 is thus a judgment by a court where the relevant property is situate adjudicating on its title or disposition as against the whole world (and not merely as between parties or their privies in the litigation before it)'.

Lord Mance cited the definition in *Stroud's Judicial Dictionary*:[127]

'A judgment in personam binds only the parties to the proceedings as distinguished from one in rem which fixes the status of the matter in litigation once for all, and concludes all persons'.

However, there is some doubt as to whether judgments in personam that are ancillary to divorce decrees, such as lump sum orders or variations of settlements, are treated as in personam judgments for the purposes of determining whether the foreign court had jurisdiction. In the English case of *Phillips v Batho*[128] the plaintiff was the petitioner in Indian divorce proceedings and the defendant was the co-respondent. The defendant was not resident in India at the time of the suit and did not submit to the jurisdiction. The Indian court awarded damages against the defendant for adultery. The plaintiff sought to enforce the damages award in England. Scrutton J recognised that if the Indian judgment were treated as a judgment in personam against the defendant, it would not be actionable in England because the Indian court had no jurisdiction in personam over the defendant. Scrutton J, however, allowed the Indian judgment to be enforced against the defendant in England on the grounds that it was ancillary to the judgment in rem dissolving the marriage. But

---

[125] *Dicey, Morris & Collins*, para 14-100; they include as examples of cases which divided English judges *Cammell v Sewell* (1860) 5 H & N 728 and *Castrique v Imrie* (1870) LR 7 HL 414.

[126] *Ali v Pattni* [2007] 2 AC 85.

[127] 7th edn (2006) at p 2029.

[128] [1913] 3 KB 25.

he confined the extension to the case where both the court pronouncing the judgment and the court enforcing it were courts of the same Sovereign, and where the court enforcing it could not itself grant the relief because it had no jurisdiction over the marriage to whose dissolution the proceedings were ancillary.

The *Phillips* judgment has been heavily criticised,[129] and not followed in New Zealand[130] or Canada.[131] Moreover, its reasoning was undermined in *Jacobs v Jacobs*[132] where it was held that damages for adultery were not necessarily ancillary to a decree of divorce. But it has apparently been applied in Bermuda in relation to a lump sum matrimonial award from New Hampshire.[133]

Notwithstanding the doubt about *Phillips v Batho*, there can be little doubt that in most trust jurisdictions[134] an English order varying a trust whose assets were in the jurisdiction at the time would be regarded as an order in rem, capable of being recognised elsewhere at common law. But to the extent that the assets are already offshore (as is commonly the case) this rule will be of no assistance.

In relation to the first situation (the in personam judgment) the court in common law jurisdictions will recognise the court of the foreign country concerned as having jurisdiction to give that judgment in the following four cases:[135]

(a) if the judgment debtor was, at the time the proceedings were instituted, present in the foreign country;[136]

(b) if the judgment debtor was claimant (or counterclaimant) in the foreign proceedings;[137]

(c) if the judgment debtor (being defendant) voluntarily appeared in the proceedings;[138]

---

[129] *Cheshire and North's Private International Law* (12th edn), p 363; *Dicey, Morris & Collins* (14th edn), para 14-085.

[130] *Redhead v Redhead* [1926] NZLR 131.

[131] *Patterson v D'Agostino* (1975) 58 DLR (3d) 63.

[132] [1950] P 146

[133] *Ellefsen v Ellefsen*, Sup Ct Civil 1993: 202. However it seems that the husband participated in the New Hampshire proceedings.

[134] It may well be different in jurisdictions where the beneficiary is regarded as only enjoying a personal right against the trustee, as is the case in Scotland, India, and elsewhere.

[135] *Dicey, Morris & Collins*, r 36.

[136] *Carrick v Hancock* (1895) 12 TLR 59; *Littauer Glove Corporation v FW Millington (1920) Ltd* (1928) 44 TLR 746; *Vogel v RA Kohnstamm Ltd* [1973] QB 133; *Adams v Cape Industries plc* [1990] Ch 433, CA; *cf Sfeir & Co v National Insurance Co of New Zealand* [1964] 1 Lloyd's Rep 330 (a case on the 1920 Act); Read, pp 148–151.

[137] *Burpee v Burpee* [1929] 3 D.L.R. 18 (BC); Read, p.160.

[138] *De Cosse Brissac v Rothbone* (1861) 6 H & N 301, as explained in *Schibsby v Westenholz*

(d) if the judgment debtor (being defendant) had before the commencement of the proceedings agreed in respect of the subject matter of the proceedings to submit to the jurisdiction of that court (or the courts of that country).[139]

In substance, they come down to two propositions: either the defendant in the foreign court was present there when the proceedings were brought (and thus was within the 'territorial' jurisdiction of the court) or the defendant submitted in some way to the jurisdiction of the foreign court. As stated above, in England and Wales there are no 'domestic rules of jurisdiction' which can be applied at international level, and (for the avoidance of doubt) we add that the US notion of 'sufficient minimum contacts' between the subject matter of the action and the foreign court is not part of English common law.

There is, however, one rule of exclusive jurisdiction which is relevant. The English court holds that the courts of a particular country have no jurisdiction to adjudicate on the title to, or right to possession of, any immoveable property situated outside that country. This is a rule which applies (with limited exceptions)[140] to the English court as it applies to foreign courts.[141]

It should also be made clear that the court in common law jurisdictions will not regard a foreign court as having had jurisdiction over the defendant if the bringing of proceedings was contrary to an agreement under which the dispute in question was to be settled otherwise than by proceedings in the court of that country, and the defendant did nothing to submit to the jurisdiction of that court.[142] Nor will the foreign court be regarded as having jurisdiction against a person who under the rules of public international law was entitled to immunity from the jurisdiction of the court of that country and that immunity was not waived.[143]

(1870) LR 6 QB 155, 162; *Voinet v Barrett* (1885) 55 LJQB 39, CA; *Guiard v de Clermont* [1914] 3 KB 145; *SA Consortium General Textiles v Sun & Sand Agencies Ltd* [1978] QB 279, CA); *Jet Holdings Inc v Patel* [1990] 1 QB 335, 341, CA; and cf *Rich (Marc) & Co AG v Società Italiana Impianti PA, The Atlantic Emperor (No 2): C-190/89* [1992] 1 Lloyd's Rep. 624, 633, CA.

[139] *Bank of Vallée v Dumergue* (1849) 4 Exch 290; *Australasia v Harding* (1850) 9 CB 661; *Bank of Australasia v Nias* (1851) 16 Q.B. 717; *Kelsall v Marshall* (1856) 1 CBNS 241; *Copin v Adamson* (1875) 1 ExD 17, CA; *Feyerick v Hubbard* (1902) 71 LJKB 509; *Jeannot v Fuerst* (1909) 25 TLR 424; *Blohn v Desser* [1962] 2 QB 116; *Vogel v RA Kohnstamm Ltd* [1973] QB 133; *SA Consortium General Textiles v Sun & Sand Agencies Ltd* [1978] QB 279, CA.

[140] Eg the Civil Jurisdiction and Judgments Act 1982, s 30.
[141] *Dicey, Morris & Collins*, r 40.
[142] *Dicey, Morris & Collins*, r 37.
[143] *Dicey, Morris & Collins*, r 38.

8.4.2.2 The law applied by the foreign court

In considering the recognition or enforcement of the foreign judgment in a common law system, the court in common law systems will not be concerned with how the foreign court dealt with the matter, or which law it applied,[144] in the absence of fraud (either on the part of one of the parties, or on the part of the court,[145] or breach of natural justice.[146] In particular, a foreign judgment cannot be impeached in the court in common law systems on the grounds that the court which gave it was not competent to do so according to the law of that foreign country.[147]

8.4.2.3 Public policy

Of course public policy has an important role to play here.[148] Some of the main heads which are applicable have already been set out. They are reflected in the rules requiring that a foreign court should have jurisdiction according to the rules set out above, that the foreign court has no jurisdiction in certain cases (notably land outside the jurisdiction, diplomatic or other immunity, non-jurisdiction agreements) and also where the judgment has been obtained by fraud, in breach of natural justice, or its enforcement would be contrary to public policy. An example of the last of these is the rule that the courts in common law systems will not enforce foreign tax or criminal liabilities.[149]

8.4.3 The enforcement of ancillary relief orders in relation to foreign trustees

In examining this question, a number of discrete situations must be considered. But it is worth making the general point that the question for the trust court is whether to enforce or recognise the judgment of the divorce court; it is not to ask whether the latter judgment was right.[150] In ordinary circumstances the trust court will not retry the case. Thus, for example, if a trust (document) is held to be a sham by the divorce court, the trust court will not hear argument on whether it was right to do so.[151]

8.4.3.1 Where the divorce court ordering ancillary relief orders a lump sum payment

The court may not need to go so far as to conclude that a trust is a sham and that in reality the assets all belong beneficially to one spouse alone.

---

[144] *Dicey, Morris & Collins*, r 41; see *Re B Trust* 2006 JLR 562, para 15.

[145] *Dicey, Morris & Collins*, r 43.

[146] *Dicey, Morris & Collins*, r 45.

[147] *Dicey, Morris & Collins*, r 42(2).

[148] *Dicey, Morris & Collins*, r 44.

[149] *Dicey, Morris & Collins*, r 3.

[150] See *Re B Trust* 2006 JLR 562, para 15.

[151] *CI Law Trustees Ltd v Minwalla*, sub nom *Re Fountain Trust* [2005] JRC 099, para 25.

Nor need the trustees be a party to the ancillary relief application. Even in the case of a genuine trust, properly administered, the court may yet conclude that the circumstances are such that the trust assets should be regarded as *resources* which may be available to a spouse in appropriate circumstances, whether the trust is a fixed trust[152] or a discretionary one.[153] In particular, if a spouse is a beneficiary of a discretionary trust in an offshore jurisdiction, and the trustees have hitherto looked with favour upon any requests made from time to time by the spouse by income or capital, then the court is very likely on a divorce to treat the assets of that trust as assets 'available to' the spouse and so take them into account in deciding what orders should be made for the distribution of assets on divorce.[154]

This may go to the extent of making an order for payment of a sum by one spouse to another, which the spouse ordered to pay cannot in fact pay out of his or her own resources, but can only pay with the assistance of the trustees. This may in turn mean that spouses are actually committed to prison because of a failure to pay sums they had been ordered to pay, which could have been obtained from the trustees, but which the spouse in question refused to do.[155] On the other hand, the trustees of a discretionary trust, faced with the order against one of their beneficiaries to pay a sum beyond his or her means, may very well properly form the view that it is in the best interests of the beneficiary to make the payment on his behalf, and the offshore trust court asked for its approval may well give it.[156] For example, where the spouse beneficiary is a professional person, the spectre of bankruptcy may act as a powerful incentive. The trustees may well consider that it is in the interests of the spouse beneficiary not to be made bankrupt, and provide the funds needed to avoid this.

A question arises as to how far a foreign court order against one spouse to pay the other a sum of money calculated by reference to (inter alia) trust assets in the enforcing jurisdiction should be treated, for enforcement purposes, as if it were an order purporting to vary or have other direct effect on those trust assets. This is discussed further below.

---

[152] *Calder v Calder* [1975] 6 Fam Law 242, CA (husband had expectations on death of life tenant).
[153] *Browne v Browne* [1989] 1 FLR 291, CA.
[154] *Thomas v Thomas* [1995] 2 FLR 668, CA; *J v M* 2002 JLR 330, RCt; *Charman v Charman (No 4)* [2007] EWCA Civ 503. See further Appendix 2 below.
[155] See eg *Browne v Browne* [1989] 1 FLR 291, CA (but the order was suspended on terms, and by the time of the appeal the funds had arrived from Jersey).
[156] See eg *Re X Trust* 2002 JLR 377.

8.4.3.2   *Where the divorce court ordering ancillary relief holds that the foreign trust is a sham*

This is not the place for discussion about the doctrine of sham in relation to trusts.[157] But it is necessary to say something about the effects of such a sham. English divorce judges persist in saying that a trust which is held to be a 'sham' is void,[158] or at any rate liable to be set aside.[159] This betrays at best linguistic confusion,[160] at worst a serious misunderstanding of trust law.[161] Where S transfers legal ownership of assets to T apparently on the terms of a trust document or other assertion (e g orally or by gesture), but the reality is that it is a bare trust for S, then, subject to the effect of any relevant formalities rules, the *trust document or other assertion* is a sham (because it does not tell the truth), and the *true transaction* is a bare trust for S. The true transaction is not void, or liable to be set aside: it is what it is, in this case a resulting trust. The false *trust document or other assertion* is, to the extent of the falsity, nothing at all, a thing written in water that has no effect. If, on the other hand, S purports to transfer legal ownership of assets to T, apparently on the terms of a trust document or other assertion, but the reality is that S remains legal owner, T is at best the agent of an undisclosed principal and (in that case) there is no trust at all. Then, and only then, does it make sense to talk of a sham trust being 'void' (but not voidable: that makes no sense at all). But this latter case is extremely rare, if only because of property registration statutes which give translocative effect to the registration of the 'trustee' as new owner, whatever the parties' true intentions.[162] The usual sham trust case in ancillary relief applications is the former, ie a bare trust for the settlor, made out to appear to be a more complex trust for the family.[163]

In *Minwalla v Minwalla*,[164] the wife sought ancillary relief against the husband, who had at an earlier stage created a Jersey trust. The Jersey trustees did not take part in the substantive English proceedings, but had submitted to the jurisdiction in assuring the (English) court that they would abide by any order made. The court having heard argument on behalf of the wife concluded that the Jersey trust was a sham, and treated

---

[157] See Chapter 6 at **6.2.3.1.5** above, and also e g Mowbray [2000] PCB 28, 105; Hayton (2004) 8 JL Rev 6; Russell (2007) 5 TQR 5.

[158] *A v A* [2007] EWHC 99 (Fam), para 55.

[159] *Minwalla v Minwalla* [2005] 1 FLR 771, FD.

[160] See the seven different meanings of sham discussed in *A v A* [2007] EWHC 99 (Fam), para 15.

[161] The problem stems from the fact that the main authorities on the doctrine of sham are not about trusts at all, but instead about commercial transactions which were alleged to be pretences: *Snook v London and West Riding Investments Ltd* [1967] 2 QB 786 at 802; *Hitch v Stone (Inspector of Taxes)* [2001] EWCA Civ 63, [2001] STC 214.

[162] See e g Land Registration Act 2002, s 58(1).

[163] There is a third case, where S transfers assets to T ostensibly on trust for A but in reality on trust for B. Here again, subject to formalities rules, the true transaction is a trust for B; the trust document or other source of the ostensible trust for A is the sham. But this third case is also rare in ancillary relief litigation, and is not considered further here.

[164] [2005] 1 FLR 771, FD.

its assets as belonging beneficially to the husband. It therefore ordered the husband to transfer significant trust assets to the wife, and the trustees to facilitate such transfer by treating the wife as beneficial owner of certain assets. The trustees thereupon applied to the Jersey Royal Court for directions as to how they should respond to the English judgment.[165]

Counsel for the wife in *Minwalla* urged upon the Royal Court that the English judgment ought to be recognised and enforced on two alternative bases:

(i)   pursuant to the provisions of the Judgments (Reciprocal Enforcement) Jersey Law 1960; or

(ii)   as a matter of comity.

The reciprocal enforcement provisions in Jersey apply only to money judgments, whereas the English court order in *Minwalla* was an order addressed to the trustee requiring it in effect to transfer assets to the wife. The Jersey court therefore held that the English judgment was not enforceable in Jersey under the first of the above two alternatives.

With regard to the second possible basis of enforcement, the Royal Court laid particular emphasis on the fact that the trustee had submitted to the jurisdiction of the English court.[166] They had asserted in the English proceedings through their counsel that they would abide by any order or declaration made by the English court. They had also taken part in the final English ancillary relief hearing limited so as to make representations regarding costs. The court therefore held that there could be no unfairness as a matter of comity if the English judgment were enforced against the trustee in Jersey. The Jersey court was also clearly influenced by the extraordinary lengths that Mr Minwalla had gone to in order to conceal his assets from both his wife and the English divorce court.

8.4.3.3   *Where the divorce court ordering ancillary relief purports to vary the foreign trust directly*

Strictly speaking, variation of a foreign trust is not of itself *enforcement* of an ancillary relief order: it is only *the order itself*. But the divorce court in the common law world typically has statutory power to vary a marital settlement.[167] For English law the critical provision is s 24(1)(c) of the MCA 1973, which refers to 'any ante-nuptial or post-nuptial settlement ... made on the parties to the marriage'. The English courts have taken an

---

[165]   See *CI Law Trustees Ltd v Minwalla*, sub nom *Re Fountain Trust* 2005 JLR 359.

[166]   Cf *FM v ASL Trustee Company Ltd* [2006] JRC 020A, another divorce case, where the trustee (following directions from the court) did not submit to the English jurisdiction, but the Jersey court still gave effect to the English judgment varying the trust.

[167]   For more detail, see Chapter 5.

expansive view of what is such a settlement.[168] It includes a trust governed by foreign law,[169] one conferring discretion on the trustees,[170] the acquisition by the parties of a matrimonial home in joint names,[171] and even (until the law was subsequently amended[172]) some pension arrangements.[173] Moreover the settlement does not have to have been made by the parties, only on them[174] (even by will[175]) or even on only one of them.[176] A settlement which once fell within the scope of the provision may still be varied even if the spouses have been removed as beneficiaries by the date of the hearing.[177]

But the equivalent law in offshore jurisdictions, even if based on English law, may not be so expansive. For example, in Jersey, the phrase 'post-nuptial settlement'[178] has been construed more narrowly than in England, and must be referable to the marriage in question, conferring benefits on the parties qua husband and wife.[179] This may lead to arguments based on lack of symmetry between the law of the divorce jurisdiction and that of the trust jurisdiction.[180]

Moreover, courts in offshore jurisdictions are nowadays keen to defend their trust industries against what they may see as undue interference by other states. Thus, for example, in one Jersey case[181] the judge stated:

> 'The court regards it as unlikely that an English court would so exceed the normal bounds of comity as to purport to vary a settlement governed by Jersey law, administered in Jersey by Jersey trustees and which had no connection with England save that some of the beneficiaries resided there'.

And in another:[182]

---

[168] See *Prinsep v Prinsep* [1929] P 225; *Brooks v Brooks* [1996] AC 375, HL.

[169] *Nunneley v Nunneley and Marrian* (1890) 15 PD 186; *Forsyth v Forsyth* [1891] P 363; *Goff v Goff* [1934] P.107, 111.

[170] *Marsh v Marsh* (1877) 47 LJP 34; *Vallance v Vallance* (1907) 77 LJP 33.

[171] *Brown v Brown* [1959] P 86, [1959] 2 All ER 266, CA; *Dinch v Dinch* [1987] 1 All ER 818, [1987] 1 WLR 252, HL.

[172] By the Welfare Reform and Pensions Act 1999, with effect from 1 December 2000. But there is now provision for so called 'pension-attaching' orders under ss 25B–25D, and for 'pension-sharing' orders under ss 21A, 24B, 24C and 24D.

[173] *Brooks v Brooks* [1996] AC 375, [1995] 3 All ER 257, HL.

[174] *Paul v Paul and Farquhar, sub nom St Paul v St Paul and Farquhar* (1870) LR 2 P &D 93; *E v E (Financial Provision)* [1990] 2 FLR 233.

[175] S 24(1)(c).

[176] *Melvill v Melvill and Woodward* [1930] P 99.

[177] *Compton (Marquis of Northampton) v Compton (Marchioness of Northampton) and Hussey* [1960] P 201, [1960] 2 All ER 70; *Charalambous v Charalambous* [2004] 2 FLR 1093, CA.

[178] Under the Matrimonial Causes (Jersey) Law 1949, Art 27.

[179] *J v M* 2002 JLR 330, paras 13–14; see also *Re the B Trust* 2006 JLR 562, paras 9–11; Harris (2007) 11 JGLR 184, para 24–25.

[180] See e g *Re the B Trust* 2006 JLR 562, paras 12–13.

[181] *Re Rabaiotti 1989 Settlement* 2000 JLR 173.

[182] *CI Law Trustees Ltd v Minwalla, sub nom Re Fountain Trust* 2005 JLR 359, para 27.

'[A]s a general rule ... it would be an exorbitant exercise of jurisdiction for a foreign court to purport [...] to vary the terms of a Jersey settlement ...'

On the other hand, the offshore court will not simply ignore the decision of the divorce court, as 'that court will have investigated the matter fully and will have made a decision intended to achieve a fair allocation as between the spouses'.[183]

Caution must be exercised here. What the Jersey court regarded as exorbitant jurisdiction was that claimed by an English court purporting to vary a *Jersey* law trust of which both the trustees and the trust administration *were based in Jersey*. Although the power contained in offshore jurisdictions' matrimonial laws to vary marriage and post-nuptial settlements is sometimes expressed to extend to trusts governed by foreign law,[184] this does not necessarily mean asserting jurisdiction over trustees and administration, or for that matter assets, *situated in a foreign country*. Trustees in offshore jurisdictions such as Jersey frequently hold assets on trusts governed by another law. Yet the English Court of Appeal has held that in the case of a marital settlement the court enjoys just such a power to vary the foreign law trust with foreign trustees and administration where by its own rules it has jurisdiction over the *parties to the marriage*, even though it has none over the *foreign trustees*.[185]

Thus in one recent English ancillary relief case,[186] the husband had for over seven years failed to pay any part of the £5m ordered to be paid to the wife, but accepted that his Jersey trust (with Jersey trustees), though in form a proper discretionary trust, was to be treated as his alter ego. Despite the warnings from the Jersey courts, the judge held that this was an appropriate case for the English court to order a variation of the trust in favour of the wife, so as to secure to her the payments which had not been made by the husband.[187]

But what happens in England is of course only half the equation. The next question is, what happens thereafter in the offshore jurisdiction? The problem is that there is no satisfactory authority on the question of recognition at common law.[188] In another recent Jersey case[189] the Royal Court had to consider the effect of a variation by the English divorce court under s 24(1)(c) of the MCA 1973. The application was heard just

---

[183] *Re H Trust* 2006 JLR 280, para 16; cf *Compass Trustees Ltd v McBarnett* 2002 JLR 321, para 8.

[184] Matrimonial Causes (Jersey) Law 1949, art 27; Matrimonial Causes (Guernsey) Law 1939, s 45; see *J v M* 2002 JLR 330; *Re the X Trust* 2002 JLR 377; Hanson [2005] Fam Law 36.

[185] *C v C (variation of post-nuptial settlement: company shares)* [2003] 2 FLR 493, criticised by Harris (2005) 120 LQR 16.

[186] *Mubarak v Mubarik* [2007] EWHC 220 (Fam).

[187] The question whether this is a proper way of enforcing payment of a lump sum order is discussed briefly later.

[188] *Cf Colliss v Hector* (1875) LR 19 Eq 334 (a rather special case, however).

[189] *Re B Trust* 2006 JLR 562.

after the coming into force of amendments to the Jersey trusts law which for the first time[190] provided a bar to enforcement in Jersey of foreign orders affecting Jersey law trusts. The court was critical of the drafting of the new provisions (which are discussed in more detail later), calling them 'obscure' and 'circular'. But, ultimately, the court was prepared to direct that the variation should (mostly) be given effect to by the Jersey trustees, albeit on the basis of 'comity', the effect of which it held was not excluded by the new provisions. It should be noted that the Jersey court in such cases does not purport to vary the trust itself.[191] No reference was made to the common law rule recognising in rem judgments where the assets concerned were within the jurisdiction of the court making the order at the time it was made.[192]

8.4.4   The impact of 'comity'

In the past the Royal Court of Jersey has frequently[193] relied on 'comity' as the basis of the enforcement of foreign judgments otherwise than pursuant to the statutory procedure.[194] Given the restricted nature of the statutory jurisdiction,[195] the desire to find another way to do justice in those cases where it does not apply is understandable. But the enforcement of foreign judgments is based on rules – even discretionary ones – whereas 'comity' is simply a policy underlying relevant rules. The English common law in the nineteenth century adopted the theory of obligation to explain enforcement of foreign judgments, that is, 'the judgment of a court of competent jurisdiction over the defendant imposes a duty or obligation on him to pay the sum for which the judgment is given, which the courts in this country are bound to enforce'.[196] This has also been stated by the Privy Council to be the basis of common law enforcement of foreign judgments in Jersey,[197] but so far it has not been followed by the local courts.[198]

---

[190] Except for legislation dealing with the enforcement of forced heirship claims, which had been introduced as early as 1989.

[191] *Re B Trust* 2006 JLR 562, para 16. Cf *FM v ASL Trustee Company Ltd* [2006] JRC 020A, para 12.

[192] The trust assets were shares in a Jersey company which in turn held English real property.

[193] See eg *Re Dagless* (1973) 260 Ex 401; *Lane v Lane* 1985-86 JLR 48; *Cadwell v Cadwell* (1989) 17 TLI 152; *Solvalub Ltd v Match Investments Ltd* 1996 JLR 361; *Compass Trustees Ltd v McBarnett* 2002 JLR 321; *Re First National Bank of Granada Ltd* 2002 JLR N[7]; *SP v AJP* 2002 JLR N[15]; *Re Bald Eagle Trust* 2003 JLR N[16]; *CI Law Trustees Ltd v Minwalla*, sub nom *Re Fountain Trust* 2005 JLR 359; *FM v ASL Trustee Company Ltd* [2006] JRC 020A; *Re H Trust* 2006 JLR 280; *Re B Trust* 2006 JLR 562.

[194] That is, the Judgments (Reciprocal Enforcement) (Jersey) Law 1960, in ordinary cases: there is a special regime for cross-border assistance in insolvency cases.

[195] The 1960 Law applies only to 'final and conclusive' judgments and orders *for a sum of money*, and only to judgments and orders of courts from the UK and from Guernsey and the Isle of Man.

[196] *Schibsby v Westenholz* (1870) LR 6 QB 155, 159.

[197] *Showlag v Mansour* [1995] 1 AC 431, 440.

[198] It is right to say there is some common law support for a comity-like approach (but stricter, depending on substantial reciprocity) in the recognition of foreign matrimonial

The point appears most recently in *Re B Trust*,[199] a case which came before the Royal Court in Jersey on 27 October 2006 (the day after the coming into force of the amended Jersey trusts law).[200] Inter alia, the court commented that certain paragraphs of new Art 9[201] were 'rather obscure'.[202] Importantly, in understanding the extent to which the new Jersey law will protect trusts from a variation order under the MCA 1973, s 24, the court said the following:

> 'If the purpose of the amended article 9 really is to protect trust assets to the extent that a manipulative spouse can evade the enforcement of a carefully considered judgment designed to do justice between husband and wife on divorce, that would seem to us to be a very unhappy state of affairs. But fortunately we do not consider it to be the effect of these statutory provisions nor, we trust, do we believe it to be the intention of the legislature.'[203]

They also said of Art 9 that they were 'quite clear what they do not mean and that they do not exclude the application of the doctrine of comity'.[204] The court was of the opinion that it would:

> 'take very clear and express words to persuade us that the legislature intended to deprive this court of the flexibility to do justice in a wide range of cases on the basis of a principle of almost universal applicability'.[205]

Despite these comments, the Bailiff expressed 'the hope however that English courts might in future exercise judicial restraint before asserting a jurisdiction pursuant to s 24 of the Matrimonial Causes Act 1973 to vary a Jersey trust'.[206] He continued:

> 'This court has shown itself sensitive (long before the enactment of the Trusts Law Amendment) to perceived interference with its jurisdiction to supervise Jersey trusts. Such sensitivities were expressed in *Lane v Lane* 1985-86 JLR 48, *Re Rabaiotti 1989 Settlement* 2000 JLR 173, and in *Re The Fountain Trust* 2005 JLR 359, to name but a few cases in which these considerations have arisen.'[207]

However:

---

orders *affecting status: Travers v Holley* [1953] P 246, 257; *Indyka v Indyka* [1969] 1 AC 33. But it has been rejected by English courts outside that field: *Re Trepca Mines Ltd* [1960] 1 WLR 1273.
[199] 2006 JLR 562.
[200] *Re B Trust* 2006 JLR 562.
[201] Set out and considered below.
[202] 2006 JLR 562, para 14.
[203] 2006 JLR 562, para 13.
[204] 2006 JLR 562, para 18.
[205] 2006 JLR 562, para 18.
[206] 2006 JLR 562, para 30.
[207] 2006 JLR 562, para 30.

'The jealousy with which the court guards its supervisory jurisdiction over Jersey trusts does not mean that it is insouciant of the reasoned decisions of other courts exercising a matrimonial jurisdiction.'[208]

Hence it seems clear that, although the Jersey courts will be willing to give directions to trustees so as to give effect to a foreign variation of a trust in the interests of fairness, justice and comity, they are extremely keen to assert their own independence. In fact it has been persuasively argued that comity is not a firm rule forming part of Jersey law at all.[209] It may not mean any more than respect. The Jersey court will direct trustees to implement a s 24 order but only when they decide that it is what they think should be done – not when the English court tells them to do so. Thus, in *Re B* for example, the Jersey court declined to give effect to a part of the English order.[210] The Royal Court concluded its decision in *Re B Trust* by calling upon the English courts (having calculated their award on the basis of the totality of the assets available to the parties) 'to exercise judicial restraint[211] and to refrain from invoking their jurisdiction under the Matrimonial Causes Act to vary the trust' and instead to 'request this court to be auxiliary to them',[212] as had happened in at least one earlier case.[213] Only time will tell if the English court pays heed to this request, and how Jersey and other jurisdictions will react if the English court does not.

But the portents are not at present very promising. An issue raised earlier (but not then resolved) was how far we can properly distinguish the case of variation from that where the English court merely identifies the assets of a foreign trust as resources available to one of the divorcing spouses, so that the order made is one (at this stage, at least) against that spouse alone, to pay or transfer a sum of money. In such a case, there is no order made against the foreign trustees or biting or purporting to bite on the trust assets. Thus, as the Court of Appeal put it recently in *Charman v Charman (No 4)*:[214]

'[Counsel for the husband] submits that, if this court were to dismiss the part of the appeal referable to Dragon, it would send a message to the off-shore world that, in family cases, trusts do not matter. It will by now be clear that we send no such message.[215] He draws our attention to the

---

[208] 2006 JLR 562, para 31.
[209] Harris (2007) 11 JGLR 184.
[210] 2006 JLR 562, paras 25–29.
[211] The second mention of this phrase in the judgment.
[212] 2006 JLR 562, para 32. The Jersey courts have often taken this position in the past in civil litigation: see *eg Johnson Matthey Bankers Ltd v Arya Holdings Ltd* 1985-86 JLR 208, RCt; *Solvalub Ltd v Match Investments Ltd* 1996 JLR 361, Jersey CA.
[213] *Compass Trustees Ltd v McBarnett* 2002 JLR 321, paras 8, 11, 20 (though there the Jersey court did not vary under the Jersey equivalent of MCA 1973, s 24, but instead gave directions under s 47 of the 1984 Law).
[214] [2007] EWCA Civ 503, para 58. See further Appendix 2.
[215] Though this is the same court that airbrushed the trust out of the history of marital property in England and Wales: see the quotation at the beginning of this chapter.

decision of the Royal Court of Jersey in *In re Fountain Trust* 2005 JLR 359, in which it observed, at [18], that an assumption of jurisdiction by a judge of the Family Division in England to declare a Jersey trust to be a "sham", such as had there occurred, would generally be exorbitant. We agree with the Royal Court's observation. Mr Boyle also draws our attention to the decision of the same court in *In the matter of the B Trust*, as yet unreported, [2006] JRC 185.[216] There, at [32], an important suggestion was made, namely that, when a party applied to it for variation of an off-shore settlement, the English court should give serious consideration to declining to exercise its jurisdiction on the basis that, after conducting the substantive enquiry, it should instead invite the off-shore court, provided of course that the latter is invested with the appropriate jurisdiction, to act as an auxiliary to it in regard to any proposed variation. But the wife in the present case has been, relatively speaking, in a fortunate position. She cannot and does not allege that Dragon is a sham. She does not, and does not need to, apply for variation of Dragon. For she has the evidence with which to identify the assets of Dragon as part of the husband's resources.'

It will be noted that, in this passage, the Court of Appeal expressly agreed with the comment of the Jersey court that the English court finding the Jersey trust to be a 'sham' could be described as an 'exorbitant' exercise of jurisdiction. But, on the other hand, it expressed no such sentiment in discussing what it described as the Jersey court's 'important suggestion' of leaving any variation of the foreign trust to the foreign court. The opposition is striking, and the inference may be that the English courts consider themselves under no limits in this respect.

It was also rather disingenuous of the Court of Appeal to dismiss so lightly the point made by counsel, on the basis that the wife did not need to apply for a variation of the trust in question. The true position was that she did not need to apply for such a variation *at that stage*. However, if the judgment against the husband were to remain unsatisfied, then, like the wife in *Mubarak*[217] she might well consider applying to the court for a variation under s 24(1)(c) of the MCA 1973, as a roundabout means of achieving recovery of the judgment debt.[218]

Here the court orders the husband to pay to the wife a sum of money calculated, not on the basis of the husband's own assets, but expressly on the basis of assets which legally and beneficially do *not* belong to the husband (for – as the court says – no 'sham' is found). Instead, the assets

---

[216] Now reported at 2006 JLR 562.

[217] [2007] EWHC 220 (Fam).

[218] The two stages are of course technically different, and a litigant who has obtained a lump sum order with an application for variation having been dismissed is not supposed to be able to come back for a second bite at the cherry. But the English divorce court has long been in the vanguard in cutting through technical distinctions in order to attack the substance when it feels like doing so: see e g *Mubarak* itself, at paras 78–125. For the future, a practice might, for example, develop of the English court *staying* an application for variation until the lump sum order has been satisfied, rather than dismissing it outright. Then, if the order were not met the court could revive the variation application.

concerned belong (at law) to the trustees, on trust for many other persons, including children and unborn beneficiaries. At the very least, this order is calculated to put (and in practice will put) pressure on the trustees to decide to allocate these assets in a way which otherwise they would not have done. The unspoken threat from the Court of Appeal is that actually implemented in *Mubarak*, and – in deafening silence – not disclaimed here, that is, to vary the foreign trust in the wife's favour.

For the court then to assert that in making the original order it is not thereby interfering in any way with the foreign trustees (and hence need not consider the sensibilities of the foreign court concerned) is pure sophistry. In itself there is nothing inherently wrong with a political decision to enact a legal rule that says that assets not belonging to a spouse, but which are readily available to him, can be taken into account in deciding how much to order him or her to pay to the other. But it is necessary to be honest about the *effects* of so doing, and in particular whether the order in a particular case would have such extra-territorial effect that either it should be left to the foreign court to make, or should at least be made conditional on approval by that court (as is, for example, the case with freezing orders in civil litigation).[219] It is a pity that the English court did not at least acknowledge the substantive issue for what it was, and act accordingly.

8.5   OFFSHORE LEGISLATION – ASSET PROTECTION

Finally, there is the important question of legislation passed in the offshore jurisdictions which seeks to protect assets settled in those jurisdictions against orders made in home jurisdictions which in some way, shape or form attack those trusts.[220] In a sense such legislation could be described as generally anti-creditor legislation. For this purpose it does not much matter whether the creditor concerned is a commercial creditor of the settlor, a person entitled to inherit the property of the deceased settlor, or the disgruntled former spouse of the settlor. In each case there is a claim on the settlor, but the settlor has transferred assets away from himself or herself to trustees. Offshore jurisdictions have enacted anti-creditor legislation of different kinds. Some have restricted themselves to legislation which is intended to protect against claims arising from forced heirship.[221] Others have done so in relation to both forced heirship and matrimonial claims.[222] Still yet others have done it in relation to all including commercial claims.[223] Moreover, in more recent times the scope of some such legislation has expanded to cover cases where the 'creditor' has a claim, not against the *settlor* of the *trust*, but

---

[219] See *Civil Procedure 2007*, Pt 25 Practice Direction 'Draft freezing order', para 19.

[220] See eg the Trusts Law (Revised 1998), ss 90–93, of the Cayman Islands.

[221] Eg Guernsey (and, until 2006, Jersey).

[222] Eg the Cayman Islands.

[223] Eg the Cook Islands.

against one of its *beneficiaries*. The particular stance of an individual jurisdiction must depend on political choices to be made there as to what kind of business it wishes to attract.

Where legislation intended to protect trusts in that jurisdiction against claims arising from matrimonial proceedings is concerned, the question to be asked is, what exactly is the legislation aiming to protect against? What other things is the legislation *not* intending to protect against? For example, it would be rare to find a jurisdiction whose anti-creditor legislation sought to protect the settlor against the allegation that the trust was a sham.[224] If documents are created to dress up the situation and make it appear that there is a trust when there is not, or (more likely) that there is a complex trust when there is only a simple one, it would be a bold jurisdiction which said that the *appearance* of the trust was, in that jurisdiction at least, to be treated as the reality. (Plainly it would not be so treated elsewhere.)[225] On the other hand it may be that the legislation is intended to protect against a claim being made under the order of the foreign court to some assets which the settlor used to have but which have been transferred into trust and (let us say) a certain period of time has elapsed. This would be a kind of limitation provision.

Whether the particular legislation achieves its objective must depend again on a number of factors. First and foremost amongst these will be the wording actually used. It is not uncommon to find that the wording used does not cover all the possible ramifications, simply because nobody thought of them all at the time of the enactment of the legislation. That is the nature of lawmaking. It is a static process, compared to the dynamic process of case development. If the legislation indeed achieves its objective, it may mean that assets that are within the offshore jurisdiction are protected from the claims of the other spouse in the home jurisdiction. But that is not always the case. In some situations it may be that assets are not in the trust jurisdiction at all but in the home jurisdiction[226] or in some third jurisdiction and it may be possible for the order of the home court to be enforced directly there or in the third jurisdiction. That will depend on other features such as whether or not there are conventions or treaties which apply to the recognition and enforcement of judgments. The question is whether the home court – say, English – can effectively vary a trust governed by a foreign law with anti-matrimonial order legislation – say, Caymanian, when the trust assets are not within the home jurisdiction (whether in Cayman or otherwise). At least one English case has now gone this far, and it is now necessary to

---

[224] Cf the 'reserved powers' provisions found in many offshore jurisdictions nowadays, which do not, however, go quite so far.

[225] Cf Hanson and Renouf [2005] Fam Law 794, 795–797.

[226] Cf *C v C (variation of post-nuptial settlement: company shares)* [2003] 2 FLR 493.

wait for the foreign court's own view of this.[227] But in the interim we can examine the relevant statutory provisions for ourselves.

One legislative model has proved particularly influential. This is that of the Cayman Islands. A number of offshore jurisdictions line up behind the Cayman approach. They include the Bahamas,[228] the Isle of Man,[229] the Cook Islands,[230] the Turks and Caicos Islands,[231] Anguilla[232] and the Marshall Islands.[233] Jersey became the latest country to be added to the list having enacted the Trusts (Amendment No 4) (Jersey) Law 2006 which came into force on 26 October 2006.

8.5.1 Cayman

The wording of the relevant sections of the Cayman legislation is:

'90. All questions arising in regard to a trust which is for the time being governed by the laws of the Islands or in regard to any disposition of property upon the trusts thereof including questions as to—

(a) the capacity of any settlor;

(b) any aspect of the validity of the trust or disposition or the interpretation or effect thereof;

(c) the administration of the trust, whether the administration be conducted in the Islands or elsewhere, including questions as to the powers, obligations, liabilities and rights of trustees and their appointment and removal; or

(d) the existence and extent of powers, conferred or retained, including powers of variation or revocation of the trust and powers of appointment, and the validity of any exercise thereof,

are to be determined according to the laws of the Islands, without reference to the laws of any other jurisdictions with which the trust or disposition may be connected:

Provided that this section—

(i) does not validate any disposition of property which is neither owned by the settlor nor the subject of a power in that behalf vested in the settlor, nor does this section affect the recognition of foreign laws in determining whether the settlor is the owner of such property or the holder of such a power;

(ii) takes effect subject to any express contrary term of the trust or disposition;

(iii) does not, as regards the capacity of a corporation, affect the recognition of the laws of its place of incorporation;

---

[227] *Mubarak v Mubarik* [2007] EWHC 220 (Fam). *Charalambous* was actually about whether the Court *in principle* had the power to vary.

[228] Trusts (Choice of Governing Law) Act 1989, s 7(1)(a).

[229] Trusts Act 1995, s 5(b)(i).

[230] International Trusts Act 1984, s 13H(1)(a).

[231] Trusts Ordinance 1990, s 13(1)(a).

[232] Trusts Ordinance 1994, s 62(1)(a).

[233] Trust Act 1994, s 39(1)(a).

(iv)   does not affect the recognition of foreign laws prescribing generally (without reference to the existence or terms of the trust) the formalities for the disposition of property;

(v)   does not validate any trust or disposition of immovable property situate in a jurisdiction other than the Islands which is invalid according to the laws of such jurisdiction; and

(vi)   does not validate any testamentary trust or disposition which is invalid according to the laws of the testator's domicile.

91. Subject to the same provisos as are set out in paragraphs (i) to (vi) of section 90, it is expressly declared that no trust governed by the laws of the Islands and no disposition of property to be held upon the trusts thereof is void, voidable, liable to be set aside or defective in any fashion, nor is the capacity of any settlor to be questioned, nor is the trustee, any beneficiary or any other person to be subjected to any liability or deprived of any right, by reason that—

(a)   the laws of any foreign jurisdiction prohibit or do not recognise the concept of a trust; or

(b)   the trust or disposition avoids or defeats rights, claims or interests conferred by foreign law upon any person by reason of a personal relationship to the settlor or by way of heirship rights, or contravenes any rule of foreign law or any foreign judicial or administrative order or action intended to recognise, protect, enforce or give effect to any such rights, claims or interests.

92. An heirship right conferred by foreign law in relation to the property of a living person shall not be recognised as—

(a)   affecting the ownership of immovable property in the Islands or movable property wherever situate for the purposes of paragraph (i) of section 90 or for any other purpose; or

(b)   constituting an obligation or liability for the purposes of the Fraudulent Dispositions Law (1996 Revision) or for any other purpose.

93. A foreign judgment shall not be recognised, enforced or give rise to any estoppel insofar as it is inconsistent with section 91 or 92.'

Section 87 provides two important definitions, amongst others:

"'heirship right" means any right, claim or interest in, against or to property of a person arising, accruing or existing in consequence of, or in anticipation of, that person's death, other than any such right, claim or interest created by will or other voluntary disposition by such person or resulting from an express limitation in the disposition of the property to such person;

"personal relationship" includes every form of relationship by blood or marriage, including former marriage, and in particular a personal relationship between two persons exists if—

(a)   one is the child of the other, natural or adopted (whether or not the adoption is recognised by law), legitimate or illegitimate;

(b)   one is married to the other (whether or not the marriage is recognised by law);

(c)   one cohabits with the other or so conducts himself or herself in relation to the other as to give rise in any jurisdiction to any rights, obligations or responsibilities analogous to those of parent and child or husband and wife; or

personal relationships exist between each of them and a third person, but no change in circumstances causes a personal relationship, once established, to terminate ...'

This legislation thus does four things. First, s 90 provides for Cayman law to govern all relevant aspects of a Cayman law trust. This includes questions of validity, interpretation and so on. Secondly, s 91 makes plain that a Cayman law trust is not attackable because of foreign rules relating to inheritance or any personal relationship (including marriage), and nor is a trustee (or indeed anyone else) to be liable personally to anyone as a result. This second rule does not appear in all the camp followers' laws, but in fact it is crucial. It is not enough to pick a choice of law rule: it is necessary also to ensure that trustees and others involved in the transaction are free from all collateral attack. Otherwise the attacker, thwarted at the front door, simply runs round to the back of the house and breaks in there. Indeed, this further rule in Cayman law was only added in 1995,[234] after some particularly heavy international trust litigation. This was based in part on forced heirship rules in the settlor's jurisdiction, in the course of which the trustee was threatened with personal liability for conspiracy. Thirdly, s 92 prevents any argument that any rights to inherit from another can during the life of the de cujus have any personal or proprietary effects[235] (at least in relation to certain property). Lastly, s 93 makes clear that if the Cayman court cannot do something because of s 91 or s 92, then no other court elsewhere can do it and expect the Cayman court to give effect to that decision.

As elsewhere, however, the Cayman provisions do not protect the trustee where the settlor had no title or power to transfer the property in the first place. On the other hand, these rules extend the protection to forced heirship claims, and beyond, to protect the trustee in cases where the rights in question arise (and hence the problem arises) out of marriage, or indeed out of any other personal relationship.

8.5.2 Jersey

The new Jersey legislation, which came into effect on 26 October 2006, is worded slightly differently, but the overall effect is much the same:

---

[234] Trusts (Foreign Element) (Amendment) Law 1995, s 5, now consolidated as the Trusts Law (1998 Revision), s 91.

[235] In fact this provision is prophylactic, because such rights take effect only on death, and during the life of the de cujus do not have any such effect even according to their proper law: after all, the possible heirs of the de cujus may die in his lifetime, or he may die a national or a resident of a different state.

'9   Extent of application of law of Jersey to creation, etc of a trust

(1) Subject to paragraph (3), any question concerning—

(a)   the validity or interpretation of a trust;

(b)   the validity or effect of any transfer or other disposition of property to a trust;

(c)   the capacity of a settlor;

(d)   the administration of the trust, whether the administration be conducted in Jersey or elsewhere, including questions as to the powers, obligations, liabilities and rights of trustees and their appointment or removal; or

(e)   the existence and extent of powers, conferred or retained, including powers of variation or revocation of the trust and powers of appointment and the validity of any exercise of such powers,

shall be determined in accordance with the law of Jersey and no rule of foreign law shall affect such question.

(2) Without prejudice to the generality of paragraph (1), any question mentioned in that paragraph shall be determined without consideration of whether or not—

(a)   any foreign law prohibits or does not recognise the concept of a trust; or

(b)   the trust or disposition avoids or defeats rights, claims, or interests conferred by any foreign law upon any person by reason of a personal relationship to the settlor or by way of heirship rights, or contravenes any rule of foreign law or any foreign judicial or administrative order or action intended to recognize, protect, enforce or give effect to any such rights, claims or interests.

(3) The law of Jersey relating to–

(a)   *légitime*; and

(b)   conflicts of law,

shall not apply to the determination of any question mentioned in paragraph (1) unless the settlor is domiciled in Jersey.

(4) No foreign judgment with respect to a trust shall be enforceable to the extent that it is inconsistent with this Article irrespective of any applicable law relating to conflicts of law.

(5) The rule *donner et retenir ne vaut* shall not apply to any question concerning the validity, effect or administration of a trust, or a transfer or other disposition of property to a trust.

(6) In this Article—

"foreign" refers to any jurisdiction other than Jersey;

"heirship rights" means rights, claims or interests in, against or to property of a person arising or accruing in consequence of his or her death, other than rights, claims or interests created by will or other voluntary disposition by such person or resulting from an express limitation in the disposition of his or her property;

"*légitime*" and "*donner et retenir ne vaut*" have the meanings assigned
to them by Jersey customary law;
"personal relationship" includes the situation where there exists, or
has in the past existed, any of the following relationships between a
person and the settlor—

(a)   any relationship by blood, marriage or adoption (whether or not
        the marriage or adoption is recognised by law);
(b)   any arrangement between them such as to give rise in any
        jurisdiction to any rights, obligations or responsibilities analogous
        to those of parent and child or husband and wife; or
(c)   any personal relationship between the person or the settlor and a
        third person who in turn has a personal relationship with the
        settlor or the person as the case may be.

(7) Despite Article 59, this Article applies to trusts whenever constituted or
created.'

Thus, it will be seen that Art 9(1) corresponds to s 90 of the Cayman law,
Art 9(2) to s 91, and Art 9(4) to s 93. Article 9(3) is more problematic. It
has no equivalent in the Cayman law, but was no doubt intended to
ensure that foreign domiciliaries did not have the benefit of Jersey's
ordinary conflict of laws rules. Unfortunately, it was poorly drafted, a fact
brought out in the recent articles on the subject by Harris[236] and
Hochberg[237] respectively, and by the decision of the Royal Court of Jersey
in *Re B Trust*[238] (discussed below).

Despite this legislative activity, some of the key parts of the Caymanian
trust law (as mirrored in the new Jersey trust law and in the trust law of
other jurisdictions) remain unclear both in meaning and effect. One
important obscurity relates to variations imposed on foreign 'nuptial
settlements' by matrimonial legislation such as s 24 of the (UK) MCA
1973. In the Cayman law, as in the new Jersey law, there is provision for
the non-recognition or enforcement of a foreign court judgment to the
extent that it is inconsistent with s 91 or s 92 (in Cayman law) or with
Article 9 (in Jersey law). We may note here that the Jersey provision is
actually wider than the Cayman one, as it applies to *any* provision in
Art 9, thereby including the Jersey equivalent to s 90, whereas the s 93
applies in terms only to ss 91 and 92, and *not* s 90. This complicates
matters slightly.

Would an English judgment imposing such a variation be so inconsistent?
It appears not. There is nothing in Cayman's ss 91 and 92 with which the
English variation judgment would be inconsistent. So far as s 90 is
concerned, s 93 does not assist the trustees anyway. If enforcement of the
English judgment is to be refused, it will be on the basis that any
judgment applying, as the lex causae of this litigation, a law other than

---

[236]   (2007) 11 JGLR 9.
[237]   (2007 11 JGLR 20.
[238]   2006 JLR 562.

that of Cayman is inconsistent with s 90 and hence is against public policy. Given that s 93 could have included a reference to s 90, but did not, that argument is rather weaker than it might be.

But the Jersey equivalent (Art 9(4)) *does* help the trustees in relation to Art 9(1), and it is necessary to examine its provisions more closely. The English judgment would not touch on any 'aspect of the validity of the trust or disposition or the interpretation or effect thereof'; for the judgment does not purport to pronounce on any of these things. Nor would it touch on 'the administration of the trust', nor again would it involve 'questions as to the powers, obligations, liabilities and rights of trustees ...' All questions as to 'the functions, appointment and removal of trustees and enforcers' of the trust will probably remain unaffected by the variation. It cannot relate to the existence or exercise of 'powers of variation or revocation of the trust', because these are powers conferred or retained by the trust itself, ie *internal* to the trust, rather than imposed from outside by the general law (and a *foreign* law at that).

Of course, it will be said, it is not for an English trust lawyer to interpret these novel provisions. It is for the local judges. They will surely construe these words in the way that best protects their trust industry – here, perhaps, in a generous way. And thus these provisions will protect local trusts. But even if the local courts are tempted to give in to this special pleading (which is by no means certain),[239] the ultimate court of appeal for these offshore jurisdictions does not sit by the sleepy lagoon in the sunshine. Instead, it sits in the cold hard light (and probably rain) of Downing Street in London: the Judicial Committee of the Privy Council. These judges, mostly senior British judges of perhaps more conservative outlook than the legislators in offshore islands, and insulated from political pressure to a greater extent than their offshore colleagues, are not brought up to regard offshore trust jurisdictions as especially deserving of generous interpretative treatment, and they are unlikely to be so tender as the local judges in construing innovative trust legislation.[240] The consequence is that s 93 probably will not automatically render the English variation judgment ineffective in Cayman, nor Art 9(4) similarly in Jersey.

8.5.3　Guernsey

In July 2007 a new trusts law was approved by the Guernsey States to replace the Trusts (Guernsey) Law 1989. This contains provisions similar – but not identical – to those in the Cayman and Jersey laws that we have

---

[239] For an extreme example of the legislators forgetting to take the judges with them, and living to regret it, see the two *South Orange Grove* cases, *No 1* (1995) 15 TLI 41, and *No 2* (1996) 1 OFLR 3, Cook Islands CA.

[240] Compare eg *Douglas v Pindling* [1996] AC 890, 894, 901–902, PC (Bahamian banking secrecy legislation read down to anodyne level).

been considering. The differences are or may be crucial to the question of enforcement of a foreign variation order, and we must consider the text carefully:

'14(1) Subject to the terms of the trust, all questions arising in relation to a Guernsey trust or any disposition of property to or upon such a trust, including (without limitation) questions as to—

(a) the capacity of the settlor,

(b) the validity, interpretation or effect of the trust or disposition or any variation thereof,

(c) the administration of the trust, whether it is conducted in Guernsey or elsewhere, including questions as to the functions, appointment and removal of trustees and enforcers,

(d) the existence and extent of any functions in respect of the trust, including (without limitation) powers of variation, revocation and appointment, and the validity of the exercise of any such function,

are to be determined according to the law of Guernsey without reference to the law of any other jurisdiction.

In this subsection "the law of Guernsey" does not include the other Guernsey rules of private international law.

(2) Subsection (1) —

(a) does not validate any disposition of property which is neither owned by the settlor nor the subject of a power of disposition vested in the settlor,

(b) does not affect the recognition of the law of any other jurisdiction in determining whether the settlor is the owner of any property or the holder of any such power,

(c) is subject to any express provision to the contrary in the terms of the trust or disposition,

(d) does not, as regards the capacity of a corporation, affect the recognition of the law of its place of incorporation,

(e) does not affect the recognition of the law of any other jurisdiction prescribing (without reference to the existence or terms of the trust) the formalities for the disposition of property,

(f) does not validate any trust or disposition of real property situate in a jurisdiction other than Guernsey which is invalid under the law of that jurisdiction, and

(g) does not validate any testamentary disposition which is invalid under the law of the testator's last domicile.

(3) No Guernsey trust, and no disposition of property to or upon such a trust, is void, voidable, liable to be set aside, invalid or subject to any implied condition, nor is the capacity of any settlor, trustee, enforcer, trust official or beneficiary to be questioned, nor is any settlor, trustee, enforcer, trust official, beneficiary or third party to be subjected to any obligation or liability or deprived of any right, claim or interest, by reason that—

(a) the laws of any other jurisdiction prohibit or do not recognise the concept of a trust, or

(b) the trust or disposition—

(i)   avoids or defeats or potentially avoids or defeats rights, claims, interests, obligations or liabilities conferred or imposed by the law of any other jurisdiction on any person—

(A)   by reason of a personal relationship to a settlor or any beneficiary, or

(B)   by way of foreign heirship rights, or

(ii)   contravenes or potentially contravenes any rule of law or any judicial or administrative judgment, order or action of any other jurisdiction intended to recognise, protect, enforce or give effect to any such rights, claims, interests, obligations or liabilities, whether by seeking to invalidate the trust or disposition or by imposing on a settlor, trustee, enforcer, beneficiary or third party any obligation or liability or otherwise.

(4) Notwithstanding any legislation for the time being in force in relation to the recognition or enforcement of judgments, no judgment or order of a court of a jurisdiction outside Guernsey shall be recognised or enforced or give rise to any right, obligation or liability or raise any estoppel if and to the extent that—

(a)   it is inconsistent with this Law, or

(b)   the Royal Court, for the purposes of protecting the interests of the beneficiaries or in the interests of the proper administration of the trust, so orders.

(5) This section applies—

(a)   whenever the trust or disposition arose or was made,

(b)   notwithstanding any other provision of this Law.

(6) In relation to a Guernsey trust or any disposition of property to or upon such a trust, the law of Guernsey relating to légitime and the rights of a surviving spouse apply only where the settlor is domiciled there.'

It will be seen that clause 14(1)(b) clearly goes further than the Jersey or Cayman laws, and covers *any* variations of the trust (ie even those imposed by the court), requiring them to be determined according to Guernsey law. Then, clause 14(4) (going even further than Jersey's Art 9(4)) will prevent recognition or enforcement of the English judgment varying the trust under English law as inconsistent with 'this Law'. Assuming that the Privy Council sanctions this new law, and that the English courts continue their 'long-arm' approach to foreign trusts where ancillary relief applications are concerned, it can only be a matter of time before other jurisdictions consider making similar changes to their laws.

It was noted earlier that the attitude of the English divorce court in earlier times was not to make an ancillary relief order over foreign property, even where it technically had jurisdiction to do so, 'where any order that it might make would be wholly ineffective'.[241] Those cases tended to

---

[241] *Tallack v Tallack and Broekema* [1927] P 211; *Goff v Goff* [1934] P 107; *Wyler v Lyons* [1963] P 274.

concern property in civil law countries where trusts were in any event unknown. In more recent times the English court has found that its orders have usually been recognised or implemented in the offshore trust jurisdictions, at least partly because they are mostly former British colonies or dependencies with similar matrimonial laws, and with judges educated in the common law tradition. But the growth in offshore and other foreign legislation forbidding the recognition or enforcement of trust variation orders must put all that in question. If offshore trust jurisdictions will not recognise or enforce its orders, surely the English court should not make them in the first place, as 'wholly ineffective'.

8.6 CONCLUSION

The world is a global village, and family litigation, just like other kinds, is increasingly international in scope and effect. In the nineteenth century the Pax Britannica bestrode the world as a function of the British Empire. In the twentieth century it was the turn of the long-arm Lex Americana to export itself everywhere, as an outward manifestation of the Americanisation of world business. Money talked. But the Americans, like the British before them, have learned that the natives are increasingly restless. They do not like having other people's law forced down their throats. Much more is therefore now done by international agreements, employing more or less standard conflict of laws machinery, in which everyone wins and loses something. Some aspects of family litigation, dealing with the abduction of children, say, or the collection of maintenance payments, have been the subject of such agreements. But ancillary relief orders involving trusts have proved particularly attractive to the 'We know best for everyone' school of judging, and particularly resistant to attempts to rein it in.

There can be little doubt that matters cannot go on as they are. The Court of Appeal, in deciding the case from which an extract is set out at the beginning of this chapter, added its weight to the clamour for review and possible reform.[242] But there must not only be domestic reform. There must be international agreement. Otherwise the drawbridges will start to go up round the world, and judicial and other legal co-operation will be threatened. Above all, the Family Division judges must appreciate that they do not have a world monopoly of wisdom and justice, and that their colleagues in other countries, with different values and different rules to apply, are as likely to be 'right' in refusing to enforce English judgments as they are to be in making them.

---

[242] *Charman v Charman (No 4)* [2007] EWCA Civ 503, para 126. See further Appendix 2.

APPENDIX 1

USEFUL LINKS AND WEBSITES

GENERAL

- www.withersworldwide.com
- www.worldlii.org
- www.assetprotectionbook.com
- www.findlaw.com
- www.international-divorce.com
- www.lexis.com

AUSTRALIA

- www.austlii.edu.au
- www.familycourt.gov.au
- www.familylawsection.org.au

BAHAMAS

- www.stepbahamas.org
- www.lexbahamas.org
- www.bahamas.gov.bs
- www.conyersdillandpearman.com
- www.caricomlaw.org (Caribbean Community Secretariat)

BVI

- www.bvifsc.vg (BVI Financial Services Commission)

CAYMAN

- www.mondaq.com

GUERNSEY/JERSEY

- www.jerseylegalinfo.je

- www.guernseybar.com

HONG KONG

- www.hkii.hk

- www.hkreform.gov.hk

- www.info.gov.uk

- www.judiciary.gov.hk

- www.legislation.gov.hk

- www.doj.gov.hk (Department of Justice)

SINGAPORE

- www.sal.org.sg (Singapore Academy of Law)

- www.scwo.org.sg (Singapore Council of Women's Organisations)

- www.subcourts.gov.sg

- www.familycourtofsingapore.gov.sg

- www.lawnet.com.sg

- www.lawonline.com.sg

- www.lawsociety.org.sg

- www.statutes.agc.gov.sg

USA

- www.state.ca.us

- www.martindale.com

- www.leginfo.ca.gov

- www.nycourts.gov

- www.california-divorce.com

- www.cga.ct.gov

- www.courtinfo.ca.gov

- www.courts.state.ny.us

- www.ctbar.gov

- www.divorcesource.com

- www.legaltips.org/california

APPENDIX 2

KEY EXTRACTS FROM FAMILY LAW REPORTS

CHARMAN v CHARMAN

[2005] EWCA Civ 1606, [2006] 2 FLR 422, CA

Court of Appeal

Sir Mark Potter P, Wilson and Lloyd LJJ

20 December 2005

Ancillary relief – Letters of request – Assets in offshore trust – Conjectural documents – Fishing expeditions – Jurisdiction of court to order letters of request

The husband appealed against two orders made in ancillary relief proceedings following an application by the wife for the issue of a letter of request to the Bermudian courts. Both orders were designed to elicit material about a discretionary trust established by the husband. The trust was originally situated in Jersey but the husband had procured its transfer to Bermuda, when he himself had relocated there. The beneficiaries of the trust were the husband, the wife, their children and the husband's remoter issue. The husband was the only person who had put assets into the trust. Since its establishment it had been operated as an interest in possession settlement. The wife valued the trust assets at £67m. The central question was whether the trust was a financial resource of the husband for the purpose of s 25(2)(a) of the Matrimonial Causes Act 1973. The letter of request ordered by the judge was that the husband's Bermudian solicitor, who was a director of the sole trustee, be asked to produce trust accounts, trust deeds, resolutions and letters of wishes, to state to what extent the trustee consulted with the husband about prospective policy decisions and the extent to which the trustee had discussed the possible collapsing of the trust and changing the husband's letter of wishes, and to provide details of communications with the husband's accountant, himself the subject of the second order. The accountant was ordered to produce documents relating to advice or discussions concerning the trust. The husband raised a number of objections to the orders, in particular that the application was a 'fishing' expedition and that the documents sought were conjectural only and therefore their production was not permitted by s 2(4)(a) of the Evidence (Proceedings in Other Jurisdictions) Act 1975.

Held – dismissing the appeal, save for a minor modification to the letter of request –

(1)   The central question, whether the trust was a financial resource of the husband for the purpose of s 25(2)(a) of the 1973 Act, should be expressed in terms of whether the trustee would be likely to advance the capital immediately or in the foreseeable future rather than whether the husband had 'effective control' over the trust. Since a trustee would usually be acting entirely properly if, after careful consideration of all the relevant circumstances, it resolved in good faith to accede to a request by the settlor for the exercise of his power of advancement of capital, whether back to the settlor or to any other beneficiary (see paras [12], [13]).

(2)   Insofar as they sought the production of documents, the orders for the letter of request and for the inspection appointment could not lawfully have been made if they represented a 'fishing' expedition. Insofar as the letter of request sought the taking of oral evidence, it would be preferable to conduct the initial appraisal by asking whether the intention was to obtain the solicitor's evidence for use at trial and there was reason to believe that he had knowledge of matters relevant to issues at trial. Different principles did not apply in financial proceedings following divorce from those applied in other types of proceeding. Neither the application in respect of the solicitor, nor that in respect of the accountant constituted a 'fishing' expedition. The wife had made a particularised allegation regarding the advancement of capital and was seeking to elicit evidence in support of that allegation. The request was not part of a search for material that might enable the wife to raise an allegation (see paras [37], [38], [39]).

(3)   In financial proceedings following divorce there was no need to limit the production of documents by a non-party to those documents whose existence could be proven. Whilst such a limitation might make sense in ordinary civil litigation, it could not be regarded as mandatory in a special type of proceeding where it would largely render ineffective the jurisdiction to secure the production of documents. A wife would seldom have the requisite knowledge to prove the existence of a document. This conclusion was reinforced by s 25 of the 1973 Act, which imposed a quasi-inquisitorial role on the courts to investigate issues in ancillary relief litigation and that duty could not be disabled by any fetter upon the court's ability to extract relevant documents from a non-party not expressly mentioned by s 2(4) of the 1975 Act. Such an approach was also consistent with the Family Proceedings Rules 1991, r 2.51(B), which required the court to ensure that the parties were on an equal footing. One of the aims of the Rules was to encourage a 'cards on the table' approach (see paras [46], [47], [48], [72]).

(4)   An inspection appointment could only be ordered in respect of a document inspection where it appeared necessary for the fair disposal of the application or for saving costs, and the same principle applied to a letter of request for the production of documents. The judge was correct to conclude that the production of documents was necessary (see para [50]).

(5)   In financial proceedings following divorce where the court was asked to consider whether to order an inspection appointment, or to order the issue of a letter of request for the production of documents, it was obliged to exercise its power in a way that was proportionate to the sums involved, the importance of the

case, the complexity of the issues and the financial position of each party. In view
of the sums involved it was clearly appropriate to grant the order (see para [52]).

(6)   The order was not be oppressive since both the solicitor and the accountant
were professionals (see para [55]).

(7)   The judge's request that the solicitor be required to divulge communications
between the accountant and the trustee was wider than the extent of the
obligation to divulge communications between the husband and the trustee and
was too wide. It was to be modified so that the two obligations ran parallel to one
another (see para [56]).

(8)   Whilst traditionally trustees were regarded as entitled to refuse to disclose to
beneficiaries any document that bore on their reasons for taking a particular
decision in the exercise of their discretion over trust income or capital, no such
decision had been taken in the instant case beyond the appropriation of income to
the husband. Accordingly, the general proposition against disclosure of the trust
accounts did not apply. Furthermore, it was not true to say that a discretionary
beneficiary did not have sufficient interest to be entitled to disclosure. The trustee
would not be bound to succeed in persuading the Bermudian court, should it seek
to do so, that the evidence ought not to be ordered to be given, such that it would
be pointless to order that the letter of request be issued (see paras [64], [65], [66]).

Statutory provisions considered
Matrimonial Proceedings and Property Act 1970, s 5
Matrimonial Causes Act 1973, s 25(2)(a)
Evidence (Proceedings in Other Jurisdictions) Act 1975, s 2
Rules of the Supreme Court 1965 (SI 1965/1776), Ords 38, 39, rr 1, 2, 3(3), 9, 14
Family Proceedings Rules 1991 (SI 1991/1247), rr 1.3, 2.51B, 2.61B(7)(a), 2.62(7)
Civil Procedure Rules 1998 (SI 1998/3132)
Bermudian Evidence Act 1905
Gibraltarian Evidence Ordinance

Cases referred to in judgment
Asbestos Insurance Coverage Cases, Re [1985] 1 WLR 331, [1985] 1 All ER
    716, HL
B v B (Matrimonial Proceedings: Discovery) [1978] Fam 181, [1978] 3 WLR 624,
    [1979] 1 All ER 801, FD
Browne v Browne [1989] 1 FLR 291, CA
D v D (Production Appointment) [1995] 2 FLR 497, FD
First American Corporation v Zayed [1999] 1 WLR 1154, [1998] 4 All ER 439, CA
Frary v Frary and Another [1993] 2 FLR 696, CA
Khanna v Lovell White Durrant [1995] 1 WLR 121, [1994] 4 All ER 267, ChD
Letterstedt v Broers (1884) 9 App Cas 371, PC
Morgan v Morgan [1977] Fam 122, [1977] 2 WLR 712, (1976) FLR Rep 473, [1977]
    2 All ER 515, FD
Netbank v Commercial Money Center [2004] Bda LR 46, Berm SC
Panayiotou v Sony Music Entertainment (UK) Ltd [1994] Ch 142, [1994] 2 WLR
    241, [1994] 1 All ER 755, [1994] EMLR 229, ChD
Parra v Parra [2002] EWCA Civ 1886, [2003] 1 FLR 942, CA

Schmidt v Rosewood Trust Ltd [2003] UKPC 26, [2003] 2 AC 709, [2003] 2 WLR
   1442, [2003] 3 All ER 76, PC
State of Norway's Application, Re [1987] QB 433, [1986] 3 WLR 452, [1989]
   1 All ER 661, CA
State of Norway's Application (No 2), Re [1990] 1 AC 723, [1989] 2 WLR 458,
   [1989] 1 All ER 745, HL
The Esteem Settlement, Re [2004] WTLR 1, [2004] JRC 92, Jersey RC
W v W (Disclosure by Third Party) (1981) 2 FLR 291, FD
*Westinghouse Electric Corporation Uraniam Contract Litigation MDL Docket 235
   (No 2), Re* [1978] AC 547, [1978] 2 WLR 81, [1978] 1 All ER 434, HL
White v White [2001] 1 AC 596, [2000] 3 WLR 1571, [2000] 2 FLR 981, [2001]
   1 All ER 1, HL
Zakay v Zakay [1998] 3 FCR 35, Gib Sup Ct

Barry Singleton QC and Deborah Eaton for the appellant
Martin Pointer QC, Daniel Hochberg and James Ewins for the respondent

Cur adv vult

WILSON LJ:

[1]   This appeal requires us to identify the principles by reference to which a court should determine an application in proceedings for financial relief ancillary to divorce for:

(a)   an order (under Ord 39, rr 1 and 2 of the Rules of the Supreme Court 1965 (the 1965 Rules), superseded for other civil proceedings but presently still applied to family proceedings by r 1.3 of the Family Proceedings Rules 1991 (the 1991 rules)) for the issue of a letter of request to the authorities of a foreign country to take a person's evidence; and
(b)   an order (under r 2.62(7) of the 1991 Rules) that a person should attend before the court at an inspection appointment and there produce documents.

[2]   A husband appeals against orders of each of these types made on the application of his wife by Coleridge J on 20 October 2005.

[3]   In 1976, when neither had significant resources, the parties were married. They lived in England and had two children, now adult. In 2003 the husband took up residence in Bermuda and separated from the wife, who has remained resident in England. In June 2004 she issued a petition for divorce, which included an application for ancillary relief. In January 2005, Coleridge J refused the application of the husband, who in August 2004 had himself issued proceedings for divorce in Bermuda, for a stay of the wife's petition, which has thus proceeded to the grant in April 2005 of a decree nisi of divorce. The wife's claim for ancillary relief is due to be heard by Coleridge J over 7 days in February 2006.

[4]   During the marriage the husband made a fortune in the insurance market in the City of London. He concedes that the assets which fall for division in the proceedings, 'the relevant assets', amount to £59m. But the wife contends that the relevant assets are £126m. The difference (£67m) represents the assets of a trust

now situated in Bermuda, namely Dragon Holdings Trust, 'Dragon'. At the hearing in February 2006 the husband will contend that, whatever their size, the wife should be awarded substantially less than an equal share of the relevant assets by virtue of his exceptional contribution to their creation. Nevertheless, in the light of the decision of the House of Lords in *White v White* [2001] 1 AC 596, [2000] 2 FLR 981 that the court should cross-check its provisional award against the yardstick of equal division and of the fact that, even if that yardstick were found inapt, the award might well be cross-checked against the yardstick of some lesser percentage of the relevant assets, the difference between £59m and £126m might well make a substantial difference to the award.

[5] The orders under appeal were both designed to elicit 'material' about Dragon for consideration at the forthcoming hearing. At this stage I use that neutral word. The sole trustee of Dragon is Codan Trust Company Ltd, a Bermudian company linked to Conyers, Dill and Pearman, the well-known firm of solicitors in Bermuda. Mr Anderson, a partner in the firm, is a director of Codan. The letter of request is to the Bermudian court to cause Mr Anderson to be orally examined, and to produce documents, concerning specified matters, which I will describe in para [20], below, in relation to Dragon. The husband's long-standing accountant in England is Mr Clay. The order for the inspection appointment is for Mr Clay to attend court in London and there to produce documents, specified in terms which I will quote in para [21], below, in relation to Dragon.

[6] Dragon is a discretionary trust in largely conventional terms which was created under the law of Jersey in 1987 and of which the husband was the settlor. He alone has placed assets into it. Its beneficiaries are defined as the husband, the wife, their two children, any future child or remoter issue of the husband, charities and such other persons as the trustees might add. The trustees have power to distribute capital as well as income to any beneficiary. At the time of Dragon's creation the husband wrote a letter of wishes to the trustee, then a Jersey trust company, in the following terms:

'You may find it helpful to know my wishes regarding the exercise of your powers and discretions over the funds of the ... Settlement. I realise of course that these wishes cannot be binding on you.

My real intentions in establishing the Settlement are to protect and conserve certain assets for the benefit of myself and my Family.

During my lifetime it is my wish that you consult me with regard to all matters relating to the investment or administration of the Fund and thereafter you should consult my wife in like manner. If my wife survives me, it is my wish that the fund should be administered primarily for her benefit and that she should have access to capital, if necessary. If both of us are dead, my children are to be treated as the primary beneficiaries and I hope you will consult my executors and their guardians. Should anything happen to the entire family, then the funds subject to the Settlement should follow my estate.

Insofar as is consistent with the terms of the Settlement I wish to have the fullest possible access to the capital and income of the Settlement including the possibility of investing the entire Fund in business ventures undertaken by me.

If circumstances should change in any way I will write you a further letter.'

[7] Between 1992 and April 2003 a second Jersey Trust company acted as Dragon's sole trustee. It has stated as follows:

'... throughout the whole of our trusteeship of the Trust, we held the income of the Trust for [the husband] absolutely and regarded the Trust as an interest-in-possession trust. The capital and income were held in segregated accounts and accumulated income either distributed to [the husband] or left in the accumulated income account to be distributed to him at a later date.'

The husband states that distributions to him out of the accumulated income account ceased in 1997. There has been no distribution to any other beneficiary at any time.

[8] In April 2003, soon after he had ceased to be resident in the UK and had taken up residence in Bermuda, the husband exercised his power to change the trustee to Codan; and the proper law of the trust was changed to Bermuda. Weeks earlier he had had two meetings with Mr Clay. At the first meeting Mr Clay, according to his note, expressed concern at the central control of Dragon which the new Bermudian trustee might exercise; suggested that the husband should draft a fresh letter of wishes as soon as the change of trustee had taken place; questioned whether, in the event of the husband's death, too much control would be in the hands of the new trustee; and advised the husband to consider whether to arrange further protection so as 'to ensure that his wishes were actually carried out'. At the second meeting, Mr Clay, according to his note, suggested that, while the husband was non-resident in the UK, Dragon should or might be collapsed.

[9] Following its appointment as trustee, Codan resolved to follow its predecessor by appointing Dragon's income to the husband for life and thus, subject to any distribution to him, by adding it into the accumulated income account held for him absolutely. They formally resolved to regard Dragon 'as an interest-in-possession trust'.

[10] In May 2004 the husband sent a letter of wishes to Codan. In it he said:

'During my lifetime, I would like you to treat me as the primary beneficiary, although I expect that you will consider the interests of the other immediate family beneficiaries as appropriate from time to time. I acknowledge that you have appointed the annual income to myself as a life interest disposition, as had the previous trustees.

After my death, and if they survive me, I would wish you to treat my children as primary equal beneficiaries per stirpes

...

I may amend these wishes from time to time to take account of changing circumstances.'

[11] In June 2004 the husband sent a written instruction to Codan in relation to the accumulated income held to his order. It was to the effect that, subject to one specific disbursement in order to defray costs associated with a company owned by him, the accumulated income then held for him, and, unless he were to instruct otherwise, all income to be appointed to him in the future, should be paid back into the trust. The husband states that Codan does not appear to have acted upon this instruction.

[12] There has been some debate at the hearing of this appeal as to the nature of the central question which, in this not unusual situation, the court hearing an application for ancillary relief should seek to determine. Superficially the question is easily framed as being whether the trust is a financial 'resource' of the husband for the purpose of s 25(2)(a) of the Matrimonial Causes Act 1973 (the 1973 Act). But what does the word 'resource' mean in this context? In my view, when properly focused, that central question is simply whether, if the husband were to request it to advance the whole (or part) of the capital of the trust to him, the trustee would be likely to do so. In other cases the question has been formulated in terms of whether the spouse has real or effective control over the trust. At times I have myself formulated it in that way. But, unless the situation is one in which there is ground for doubting whether the trustee is properly discharging its duties or would be likely to do so, it seems to me on reflection that such a formulation is not entirely apposite. On the evidence so far assembled in the present case, as in most cases, there seems no reason to doubt that the duties of the trustee are being, and will continue to be, discharged properly. In his written argument in this court, Mr Pointer QC, on behalf of the wife, at one point referred to the possible 'unity of interest' between the husband and Codan; and in his written argument before the judge he tentatively described Codan as 'quasi-agents' of the husband. Both phrases imply that Codan is not asserting, or would not assert, the independence that its duties require of it; and, in my view, on the present evidence, it was wise of Mr Pointer in oral argument to withdraw them. A trustee – in proper 'control' of the trust – will usually be acting entirely properly if, after careful consideration of all relevant circumstances, he resolves in good faith to accede to a request by the settlor for the exercise of his power of advancement of capital, whether back to the settlor or to any other beneficiary.

[13] Thus in effect, albeit with one small qualification, I agree with the suggestion of Butler-Sloss LJ in this court in *Browne v Browne* [1989] 1 FLR 291 at 239D–E that, in this context, the question is more appropriately expressed as whether the spouse has 'immediate access to the funds' of the trust than 'effective control' over it. The qualification relates to the word 'immediate'. In that case the trial judge knew that, if he were to proceed also to order the wife to pay the husband's costs, she would be unable to comply with his orders for her swift payment of a lump sum and costs without recourse to the off-shore trusts over which he found her to have 'effective control': see 295B–C. So the question in that case was whether her access to their funds was immediate. In principle, however, in the light of s 25(2)(a) of the 1973 Act, the question is surely whether the trustee would be likely to advance the capital immediately or in the foreseeable future.

[14] It is obvious that in the present case there is a contingent subsidiary question, albeit of less potential significance. Were it not to be persuaded that Codan would be likely to accede to a request by the husband for advancement of the capital to him, the court would need to consider whether at any rate the income of the trust is being made available, and would be likely to continue in the foreseeable future to be made available, for deployment at the husband's direction.

[15] If such be the central question, and indeed the contingent subsidiary question, for determination in relation to Dragon, what is the stance, at this stage necessarily provisional, of each party in relation to them?

[16] The wife's stance is that, in the light of the husband's status as its settlor, of his subsisting status as a beneficiary able to receive an advancement of capital and of the contents of his two letters of wishes, the court should not hesitate before answering the central question affirmatively, with the result that the subsidiary question does not arise.

[17] The husband's stance needs closer study:

(a) Under cover of his solicitors' letter dated 27 August 2004 the husband made his first presentation of assets in the proceedings. In what was entitled a 'Schedule of Matrimonial Assets' he included three categories, namely his own assets, jointly held assets and trust assets, and he estimated the total value of assets in all three categories at £83,000,000. He appended a note that the schedule included neither his 'Children's Settlement' nor another trust 'as neither party has financial interest in these trusts'. It is agreed that the 'trust assets' which he included in the total either comprised, or at least included, the assets of Dragon. It seems to me highly arguable that, by that schedule, the husband was conceding that the capital assets of Dragon would be likely to be made fully available to him upon request. But, if such was an unintended misrepresentation, he is entitled to say so. And, by letter dated 20 September 2004, his solicitors wrote that the assets of Dragon had been included in the schedule only for convenience and that he neither controlled them nor regarded them as his.

(b) In January 2005, when he gave oral evidence in support of his application for a stay of the English divorce proceedings, the husband's case in relation to Dragon began more clearly to emerge. His case has now been encapsulated by the description of Dragon as a 'dynastic' trust. In relation to its creation he said:

> 'I deeply wanted to establish a legacy for my future generations because I felt it was the most wonderful thing that I could ever do to ensure not only the longevity of my name but also my reputation and my standing in the future generations of offspring.'

(c) In March 2005 the husband complied with his duty under r 2.61B(7)(a) of the 1991 Rules to file a concise statement of the issues between him and the wife. Echoing almost word for word the statement of issues already filed on her behalf, he identified the following issue:

> 'To what extent, if any, are the assets of [Dragon] to be regarded as matrimonial assets to which the court should have regard?

I have no need or desire for future distributions.'

In an affidavit sworn in August 2005 he amplified this case and added:
(d)   The wife's solicitor considered, in my view reasonably, that the husband was sitting on the fence. By letter dated 15 September 2005 she asked his solicitor to state whether the husband conceded for the purpose of the application for ancillary relief that the assets of Dragon were resources which were and would be available to him. By letter dated 19 October his solicitor replied:

> 'In 1987 my client wished to create a structure whereby the wealth that he had generated and expected to generate for the future was perpetuated and would benefit future generations. For this purpose he established the Trust ...
>
> My client has explained how the first Letter of Wishes came to be signed. Of course at that stage in my client's career, although he might have been confident of success, he could not actually know that he would succeed to the extent that he has, and particularly that things would not go wrong with the result that he would need to ask that the trustees consider making provision for the immediate family. Nevertheless his confidence proved to be well-founded ...
>
> You write that my client "*has exercised and continues to exercise control over the trust*" ... I accept that in the circumstances that have arisen, namely the change in treatment to an interest in possession trust, my client can be said to "control" the income. However, I suspect that you are trying to elevate the fact that the trustees have been willing to invest the trust assets into ventures in which my client was involved into an argument that this means that he controls the Trust ...
>
> The very reason that the Trust was established was to hold an interest in Charman Underwriting. It is neither surprising nor unusual for trustees to accede to a settlor's request to invest in an enterprise in which he is involved. It is certainly not evidence of control. Furthermore the Trust has made a great deal of money from my client's requests that the trustees invest in his business activities, far more, I believe, than it might have made by a more conventional investment approach ...
>
> My client has explained that he does not really understand the background to the change in treatment of the trust from a discretionary trust to an interest in possession trust.
>
> The fortunate result for your client of this practical change in treatment is that my client's ability to call for income from the Trust will be taken into account in these proceedings. Nevertheless he will ask the Court also to have regard to the fact that he has never actually received income, except in the very particular circumstances outlined above, and in his evidence, that there have not been any payments out of income since 1997 and that his treatment of the Trust, as against

the decision that appears to have been taken in this regard by the trustees, has been consistent with his initial intention that this fund, as to both income and capital, should not be for him or his immediate family.

He does not accept that the capital should be taken into account in these proceedings.'

By that letter, written on the day prior to the hearing before the judge, the husband appeared to climb down from the fence. On the central question, namely as to the availability to him of the capital of Dragon, he definitely adopted a negative stance. I confess that – perhaps too quickly – I had read his stance in relation to the contingent subsidiary question, namely as to the availability to him of its income, as an affirmative concession. But Mr Singleton QC, on his behalf, asserts that a careful reading of the letter shows the opposite; and I proceed on that basis.

[18] Mr Singleton's arguments to the judge in opposition to the applications for the orders under appeal were identical to his arguments to this court. Re-arranged and slightly reformulated, they were and are as follows:

(a)   the applications are in aid of a 'fishing' expedition and thus impermissible;
(b)   insofar as the applications are for the production of documents the very existence of which the wife cannot prove, they are impermissible;
(c)   the orders are unnecessary and thus impermissible;
(d)   the orders are disproportionate and so should in the exercise of discretion be refused;
(e)   the orders are oppressive, particularly in relation to Mr Anderson, and so should in the exercise of discretion be refused; and
(f)   at least in part the orders go too wide and should be cut down.

[19] Having identified the central issue much as I have sought to do, the judge said as follows:

'The point is made by Mr Singleton ... that surely the wife has enough to advance this case in argument. That is to say, surely there are enough documents and answers to questionnaires so far in existence, which support [her] case ...

But I remain uneasy about it, and ultimately it is for me to decide whether or not, as the trial judge, there is sufficient evidence before me at the moment to enable me to come to a clear conclusion on this centrally important, if not pivotal, issue as matters currently stand. I do not wish to be reduced to conjecture based on inadequate evidence if there is more which could be of real assistance.

If this had not been a central issue in the case and if the sum of money involved had not been of the order that it is, or the proportion that it is of the overall total, I would tend to agree with Mr Singleton, that there was enough already and this was perhaps a disproportionate procedural step to take. But the resolution of this issue could impact on the result to the extent of millions, or even tens of millions, of pounds. The court should make a decision that is determinative of an issue of that gravity on the basis of the best possible evidence… It may be that there is nothing else. If so, that too may be relevant. It may be that there are documents and communications between the husband and the trustees that deal with his intentions, past present or future. If so, I need to see them.'

[20] The letter of request ordered by the judge was that Mr Anderson should be asked specified written questions annexed to the letter and, where applicable, be required to produce documents specified in the annexe. In summary the request was for him to be required to:

(a)   produce trust accounts for the two most recent completed years;
(b)   produce any trust deeds, written resolutions and letters of wishes, other than identified documents of each class already disclosed by the husband;
(c)   state whether it was the practice of the trustee to consult the husband, and/or to be guided by him, about prospective policy decisions, whether as to investment, distribution or otherwise, and, if so, give full details and produce all relevant documents;
(d)   state whether the trustee and the husband had discussed the possible collapse of the trust or change in the expression of his wishes and, if so, give full details and produce all relevant documents; and
(e)   state whether there had been any communications between Mr Clay and the trustee 'regarding the trusts' and, if so, give full details and produce all relevant documents.

The letter also requested that the wife's representative be permitted orally to ask – and impliedly that Mr Anderson should be required to answer – supplementary questions in order to elicit the clearest possible account of the above matters.

[21] The order for the inspection appointment obliged Mr Clay to produce to the court:

'any documents … containing evidence of any advice given to, discussions with or communications from, [the husband], relating to the past, present and future treatment of the trust funds or which bear upon the conception, creation and possible ultimate dissolution of [Dragon]…'

Preface to the arguments

[22] In the determination of this appeal it may be helpful to reflect first on the pattern of orders available to the court in proceedings for financial relief following divorce for causing persons who are not parties to the proceedings to produce documents and/or to give oral evidence in advance of the substantive hearing.

Documents to be produced by a person in England and Wales:

[23] (a) The appropriate form of order, as was made (rightly or wrongly) in the present case, is that the person should attend an inspection appointment. By virtue of r 2.62(7) of the 1991 Rules, the order can require him to produce 'any documents to be specified or described in the order, the inspection of which appears to the court to be necessary for disposing fairly of the application for

ancillary relief or for saving costs'. By virtue however of para (8) of the rule, no person can be compelled under (7) to produce a document which he could not be compelled to produce at the substantive hearing. It is clear, therefore, that, while the court has to be satisfied that inspection of the document is necessary for disposing fairly of the application or for saving costs, the court should nevertheless exercise its discretion to refuse production if application of the general principles for setting aside a writ of subpoena to produce documents (as unfortunately the continuing link with the 1965 Rules requires such a summons to be described) leads to that result. (b) The order for an inspection appointment is not an order for the person to give oral evidence. Nevertheless it has become the practice for the person attending it to be asked any question necessary to enable the inspection to proceed effectively, for example, if it is not clear from the face of a document produced, to identify its source or how it relates to another document or whether a document is missing and, if so, why. I consider that it is permissible to require answers to such questions. In *Frary v Frary and Another* [1993] 2 FLR 696, at 703B, Ralph Gibson LJ thought so too.

Oral evidence to be given by a person in England and Wales

[24]   Although it is usually desirable that a person should produce documents in advance of the substantive hearing, it is usually undesirable that he should give oral evidence in advance of it. At that stage the parties and the judge are likely to lack the requisite overview necessary for their focused questioning and his focused listening. So, if a person is in England and Wales, the procedure of choice will be to seek authority, pursuant to Ord 38, r 14 of the 1965 Rules, to issue a writ of subpoena to attend the substantive hearing and give oral evidence. Nevertheless there are exceptional cases in which it will be appropriate for such a person to be required to give oral evidence in advance of the substantive hearing. It may well be that a subpoena to attend and give oral evidence can lawfully be made returnable prior to the substantive hearing. In *Khanna v Lovell White Durrant* [1995] 1 WLR 121, at 127C, Sir Donald Nicholls V-C, as he then was, left the point open; but the logic behind his decision tends that way. Alternatively an order can be made under Ord 39, r 1 of the 1965 Rules for a deposition to be taken of a person's oral testimony before an examiner, with a view to its reception into evidence under Ord 38, r 9.

Documents to be produced by a person abroad

[25]   The appropriate form of order, as was made (rightly or wrongly) in the present case, is for the issue pursuant to Ord 39, rr 1 and 2 of the 1965 Rules of a letter of request to the relevant judicial authorities to cause the person to be required to produce the documents.

Oral evidence to be given by a person abroad

[26]   Since such a person cannot be compelled by subpoena to attend the hearing and give oral evidence, the appropriate form of order, as was made (rightly or wrongly) in the present case, is for the issue, pursuant to the same rules, of a letter of request to cause the person to be required to answer written questions under Ord 39, r 3(3) and/or oral questions.

[27] There is no logical reason why the principles by reference to which the court determines whether, and if so to what extent, to require a person who is not a party to the proceedings to produce documents or to give oral evidence should differ according to whether he is in England and Wales or abroad. Both sides agree upon that. Indeed, in *Panayiotou v Sony Music Entertainment (UK) Ltd* [1994] Ch 142 (the *George Michael* case), at 152C, Sir Donald Nicholls V-C upheld that proposition. Thus the principles determinative of an application for an order for an inspection appointment referred to in para [23] above will be same as those determinative of an application for an order for the issue of a letter of request of the type referred to in para [25]. Equally the principles determinative of an application to set aside a writ of subpoena referred to in para [24] will be the same as those determinative of an application for an order for the issue of a letter of request of the type referred to in para [26].

[28] But in the *George Michael* case Sir Donald Nicholls V-C went further than that. In the same passage at 152C he held that the principles determinative of an application for an order for the issue of a letter of request in respect of documents or of oral evidence ('an outgoing request') were the same as those determinative of an application for an order giving effect to a letter of request received from a foreign court in respect of documents or of oral evidence ('an incoming request'). Thus, according to him, the principles were identical in relation not only to subpoenas and to outgoing requests but also to incoming requests. Mr Singleton commends this approach. But, for a reason which it is easy to understand, Mr Pointer does not accept it. The reason is that, as I will explain, the court's approach in ordinary civil litigation to whether to give effect to an incoming request is governed by statute and is restrictive and, were such an approach necessarily to apply to an outgoing request and were it also to apply to proceedings for financial relief following divorce, Mr Pointer's defence of the orders under appeal would largely fail.

[29] In my opinion, however, Sir Donald Nicholls V-C was clearly correct to equate the principles apt to the issue of an outgoing request with those apt to the giving of effect to an incoming request. It would be unconscionable for the English court to make an outgoing request in circumstances in which, had it been incoming, it would not give effect to it; nor could the foreign court reasonably be expected to give effect to the English court's request in such circumstances. 'Do unto others as you would be done by', as Lord Denning MR reminded us, in this context, albeit obiter, in *Re Westinghouse Electric Corporation Uraniam Contract Litigation MDL Docket 235 (No 2)* [1978] AC 547 at 560H.

[30] It is thus necessary to address the principles by which the English court decides whether to give effect to an incoming request. The principles are set out in, or at least derived from, the Evidence (Proceedings in Other Jurisdictions) Act 1975 (the 1975 Act). Section 2 provides:

'(1) ... the High Court ... shall ... have power ... by order to make such provision for obtaining evidence... as may appear to the court to be appropriate for the purpose of giving effect to the request in pursuance of which the application is made; ...

(2) ... an order under this section may, in particular, make provision—

(a)   for the examination of witnesses, either orally or in writing;
(b)   for the production of documents; ...

(3)   An order under this section shall not require any particular steps to be taken unless they are steps which can be required to be taken by way of obtaining evidence for the purposes of civil proceedings in the court making the order ...

(4)   An order under this section shall not require a person—

(a)   to state what documents relevant to the proceedings to which the application for the order relates are or have been in his possession, custody or power; or
(b)   to produce any documents other than particular documents specified in the order as being documents appearing to the court making the order to be, or to be likely to be, in his possession, custody or power.'

'Fishing'

[31]   It will be noted that s 2(4) of the 1975 Act is mandatory, so it narrows the jurisdiction rather than informs the exercise of the discretion conferred by the section. There is no doubt that, in the words of Lord Fraser of Tullybelton in *Re Asbestos Insurance Coverage Cases* [1985] 1 WLR 331, at 337E, 'it is to be construed so as not to permit mere 'fishing' expeditions'.

[32]   In *Re State of Norway's Application* [1987] QB 433 (*Norway I*), this court, by a majority, set aside on the ground of 'fishing' an order made pursuant to a Norwegian request for oral evidence to be taken from two London bankers alleged to have such knowledge of the affairs of the deceased as was relevant to an issue in the Norwegian court as to his estate's liability to pay tax. At 482C–F, Kerr LJ said:

' ... although "fishing" has become a term of art for the purposes of many of our procedural rules dealing with applications for particulars of pleadings, interrogatories and discovery, illustrations of the concept are more easily recognised than defined. It arises in cases where what is sought is not evidence as such, but information which may lead to a line of inquiry which would disclose evidence. It is the search for material in the hope of being able to raise allegations of fact, as opposed to the elicitation of evidence to support allegations of fact, which have been raised bona fide with adequate particularisation ... It is perhaps best described as a roving inquiry, by means of the examination and cross-examination of witnesses, which is not designed to establish by means of their evidence allegations of fact which have been raised bona fide with adequate particulars, but to obtain information which may lead to obtaining evidence in general support of a party's case.'

At 482H–483B, Kerr LJ gave an example of what he meant: namely that, if raised with adequate particularisation, a question whether X was the settlor of a trust would be legitimate but that, if the answer was negative, a supplementary question as to 'who, then, was it?' would be 'fishing'.

[33] The request in *Norway I* was therefore only for oral evidence to be taken, not for documents to be produced. Doubt has subsequently been cast as to whether this court was right to apply the concept of 'fishing' to a request for oral evidence. Section 2(4) of the 1975 Act is, after all, confined to documents. In *Re State of Norway's Application (No 2)* [1990] 1 AC 723, at 781G, Woolf LJ in this court expressed 'difficulty in applying the concept of fishing to a request that a witness should be required to give oral evidence'. When the House of Lords determined appeals from each of the two decisions of this court in *Norway*, it declined to comment on this peripheral issue: per Woolf LJ in the Court of Appeal at 810F–G.

[34] In *First American Corporation v Zayed* [1999] 1 WLR 1154, at 1162G, Sir Richard Scott V-C (as he then was) with whom the other members of this court concurred, agreed with Woolf LJ. In the *Zayed* case there were proceedings in the District of Columbia against defendants accused of conspiring with BCCI to obtain control of the claimants by fraud. The request was for oral evidence to be taken from officers of BCCI's accountants in London. The court held that:

(a) in relation to a request for oral evidence there was no jurisdictional limitation in respect of 'fishing' (see 1164B of *Zayed*);

(b) *Norway I*, properly regarded, demonstrated that, *as a matter of discretion*, a request for oral evidence should be refused if the intention was to obtain information rather than evidence for use at trial (see 1164D);

(c) if, however, the intention was to obtain evidence for use at trial and there was reason to believe that the person had knowledge of matters relevant to issues at trial, the request should not be refused on the ground of 'fishing' (see 1164F); and

(d) the request satisfied those tests but should nevertheless be refused as being oppressive because the claimants had alleged that the accountants had been complicit in the fraud and might well use their proposed evidence in later proceedings against them (1168F).

[35] In the present case the request to the Bermudian court is both for the production of documents and for the taking of oral evidence. The nexus between the two was, as it happens, recently considered by Kawaley J in a valuable judgment in the Supreme Court of Bermuda in *Netbank v Commercial Money Center* [2004] Bda LR 46. Before him was an issue as to the enforcement of a letter of request from Ohio for oral evidence to be taken from employees in Bermuda of an insurance company. Into the island's Bermudian Evidence Act 1905 had been inserted provisions identical to those in the British Evidence (Proceedings in Other Jurisdictions) Act 1975. At 11 the judge observed:

'Typically, perhaps, oral examination relates almost exclusively to the requested documents, so, if the documents are not properly sought, oral examination falls away.'

In that, in the case of *Netbank*, the request was only for oral evidence Kawaley J, choosing to adopt the approach commended in *Zayed*, held that he had a discretion, which he proceeded to exercise.

[36] I respectfully agree with Kawaley J about the typical case. In the present case the request for documents is certainly important. Nevertheless, in the light, in

particular, of the likely extent of Mr Anderson's personal, oral dealings with the husband and of the court's need to focus upon the willingness of the trustee to comply with the husband's wishes, including meeting his asserted needs, I regard the request for him to be required to give oral evidence as free-standing.

[37]　Thus in my view:

(a)　insofar as they seek production of documents, the orders for the letter of request and for the inspection appointment could not lawfully have been made if they represent an attempt to go 'fishing'; and

(b)　insofar as the letter of request seeks the taking of oral evidence, it may be preferable to conduct its initial appraisal not by reference to 'fishing' but by asking, perhaps in effect only slightly differently, whether the intention is to obtain Mr Anderson's evidence for use at trial and there is reason to believe that he has knowledge of matters relevant to issues at trial.

Furthermore, whether or not it was apt to the particular case before him, the analysis of 'fishing' made by Kerr LJ in *Norway I* cannot, in my view, be bettered and should at any rate be applied to the court's appraisal of the request for production of documents.

[38]　It follows that, in this area of the case, I would not accept that different principles apply in financial proceedings following divorce from those which apply elsewhere. In this regard I refer to the decision of Dunn J in *B v B (Matrimonial Proceedings: Discovery)* [1978] Fam 181. Before him was a wife's application in financial proceedings for disclosure by the husband, rather than by a non-party. At 191E–H, the judge said:

'It is another feature of such proceedings that one party, usually the wife, is in a situation quite different from that of ordinary litigants. In general terms, she may know more than anyone else about the husband's financial position … She may … know, from conversations with the husband in the privacy of the matrimonial home, the general sources of his wealth and how he is able to maintain the standard of living that he does. But she is unlikely to know the details of such sources or precise figures, and it is for this reason that discovery now plays such an important part in financial proceedings in the Family Division.

Applications for such discovery cannot be described as "fishing" for information, as they might be in other divisions. The wife is entitled to go "fishing" in the Family Division within the limits of the law and practice.'

The judge's first paragraph is, if I may say so, important; and I will return to it at para [47], below. But his reference to an entitlement to go 'fishing' might have caused confusion. I believe that he meant to convey only that, by a request for an order for disclosure, a wife is entitled to seek to ensure that a husband complies with his duty to make full and frank disclosure of all his resources. The passage does not, and could not, confer upon a spouse a licence to go 'fishing' for documents against a non-party.

[39]　In my view the order for the letter of request and the order against Mr Clay clearly pass the tests set out at para [37], above. Albeit not set out in any pleading,

the wife makes a particularised allegation that, if requested, Codan would make the capital of Dragon available to the husband. He denies the allegation. As both parties have formally recognised, this raises an issue in the proceedings. By means of the request, the wife wishes to elicit evidence in support of the allegation for use at the forthcoming hearing. To the evidence in support of it already before the court she wishes to add further evidence as to the husband's past dealings with the trustee. Pre-eminently Mr Anderson has knowledge of those dealings; but so also to a significant extent does Mr Clay. The request is not part of a search for material which might enable the wife to raise an allegation. So she is not 'fishing' for the documents. Equally the request for Mr Anderson to give oral evidence also passes its initial test; at any rate, inasmuch as this appears to be a matter of discretion, the judge did not err in having in effect so held.

[40] The case of *Zakay v Zakay* [1998] 3 FCR 35, decided by Schofield CJ sitting in the Supreme Court of Gibraltar, holds a mirror to the present case in various respects; and it is very instructive. In financial proceedings in England following divorce the wife alleged – and the husband denied – that he was the beneficial owner of shares held by a Gibraltarian trust company. The English judge ordered the issue of a letter of request to the Gibraltarian court that an officer of the trust company be required both to give oral evidence identifying the beneficial owner of the shares and to produce all documents in relation to such ownership. Before Schofield CJ, the officer sought to set aside an order in Gibraltar which had in both respects given effect to the request. The chief justice had to apply provisions of Gibraltar's Evidence Ordinance identical to those in s 2 of the English Evidence (Proceedings in Other Jurisdictions) Act 1975. He refused to set aside the order. At 42B–C, Schofield CJ said:

> 'the documents requested for production in this case are narrowly confined to the single issue they are aimed to support. The documents are more than likely in the possession of the applicant and are readily identifiable. Of course, it is impossible for the petitioner to know the specific identity of individual documents. But the applicant is being asked a specific question and is being asked to produce the documents to prove his answers. That is not a fishing expedition in the sense of casting a line in the hope that something will be caught: the fish has been identified and the court is endeavouring to spear it.'

The vivid development of the metaphor applies neatly to the present case.

Documents not proved to exist

[41] Section 2(4) of the 1975 Act has been authoritatively construed as going further than to prohibit 'fishing' for documents against non-parties.

[42] In *Re Westinghouse Electric Corporation Uraniam Contract Litigation MDL Docket 235 (No 2)*, cited above, the House of Lords held that incoming letters of request from Virginia should not be given effect in that they had become an attempt to abuse the process of the English court. At 610E, however, Lord Wilberforce observed that the reference in s 2(4)(b) to 'particular documents

specified in the order' excluded a request for a class of documents. And, at 635G, Lord Diplock construed the phrase as meaning 'individual documents separately described'.

[43] In the *Asbestos Insurance* case, cited above, the House of Lords allowed an appeal by a London insurance brokerage company which in the courts below had been ordered to produce documents pursuant to a letter of request issued by a Californian court in proceedings brought by manufacturers of asbestos against their insurers. At 337H, Lord Fraser of Tullybelton, who made the only substantive speech, departed somewhat from the dicta in *Westinghouse* by suggesting that a compendious description of specific documents would suffice. But at 338B–C he added an important rider. For he construed s 2(4)(a) of the 1975 Act – which prohibits a person from being required to state what documents relevant to the proceedings are in his possession – as meaning that the request could seek production only of actual documents, ie of documents which, on the evidence, existed or had existed, rather than of conjectural documents, ie of documents which might or might not have existed.

[44] In the *George Michael* case, cited above, the singer claimed that his contract with the defendant was in restraint of trade and that he should thus not be bound by it; and in that regard he asked the court to order the issue of a letter of request to the New York court to order the production of documents by officers of companies associated with the defendant. Having determined that the principles applicable to the issue of an outgoing request equated with those applicable to the giving effect to an incoming request, Sir Donald Nicholls V–C held, at 153F–154B, that the request had not only to avoid falling foul of the prohibition on 'fishing' but also to be confined to particular documents, albeit perhaps compendiously described (indeed – as he added – description itself being 'a matter of degree'), and indeed to documents which the court was satisfied existed or had existed. He refused part of the singer's application by reference to these criteria.

[45] Here, in my view, we detect the high water-mark of the husband's appeal in the present case. Even if the orders under appeal can, as in my view they can, be construed as seeking the production of 'particular documents specified in the order', Mr Pointer accepts that in various respects they seek only 'conjectural documents', ie documents which he cannot (at this stage) prove to exist or to have existed. If, in financial proceedings following divorce a requirement to a non-party to produce documents is to be limited to those which the applicant can prove to exist, this appeal must largely succeed.

[46] In my view there is no need – or room – for any such limitation in deciding whether to order a non-party to produce documents in financial proceedings following divorce. No doubt the limitation makes perfect sense in ordinary civil litigation, in particular commercial litigation. But it is born of a construction of s 2(4)(a) of the 1975 Act – namely that a prohibition against requiring a person to state what relevant documents he holds includes a prohibition against requiring him to state whether he holds a relevant *and specified* document or class of documents – which cannot be regarded as mandatory in a special type of proceeding in which it would largely deprive the jurisdiction to secure the production of documents of its efficacy.

[47] In my experience – plentiful in relation to inspection appointments, although exiguous in relation to letters of request – the wife will very seldom have the knowledge with which to prove the existence of a document which, if it does exist, may have a crucial bearing on the outcome of her financial application. In *B v B*, in the passage which I have quoted at para [38], above, Dunn J said as much. In this regard it is at the very least of interest to note that, in *Zakay*, in the passage which I have quoted at para [40], above. Schofield CJ, to whom the *George Michael* case had been cited, observed that 'of course, it is impossible for the petitioner to know the specific identity of individual documents'; he clearly held that the Gibraltarian equivalent of s 2(4)(a) of the 1975 Act presented no impediment to his giving effect to the English request, notwithstanding the absence of proof of existence of the documents. Indeed, as Coleridge J correctly observed in the passage quoted at para [19], above, it may be relevant for the court to learn, if it be the case, that there is no such document in the possession of a trustee or of an accountant of the type specified in his orders.

[48] This conclusion is fortified by the statutory duty cast upon the courts of England and Wales (and of a number of related jurisdictions) in determining an application for financial relief following divorce. Introduced by s 5 of the Matrimonial Proceedings and Property Act 1970, the duty is now cast by s 25 of the Matrimonial Causes Act 1973 (1973 Act) as follows:

'(1)   It shall be the duty of the court in deciding whether to exercise its powers ... and, if so, in what manner, to have regard to all the circumstances of the case...

(2)   ... the court shall in particular have regard to the following matters – (a) the ... financial resources which each of the parties to the marriage has or is likely to have in the foreseeable future...'

[49]   In *Parra v Parra* [2002] EWCA Civ 1886, [2003] 1 FLR 942, Thorpe LJ in this court observed at para [22]:

'The quasi-inquisitorial role of the judge in ancillary relief litigation obliges him to investigate issues which he considers relevant to outcome even if not advanced by either party. Equally, he is not bound to adopt a conclusion upon which the parties have agreed.'

The court's 'quasi-inquisitorial role' stems from s 25 of the 1973 Act. Insofar as it is its independent duty to have regard to a spouse's resources, the court cannot be disabled from discharging it by any substantial fetter upon its ability to extract relevant documents from a non-party not expressly mandated by the words of s 2(4) of the 1975 Act. Thus in *D v D (Production Appointment)* [1995] 2 FLR 497, Thorpe J (as he then was) in deciding to set a wide boundary around the scope of the documents which he was ordering the wife's accountant to produce at (as it is now called) an inspection appointment, said, at 500A–B:

'If the boundary is set narrow, there is the risk that information as to the nature and extent of the [wife's] financial circumstances may be lost to the detriment of the husband and to the obstruction of the court in its duty to carry out the s 25 exercise as between the husband and the wife.'

Necessity

[50] As explained in para [23](a), above, an inspection appointment can be ordered only in respect of a document inspection of which appears 'necessary' for disposing fairly of the application or for saving costs; and, as explained in para [27], above, the same principle applies to a letter of request for the production of documents. In my view the judge was correct to conclude that, in both cases, the threshold of necessity was crossed. There is something inherently unconvincing about Mr Singleton's submission that the wife is already in possession of quite enough ammunition to deploy in respect of the central issue as to Dragon. For, if her ammunition is so powerful, why is the husband continuing to reject her argument so stoutly? I cannot fault the reasoning of the judge set out in para [19], above.

Proportionality

[51] Rule 2.51B(3) of the Family Proceedings Rules 1991 provides that, when exercising any power given to it under the rules for financial relief following divorce, the court must seek to give effect to the overriding objective. Rule 2.51B(1) defines the overriding objective as enabling the court to deal with cases justly. Rule 2.51B(2) provides:

'Dealing with a case justly includes, so far as is practicable—

...

(c)   dealing with the case in ways which are proportionate – (i) to the amount of money involved; (ii) to the importance of the case; (iii) to the complexity of the issues; and (iv) to the financial position of each party; ...'

In that the power to order an inspection appointment arises under such rules, the court must therefore seek to exercise it in a way which is proportionate to the four specified factors. By analogy, the same requirement applies to the power to order the issue of a letter of request for the production of documents in such proceedings. A clear failure to observe such proportionality will vitiate the resultant exercise of discretion whether to make either such order.

[52] The costs generated by the orders referable to Mr Anderson and, to a lesser extent, to Mr Clay will be significant; and the wife accepts that, without prejudice to her aspiration to obtain an order for costs inclusive of them against the husband at the end of the proceedings, she must meet their costs insofar as they are reasonable. Nevertheless I unhesitatingly accept Mr Pointer's submission – and I cannot improve upon his formulation of it – that 'any question of proportionality is overcome by the magnitude of the trust assets in question'.

Oppression

[53] Any civil court asked to order a person to divulge material, whether documentary or oral, in proceedings to which he is not a party must consider whether, as a matter of discretion, the order would be so oppressive upon him as to outweigh the likely value of the material in determination of the case. In this respect I exclude pleas of confidentiality or of privilege which require separate appraisal. In the majority of cases oppression of such weight will scarcely be arguable. But in the present case Mr Singleton does argue that, at least upon Mr Anderson if not also upon Mr Clay, the orders of the judge are so oppressive that they should not have been made.

[54] There is no doubt that in financial proceedings following divorce the 'oppression' argument, which of course is available not only to the party to the proceedings who may initially respond to the application but also – and in particular – to the non-party when he appears before the court pursuant to order, will sometimes prevail. A wife's father, ordered to explain, with documentation, his testamentary intentions towards her, may well be able successfully to invoke it: as in *Morgan v Morgan* [1977] Fam 122, (1976) FLR Rep 473. A spouse's wealthy cohabitant, ordered to produce evidence not just as to the support provided by her (or him) to the spouse but as to her (or his) overall resources, may be able successfully to invoke it: as in *Frary v Frary*, cited above. Even a spouse's creditor may have a live argument as to oppression which the court must weigh: as in *W v W (Disclosure by Third Party)* (1981) 2 FLR 291.

[55] But how strong is such an argument in relation to the trustee of one of the family's trusts or indeed to a spouse's accountant? These are professionals, whose personal privacy the proposed orders would in no sense invade. 'It must always be borne in mind', said Lord Blackburn in *Letterstedt v Broers* (1884) 9 App Cas 371, at 386, 'that trustees exist for the benefit of those to whom the creator of the trust has given the trust estate'. Granted that the company of which he is an officer is trustee of a trust of which the beneficiaries are not only the husband and wife but also the children, issue etc, what nevertheless is more obvious than that Mr Anderson should impart such knowledge, and produce such documents in his possession, as are relevant to the debate in court as to the fair outcome of the financial dispute between the settlor (a beneficiary) and his wife (also a beneficiary)? Oppressive upon Mr Anderson and Mr Clay? Why? I cannot understand that point, even when articulated by Mr Singleton.

Excessive width

[56] The only part of the judge's request, as summarised in para [20], above, which is appealably too wide – and was quickly conceded to be so by Mr Pointer in this court – relates to the request, summarised at para [20](e), that Mr Anderson be required to divulge communications between Mr Clay on behalf of the husband and the trustee defined by a formula wider than the formulae defining the communications to be divulged between the husband himself and the trustee. Mr Pointer concedes that the request referable to communications with Mr Clay should be so modified as to run parallel with those referable to communications with the husband himself. At first I also doubted whether communications between the husband and the trustee, if any, about prospective investment decisions, referred to at para [20](c), above, would illumine the answer to the central (or indeed the subsidiary) question. On balance, however, I have been persuaded by Mr Pointer that the way in which any such communication has been phrased might so illumine it and that at any rate the exercise of the judge's

discretion in that regard cannot be impeached. In my view there is no appealably excessive width in the terms of the order for Mr Clay's attendance at the inspection appointment.

Conclusion

[57] Subject to the minor modification to the letter of request identified in para [56], above, I would dismiss the appeal.

LLOYD LJ:

[58] I agree with everything that my Lord, Wilson LJ has said in his judgment. I add only the following points.

[59] Mr Singleton opened the appeal to us as raising an issue of principle, namely whether the issue of letters of request is governed by different principles in the Family Division from those which apply in ordinary civil litigation in the Chancery Division and the Queen's Bench Division. He is right to submit that the principles on which the issue of subpoenas are issued, outgoing letters of request issued and incoming letters of request implemented are the same in all Divisions of the High Court. However, the nature of the issues in proceedings in the Family Division, at any rate in ancillary relief proceedings, is very different from those which arise in ordinary civil proceedings, not least because of the impact of s 25 of the 1973 Act. Accordingly it does not seem to me that it is surprising, or that it reveals a difference of underlying principle, that orders made in ancillary relief proceedings should produce what appear to be different results in practice from those that would obtain in ordinary civil litigation in the other Divisions. I am satisfied, for the reasons given by my Lord, that the object of the letter of request (like that of the inspection appointment) in the present case is, in the words of Sir Donald Nicholls V-C in the *George Michael* case, at 151, 'to compel the witness to produce evidence directly material to the issues in the case'.

[60] The Dragon Holdings Trust is a wide discretionary settlement whose only unusual feature, by the standards of normal English settlements of this kind, is that the settlor and his wife are beneficiaries. Their exclusion from an English settlement made by a UK-resident settlor would be desirable having regard to UK income tax legislation. Under this settlement, however, it is open to the trustee to appoint all or part of the capital to the settlor under cl 4(b). Moreover, there is, on the face of it, no reason to suppose that, if they were to do so, they would not be acting entirely properly as trustees and in accordance with the obligations incumbent on them as regards the exercise of discretionary powers. It is, therefore, unnecessary for the petitioner, wishing to establish that the respondent has access to the trust funds, in the sense described by Wilson LJ, above, at para [13] of his judgment, to allege any improper conduct or attitude on the part of the trustees. It was unwise to use language which implied that such a case was made (see para [12], above, of the judgment of Wilson LJ).

[61] There is no doubt that trustees can properly take into account any expression of wishes, formal or otherwise, on the part of the settlor as to how they should exercise their discretionary powers, and indeed that they should have regard to any such wishes expressed to them. Hitherto the only decision that the

trustees have taken as regards the disposition of any part of the fund is to treat the settlor as entitled to the income as it arises. This can be done without any formality under cl 3(b). It seems that this has been done throughout the life of the trust. The respondent says that he has not received any distribution since 1997, but it seems clear that this is of his own choice. Wilson LJ describes at para [11] what seems to be the latest position. What the position is in a formal sense may only be apparent once the trust accounts are seen, but it must be right to regard the respondent as having immediate access to the income of the fund. The fact (if it be so) that he has added it back from time to time to the trust fund does not alter the fact that it was, and for the time being remains, his to give away or to take for himself.

[62] It seems to me that, as the effective income beneficiary, the respondent must be entitled to see the accounts of the trust. We were told that some have been produced and disclosed but that he does not have the most recent accounts. On enquiring as to the attitude of the trustees to requests for production of documents, we were shown a response by the respondent to a questionnaire by the petitioner in which she asked, among other things, for a very widely described category of communications between the respondent and the successive trustees. He said that he had no such documents in his possession. He also said that his solicitors had asked the present trustee to produce the information requested, without result. The trustee's response was given as follows:

'They responded that they are not willing to produce these documents from their files as neither the Respondent nor the Petitioner has a right to these documents and they do not consider it to be in the interests of the trust for the trust to participate in a discovery procedure in the English court.'

[63] That request was put much more broadly than the letters of request which the judge has ordered to be issued. However, it may be that the trustee will respond along these lines if the Bermudian court accedes to the letters of request by ordering the trustee to produce documents and answer questions relating to them. If objection is taken by the trustee, it will be for the court in Bermuda to rule on it, by reference to the particular points taken as regards the particular obligations sought to be imposed as regards the production of documents and the giving of oral evidence. Nothing that this court says can, or should be taken as intended to, pre-empt or anticipate the decision of that court on whatever points are taken before it. Nevertheless, if the Bermudian court would be bound to recognise the validity of that objection on the part of the trustee it could be futile to issue the letters of request. It seems to me proper, therefore, to give some thought to whether such an objection would be bound to succeed.

[64] Traditionally, under the English law of trusts, trustees have been regarded as entitled to refuse to disclose to beneficiaries any document which bears on or might reveal their reasons for taking a particular decision in the exercise of a discretion over income or capital. However, inasmuch as there has been no such decision in the present case, except the appropriation of income to the respondent, of which neither the fact nor the propriety is in doubt, it does not seem to me that this proposition is likely to be relevant. Apart from documents of this nature, there is no general exception from the principle that a trustee must disclose accounts and other documents relating to the trust to a beneficiary. There are references in the books to other exceptions, such as where there is a conflict of

some kind between the interests of the trust, the beneficiaries as a whole and the trust fund on the one hand and those of the beneficiary seeking the information on the other, but no such point arises here.

[65] Another proposition that might have been advanced is that neither the respondent nor the petitioner is, in practice, more than a discretionary beneficiary, and that as such they are not entitled to see documents, even if a beneficiary having a vested interest of some kind, such as those who would receive capital in default of appointment, under cl 3(e), might be so entitled. Whether that is a fair classification of the respondent's position, he being the effective income beneficiary, is another matter. Even if it is, however, in the light of the decision of the Privy Council in *Schmidt v Rosewood Trust Ltd* [2003] UKPC 26, [2003] 2 AC 709, the proposition that a discretionary beneficiary does not have a sufficient interest to be entitled to disclosure does not hold good.

[66] If such a question were to arise in England in litigation between a beneficiary and the trustees, the court's decision would be taken after considering the sort of factors discussed by Lord Walker in *Schmidt* at para 54. Of course, the question which will arise, if the trustees raise it, in Bermuda on an order made to give effect to the letters of request (or on the question whether such an order should be made or, having been made, should be set aside) does not arise in litigation between a beneficiary and the trustees seeking disclosure. On the contrary, as Wilson LJ has explained, the question is whether the trustee should be required to provide the documentary and oral evidence in question for the purposes of and, in effect, as a witness in the course of a trial as between the petitioner and the respondent. One can see that, if the point is taken, cases concerning litigation between beneficiaries and trustees might be seen as relevant by way of analogy. All I need say for present purposes is that it does not seem to me that, if the trustee were to take such a point, it would be bound to succeed in persuading the court in Bermuda that the evidence ought not to be ordered to be given, so that it would be pointless to order that the letters of request be issued.

[67] The only other point I wish to add is this. The trustee's decisions ought to be made having regard to the best interests of the beneficiaries. In the absence of this evidence from the trustee, the judge at trial in England will have to draw inferences as to the likelihood that the respondent has access to the trust fund. In the nature of things the inferences drawn might not be accurate. If they are not accurate, they would be likely to lead to one or other of the petitioner and respondent, both of whom are beneficiaries, being treated on a false basis by the English court. In those circumstances, it seems to me that it could be open to the trustee to regard it as being positively in the interests of the beneficiaries that it should provide the evidence sought.

[68] For those reasons, and for those given by Wilson LJ, I too would dismiss this appeal, save for the narrowing of the category of material referred to in question 14.

SIR MARK POTTER P:

[69] I agree with both judgments and would only add this.

[70] This case has a number of features frequently encountered in ancillary relief claims by a wife whose highly successful former husband has, during the marriage, built up very substantial funds in a tax haven off-shore in the form of a discretionary trust administered by trustees endowed with discretion of the widest kind to administer the trust for the benefit of the beneficiaries including the settlor. The features of such a trust and the powers of its trustees have recently been clearly and helpfully described in a decision of the Royal Court of Jersey in *Re The Esteem Settlement* [2004] WTLR 1, particularly at paras 163–167.

[71] It is in the nature of such cases that, until the occasion of marriage breakdown and divorce, the wife has been content to leave the task of wealth creation to the husband as well as the arrangements for the protection of the family fortunes. Often the wife will be ignorant, or at any rate have minimal knowledge, in respect of such arrangements, save for knowledge that there is a substantial off-shore family trust administered by off-shore trustees in consultation with the husband or his accountant and a likelihood that the husband has immediate access to the trust funds in the *Browne v Browne* [1989] 1 FLR 291 sense. If, in ancillary proceedings following divorce, the court is to achieve a fair division or adjustment of the parties' assets in a situation where the wife is ignorant of the true asset position and dependent on the frankness and cooperation of a now disaffected and resistant husband, the issue of a letter of request addressed to the courts of the jurisdiction in which the discretionary trust is situate is a valuable means by which to obtain the necessary information. In my view, therefore, the court should in principle be receptive to an application by the wife in such a case where there is good reason to suppose that evidence of assistance to the court in its 'quasi-inquisitorial' role under s 25 of the 1973 Act may thereby be obtained.

[72] It is, after all, stated in r 2.51B(1) of the 1991 Rules that the ancillary relief rules have 'the overriding objective of enabling the court to deal with cases justly'. Rule 2.51B(2) goes on to say that dealing with a case justly includes, so far as it is practicable '(a) ensuring that the parties are on an equal footing'. It has often been said that one of the aims of the 1991 Rules, like the Civil Procedure Rules 1998, is to encourage a 'cards on the table' approach. In exercising its power and discretion to issue letters of request in appropriate cases under the provisions of RSC Ord 39, rr 2 and 3, the court should in my view be astute to assist a wife where, without such assistance, the cards of the husband are likely to remain face down and the true extent of his assets undisclosed.

[73] The essence of Mr Singleton's submissions rests upon the observations of Sir Donald Nicholls V-C in *Panayiotou v Sony Music Entertainment (UK) Ltd* [1994] Ch 142 (the *George Michael* case). That was a case where the issue of the letter of request was in order to obtain the production of a number of documents relevant to the issues in the action and it was acknowledged that, where the request was not a disguise for seeking discovery of documents, it was appropriately sought. However, in relation to particular documents sought, the Vice-Chancellor stated at 153F–154A as follows:

'I approach this application, therefore, on the footing that the plaintiffs are not entitled to seek what is in substance discovery. The letter for request must be confined to particular documents, although these may be described compendiously, as with the letters in *Lee v Angas* L.R.2 Eq. 59, 63.

I preface consideration of the documents sought by noting that particularity of identification or description is a matter of degree. The description used, moreover, may be important in another way: it may throw light on the purpose for which the documents in question are sought. The court should be astute to see that what is essentially a discovery exercise, whereby the applicant is seeking production of documents with a view to ascertaining whether they may be useful rather than with a view to adducing them in evidence as proof of some fact, is not disguised as an application to produce particular documents. Where an applicant has not seen the documents sought and does not know what they contain, the application can the more readily be characterised as a discovery exercise. Further, to be the subject of a letter of request the document must be admissible in evidence; it must be directly material to an issue in the action ...'

[74]   So far, so good. However, the Vice-Chancellor went on to say:

'... and the court must be satisfied that it does exist or did exist, and that it is likely to be in the possession of the person of whom production is being sought. Actual documents are to be contrasted with conjectural documents, which may or may not exist; see Lord Fraser in the *Asbestos* case [1985] 1 WLR 331, 338.'

[75]   It is these words which are relied on by Mr Singleton. He submits that they govern this case, and as such are fatal to the wife's application. If he is right, that seems to me a most unsatisfactory situation. It means that, although it would be legitimate as a matter of practice and procedure in this country to call Mr Anderson and ask him in the course of his evidence whether a certain document or class of documents exists and, if so, to produce them (they being material and admissible evidence), there is no power by means of letters of request to ask a foreign court to assist in that respect, if willing under its own rules of practice or procedure, to do so. While there may well be good reason in practice why that should be the position in inter parties litigation elsewhere than in the Family Division, it does not seem to me appropriate, unless it is unavoidable, to adopt the same approach in relation to financial proceedings following divorce, both for the reasons given by Wilson LJ at paras [46]–[49], above, and because of the overriding need to do justice between parties in an unequal position to which I have referred at the beginning of this judgment. None of the authorities to which we have been referred involved, or focused upon, the position in relation to ancillary relief claims in family cases.

[76]   The question whether the wording of s 2(4)(b) of the 1975 Act, which precludes the court from ordering production of documents 'other than particular documents specified in the order as being documents appearing to the court making the order to be or likely to be in his possession', precludes an order in this case is a different one from the question whether the request is objectionable as 'fishing' or a disguised exercise in pre-trial discovery. It is a separate and narrower question. As Sir Donald Nicholls V-C observed in the *George Michael* case at 152B:

'Paragraph (a) excludes discovery. Paragraph (b) narrows the ambit of the order even further.'

[77]   So far as the form of the requests in this case is concerned, they have been compressed and summarised at para [20] of the judgment of Wilson LJ, above. However, they appear fully set out in Annexe 1 to the letter of request, which clearly identifies the documents or class of documents required to be produced on the premise of a positive reply to questions requested to be addressed to Mr Anderson. I am satisfied that the documents are sufficiently identified and described to satisfy the requirement for particularity set out in s 2(4)(b) of the 1975 Act and that they are likely to be in Mr Anderson's possession.

[78]   Thus the critical question is whether the fact that the documents are 'conjectural', in the sense that at this stage the court cannot (prior to the examination of Mr Anderson) be satisfied that they do or did exist, should be fatal to the wife's application. For the reasons already given by Wilson LJ, I do not think it should. I would dismiss the appeal.

Appeal dismissed.

Solicitors: *Withers LLP* for the appellant
               Manches for the respondent

ROBERT CROSSLEY
Law Reporter

CHARMAN v CHARMAN (No 2)

[2006] EWHC 1879 (Fam), [2007] 1 FLR 593, FD

Family Division

Coleridge J

27 July 2006

Financial provision – Application of the guidelines in the Matrimonial Causes Act 1973 –Unequal division – Exceptional contribution – Meaning and relevance of conduct – Whether discretionary trust intended to create dynastic wealth to be included in matrimonial property

When the husband and wife married in 1976, aged 23 and 22 respectively, they had no assets of any value and lived, initially, with the wife's parents. By the time they separated 30 years later, the husband had generated wealth to the tune of £150–160m. £6m of that was in the wife's name, £30m or more was in a trust for the parties' two adult children and the remaining £125m or so was either in the husband's ownership or in the Dragon Holdings Trust. Both parties had lavish homes. The wife sought capital provision bringing her fortune up to at least 45% of the total value of the assets owned by herself, the husband and the Dragon Trust – a total of around £59m. She argued that the marriage had been a long one, that all the wealth had been generated from scratch, that she had played a full part as wife and mother and that, if the court were to take into account the husband's special contribution in generating the wealth, she would accept a division of 45:55. The husband offered to pay her a sum which would bring her assets up to £20m. He asserted: that the assets owned by the Dragon Trust should be left entirely out of account because they had been deposited by him as part of his intention to found a 'dynastic trust' for the benefit of as yet unborn members of the family; that the court should not use a split of 50:50 as a starting point; that the wife's award should reflect the fact that she failed to support him in business endeavours during the marriage and, latterly, refused to move with him to Bermuda; that the wife's calculations of assets did not take proper discounts (to reflect the lack of marketability of some investments) into account; and that, in any event, he had made a stellar contribution which should be recognised by a special premium in the post-marriage division.

Held – awarding the wife a total of about £48m (just under 37% of the total) and the husband just over 63% –

(1) Although the marriage was a long one with both parties playing their full part and all the wealth effectively being created during its subsistence, the case fell into that very small category where, wholly exceptionally, the created wealth was of extraordinary proportions and arose from extraordinary talent and energy. Each party to a marriage was entitled to a fair share of the available property and the search was always for what fairness required in the particular case.

Nonetheless, the yardstick of equality was to be applied as an aid not a rule. Taking everything into account the assets were to be divided as above (see paras [127] and [128]).

(2) Under the balancing exercise of s 25 of the Matrimonial Causes Act 1973, the assets in the Dragon Trust were a resource and part of the main schedule of assets for consideration (a spouse could not remove half of the assets accumulated during a marriage without the consent of the other on the basis of a letter of dynastic wishes); in relation to s 25(2)(g), lesser misconduct, as alleged here, could not be allowed to seep into any case; when considering contributions under s 25(2)(f), the source of the assets may be taken into account but its importance will diminish over time. If the assets were not generated by the joint effort of the parties or were 'family' assets, then the duration of the marriage may justify a departure from the yardstick of equality. The nature and source of the property and the way the couple have run their lives may be taken into account in deciding how it should be shared. Thus conduct and contribution were opposite sides of the same coin – conduct was apt to describe not only misconduct but any conduct which stared the court in the face and could not be ignored without creating unfairness. The husband's extraordinary talent had, exceptionally and in fairness, to be taken into account (see paras [58], [109], [111]).

Per curiam: a tariff of percentage bands which decreased as the size of extraordinary fortunes increased might prove to be a helpful guidance and, ultimately, no less fair than the current expensive uncertainty (see para [136]).

Statutory provisions considered
Matrimonial Causes Act 1973, ss 1(2)(b), 23, 25
European Convention for the Protection of Human Rights and Fundamental Freedoms 1950, Protocol 1, Art 1

Cases referred to in judgment
Conran v Conran [1997] 2 FLR 615, FD
Cowan v Cowan [2001] EWCA Civ 679, [2002] Fam 97, [2001] 3 WLR 684, [2001] 2 FLR 192, CA
Esteem Settlement, Re [2004] WTLR 1, Jersey RC
G v G (Financial Provision: Equal Division) [2002] EWHC 1339 (Fam), [2002] 2 FLR 1143, FD
Kokosinski v Kokosinski [1980] Fam 72, [1980] 3 WLR 55, (1980) 1 FLR 205, [1980] 1 All ER 1106, FD
Lambert v Lambert [2002] EWCA Civ 1685, [2003] Fam 103, [2003] 2 WLR 631, [2003] 1 FLR 139, [2003] 4 All ER 342, CA
Miller v Miller; McFarlane v McFarlane [2006] UKHL 24, [2006] 2 AC 618, [2006] 2 WLR 1283, [2006] 1 FLR 1186, [2006] 3 All ER 1, HL
Sorrell v Sorrell [2005] EWHC 1717 (Fam), [2006] 1 FLR 497, FD
White v White [2001] 1 AC 596, [2000] 3 WLR 1571, [2000] 2 FLR 981, [2001] 1 All ER 1, HL

Martin Pointer QC, James Ewins and *Rebecca Bailey Harris* for the wife
Barry Singleton QC, Deborah Eaton and *Deepak Nagpal* for the husband

Cur adv vult

COLERIDGE J:

Introduction

[1] In the recent House of Lords decision in the case of *Miller v Miller; McFarlane v McFarlane* [2006] UKHL 24, [2006] 2 AC 618, [2006] 1 FLR 1186 (*Miller/McFarlane*) Baroness Hale considered that the size of the fortune in the *Miller* case (about £17.5m) put it in the category of a 'very big money case' (para [149]). Adopting a similar categorisation for this case leads to a description, perhaps, of a 'huge money case'. The overall assets even on the most pessimistic presentation exceed £100m.

[2] John Charman (the husband) and Beverley Charman (the wife) are only 5 months apart in age. They are both 53. They met at school as teenagers in 1969/70. In 1973 when they were about 20 they became engaged. By then they were both working. They married in 1976 when the husband was 23 and the wife 22. They made their first home with the wife's parents but within months moved into their own home. When they married, apart from their respective earning capacities, they had no assets of any particular value.

[3] In November 2003, 30 years after they became engaged, the husband and wife separated. By the time the hearing of this application began in February 2006, by the wife's calculation, the husband had generated wealth to the tune of £150–160m although by then it was by no means all in his name. So, for example, nearly £6m of that sum was in wife's name. £25m–£30m (or may be more) was held in a trust for the parties' children. The remaining £125m or so was either in the husband's ownership (about £56m) or in a trust called the Dragon Holdings Trust (£68m) (the Dragon Trust).

[4] This application by the wife seeks capital provision bringing her fortune up to at least 45% of the total value of the assets owned by herself, the husband and the Dragon Trust. In round terms that is just about £53m on top of her present £6m, ie a total of £59m. The husband does not accept the wife's calculations and has offered to pay the wife a sum to bring her assets up to a total of £20m. So simple arithmetic shows that about £40m turns on the resolution of the various significant issues in the application. That, as I say, even by today's standards in this division, makes the common but unattractive description, 'big money case,' something of an understatement so far as this application is concerned.

[5] The wife's case is the now familiar one. She says this was a long marriage during which all the wealth (however now held) was generated from scratch. She played her full part as wife and mother (of two now adult sons). Fairness dictates that the fortune generated during their marriage (apart from the sum set aside in trust for the children) should be split 50:50. However, in deference to very recent authority she is prepared to accept a 45/55% split to recognise what has come to be called the husband's special/stellar contribution to the generation of the wealth if, despite her submissions, the court were to hold that in this case that is a factor properly to be taken into account in the divisionary process.

[6] The husband resists the application, defending his position on every front.

[7]　First, he asserts that the assets owned by the Dragon Trust should be left entirely out of account because they were deposited there by him as part of his long-term plan and intention to found a 'dynastic trust' for the benefit of as yet unborn members of the family (the children having been already provided for by their own trusts).

[8]　Secondly, whatever the recent authorities may or may not say, he does not accept a 50:50 starting point/cross check. He says the court should proceed from the position that the wife is entitled to nothing except as ordered by the court and the court should not be deflected from an incremental approach by talk of any particular percentage entitlement, let alone 50:50. Since *Miller/McFarlane* he also invites the court to consider carefully whether all the assets in the case really fall into the same category for allocation between the parties. The business assets are to be looked at differently, he says.

[9]　Thirdly, he says the wife's award should reflect or be reduced by the fact that she failed to support him in his business endeavours during the marriage and, as part and parcel of that argument, at the end of the marriage refused to move with him to the tax haven of Bermuda to avoid a massive potential Capital Gains Tax claim. She should not anyway benefit from that tax saving, he says.

[10]　Fourthly, he says that the wife's calculations of the wealth take no account of proper discounts which should be applied to the valuation of his assets to reflect the lack of marketability of some of the investments he and the Trust hold in Axis, the insurance company he has built up since 2001.

[11]　Fifthly, and in any event, he asserts that he has made a special/stellar contribution which should lead the court to award him a special bonus/premium in the post-marriage division. Thus, departure from equality is fully justified.

[12]　Those are the significant issues between the parties. Plainly the resolution of each one either way could carry expensive financial implications. I shall decide them as they arise during the course of this judgment. Finally he asserts that taking assets from him, potentially, infringes his rights to enjoy his possessions is breach of his 'Human Rights'.

The hearing and the evidence

[13]　The hearing lasted a total of 9 days and had a number of unusual features. In the first place, it was divided into two parts (in February and May) because it was anticipated, rightly, that House of Lords decisions in the pending cases of *Miller/MacFarlane* might throw some much needed light onto the proper approach to the 'conduct' and 'special contribution' debates which have been bedevilling these cases since *Cowan v* Cowan [2001] EWCA Civ 679, [2002] Fam 97, [2001] 2 FLR 192. This was in the context that the wife had made a written concession that she would not contend for a greater share than 45% of the assets if 'special contribution' as a concept survived the *Miller/MacFarlane* decisions. Accordingly it was agreed that judgment should be reserved following the hearing in February until the House of Lords had delivered their decision. Further written and oral submissions followed the House of Lords delivering their decision on 24 May 2006.

[14]   Secondly, and unusually, every word of the final hearing was professionally transcribed and produced in written form within hours of its being spoken by a witness, counsel or myself. This was a luxury which very few cases require or can stand but in this case, for reasons which will be apparent, it was helpful.

[15]   The evidence was partly written and partly oral. The written evidence (Forms E, statements, reports from experts and numerous assorted documents) was contained in 14 coloured lever arch files provided to the court.

[16]   Many other documents (13 other files) which had arisen during the interlocutory stages of the case were not included in the main trial bundles provided to the court in the interests of manageability. Instead a useful innovation was employed during the trial. It was Bundle N known as the 'Elevation bundle'. This contained other documents not included in the main bundles but 'elevated' there during the course of the hearing by one side or the other as a result of reference being made to them in examination or submission. Its lettered dividers matched the unused bundles so that their origin could be identified. By the end of the hearing it was about one-third full. So far as the advocates are concerned, such a bundle has an advantage over a more conventional core bundle because it does not alert the opposition to the presence of a forensic man-trap lying inconspicuously in the long grass of the more peripheral written material. Whilst the element of surprise is nowadays regarded as a device to be discouraged in the interests of promoting settlement, occasionally it can still be useful and legitimate providing the documents have at the appropriate stage been disclosed.

[17]   The oral evidence was from the wife, husband, forensic accountants and a pension expert. At the start of the hearing there were four other supporting witnesses on the witness template. Two for the wife (dealing with her supportive role as the wife of a business man) and two for the husband (dealing with his extraordinary skills in the world of high risk insurance). In the end, I having read them and given a sotto voce judicial hint, none of them was called. I doubted whether further oral examination of these witnesses would advance either case on the points about which they could speak given that there was no competing evidence on the points.

[18]   No mention of the material provided to me would be complete without reference to the written opening and closing statements/memoranda/submissions (and chronologies) provided by the teams of counsel and solicitors for both parties at the beginning and end of both parts of the hearing. They, together with the multi coloured asset and other schedules (in the husband's case laminated for durability in the style of a restaurant menu) have been simply invaluable.

The wife and husband

[19]   Before coming to the background to this application in detail I shall say something of the parties. Common to both of them was an immense feeling of hurt and pain surrounding the marriage breakdown which, I detected, still lingers. As a result extraneous issues/evidence found their way into the application which have caused added bitterness. Both sides blame the other for the fact that the children have become involved. The husband is genuinely bemused that the wife should regard his £20m offer as anything other than reasonable, even generous.

Her refusal to compromise on his terms has led him to deploy every available point to protect what he regards as his wealth generated entirely by his efforts. In the narrow, old fashioned sense that perspective is understandable if somewhat anachronistic. Nowadays it must attract little sympathy.

[20]   It has also meant that the court has been asked to examine closely aspects of the psychological dynamic of the marriage partnership in a way nowadays almost unheard of. At times the hearing almost took on the form of a defended divorce. I mention this now (as well as later) because it explains the husband's approach to the case and affected too his evidence.

[21]   Both wife and husband were careful witnesses. She is a quiet, even reticent, woman but steady and determined. The husband is a dynamic, energetic, self-made entrepreneur. Both are utterly different in their personality and approach to the priorities of life. Neither approach can possibly be said to be right or wrong, good or bad. Both are equally valid but of course their very difference created tension and conflict within this long marriage which unresolved and without compromise on both sides has eventually led to its destruction.

[22]   I find, where there is a difference of recollection, that the wife is to be preferred. That is especially so where the detailed events and conversations relating to the ending of the marriage and the husband's move to Bermuda are concerned. His written evidence on these points is less reliable and in his oral evidence he, from time to time, accepted that.

The background and chronology

[23]   Both sides have produced detailed chronologies and summaries of the background drawn from the statements and documents. There is little distinction, other than emphasis, to be drawn between them. I am not going to set out the whole history of the marriage at such length. They can be taken to be part of my consideration of the whole background picture. Accordingly I shall only now mention dates and facts which are required so that this judgment can be free standing.

[24]   The husband was born in 1952 and the wife in 1953 so both are now 53. As I have indicated they met in 1969/1970 and started working in 1971 having left school. The husband soon found a position as a junior in the marine box at Sturge underwriters at Lloyd's. The wife worked for Legal and General. In 1972 she became a civil servant. In 1973 the parties became engaged. In 1975 the husband became a deputy marine underwriter.

[25]   The parties married on 28 February 1976. They owned almost nothing and went to live with the wife's parents. Later that year they bought a small house in Strood, Kent for £14,500 on a mortgage.

[26]   The house in Strood was the first of four homes ending in the purchase in 1987 of Dell House, Sevenoaks, Kent. This was their home until separation in 2003.

[27]   The husband returned to Sturge as a deputy underwriter in 1977. In 1981 he moved to a position with Scottish Lion Insurance, a company owned by the wealthy Tung family of Hong Kong. The husband maintains that his approach to both business and family matters was considerably affected by his contact with that family. He explained that both in his written and oral evidence.

[28]   In 1986 the husband returned to Lloyd's and acquired the Posgate & Denby syndicate for £700,000 using borrowed money. He became an underwriting member of Lloyd's by virtue of a charge over the party's then matrimonial home Cherry Bank, Bearsted, Kent. The husband maintains that the wife was a little slow to embrace his requirement for the use of the jointly owned home as collateral. The wife admits that she took about 24 hours to make up her mind before signing. Her caution, if such it be, in this respect seems to me to be reasonable, prudent and proportionate given the state of the parties' finances at the time. However the husband's criticism of the wife in this regard is a nice illustration of their difference of approach to life generally.

[29]   Six years after the marriage, in May 1982, Nicholas the eldest son was born, so he is now nearly 24. Michael was born in April 1987 and so is 19. The wife ceased paid employment prior to the birth of Nicholas. She has not since resumed a paid position. In 1994 she became a lay magistrate and is now a chairman of her local bench.

[30]   Charman Underwriting Agencies Ltd was formed in 1986. This was the start of the transformation of the parties' financial circumstances. Dell House was bought the following year for £475,000.

[31]   On 16 November 1987, the husband created the two main trusts in this case; the Dragon Holdings Trust and the JR Charman Children's Settlement. The husband explained to me that he hoped and intended to generate substantial asset value and these vehicles were a natural part of the planning. Both settlements were established at that time in Jersey.

[32]   In 1994, as a result of the restructuring undertaken at Lloyds, Tarquin was formed and 25% of Charman Underwriting was sold to Tarquin Ltd, by way of an exchange of shares. Each of the husband, the Dragon Holdings Trust and the Children's Settlement disposed of part of their respective shareholdings in Charman Underwriting.

[33]   In November 1995, the balance of the shares in Charman Underwriting were sold to Tarquin Ltd for a combination of cash and further shares in Tarquin.

[34]   In 1998 Tarquin Ltd was sold to Ace, a large international Bermuda incorporated insurance company listed on the New York Stock Exchange, for about $575m (£350m). The husband became a director of Ace and the senior executive outside the USA, based in the UK. Consequently, the husband, the Dragon Holdings Trust and the Children's Settlement all became the holders of substantial blocks of shares in Ace Ltd.

[35]   In October 2000 the Children's Settlement sold 502,000 shares in Ace for £13.4m. Apart from that disposal, the husband and the trusts retained their

holdings in Ace; and in fact received additional shares over the 5 years from 1998 under a combination of a dividend re-investment plan, the award of additional shares and the exercise of options.

[36]   In March 2001 the husband left Ace Ltd. It seems that there was a clash of management styles between the husband and two other directors. The consequence was that the husband was summarily removed from his position. The husband was distressed by the circumstances in which he came to be removed from that company and as is often the case when parties to a marriage face a common threat, they drew close. The wife gave the husband considerable emotional support at the time.

[37]   It is the husband's contention that he was unfairly dismissed by Ace and certainly by 16 May 2001 the husband had negotiated severance terms of a total value of £4.2m.

[38]   During this time (ie in the months before '9/11') the husband was approached by Marsh & McLennan to set up a new global insurance company based in Bermuda.

[39]   Axis Specialty Ltd was incorporated in Bermuda on 8 November 2001. '9/11' accelerated the setting up and development process and it formally began trading on 20 November 2001. The husband was appointed CEO and was paid a founder's fee of $2.5m.

[40]   Axis was launched with funding of $2.5b, of which $200m was from Marsh & McLennan itself and the balance from finance houses in New York. The husband invested $20m partly from the Dragon Holdings Trust and partly from the Children's Settlement.

[41]   The husband's employment had for years entailed him spending much time abroad. But following the decision to launch the new insurance company this increased. There is some dispute about events and conversations at this time but I find that in October 2001 (at a time when they were on holiday in Venice) he told the wife that he would be travelling to Bermuda each week but only for about 6 months during the period the business was being set up . In fact he spent about 3 days a week there from autumn 2001.

[42]   During 2002 the husband's absences abroad were the cause of real tension between the parties and in late 2002 he told her he intended to limit his travelling to Bermuda to once a month. However, from then onwards in fact he spent most of his time abroad. By January 2003 the husband had evidently decided that he was no longer resident in the UK for tax purposes for, when he reported the date of his change of residence to the Inland Revenue, he gave that as 27 January 2003.

[43]   Meanwhile the development of Axis proceeded apace. On 9 December 2002, Axis Holdings Ltd was formed as the new holding company.

[44]   The husband and the Trust were still considerable shareholders in Ace. In a programme of disposals from February 2003 to February 2004 those shares were all liquidated. The summary table prepared by the wife's team shows the position nicely:

Vendor	No of shares in Ace Ltd that are sold	Sale proceeds in cash £
H	1,073,500	22,163,333.28
Dragon Holdings Trust	1,720,805	36,792,945.00
Children's Settlement	261,037	5,575,750.32
Total		£59,532,028.60

[45]   As part of his decision to move abroad the husband arranged to export the family trusts from Jersey to Bermuda. In February 2003 Conyers Dill and Pearman, Bermuda attorneys, were formally instructed to effect the shift which took place in April 2003. The wife remained in ignorance of these emigration plans and steps until May 2003.

[46]   In July 2003 Axis Capital Holdings Ltd was floated on the New York Stock Exchange.

[47]   Somewhat inconsistent with the husband's apparent emigration plans, in September 2003 the parties agreed to buy another, larger house in Sevenoaks which they had both always had an eye on, Stormont Court. On 24 September 2003 the parties agreed to buy it for £3.5m. In October 2003, in the course of discussion about the husband's absences, he told her he did not want to live in Bermuda.

[48]   Despite these conversations, on 14 November 2003 the husband told the wife by telephone that he regarded the marriage as over. He told her that he had established his residence in Bermuda and that he was not coming back to the UK. This was confirmed in writing on 26 November 2003 and, on the same day, the wife told the owners of Stormont Court that the purchase would not proceed.

[49]   The husband seeks to rely on the failure of the wife to remove with him to Bermuda at the end of the marriage and her attitude to his work during the marriage. However, many of the facts relating to these matters are very much in issue. I shall resolve those issues, to the extent necessary, later in this judgment when dealing with the relevance of conduct/contribution within the s 25 analysis.

[50]   The wife filed a petition for divorce (s 1(2)(b) of the Matrimonial Causes Act 1973) in London on 28 June 2004 and the correspondence between the parties' respective London solicitors began in July.

[51]   However, the husband preferred the divorce to take place in Bermuda and to that end filed a petition there on 26 August 2004. The following day he filed an Answer here, seeking a stay of the English proceedings. The wife sought a '*Hemain*' undertaking which was not forthcoming and indeed the husband then took numerous steps to progress the Bermuda suit. This early skirmishing (the details of which now no longer matter) ended in an application by the wife for a *Hemain* injunction which I heard and granted on 24 September 2004. Since that time I have heard all interlocutory applications (save for the FDR) including one by the husband that I should recuse myself.

[52]   On 11 February 2005, I refused the husband's application for a stay of the English proceedings and I also dealt with the wife's application for maintenance pending suit. I gave the husband the option of paying at the rate of £360,000 p a or of paying £5m on account instead. He chose the latter course and this is source of the sum of capital which the wife still has. In my judgment this optional approach is the best way of dealing with interim provision in these very large cases.

[53]   The only other interlocutory step of significance was the wife's application for the issue of letters of request directed ultimately to the trustees in Bermuda to investigate the husband's assertion that the Dragon Trust was and had always been considered to be a 'dynastic trust' and so, arguable in a different category from the other resources of the husband.

[54]   On 20 October 2005, despite the husband's vigorous resistance, I granted the request. He appealed to the Court of Appeal but the appeal was dismissed by a series of reserved, detailed and closely reasoned judgments. However, all this forensic activity was to no avail because the judge in Bermuda, Bell J, somewhat churlishly in my view, declined to assist the English Court in the face of opposition from the trustees. He would not order/permit the production of documents by the trustees. He thus rendered any examination of the trustees largely nugatory. There was no time before this hearing for an appeal to be heard in Bermuda against that rather parochial decision of the Bermuda judge.

[55]   Finally, on 6 February 2006 the husband announced that he would retire when he is 55 'as a direct result of the legal action taken by the wife'. That would be 2008. A press release followed to like effect. It remains to be seen whether the husband in the end will adhere to that expressed intention. It is an indication of the underlying strength of Axis that the husband's announcement of his departure has had no adverse affect on its share price.

[56]   So, as matters now stand, the husband is based in Bermuda and America but still travelling extensively. He has formed a relationship with another woman. That may have been the catalyst for the final ending of the marriage but it was not the cause of its breakdown. The husband has bought two large homes in America; Atlanta and Palm Beach. He also rents a property in Bermuda.

[57]   The wife remains in Sevenoaks in Dell House. There is no dispute that she should keep it. Nicholas is studying at Birkbeck College in London, his younger brother, Michael is working with his father in Bermuda.

The statutory 'balancing exercise'

[58]   Section 25 of the Matrimonial Causes 1973 rules the day. And despite the endless judicial gloss which is applied to it year in and year out at every level it is always best to start and end in that familiar section. The first consideration is as always the children but they are so amply provided for that they call for no special mention.

[59]   For some mysterious reason the final figure for the Children's Trust has not been forthcoming despite the husband having, apparently, recently asked for it.

The wife calculates it by updating previous disclosure at about £37.7m. The latest actual disclosure put it at nearer £26m. Either way the adult children's financial needs for the rest of their lives need form no part of the main debate between the husband and wife.

[60]   The obvious starting point for all these applications is the financial position of the parties now. I turn to consider the assets one by one and the issues attendant upon them

The parties resources (assets, liabilities, earning capacity): Section 25(1)(a)

[61]   I have referred to the excellent schedules produced by the diligence of counsel and provided to me in hard copy and electronically. For convenience, as an index, I shall use the pro forma provided to me at the conclusion and headed 'Judge's Asset schedule' and work down it item by item. The value of some of the assets and differences between the parties are, in the context of the huge figures in this case very small. I shall avoid hair splitting and nit-picking (as indeed parties in these cases should endeavour to do). Swings and roundabouts are always present. The completed schedule will be attached to this judgment.

[62]   Dell House. A recent valuation by the agreed valuer asserts £2.75m as the current value. The husband thinks that is on the low side. He may be right but in the context of the figures in this case the difference is immaterial. I shall use the valuer's figure.

The husbands American properties: Palm Beach and Atlanta

[63]   The husband proposes the original 2004 purchase prices. The wife wants to adjust them by applying published local house price indices. The husband's figures are, unlike many of the figures in the case, hard numbers. I adopt them unchanged. House price indices are only the broadest of guides based on averages. Having seen the photographs I doubt these houses are very average.

[64]   Willicombe House. This is a property occupied by the wife's parents. It has an agreed value of £575,000. The wife wants to discount that to take account of her mother's age and because she says it is not readily available to her. I shall be considering discounts for lack of immediate saleability in the context of the Axis interests later. Where, as here, there is no pressing need to liquidate assets, discounts need, I consider, to be approached with caution in this jurisdiction. The wife will extract full value in the fullness of time. No discount is warranted here.

[65]   The figures for the bank accounts and smaller investments are not in dispute. The wife's current bank balance derives from the interim arrangement forming part of the order of 11 February 2005. I have included the figures as they appear on the schedule. The figure for the husband's tax liabilities is now also not in dispute (subject to para [94], below); £1,835,000. There is the familiar argument about adding back the paid legal costs. Where they form, as a proportion of the whole financial cake, a significant tranche that may make good sense especially where the bills are very different. The costs in this case are, of course, very high but not as a proportion of the whole. I have decided therefore to ignore them.

Personal possessions

[66] The husband's opening position was that a figure of £692,375 should be included as part of the wife's assets to take account primarily of the value of the contents of Dell House, her jewellery and the car. The wife suggested these figures should be ignored in the conventional way. However, each has reversed their position, because as a result of last minute disclosure during the hearing it became apparent that the husband had spent £2.4m on furnishing his houses and buying jewellery etc. Unsurprisingly he would now prefer to adopt the wife's original suggestion! The figures are now too large just to be ignored. Ignoring cars, a reasonable figure for furniture, bearing in mind these are insurance values or purchase prices, for the wife is £400,000 and for the husband £1,250,000.

Pensions

[67] Relatively speaking, the values are not very significant in this case and I think with a bit more give and take on each side figures should have been capable of agreement. The husband has a pension entitlement (SERA) by virtue of his employment with Axis together with a further pension from previous employment with an agreed value of £271,000. The SERA is in the nature of a contractual income entitlement. So both sides have advanced valuations of the expected income stream. I heard live evidence on the matter. It all boils down to the rate of return to be applied to an imaginary capital fund which would produce this income (the discount rate). The higher the return, the lower the value of the fund. By this route the husband now (his expert moved during the hearing) contends for a discount rate of 10% producing a value of £1,906,898. The wife's 7% produces £2,437,215. The contentions on both sides are all completely theoretical but equally well-reasoned and arguable. I hope I shall be forgiven for splitting the difference. I shall take the figure of £2,442,000 including the agreed extra figure of £271,000.

2005 bonus

[68] This had been earned but not paid by the time of the hearing. I suspect by now it has been paid. It is in sterling terms £785,000. The husband asserts that it should be ignored as it is income not capital. But the husband has a salary in excess of £702,000 as well as stock awards. Distinction between income and capital when the figures are this large is artificial. I shall include it.

Accumulated income from Dragon Trust

[69] This is income which on any view can be called for by the husband because the trustees have always allocated him the income albeit that he has not historically (except for very small amounts) called for it or needed it. If, of course, at the end of the day I include the whole of the Dragon Trust assets in the overall amount for division it makes no difference where on the schedule this sum of £4,045,000 is included. However, if a distinction is to be drawn then, says the wife, this amount is the husband's anyhow. I think it is properly regarded as in a slightly different category from the rest of the trust assets so I shall include it on this part

of the schedule as an asset of the husband. It might have added significance if enforcement of an order becomes seriously problematic.

Axis interests and the Dragon Trust

[70] This is where the really significant financial/valuation issues repose. The husband contends for the exclusion of the entirety of the value of the assets held by the Dragon Trust. On his figures that is in excess of £57,000,000 (ignoring notional 'Bermuda' tax savings). By the wife's calculations it would exclude just under £68m, i e over half the assets in the case. Within both those Dragon figures there are agreed non Axis assets of £39,397,000.

[71] I shall deal with that issue now because if Dragon is to be left out of account the valuation debate relating to the value of the Axis interests becomes altogether less important to the overall outcome.

[72] It has been the husband's contention from early in the proceedings that Dragon assets should be ignored. He says they are in a different category from the rest of his assets and have always been so regarded by himself. And, furthermore, he says, the trustees have known about his views throughout. I do no justice to the detailed and careful arguments advanced for (and against) the husband's case that Dragon was a dynastic trust and should, accordingly be ring-fenced from consideration by the court. Mr Singleton amplifies them fully on pp 3–8 of his closing submissions. Mr Pointer sets out on p 103 et seq (a)–(v) and pp 109–111 of his submissions his detailed refutation of the husband's position. This judgment will not benefit from extensive reproduction of the arguments. I have the points on both sides fully in mind.

[73] At the end of the day I have come to the conclusion that the husband's arguments fail both on the facts and as a matter of principle.

[74] On the facts: the evidence far from supporting the husband's case seems to me to undermine it. The failure to indicate any such dynastic plan on the face of any of the letters of wishes drafted at any time since Dragon's inception is, quite frankly, incredible if it underlay the trust's true purpose. At all times the trust has been in the hands of paid professional offshore trustees. Would they have allowed this fundamental matter to have remained undocumented? I think not. I reproduce a short passage of the transcript:

'Q.   As you told the judge a year ago, your view always was that you were not going to see old bones?
A.   Sorry, what did you say?
Q.   You never thought you would live to an old age?
A.   No, I said I had never expected longevity because my father died when he was 45. I never expected that longevity was something that I could rely on.
Q.   That is what I am saying to you.
A.   No, that's not. It meant I had a great regard for every day that I woke up and lived my life.
Q.   There is nothing there about ongoing generations, is there?
A.   No, I didn't think that there needed to be. I've said it time and time again.

Q   How on earth was anybody going to understand that this was your abiding
           ambition then?
A.   The greatest risk I faced, my Lord, is the fact that I died, and I was far too
           busy trying to create value to worry about my demise.
Q.   You cannot have cared too much about –
A.   I did care.
Q.   – your ambition, because it is an extraordinary – I do not mean that in a
           disbelieving sense – it is an extraordinary ambition to wish to leave half
           your fortune to people who are yet to be born.
A.   But, my Lord –
Q.   That would not be the natural behaviour of people left behind if you were
           to fall under a bus or crash into the sea to think, "Well, we are not going to
           benefit his heirs, we are going to hold it all and keep it away from them".
A.   But that was my intent, my Lord.
Q.   You kept it to yourself though.
A.   I did, I am afraid. That is what I said yesterday, if I had known that I would
           be sitting here today and poring over documents that have been produced
           over the last –
Q.   That is not much of an answer. That is really not much of an answer,
           Mr Charman. Nobody in the world knew that this was an ambition of
           yours, it was not written down anywhere. How was anybody going to act to
           bring about this intention? It is no good harbouring some deep intention if
           no one in the world knows about it, is it?
A.   At that time that was a risk I was prepared to take, my Lord.
Q.   It is not only that time, it is throughout the entire life of the trust?
A.   No, I had told Alec Anderson when I went to Bermuda – my Lord, if you
           go back to Codan, I had a very limited number of discussions with Codan.'

[75] I am bound to say having now heard and read everything about Dragon I
remain sceptical about the husband's actions or lack of them. Nor do I readily
accept the husband's plea when I contemplate the Herculean struggle put up by
him and his team to *prevent* co-operation from the very people who, in all normal
circumstances would have been expected to support it. His eleventh hour change
of heart and approach to the trustees (on the eve of the trial) in Bermuda was also
unconvincing. So if the husband harboured this as a settled and real intention
from the outset, the lack of a single piece of supporting documentary evidence
from any quarter is truly remarkable. Mr Pointer stresses the absence of any of the
steps which the husband could have taken along the way to make sure that this
intention was realised. None of them was very complex. Indeed only a little simple
drafting was required.

[76] The wife also knew nothing of this plan. I am satisfied having heard her
evidence that she would not have deliberately concealed this if she had heard of it.
Her evidence is straightforward and her recollection good.

[77] So I find that, on the facts, this part of the husband's case fails. These assets
are no more 'dynastic' than any other part of the husband's immense fortune
which will inevitably be handed on for many generations to come after 'he has
shuffled off this mortal coil' (*Hamlet*).

[78] But even if I had been persuaded of the existence of this as a settled, even documented intention I am doubtful in the circumstances of this case whether, of itself, it would have been very influential in the result.

[79] The test is whether the assets in the trust should be regarded by the court as a 'resource'. That is a very broad definition. These assets are held in a discretionary trust in conventional form. I will not repeat the very helpful descriptive analysis of such a trust in the Jersey High Court adopted by Potter P in his judgment dismissing the husband's appeal against my order relating to letters of request.[1] (See *Re Esteem Settlement* [2004] WTLR 1). It is a very useful description of general application in cases like this. And as Lloyd LJ on the same occasion pointed out the assets in the trust 'could be available to him on demand without being his money', as Mr Singleton was constrained to agree.

[80] So even if the husband had got home on the facts, for the Court simply to have ignored the assets would have been, I consider, wrong and, in my experience, entirely novel.

[81] Can a spouse remove from consideration under s 25 of the Matrimonial Causes Act 1973, at the stroke of, for example a letter of wishes, half the assets accumulated during a marriage without the consent of the other spouse? At the end of a marriage of this length for a spouse to be excluded from benefit by such an informal arrangement even if consensual and created at the time when the marriage was sound would be grotesquely unfair. He or she must be able to say, surely, in such circumstances:

> 'whatever may have been your/our intentions then, now that the marriage is over I have changed my mind and these assets must be on the table for consideration like all the others. I will decide following receipt of my portion what I want to do with them and whom I want to benefit now and in the future.'

[82] So in the end I am persuaded by Mr Pointer's arguments and all the assets in the Dragon Trust will remain well and truly on the main schedule.

[83] I turn to the valuation of Axis shares, option and warrants within and without Dragon. Both sides have employed the services of household-name accountancy firms to assist them. Price Waterhouse Coopers (PwC) for the wife and KPMG for the husband. The extent of the overall difference between them is almost exactly £20m. It is nicely illustrated on a schedule which I shall annex to this judgment (Sch 1) entitled 'Comparison of experts' reports and conclusions as to valuation' which was prepared jointly by junior counsel. It highlights the different discounts contended for by each side.

[84] In support of the arguments proposed by each side I have careful written submissions. Mr Pointer in his opening note summarises the main differences between the experts and the competing contentions from p 29. I annex an edited version (Schedule 2)[2] (Clokey from PwC was the wife's valuer (assisted by Tim

---

[1]   Editor's note: see *Charman v Charman* [2005] EWCA Civ 1606, [2006] 1 WLR 1053, [2006] 2 FLR 422.

[2]   Editor's note: Schedule 2 is reproduced at the end of the judgment.

Lawrence formerly of that firm). Nicholas Andrews and Andrew Collard from KPMG were the valuers for the husband).

[85] The approach to valuation issues in this Division is and always has been to look at the reality of the situation in any given case. For decades the court has set its face against hypothetical valuations produced for different purposes (income tax, probate etc). Any other approach is, quite simply, unfair. Indeed the rigid adoption of cash equivalent transfer values (CETVs) in pension cases sometimes has that effect, albeit that it is expedient for other reasons. Of course this often leads to spirited debate. So where for instance a case proceeds on the basis that a sale at less than true market value is inevitable to satisfy a likely court order then discounts at high levels are often appropriate. But where a sale can be avoided or delayed to enable full value to be extracted over a reasonable time that too must, in fairness, be properly reflected in valuation.

[86] For that reason I reject the approach adopted by KPMG as being hypothetical and prefer PwC as being specific to the facts of this case. Exactly the same kind of considerations apply when looking eg at discounts for valuation of minority interest in private companies. Sometimes they apply, sometimes, especially in family situations, they do not. See *G v G (Financial Provision: Equal Division)* [2002] EWHC 1339 (Fam), [2002] 2 FLR 1143.

[87] I shall adopt the share price current at the time of the February hearing because as it turns out the figure of $29.50 is a reasonable mid price. As a preliminary matter it is also important to remember that Axis is a company whose stock is quoted on the New York Stock Exchange. This is not a case about private company holdings where the 'top line' is in issue before discounts are applied. So all the shares are (subject to particular time restriction) freely tradable and, in time therefore also, the shares generated by the exercise of options. Great care therefore needs to be taken when discounting from readily available market value.

[88] As to the discounts for delay or restriction on sale; I heard no rational basis for the huge discounts (60% and 70%) contended for by KPMG. They accepted they were in effect plucking figures out of the air. I did not understand their methodology at all. I reject it and prefer PWC's more measured approach.

[89] As for the CEO selling discount, those arguments must, I consider, nowadays normally be regarded as 'old hat'. There was a time when CEOs in the divorce courts were a rarity, and the prospect of their having to find cash to meet settlements for wives was enough to send a shiver down the stock market's spine. Expert evidence was often led to predict the affect on a share price in the CEO's company of a sale following divorce. All recent evidence and experience shows that this is no longer the case. CEO's are now, sadly, frequenters of these courts and with the most minimal of careful public relations prior to a sale, it is of no moment so far as the stock market is concerned. The recent *Sorrell* case (*Sorrell v Sorrell* [2005] EWHC 1717 (Fam), [2006] 1 FLR 497), amongst others, illustrates this. I would like to hope that these arguments are now anachronistic and can be confined to forensic history. If that is removed from the discount debate there is really nothing between the experts so far as volume discounts are concerned.

[90] The attempt by KPMG to apply a further discount for the departure of the 'key-man' cannot possibly now be sustained given the husband has announced his

departure and the market responded by increasing the share price. I again remind myself that this is a huge publicly quoted company where the departure of one man is self-evidently unlikely to rock the boat.

[91]   Overall, I far preferred the evidence of Mr Clokey on all valuation issues at stake. His approach and discounts seemed carefully considered, rational and fair in contrast to KPMG where I had the distinct impression that straws were being clutched at every opportunity to depress the figures artificially. I shall adopt the PwC figures and have included them on the main schedule. Their overall value within and without Dragon is £73,117,406 broken down as appears on the schedule.

[92]   The husband seeks inclusion on the assets schedule, by way of a deduction, of the potential (not actual) liability to tax which he asserts was saved by his emigration to Bermuda. He says the wife should not be allowed to benefit from that saving (both in relation to his assets or those in Dragon) because she did not make the move and accompany him. If there is anything in that argument the place for it is in relation to consideration of matters of conduct which I will revert to below. It is not a true monetary deduction at this stage of the s 25 exercise. I shall remove it for now from the schedule.

[93]   The assets schedule (annexed as Sch 3) thus far reveals a grand total of all resources of £131,323,000 broken down as to £6,634,000 in the wife's name, £56,564,000 in the husbands name and £68,125,000 in Dragon.

[94]   At the 59th minute of the 11th hour, namely about a week ago the husband sought to make an application to admit new evidence about a potentially much higher level of income tax which might be chargeable on his Axis interests; the restricted shares and the share options. The further liability was estimated at a little under £11m. I heard the application over the telephone as I was on circuit. It was vigorously opposed by the wife. The liability had apparently been overlooked by the husband's accountancy team until the end of June. No explanation was forthcoming. I refused the application on the basis that it seemed to me almost inevitable that it would lead to a very significant further delay in delivery of judgment as the liability was far from conceded. However, I indicated, and the wife accepted, that if in fact in the end there is indeed a further UK tax charge referable to these interests when realised, a mechanism should be provided to enable the husband to recoup a portion of the actual tax paid (when it is paid) by him to the Inland Revenue. I shall so provide.

Earning capacity

[95]   The husband, additionally, has a very significant, indeed he would assert extraordinary, earning capacity. I cannot ignore it.

[96]   There is no doubt that even if the husband's fortune were to evaporate or disappear in a puff of smoke, with his expertise, experience and reputation built up during the period of the marriage he would be hugely in demand and capable of supporting himself and amassing further surplus wealth easily. This factor is specifically mentioned in s 25(2)(a) of the Matrimonial Causes Act 1973 and has given rise to many of the recent cases where exceptional earnings have been

reflected in ongoing income provision even where an equal division of capital has been accepted. The wife in this case sensibly and rightly does not seek either to value the husband's earning capacity (an exercise occasionally performed, I understand, in some of the more enthusiastic American states!) nor does she aspire to ongoing income support in the context of the huge figures in this case. However, she is entitled, in my judgment, to pray its existence in aid in support of her case for an equal (or near equal division) of capital. It is in a very real sense, a valuable resource acquired during the marriage. So it cannot be ignored, but a little caution is called for.

[97] The husband has indicated that his days of working at this rate are coming to an end. He has indicated a retirement date, disenchanted as he is by the demands and strain of this litigation. For a man of his age, wealth and work record to say, for whatever reason, that he does not envisage working much longer cannot be unreasonable. So overall his earning capacity may not have a very significant present value.

The parties' respective financial needs and their standard of living (s 25(b) and (c) of the Matrimonial Causes Act 1973)

[98] These two factors call for only scant attention in this case for quite obvious reasons. Even on the basis of the husband's open offer the wife's 'needs' could be met at the standard of living which she has become used to particularly in the last 5 years but to a lesser extent in last 10. The remaining fortune in the husband's hands even on his own figures and ignoring Dragon would be much more than that. It is not suggested that either spouse should want for anything financially. They each spend at an enormous rate. And why not given their resources? During 2005 the husband spent (even excluding his expenditure on refurnishing and legal fees) in excess of £2m. They both have lavish homes, photographs of which I have seen. In this case, in the end, the result is not really going to be determined by reference to these two factors. Other factors elbow them aside.

The conduct of each of the parties if that conduct is such that it would in the opinion of the court be inequitable to disregard it (s 25(2)(g), Matrimonial Causes Act 1973)

[99] In this regard, at this stage of the judgment, I am referring to what is conventionally regarded as falling within this subsection, ie domestic misconduct. Mr Singleton QC relies on it in a more positive sense for the husband as well. I will explore that interpretation further below.

[100] This factor has given rise to much heated debate. The husband has said throughout that he is not relying on it (see his Form E (E127), schedule of issues (E161) and his counsel's opening at p 18). The wife asserts however that he is trying to sneak it in by the back door by relying on two discrete issues; her alleged failure to support him in his business endeavours and her alleged refusal to move to Bermuda to avoid tax at the end of the marriage.

[101] These allegations are indeed relied on by the husband albeit in the context of his complete acceptance that in her role as homemaker and mother she could not be criticised.

[102] The generous arguments for and against these positions are set out by the parties' respective counsel in their first written submissions (the wife at pp 91–102 and the husband at pp 15–27). I am not going to repeat them at length. Having read and heard the evidence and considered the arguments, I substantially agree with the wife's case on these matters.

[103] In the first place, as I made clear during the hearing, in my view these allegations cannot be dressed up as anything but 'conduct'. The husband invites me to include them fully in the financial reckoning. They are not just the conventional 'side-swiping' which is sometimes included as (irrelevant) colour in affidavits. I agree with Mr Pointer QC that they should have been asserted fully as 'conduct' from the outset. However, as the evidence for the precise allegations was set out early on I did not, in the end, prevent the husband from seeking to advocate them at the hearing. But this approach did create a real risk that the wife was not given a proper opportunity to deploy other allegations in response when the court was delving into these two discrete issues.

[104] In any event, as a matter of fact, preferring the evidence of the wife on disputed matters as I do, especially in relation to the events surrounding the final ending of the marriage, I do not find that the wife failed to provide the husband with support in his business endeavours. She supported him perfectly reasonably within the context of his career and their marriage whilst perhaps not to the extent he would have ideally liked and whilst not according those endeavours the priority which the husband attached to them. The evidence of the wife and her witnesses, I find, provides no basis for the husband to establish that the wife's behaviour in this regard was of a character which requires me to have 'regard' to it in this respect.

[105] Furthermore I do not find, as a matter of fact, that she refused, in the end to move to Bermuda. She certainly protested, as she was fully entitled to, that she did not want to move there, but I am satisfied that eventually she was resigned to do so. When she suggested a compromise of a trial period of 2 years the husband did not take her up on it. By this time he regarded the marriage as over for other reasons and, I think, had by then embarked on another relationship. Two passages in the oral evidence (amongst many others) seemed to me to be telling. The first, reproduced from the transcript:

'Q.   I understand.

A.   I did not change those tax laws in 1998. When I tried to explain the situation to Beverly and that just so great a proportion of the wealth that I had worked so hard over such a long period of time to create was going to be seised and her answer was: "Well, just go and pay the tax".

Q.   I totally understand that from your point of view as the one who worked hard to generate it, that was an anathema.

A   Yes, my Lord.

Q.   But can you for a moment put yourself in her position?

A.   I have always tried to put myself in her position, my Lord, and that is why continuously I try to find alternatives, but I did try to find alternatives for the sake of the family, but it is very difficult when the only debate is the fact that Beverley was not going to move from England.

Q.   I do see you both had your very, very clear views about it. What I have to decide is whether or not one person's view was inherently less reasonable than the other person's view viewed from the particular standpoint that they were at and whether, in any event, that amounts to some factor which affects the result of this case.

Q   (Mr Pointer):You agree at any rate, Mr Charman, that in about October 2003 Mrs Charman at the pizza restaurant in Sevenoaks suggested that she would come out to Bermuda for two years and see if you and she could make it work?

A.   I don't remember that at all, my Lord. I am sorry. I just don't remember ...

Q   (Mr Justice Coleridge): The tragedy of this case seems to me to be that there was this enormous blockage between you on this point, and there was need for compromise on both sides and when it came to the compromise, or the possibility of compromise, it was all too late. Is that fair?

A.   Yes, it is fair, my Lord.'

The second passage I also reproduce in full from the transcript:

'Q   (Mr Justice Coleridge): I heard the evidence and I can see what is written here. What I want to understand is this, and certainly by February 2004 there is nothing left to discuss, I appreciate that, and you have this terrible meeting between the two of you first the night before and then in your hotel room as you are about to leave the country. What she has said is that in fact at no time was there ever a stage where you said: "If you won't come to Bermuda then you must regard the marriage as over".

A.   No, that's true.

Q.   It died, did it not? It withered. You knew this was a block that she could not get over, and you took the decision really, did you not, that you were going to have to get on with your life in Bermuda.

A.   Yes.

Q   (Mr Pointer): You know that she says that in the autumn of 2003 she suggested buying a house in Bermuda and giving a try for a couple of years, do you not?

A.   Yes, she said that.

Q.   Do you agree she said that?

A.   Sorry? Well, show me where she said it.

Q.   Of course. It is at E 355. The actual passage is over the page at 356. That is the passage leading up to it in para 48:

> "In the autumn of 2003 I suggested to John we buy a property in Bermuda and try living there for a couple of years."

You accept that she said that, do you not?

A.   I don't remember it but if she said she said it then I'm sure she said it.

Q.   Is the reality that by the autumn of 2003 you had formed the view that the marriage was over?

A.   Yes.'

[106] I ask myself whether, even if the husband's version of the events surrounding the move to Bermuda had been correct it would amount to 'conduct' of sufficient quality and gravity to impact on the result. The husband's protestations of lack of support seem to me to proceed from the assumption that a wife in this wife's circumstances should always subjugate her life to the wealth generating party's demands and views. That seems to me to relegate the wife to a

somewhat 'Victorian' and subservient role. A wife who fulfils the customary role of mother and home-maker must surely be entitled, nowadays, to make a life of her own whilst the husband is at work. That was what this wife did; she had her family (children and parents) and was heavily involved in her local magistracy. When it came to having to decide her priorities in life hers were driven by more than money. Surely she could not be criticised for that? The parties had already amassed wealth measured at between £80m and £100m. To have refused to move offshore to save the potential tax, payment of which could not possibly impact on their daily lives or the future security of their children despite its size, seems to me to be a perfectly tenable point of view, domestically speaking.

[107]   So, in relation to this aspect of the husband's case I find that, far from it being 'inequitable to disregard it', I find it would be 'inequitable to' regard it.

[108]   The whole of this section of this judgment (paras [97]–[105]) was written before the delivery of the *Miller/McFarlane* speeches. Does it require amendment in the light of them? I do not think so. Lord Nicholls of Birkenhead, Baroness Hale of Richmond and Lord Mance were, at least on this issue, of one mind. The only domestic misconduct which falls under s 25(2)(g) of the Matrimonial Causes Act 1973 is that which fulfils the statutory criterion as being of a seriousness where 'it would in the opinion of the court be inequitable to disregard it'. Per Lord Nicholls of Birkenhead, at para [65]:

> 'Parliament has drawn the line. It is not for the Courts to redraw the line under the guise of having regard to all the circumstances of the case. It is not as though the statutory boundary line gives rise to injustice. In most cases fairness does not require consideration of the parties' conduct. ... Where, exceptionally, the position is otherwise, so that it would be inequitable to disregard one party's conduct, the statute permits that conduct to be taken into account.'

[109]   Lesser misconduct cannot be allowed to seep into this or any case. Furthermore if it is to be relied on it should be clearly included and asserted at the first opportunity in the appropriate box on the Form E. It invariably raises the temperature in a case and the court needs to be alive to it from an early stage.

Contributions (subsection (f))

[110]   I deal with this factor last because there is an overlap with the further interpretation of 'conduct' as foreshadowed above in para [99].

[111]   For the past nearly 5 years, since *White v White* [2001] 1 AC 596, [2000] 2 FLR 981, courts at every level have been wrestling with the question of whether or not in departing from equality and striving for fairness it is proper to take into account and give weight to exceptional wealth creation by one spouse. In reading and re-reading all the now familiar authorities, attempting to expose and explain the underlying principles, one is reminded of a frenzied butterfly hunter in a tropical jungle trying to entrap a rare and elusive butterfly using a net full of holes. As soon as it appears to have been caught it escapes again and the pursuit continues.

[112] After the four speeches in the recent lengthy House of Lords decision I cannot think anything more can usefully be said on the subject. The courts at first instance must now try to apply the variously expressed principles, encapsulated by Bodey J, in *Lambert v Lambert* [2002] EWCA Civ 1685, [2003] Fam 103, [2003] 1 FLR 139 and repeated by Lord Nicholls of Birkenhead, at para [68]:

> 'The answer is that exceptional earnings are to be regarded as a factor pointing away from equality of division when, but only when, it would be inequitable to proceed otherwise. The wholly exceptional nature of the earnings must be, to borrow a phrase more familiar in a different context, gross and obvious. Bodey J encapsulated this neatly when sitting as a judge of the Court of Appeal in *Lambert v Lambert* [2003] Fam 103, 127, para 70. He described the characteristics or circumstances which would bring about a departure from equality:
>
>> "[However,] those characteristics or circumstances clearly have to be of a wholly exceptional nature, such that it would very obviously be inconsistent with the objective of achieving fairness (ie it would create an unfair outcome) for them to be ignored."'

[113] Baroness Hale of Richmond preferred to explore the principles of unequal division by reference to those underlying the matrimonial property regime leading up to and now enshrined in the Matrimonial Causes Act 1973. From para [149] of her speech she pointed up the competing analyses:

> '[149]   The question, therefore, is whether in the very big money cases, it is fair to take some account of the source and nature of the assets, in the same way that some account is taken of the source of those assets in inherited or family wealth. Is the "matrimonial property" to consist of everything acquired during the marriage (which should probably include periods of pre-marital cohabitation and engagement) or might a distinction be drawn between "family" and other assets? Family assets were described by Lord Denning in the landmark case of *Wachtel v Wachtel* [1973] Fam 72, at 90:
>
>> "It refers to those things which are acquired by one or other or both of the parties, with the intention that there should be continuing provision for them and their children during their joint lives, and used for the benefit of the family as a whole."

> Prime examples of family assets of a capital nature were the family home and its contents, while the parties' earning capacities were assets of a revenue nature. But also included are other assets which were obviously acquired for the use and benefit of the whole family, such as holiday homes, caravans, furniture, insurance policies and other family savings. To this list should clearly be added family businesses or joint ventures in which they both work. It is easy to see such assets as the fruits of the marital partnership. It is also easy to see each party's efforts as making a real contribution to the acquisition of such assets. Hence it is not at all surprising that Mr and Mrs McFarlane agreed upon the division of their capital assets, which were mostly of this nature, without prejudice to how Mrs McFarlane's future income provision would be quantified.

[150] More difficult are business or investment assets which have been generated solely or mainly by the efforts of one party. The other party has often made some contribution to the business, at least in its early days, and has continued with her agreed contribution to the welfare of the family (as did Mrs Cowan). But in these non-business-partnership, non-family asset cases, the bulk of the property has been generated by one party. Does this provide a reason for departing from the yardstick of equality? On the one hand is the view, already expressed, that commercial and domestic contributions are intrinsically incommensurable. It is easy to count the money or property which one has acquired. It is impossible to count the value which the other has added to their lives together. One is counted in money or money's worth. The other is counted in domestic comfort and happiness. If the law is to avoid discrimination between the gender roles, it should regard all the assets generated in either way during the marriage as family assets to be divided equally between them unless some other good reason is shown to do otherwise.

[151] On the other hand is the view that this is unrealistic. We do not yet have a system of community of property, whether full or deferred. Even modest legislative steps towards this have been strenuously resisted. Ownership and contributions still feature in divorcing couples' own perceptions of a fair result, some drawing a distinction between the home and joint savings accounts, on the one hand, and pensions, individual savings and debts, on the other (*Settling Up*, para 128 earlier, chapter 5). Some of these are not family assets in the way that the home, its contents and the family savings are family assets. Their value may well be speculative or their possession risky. It is not suggested that the domestic partner should share in the risks or potential liabilities, a problem which bedevils many community of property regimes and can give domestic contributions a negative value. It simply cannot be demonstrated that the domestic contribution, important though it has been to the welfare and happiness of the family as a whole, has contributed to their acquisition. If the money maker had not had a wife to look after him, no doubt he would have found others to do it for him. Further, great wealth can be generated in a very short time, as the *Miller* case shows; but domestic contributions by their very nature take time to mature into contributions to the welfare of the family.

[152] My lords, while I do not think that these arguments can be ignored, I think that they are irrelevant in the great majority of cases. In the very small number of cases where they might make a difference, of which *Miller* may be one, the answer is the same as that given in *White v White* [2001] 1 AC 596 in connection with pre-marital property, inheritance and gifts. The source of the assets may be taken into account but its importance will diminish over time. Put the other way round, the court is expressly required to take into account the duration of the marriage: section 25(2)(d). If the assets are not "family assets", or not generated by the joint efforts of the parties, then the duration of the marriage may justify a departure from the yardstick of equality of division. As we are talking here of a departure from that yardstick, I would prefer to put this in terms of a reduction to reflect the period of time over which the domestic contribution has or will continue (see Bailey-Harris, "*Comment on GW v RW (Financial Provision: Departure from Equality)*" [2003] Fam Law 386, at 388) rather than in terms of accrual

over time (see Eekelaar, "*Asset Distribution on Divorce – Time and Property*" [2003] Fam Law 828). This avoids the complexities of devising a formula for such accruals.

[153] This is simply to recognise that in a matrimonial property regime which still starts with the premise of separate property, there is still some scope for one party to acquire and retain separate property which is not automatically to be shared equally between them. The nature and the source of the property and the way the couple have run their lives may be taken into account in deciding how it should be shared.'

[114] Both speeches support the concept of exceptional wealth creation as a potentially relevant factor in the discretionary exercise. Inevitably these speeches will provide fertile areas for creative advocacy in the years ahead but it is prudent to remember that they are explanations of and expansions upon the statute not the statute itself.

[115] Further, as it now seems to be agreed that conduct and contribution are opposite sides of the same coin (per Lord Mance, at para [164]), or of the same species, the tests for their inclusion must surely be identical. As Mr Singleton QC pointed out, in my view rightly, in his original written closing submission it has long been recognised that in fact conduct has no limiting words and is apt to describe not only misconduct (as set out above) but, indeed, any conduct of a spouse which stares the court in the face and cannot be ignored without creating unfairness. The elephant in the room; incapable of definition but easy to recognise.

[116] Mr Singleton QC argues:

'Although conventionally s 25(2)(g) is often employed in relation to negative behaviour, there is nothing in its language that requires such a restrictive interpretation. This proposition is confirmed by Wood J in *Kokosinski v Kokosinski* [1980] Fam 72, at 83E:

"It is argued, and indeed it is true, that the factor of 'conduct' has for the most part been used in order to cut down the amount of financial relief which the court might otherwise have awarded to a party, and not for the purpose of increasing that amount. In my judgment there is nothing in the language of the section itself which supports this restricted view. My initial approach, therefore, is that any such restriction is unwarranted. I then turn to authority."

Having reviewed the authorities, Wood J concluded at 85F:

"I find nothing therefore in the authorities to suggest that a broad and general approach to the words 'conduct' and 'in all the circumstances of the case' is undesirable or wrong."'

[117] So, in the end, is a departure from equality applicable in this case? Or as Mr Singleton QC would have it, are the husband's extraordinary talent and the nature/value of the assets so generated, factors which, adopting his incremental

approach, lead to a figure which happens to be much less than one half. In the end I doubt whether the differing approaches lead to a different result.

[118] Whichever way it is approached it seems to me this factor must, exceptionally and in fairness, be taken into account in this case. Whether the husband's remarkable abilities in the insurance world, his energy and wealth creation (as I have summarised above and as fully described in his affidavits, those of his witnesses and in argument) are 'conduct' or 'a contribution to the welfare of the family' in the broadest sense their product is wholly exceptional, 'gross and obvious'. I am not impressed in this particular case by the arguments about when the wealth arose; Axis was well and truly under way by the time of the separation and a natural extension of the husband's previous business activities. Also attempts at categorisation of the assets hinted at by Baroness Hale of Richmond are fraught with difficulty after a marriage of this length as she recognises. It leads inevitably to the kind of ring-fencing arguments which surrounded the Dragon assets issue.

[119] However, I consider that one way or another this factor weighs and departure from equality is fair. So far so good.

[120] From the summit of the mountain, the House of Lords has pronounced some of the principles which underlie the 'special contribution' issue. They are silent on how to apply them. Indeed whilst disagreeing with the lower courts in *Miller* they did not alter the award. For those of us rootling around in the foothills trying to translate these principles into figures, this final stage is the more difficult part of the exercise.

[121] Mr Pointer QC concedes the small reduction to which I have made reference but urges great caution in moving away from 50% in case discrimination starts creeping in. Mr Singleton QC rebuts wholly the simple departure from equality approach. In his written submissions he says ...

> 'The proper approach is for the Court to consider all the factors in s 25 and determine a fair outcome. The court must cross-check its provisional award against the yardstick of equality to ensure that in the event of an unequal division there are good reasons to justify the difference. The quantification of the provisional award is both a cumulative/incremental approach. The court should look at each of the factors and weigh them into the balance. What the Court cannot do is to assume that the parties (in a long marriage where the resources exceed their needs) are each going to receive 50% and then determine if there is any reason why they should not. Apart from being contrary to *White*, that approach creates a real risk that each of the factors will not be given the proper consideration that the statute requires.'

[122] At this stage discretion must rule and I am tempted to call for the assistance of the jury. Most of the factors within s 25 of the Matrimonial Causes Act 1973 have a direct pecuniary impact capable of some calculation. (That of course was the great advantage of the pre-*White*/*Duxbury* approach albeit that unfairness was a not uncommon result in cases of this magnitude). But the exercise of inclusion /adjustment for the factor of special contribution is more akin to the 'calculation' of general damages in a personal injury or defamation case. Or possibly arguments about contributory negligence. There is no real rhyme or reason to the figures awarded for, say, a broken leg or paraplegia and, similarly, try as I do, I can find little hard ground once the self-justifying fairness of 50:50 is departed from.

[123]   This problem has in fact been with us far longer than just in the post *White* era. It is most instructive to reread the thoughts of the then Wilson J, one of the supreme specialist practitioners in this field throughout the whole of the post 1971 era. In *Conran v Conran* [1997] 2 FLR 615 he similarly struggled when increasing the wife's award on account of her 'outstanding contribution' in that case. He said, at 623:

> 'Section E: The Law
>
> Mr Coleridge QC on behalf of the husband accepts that, if this wife has made an outstanding contribution, it must be reflected in the award. The questions are: by what process of thought should it be reflected and, of course, to what extent?
>
> There seem now to be alternative processes of thought by which a wife's contribution should be reflected; but I doubt that they lead to a different result and so the point, though interesting, is academic.'

Then, at 627:

> 'Section G: Conclusion
>
> I must now conduct an overarching review of all relevant factors in accordance with the subsection. The scale of the husband's wealth and the standard of living during the marriage are already reflected in the figure for the wife's reasonable requirements. But what in particular are not there reflected are the subsistence of the marriage for no less than three decades and the contributions of both parties to the welfare of the family.
>
> I find it far from easy to reflect the wife's outstanding contribution in monetary terms. Nor is there even a reported case vaguely analogous to this. All that I can do is recall the detail of the wife's contribution set out in Section D; to apply to it some general considerations; and to trust that I have the instinct and experience to allow justly for it in the ultimate figure.'

And finally, at 628:

> '... That said, it would be absurd to conclude that the wife played anything approaching an equal role with the husband in the actual generation of his wealth or indeed to seek to ascribe any particular fraction of it to her contribution. That is why I have no appetite for awarding the wife a particular fraction of the joint wealth or even, which would be just legitimate on the authorities, for cross-checking an award, conceived otherwise, against such an approach. It crossed my mind to uplift the wife's reasonable requirements by some fraction of those requirements and to survey whether the result seemed fair; but, when I came to articulate the logic of such an exercise, I began to flounder.

The fact is, as Thorpe LJ has so well demonstrated in *Dart* at 293F–295B, that every fractional approach is inconsistent with the wide discretion under the Act; a discretion which in my opinion will have served better than any possible alternative provision the interests of those who since 1971 have suffered the heartbreak of arrival at our divorce court.

After protracted thought – and, let me confess, regular commuting between £10m and £11m – I have come to the conclusion that the award should bring the wife's wealth to £10.5m.

Accordingly the husband will pay her a lump sum of £6.2m.'

[124] At the end of the day I doubt whether I am carrying out any different process from Wilson J in *Conran*. Of course since *White* fractions and yardsticks are now permissible but otherwise I am driven to conclude plus ca change.

[125] If adjustment is appropriate, especially in these huge money cases, I think, it should be meaningful and significant and not a token one. It either means something and the court should so mark it or it does not (compare, for example contributory negligence). The sharp carving knife rather than the salami slicer is the appropriate tool. Having said that any adjustment should not be so great as to actually impact on the wife's standard of living where, as here, no conduct of the wife's is relevant other than it being conceded that she was a fully attentive wife and mother. But reduction in living standard is highly unlikely in this class of case, given that what is being divided up is the surplus fat in the case, way over and above any amount required to meet the payee spouse's needs.

Human rights

[126] Many of the arguments deployed by and on behalf of the husband by his legal team are both interesting and, as I have accepted, compelling. However the suggestion that a lump sum order made pursuant to s 23 and s 25 of the Matrimonial Causes Act 1973 (as expounded upon by the House of Lords) and following a 9-day hearing with the fullest and most skilful representation, in some way breaches the husband's right to 'peaceful enjoyment of his possessions '(per Art 1 of Protocol 1) is, in my judgment, frankly absurd. I entirely agree with Mr Pointer's QC exposition in this regard. These 'Human Rights' arguments have never yet been successfully deployed in these applications. I hope this is the last we shall see of them.

Conclusions

[127] This was a long marriage where the parties started with nothing and all the wealth was effectively created, I find, during its subsistence. Both played their full part in the marriage. However this is a case, in that very small category, where, wholly exceptionally, the wealth created is of extraordinary proportions from extraordinary talent and energy. Taking everything properly into account, I have decided, after much deliberation ('regular commuting' per Wilson J), to transfer the husband's interest in Dell House to the wife and additionally order him to pay her a lump sum of £40m (in addition to her present assets). She will exit the marriage with a total of about £48m including the assets already in her name. In percentage terms that is just under 37% of the total. The husband will accordingly retain just over 63%. I fully intend the difference which also reflects the fact that the wife is getting cash (if she wants it) and the husband will continue to operate and have a significant stake in one of the most risky fields; high risk insurance.

[128] The figure that I have arrived at will provoke one of two responses. There will be those who say that provision to this wife (or probably any wife) at this level is far and away more than she needs and far and away more than she has earned or is entitled to whatever the principles. To those I respond by drawing attention to Lord Nicholls of Birkenhead's remarks at para [9] of his speech in *Miller/McFarlane*:

> 'The starting point is surely not controversial. In the search for a fair outcome it is pertinent to have in mind that fairness generates obligations as well as rights. The financial provision made on divorce by one party for the other, still typically the wife, is not in the nature of largesse. It is not a case of "taking away" from one party and "giving" to the other property which "belongs" to the former. The claimant is not a suppliant. Each party to a marriage is entitled to a fair share of the available property. The search is always for what are the requirements of fairness in the particular case.'

But there will be an equally vociferous response from those who say that after a marriage of this length and quality, where all the wealth has been created during its subsistence, there is no reasonable justification for this wife (or any such wife) receiving less than half of the fruits of their combined but different efforts. To those I respond by drawing attention to Lord Nicholls of Birkenhead's remarks at para [16] of his speech:

> '[16] A third strand is sharing. This "equal sharing" principle derives from the basic concept of equality permeating a marriage as understood today. Marriage, it is often said, is a partnership of equals. In 1992 Lord Keith of Kinkel approved Lord Emslie's observation that "husband and wife are now for all practical purposes equal partners in marriage": *R v R* [1992] 1 AC 599, 617. This is now recognised widely, if not universally. The parties commit themselves to sharing their lives. They live and work together. When their partnership ends each is entitled to an equal share of the assets of the partnership, unless there is a good reason to the contrary. Fairness requires no less. But I emphasise the qualifying phrase: "unless there is good reason to the contrary". The yardstick of equality is to be applied as an aid, not a rule.'

And to both responses I draw attention to Baroness Hale of Richmond's illustration of this dilemma in paras [150]–[151] of her speech (at para [113], above).

[129] The decision to which I have arrived seeks to accord proper weight to all these principles and, taking into account all the circumstances, be fair to both parties.

[130] If the further tax charge to which I referred in para [94] is payable then, when it is paid, the wife will pay the husband a lump sum equal to 36% of such tax. It goes without saying that the clearest possible accountancy evidence would

need to be produced to the wife before any such lump sum would be payable. If there were to be a dispute I would have to adjudicate.

[131]   I will listen to further submissions about the timing of payment etc but I would hope that the husband has already in hand the wherewithal to pay most of the sum; at the very least the amount he has offered.

And finally

[132]   Cases of this magnitude (in excess of say £30m) are rare but regular in this division nowadays. Mostly they are settled by negotiation (sometimes with court assistance) and the court merely approves the final order. However the sums involved and at stake make the cost of the litigation although very high, relatively proportionate, so full contests result. The parties need all the help they can get from previous authority to assist in negotiation. In a field as discretionary as this one it is often hard to provide real guidance which limits rather than promotes debate. Pandora is constantly vigilant for opportunities to unlock the box. With the arrival of *Miller/McFarlane* I hear the rattling of keys.

[133]   As I have demonstrated in this case, in the end, whatever the underlying principles they have to be translated into £s. But this is not the only field of law where such an exercise is undertaken; the common law has lived with it for centuries when awarding general damages. The criminal law undertakes something similar in the sentencing field. In both those areas the courts have been driven to resort to tariffs recognising that there is, in truth, no right or wrong answer and the compromise of unrestrained judicial discretion is justified in the public interest (see e g *Guidelines for the assessment of General Damages in Personal Injury Cases* (OUP, 2006) compiled for the Judicial Studies Board) and to aid compromise.

[134]   I therefore begin to wonder whether some kind of generally accepted tariff is not called for in this area of very big/huge money too? As Mr Pointer QC was constrained in the end to concede in argument, if this case did not attract an unequal split it is hard to think of one which would. Very similar factors and considerations almost always apply in other cases of self-made wealth of similar magnitude. Extraordinary energy, extraordinary entrepreneurial or other wealth generating skill, combined with the sheer size of the fortune, inundate the picture and have a tendency to overwhelm the s 25 exercise however carefully performed.

[135]   Tariffs are a bit crude and purists would protest that this is an incursion into the hallowed s 25 exercise but are they, in the end, likely to produce a less fair result than any other unscientific exercise of judicial discretion? And they have the advantage of increased certainty. Of course they are non-binding and only guidance. Section 25 would continue to prevail.

[136]   I forbear from suggesting one at this stage in this case lest it be thought I have applied it to arrive at my decision. I have not. But a tariff of percentage bands which decreased as the size of these extraordinary fortunes increased might prove to be helpful guidance and, ultimately no less fair than the current expensive uncertainty.

Order accordingly.

Solicitors: *Manches* for the wife
               Withers for the husband

SCHEDULE 2

Valuations and Discounts Re AXIS interests

See judgment, at para [84].

(48)   *General points*

The first substantive difference between the experts relates to their overall approach to the valuation of H's interest in the shares, options and warrants relating to Axis (V1:242: para 10). This difference is of central importance as it affects the experts' approach to many other aspects of their valuations.

(49)   Clokey sets out to estimate what he terms the 'economic value' of H's interests, which he defines at V1:145 at para 2.16 as representing 'the compensation [H] would require in exchange for not owning the asset, including compensation for any indirect consequences'. This thesis may be broken down as follows:

(i)   Clokey's approach assumes that H is a rational investor (V1:151; para 4.5) who would, in realising his assets, do so in an orderly way rather than by an immediate forced sale (V1:151; para 4.3 and V1: 153; para 4.13) so far as possible.
(ii)   It is also premised on the assumption that H does not need to realise all his assets now (V1:152; para 4.7).
(iii)   Thus, it is assumed that where there would be a financial penalty in realising an asset now, such realisation is delayed to minimise such penalty (see V1:153; para 4.14), and a discount is applied to reflect the delay, rather than assuming that H would realise all his assets now and take the immediate and substantial knock on the price achieved.
(iv)   It is a further consequence of this approach that no attempt is made to put an artificial immediate value (using, for example, a rigid Inland Revenue valuation formula) on assets that after a period of time can be realised for a more readily ascertainable sum (V1:151; para 4.4).

(50)   KPMG use what they choose to call a 'fair market value approach' which actually means the assumption that there is an immediate sale of the assets (V1:62; para 1.5.1). Their approach follows the same lines as when assets are valued for tax purposes in this or other jurisdictions and adopts the tax/Inland Revenue definition of 'fair market value'. Thus:

Where no immediate sale is possible, a discount is applied to reflect that: formulae from the Inland Revenue or other tax authorities are adopted to provide notional immediate values where immediate sale is not possible. KPMG further suggest that: (i) Clokey's method is not normally applied in matrimonial cases, (ii) has been overruled (from an Inland Revenue perspective) by the Finance Act 2003, and (iii) is inconsistent with the approach applied to, say, the former matrimonial home (V1:410; para 2.2.2 et seq).

(51)   In considering assets of the relative complexity of the Axis interests, it is clear that any attempt to determine a value, as at today's date, of assets that cannot be realised for a period of time is going to include a element of speculation (the only certainty being that any figure fixed upon today will not be what is finally realised in the course of time). Nonetheless, every effort should be made to alight upon the most accurate estimated values.

(52)   It is further clear that different assets will require a different approach: for example assessing the current value of the piece of real estate is a wholly different exercise from valuing a current interest in a derivative asset, itself subject to the vagaries of the market and the approach to one cannot be criticised solely on the basis that it differs from the approach taken to another.

(53)   Secondly, the experts agree that were H to sell his interests in Axis shares, bearing in mind his position as the CEO and the restrictions of share sales that that necessitates, the appropriate route for such a sale would be what is referred to as a s 144 'dribble out' approach (see KPMG at V1:119; at para 5.6.2 and Clokey at V1:149; para 3.9). However, a s 144 sale is limited by the average weekly trade figure in Axis shares (the Trading Volume Formula (see KPMG at V1:94; para 5.3.4 and Clokey at V1:154; para 4.18(a)). and in this regard the experts differ:

–   Clokey, assuming H to be a rational investor and not hypothesising an immediate sale, does not consider that H will be hindered by this limitation, which in any event he calculates at 4.1 million shares (Vi:154; para 4.18 et seq);
–   KPMG state that the figure is 3.5 million shares, and apply a discount based upon the delay that will be suffered by an attempt immediately to sell more that 3.5 million shares (V1:94; para 5.3.4 and V1: 418: para 2.2.37).

(54)   This affects the period over which any shares could be sold, and thus the discounts for delayed sale which the experts apply.

(55)   *Shares*

The first significant difference is the share price adopted by the experts (V1:244; para 14):

–   Clokey adopts the mid-market closing price (V1:170; para 5.7 et seq). This is the price that one finds in the newspapers or other records of the share's price at a particular date – it is the standard price to which any applicable discounts are generally applied.
–   KPMG use the bid price (V1:90; para 5.2.11). This is based on the premise that H would be a seller, not a buyer.
–   However, KPMG are constrained to acknowledge, in their second report, that the adoption of the bid-price may require a 1% adjustment to their figures in certain cases (V1:434; para 2.2.104) on the basis that published discounts are generally applied to the mid-market price.

(56)   There are several discounts considered by the experts as applicable to the valuation of the shares. They are:
       discount for delay or restriction on sale;

the CEO selling discount; and
the volume or blockage discount.

(57) As to the discount for delay or restriction on sale:

(i)   Clokey proposes a discount of 5% pa for the restricted shares (V1:159; para 4.30). This extrapolates, because of the different periods, to 9.7%, 14.8% and 19.9% respectively to the three blocks of restricted shares (C3:867); and 5% for the shares underpinning the warrants (V1:158; para 4.30), on the basis that these shares cannot be sold for 12 months.

(ii) KPMG propose discounts of 60% and 70% to the three blocks of restricted shares and a 25% discount to the shares underpinning the warrants (V1:94; para 5.3.7 et seq and C3:843). However, these percentages include the discounts relied upon under the following two headings as well. KPMG respond to Clokey's arguments at (V1:422; para 2.2.54 et seq), acknowledging that Clokey's figure is within the range used in their own dealings with the Inland Revenue, but nonetheless produce a figure of 25% relying heavily, it would seem, on the US tax case of Adair (V2:689 et seq).

(58) As to the CEO selling discount:

(i)   Clokey concludes that this discount cannot be meaningfully distinguished from the volume or blockage discount (see below) (V1:163; para 4.44); he concludes that applicable total discount under those combined heads is 2% (V1:168; para 4.60);

(ii) KPMG assert that the appropriate discount for a sale of shares by a CEO (ie the effect on the market of the CEO selling a large number of shares) is 5% to 10% (V1:102; para 5.3.31 and V1:424; para 2.2.61 et seq).

(59) As to the volume or blockage discount:
      Clokey – see CEO discount above.

(i)   KPMG take the view that a volume or blockage discount is applicable (V1:102; para 5.3.32ff) and their conclusion is 1% to 4% (V1:432; para 2.2.98);

(ii) KMPG then treat their figures for CEO and volume/blockage discounts in combination and then arrive at an aggregate 10% (V1:432; para 2.2.98).

(60) *Options*

A number of differences between the experts are apparent in their valuation of H's options to purchase Axis shares.

(61) There are two elements to the value of the options: the 'intrinsic value' (that is simply the current share price minus the option price, ie the profit margin); but also the 'time or potential value' which is the value ascribed to the benefit H derives from the fact that he can retain the options until their expiry, with no risk as to the price, but retaining the right to purchase (and then sell) at any time within the option period.

(62) As to the valuation of the options Clokey approaches the valuation as follows:

He uses the binomial valuation model (this is the same valuation model as is then adopted by KPMG) (V1:174; para 5.19);

there are minor differences between the experts in the data put into that model but Clokey (and Lawrence) do not consider that these differences merit further consideration (V1:175; para 5.20(b)) save as to the date of exercise of the options, which Clokey assumes to be the end of the option period (V1:173; para 5.14(e));

Clokey runs the model having discounted the share price by 2% (being the figure he adopts for the CEO/volume or blockage discount) and reaches a single aggregate valuation (C3:867) for each of the options, ie a value which includes the intrinsic value which is calculated using the same assumptions as set out under 'Shares' above.

(63) KPMG approach the valuation as follows:

they too use the binomial model (V1:71; para 3.3.2);

they assume that H will exercise his options half way between now and the expiry of the term (V1:77; para 3.6.70);

Having run the model, they then apply a further 60 to 70% (say 65%) discount to the potential element of the value of the basis that the lack of marketability would justify such a discount for tax purposes (V1:74; para 3.5.6); the rationale here is that since the options cannot be transferred (in accordance with their rules) and the potential value attaches to the option rather than the underlying share, there is strictly no market value at all. However, KPMG are again obliged to concede that this does not reflect the reality, which is that the options will become exercisable in due course and the shares marketable in the future (V1:73; para 3.5.3).

(64) The most significant issue as to the valuation of the options is the impact of the date upon which the experts assume that H will exercise his options:

–   Clokey explains the economic theory behind his approach (V1:152; para 4.9), justifying the assumption that H will retain the options to the expiry of their respective terms. In simple terms the theory states that in the case of options where the holder does not receive dividends until the option is exercised (which these are) it is always advantageous to retain options for the maximum period unless the loss of dividends suffered on the unexercised options is so great as to outweigh the benefit of retaining the options. With an agreed dividend yield of 2%, the benefit of retention clearly outweighs the dividend loss.

–   KPMG adopt what they assert to be a 'fair value' approach based, they say, upon international accounting practice (but in fact used predominantly for tax related purposes) (V1:416; para 2.2.33) and assume a disposal at the middle of the term.

–   KPMG further suggest that Clokey's approach assumes that H will remain an executive of Axis until the expiry of the final term (ie 2015).

(65) *Warrants*

The valuation of the warrants involves similar considerations to the valuation of options, which will not be repeated here. The summary of the position is:

–   Clokey incorporates in the binomial model (i) the 2% CEO/volume discount
     to obtain an aggregate value; and (ii) a 5% restriction on sale discount to
     represent the 12 months holding period during which the shares cannot be
     sold after the exercise of the warrants, and thus produces an aggregate value
     (ie including the intrinsic and time/potential values of the warrants);
–   This underlying share price may need to be modified in the light of the
     effect of H's retirement announcement on the CEO/volume discount.
–   KPMG apply the same 60–70% discount to the potential/time value, and a
     25% delay or restriction on sale discount to the underlying shares (V1:105;
     Table 8).

(66)   *Personal contribution, or Key Man*

The key man argument put forward on behalf of H is an attempt to derive a
notional discount to all the Axis interests in which H (including Dragon) has an
interest. The discount figure argued for is 7.5%.

(67)   The argument is not that the interests are in fact worth 7.5% less, but that W
is not entitled to any share of 7.5% of their value. Thus its similarity to an
exceptional contribution argument is obvious.

(68)   The argument which **KPMG** were instructed to consider (V1:57; para 1.1.5)
is presented on the following basis:
     H has made a personal contribution to Axis (V1:112; para 6.2.2 et seq);
     The value of that contribution is hard to measure (and could well be
     temporary) (V1:125; para 6.2.16);
     That H's departure from Axis is not readily foreseeable (V1:125;
     para 6.2.17) and thus the market expects that he will continue to provide his
     services for the foreseeable future;
     It may take up to 3 years to replace H, and thus dividing his 'key man'
     insurance over 2 to3 years' profits provides a benchmark percentage of 4.2%
     (V1:126; para 6.2.21);
     A figure in the range 5 to 10% is appropriate.

(69)   We will say that the basis for this argument has been completely
undermined by H's announcement of his retirement and consequential effect on
the Axis share price.

The reports show that KPMG were expressly instructed to consider 'the
additional discount relating to the market expectation that [H] will continue to
provide his services to Axis for the foreseeable future', considering in particular,
(a) the impact were he to leave and (b) the impact of a share sale to fund a divorce
settlement (V1:57; para 1.1.5).

–   H announced his retirement, due to the pending divorce proceedings, on
     7 February 2006 after the close of trading;
–   The fact of H's departure is now not only foreseeable, but plainly in the
     public domain and must therefore be expressed in the share price;
–   Axis shares opened up 6.1% the following day; and

– In any event, H has given Axis nearly 3 years' notice of his retirement, which allows for the appointment of replacement CEO even on the most pessimistic timetable suggested by KPMG whilst H remains in office and 'fully committed to the company'.

CHARMAN v CHARMAN (No 3)

[2006] EWCA Civ 1791, [2007] 1 FLR 1237, CA

Court of Appeal

Sir Mark Potter P, Thorpe & Wilson LJJ

11 December 2006

Appeal – Conditions – Security for outstanding element of award – No current breach of order – Relevance of pre-judgment events

Costs – Security for costs – Costs of appeal – Security for outstanding element of award – No current breach of order – Relevance of pre-judgment events

The husband, a resident of Bermuda, had placed considerable pressure, including financial pressure, on the wife to accede to his various demands in the financial relief proceedings. At the conclusion of the proceedings, as part of a total settlement of £48m, the husband was ordered to pay the wife a lump sum of £40m, £12m of which was to be paid on or before 31 August 2006. When the husband failed to pay £4m of the £12m by the due date, the wife was granted a freezing order up to the value of the outstanding liability. The husband was granted an extension of time in which to pay the outstanding £4m; the court also directed that he was to pay the remaining £28m on or before 1 March 2007. The judge, noting that in making arrangements for payment, the husband had taken a 'somewhat cavalier' attitude towards the order, expressed uneasiness about whether or not the husband was going to make the final payment and renewed the freezing order. The husband paid the outstanding £4m by the revised deadline, but did not pay any interest. The husband was given permission to appeal against the judge's award, and was granted a stay of execution in respect of the remaining £28m. The wife applied to the court, arguing that the permission to appeal ought to be subject to a condition that the husband provide security for the outstanding £28m plus interest and also to a condition that the husband provide security for the wife's costs of the appeal.

Held – granting security for costs but otherwise dismissing the application –

(1) Events pre-judgment were merely background; it was events post-judgment which were of concern to the appellate court, in particular whether there had been a failure to pay under the judgment and whether there was reason to suppose that if the appeal failed the judgment would not be paid and, if so, whether the judgment was amenable to the normal procedures for enforcement. The court would not assume that the husband's determination to protect what he regarded as his wealth generated entirely by his own efforts would necessarily extend to refusal to pay under a judgment of the Court of Appeal if his appeal were unsuccessful. The husband should not be treated as in breach of any order of the court at this stage and his likely failure to make payment on 1 March should not be regarded as a compelling reason to make an order for security. The difficulty of enforcement in Bermuda had not been sufficiently established to justify an order

for security; while the husband might raise difficulties over payment, his conduct did not necessarily demonstrate that he would disobey the court's order when eventually made, and there was a lack of evidence that enforcement processes in Bermuda were likely to prove abortive (see paras [28]–[30], [37], [38]).

(2)   However, security for costs in the sum of £225,000 would be ordered under Part 25.13(2)(a) of the Civil Procedure Rules 1998 on the basis that the husband was resident outside the jurisdiction, not in a Brussels or Lugano Contracting State (see paras [40], [42]).

Statutory provisions considered
Matrimonial Causes Act 1973, s 25
Civil Procedure Rules 1998 (SI 1998/3132), Part 25.13(2)(a), rr 25.15, 25.13(2)(a), 25.13(2)(g), 52.9(1)

Cases referred to in judgment
Barings plc v Coopers & Lybrand [2002] EWCA Civ 1155, [2002] All ER (D) 278 (Jul), CA
Bell Electric v Aweco Appliance Systems GmbH & Co KG [2002] EWCA Civ 1501, [2003] 1 All ER 344, CA
Hammond Suddards v Agrichem International Holdings Ltd [2001] EWCA Civ 2065, [2001] All ER (D) 258 (Dec), CA
Miller v Miller; McFarlane v McFarlane [2006] UKHL 24, [2006] 2 AC 618, [2006] 2 WLR 1283, [2006] 1 FLR 1186, [2006] 3 All ER 1, HL

Martin Pointer QC and James Ewins for the applicant wife
Barry Singleton QC and Deborah Eaton and Deepak Nagpal for the respondent husband

Cur adv vult

SIR MARK POTTER P:

[1]   This is an application by the respondent wife in relation to an appeal by the appellant husband from a judgment and order of Coleridge J made on 27 July 2006 in ancillary relief proceedings. The judge ordered the husband to pay £40m to the wife which, when added to almost £8m of assets held by her, made overall capital provision for the wife of £48m, which sum amounted to 37% of the total assets available, which the judge held amounted to £131m.

[2]   In round terms, that figure was made up of the wife's assets, £57m worth of assets held by the husband and £68m worth of assets held by a Bermuda-based trust called Dragon Holdings Trust (Dragon). Those funds had been built up over the years by the husband in his extraordinarily successful career in the global insurance industry.

[3]   The proceedings have been notable not only for the size of the sums involved but for the determined resistance of the husband to the claims of the wife in what the trial judge described as his deployment of every available point to protect what he regards as his wealth generated entirely by his own efforts.

[4] The order of 27 July 2006 provided for payment to the wife of a lump sum of £40m; as to £12m on or before 31 August 2006 and as to the balance of £28m as should be directed by the court at a hearing to take place on 23 October 2006. The order provided that at that subsequent hearing the court would consider the date for payment of any remaining instalment of the lump sum; the interest on the lump sum payable by the husband from the date of the July order; provision by the husband of documentation relating to his extant tax liabilities arising from his employment by a company called Axis in which he held shares and options worth millions of pounds, in relation to which the wife was to be subject to a liability to pay 36% of the amount of tax due, subject to a maximum contribution; and, finally, the husband's intended application for permission to appeal.

[5] The husband failed to pay £4m of the £12m ordered to be paid by 31 August 2006.

[6] On 13 September 2006, the wife obtained a freezing order in respect of the husband's assets, whether held in or outside the jurisdiction, up to the value of his outstanding liability.

[7] On 23 October 2006, Coleridge J extended the time for payment of £4m to 14 November 2006 and ordered payment of the balancing lump sum instalment of £28m on or before 1 March 2007, with interest to run on those sums at the rate of 8%. He renewed the freezing injunction in a form modified to also cover sums outstanding from the husband on account of costs. On that occasion also, the judge refused the husband's application for permission to appeal the order of 27 July. The timing of the payment of £28m was then ordered and various other directions made by the judge.

[8] In giving judgment, the judge observed that he considered that, in making arrangements for payment under his judgment of July 2006, the husband had taken a 'somewhat cavalier' attitude towards the order the judge had made, and that he appeared now to be going out of his way to contest every aspect of that order, such that the judge felt uneasy about whether or not he was going to pay even if he was eventually given leave to appeal.

[9] On 7 November 2006, the husband lodged a notice of appeal, accompanied by a very full skeleton argument – so called, although it ran to 233 paragraphs and 67 pages. On 16 November 2006, Wilson LJ granted unlimited leave to appeal and granted a stay of execution in respect of the requirement to pay to the wife the balancing lump sum instalment of £28m plus the interest due on that sum at the rate of 8% on 27 July 2006 to the date of payment (such sum being over £1.3m as at 1 March 2007). Wilson LJ directed that the order for a stay should not come into effect in the event that the wife should, prior to 30 November 2006, have issued and served an application to show cause why it should not do so, and that the wife should, in any event, have permission at any time to apply on notice to the husband for a further order in respect of the stay.

[10] By way of background, the principal matter in dispute between the parties below was whether or not the assets held by Dragon should be taken into account as part of the husband's assets. He contended that his intention was always that this trust should benefit future generations of the family and was not intended to benefit himself, his wife or the children for whom he had made separate provision.

[11]   The wife's case was that this was an insincere assertion, that the assets in Dragon were, and were intended to be, available to the husband whenever he wished and should be fully brought into account. The judge accepted the wife's case. He comprehensively rejected the husband's case as to the purpose of Dragon, either as originally intended or subsequently treated. He found that the assets were held on a discretionary trust in conventional form and were in fact available to the husband on demand if he chose to make such demand. He therefore treated the assets in Dragon as properly to be included in the husband's schedule of assets for the purposes of the Sch 25 application, thus producing the figures to which I have referred.

[12]   So far as the grounds of appeal are concerned, there is and can realistically be no direct challenge to the judge's finding of fact as to the purpose of Dragon or, at least at first sight, the availability to the husband of the assets within it to meet the wife's claim.

[13]   The way in which the judge treated Dragon is, nonetheless, the subject of a challenge in the appeal which is articulated in the grounds as: (1) the failure to treat Dragon as a 'non-family asset' or the husband's interest in Dragon and his income therefrom as a 'non-family' asset. It is also asserted in the skeleton argument in support of the appeal that the judge wrongly ignored or brushed aside the status of Dragon as a trust and that he should not have made assumptions as to the trustees' willingness to advance sums to the husband to meet his liability.

[14]   Apart from that ground, there are two principal grounds to be advanced in the appeal which are of general importance and, when heard, will constitute the first examination and application by this court in a 'big money' case of the principles expounded by the House of Lords in the cases of *Miller v Miller; McFarlane v McFarlane* [2006] UKHL 24, [2006] 2 AC 618, [2006] 1 FLR 1186. They relate to the question of:

(1)   the general approach of the judge and whether he was correct (as he did) to use a starting point of 50% for the wife's share of assets, thereafter discounting the wife's entitlement on account of various factors considered, or whether he should, as the husband contends, have built up the wife's award incrementally by reference to the individual factors set out in s 25 of the Matrimonial Causes Act 1973;

(2)   the husband's 'special contribution' to the assets built up during the marriage. It is said that, rather than treating that contribution as an individual discounting factor, the judge should have analysed the extent to which it had resulted in the generation of resources and how that should be reflected in determining the wife's award. No doubt it will be contended that the fruits of that special contribution reside in the Dragon Trust.

[15]   In addition to the three heads I have mentioned, namely General Approach, Special Contribution and Non-family Assets, there are a number of grounds of appeal of a more limited, partly discrete, and partly overlapping nature. On this application, the wife does not challenge the grant by Wilson LJ of permission to appeal on the above matters. She further concedes that the question of costs below, subject of the appeal, may well require to be revisited should the husband succeed in the appeal. However, she seeks an order that the remaining grounds of appeal be struck out. I shall turn in a moment to that aspect of the application.

[16]   I turn first to the terms of the application before us. Under para 1, pursuant to r 52.9(1) of the Civil Procedure Rules 1998 (CPR), the wife seeks that the grounds of permission to appeal be made subject to a condition that the husband provide security to the wife for the outstanding balance of the lump sum payable to the wife, namely the £28m plus interest, ordered to be paid by 1 March 2007 and some £1.39m accrued at the rate of 8% on the £12m so far paid; and, in consequence, that the contingent stay provided for by Wilson LJ granting permission to appeal should not come into effect.

[17]   Under para 2 of the application the wife seeks that various grounds of the appeal other than the three main heads of appeal, to which I have referred, should be struck out.

[18]   Third, she seeks, pursuant to rr 25.15, 25.13(2)(a) and 25.13(2)(g) of the CPR, that the husband provide security for the wife's costs of the appeal. Rule 52.9(1) and (2) of the CPR read as follows:

> '(1)   The Appeal Court may
>   (a)   strike out the whole or part of an appeal notice;
>   (b)   set aside permission to appeal in whole or in part;
>   (c)   impose or vary conditions upon which an appeal may be brought.
> (2)   The Court will only exercise its powers under paragraph (1) where there is a compelling reason for doing so.'

[19]   There is a cautionary note at para 52.9.2 of Vol I of *The White Book Service 2006, Civil Procedure* (Sweet & Maxwell, 2006) which expresses the need for a 'compelling reason' to be demonstrated by a respondent seeking to impose a condition on a permission to appeal already granted. The note refers to various decisions of this court in the early life of the rule which appeared to indicate that, where permission to appeal had been granted by a single Lord Justice, the rule was simply there to cater for cases where the Lord Justice had overlooked some decisive authority or statutory provision or had, in some material way, been misled at the stage of his consideration. Such limitation is imposed for the purpose of avoiding tactical skirmishing and interlocutory satellite litigation once permission has been granted.

[20]   Laws LJ stated in *Barings plc v Coopers & Lybrand* [2002] EWCA Civ 1155, [2002] All ER (D) 278 (Jul), at para [43]:

> 'It seems to me to be of the highest importance that this court should ... discourage the bringing of satellite litigation under the guise of an application under CPR Part 52, r.9. The rule is there to cater for the rare case in which the lord justice granting permission to appeal has actually been misled. If he has, the court's process has been abused and that is of course a special situation. There may also be cases where, as Longmore LJ indicated in *Nathan v Smilovitch* [2002] EWCA Civ 759, [2002] All ER (D) 573 (May) some sizeable authority or statute has been overlooked by the lord justice granting permission. But where such a state of affairs is asserted,

the learning in question must in my view be plainly and unarguably decisive of the issue. If there is anything to argue about, an application to set aside the grant of permission will be misconceived.'

That statement has continued to govern applications of the kind before us.

[21] Subsequent decisions, and in particular those in *Hammond Suddards v Agrichem International Holdings Ltd* [2001] EWCA Civ 2065, [2001] All ER (D) 258 (Dec) and *Bell Electric v Aweco Appliance Systems GmbH & Co KG* [2002] EWCA Civ 1501, [2003] 1 All ER 344, referred to at para 52.9.4, show that an order may properly be made in a situation where the appellant has: (1) been ordered to pay an amount at trial and has deliberately failed to do so; and (2) it is clear, either explicitly from statements made on behalf of the appellant as in *Bell Electric* or by reason of the conduct of the appellant as in *Hammond Suddards*, that he will resist or avoid enforcement of the judgment if his appeal is unsuccessful.

[22] The application by the wife in para (2) of the application to strike out various grounds of the appeal seems to me to be governed by the remarks of Laws LJ which I have quoted, and I turn to deal with it now.

[23] The grounds sought to be struck out are grounds 2 and 3, which relate to the treatment of Dragon. It seems clear to me that they interrelate with the 'family/non-family assets' point and proper treatment of the Dragon assets in that respect. There is no good ground for striking out those items. Ground 4 relates to the value of the financial instruments in Axis Capital Holdings held by the husband and Dragon, and concerns a dispute between the valuers. Ground 5 asserts a procedural and substantive error by the judge in calculating the husband's tax liability. Ground 6 relates to timing of the judge's order for payment of the lump sum. Ground 7 relates to the rate of interest ordered by the judge. Ground 8 relates to the judge's extension of the freezing injunction.

[24] I would accept, on the limited consideration which I have given the matter, that there appears to be nothing in grounds 6–8 and not much more in grounds 4 and 5. However this application is not the point at which to hear argument on these questions. It may well be that the matters will not be pursued to any significant extent at the hearing in the face of a court by then familiar, and well prepared to deal, with the arguments. But in the light of the broad grant of permission to appeal, it is not appropriate, in my view, to consider and resolve the arguability of the points here.

[25] The second subparagraph of para 2 of the application includes an application to strike out that part of the notice of appeal in respect of Coleridge J's order of 23 October 2006, which seeks the discharge of his order freezing the assets of the husband unless and until he provides security by payment of his outstanding liability into court. It seems most unlikely to me that such an appeal will succeed. However the matter is not unarguable and again it seems clear to me that it would be wrong to litigate that matter at this stage.

[26] Accordingly, I would refuse the leave sought in para 2 of the application.

[27]   Turning to para 1 of the application, the applicant's reasons for seeking the condition as to security are put as follows. First, reliance is placed upon the hard-nosed manner, if I may so term it, in which the husband has conducted the proceedings prior to trial and the various steps he took and the resulting financial pressure which, it is said, he placed upon the wife in the course of the proceedings, designed, first, to achieve the hearing of the proceedings in Bermuda which the husband plainly thought to be in his own interests, and, second, to make the wife buckle and accept settlement at a figure offered by the husband. Reliance is also placed on the husband's opposition to the issue of Letters of Request in Bermuda in order to prevent inquiry into the conduct of Dragon relating to the question of whether or not it danced to his tune. Lastly, an unpleasant and oppressive letter was written by the husband directly to the wife seeking to dissuade her from pursuing her claim which was alleged to involve risk to the husband of bankruptcy and a drop in the value of his Axis shares and a number of other adverse effects, none of which bore examination or proved justified by events.

[28]   In this respect, and in the light of the authorities, I do not think it helpful to concentrate on events pre-judgment and, in particular, steps taken by the husband with a view to obtaining as low an award as he could or some other result satisfactory to him, as an indication whether security is appropriate post-judgment. It seems to me that, at best, that is background and what the court is concerned with is the extent to which the husband can be shown to be in breach of the trial judge's order and bent on non-compliance with any judgment of the Court of Appeal.

[29]   I am content to accept the view of the judge that the husband's attitude pre-judgment stems from his determination to protect what he regards as his wealth generated entirely by his own efforts, without assuming that such determination will necessarily extend to refusal to pay under a judgment of the Court of Appeal if his appeal is unsuccessful.

[30]   It is events post-judgment which are, on the authorities, of concern to this court, in particular, whether: (1) there has been a failure to pay under this judgment; and (2) whether there is reason to suppose that if the appeal fails the judgment will not be paid and, if so, whether the judgment is amenable to the normal processes of enforcement, whether here or abroad. So far as (1) is concerned, there was a failure by the husband to pay the sum of £12m by 31 August 2006, he paying only £8m. On return of the matter before Coleridge J, however, those moneys were paid once the date had been extended to 14 November and the date for payment of the balancing lump sum was set at 1 March 2007.

[31]   So far as that balance is concerned, the stance of the husband (see, in particular, paras 20–21 of Mr Singleton's skeleton argument) is that, whereas it may be that he will have sufficient available assets to meet the order on 1 March without taking account of the Dragon assets, he may not. And, in any event, he should not be obliged to realise these assets because the risk of injustice to him of being required to realise his assets by that date, if in fact he is entitled to succeed in his appeal and exclude from his assets the assets of the Dragon Trust, is greater than any hardship to the wife, if she is successful, of having to wait for a matter of weeks or months before payment.

[32] In this context, therefore, there is no breach of the order as at this date; however, the wife relies on the likelihood of the breach of order once 1 March 2007 arrives, which, the wife says, would justify an order for security that such sum should be paid. In that respect the wife does have the limited comfort, if not the security, of the freezing order covering the sums ordered to be paid.

[33] So far as concerns the question of the amenability of the husband to enforcement in Bermuda should the wife succeed in resisting his appeal, this raises two further questions: whether there is compelling reason to think that the husband will oppose enforcement in Bermuda and, if so, whether it is likely that the Bermudan authorities will refuse to recognise and enforce the judgment once upheld by the Court of Appeal.

[34] The matter has been argued before us at length by Mr Pointer QC and Mr Singleton QC. The husband's stance is as follows. While he has neither stated, nor instructed Mr Singleton to state on his behalf, that he will comply with the order for payment on 1 March, he should not be put to that particular sword. He says that, as of today, he is in compliance with the order of the court. While he may, but is unlikely to be, in a position to comply, by disposal or securing of his personal assets against payment of that sum, it is in principle wrong that he should have to do so, because he would then be in, effectively, a zero-asset position, leaving out of account the assets in Dragon, which, as he contends in the appeal, are not his, nor are they family assets, and should have been left out of account by the judge.

[35] Mr Singleton says on his behalf that by his actions, despite being late in the payment of £4m at one stage, he has recognised that he must comply with orders of the court but submits that he should not either have to pay the balance, or to dispose of or pledge all his assets to do so, before the outcome of the appeal, due to be heard only a week after the date for payment, when a successful outcome to this appeal might expunge his liability or, at any rate, very considerably reduce it. In these circumstances he should be permitted to pursue the appeal process before paying or being required to provide security. These seem to me powerful arguments. There is considerable dispute as to the value of the husband's personal assets, leaving out of account the Dragon assets. What is clear is that, if he is to make payment by 1 March, it will only be by realising shares and options in a manner which may trigger tax payments which might otherwise be deferred for years. Given that permission to appeal has been granted, there seems to me to be an undesirable tension between requiring the husband to meet his obligation by disposition of assets in a forced manner when the possible outcome might render such disposition unnecessary.

[36] Against this position, Mr Pointer adopted a secondary position. He submitted that even if Mr Singleton is right in principle, in practice the husband has what he describes as liquid resources, out of which a partial or token payment could be made or secured, amounting to some £8.8m, plus a bonus expected to be paid in 2006, the amount of which is also uncertain (see the items at para 18 of Mr Pointer's skeleton argument), plus a further figure of £2.3m, being the balance of a share sale in relation to Axis shares. It is right, however, to observe that £5m of the £8.8m is the value of properties in Atlanta and Florida which would require realisation, and the borrowing against them has another complication which has been made clear in an exchange between the husband's solicitor and his bankers which has been placed before us. Mr Pointer suggests that some form of security should be ordered, if only by way of a charge on the properties, a point made by him in reply.

[37]   Having considered the matter with care, I do not think that a position has been demonstrated in which the husband should be treated as in breach of any order of the court at this stage or that his likely failure to make payment on 1 March, which does seem on the cards, should be regarded as a compelling reason to make an order for security in the circumstances of this case.

[38]   Finally, I do not think that the second concern in cases of this kind, namely the difficulty of enforcement should the husband refuse to pay the judgment if upheld by the Court of Appeal, has been sufficiently established. Like the judge, I fear that the husband may raise difficulties but I do not think that his conduct to date necessarily demonstrates that he will disobey the court's order when eventually made. Even if he does, we lack any evidence before us that enforcement processes in Bermuda are likely to prove abortive.

[39]   Accordingly, I would refuse the application under para 1.

[40]   So far as the application for security for costs is concerned, the case seems to be plainly one where security for costs should be ordered under Part 25.13(2)(a) of the CPR, namely that the husband is resident out of the jurisdiction but not resident in a Brussels or Lugano Contracting State. The matter is put also under subpara (g) of that rule, namely that the appellant has taken steps in relation to his assets that would make it difficult to enforce an order for costs against him. That is disputed by the husband but it is unnecessary to decide. Suffice it to say that, in my clear view, the wife should be protected against the costs of the appeal. The amount in which security is sought is set out in summary form in a costs estimate provided to us and the estimated total of the costs is £227,000. The detailed make-up, in the sense of the individual items listed in that costs estimate, has not been attacked by Mr Singleton. He says that, on an earlier occasion, the estimate of costs was much lower. However we understand from Mr Pointer that, at the stage that estimate was given, the appeal was assumed to be a one-day appeal and the detail of the grounds had not been anticipated.

[41]   In those circumstances, while I am bound to say that the amount sought appears to be high, because we lack any assistance in relation to the appropriateness of the time involved or the rates charged, I do not think it right to reduce the sum to any substantial extent by way, as it were, of informal taxation.

[42]   I would order that the husband provide security for the costs of his appeal in the sum of £225,000, to be paid into court by a date which it seems to me should appropriately be set at 31 December; but in relation to that, no doubt, submissions can be made. The order providing for such payment should allow, in my view, for some alternative means of security provided that it is acceptable to the respondent's solicitors.

THORPE LJ:

[43]   I agree.

WILSON LJ:

[44]   I also agree.

Applications refused. Security for costs be provided by respondent in sum of £225,000.

Solicitors: *Manches* for the applicant wife
               Withers for the respondent husband

PHILIPPA JOHNSON
Law Reporter

CHARMAN v CHARMAN (No 4)

[2007] EWCA Civ 503, [2007] 1 FLR 1246, CA

Court of Appeal

Sir Mark Potter P, Thorpe and Wilson LJJ

24 May 2007

Financial relief – Divorce – Special contribution – Sharing principle – Conflict between distributive principles – Attribution of trust assets to husband

The parties had been married for almost 28 years, having met as teenagers; they were both now 54 years old. There were two children, now aged 24 and 20. At the time of the marriage neither party had any capital assets. The wife had worked as a civil servant until late into her first pregnancy; the husband had begun as a junior clerk at Lloyds and thereafter enjoyed dramatic success in the insurance industry. The family lived together in England for about 25 years; thereafter the husband began to spend significant periods in Bermuda, where he was setting up a new global specialist insurance business. The wife resisted pressure to move to Bermuda, but eventually agreed to do so when the husband became non-resident in the UK for tax purposes. However, the husband then informed the wife that the marriage was at an end. At the hearing of the wife's application for ancillary relief on divorce, the judge found that the parties' assets amounted to £131m, including £68m in an off-shore discretionary trust created by the husband upon an expression of wish that during his lifetime he should be its primary beneficiary. There was a separate trust set up for the children, containing assets of at least £30m, which the judge did not treat as part of the assets to be divided. The wife conceded a special contribution by the husband in the generation of the fortune, and sought 45% of the matrimonial assets. The husband was offering the wife £20m. The judge awarded the wife £48m, 36.5% of the assets, basing his departure from equality both on special contribution by the husband, and on the greater risks inherent in the assets remaining with the husband. Under a further order, if the husband was required to make specified tax payments (estimated by the husband at £11m) the wife should contribute 36% of such payments (up to £3.5m). The husband appealed, on the basis that the judge had made insufficient allowance for the husband's special contribution, in particular that the methodology employed by the judge had been flawed because the judge had begun with a hypotheses of equal division, and then factored the husband's special contribution into the equation by way of discount, whereas he should have proceeded through s 25 of the Matrimonial Causes Act 1973, allowing for the husband's special contribution within that exercise. Further, the husband appealed against the judge's treatment of the trust assets as financial resources of the husband, and thus fit for inclusion in the computation of the parties' assets, because the trust was a dynastic trust intended for the benefit of future generations. The husband argued that the judge had failed to ask himself the necessary question, namely whether, if the husband were to request the trustee to advance himself the whole of the assets, the trustee would be likely to do so.

Held – dismissing the husband's appeal –

(1) In *Miller v Miller; McFarlane v McFarlane* [2006] UKHL 24 the House of Lords had identified three main distributive principles: need (generously interpreted), compensation and sharing. The yardstick of equality of division, identified by the House of Lords in *White v White*, had filled the vacuum that resulted from the abandonment of the criterion of 'reasonable requirements', but had now developed into the 'equal sharing principle'. Under the 'sharing principle', property should be shared in equal proportions unless there was good reason to depart from such proportions, therefore departure from equality was not departure from the principle, but took place within the principle (see paras [64], [65], [68])

(2) Since *Miller* and the development of the yardstick into the sharing principle, the court's consideration of the sharing principle no longer had to be postponed until the end of the process. The sharing principle could not, however, be a true starting point; as the judge had stated, the starting point of every enquiry in an application for ancillary relief was the financial position of the parties and was always in two stages: first computation and then distribution. Although it might be convenient for the court to consider some of the matters set out in s 25(2) other than in the order set out in the section, a court should first consider, with whatever degree of detail was apt to the case, the matters set out in s 25(2), namely the property, income (including earning capacity) and other financial resources. Irrespective of whether the assets were substantial, likely future income must always be appraised for, even in a clean-break case, such appraisal might well be relevant to the division of property that best achieved the fair overall outcome (see paras [65], [67]).

(3) Notwithstanding some remarks in *Miller*, and subject to the exceptions identified in that case, the sharing principle applied to all the parties' property, but to the extent that property was non-matrimonial there was likely to be better reason for departure from equality. The distinction put forward by Baroness Hale of Richmond in *Miller* between unilateral assets and other matrimonial property was for use in cases in which the marriage was short; its application in a case such as the present would be deeply discriminatory and gravely undermine the sharing principle (see para [66]).

(4) Each of the three distributive principles identified by the House of Lords in *Miller* could be collected from s 25 of the Matrimonial Causes Act 1973: the principle of need required consideration of the financial needs, obligations and responsibilities of the parties, the standard of living enjoyed by the family, the age of the parties and any physical or mental disability of either; the principle of compensation related to prospective financial disadvantage which some parties faced upon divorce as a result of decisions taken for the benefit of the family during the marriage; and the principle of sharing was dictated by reference to the contributions of each party to the welfare of the family, to the length of the marriage and, in an exceptional case, to the conduct of a party. However, it was as unnecessarily confusing to present a case of contribution as a positive type of conduct, which it would be inequitable to disregard, as it was to present a case of conduct as a negative or nil type of contribution (see paras [69]–[72]).

(5)   Any irreconcilable conflict between the result suggested by one of the three principles, needs, sharing and compensation, and that suggested by another, must be answered by application of the criterion of fairness: when the result suggested by the needs principle was an award greater than the result suggested by the sharing principle, the former should in principle prevail; when the result suggested by the needs principle was an award of property less than the result suggested by the sharing principle, the latter should in principle prevail; irreconcilable conflict between the compensation principle and one of the others would be left for another case (see para [73]).

(6)   In cases of very substantial matrimonial property it might be immediately apparent that the result of applying the sharing principle would immediately subsume the result of applying the principles of need and of compensation. In such circumstances the judge might well first consider distribution by reference to the sharing principle, and then shortly refer to the other principles. It was not the case that consideration of the discount from equality should play no part in the distributive exercise: a discount was nothing other than a departure from equality. The judge had in fact adopted a serial approach, considering all the factors set out in s 25, insofar as they were relevant, including the husband's special contribution, arriving at a figure of £48m for the wife, noting that this was 37% of the total assets, and concluding that such departure from equality was justified. That was a valid approach, but the judge would have been entitled to consider percentages at an earlier stage (see para [76]).

(7)   The court did not agree with the approach suggested by Mance LJ in *Cowan v Cowan* [2001] EWCA Civ 679 of sharing the surplus of the assets after needs had been satisfied; in the large cases, it was probable that sharing, whether equal or not, would cater automatically for needs. There was also the grave practical objection that an approach that invited expensive concentration upon the value of assets and also elaborate presentation of needs would be the worst of both worlds (see para [77]).

(8)   Special contribution had inevitably survived *Miller*, because the statutory requirement to consider contributions by each party to the welfare of the family would be inconsistent with a blanket rule that past contributions to its welfare must be accorded equal weight. However, the House of Lords had heavily circumscribed the situations in which it would be appropriate to find that one party had made a special contribution. The notion of special contribution could, in principle, take a number of forms, non-financial as well as financial, but in practice, for practical reasons, special contribution claims had thus far arisen only in cases of substantial wealth generated by a party's success in business during the marriage. In such cases the court would have regard to the amount of the wealth, which in some cases would be so extraordinary as to make it easy for the party who generated it to claim an exceptional and individual quality which deserved equal treatment; often, however, he or she would need independently to establish such a quality, whether by genius in business or in some other field. Sometimes, by contrast, it would immediately be obvious that substantial wealth generated during the marriage was a windfall, not the product of a special contribution. Neither in its method nor in its result had the judge's treatment of the husband's special contribution been vulnerable to appeal (see paras [79], [80], [91]).

(9)   Notwithstanding a suggestion by Baroness Hale of Richmond in *Miller* that the generation of wealth should not always qualify as a contribution to the welfare of the family, the usual conclusion, applicable in this case, was that wealth generated by a party during a marriage was the product of a contribution on his or her part to the welfare of the family. In any event, a party's property did not fall outside the court's redistributive powers in ss 23–25 of the Matrimonial Causes Act 1973 just because it was not the product of a contribution within the meaning of s 25. The distinction put forward by Baroness Hale of Richmond in *Miller* between unilateral assets and other matrimonial property was for use in cases in which the marriage was short, and had not been commended for use in other cases. Its application in a case such as the present would be deeply discriminatory and gravely undermine the sharing principle (see paras [81], [83]).

(10)   The court was unable to identify any figure as a guideline threshold for a special contribution; a party's claim to have made a special contribution ought not to succeed by reference to something interpreted as effectively a presumption deriving from the court's identification of a threshold figure. However, the court was prepared to respond to the judge's call for guidance on the appropriate range of percentage adjustment to be made in which departure from equality was justified, although it ought to be borne in mind that fair despatch of some cases might require departure from the proposed range: it was hard to conceive that, where such a special contribution was established, the percentages of division of matrimonial property should be nearer to equality than 55%–45%; but also, following a very long marriage, fair allowance for special contribution within the sharing principle would be most unlikely to give rise to percentages further from equality than 66.6%–33.3%. If the contribution was special, it followed that it was unmatched, and, in principle, the greater the wealth the greater the extent to which it was unmatched, and to which it called for an unequal division under the sharing principle (see paras [87]–[90]).

(11)   The judge's rejection of the husband's dynastic argument had been inevitable, given: the obvious fiscal purpose behind the trust; the husband's inclusion of himself as a named beneficiary; his power to replace the trustees; the contents of his letters of wishes; the absence of any documentary evidence to support his argument; the inference to be drawn from his attempts to prevent the wife having access to trust documents, and other factors (see para [47]).

(12)   Before attributing all the trust assets to the husband, the judge had to have been satisfied that the trustees would have advanced those assets to the husband if he had asked them to do so. The judge had rightly asked himself the question whether the trust assets were a 'resource', 'resources' being the portmanteau word used in s 25(2)(a), and, although he had made no express finding that the trustees would be likely to advance all the capital of the trust to the husband upon request, by his references to authorities and to counsel's arguments it was quite clear that he had effectively made such a finding. It was a perfectly adequate foundation for the aggregation of trust assets with a party's personal assets for the purposes of s 25(2) that they should be likely to be advanced to the party in the event only of 'need', and on the husband's own argument the order made created a need for capital out of the trust (see paras [48], [50], [51], [53]).

(13)   Prior to *White* the elaborate enquiry in the present case as to the status of the trust assets would probably have been unnecessary, but since the advent of

reference to proportions, the focus of the court had largely shifted from needs to computation of resources. Wherever such an enquiry had to be made, it was essential that the court bring to the task a mixture of worldly realism and respect for the legal effects of trusts, the legal duties of trustees and, in the case of off-shore trusts, the jurisdictions of the off-shore courts. In the circumstances of the case it would have been a reproachful emasculation of the court's duty to be fair if the assets that the husband had built up in the trust during the marriage had not been attributed to him (see para [57]).

Per curiam: remarks by Baroness Hale of Richmond in *Miller* at para [154] were said to permit argument that a party's earning capacity was itself an asset to which the other had contributed and which might to some extent be subject to the sharing principle; this seemed an area of complexity and potential confusion which it was unnecessary to visit (see para [67]).

Per curiam: the court surveyed legal developments in ancillary relief, noting that in big money cases the *White* factor had more than doubled the levels of award and that many said that London had become the divorce capital of the world for aspiring wives. *Miller* had not been received by practitioners as a decision that introduced the benefit of predictability and improvement of the prospect of compromise; if so, it was highly unfortunate. Arguably the English statute was in need of modernisation in the light of social and other changes, as well as in the light of experience. The court called for a Law Commission review of the state of English and international law concerning the property consequences of marriage and divorce (see paras [106]–[126]).

Statutory provisions considered
Divorce Reform Act 1969
Matrimonial Proceedings and Property Act 1970, s 5
Matrimonial Causes Act 1973, ss 23, 24(1)(c), 25(2)
Matrimonial and Family Proceedings Act 1984, s 3
Family Law (Scotland) Act 1985
Lugano Convention on Jurisdiction and the Enforcement of Judgments in Civil and Commercial Matters (1988) OJ L 319/9
Council Regulation (EC) No 44/2001 of 22 December 2000 on jurisdiction and the recognition and enforcement of judgments in civil and commercial matters
Council Regulation (EC) No 2201/2003 of 27 November 2003 concerning jurisdiction and the recognition and enforcement of judgments in matrimonial matters and in matters of parental responsibility, repealing Regulation (EC) No 1347/2000 (Brussels II Revised) (2003) OJ L 338/1
New Zealand Property (Relationships) Act 1976
New Zealand Family Proceedings Act 1980

Cases referred to in judgment
B Trust, Re [2006] JRC 185, Jersey RC
Bentinck v Bentinck [2007] EWCA Civ 175, [2007] All ER (D) 76 (Mar), CA
Charman v Charman [2005] EWCA Civ 1606, [2006] 1 WLR 1053, [2006] 2 FLR 422, CA
Cowan v Cowan [2001] EWCA Civ 679, [2002] Fam 97, [2001] 3 WLR 684, [2001] 2 FLR 192, CA

Duxbury v Duxbury (Note) [1992] Fam 62, [1991] 3 WLR 639, [1987] 1 FLR 7, [1990] 2 All ER 77, CA
Fountain Trust, Re [2005] JLR 359, Jersey RC
H Trust, Re [2006] JRC057, Jersey RC
Lambert v Lambert [2002] EWCA Civ 1685, [2003] Fam 103, [2003] 1 FLR 139, [2003] 4 All ER 342, CA
Letterstedt v Broers (1884) 9 App Cas 371, (1884) 53 LJPC 44, [1881–1885] All ER Rep 882, PC
McFarlane v McFarlane; Parlour v Parlour [2004] EWCA Civ 872, [2005] Fam 171, [2004] 3 WLR 1480, [2004] 2 FLR 893, [2004] 2 All ER 921, CA
Miller v Miller; McFarlane v McFarlane [2006] UKHL 24, [2006] 2 AC 618, [2006] 2 WLR 1283, [2006] 1 FLR 1186, [2006] 3 All ER 1, HL
Moore v Moore [2007] EWCA Civ 361, [2007] All ER (D) 158 (Apr), CA
O'D v O'D [1976] Fam 83, [1975] 3 WLR 308, (1975) FLR Rep 512, [1975] 2 All ER 993, CA
Preston v Preston [1982] Fam 17, [1981] 3 WLR 619, (1981) 2 FLR 331, [1982] 1 All ER 41, CA
S v S [1977] Fam 127, [1976] 3 WLR 775, [1977] 1 All ER 56, CA
S v S (Divorce: Distribution of Assets) [2006] EWHC 2793 (Fam), [2006] All ER (D) 137 (Nov), FD
Skeats' Settlement, Re; Skeats v Evans (1889) 42 Ch D 522, (1889) 58 LJ Ch 656, (1889) 37 WR 778, [1886–1890] All ER Rep 989, ChD
SRJ v DWJ (Financial Provision) [1999] 2 FLR 176, CA
The Esteem Settlement, Re [2004] WTLR 1, [2004] JRC 92, Jersey RC
W v W [2001] Fam Law 656, FD
Wachtel v Wachtel [1973] Fam 72, [1973] 2 WLR 366, [1973] 1 All ER 829, CA
White v White [2001] 1 AC 596, [2000] 3 WLR 1571, [2000] 2 FLR 981, [2001] 1 All ER 1, HL

Barry Singleton QC, Alan Boyle QC, Deborah Eaton, Deepak Nagpal and *Dakis Hagen* for the appellant husband
Martin Pointer QC, Christopher Nugee QC, James Ewins and *Andrew Mold* for the respondent wife

Cur adv vult

SIR MARK POTTER P:

[1]   This is the judgment of the court.

Section A: Introduction

[2]   Mr Charman, whom it will be convenient to describe as 'the husband', notwithstanding pronouncement of a decree absolute of divorce, appeals against an order made on 27 July 2006 by Coleridge J in the Family Division of the High Court[1] upon an application for ancillary relief brought in the divorce proceedings by Mrs Charman, whom it will be convenient to describe as 'the wife'. The judge found that the parties' assets amounted to £131m, of which, upon the agreed basis

---

[1]   Editor's note: see *Charman v Charman (No 2)* [2006] EWHC 1879 (Fam), [2007] 1 FLR 593.

that the husband would transfer to her his interest in the matrimonial home, the wife held £8m and the husband held £123m. The judge's order was that in full settlement of all her claims the husband should pay to the wife a lump sum of £40m, thereby providing her with assets amounting to £48m (or 36.5% of the parties' assets) and providing him with assets amounting to £83m (or 63.5% of them). Of the lump sum which he was ordered to pay, the husband has paid £12m but pending determination of this appeal he has not been required to pay the balance. His contention is that the judge was wrong to award the wife a lump sum of as much as £40m and, in particular, that the methodology which he deployed in arriving at such an award was flawed. The husband contends that the judge should have awarded the wife either a lump sum of £12m, namely the sum which he has already paid and by which her assets have been increased to £20m, or, at most, a lump sum of £20m, in which case he would be required to pay her a further £8m so as to increase her assets to £28m. The wife defends the judge's order and does not cross-appeal.

[3] The judge, however, made a further order, which he described as being for a reverse contingent lump sum, namely that if the husband was required to make specified payments to Her Majesty's Revenue and Customs, estimated by the husband at £11m, the wife should contribute thereto by way of repayment to him of – in simple terms – 36% of all such payments or £3.5m, whichever was the lower. In his computation of the parties' assets the judge made no allowance for these tax liabilities, which the husband had drawn to his attention very late; but, were they to be required to be paid, it is unlikely in view of the terms of this further order that any significant alteration would fall to be made to the percentages (as opposed to the figures) set out above.

[4] Although higher lump sum orders have been made by consent, the judge's order is believed to be the highest award ever made on determination of a contested application for ancillary relief in divorce proceedings in England and Wales.

[5] While contending that she had made an important contribution to the welfare of the family to which the judge should have regard under s 25(2)(f) of the Matrimonial Causes Act 1973 (the Act), the wife in effect conceded below that the husband's contribution had been of such significance as to justify his departure from the marriage with a greater proportion of the assets than should be awarded to her. We will follow the convention of describing such a contribution as 'a special contribution'. By reference thereto, the wife suggested a division of 55%–45% in the husband's favour. The wife's concession was that the husband's special contribution lay in the generation by his skill and effort during the marriage of the entire fortune of £131m for the welfare of the family. The judge endorsed the wife's concession of a special contribution but, in the end, following review of numerous factors, he favoured the result which represented a division of 63.5%–36.5% in the husband's favour. It is clear that he favoured such disparity by reference principally to the husband's special contribution, but also to what he considered to be the greater risks inherent in the assets remaining with the husband than those inherent in the assets awarded to the wife.

[6] The husband's first main ground of appeal is that by his order the judge made insufficient allowance for his special contribution; and that he made insufficient allowance for it because he approached it in the wrong way. It will be

seen, therefore, that the appeal primarily raises questions not as to the circumstances in which a spouse's contribution should be regarded as special but as to the manner in which, by his reasoning, a judge should make allowance for such a contribution. In this regard Mr Singleton QC, on behalf of the husband, contends first that the judge began with a hypothesis of equal division and then factored the husband's special contribution into the equation by way of a discount; and second that he was wrong to do so. Mr Singleton further contends that the proper approach should have been for the judge to allow for the husband's special contribution in the course of the exercise mandated by s 25(2) of the Act and that, had he done so, then, after conducting the necessary cross-check against the yardstick of equality (subject, however, to the agreed conclusion that the yardstick was at any rate to some extent inapt to the case), the awards would have been of £20m or at most £28m to the wife, inclusive of her existing assets, and (subject to the second main ground of appeal) of £111m or £103m to the husband. Mr Singleton's contentions require us to consider and interpret some of the guidance to the quantification of awards of ancillary relief, especially where the assets are large, given by the House of Lords in *White v White* [2001] 1 AC 596, [2000] 2 FLR 981 and, in particular, in *Miller v Miller; McFarlane v McFarlane* [2006] UKHL 24, [2006] 2 AC 618, [2006] 1 FLR 1186. The latter decision was given only 2 months prior to delivery of the judgment of Coleridge J.

[7] The husband's second main ground of appeal is that the judge erred in computing the total assets at £131m, within which the judge included £68m held within an off-shore discretionary trust known as The Dragon Holdings Trust (Dragon). The husband had set up Dragon in 1987 upon an expression of wish to the trustee that during his lifetime he should be its primary beneficiary. Although it is a subsidiary contention of the husband that the assets of Dragon should have been computed at less than £68m, the second main ground of appeal is that the judge fell into error in regarding the assets of Dragon, whatever their size, as 'financial resources' of the husband for the purpose of s 25(2)(a) of the Act and thus as fit for inclusion at all in the computation of the parties' assets. Mr Boyle QC, who in this appeal appears together with Mr Singleton on behalf of the husband but did not do so below, submits that in this regard the judge failed to ask himself the necessary question, namely whether if the husband were to request it to advance to him the whole (or part) of the assets of Dragon, its trustee would be likely to do so. Mr Boyle further submits that, had he asked himself that question, the judge could reasonably have answered it only in the negative. Put another way, his submission is that, if the judge asked himself that question and answered it in the affirmative, it was not open to him to do so. Mr Boyle therefore primarily contends that no part of the assets of Dragon should have been included in the computation of the parties' assets. He makes, however, three fall-back suggestions, to which we will refer in para [56], below.

[8] Mr Nugee QC, who in this appeal appears together with Mr Pointer QC on behalf of the wife, but who again did not do so below, accepts that it was necessary for the judge to ask himself the question identified by Mr Boyle. That being so, our task is to discern, in the light of the nature of the submissions below and the resulting form of the judgment, whether he did so; if he did so, whether he did so affirmatively; and, if he did so affirmatively, whether it was open to him to do so. In particular we need to place the judge's treatment of the issues in relation to Dragon in the context of the nature of the arguments put before him, particularly by Mr Singleton. Mr Nugee contends that the thrust of the husband's

case as presented in this appeal is entirely different from that of his case as put before the judge; that some of Mr Boyle's arguments in this area were never articulated before the judge at all; that it is improper, or at least unsatisfactory, that they should first be raised in this court; and indeed that some are included in a proposed amendment to the grounds of appeal filed only days prior to the hearing of the appeal, for which permission has not yet been granted and should be refused.

[9] There are in effect three further, subsidiary grounds of appeal. But they are of less general interest and we can address them shortly without the need for introduction here.

Section B: Current circumstances

[10] The wife is aged 54. She lives in the former matrimonial home in Kent. It is worth £3m. She has no paid employment and sits as a magistrate.

[11] The husband is also aged 54. He is not ordinarily resident in the UK and mainly resides in a rented home in Bermuda, where he claims to be domiciled. He owns two further homes in the USA, which are together worth £5m. He is President and Chief Executive Officer of Axis Capital Holdings Ltd (Axis), which is quoted on the New York Stock Exchange and is the holding company for a global group of specialist insurance and reinsurance companies. His salary and bonus amount to about £2m pa. A week prior to the substantive hearing before the judge, he caused Axis to issue a press release which announced that, as a result of the proceedings brought against him by the wife, he would retire on 31 December 2008. Whatever the merit of the reason given, it is, as the judge found, not unreasonable for the husband to retire at the age of 56 in the light of the size of the wealth which he has generated and which, whatever the outcome of this appeal, will be available to him. But, whether logical or otherwise, the husband's arresting public assertion of a direct link between the wife's application for ancillary relief and his proposed retirement illustrates his indignation at the wife's prosecution of her application and its result to date. Having heard his oral evidence at length, the judge found that the husband was genuinely bemused that the wife should regard his offer that she should leave the marriage with £20m as anything other than reasonable or, indeed, generous. The husband's indignation has an intensity which has rendered this litigation hard-fought at every turn and which, we fear, will continue to do so until whatever is properly payable to the wife under English law has been paid in full.

[12] There are two children of the family, both boys, aged 24 and 20. In 1987, when he created Dragon, the husband created the JR Charman children's settlement for the two boys. It has assets now worth at least £30m, which the judge naturally excluded from his computation of the parties' assets.

Section C: The history

[13] The parties met in 1970, when they were each aged about 17 and in the sixth forms of their schools in Rochester, Kent. They became engaged in 1973 and were married in 1976. In 1971 the husband, in effect unqualified, had gone to work as a junior clerk in an underwriting agency at Lloyd's of London and in 1975 he had

accepted an invitation to take a more senior position in another agency at Lloyd's. The wife was working as an inspector in what is now the Department for Work and Pensions. To the marriage they brought their earning capacities but at that time they had in effect no capital assets.

[14] Thereafter the wife continued to work full-time until late in her first pregnancy in 1982.

[15] Until 1981 the husband's career at Lloyd's continued to flourish dramatically. Then for 5 years he worked instead in a senior capacity, and for very substantial reward, in a marine insurance company based in London and owned by Mr CH Tung of Hong Kong, whom the husband regards as his mentor. In 1986 the husband returned to Lloyd's: at a price of £700,000 he bought an underwriting agency which was in disarray and he operated it through what became Charman Underwriting Agencies Ltd (Charman), of which he was the chief executive. During the following 10 years he turned the syndicate which Charman managed into the largest and most profitable at Lloyd's. In 1994/1995, convinced of the importance of attracting corporate investment both for his agency in particular and for Lloyd's in general, the husband caused Charman's holding company to be sold to a newly created company, Tarquin plc; and he and the trustees of Dragon and of the children's settlement, all of whom had substantial shareholdings in Charman, received in lieu significant amounts of cash and, in all, one third of the shares in Tarquin, for which he continued to work as he had for Charman.

[16] By then Lloyd's was facing grave difficulties. The husband, who was appointed senior deputy chairman of Lloyd's, was one of a few senior figures who had the drive, ingenuity and courage to devise and implement the series of complex initiatives which saved it. He says that in 1997, after it had in effect been saved, he became disillusioned with Lloyd's because in his view it was beginning to retrench rather than continuing to pursue further radical reform. In 1998 he caused Tarquin to be sold at a record price to Ace Ltd, a global insurance company based in Bermuda with existing interests at Lloyd's; and the husband, Dragon and the children's settlement exchanged their shares in Tarquin for stock in Ace worth a total of US$133m. In due course the husband's work, as a director of Ace and its senior executive outside the US, embraced more than its interests at Lloyd's; the dimensions of his work became international.

[17] In March 2001 the husband suddenly left Ace. He had been outvoted by his co-directors and summarily dismissed, which gave rise to litigation and his negotiation of a substantial severance package and a company apology. The judge found that, at this time of unexpected adversity, the parties grew close and the wife gave the husband considerable emotional support. The husband, Dragon and the children's settlement retained their shareholdings in Ace, the value of which had grown substantially since 1998, until sale of them took place in stages between February 2003 and February 2004 at a total price of £60m. As we will explain, the husband became non-resident in the UK for tax purposes on 27 January 2003; and there were substantial advantages in delaying disposal of the shares in Ace until after he had done so.

[18] In May 2001 the husband embarked on plans to establish a new global specialist insurance business. Paradoxically the '9–11' terrorist attacks enabled him

to accelerate and enlarge his plans; and in November 2001 the first Axis company was incorporated in Bermuda. Within a few weeks it had attracted investment in the USA of US$2.5 billion. The husband at once took his present position of President and Chief Executive. The Axis holding company was floated in 2003; and the growth of the group's capital, turnover and profit has been rapid and remarkable.

[19] From autumn 2001, when Axis began to operate, the husband rented a home in Bermuda and began to spend about half of each week there. He promised the wife that he would do so only for about 6 months, while he set up the business. But after the 6 months he continued to do so; indeed during 2002 he increased the amount of time spent in Bermuda and elsewhere abroad. In consequence the marriage came under strain. The wife was on any view reluctant to move from the parties' fourth and final matrimonial home in Kent offshore, whether to Bermuda or otherwise; but the judge rejected the husband's criticisms of her in this regard. Both parties were worried about their younger son, then aged 15, whose education in England was not proceeding well; the wife considered that it was important for him that she should continue to reside in England. Furthermore her elderly parents lived nearby and needed her attention. She was also reluctant to resign as a magistrate.

[20] But taxation as well as business considerations were leading the husband to favour abandonment of his residence in the UK. In particular, as a result of changes introduced in the UK in 1998, disposals of Ace (and other) shares not only by him but also by the two trusts of which he was the settlor would thenceforward attract Capital Gains Tax unless he were non-resident. Even as early as January 2002 he was considering abandoning his residence and indeed his domicil in the UK. Eventually in April 2003 he notified the Inland Revenue that on 27 January 2003 he had ceased to be resident and ordinarily resident in the UK. He did not tell the wife of his cessation of residence until May 2003; and she was then alarmed to be told that the fiscal advantages would be lost if he were to spend more than 90 days a year in the UK for the following 5 years. The judge, who generally preferred the evidence of the wife to that of the husband when in conflict, and in particular did so in relation to disputed events surrounding the end of the marriage and to their discussions about moving to Bermuda, found that in 2003 the wife became resigned to her moving to Bermuda in order to save the marriage; that in October 2003 she proposed to the husband that she should join him there for a trial period of 2 years; but that by then the husband, who, so the judge tentatively found, had by then already embarked on another relationship, did not accept the proposal. In November 2003 the husband told the wife that the marriage was at an end: it had endured for almost 28 years.

Section D: Proceedings between the parties

[21] On 28 June 2004, the wife issued a petition for divorce in England. On 14 July 2004, without prior notice, it was served on the husband in Bermuda. On 26 August 2004 he issued a petition for divorce in Bermuda and on the following day he applied for a stay of the English suit so that the divorce might proceed in Bermuda. On 24 September 2004, after he had taken steps to progress the suit in Bermuda as fast as possible, Coleridge J ordered him not further to proceed with the suit in Bermuda until after his application for a stay of the English suit had been determined.

[22]   On 28 January 2005, Coleridge J heard the husband's application for a stay and by order dated 11 February 2005 he dismissed it. In effect the husband's principal argument in support of his application related to Dragon, which by then had a Bermudian corporate trustee, namely Codan Trust Company Ltd (Codan), and was governed by Bermudian law. His argument was that it was inevitable that, as part of her claim for ancillary relief, the wife would apply under s 24(1)(c) of the Act for an order for variation in her favour of Dragon, which he conceded to be a post-nuptial settlement; that the law of ancillary relief in Bermuda was closely modelled on that in England and Wales and gave the Bermudian court jurisdiction to entertain such an application; that, unless (which was unclear) Codan, as trustee of Dragon, should voluntarily participate in any application for variation made to the English court, there were grave doubts as to whether any such order by that court would be enforceable against it in Bermuda; and that, by contrast, there would be no difficulty about enforcement against it of any such order made in Bermuda. The wife's response, which the judge described as unsurprising, was that her intention was not to apply for an order for variation of Dragon but, rather, to contend that its assets constituted a resource of the husband which should be brought into account in computation of the lump sum for which she had applied in the English proceedings. The wife thus cut away much of the ground from under the husband's feet in relation to the stay; and, having referred to all the other factors relevant to the choice of forum, the judge concluded that the 'case is as English as Tunbridge Wells'.

[23]   Thus the wife's suit in England proceeded to decree nisi in April 2005 and both parties sought to assemble their case in relation to her application to the English court for ancillary relief. To the wife's argument that the assets of Dragon were a resource of the husband because Codan would be likely to make them available to him if he were so to request, the husband countered with an argument that, in setting it up in 1987 and ever thereafter, he had intended that the assets of the trust should be held for the benefit of his issue yet unborn and, in short, that it was a 'dynastic' trust, the assets of which should not be aggregated with his own.

[24]   The wife, by her advisers, took the view that the merits of the rival arguments in relation to Dragon might well be illumined by documents which were or might be in the possession of Codan and by its answers to specified questions, both relating primarily to the content of the historical dealings between the husband and Mr Clay, his English accountant, on the one hand and the successive trustees on the other. The husband, by his solicitors, alleged that, notwithstanding what he said had been his own request to it to co-operate in this regard, Codan was not prepared to do so. Thus in July 2005 the wife applied to the English court for an order for the issue of a letter of request to the Bermudian court to require Mr Anderson, a director of Codan, to produce specified documents and give oral answers under oath to specified questions for use in the English proceedings. As the Royal Court of Jersey recently pointed out in *Re H Trust* [2006] JRC057, at para [18], the provision of information relating to a family trust by its offshore trustee to a court in England charged with adjudicating a claim for ancillary relief is in principle desirable and does not represent any submission on the part of the trustee to its jurisdiction. In the event, however, rather than supporting the wife's application, the husband strongly opposed it. Indeed, when by order dated 20 October 2005, Coleridge J nevertheless granted the application, the husband appealed to this court. On 20 December 2005, by a

constitution of this court of which two of us were members, the appeal was dismissed: see *Charman v Charman* [2005] EWCA Civ 1606, [2006] 1 WLR 1053, [2006] 2 FLR 422.

[25] Meanwhile the letter of request had been issued and, on an application by the wife without notice to Codan, Bell J in the Supreme Court of Bermuda had ordered Mr Anderson to attend before an examiner in order to disclose the documents and answer the questions specified in the letter. But Codan had applied to set the order aside; and the hearing of its application was conveniently adjourned until just after the date fixed for handing down the decision of this court, namely until 22 December 2005. At that hearing Codan persuaded Bell J to set aside the entire order for disclosure on the basis that 2 days previously this court had erred in holding that in proceedings for ancillary relief a letter of request could issue in order to obtain disclosure of documents of the existence of which the applicant was not already aware. Although no one had expected the Bermudian court to rubber-stamp the request in the letter (see in particular the judgment of Lloyd LJ in this court at paras [62]–[66]), it has to be said that the reasoning adopted by Bell J, which he frankly acknowledged might lead to an unsatisfactory result, was, with great respect to him, somewhat unexpected, at least by this court; the courts of the two closely related jurisdictions, which apply analogous principles to applications for ancillary relief, usually aspire to approach issues such as those in relation to the disclosure of documents held by a third party in the same way. The wife says that in effect there was no time for her to appeal against the decision of Bell J prior to the start of the substantive hearing before Coleridge J on 13 February 2006 and that, without disclosure of the documents, there was no point in attempting to conduct the oral examination of Mr Anderson which Bell J had continued to permit but which, unsurprisingly, he had limited to examination-in-chief.

[26] Coleridge J conducted the substantive hearing of the wife's application over some 9 days, beginning on 13 February 2006. Both parties agreed with the judge that he should then delay delivery of his judgment until after the House of Lords had given its decision in the appeals, upon which it had recently heard argument, in *Miller*. On 24 May 2006 the House gave its decision and on 21 June 2006 the judge heard further argument upon its relevant effect. On 27 July 2006 he handed down his judgment.

[27] Although we must closely scrutinise other parts of his judgment below, it is helpful here to record the judge's computation of the parties' assets, each component of which we round to the nearest million pounds:

(a) The wife

(i) Matrimonial home (proposed 100% interest)	£3
(ii) Flat occupied by her parents	£1
(iii) Bank accounts	£4
WIFE: TOTAL	£8

(b) The husband

(i) Real property in US	£5
(ii) Bank accounts	£1

(iii) Investment: Bank of New York	£10
(iv) Personal possessions	£1
(v) Pensions	£2
(vi) Accumulated income: Dragon	£4
(vii) Bonus for 2005	£1
(viii) Axis shares	£11
(ix) Axis options	£22
(x) Liabilities	(£2)
SUBTOTAL	£55

and, in Dragon,

(xi) Cash and investments other than in Axis	£39
(xii) Axis shares	£29
(xiii) Axis warrants	£12
(xiv) Liabilities	(£12)
SUBTOTAL	£68
HUSBAND: TOTAL	£123
JOINT: TOTAL	£131

[28] Having concluded that the lump sum payable by the husband to the wife should be £40m, the judge thereupon ordered the husband to pay £12m (being the amount which the husband had suggested as the total proper award) to the wife by 31 August 2006 and adjourned until 23 October 2006 determination of the date for payment of the balance. In the event the husband paid only £8m by 31 August and omitted, so the judge found at the hearing on 23 October, to give any proper explanation for his failure to have paid the remaining £4m. The judge then ordered him to pay it by 14 November 2006, which he did pay, albeit 2 days late. The judge also made an order, which we have stayed pending determination of this appeal, for the husband to pay the balance of £28m by 1 March 2007.

Section E: Dragon

(i)   The background facts

[29] In an application for ancillary relief, the court's computation of the parties' assets logically precedes its consideration of their fair distribution. We therefore turn first to the husband's second main ground of appeal, namely that the judge erred in regarding the assets of Dragon as part of his resources.

[30] Dragon was set up by a deed of trust dated 16 November 1987. The husband was the settlor. A trustee company in Jersey was the trustee; and the proper law of the trust was that of Jersey. The beneficiaries were defined as the husband, the wife (who was named), their two sons, any future children and remoter issue of the husband, such charities as the trustees might identify and such other persons as the trustees might add. In effect the trust is entirely discretionary; and the trustees have a wide power to advance capital instead of, or in addition to, income to a beneficiary, save that they cannot do so if it would 'prejudice any person entitled to any prior life or other vested interest in the Trust fund or any part ... thereof'.

[31] By two provisions of the deed, the husband went out of his way to empower the trustees to benefit one beneficiary at the expense of the others. By cl 5(e) he provided that, in exercising their powers in favour of one beneficiary, the trustees could 'ignore entirely the interests or expectations' of any of the others; and, repetitiously, by cl 12(a), he provided that the trustees could exercise their powers for the benefit of one beneficiary 'without being obliged to consider the interests of the ... others'.

[32] By cl 15(e) power was conferred on the husband to replace the trustees. The purpose behind the inclusion of this power is explained in a letter to the husband dated 13 October 1987 written by Mrs Rees, his solicitor in London, who was orchestrating the creation of the trust and corresponding with solicitors in Jersey to that end. She wrote:

> 'I put to [the solicitors in Jersey] the question of making certain of the powers exercisable only with your consent and of giving you the power to appoint new trustees. Their response was to suggest your appointment as "protector" of the settlement who would in effect have to bless all the trustees' decisions before they could be implemented. Neither I nor [your accountants] really like this as it could be argued that the protector was in effect a trustee and prejudice the off-shore status of the trusts. [Your accountants] are confident that the letter of wishes will not be ignored and, correctly drafted, would afford adequate protection. As a letter of wishes is morally binding only and [the proposed corporate trustee] an unknown entity, I would suggest that, at the very least, you should have power to appoint and remove the trustees and will so provide.'

[33] The husband's letter of wishes to the trustee, there foreshadowed by Mrs Rees, was signed and dated 18 November 1987 and was expressed as follows:

'THE DRAGON HOLDINGS TRUST Dated 16 November 1987

You may find it helpful to know my wishes regarding the exercise of your powers and discretions over the funds of the above Settlement. I realise of course that these wishes cannot be binding on you.

My real intentions in establishing the Settlement are to protect and conserve certain assets for the benefit of myself and my Family.

During my lifetime it is my wish that you consult me with regard to all matters relating to the investment or administration of the Fund and thereafter you should consult my wife in like manner. If my wife survives me, it is my wish that the fund should be administered primarily for her benefit and that she should have access to capital, if necessary. If both of us are dead, my children are to be treated as the primary beneficiaries and I hope you will consult my executors and their guardians. Should anything happen to the entire family, then the funds subject to the Settlement should follow my estate.

Insofar as is consistent with the terms of the Settlement I wish to have the fullest possible access to the capital and income of the Settlement including the possibility of investing the entire Fund in business ventures undertaken by me.

If circumstances should change in any way I will write you a further letter.'

[34] Although the deed records that the initial sum placed by the husband into Dragon was £10,000, the real purpose behind setting up the trust and indeed the children's settlement was that, using the cash thus placed into them, the respective trustees should subscribe for some of the shares in Charman for which the husband would otherwise have been entitled to subscribe and which he correctly anticipated might become very valuable. Of his potential entitlement, 25% was placed in his own name, 25% was placed in the children's settlement and 50% was placed in Dragon. In her letter dated 13 October 1987, Mrs Rees had written to the husband in relation to Dragon:

'I think [your accountants] feel that the long term inheritance tax effects of a discretionary settlement ... can be ignored because it was understood at their first meeting with you that decisions would be taken about the ultimate destination of the fund before the expiration of the first ten year period. This does not entirely accord with my understanding in our subsequent discussions when I gathered that you might well wish to leave the settlement in place until such time as the Charman shares are sold ...

It seems to emerge clearly in our discussion that a discretionary settlement is appropriate to preserve flexibility as to the ultimate disposal of the assets of that trust and that you should reserve a right to retain part of the funds; capital gains tax protection may be its only advantage but, on balance, I suggest we go ahead ...'

The capital gains tax protection of which Mrs Rees there spoke was the deferment of liability beyond the trustee's disposal of an asset for capital gain until it made a capital payment to a beneficiary.

[35] In that Charman paid a substantial dividend on its shares even in 1988, its first year of operation, Dragon at once began to receive income; and since 1993, reflective of the changes into Tarquin, thence into Ace and finally into Axis, that income has been very substantial. Between 1988 and 1998 Dragon's initial corporate trustee and its successor, another Jersey trust company which replaced it in 1992, made four distributions of income to the husband totalling £800,000. At any rate, the first such distribution, made in 1988 itself, was made pursuant to the husband's express written request. All four distributions seem to have been made for fiscal purposes. But even income which the successive trustees did not distribute to the husband was assigned to him, apparently without his knowledge; and they accumulated it for him in a bespoke account. In 2004, after it had been replaced by Codan, the second Jersey trust company wrote:

'throughout the whole of our trusteeship of the Trust, we held the income of the Trust for [the husband] absolutely and regarded the Trust as an interest-in-possession trust.'

Apart from the four payments of income to the husband, there has been no distribution out of Dragon to any of the beneficiaries. Irrespective of the trustee's partial distribution and residual accumulation of the income to and for him, the husband, as a UK resident settlor retaining a potential interest under the trust, was liable to pay UK tax referable to its worldwide income. Until 1998, and irrespective of the precise fiscal purposes behind them, the distributions appear in effect to have indemnified him in that regard.

[36] It was agreed before the judge that the wealth of Dragon had been built by its investment, in accordance with the husband's requests, in his successive business ventures. It was, therefore, his requests which led the trustee to subscribe for the shares in Charman; to exchange the shares in Charman for shares in Tarquin and cash; to exchange the shares in Tarquin for shares in Ace; to buy shares and warrants in Axis with heavy borrowings; to sell its shares in Ace for £37m in eight tranches during the 9 months in 2003 which immediately followed his cessation of residence in the UK; and to use the investment management services of the Bank of New York. In 1990 the trustee had also acceded to his request to put up the assets of the trust as security for a bank guarantee necessary for his membership as a Name at Lloyd's.

[37] By 2002 the husband had resolved to move Dragon, as well as the children's settlement, to Bermuda. In December 2002 he approached Conyers Dill and Pearman, the well-known firm of barristers and attorneys in Bermuda, who offered him the services of their trust company, namely Codan. The husband thus caused the second Jersey trust company to resign as trustee of Dragon in favour of Codan with effect from 4 April 2003; and Codan thereupon exercised its power to change the proper law of the trust from that of Jersey to that of Bermuda.

[38] Meanwhile Mr Clay had sought to advise the husband to take steps to ensure that the move of Dragon to Bermuda did not lead to any loss of control over Dragon on his part. At a meeting between them on 7 March 2003, in the words of a memorandum of it made by Mr Clay:

'[Mr Clay] raised his concerns at the possible central control that may be exercised by the new Bermudan Trustees and that it was firstly critical for [the husband] to draft a Letter of Wishes as soon as the transfer from Jersey to Bermuda had taken place. Secondly, in the event of [the husband's] death, [Mr Clay] raised concerns that too much control would be in the hands of the Bermudan Trustees and that [the husband] needed to reflect on whether further protection should be arranged to ensure that his wishes were actually carried out.

[The husband] ... had met recently with [Mr] Anderson to review the management arrangements for the two trusts and he was quite comfortable with [Mr] Anderson's approach. However, it was agreed that [Mr Clay] should remind [the husband] to draft a Letter of Wishes for each Trust.'

At that time Mr Clay seems to have been under the impression that the husband's non-residence in the UK might not endure beyond the requisite 5 years. At a further meeting with the husband on 25 March 2003, Mr Clay, according to the latter's memorandum, suggested that Dragon should be 'collapsed' while the husband was non-resident; and in a memorandum dated June 2003, which he prepared for the use of Codan, Mr Clay suggested that it 'should consider whether it is appropriate "to bust" [Dragon] prior to [the husband] returning to the UK'.

[39] On 19 April 2004 Codan passed a written resolution in respect of Dragon. After noting that its predecessor had held its income on behalf of the husband and, albeit informally, had regarded it as an interest-in-possession trust, Codan formally resolved to regard it likewise and confirmed that it was exercising its power to appoint the income of the trust to the husband for life with effect from 4 April 2003 and so would accumulate it for him and periodically distribute it to him.

[40] By letter addressed to Codan dated 13 May 2004, ie after the breakdown of the marriage but prior to the issue of divorce proceedings, the husband wrote a fresh letter of wishes in relation to Dragon. The main change was that he excised the request made in 1987 that, following his death, the trust should be administered primarily for the benefit of the wife. He wrote:

'During my lifetime, I would like you to treat me as the primary beneficiary, although I expect that you will consider the interests of the other immediate family beneficiaries as appropriate from time to time. I acknowledge that you have appointed the annual income to myself as a life interest disposition, as had the previous trustees.

After my death, and if they survive me, I would wish you to treat my children as primary equal beneficiaries per stirpes.

I would like my children to receive income only up to the age of 30, unless otherwise agreed by the Trustee. I would like you to consider making half the capital of the presumptive share of each of my children available to them at the age of 30. At the age of 40, I would like you to consider making the whole of the capital of their share available to them.'

[41] On a date ostensibly in June 2004, the husband wrote to Codan in connection with its recent appointment to him of the income of Dragon. Subject to a direction for defrayment out of the income of an apparently small recurring expense referable to the management of his personal investment company, the husband instructed Codan to add back into Dragon all the accumulated income held for him and, subject to any contrary instruction, all future income otherwise to be held for him. The accumulated fund which the husband thereby – after the end of the marriage – chose to resettle into Dragon was £4m and, as can be seen in para [27], above, the judge notionally deducted it from the assets of Dragon and restored it into the list of the husband's personal assets. A subsidiary ground of appeal is that the judge was wrong to conduct that notional exercise. In the event, however that, upon the second main ground of appeal, we were to determine that the judge was entitled to regard the assets of Dragon as part of the husband's resources, we would not address this ground because the precise place in the list for inclusion of the £4m would be irrelevant.

[42] On 27 August 2004, being the day after he had filed his petition in Bermuda, the husband, by his English solicitors, made a proposal to settle the wife's financial claims; and, in order that her solicitors could advise her upon it, his solicitors sent to them what in their covering letter they described as 'a summary

schedule of his worldwide resources'. The schedule was itself headed 'Schedule of Matrimonial Assets' and on four pages it set out first the husband's assets totalling £27m, then jointly owned assets totalling £4m and finally trust assets, being the assets of Dragon, totalling £52m, ie together totalling £83m. A note was appended that the summary did not include the children's settlement because neither party had a financial interest in it. The schedule had been prepared by Mr Clay; and the husband did not see it prior to his solicitors' despatch of it to the wife's solicitors. He asserts that it was an entirely inappropriate, confused and unauthorised treatment of the assets of Dragon as part of the 'matrimonial assets' and of 'his worldwide resources' on the part of Mr Clay and his solicitors.

(ii) The argument before the judge

[43] The husband's primary argument before the judge in relation to Dragon was very different from the primary argument which he now seeks to advance in this appeal. In shorthand, as endorsed on the Schedule of Assets furnished on his behalf to the judge, his case was 'Trust dynastic and should not be taken into account'. Or, as Mr Singleton QC wrote in his opening submissions to the judge:

'The most important features of the trust are:

(1)   H's case is that this trust was set up to provide for the future generations of H's family.
(2)   H has made it clear that he has no wish to benefit from the trust.
(3)   H has had minimal communication with the trustees, which tends to support his case as to intention.
(4)   There have been few actual distributions to H, and none at all for the last 7 years.'

We hasten to add that Mr Singleton did also submit that the court could not conclude that the trustees (in the words of his opening submissions) 'will do what H says or asks as regards distribution, rather than investment' or (in the words of his closing submissions) 'will simply accede to any request made by H that they should advance a huge chunk of the fund'. But this submission was rolled up as part of Mr Singleton's fundamental argument: the thrust of it was that, because the husband had created Dragon in order to put assets aside there for the benefit of his issue yet unborn, rather than himself (or the wife), it would not be reasonable to expect him to request the trustees to advance capital to him nor, were he to do so, to expect the trustees to accede to the request. Ironically it was Mr Pointer who, in his written closing submissions to the judge, teased the two issues apart more clearly:

'In the end, the fundamental issue ... in respect of the Dragon Holdings Trust is whether or not H has demonstrated to the satisfaction of the court that it is a dynastic trust, having a different quality from an ordinary offshore trust, such that the court's approach should therefore be divergent from the norm.

A secondary issue may be said to arise in the circumstances of this case, namely whether, were H to invite the trustees to distribute some or all of the funds within the Dragon Holdings Trust to him absolutely, they would comply with that invitation.'

[44] Both parties gave written and oral evidence to the judge in relation to 'the fundamental issue', namely the dynastic issue. The husband averred that he had always intended Dragon to be a legacy for future generations of his family. The wife averred, by contrast, that she had always understood that Dragon was a family trust in which the husband, she and the boys had a continuing interest and that its assets were never beyond his control in that, were he to need them or want access to them, arrangements would be made accordingly.

[45] In the event the judge preferred the case of the wife to that of the husband in relation to the dynastic issue. In particular the judge found that:

(a)   the husband's letters of wishes both in 1987 and in 2004 were inconsistent with an intention to create a dynastic trust;
(b)   there was no evidence, in particular no documentary evidence, corroborative of the husband's own evidence in support of his case;
(c)   the husband had conducted a 'Herculean struggle' to prevent Codan from giving evidence in circumstances in which, had Dragon been dynastic, it would be likely to have been able to produce evidence from its files to that effect; and
(d)   the wife, whose recollection was good, had known nothing of any dynastic intention on the part of the husband.

[46] Then the judge proceeded as follows:

'[78]   But even if I had been persuaded of the existence of this as a settled, even documented, intention I am doubtful in the circumstances of this case whether, of itself, it would have been very influential in the result.

[79]   The test is whether the assets in the trust should be regarded by the Court as a "resource". That is a very broad definition. These assets are held in a discretionary trust in conventional form. I will not repeat the very helpful descriptive analysis of such a trust in the Jersey High Court adopted by Potter P in his judgment dismissing the husband's appeal against my order relating to letters of request. (See *Re Esteem Settlement* [2004] WTLR 1). It is a very useful description of general application in cases like this. And as Lloyd LJ on the same occasion pointed out the assets in the trust "could be available to him on demand without being his money", as Mr Singleton was constrained to agree.

[80]   So even if the husband had got home on the facts, for the Court simply to have ignored the assets would have been, I consider, wrong and, in my experience, entirely novel.

...

[82]   [I]n the end I am persuaded by Mr Pointer's arguments and all the assets in the Dragon Trust will remain well and truly on the main schedule.'

(iii)   The argument before us

[47]   Mr Singleton tells us that, notwithstanding what he acknowledges to be great difficulty in his way, he aspires to persuade us to set aside the judge's finding that Dragon is not a dynastic trust. The point is not clearly raised in the grounds of appeal, even as now proposed to be amended. Mr Singleton's only point is that, had he reminded himself of the absence of distributions out of Codan since 1998, the judge would have been compelled to make the contrary finding. But since then the husband has had no need for distributions and has not asked for them; indeed until 2003 distributions of capital were, from a fiscal perspective, firmly to be avoided. We consider that the judge's rejection of the husband's dynastic argument was inevitable. The obvious fiscal purpose behind Dragon; indeed its status, in Mr Singleton's own words in this appeal, as a 'key component in [the husband's] overall financial and tax planning'; the husband's unusual inclusion of himself in the deed as a named beneficiary; the terms of the letter of Mrs Rees dated 13 October 1987; the content of each of his letters of wishes; Mr Clay's suggestion in 2003 that the husband should collapse the trust; the first presentation of Dragon on the husband's behalf in the proceedings as being part of his resources; the absence of any documentary evidence to support his argument; the inference to be drawn from his attempts to prevent the wife's access to documents on Codan's file; and her own convincing, contrary evidence. All these in effect compelled the judge's conclusion.

[48]   The primary argument now put before us on behalf of the husband is that the judge failed to resolve the 'secondary issue' which Mr Pointer on behalf of the wife had purported to identify for him, namely the issue as to the likelihood of advancement. On any view the argument lacks forensic integrity because it was never separately identified on behalf of the husband. Strictly, there was no separate 'issue' for the judge to resolve. Nevertheless we agree with both counsel that, before he attributed all the assets of Dragon to the husband, the judge had to be satisfied that, if so requested by the husband, Codan would be likely to advance them to him: in the judgments in this court on the husband's appeal against the order for issue of the letter of request, in particular at para [12], such had been confirmed as the central question generally arising in such cases.

[49]   The first question is, therefore, whether the judge made a finding that, if requested, Codan would be likely to advance all the assets of Dragon to the husband. Mr Boyle submits that the judge never even addressed that question. The second question, which arises if, contrary to Mr Boyle's submission, the judge made such a finding, is whether it was open to him to do so.

[50]   The answer to the first question is to be found in the paragraphs of the judge's judgment set out at para [46], above. We analyse them as follows:

(a)   The judge asked himself whether the assets in Dragon were a 'resource'. Mr Boyle's submission that such was not the test is misconceived: it is the overarching test because the word 'resources' is the portmanteau word used in s 25(2)(a) of the Act.

(b)   Then the judge turned to consider the matter in the context of discretionary trusts. First he referred to the decision of the Royal Court of Jersey in *Re*

The Esteem Settlement [2004] WTLR 1 as containing a very helpful descriptive analysis of such a trust. Part of that court's analysis is as follows, at para [166]:

> '... one would expect to find that in the majority of trusts, there had not been a refusal by the trustees of a request by a settlor. This would no doubt be because, in the majority of cases, a settlor would be acting reasonably in the interests of himself and his family. This would particularly be so where there was a small close-knit family and where the settlor could be expected to be fully aware of what was in the interests of his family.'

Then the judge referred to the observation of Lloyd LJ in the course of argument upon the husband's previous appeal to this court that the assets in Dragon 'could be available to [the husband] on demand without being his money'.

(c) Ultimately the judge declared himself persuaded by Mr Pointer's arguments, to which he had earlier referred albeit in part only by cross-reference to Mr Pointer's written submissions, and concluded that all the assets in Dragon should be attributed to the husband. Mr Pointer had articulated one additional argument, which we consider in para [55], below, specifically in relation to the likelihood of advancement. But, just as Mr Singleton's argument in relation to the likelihood of advancement was rolled up as part of his argument in relation to the dynastic issue, so were all Mr Pointer's arguments in response, save for that one addition: they related to features of the evidence which, because, according to Mr Pointer, they suggested that its capital would be likely to be advanced to the husband, demonstrated that Dragon was not dynastic. In accepting those arguments the judge accepted their premises as well as their conclusions.

(d) Indeed the judge indicated that, had it been necessary, he would have considered going further than Mr Pointer had asked him to go. For he observed that, even had he found that Dragon was dynastic, it was doubtful whether he would have declined to attribute its assets to the husband. It was only an aside: but the construction which we place upon it is that the judge considered that, whatever the husband's historical intentions in relation to Dragon, it would be likely that, in the changed circumstances of his need to discharge obligations following divorce, its trustee would advance its capital to him.

[51] The judge would certainly have obviated energetic argument upon this appeal if he had expressly found that Codan would be likely to advance all the capital of Dragon to the husband upon request. But for the reasons set out at para [50], above, it is obvious that the need to address such a question was in the forefront of his mind. We are quite clear that he effectively made such a finding; nor, in the light of the way in which Mr Singleton had presented his case, do we significantly criticise the judge for omitting to spell it out.

[52] We turn to the second question, namely whether it was open to the judge to find a likelihood of advancement. Mr Boyle's brief in this regard has proved scarcely arguable. He describes as his 'keynote' point the absence of a track record

of advancement; but we have explained in para [47], above, why we do not regard such absence as significant. Mr Boyle needs to confront in particular the following facts:

(a)   the husband was the settlor of Dragon;
(b)   its wealth represents the fruits of investment at his request in companies which, substantially as a result of his talents, became very successful;
(c)   until after the breakdown of the marriage the operative letter of wishes was that he should 'have the fullest possible access to the capital and income of the Settlement'; and
(d)   even today, following despatch of the fresh letter, his expressed wish is to be treated as the primary beneficiary.

[53]   Mr Boyle's response to his difficulties is in part disarmingly frank. He accepts that the judge was required to look at the reality of the situation and that trustees of such trusts can generally be expected to respond favourably to reasonable requests made of them by settlors and to comply with any expression of wishes on their part. Mr Boyle even concedes that, if disaster struck the husband's business and he fell into real financial difficulty, Codan could properly make available to him a large sum of capital. But, so Mr Boyle contends, such a hypothesis is inapt because the husband has had no 'need' for any capital out of Dragon. Our reaction to that contention is two-fold. First, it is in law a perfectly adequate foundation for the aggregation of trust assets with a party's personal assets for the purposes of s 25(2)(a) of the Act that they should be likely to be advanced to him or her in the event only of 'need'. Secondly, the contention is inconsistent with another area of the husband's argument, which is to the effect that, although his personal assets computed by the judge at £55m exceed the lump sum award of £40m, the judge must have expected him to have recourse, directly or indirectly, to the assets of Dragon, particularly its cash and investments other than in Axis, for the purposes of satisfying the order and that indeed the order can only reasonably be satisfied in that way. If so, why then does the husband not have a 'need' for capital out of Dragon in order to assist him to discharge his legal obligations? Mr Boyle is driven to respond with the suggestion that, because the moment at which the judge considered whether to attribute the assets of Dragon to him was prior to the making of any order against the husband, the husband had had no need for them at that critical moment. This is chop-logic of the most specious kind, as all those who have discharged their liabilities to ex-spouses without court orders will readily understand.

[54]   His back to the wall, Mr Boyle seeks to raise questions as to how Codan would respond to a request by the husband for advancement and suggests that they remain unanswered. In circumstances in which the judge made a finding, unchallenged in this appeal, that the husband had put up 'a herculean struggle' in order to prevent Codan from giving evidence in the proceedings, it was inevitable that there would be no express presentation to the court of its likely response. At first, for example, Mr Boyle submitted that in the event of such a request Codan would be 'bound' to consider the interests of the other beneficiaries. As he now accepts, the submission is incorrect: see the provisions of the deed referred to in para [31], above. That Codan would, however, *wish* to consider the interests of the other beneficiaries, albeit probably only briefly, we have no doubt. Mr Boyle also refers to the prohibition in the deed of trust against any such exercise of the power of advancement as would prejudice any person entitled to a prior life interest in

the fund. He refers to the resolution in 2004 by which the husband's life interest was formally confirmed and suggests, in our view casuistically, that an advancement of capital to him would prejudice him qua life tenant. More broadly, Mr Boyle argues that, faced with a request for advancement, Codan would be likely to apply for directions to the Bermudian court or seek the advice of Bermudian counsel; and the argument is prelude to a long presentation on his part, including references for example to Bermudian statute and to cases determined in the Royal Court of Jersey, of the terms in which the Bermudian court might respond to any such application or counsel might advise. In the light of the strength of the wife's case on the likelihood of advancement to the husband of the assets in Dragon for the reasons mainly set out in para [52], above, as well as of Mr Boyle's own concessions in that regard set out in para [53], above, it would be difficult for the husband at any stage of the proceedings convincingly to have raised a spectre that, even if approached, the Bermudian court or Bermudian counsel would find reason to frustrate a proposed advancement to him. But there is another reason why we should draw a line across this argument: it was never raised before the judge; the evidence of foreign law was never placed before him; he made no reference to the argument; it does not figure in the pleaded grounds upon which the husband has secured permission to appeal nor even in the skeleton argument in support of them; and it was first raised in a supplementary skeleton argument dated 11 working days prior to the hearing of the appeal. In short the argument is brought too late in any event.

[55]

(a)   We advert briefly to Mr Pointer's additional argument to the judge in favour of the likelihood of advancement, to which we referred in para [50](c), above. The argument was that, given the husband's express power to replace the trustees of Dragon, he could replace a trustee who declined to accede to a request for advancement with one who would accede to it. This was not one of the arguments of Mr Pointer which the judge expressly articulated and accepted. But it was one of the arguments which, in para [82] of his judgment (set out in para [46], above), the judge accepted by reference.

(b)   It was hardly surprising that Mr Pointer should argue – and that the judge should accept – that the husband's power to replace the trustees was indicative of the likelihood of advancement. The power had been inserted at the suggestion of Mrs Rees expressly in order to make it even more likely that the trust would be administered in accordance with the husband's letters of wishes.

(c)   The submission of Mr Boyle, however, is that, as established in *Re Skeats' Settlement; Skeats v Evans* (1889) 42 Ch D 522 the power to replace trustees is fiduciary and that therefore the husband cannot lawfully exercise it by way of response to a refusal by a trustee to accede to his request for advancement. Mr Nugee, for his part, accepts that it was held in *Skeats' Settlement* that the power is fiduciary and, for the purposes of this appeal, he accepts that we should treat the case as having been correctly decided.

(d)   Again, Mr Boyle's point was never made to the judge and thus *Skeats' Settlement* was not drawn to his attention. Indeed the point was introduced into the argument on this appeal only on the first day of the hearing. Had it been made to the judge, he might well have elected not to adopt Mr Pointer's additional argument even by reference. There is a wealth of other material which justifies the judge's finding as to the likelihood of advancement. But the judge might alternatively have held, as Mr Nugee has in passing invited us to hold, that it may be simplistic to conclude that, just because it is fiduciary, the power is irrelevant to the likelihood of advancement.

(e)   In this respect Mr Nugee invites us to be realistic; and it is an invitation which, in exercising its jurisdiction in relation to ancillary relief, it is in principle particularly appropriate for the court to accept. Mr Nugee submits that, realistically, a settlor with a power to replace trustees will be unlikely to allow a point to be reached at which his exercise of it would become unlawful as being in breach of his duty to act in good faith. In proposing inclusion of the power as an extra safeguard for the husband Mrs Rees, for example, would not have been contemplating its unlawful exercise. It is well settled that lack of harmony between a beneficiary and a trustee can be a lawful ground for the latter's replacement: see *Letterstedt v Broers* (1884) 9 App Cas 371, at 386, cited in *Re The Esteem Settlement* [2004] WTLR 1, at para [165]. A settlor with a power to replace trustees, says Mr Nugee, will be wise to ask himself from time to time, and well in advance of any actual request for advancement, whether, in the light of his continuing dealings with the trustee, he is or remains – to adopt the word used in the memorandum of the husband's meeting with Mr Clay on 7 March 2003 – 'comfortable' with the trustee. If the two of them do not see eye to eye, then it is likely to be in the interests of the beneficiaries of the trust of which he is the settlor, and therefore to be lawful, for him to replace the trustee by virtue of the principle in *Letterstedt*.

(f)   There is no need for us to decide this peripheral issue. It has arisen very late and has not been fully argued on either side. We consider that exploration of the difficult interface between the likely exercise of powers in the real world and what must for the court be the dominant requirements of the law is better left to another occasion.

[56] From the foot of his argument that it was not open to the judge to make a finding as to the likelihood of advancement to the husband of all Dragon's assets, Mr Boyle has proceeded to suggest how the judge should properly have treated its assets. Although in the event this section of his argument is academic, it is nonetheless helpful for us to notice it. Without prejudice to the husband's basic contention that none of the assets of Dragon should have been attributed to him, Mr Boyle makes three alternative fall-back suggestions:

(a)   The court should have attributed to the husband the capitalised value of the interest in the future income of the trust which in 2004 Codan formally appointed to him for life. No doubt if it had been inappropriate to attribute all the trust assets to him, it would have been appropriate to conduct that exercise and also somehow to weigh the value of Codan's power to advance capital to him. Before the judge, as part of a fall-back position of his own, Mr Pointer sought to conduct just such an exercise and produced capitalised figures of £15m or £34m. At that time, however, the unqualified response of Mr Singleton was that the exercise was inappropriate; and in the event the judge had no need to address the issue. We consider that Mr Boyle's commendation of the exercise, first articulated 11 days prior to the hearing of this appeal, is another example of the husband's cynical deployment at different stages of these proceedings of contradictory arguments, dictated only by whether they seem to suit his book at that stage.

Even if it had been open to him to present his current argument to this court at so late a stage, the husband must realise that contradictory arguments cannot both be valid and that a litigant who advances them forfeits a degree of forensic credibility.

(b)   Alternatively such component of the court's award to the wife as was referable to the assets in Dragon should have been the capitalised value of the life interest which (so the argument runs) would probably have been granted to her in some of those assets in the event that she had applied to the English court for an order for variation in her favour of Dragon as a post-nuptial settlement. This argument is specifically set out in the late proposed amendment to the grounds of appeal for which the husband seeks our permission; and for six reasons we find the argument extraordinary. First, there is a fundamental conceptual confusion in linking the court's duty in every application for ancillary relief to inquire into the extent of a party's resources with its power to redistribute assets which are not the resources of only one party but are susceptible to redistribution because they are held in a settlement which is nuptial. Secondly, although Mr Boyle now argues that, in cases in which there is no track record of distributions of capital out of a settlement, an application to vary it should be strongly encouraged, it was the husband's principal argument on his application for a stay of the English suit that the doubts about the enforceability in Bermuda of an English order for variation of settlement were such that the wife could not sensibly apply for it in England. Thirdly, because the husband never asked the judge to assess the outcome of a hypothetical application to vary, he never did so. Fourthly, it is impossible to discern the size of the fund which would have been taken out of Dragon for the wife by way of variation, interrelated, as it would be, with the outcome of a second hypothetical exercise, namely assessment of the size of the award to the wife out of the husband's personal assets by way of a lump sum. Fifthly, we see no reason to accept that, just because after the breakdown of the marriage Codan formally assigned to the husband a life interest in Dragon, the result of an application to vary it would have been provision for the wife only of a life interest, albeit presumably subject to a power in her trustees to advance capital to her; our instinct, on the contrary, is that on the facts of this case outright provision would have been more likely. Sixthly, this argument, too, was first raised 11 days before the hearing of the appeal. In all these circumstances we refuse permission to amend the grounds of appeal so as to include it. [We have already considered the other, more general, proposed amendments, including the suggestion, which we regard as inherent in the issue as to the likelihood of advancement upon request, that the judge's order placed undue pressure on Codan; the convenient course is to grant permission to amend in these other respects].

(c)   Alternatively the court should attribute one third of the assets of Dragon to the husband. Mr Boyle first raised this argument on the second day of the hearing and at the conclusion of his oral submissions. The one third fraction is, so Mr Boyle suggests, a fair but necessarily conservative reflection of all the features relative to the nexus between the husband and Dragon. We can discern no logical path to the fraction; and the argument would have found no favour with us at all.

[57]   For reasons of policy we are pleased to find ourselves able to uphold the judge's attribution to the husband of all the assets in Dragon. Although the list of

matters to which, upon an application for ancillary relief, the court must have regard pursuant to s 25(2) of the Act presently remains unchanged, the decision in *White* alters the necessary extent of the focus upon some of those matters in cases of substantial wealth. The needs of the parties remain to be considered, but in many cases focus upon them has waned as a result of an early conclusion that they will on any view be met as part of the outcome of other aspects of the requisite exercise. As a result of the advent of reference to proportions, the focus has largely shifted to computation of resources. Prior to the decision in *White v White* [2001] 1 AC 596, [2000] 2 FLR 981 the elaborate inquiry in the present case as to the attributability of the assets in a trust to a party as part of his or her resources would probably have been unnecessary. But, whenever it is necessary to conduct such an inquiry, it is essential for the court to bring to it a judicious mixture of worldly realism and of respect for the legal effects of trusts, the legal duties of trustees and, in the case of off-shore trusts, the jurisdictions of off-shore courts. In the circumstances of the present case it would have been a shameful emasculation of the court's duty to be fair if the assets which the husband built up in Dragon during the marriage had not been attributed to him.

[58]   Mr Boyle submits that, if this court were to dismiss the part of the appeal referable to Dragon, it would send a message to the off-shore world that, in family cases, trusts do not matter. It will by now be clear that we send no such message. He draws our attention to the decision of the Royal Court of Jersey in *Re Fountain Trust* [2005] JLR 359, in which it observed, at para [18], that an assumption of jurisdiction by a judge of the Family Division in England to declare a Jersey trust to be a 'sham', such as had there occurred, would generally be exorbitant. We agree with the Royal Court's observation. Mr Boyle also draws our attention to the decision of the same court in *Re B Trust* [2006] JRC 185. There, at para [32], an important suggestion was made, namely that, when a party applied to it for variation of an off-shore settlement, the English court should give serious consideration to declining to exercise its jurisdiction on the basis that, after conducting the substantive inquiry, it should instead invite the off-shore court, provided of course that the latter is invested with the appropriate jurisdiction, to act as an auxiliary to it in regard to any proposed variation. But the wife in the present case has been, relatively speaking, in a fortunate position. She cannot and does not allege that Dragon is a sham. She does not, and does not need to, apply for variation of Dragon. For she has the evidence with which to identify the assets of Dragon as part of the husband's resources. Nor do we read the decision of Bell J in Bermuda on 22 December 2005 as any indication that the courts of Bermuda will not be disposed to help to ensure, within the parameters of its laws, that whatever may ultimately be awarded to the wife in these proceedings will be duly paid.

Section F: Special contribution

(i)   The structure of the judge's judgment

[59]   After introducing the case and setting out background matters, the judge entitled a section of his judgment,[2] 'The Statutory "Balancing Exercise"' and in it said, at para [58]:

---

[2]   *Charman v Charman (No 2)* [2006] EWHC 1879 (Fam), [2007] 1 FLR 593.

'Matrimonial Causes Act 1973, s 25 rules the day. And, despite the endless judicial gloss which is applied to it year in and year out at every level, it is always best to start and end in that familiar section. ... The obvious starting point for all these applications is the financial position of the parties now.'

[60] Thereupon there were sections of the judgment in which the judge addressed:

(a) The parties' resources in the form of their assets and liabilities and, in the case of the husband, his earning capacity.

(b) The parties' needs and standard of living during the marriage. This section, however, comprised only one paragraph ([98]), as follows:

> 'These two factors call for only scant attention in this case for quite obvious reasons. Even on the basis of the husband's open offer the wife's "needs" could be met at the standard of living which she has become used to ... The remaining fortune in the husband's hands even on his own figures and ignoring Dragon would be much more than that. It is not suggested that either spouse should want for anything financially. They each spend at an enormous rate. And why not given their resources? ... [I]n the end, the result is not really going to be determined by reference to these two factors. Other factors elbow them aside.'

(c) The husband's contention (or what the judge held to be the true nature of the husband's contention) that, in two respects including that to which we will refer in para [95], below, the wife had been guilty of conduct which it would be inequitable to disregard. The judge rejected that contention.

(d) The contributions of the parties. The judge began his analysis as follows, at para [111]:

> 'For the past nearly 5 years, since *White*, courts at every level have been wrestling with the question of whether or not in departing from equality and striving for fairness it is proper to take into account and give weight to exceptional wealth creation by one spouse.'

Then he cited passages in the speeches of Lord Nicholls of Birkenhead and Baroness Hale of Richmond in *Miller*; noted the conclusion in *Miller* that the criteria by which the court decided whether to take conduct and special contribution into account were identical; addressed the suggestion that special contribution was a species of conduct; and continued as follows, at para [117]:

> 'So, in the end, is a departure from equality applicable in this case? Or, as Mr Singleton QC would have it, are the husband's extraordinary talent and the nature/value of the assets so generated, factors which, adopting his incremental approach, lead to a figure which happens to be much less than one half? In the end I doubt whether the differing approaches lead to a different result.

Whichever way it is approached it seems to me this factor must, exceptionally and in fairness, be taken into account in this case. Whether the husband's remarkable abilities ..., his energy and wealth creation ... are "conduct" or a "contribution to the welfare of the family" in the broadest sense their product is wholly exceptional, "gross and obvious ..."

[O]ne way or another this factor weighs and departure from equality is fair. So far so good.

... [T]he House of Lords has pronounced some of the principles which underlie the "special contribution" issue. They are silent on how to apply them. For those of us ... trying to translate these principles into figures, this final stage is the more difficult part of the exercise.

Mr Pointer QC concedes the small reduction to which I have made reference but urges great caution in moving away from 50% in case discrimination starts creeping in. Mr Singleton QC rebuts wholly the simple departure from equality approach [and] says "the proper approach is ... to consider all the factors in s 25 and determine a fair outcome. The court must cross-check its provisional award against the yardstick of equality to ensure that in the event of an unequal division there are good reasons to justify the difference. The quantification of the provisional award is both a cumulative/incremental approach ... What the court cannot do is to assume that the parties (in a long marriage where the resources exceed their needs) are each going to receive 50% and then determine if there is any reason why they should not"

...

I can find little hard ground once the self-justifying fairness of 50/50 is departed from ...

If adjustment is appropriate, especially in these huge money cases, I think it should be meaningful and significant and not a token one ...'

[61] Then followed a section entitled 'Conclusions'. The judge said:

'This was a long marriage where the parties started with nothing and all the wealth was effectively created ... during its subsistence. Both played their full part in the marriage. However this is a case, in that very small category, where, wholly exceptionally, the wealth created is of extraordinary proportions from extraordinary talent and energy. Taking everything properly into account, I have decided, after much deliberation ..., to transfer the husband's interest in [the home] to the wife and additionally order him to pay her a lump sum of £40m (in addition to her present assets). She will exit the marriage with a total of about £48m including the assets already in her name. In percentage terms that is just under 37% of the total. The husband will accordingly retain just over 63%. I fully intend the difference, which also reflects the fact that the wife is getting cash (if she wants it) and

the husband will continue to operate and have a significant stake in one of
the most risky fields; high risk insurance.'

[62]   To his judgment the judge added a postscript in which he recognised the
current uncertainty of outcome in this type of case and raised the possibility that,
by way of guidance which would not erode the width of the discretion invested in
trial courts by s 25 of the Act, the court might suggest, by way of departure from
50–50, a tariff of percentages related to the size of such wealth as might qualify as
a special contribution.

(ii)   The statutory exercise expounded in Miller

[63]   The best way for us to address Mr Singleton's attack on the judge's
treatment of the husband's special contribution is to do so by reference to our
interpretation of what is now the proper approach to a case of alleged special
contribution, first considering the general nature of the statutory exercise. Two
objectives will govern what we say. The first is to be loyal to what we understand
to be the spirit as well as the letter of such guidance on the topic as has been given
by the House of Lords in *White v White* [2001] 1 AC 596, [2000] 2 FLR 981 and
Miller v Miller; McFarlane v McFarlane [2006] UKHL 24, [2006] 2 AC 618, [2006]
1 FLR 1186, whether or not it is part of the reasoning behind those actual
decisions. We say so because there is no doubt that, under that guidance, the
House has left much for the courts to develop. The second is to express ourselves
as clearly and simply as the subject allows.

[64]   'The yardstick of equality of division', first identified by Lord Nicholls of
Birkenhead in *White* at 605G and 989 respectively, filled the vacuum which
resulted from the abandonment in that decision of the criterion of 'reasonable
requirements'. The origins of the yardstick lay in s 25(2) of the Act, specifically in
s 25(2)(f), which refers to the parties' contributions: see the preceding argument of
Lord Nicholls of Birkenhead at 605D-E. The yardstick reflected a modern,
non-discriminatory conclusion that the proper evaluation under s 25(2)(f) of the
parties' different contributions to the welfare of the family should generally lead
to an equal division of their property unless there was good reason for the division
to be unequal. It also tallied with the overarching objective: a fair result.

[65]   Although in *White* the majority of the House agreed with the speech of
Lord Nicholls of Birkenhead and thus with his description of equality as a
'yardstick' against which tentative views should be 'checked', Lord Cooke,
at 615D and 999 respectively, doubted whether use of the words 'yardstick' or
'check' would produce a result different from that of the words 'guideline' or
'starting point'. In *Miller* the House clearly moved towards the position of
Lord Cooke. Thus Lord Nicholls of Birkenhead, at paras [20] and [29], referred to
the 'equal sharing principle' and to the 'sharing entitlement'; those phrases
describe more than a yardstick for use as a check. Baroness Hale of Richmond
put the matter beyond doubt when, referring to remarks by Lord Nicholls of
Birkenhead at paras [29], she said, at para [144]:

'I agree that there cannot be a hard and fast rule about whether one starts with equal sharing and departs if need or compensation supply a reason to do so, or whether one starts with need and compensation and shares the balance.'

It is clear that the court's consideration of the sharing principle is no longer required to be postponed until the end of the statutory exercise. We should add that, since we take the 'the sharing principle' to mean that property should be shared in equal proportions unless there is good reason to depart from such proportions, departure is not *from* the principle but takes place *within* the principle.

[66] To what property does the sharing principle apply? The answer might well have been that it applies only to matrimonial property, namely the property of the parties generated during the marriage otherwise than by external donation; and the consequence would have been that non-matrimonial property would have fallen for redistribution by reference only to one of the two other principles of need and compensation to which we refer in para [68], below. Such an answer might better have reflected the origins of the principle in the parties' contributions to the welfare of the family; and it would have been more consonant with the references of Baroness Hale of Richmond in *Miller* at paras [141] and [143] to 'sharing ... the fruits of the matrimonial partnership' and to 'the approach of roughly equal sharing of partnership assets'. We consider, however, the answer to be that, subject to the exceptions identified in *Miller* to which we turn in paras [83]–[86], below, the principle applies to all the parties' property but, to the extent that their property is non-matrimonial, there is likely to be better reason for departure from equality. It is clear that both in *White*, at 605F–G and 989 respectively, and in *Miller*, at paras [24] and [26], Lord Nicholls of Birkenhead approached the matter in that way; and there was no express suggestion in *Miller*, even on the part of Baroness Hale of Richmond, that in *White* the House had set too widely the general application of what was then a yardstick.

[67] Even if, however, a court elects to adopt the sharing principle as its 'starting point', it is important to put that phrase in context. For it cannot, strictly, be its starting point at all. As Coleridge J himself stated in the passage cited in para [59], above, the starting point of every inquiry in an application of ancillary relief is the financial position of the parties. The inquiry is always in two stages, namely computation and distribution; logically the former precedes the latter. Although it may well be convenient for the court to consider some of the matters set out in s 25(2) other than in the order there set out, a court should first consider, with whatever degree of detail is apt to the case, the matters set out in s 25(2)(a), namely the property, income (including earning capacity) and other financial resources which the parties have and are likely to have in the foreseeable future. Irrespective of whether the assets are substantial, likely future income must always be appraised for, even in a clean break case, such appraisal may well be relevant to the division of property which best achieves the fair overall outcome. We appreciate that remarks of Baroness Hale of Richmond in *Miller*, at para [154], are also said to permit argument that a party's earning capacity is itself an asset to which the other has contributed and which might to some extent be subject to the sharing principle; this seems to us an area of complexity and potential confusion which in this case it is unnecessary for us to visit.

[68] In *Miller* the House unanimously identified three main principles which together inform the second stage of the inquiry, namely that of distribution: 'need (generously interpreted), compensation, and sharing', per Baroness Hale of Richmond at para [144]; and see, similarly, Lord Nicholls of Birkenhead at paras [10]–16]. The three principles must be applied in the light of the size and nature of all the computed resources, which are usually heavily circumscribing factors.

[69] It is worthy of note that, although two of them are not expressly mentioned, each of the three distributive principles can be collected from s 25(2), or at any rate from s 25(1) and (2), of the Act and that each of the matters set out in subs (b)–(h) of s 25(2) can conveniently be assigned to one or another of the three of them.

[70] Thus the principle of need requires consideration of the financial needs, obligations and responsibilities of the parties (s 25(2)(b)); of the standard of living enjoyed by the family before the breakdown of the marriage (s 25(2)(c)); of the age of each party (half of s 25(2)(d)); and of any physical or mental disability of either of them (s 25(2)(e)).

[71] The principle of compensation relates to prospective financial disadvantage which upon divorce some parties face as a result of decisions which they took for the benefit of the family during the marriage, for example in sacrificing or not pursuing a career: per Lord Nicholls of Birkenhead in *Miller* at para [13], Lord Hope of Craighead, at para [117], and Baroness Hale of Richmond, at para [140]. But the principle goes wider than that. As long ago as 1976 this court decided that, where the marriage was short, it was relevant to consider whether a party had suffered financial disadvantage arising out of entry into it: see *S v S* [1977] Fam 127, at 134C, albeit that the consideration was there directed to restriction rather than augmentation of the award. Equally, in respect of disadvantage arising out of exit from the marriage, s 25(2)(h) requires the court to consider any loss of possible pension rights consequent upon its dissolution. Even disadvantage of the type to which reference was made in the speeches in *Miller*, ie that stemming from decisions taken during the marriage, had been held in this court to be relevant before it became the driver for a principle of compensation: per Hale J (as she then was) in *SRJ v DWJ (Financial Provision)* [1999] 2 FLR 176, at 182E, and per Thorpe LJ in *Lambert v Lambert* [2002] EWCA Civ 1685, [2003] Fam 103, [2003] 1 FLR 139, at 122G and 158 respectively. In cases in which it arises, application of the principle of compensation is an appropriate contribution to the fair result.

[72] The inquiry required by the principle of sharing is, as we have shown, dictated by reference to the contributions of each party to the welfare of the family (s 25(2)(f)); and, as we make clear in para [85], below, the duration of the marriage (the other half of s 25(2)(d)) here falls to be considered. Also conveniently assigned to the sharing principle, no doubt dictating departure from equality, is the conduct of a party in the exceptional case in which it would be inequitable to disregard it (s 25(2)(g)). Mr Singleton argued to the judge that the husband's generation of substantial wealth was not only a special contribution on his part to the welfare of the family but conduct which it would be inequitable to disregard. We think, however, that it is as unnecessarily confusing to present a case

of contribution as a positive type of conduct as it is to present a case of conduct as a negative or nil type of contribution: see *W v W* [2001] Fam Law 656.

[73] Then arises a difficult question: how does the court resolve any irreconcilable conflict between the result suggested by one principle and that suggested by another? Often conflict can be reconciled by recourse to an order for periodical payments: as for example in *McFarlane*, per Baroness Hale of Richmond, at para [154]. Ultimately, however, in cases in which it is irreconcilable, the criterion of fairness must supply the answer. It is clear that, when the result suggested by the needs principle is an award of property greater than the result suggested by the sharing principle, the former result should in principle prevail: per Baroness Hale of Richmond in *Miller* at paras [142] and [144]. At least in applying the needs principle the court will have focussed upon the needs of both parties; analogous focus on the respondent is not present in the compensation principle and we leave for another occasion the proper treatment of irreconcilable conflict between that principle and one of the others. It is also clear that, when the result suggested by the needs principle is an award of property less than the result suggested by the sharing principle, the latter result should in principle prevail: per Lord Nicholls of Birkenhead in *Miller*, at paras [28] and [29], and Baroness Hale of Richmond, at para [139].

(iii)   Criticisms of the judge's approach to the exercise

[74] As we have seen, Mr Singleton suggested to the judge that his approach to identification of the award to the wife should be 'incremental'; and before us his general complaint is that the judgment is flawed because its approach was not 'incremental'. Instead of progressively building up the total award by reference to the factors in s 25(2), the judge, says Mr Singleton, wrongly used a 'top-down' approach, took equality as his starting-point and sought to identify the discount appropriate to the husband's special contribution.

[75] In oral argument, Mr Singleton has been constrained to concede that the word 'incremental' is inapt. In context it implies that the court adds to the proposed award by reference to the different factors in s 25(2); such is an unhelpful, indeed unworkable, mischaracterisation of the statutory exercise. We understand Mr Singleton's real complaint to be that the judge's approach was not what one might call 'serial': namely that the judge failed to work through s 25(2) line by line; to arrive, by reference in particular to the husband's special contribution, at a provisional quantified award to the wife; and then to cross-check it against the yardstick of equality.

[76] There are three answers to Mr Singleton's general complaint:

(a)   In our view, the judge adopted the very approach which Mr Singleton complains that he failed to adopt. After observing that s 25 'rules the day', the judge serially considered all the factors there set out insofar as they were relevant, including in particular the husband's special contribution; concluded that the wife's assets should be increased to £48m; noted that such amounted to just under 37% of the total assets; and concluded that such departure from equality was justified.

(b)   Such was indeed a valid approach for the judge to adopt. But in *Miller* sharing became a principle: see para [65], above. The judge would have been entitled to consider percentages other than at the tail-end of his reasoning. There are cases in which, whatever the effect to be given in a rare case to a special contribution, the result of applying the sharing principle will subsume the result of applying the principles of need and (if engaged) of compensation. In cases of very substantial matrimonial property such a result may be as immediately apparent as it is from here in these courts that the dome of St Paul's rises higher than the steeple of St Bride's. In such circumstances, of which this case is an example, a judge might well first consider distribution by reference to the sharing principle and then shortly refer to the other principles. In *Miller*, Lord Nicholls of Birkenhead suggested, at para [29], that, in cases in which the assets were substantial, it would be 'generally a convenient course' to consider sharing before needs in that the latter would be likely to be subsumed in the former. Even prior to *Miller* it often became difficult in substantial cases for the court sensibly to maintain that it should not consider percentages until it had provisionally quantified an award by reference to other processes of reasoning. For it seemed pointless to undertake an elaborate process of provisional quantification if such then had to be abandoned by reference to percentages. But, to the extent that the yardstick constrained it to approach the matter in that way, *Miller* has released the court from the constraint.

(c)   We do not accept Mr Singleton's argument that consideration of a 'discount' from equality should play no part in the distributive exercise. Both when it was a yardstick and now that it is a principle, the concept was and is that property should be shared equally in the absence of good reason for departure from equality. A discount is nothing other than a departure from it.

[77]   (a) Mr Singleton levels an alternative complaint about the methodology of the judge's judgment. The judge, he says, should have proceeded as follows:
   (i)   calculate the wife's needs, say at £20m;
   (ii)   calculate the husband's needs, say at £29m;
   (iii)   deduct the joint needs of say £49m from the total assets (wrongly) computed by the judge at £131m and reach a surplus of £82m;
   (iv)   distribute the surplus fairly between the parties, say 10%, or £8m, to the wife and the balance to the husband; and
   (v)   thus award the wife £28m (inclusive of her existing assets).

(b)   Mr Singleton justifies this approach, which in this court he has to establish as being the only approach properly open to the judge, by reference largely to the judgment of Mance LJ in this court in *Cowan v Cowan* [2001] EWCA Civ 679, [2002] Fam 97, [2001] 2 FLR 192. Mance LJ there concurred in allowing a wife's appeal by increasing her award to £4.4m inclusive of her existing assets. In the view of two of the members of the court the proper approach was to survey the factors in s 25(2), to cross-check the result against the yardstick of equality, to note that the result instead represented a division of 38%–2% and to conclude that in the unusual circumstances such was a proper departure from equality. Mance LJ, however, observed, at para [169], that the wife's needs had been assessed at £3m; that, if allowance for the husband's needs was made in an equivalent sum, there was a surplus of £5m; that the proposed award gave the wife

25% of the surplus; and that such seemed fair. We note that, in his speech in *Miller*, Lord Mance did not refer to this approach.

(c)   With respect to Lord Mance, we do not agree with the suggested approach. Although there are isolated references in *Miller* to sharing 'the residue' (per Lord Nicholls of Birkenhead, at para [29]) and 'the balance' (per Baroness Hale of Richmond, at para [144]), we consider that, had it wished to endorse the approach suggested by Mance LJ in *Cowan*, the House would have made its view very much clearer. On the contrary the thrust of the decisions in *White* and certainly in *Miller* itself is that the court should apply the sharing principle not just to part but to all of the property; and thus that in these large cases it is probable that the sharing, whether equal or occasionally unequal, will cater automatically for needs. But we also have a grave practical objection: from the point of view of the proportionate despatch of these large cases, whether by negotiation or adjudication, a system which invited not only, as now, expensive concentration upon the value of assets but also elaborate presentations of needs – the height of one budget no doubt being said to be entirely reasonable and the height of the other entirely unreasonable – would be the worst of both worlds.

(iv)   Special contribution

[78]   Coleridge J postponed delivery of his judgment until after publication of the determination of the House of Lords of the appeal in *Miller*. He did so not least because the wife's concession that the husband had made a special contribution which should lead to a departure, albeit modest, from equal division of the property was expressed to be conditional upon the 'survival' in *Miller* of the possibility of a special contribution for the purposes of the exercise required by s 25 of the Act.

[79]   It was inevitable, so it seems to us, that the notion of a special contribution should have 'survived' the decision in *Miller*. The statutory requirement in every case to consider the contributions which each party has made to the welfare of the family, as well as those which each is likely to make to it, would be inconsistent with a blanket rule that their past contributions to its welfare must be afforded equal weight. Nevertheless the difficulty attendant upon a comparison of their different contributions and the danger of its infection by discrimination against the home-maker led the House in *Miller* heavily to circumscribe the situations in which it would be appropriate to find that one party had made a special contribution, in the sense of a contribution by one unmatched by the other, which, for the purpose of the sharing principle, should lead to departure from equality. In this regard the House was unanimous. First it approved, at paras [67], [68] and [146], the decision of this court in *Lambert v Lambert* [2002] EWCA Civ 1685, [2003] Fam 103, [2003] 1 FLR 139, in which Thorpe LJ had ventured, at para [46], 'a cautious acknowledgement that special contribution remains a legitimate possibility but only in exceptional circumstances'. Then it reached for the criterion by which the court determines whether a party's conduct is relevant to the inquiry and suggested that it should also be applied to identification of the linked and in effect obverse feature, namely the special contribution. When, by s 3 of the Matrimonial and Family Proceedings Act 1984, Parliament had recast the reference to conduct in s 25 of the Matrimonial Causes Act 1973, it had provided in s 25(2)(g) that conduct should be taken into account if it was 'such that it would in the opinion of the court be inequitable to disregard it'. On one view that

criterion is of fair width. In practice, however, its meaning has largely been interpreted in line with the narrow criterion for determination of the relevance of conduct set by this court prior to 1984, in particular in *Wachtel v Wachtel* [1973] Fam 72, in which, at 90C, it approved the trial judge's suggestion that conduct was relevant only if it was 'obvious and gross': indeed see the current re-affirmation of this criterion by Baroness Hale of Richmond in *Miller* itself at para [145]. It is therefore in the light of the very limited ability of a party to establish a case of conduct under s 25(2)(g) that we must have regard to the statements in *Miller* both of Baroness Hale of Richmond, at para [146], that contributions should be approached in much the same way as conduct; and of Lord Mance, at para [164], as follows:

> '[S]ection 25(2)(g) recognises the difficulty and undesirability, except in egregious cases, of any attempt at assessing and weighing marital conduct. I now recognise the same difficulty in respect of marital contributions – conduct and contributions are in large measure opposite sides of a coin.'

In saying that he 'now' recognised the same difficulty, Lord Mance no doubt had in mind the wider room for special contributions which, as a member of this court, he had identified in *Cowan v Cowan* [2001] EWCA Civ 679, [2002] Fam 97, [2001] 2 FLR 192, at paras [160] and [161].

[80] The notion of a special contribution to the welfare of the family will not successfully have been purged of inherent gender discrimination unless it is accepted that such a contribution can, in principle, take a number of forms; that it can be non-financial as well as financial; and that it can thus be made by a party whose role has been exclusively that of a home-maker. Nevertheless in practice, and for a self-evident reason, the claim to have made a special contribution seems so far to have arisen only in cases of substantial wealth generated by a party's success in business during the marriage. The self-evident reason is that in such cases there is substantial property over the distribution of which it is worthwhile to argue. In such cases can the amount of the wealth alone make the contribution special? Or must the focus always be upon the manner of its generation? In *Lambert* Thorpe LJ said, at para [52]:

> 'There may be cases where the product alone justifies a conclusion of a special contribution but absent some exceptional and individual quality in the generator of the fortune a case for special contribution must be hard to establish.'

In such cases, therefore, the court will no doubt have regard to the amount of the wealth; and in some cases, perhaps including the present, its amount will be so extraordinary as to make it easy for the party who generated it to claim an exceptional and individual quality which deserves special treatment. Often, however, he or she will need independently to establish such a quality, whether by genius in business or in some other field. Sometimes, by contrast, it will immediately be obvious that substantial wealth generated during the marriage is a windfall – the proceeds, for example, of an unanticipated sale of land for development or of an embattled take-over of a party's ailing company – which is not the product of a special contribution.

[81] In *Miller*, Baroness Hale of Richmond said, at para [146]:

'Section 25(2)(f) of the 1973 Act does *not* refer to the contributions which each has made to the parties' *accumulated wealth*, but to the contributions they have made (and will continue to make) to the *welfare of the family*. Each should be seen as doing their best in their own sphere. Only if there is such a disparity in their respective contributions to the *welfare of the family* that it would be inequitable to disregard it should this be taken into account in determining their shares.'

These words have provoked lively debate upon this appeal. Like the introduction of property into a marriage at its inception (being property helpfully described by Burton J in *S v S (Divorce: Distribution of Assets)* [2006] EWHC 2793 (Fam), [2006] All ER (D) 137 (Nov), at para [28], as 'pre-matrimonial') or the introduction into it of property received during it by inheritance or gift (being property there described by Burton J as 'extra-matrimonial'), the generation of wealth during a marriage has conventionally been taken as one obvious form of contribution to the welfare of the family. Here, however, Baroness Hale of Richmond articulated a refinement, namely that the generation of wealth should not always qualify as a contribution to the welfare of the family and, in particular, perhaps that in excess of a certain level its generation should not so qualify. The dividing-line is no doubt elusive. But, if the present case were to be one in which, in excess of a certain level, the husband's wealth were not to qualify as the product of a contribution to the welfare of the family, how should the court treat the excess? Mr Singleton submits, albeit with diffidence, that the excess would not be susceptible of redistribution and so should all lie in the hands into which it has fallen, namely those of the husband. We reject that submission: a party's property would not fall outside the court's redistributive powers in ss 23–25 of the Act just because it was not the product of a contribution within the meaning of s 25(2)(f). With equal diffidence Mr Pointer submits, by contrast, that, because it is only a special contribution to the welfare of the family which justifies unequal division, the excess, not being the product of a special contribution, should fall for equal division. Such a result would, in our view, be almost absurd. The facts are that, before the judge, the case was accepted on both sides to be one in which, apart from £1m which is the subject of the third subsidiary ground of appeal, all the property, notwithstanding its size, was the product of the husband's special contribution to the welfare of the family within the meaning of s 25(2)(f); and that Mr Singleton, followed reactively by Mr Pointer, now uses this difficult passage in the speech of Baroness Hale of Richmond as a bandwagon on to which to jump. In our view the size of the property in the present case should not compel departure from the usual conclusion that wealth generated by a party during a marriage is the product of a contribution on his or her part to the welfare of the family.

[82] Next Mr Singleton submits that, in her speech in *Miller*, Baroness Hale of Richmond identified a category of cases in which property should in no way be subject to the sharing principle, notwithstanding that the principle allows in rare cases for special contributions, and that the present case falls into the category. Baroness Hale of Richmond described such cases, at para [150], as 'non-business-partnership non-family asset cases'. In *S v S (Divorce: Distribution of Assets)*, Burton J, at para [29], usefully abbreviated the description to cases of 'unilateral assets'. In summary Baroness Hale of Richmond suggested, at paras [149]–[152], that within the definition of matrimonial property a distinction fell to be made between 'family assets' and the fruits of a business in which both

parties had substantially worked, on the one hand, and the fruits of a business in which only one party had substantially worked, ie unilateral assets, on the other. The suggestion was that it was property only of the former character which was subject to the sharing principle.

[83] We hasten to correct a serious misapprehension at the heart of this submission. As we will show, Baroness Hale of Richmond put forward the distinction between unilateral assets and other matrimonial property for use in cases in which the marriage was short. And, although obiter she suggested an extension of it to another situation, namely that of the dual career to which we turn in para [86], below, she definitely did not commend the distinction for use in other cases. Its application in a case such as the present would be deeply discriminatory and would gravely undermine the sharing principle articulated, albeit embryonically, in *White* and emphatically developed in other parts of the speeches in *Miller* itself.

[84] In *Miller* the marriage endured for less than three years. The husband had assets of about £32m, of which £17m was pre-matrimonial property. Ostensibly the balance of £15m was matrimonial property; but its characterisation was complicated by the fact that it represented the value of shares in a venture which the husband joined 6 months after the marriage pursuant to plans made with a colleague prior to the marriage. By dismissal of the husband's appeal against dismissal of his appeal to this court, the decision of the House was to uphold the judge's award to the wife of £5m, ie one third of the ostensible matrimonial property.

[85] Such was the context in which the House turned to consider whether the sharing principle applied to cases in which the property had been generated during a short marriage. It was in this area that the members of the House were in substantial disagreement; and we cannot subscribe to the ingenious attempt of Burton J in *S v S (Divorce: Distribution of Assets)*, at paras [30] and [31], to reconcile their differences. We suggest with respect that, while the approach of Lord Nicholls of Birkenhead was perhaps the more logical, the approach both of Baroness Hale of Richmond, with which Lord Hoffmann agreed, and of Lord Mance was perhaps the more pragmatic. Lord Nicholls of Birkenhead, at paras [17]–[20], stressed that the sharing principle was as fully applicable to short as to long marriages and that the concept of treating unilateral assets differently from other matrimonial assets discriminated in favour of the bread-winner. He justified departure from equal sharing of the matrimonial property in *Miller* by reference, at para [73], to the amount of work done by the husband prior to the marriage referable to the venture. In a section entitled, 'The source of the assets and the length of the marriage' Baroness Hale of Richmond, at paras [147]–[152], squarely faced the conceptual difficulties inherent in the different application of the sharing principle to short marriages but considered that, on balance, perceptions of fairness justified it. Such became, at para [158], her rationale for justifying departure from equality in *Miller*. Lord Mance, at para [169], powerfully stressed the practical value of Baroness Hale of Richmond's approach, namely that it would often obviate the need to address the argument, sometimes called the 'seed-corn' argument, raised in *Miller* itself, to the effect that wealth which one of the parties ostensibly generated during the marriage was a crop of which he or she had sown the seed prior to it.

[86]   The extension of the concept of unilateral assets, suggested by Baroness Hale of Richmond in *Miller*, at para [153], was expressly endorsed by Lord Mance, at para [170]. Although *obiter*, it clearly commands great respect. It relates to the 'dual career'. The suggestion was that, where both parties had worked throughout the marriage, had pooled some of the assets built up by their efforts but had chosen to keep other such assets under their separate control, the latter, although unequal in amount, were unilateral assets which might not be subject to the sharing principle. Because of the convincing logical objections of Lord Nicholls of Birkenhead to the different treatment of unilateral assets, we would prefer, so far as it is proper for us to do so, to keep the room for application of the concept closely confined. Lord Mance offered, at para [170], the following interesting rationalisation for the suggested extension:

'Once needs and compensation had been addressed, the misfortune of divorce would not of itself ... be justification for the court to disturb principles by which the parties had chosen to live their lives while married.'

Lord Mance may there have foreshadowed future, albeit no doubt cautious, movement in the law towards a more frequent distribution of property upon divorce in accordance with what, by words or conduct, the parties appear previously to have agreed.

[87]   Mindful of the postscript to the judgment of Coleridge J to which we have referred in para [62], above, we have wondered whether, in order to help courts to perceive the circumstances in which, subject to our remarks in para [80], above, the generation of substantial wealth during the marriage might qualify as a special contribution, we should identify a threshold of wealth below which a court would be unlikely to conclude that it was the product of a special contribution. It is obvious that any such guideline would have to be laden with qualification so as to avoid any impermissible gloss on the court's duty under s 25 to assess each case on its merits. Subject to that caveat, we invited counsel to make submissions upon the threshold. Both Mr Singleton and Mr Pointer were rightly tentative. Mr Singleton suggested a threshold no higher than £40m or £50m. Five years ago, in *Lambert*, Mr Pointer had suggested a threshold of £10m, in relation to which Thorpe LJ stated, at para [46], that it was 'futile and dangerous even to attempt to speculate on the boundaries of the exceptional'. Before us Mr Pointer suggested £30m or £50m.

[88]   Like this court in *Lambert*, we find ourselves unable to identify any figure as a guideline threshold for a special contribution of this character. It would, we consider, be dangerous for us to do so. However laden with qualification, the guideline might discourage a court from discerning special contribution in the generation of wealth below the threshold in circumstances, however rare, in which it should properly do so. The greater concern, however, is the obverse risk that it might encourage a court to discern special contribution in the generation of wealth above the threshold in circumstances in which it should not properly do so. While the law recognises the concept of a special contribution in the generation of wealth, there is no doubt that, following the decision of this court in *Lambert*, approved and developed in *Miller*, it keeps the concept in very narrow bounds. We would not wish a party's claim to have made a special contribution to succeed by reference to something interpreted as effectively a presumption deriving from our identification of a threshold figure.

[89] There has been an interesting collateral discussion as to whether, if a party makes a special contribution by the generation of wealth, as a result of which the proportions of its division with the other party under the sharing principle will be unequal, the extent to which the proportions are unequal should depend upon the size of the wealth. The greater the wealth generated by one party, submits Mr Singleton, the lower should be the proportion awarded to the other. Mr Pointer disagrees. He submits that in any event the principle will yield to the maker of the special contribution more than half of the wealth; that the greater the wealth, the greater will be the amount thus yielded; and that fairness requires no further adjustment in favour of its generator. In principle we agree with Mr Singleton. If such a contribution is special, it follows that it is unmatched; and the greater the wealth, the greater is the extent to which it is unmatched and to which it calls for an unmatched, or unequal, division under the sharing principle.

[90] Although we decline to identify a threshold for the application of the principle of special contribution, we are nonetheless prepared to respond to the judge's postscript to the extent of offering guidance on the appropriate range of percentage adjustment to be made in cases in which the court is satisfied that the principle requires departure from equality; it is necessary however to bear in mind that fair despatch of some cases may require departure even from the range which we propose. As it happens, our views on this subject are by way of endorsement and development of what in this case Coleridge J has himself said. As we have recorded at the end of para [60](d), above, the judge suggested that any adjustment for special contribution of this character should be significant as opposed to token. We agree. We find it hard to conceive that, where such a special contribution is established, the percentages of division of matrimonial property should be nearer to equality than 55%–45%. Equally, in the course of Mr Singleton's application to him for permission to appeal, the judge, in referring to percentages in cases of special contribution, observed 'I think you need to be careful, after a very long marriage, to give a wife half of what you give the husband'. Arbitrary though it is, our instinct is the same, namely that, even in an extreme case and in the absence of some further dramatic feature unrelated to it, fair allowance for special contribution within the sharing principle would be most unlikely to give rise to percentages of division of matrimonial property further from equality than 66.6%–33.3%.

[91] We turn to Mr Singleton's contention that the method by which the judge allowed for the husband's special contribution was flawed. It will have become apparent in paras [76] and [77], above, that we reject the contention. In what one might now almost call the old-fashioned way, namely in accordance with *White*, the judge considered all the factors in s 25; reached a figure; and checked it against a yardstick of percentages. In the light of *Miller* he would, as it happens, have been entitled to move at an earlier stage to consider percentages. In any event this was a rare case of special contribution by the husband's generation of wealth; and the size of the wealth which he generated and contributed to the welfare of the family compelled quite a substantial departure from equality. The judge's endorsement of a departure to 63.5%–36.5% in part reflected his view that the award to the husband was of assets laden with greater risk. Mr Singleton's surmise is that the judge justified a discount against the wife of 3% in this respect; but the risk is not obviously demonstrated by the near seamless accretion of wealth by the husband as a result of his activities in the sphere of insurance throughout the marriage and we regard 3% as a maximum of what the judge must have had in mind. It is clear that the extent of the departure from equality very largely reflected the value placed by the judge upon the husband's special contribution. Such departure lies very near the middle of the range which we have suggested in para [90], above, and, in the light of the scale of his special contribution, appropriately so. Neither in its method nor in its result do we regard the judge's treatment of the husband's special contribution as vulnerable to appeal.

Section G: The three subsidiary grounds of appeal

(i)   Tax saved and tax payable

[92]   As a result of his becoming non-resident in the UK in January 2003 and, which is assumed, of his remaining non-resident until April 2008, the husband will save UK tax otherwise payable in respect both of his personal assets and of his assets in Dragon. He argued before the judge that a sum equal to the tax otherwise payable should be deducted from the amount of his personal assets and of the assets in Dragon on the basis that, in the absence of such a deduction, the wife would receive a share of assets swollen by a saving to which she had not contributed.

[93]   At the substantive hearing in February 2006 the husband adduced evidence from forensic accountants, namely KPMG, on various issues. KPMG put forward a calculation that the saving of tax referable to the husband's personal assets was £18m and to the assets in Dragon was £15m.

[94]   One problem was that, as a result of an oversight, KPMG's figure referable to the husband's personal assets was incorrect. The error was discovered long after the conclusion of the hearing in February 2006 and shortly after the judge's receipt of submissions on the effect of *Miller* in June 2006. By application made to the judge by telephone on 14 July 2006, namely a few days prior to the intended date for delivery of his judgment, Mr Singleton applied for permission to adduce fresh evidence from KPMG that the husband would at some stage become liable to pay UK tax in the sum of £11m referable to such of his shares in Axis and in particular of his options to purchase them as had been acquired prior to his becoming non-resident. The effect of this proposed evidence would have been both to reduce the amount of the tax saved referable to the personal assets from £18m–£7m and to give Mr Singleton a possibly firmer argument referable to the balance of £11m, namely that it qualified for entry on to the balance sheet as a future liability of the husband. Mr Pointer responded that he had had no time to collect the response of the wife's forensic accountants, PricewaterhouseCoopers, to the suggested liability; and that it was too late for the evidence, including no doubt their evidence by way of response, to be adduced and debated. The judge agreed that it was too late to halt delivery of the judgment in order to inquire into the size of the liability and the time at which it might accrue; he ruled that, through the mechanism of the order for a 'reverse contingent lump sum' to which we have referred in para [3], above, he would require the wife to contribute to the claimed liability by repayment to the husband only following actual future payment on his part referable to it.

[95]   In his judgment the judge rejected the husband's argument that the tax which he had saved should be deducted from the computation of his personal assets or of those in Dragon. The argument had been based on the wife's alleged unwillingness to reside with the husband in Bermuda and thus in effect to participate with him in his non-resident status in the UK. The judge rejected the argument on the facts: as we have explained in para [20], above, he found that, acting reasonably throughout, the wife was at first reluctant to move to Bermuda, but that, by the time when she had become resigned to do so and offered to do so, the husband had decided that the marriage was at an end. Mr Singleton argues that the judge mischaracterised his case against the wife as one of conduct rather than of nil contribution. In our view his argument is not only misconceived – see para [72], above – but irrelevant: for his case failed by reference to findings of fact effectively incapable of disturbance. Yet there is another reason why the appeal against the judge's treatment of the tax saved by the husband is doomed to fail: for there was of course no need for the wife to join the husband in Bermuda in order for him to save the tax. In our view it would be only if a grossly culpable refusal by the wife to take up residence in Bermuda had given rise to a tax liability that the situation would have been different.

[96] The husband also appeals against the judge's treatment of his claimed liability to tax by means of the 'reverse contingent lump sum'. His presentation of this liability to the judge was so belated that in our view the husband is in no position to complain about the pragmatic way in which, principally in order to avoid yet further delay, the judge chose to deal with it. Indeed his preferred mechanism for causing the wife to bear part of the tax liability was arguably fairer than an immediate deduction from the balance sheet of a liability which was referable primarily to options and which would not arise until the husband's exercise of them up to 8 years into the future.

(ii)   Valuation of Axis instruments

[97] KPMG valued the shares, options and warrants referable to Axis held by the husband personally and in Dragon in the sum of £53m. Pricewaterhouse-Coopers valued them in the sum of £73m. The judge adopted the latter sum. The husband contends that he thereby fell into error.

[98] The issue between the accountants was intricate and multi-faceted; but the husband has permission to complain to this court only about a general difference in their approach.

[99] The approach of KPMG was to identify the value of the instruments by reference to their 'market value', namely the likely proceeds of their immediate, orderly sale, albeit not a 'fire sale'. In fact the options and the warrants were not transferable; and some of the shares were unregistered or unvested and thus also subject to inhibitions upon sale. So in that regard the exercise commended by KPMG at once became notional or, as Mr Pointer in effect submitted, doubly notional. At all events KPMG sought to calculate what a hypothetical purchaser would pay for the instruments if able to buy them subject to their existing restrictions; and they attributed to the husband and to Dragon only the sum which, at heavy discounts, such a hypothetical purchaser would pay for them.

[100] The approach of PricewaterhouseCoopers, by contrast, was tailored to the profile of the husband and was said to be designed to identify the 'economic

value' of the instruments. They did not favour a notional marketing of non-marketable instruments. They sought to discern how, and in particular when, this husband would be likely to set about any such disposal of the instruments as in principle he had resolved to achieve. In this regard they proceeded upon an assumption that the husband had no need to realise any of the instruments immediately and that, as a rational investor, he would do so over time. They pointed for example to the shrewd retention of the shares held by the husband and by the trusts in Ace until their orderly, tax-efficient sale at his direction 2 and 3 years after his departure from it.

[101] A substantial part of Mr Singleton's challenge in this appeal to the approach of PricewaterhouseCoopers fails by virtue of the failure of his challenge to the judge's attribution of the assets of Dragon to the husband. It is clear that, although, were the assets of Dragon not to have been attributed to the husband, the award to the wife would have been substantially smaller, it would nevertheless, even on his own proposals, have exceeded his personal liquid resources, which the judge found to amount primarily to £10m at the Bank of New York. Thus, on the basis of his challenge to the attribution of the assets of Dragon to the husband, Mr Singleton has attacked the assumption of PricewaterhouseCoopers that, whether for the purposes of meeting the award to the wife or otherwise, the husband has had no need to realise any of the instruments in Axis immediately. In that his challenge has failed, his attack on the assumption must fail. In Dragon the husband holds £39m in cash and in investments other than in Axis, so he has been well able to meet the judge's award otherwise than by recourse to the sale of instruments in Axis, whether held by him personally or in Dragon.

[102] In the light of the failure of a substantial part of Mr Singleton's challenge to the approach of PricewaterhouseCoopers, we will not take long to explain why we reject the rest of it. Insofar as Mr Pointer suggests that the judge's attribution of value to the Axis instruments was a finding of primary fact, and thus particularly hard to disturb on appeal, we disagree with him. We accept nevertheless that the question for us remains whether it was open to the judge to prefer the approach to valuation on the part of PricewaterhouseCoopers. We conclude without hesitation that it was. It contained no methodological error. On the contrary, it reflected, more than did the approach of KPMG, the need for the divorce court to adopt valuations which are realistic and which, in particular, proceed from a premise that the present value of an asset in the hands of a party may sometimes differ both from its value in other hands and from such price as might be achieved in the event of its immediate sale.

(iii)   Post-separation property

[103] We turn to an argument scarcely articulated in the grounds of appeal and overlooked in Mr Singleton's substantive skeleton argument. Axis awarded a bonus of £1m to the husband for his work during the calendar year of 2005; it was paid to him in February 2006. The judge included it in his computation of the husband's assets: see para [27], above. Mr Singleton contends that the bonus was post-separation property and that, therefore, the judge was wrong to include it.

[104] In our view the bonus was clearly to be regarded as an asset of the husband. The more difficult issue, which was not clearly isolated before the judge, is whether, because it had been generated by work done by the husband not less

than 14 months after the separation and was thus probably not to be regarded as matrimonial property, the bonus was an asset which the judge should have treated differently from all the other property and of which, in particular, he should not have endorsed any percentage distribution to the wife, whether 36.5% or otherwise. This is a grey area which this court may need to survey upon a suitable appeal. We do not consider the present appeal suitable because, to leave its merits or demerits to one side, the issue is, in any event, too small to affect the outcome. In determining the amount of the lump sum to be paid to the wife, the judge elected provisionally to proceed by reference not to percentages but to a figure, namely £48m (inclusive of her existing assets). We do not accept that had he computed the matrimonial property to be less by £1m than the total assets of £131m the judge would provisionally have awarded a different figure; nor that, in checking it against the yardstick of percentages, he would have lowered his provisional award by reference to a calculation that it represented nearer 37% than 36.5% of the matrimonial property.

Section H: Result

[105]   We dismiss the appeal.

Postscript: changing the law

[106]   Section 25 of the Matrimonial Causes Act 1973 was not an innovation but the consolidation of s 5 of the Matrimonial Proceedings and Property Act 1970. The 1970 Act was the companion to the Divorce Reform Act 1969. As the courts came to apply the new law, the case of *Wachtel v Wachtel* [1973] Fam 72 was seen at the time, and is still seen to be, fundamentally important. It established, amongst other things, that the acrimonious disputes as to the causes of the breakdown of marriage, which had characterised the law of divorce prior to the 1969 Act, were not to be born again in the arena of financial disputes. However, the judicial decisions that were more profound and far-reaching were the subsequent decisions of this court in *O'D v O'D* [1976] Fam 83, (1975) FLR Rep 512 and *Preston v Preston* [1982] Fam 17, (1981) 2 FLR 331. They provided trial judges and practitioners with a method for the determination of those cases in which the available assets significantly exceeded the simple needs of the family. The applicant's reasonable requirements became the focus of the case, throughout its preparation and in its final determination. This method brought predictability and clarity, characteristics that were refined by a mechanism for capitalising the applicant's future spending requirement, a mechanism inferentially sanctioned by this court in its decision in *Duxbury v Duxbury (Note)* [1992] Fam 62, [1987] 1 FLR 7. The emphasis on the applicant's reasonable requirements as the yardstick of the award satisfied the anxiety of judges and others that we should not be drawn into the extravagance of some American states, particularly California, where very large awards were commonplace. This judicial preference for moderation ruled essentially for a generation from the mid-1970s to the year 2000. It suited the society of its day.

[107]   However the amendments introduced by the Matrimonial and Family Proceedings Act 1984 did nothing to restrict the width of the judicial discretion, whilst north of the border the Family Law (Scotland) Act 1985 introduced a statutory structure for the determination of outcome that preferred clarity and certainty over the flexibility achieved by wide judicial discretion.

[108] Dissatisfaction with the state of our law was augmented by extravagant interlocutory proceedings largely uncontrolled by the court. This led to the formation in 1992 of a group of specialist judges, practitioners and academics which, under the President's banner, proposed procedural reforms inspired by the Australian model with firm judicial control at all stages. The proposals had much in common with the civil justice reforms subsequently introduced by Lord Woolf.

[109] In advancing its proposals the committee collaborated with government officials and the collaboration was sealed by the adoption of the committee by the Lord Chancellor. The committee thus adopted was available for consultation on issues in this specialist field. The introduction of the new rules was the subject of cautious piloting and evaluation by outside consultants before their general application to all ancillary relief applications.

[110] Other issues brought to the committee concerned the enforcement of orders, routes of appeal and costs in ancillary relief. Thus the concentration of the committee was on practice and procedure rather than on primary law reform.

[111] However, in February 1998 the government announced an intention to reform s 25 of the Act as a high priority. The Lord Chancellor referred this major issue to the committee for consultation. Given its high priority, the committee was asked to submit its recommendation by the end of July 1998. The committee was particularly invited to consider the possibility of adopting in this jurisdiction the Scottish model. Although the committee was united in rejecting the Scottish option there was a divergence of view as to the alternatives.

[112] The report delivered by the committee undoubtedly influenced the proposals for reform that the government put out for public consultation in the White Paper, *Supporting Families* (1998), that autumn. The proposal was for a number of prioritised aims within an overarching objective. The government also proposed to give limited statutory force to written nuptial agreements.

[113] Subsequently the government published responses to the consultation which, although few, did not discourage progress. However the enthusiasm for reform apparently died after a single season without explanation. Indeed thereafter the government showed a marked disinclination to discuss the issue and proponents of reform experienced only frustration. Legislative inertia is not unusual in the reform of family law: see Dr Stephen Cretney, *Same Sex Relationships* (OUP, 2006). Nevertheless he concludes that reforms are ultimately better achieved by Parliament than by the judges.

[114] Was the need for reform met by the decision of the House in *White*? The decision deprived practitioners and judges of the old measure of reasonable requirements, offering instead the cross check of equality to ensure fairness and to banish discrimination.

[115] Of course these innovations were well founded on profound social change, particularly in the recognition that marriage is a partnership of equals and that the role of man and woman within the marriage are commonly interchangeable. In the majority of cases the innovations resulting from *White* were timely and beneficial.

[116] However a social change that was not perhaps recognised in that decision was the extent to which the origins and the volume of big money cases were shifting. Most of the big money cases pre-*White* involved fortunes created by previous generations. The removal of exchange control restrictions in 1979, a policy that offered a favourable tax regime to very rich foreigners domiciled elsewhere, and a new financial era dominated by hedge-funds, private equity funds, derivative traders and sophisticated off-shore structures meant that very large fortunes were being made very quickly. These socio-economic developments coincided with a retreat from the preference of English judges for moderation. The present case well illustrates that shift. At trial Mr Pointer achieved for his client an award of £48m. Before us he freely conceded that he could not have justified an award of more than £20m on the application of the reasonable requirements principle. Thus, in very big money cases, the effect of the decision in *White* was to raise the aspirations of the claimant hugely. In big money cases the *White* factor has more than doubled the levels of award and it has been said by many that London has become the divorce capital of the world for aspiring wives. Whether this is a desirable result needs to be considered not only in the context of our society but also in the context of the European Union of which we are a singular Member State, in the sense that we are a common law jurisdiction amongst largely civilian fellows and that in the determination of issues ancillary to divorce we apply the lex fori and decline to apply the law more applicable to the parties.

[117] In the case of *Cowan v Cowan* [2001] EWCA Civ 679, [2002] Fam 97, [2001] 2 FLR 192 the need for legislative review in the aftermath of the case of *White* was articulated: see paras [32], [41] and [58]. Undoubtedly the decision in *White* did not resolve the problems faced by practitioners in advising clients or by clients in deciding upon what terms to compromise.

[118] However this court adopted a cautious approach both in *Cowan* and in the later case of *Lambert*. In his submission, Mr Singleton drew attention to an article by Joanna Miles in *International Journal of Law, Policy and the Family* (2005) 19 242. He told us that he had incorporated the article in his argument for Mrs McFarlane in the House of Lords. The article criticises the earlier decision of this court in the conjoined appeals of *McFarlane v McFarlane; Parlour v Parlour* [2004] EWCA Civ 872, [2005] Fam 171, [2004] 2 FLR 893 for having declined the opportunity to identify principles underpinning the exercise of judicial discretion under the Matrimonial Causes Act 1973. The article is particularly interesting in that it demonstrates that the principles discussed in the article (needs, entitlement and compensation), were subsequently the principles identified by the House of Lords in deciding the conjoined appeals of *Miller v Miller; McFarlane v McFarlane* [2006] UKHL 24, [2006] 2 AC 618, [2006] 1 FLR 1186.

[119] The discussion in the article is founded on the statutory scheme legislated in New Zealand in the Property (Relationships) Act 1976 and the Family Proceedings Act 1980, both amended in 2001. In the article's analysis of the New Zealand experience, some emphasis is placed on the difficulty of combining needs, entitlement and compensation in one scheme.

[120] It remains to be seen whether the impact of the decision of *Miller* and *McFarlane* will be as great as has been the decision of *White* in very big money cases. There is no doubt but that specialist practitioners have not received the decision in *Miller* as one that introduces the benefit of predictability and improvement of the prospect of compromise: see the leader, *Let's Play Ancillary Relief*, from Andrew Greensmith, National Chair of Resolution, at [2007] Fam Law 203. If this is so, it is highly unfortunate.

[121] As Lord Hope pointed out in *Miller*, at para [105], the report of the Law Commission on Family Law – *The Financial Consequences of Divorce*, Law Com No 112 (HMSO, 1981), in recommending flexibility over a structured statutory scheme, added, '… that any future legislation dealing with the financial consequences of divorce should be subject to continuous monitoring and periodical reports to Parliament'. Clearly that recommendation has not been heeded. The thrust of Lord Hope's speech is to identify the need for the reform of the Family Law (Scotland) Act 1985. Arguably the English statute, in its fundamental provisions fifteen years older, is in equal need of modernisation in the light of social and other changes as well as in the light of experience.

[122] There is a limitation on the resources of even the judges of the House of Lords to conduct wide-ranging comparative studies as a prelude to establishing a new principle, or perhaps to abandoning an existing principle in what is essentially a social policy field. The Money and Property Subcommittee of the Family Justice Council at its meeting on the 20 February 2007 agreed to approach the Law Commission with the request that the reform of s 25 be included in its future work programme and the request has since been articulated in a letter to the chairman.

[123] Should this request be acted upon, careful analysis will be required of the interrelationship of our ancillary relief law with the law of other jurisdictions. Globalisation particularly affects the ultra-rich. They are unlikely to inhabit only one country. With a string of properties acquired for diverse purposes they are likely to be subject to the jurisdiction of at least two courts when the marriage falls apart. London is increasingly likely to be one of the jurisdictions. Now that London is regularly described in the press as the 'divorce capital of the world' it is inevitable that applicants will seek to achieve a London award. If there are no international conventions applicable to the dispute there will be a forum conveniens battle, often at quite disproportionate cost to the parties' assets or, more importantly, the means of one of the spouses. Even if international conventions apply, expensive struggles can still escalate. Recently in this court the case of *Bentinck v Bentinck* [2007] EWCA Civ 175, [2007] All ER (D) 76 (Mar) demonstrated the expenditure of £330,000 in legal costs despite the fact that the jurisdictional rules of the Lugano Convention on Jurisdiction and the Enforcement of Judgments in Civil and Commercial Matters (1988) OJ L 319/9 applied. Even more recently, in the case of *Moore v Moore* [2007] EWCA Civ 361, [2007] All ER (D) 158 (Apr), approximately £1.6m had been expended on the wife's endeavours to achieve a London award, rather than a Marbella award, despite the application of the Council Regulation (EC) No 44/2001 of 22 December 2000 on jurisdiction and the recognition and enforcement of judgments in civil and commercial matters (Brussels I Regulation).

[124] Any harmonisation within the European region is particularly difficult, given that the Brussels I Regulation is restricted to claims for maintenance and the

Council Regulation (EC) No 2201/2003 of 27 November 2003 concerning jurisdiction and the recognition and enforcement of judgments in matrimonial matters and in matters of parental responsibility, repealing Regulation (EC) No 1347/2000 (Brussels II Revised) (2003) OJ L 338/1 expressly excludes from its application the property consequence of divorce. In the European context this makes sense because in civilian systems the property consequences of divorce are dealt with by marital property regimes. Almost uniquely our jurisdiction does not have a marital property regime and it is scarcely appropriate to classify our jurisdiction as having a marital regime of separation of property. More correctly we have no regime, simply accepting that each spouse owns his or her own separate property during the marriage but subject to the court's wide distributive powers in prospect upon a decree of judicial separation, nullity or divorce. The difficulty of harmonising our law concerning the property consequences of marriage and divorce and the law of the civilian member states is exacerbated by the fact that our law has so far given little status to prenuptial contracts. If, unlike the rest of Europe, the property consequences of divorce are to be regulated by the principles of needs, compensation and sharing, should not the parties to the marriage, or the projected marriage, have at the least the opportunity to order their own affairs otherwise by a nuptial contract? The White Paper, *Supporting Families*, not only proposed specific reforms of s 25 but also to give statutory force to nuptial contracts. The government's subsequent abdication has not been accepted by specialist practitioners. In 2005, Resolution published a well argued report urging the government to give statutory force to nuptial contracts. The report was subsequently fully supported by the Money and Property Subcommittee of the Family Justice Council.

[125]   The European Commission is also in search of progress in this difficult area. On 17 July 2006 it published its Green Paper on *Conflict of Laws in Matters Concerning Matrimonial Property Regimes, Including The Question of Jurisdiction and Mutual Recognition*. In our jurisdiction a stakeholder group prepared a response which was subsequently considered by the North Committee but the response has been complicated by the fact that the Green Paper does not seem to fully understand our law of equitable redistribution or that we do not have a matrimonial property regime as such.

[126]   We would wish to lend our own weight to this call for a review of these matters by the Law Commission.

Order accordingly.

Solicitors: *Withers LLP* for the appellant
        Manches LLP for the respondent

PHILIPPA JOHNSON
Law Reporter

MINWALLA v MINWALLA AND DM INVESTMENTS SA, MIDFIELD MANAGEMENT SA AND CI LAW TRUSTEES LTD

[2004] EWHC 2823 (Fam), [2005] 1 FLR 771, FD

Family Division

Singer J

3 December 2004

Financial relief – Divorce – Non-disclosure – Off-shore trusts – Piercing the veil – Effect of concealing resources – International co-operation

The husband and wife had been involved in a relationship for over 15 years, and married for almost 10 years. There were no children of the marriage, but the wife had two children, aged 10 and 5 at the time the relationship began, who had been provided for by the husband at all times. From an early stage the husband had paid the wife's living expenses, and provided her with a home, acquired in the name of a Panamanian company, DM Investments SA (DM), which the husband had set up. The husband was an international businessman, with a number of property interests around the world, and the family enjoyed an extremely high standard of living. Payment for the family's personal expenses was met through DM, whose structure was eventually revised so that it became a wholly owned asset of a Jersey trust. After the marriage broke down the husband informed the wife that he had 'divested himself of all his assets' and resigned from various income-generating posts. The wife applied for and obtained a worldwide freezing injunction, which covered a hotel in Karachi and apartments in London, New York and Karachi, as well as what the wife claimed were the husband's interests in DM, and another Panamanian company, Midfield Management SA (MM), which had been involved in the purchase of the current family home. The husband's affidavits and Form E did not set out a clear statement of his assets, but asserted that his liabilities exceeded what assets there were. Specifically the husband denied any interest in either of the companies, DM or MM, or in the Jersey trust. The wife undertook a very costly investigative process in order to gather information about the husband's resources to put before the court. There was evidence that the husband had attempted not only to conceal his resources, but also to take steps to remove his assets from the jurisdiction. The husband had also instituted separate proceedings against the wife in Pakistan, and threatened to do so in a number of other forums, in relation to the worldwide freezing order. The court found that the husband had a fortune of, at a minimum, US$25m, and in all probability considerably more. The court also found that the husband had total control over both companies, and over the Jersey trust.

Held – awarding the wife £4,185,000, to include a contingent sum of £500,000 to cover actual and threatened litigation initiated by the husband in various jurisdictions –

(1) The husband's stance in relation to the court, and to the wife's claim, had been wilfully contemptuous of his obligation to make full, frank and clear disclosure in the proceedings. While the suppression of assets was not behaviour that of itself enhanced an award, the non-disclosing spouse was vulnerable to adverse inferences being drawn against him. In this case the court readily concluded that the husband had available to him ample resources with which to satisfy an award at or about the level sought by the wife (see para [45]).

(2) Where it appeared that an off-shore trust had been woven together to create a shroud designed to bury the husband's resources from view, but the husband himself pierced that veil as and when it suited him, a court exercising the ancillary relief jurisdiction would strain to see through the smoke and would set the structure aside so as to treat the resources as wholly his. This was what the parties, trustees and directors concerned should expect where fairness to both spouses depended so crucially on an accurate understanding of the realities of each party's economy (see para [1]).

(3) The shelter provided by sophisticated off-shore arrangements was dependent upon there being properly constituted corporate and trust structures in place; and there being a level of competence and of formality in the production of minutes of board meetings, powers of attorney etc, with supporting evidence for the proposition that proper consideration had been given by the trustees to the exercise of their discretionary powers (see para [51]).

(4) The Jersey trust was a sham, in that the husband had never had the slightest intention of respecting even the formalities of the trust and corporate structures that had been set up at his direction. His purpose was only to set up a screen to shield his resources from other claims or unwelcome scrutiny and investigation. The trustees had been prepared to go along almost totally passively with the way in which the husband managed the trust. The assets of the trust, namely the shares in both companies, vested in the husband as their true and sole owner (see paras [57], [58], [60]).

(5) Letters of request addressed to the Jersey courts had been used during the case, which had proved an efficacious and comparatively inexpensive method of extracting necessary information concerning off-shore trusts where the settlor or beneficiary was unwilling to provide relevant information. It was important for English courts and lawyers to bear well in mind that such assistance as letters of request could provide must be sought in accordance with the formal requirements of the Hague Convention of 18 March 1970 on the Taking of Evidence Abroad in Civil or Commercial Matters, which required, in the case of Jersey, that they be sent to Her Majesty's Attorney General for Jersey, not direct to residents of the island or to public authorities there (see paras [97], [98]).

Statutory provisions considered
Matrimonial Causes Act 1973, ss 25, 31(2)(d)
Hague Convention of 18 March 1970 on the Taking of Evidence Abroad in Civil or Commercial Matters

Cases referred to in judgment

A v A (Maintenance Pending Suit: Provision for Legal Fees) [2001] 1 WLR 605, [2001] 1 FLR 377, FD
Al-Khatib v Masry [2001] EWHC 108 (Fam), [2002] 1 FLR 1053, FD
Baker v Baker [1995] 2 FLR 829, CA
G v G (Maintenance Pending Suit: Costs) [2002] EWHC 306 (Fam), [2003] 2 FLR 71, FD
Hitch v Stone (Inspector of Taxes) [2001] EWCA Civ 63, [2001] STC 214, CA
J v V (Disclosure: Offshore Corporations) [2003] EWHC 3110 (Fam), [2004] 1 FLR 1042, FD
Midland Bank plc v Wyatt [1995] 1 FLR 696, ChD
Snook v London and West Riding Investments Ltd [1967] 2 QB 786, [1967] 2 WLR 1010, [1967] 1 All ER 518, CA
Tilley v Tilley (1980) Fam Law 89, CA
Westbury v Sampson [2001] EWCA Civ 407, [2002] 1 FLR 166, CA

Martin Pointer QC and Geoffrey Kingscote for the petitioner
The first respondent was neither present nor represented
Marcia Shekerdemian for the second, third and fourth respondents participated only in relation to costs issues affecting those parties, but did not attend the substance of the hearing

Cur adv vult

SINGER J:

[1] This judgment on a wife's ancillary relief claim touches upon a number of matters which are of importance in cases where the question is not merely the quantum of the award, but where there are issues as to the scale of resources. The first is the approach that the court should adopt where it finds (as I do here in relation to Darayus Cyrus Minwalla, familiarly known as Happy Minwalla, the husband) that a party has set out to conceal resources and obstruct proper investigation of their financial affairs, a subject only recently considered by Coleridge J in *J v V (Disclosure: Offshore Corporations)* [2003] EWHC 3110 (Fam), [2004] 1 FLR 1042 at [127] and [130]. Secondly, the virtue of international co-operation in the investigative process where the finances under review are conducted behind a web of off-shore structures. Thirdly, the approach which those involved should expect of the court where it appears that an off-shore trust with its professional trustees and associated companies with their sometimes cipher directors have been woven together to create a shroud that is designed to bury the husband's resources from view. Should the court respect the legal structure of that screen? Or, if it becomes apparent that the husband himself pierces the veil as and when it suits him, should the trustees and directors be surprised that a court exercising the ancillary relief jurisdiction will strain to see through the smoke and will set the structure aside so as to treat the resources as wholly his? For that is what he and they should expect where fairness to both spouses depends so crucially on an accurate understanding (following what should be clear and accurate disclosure) of the realities of each party's economy.

[2] The wife (W as I will call her) is 55. In 1985, when she was but 35, she was widowed. With her late husband she had two children, X and L, who are now aged 29 and 24 respectively, but were then only 10 and 5. In 1986 she met and began a

relationship with the husband (H). He is now aged 61, and was then 42. At that juncture he was still married to his third wife, D. By his first marriage the husband has one surviving son, F, who is 39. By his second marriage he has a son, T, who is 24. It would appear that at the time of the commencement of the relationship between the husband and the wife, his marriage to his third wife was continuing (although manifestly it was in difficulties). When the parties met, the husband had one son with her, J, who is now 19. In 1990 they had a second son together, HO, who is now 13.

[3]   Nevertheless there was sufficient solidity in the relationship between H and W for him, soon after they met, to buy a house in Friern Barnet for occupation by W and her two children. That property, it is agreed, was acquired in the name of a Panamanian company called DM Investments SA (hereafter DM) that had been set up by the husband in February 1985. There is a suggestion by H that at the same time as DM was formed a trust was set up in Jersey to hold the shares of the company. No documentation at all in relation to that suggested structure has been produced and it may well be that none survives, if indeed there is any truth in the suggestion. It is not disputed that in 1986 at the time that DM acquired the house in Friern Barnet, the company was acting under H's direction and control, and that that continued to be the position at the time when the trust that came to hold the shares was established (in July 1998: see below). From 1986 W and her two children have been dependants of H. The house in Friern Barnet was their family home in the UK. (It was not their only home for, as I will explain, H is an international businessman and the life that the parties led was cosmopolitan.) In 1991 the parties moved their London residence from Friern Barnet to a house in The Bishops Avenue in northwest London. By this time, it would appear, the failing marriage between H and his third wife had come to an end. In September 1992 they went through a divorce process in the Dominican Republic.

[4]   On 4 May 1994 these parties were married in Manhattan. That civil ceremony was followed by a Zoroastrian ceremony in June 1994 in London. At some point after that ceremony it came to H's attention that the divorce proceedings that he and D had undergone in the Dominican Republic may not have been valid; and so she and he went through a further set of divorce proceedings in New York, culminating in a decree on 10 March 1995. To tie their knot securely, H and W were re-married at a civil ceremony in London on 18 November 1995.

[5]   I am satisfied (indeed it is scarcely disputed) that during the period from the commencement of the parties' relationship until at least 2000 H had diverse business interests that enabled the family to enjoy a comfortable, if not opulent, lifestyle. From 1967 he had been responsible for the management of the Hotel Metropole in Karachi, erected by his late father in about 1950. From 1971 H has been employed as the local manager for Cathay Pacific in Pakistan and in Afghanistan. From 1988 to 2001 H was an Ambassador at Large for Pakistan, with a seat in the Cabinet of the Government of that country. H is the proprietor of a travel agency called 'Trade Wind Associates', which operates in the USA, Canada and the UK. He has a number of property interests around the world. The parties divided their time between Karachi, London and New York (maintaining separate establishments in each city). They have employed permanent staff in all three properties. W deposes, and I accept, that their houses were furnished to a high standard and housed valuable antiques. As she states, 'we have never wanted for anything' [B138]. And I do not doubt that while the

marriage subsisted, H was a generous provider. They travelled widely (always first class or business class) and stayed in the best hotels.

[6] Payment for their personal expenses was met through DM. The allowance that H made to W was paid by a monthly cheque drawn on an account in the name of DM.

[7] In 1998 the structure under which DM was held was revised. On 1 July 1998 the Fountain Trust (FT) was formally created. At inception the original settled property was £500 and the only named beneficiary is a charity. The trust was set up in Jersey. Once that was done, DM became a wholly owned asset of the trust.

[8] In 2000 the London base was changed. The house at The Bishops Avenue was sold and (soon after) the parties moved into an apartment in Portland Place, W1. Just as with The Bishops Avenue, extensive refurbishment was carried out, at a cost of £200,000 or thereabouts. The conveyancing file has been the subject of production procedures. The original negotiations for the purchase of the apartment were carried out in H's name. However, it transpired that the flat was already owned by a Panamanian special purpose company called Midfield Management SA (MM). This afforded the opportunity for acquisition without payment of stamp duty. The purchase was completed, therefore, by transfer of the shares in MM. These shares were acquired by FT. The funding for the purchase came as to £300,000 from moneys within DM that H diverted to FT and a mortgage of £500,000 from Standard Chartered Bank; though that mortgage was soon afterwards reduced by £200,000 which was also derived from DM.

[9] In September 2003, for reasons that are not relevant to this judgment, the marriage between the parties broke down. I record that there had been an earlier period of strain when in (it seems likely) the spring of 1998 H discovered that W had (as in her evidence to me she accepted) for some months (and mainly in absentia and by correspondence) conducted an affair. W suffered an acute sense of guilt and shame and offered to leave their marriage and abandon his support if that was what he required. She says that he accepted her promise to cut off all contact with the man concerned and wished to mend their relationship. She says she believed that they weathered this squall and that she was committed to the continuance of their marriage, until the events (about the detail of which I have heard no evidence) which led to her decision in September 2003 to bring the marriage to an end. I note that H was opposed to the divorce until the day before I pronounced decree nisi, and did not raise the allegation of adultery until his most recent affidavit which arrived with W's advisers on the eve of this hearing. I have heard evidence from W about this issue to satisfy myself (as she has) that there is in current circumstances no prospect of any relationship rekindling between W and this other man such as might impact upon the outcome of W's financial claims.

[10] W has remained from the time of that separation living in the apartment at Portland Place. H has not returned there and latterly has made his own base at the apartment in Karachi.

[11] The parties remained in dialogue both by email and by telephone. W tells me (and I accept) that orally H told her that he had 'divested himself of all his assets'; that he had resigned from his position 'as a consultant' with DM and that

payment of the household bills by that company would cease; and that he had resigned from his position at Cathay Pacific. On 11 December 2003 H sent an email to W in which he stated that he had given up his main income stream from Cathay Pacific and would wind up the few things they had asked him to do in the next month or so. He wrote that he was handing over his US business, Trade Winds and the Hotel Metropole to his sister, Mitzie. On 27 December 2003 H wrote again to W. He asserted that his arrangement with DM had been that his position was merely that of a consultant, and that he had now resigned. He claimed that he owed DM several hundred thousand dollars. The bills for utilities at Portland Place, he said, would no longer be discharged by the company. He said that two bank guarantees that had been issued by Standard Chartered were secured against the Portland Place apartment; that he did not have funds to meet the liabilities secured by those guarantees, and implied that the Bank would impose a sale of the flat. (I interpolate here that it was untrue that the guarantees were secured against the flat.) Both letters also conveyed the message that H was contemplating suicide. By mid-January 2004 letters arriving at the London flat illustrated that the arrangements H had made for payment of the household bills had indeed been terminated: the correspondence showed that all the direct debits against the DM bank account had been cancelled.

[12] All these gloomy hints, threats and prognostications jarred, from W's perception, with the financial history of their married life; and she reckoned that they were the initiation of a programme of suppression of H's true fortune, designed to minimise her financial claim against him. On 16 January 2004, therefore, W made application, without notice, to Munby J for a worldwide freezing injunction. The injunction that was granted froze H's resources up to £4m, including in particular the Hotel Metropole in Karachi, and the three apartments in New York, London and Karachi, as well as what were said to be H's interests in DM and in MM. The order contained a conventional requirement for H to disclose all his assets by affidavit within 7 days. H thereafter made two affidavits: on 23 January 2004 he purported to set out his means and on 30 January 2004 he made an affidavit answering the allegations that had been made against him by W in support of her injunction application. Neither affidavit condescended to a net summation of his assets, though the list of liabilities set out in his statement of means on 23 January 2004 was extensive. It is plain that H was describing his financial situation as parlous. (Later, in his Form E, he maintained that his liabilities exceeded his assets by some £400,000, a figure revised in his final affidavit to a deficit approaching £4m.) Furthermore, he denied any beneficial interest in DM or in MM or in FT. H claimed that he no longer had a mandate over the DM bank account, and so could not obtain bank statements. As is now known (and as I am very satisfied and will so find), that was all untrue. He asserted that he was neither a shareholder, nor director, nor in possession of any beneficial interest in either company; that he was not a trustee, nor a beneficiary of FT; that he had been the protector of that Trust, but 'only for a short time'. (That too was untrue.)

[13] H also asserted that his marriage to W had not been valid, on account of the allegedly ineffectual divorce proceedings that had taken place between him and D in the Dominican Republic. He revealed that he had on 25 November 2003 instituted proceedings in New York to annul the parties' marriage.

[14] Those were the rival contentions of the parties when the case came before me on 2 February 2004. At that hearing I continued the freezing injunction. I made directions for a hearing to take place on 14 June 2004 that should address the questions of the validity of the marriage and of forum conveniens; and of disclosure, including any application that might be made for inspection appointments or for letters of request and for the hearing of W's application for maintenance pending suit. So there was set in train the investigative process that it has been necessary for W to undertake at length and at great cost (her costs estimate to date is of the order of £400,000 of which she has so far been able to pay only £28,000 on account) in order to garner sufficient information to enable her and the court to perceive but a shadowy though not (I am sure) the full picture, of the resources that should realistically and properly be regarded as available to H.

[15] Thus it has been necessary for W to address two questionnaires to H. Neither has he answered satisfactorily. She has had to seek the issue of three sets of letters of request addressed to CI Law Trustees Ltd (CI), the professional trustee company in Jersey which supplies the trustees of FT and the directors of DM and of MM; and further letters of request directed to Standard Chartered Bank in Jersey. In order to obtain intelligible information about what had been happening in Jersey, it was necessary for there to be a 2-day hearing in Jersey, at which W was represented by Mr Kingscote, her junior counsel in this case. She has had to apply for inspection appointments against Standard Chartered Bank and EFG Bank in London; and against the conveyancing solicitors who acted for H on the purchase of The White House. A great deal of the historical information that features in this judgment is the product of that endeavour. It is conclusive of the reality to which I aspire in my appreciation of H's dealings with the assets of this so-called trust and its supposedly creature companies that in the course of the evidence that was given in Jersey they were vividly described by the Jersey-based trust operative and director of both DM and MM as H's 'personal fiefdom'. That same evidence is utterly damning of H's integrity in these proceedings, and convincingly destructive of the deceptive presentation he has attempted to foist on W and on the court.

[16] As the process has developed, the volume of information concerning H's affairs has increased, and with it more details of the steps that he was taking ahead of, at the time of, and from the breakdown of the marriage all of which were designed, as I find, to reduce or to eliminate successful enforcement of any award in favour of W on her ancillary relief claim. It is no exaggeration to describe H's stance in relation to the court and to W's claim as wilfully contemptuous of his obligation to make full, frank and clear disclosure in these proceedings so that the overall objective of fairness to both parties can be facilitated.

[17] It is now apparent, therefore, that, as early as March 2003 H had begun the process of re-arrangement of his banking facilities. The main bankers to DM were Standard Chartered Bank. The customer relationship manager there (as he is termed) was Mr Robert Mitchell. He left Standard Chartered Bank and went to join EFG Bank, which is a Swiss bank with offices in London and in Guernsey. Records produced by the EFG Bank pursuant to letters of request directed to them in Guernsey show that as early as 11 April 2003 [CC380] H was making arrangements to open a new account with that bank in Guernsey. No doubt

Mr Mitchell was keen on behalf of his new employers to attract business; but, equally, I have no doubt, H perceived that DM was an entity too closely for comfort associated with him and that its resources might be vulnerable to attack either in these proceedings (which, by then, he may well have contemplated) or in other ways. A little later, in January 2004, H is recorded as saying to Mr Rayment at Standard Chartered Bank that 'too many people know about DM Investments' [S265].

[18] Certainly it is the case that, as soon as the marriage broke down in September 2003, H swung into action. On 22 September 2003 he instructed Standard Chartered Bank, the main bankers of DM, not to send any further mail to Portland Place (the address that had until then been their mailing reference) [O289]. The same day he instructed Standard Chartered to send US$500,000 from the DM account in Jersey to EFG Private Bank [S237]. He also instructed Standard Chartered to close one of the dollar accounts that it maintained in the name of DM and send the whole of the money to the EFG Bank. On 25 November 2003 H began proceedings in New York, by which he sought a decree of nullity in respect of the parties' marriage. He relied upon the probable invalidity of the divorce proceedings that had taken place in the Dominican Republic between himself and D as rendering null the initial two ceremonies between himself and W; and thereby characterised his relationship with W as bigamous. He cynically chose to ignore the fact that there had been subsequent divorce proceedings between himself and D and a further ceremony of marriage between himself and W which was, on any view, valid if their earlier marriage ceremonies were ineffective.

[19] At the same time H developed further his relationship with EFG and the new financial structure he was forging with them. Thus, on 3 October 2003 a new service company called Jealott Investments Ltd was incorporated at the direction of H in Panama. Mr Pointer QC submits, and I accept, that the purpose of this company was to replace the historic investment function for which, in part, DM had been used. On 18 December 2003 H caused to be incorporated a further service company called Aviation International Consulting Ltd, another Panamanian company. Mr Pointer again submits, and I accept, that the purpose of this company was to perform the second of the two functions that had until then been carried out by DM, namely to receive the commission payments earned by H through his contracts with Cathay Pacific and Rolls-Royce, to which I refer below. At H's direction both companies opened bank accounts with EFG Bank. By 24 December 2003 H was giving instructions to EFG that he wished to wind-up its banking arrangements with DM (now that he had the two new companies and their accounts with EFG in place). An internal memo from Mr Mitchell of that date records that 'the client does want this account to be closed a.s.a.p. I know it could be a nuisance ... I understand the client's desire to wind the companies affairs up very urgently' [CC171]. That cryptic note by Mr Mitchell reflects the burgeoning desire of H to distance himself from that company and its resources. On 12 January 2004 H purported to resign from the board of Karachi Properties Investment Co Ltd: the company that owns the valuable Metropole Hotel in Karachi. By mid-January 2004 H had applied to Standard Chartered to borrow a further sum of £300,000 against the security of the apartment in Portland Place. He had, as I find, no need for those funds. His object was to reduce the equity in the London property, where W was living and against which her claim for a property transfer order was directed. That request

was not processed, because W had registered her rights of occupation. Between June 2003 and January 2004 H also cashed in a series of four Norwich Union policies for, in aggregate, about £216,000. The money from those policies has been expended by H and is no longer available to this court.

[20] I have recorded how on 16 January 2004 Munby J granted a freezing injunction, which was continued by me with slight adjustments on 2 February 2004. H paid scant regard to those injunctions.

[21] It is plain from the EFG Bank documentation [CC133] that by early March 2004 H was talking in terms of selling the New York flat. Indeed, by the time of the hearing before me in June 2004 W had been able to obtain particulars from the agents instructed by H in New York, demonstrating that he had been actively marketing that flat.

[22] It also has only recently become apparent from the EFG Bank documentation that in January 2004 H had given instructions for the encashment of two investment bonds, one with Norwich Union and one with Prudential that were worth together about US$750,000. The EFG and the Standard Chartered documents show that H was adamant that the bonds should be cashed, even though there was a not insignificant financial penalty for early surrender. H's directions were that the money should be placed into an account in his sole name. This was in direct breach of the orders that had been made on 16 January and 2 February 2004. Standard Chartered Bank, who had been given notice of the order of 16 January 2004, regarded that order as inhibiting the transaction that H was proposing. It appears that on 16 January 2004 H gave instructions to Standard Chartered to send all the investments held in two accounts in the name of DM to the EFG Private Bank in Guernsey. Mr Pointer submits, and I accept that it is probable, that those instructions were issued by H in reaction to the injunction that had been granted by Munby J on the same day. Because the bank was given notice of the order that had been made, they did not implement the instructions. This led, ultimately, to a tart email from Robert Mitchell to a representative of Standard Chartered Bank on 30 January. It recorded that the bank's principal (obviously a reference to H) had been expecting the transfer and was most concerned that it had not taken place. It asserted that at the time that instructions had been given to Standard Chartered, that bank had not had notice of the injunction; and that Standard Chartered had failed to act upon the instructions promptly; it sought confirmation that at the time the instructions were given the assets were 'free to transfer'; and demanded to know when Standard Chartered had received notice of the injunction.

[23] On 22 January 2004 W received a letter that purported to come from the directors of MM in Jersey. The letter stated that the directors of DM had given notice to MM terminating the licence in favour of DM to occupy the apartment at Portland Place with effect from 31 March 2004; that, accordingly, W was obliged to vacate the apartment and were she not to do so by that date she would be in illegal occupation, and steps would be taken to evict her. When W, through her solicitors, protested about this letter, H claimed, through his solicitors [E32] that he had had nothing to do with it. When, in August 2004 Nicholas Morgan the nominee director of DM came to give evidence in response to the letters of request issued in this court, he was asked about that correspondence by Mr Kingscote. It is plain from that evidence that H was 'pushing' for possession

proceedings to be instituted against W. The letter of 22 January was undoubtedly the product of a dialogue between H, the nominee directors of DM and their London solicitors. Not only was the denial in the letter of 26 January untrue, on 11 March 2004 the identical threat was repeated in another letter from the nominee director of MM.

[24] The next manoeuvre by H was to attempt to argue that the funds still held at Standard Chartered Bank in Jersey were not caught by the injunctions of 16 January and 2 February 2004, on the ground that he had no beneficial interest in FT or the two companies DM and MM. His vehicle for this argument was, again, Nicholas Morgan of CI, the corporate trustee of FT. What happened was that on 5 February 2004 Standard Chartered Bank in Jersey wrote to Mr Morgan at CI, drawing attention to the fact that they had received notice of the freezing injunction. By return of fax on the same day the compliance officer at CI replied that Mr Minwalla was not a beneficiary of FT. That letter was reinforced by a letter from Mr Morgan on 17 February 2004. By that letter he asserted that the original injunction of 16 January 2004 had been discharged on 2 February 2004. He neglected to explain that the order of 2 February 2004 made a fresh freezing injunction in like terms. The letter went on to say:

'... DM Investments SA and Midfield Management SA are both companies that are owned by the Trustees of the Fountain Trust and not by Mr Minwalla personally. We further reiterate that Mr Minwalla has not been appointed as a beneficiary of the Trust. In such circumstances if you continue to treat the accounts of the above companies as frozen until further notice, the Trustees of the Fountain Trust and the above companies themselves must reserve their position and shall look to your bank to recover any loss or damage suffered by the same as a result of your actions. In the circumstances we should be grateful to receive your urgent confirmation that you will reconsider your position and cease to freeze the relevant accounts relating to the above companies.'

[25] The letter also pressed the bank to effect the transfer of securities to the EFG Bank, ie to carry through the transaction to which I have referred above. A further letter in the same vein was written on 2 March 2004 reiterating the same threat. Fortunately, Standard Chartered reacted in a commendably responsible way to that letter from Mr Morgan. They stated:

'If, as you are suggesting, Mr Minwalla has no interest in these companies or in Fountain Trust, it seems bizarre that they are expressly mentioned in the 2 February order ...'

[26] It is apparent that the bank had taken the trouble to read in full the order of 2 February, and it had observed that, notwithstanding the blandishments and the blusters of Mr Morgan, the freezing injunction had been continued.

[27] It is unsurprising that Standard Chartered were bemused by the proposition that H had and has no interest in FT or in DM or in MM. On 16 December 2002 CI had written a letter to Standard Chartered in Jersey that was headed the Fountain Trust, and continued [T131]:

'We have introduced the above Trust to you for the purpose of opening a bank account and can confirm the following:

- We are satisfied as to the integrity and standing of Darayus Happy Minwalla, who is the Settlor and Principal Beneficiary of the above-named Discretionary Trust.
- We shall notify the Bank immediately of any changes to the Principal Beneficiary or Authorised Signatory.
- The structure of the above-named Discretionary Trust follows our standard form of Trust Deed.'

[28] CI's reference on that letter commences NSTCM, the distinctive initials borne by Mr Morgan.

[29] I struggle to see how Mr Morgan could have written such contradictory letters. I remind myself that I have not heard Mr Morgan give evidence in this case; though I do have the advantage that I have been able to read (and have indeed with mounting disquiet and astonishment read) the 126-page transcript of the evidence that he gave to the Royal Court in Jersey on 25 and 26 August 2004, and more recently on 19 November. I am satisfied that the letters from Mr Morgan in February and in March 2004 were utterly inappropriate given what emerges from his evidence as to his own state of mind concerning H's dealings by that time. I have no doubt that the letters were written by him under pressure from H, who was determined to shift his assets, so far as possible, out of DM to the new vehicles that he had constituted across the water in Guernsey. But (unless there is some very cogent explanation for his conduct) that does not warrant Mr Morgan writing letters that were quite at variance with the December 2002 letter that he had written and with the reality in respect of the trust and the two companies, as he himself knew it to be and as his evidence in August 2004 exemplified.

[30] On 27 May 2004, shortly before the hearing that had by then been fixed for 14 June 2004, a deed of appointment was executed relating to FT [BBi112]. This deed purported to add H's four sons as beneficiaries of the trust. There is no doubt that this step was taken at the instigation of H. In his evidence in Jersey, Mr Morgan accepted that this action was taken 'in the context of the matrimonial proceedings' [AA107]. I find that this was another attempt by H to impede the ancillary relief claim by W. In a letter to W's solicitors dated and received by fax today H asserts: 'I am passing on [an injunction I made on 1 December to preserve funds in accounts in Jersey] to the beneficiaries of FT, who will no doubt be appealing and filing for amendment of the same'. Similar injunctions have been in place since before the date of that deed and no application to set aside or vary has been made on their behalf, or seeking to be heard in relation to what has from the outset been W's case: that the paraphernalia of the trust and of the company structures are a sham, and that their assets have never in any real sense belonged to anyone other than H.

[31] In June 2004 the case came before me to deal with the various matters stood over from February. In order to dispose of H's unattractive plea of bigamy in response to her petition, W proposed to amend her petition to plead in the alternative the third (civil) ceremony that she had undergone with H at the Westminster Register Office, which post-dated the second divorce between H and his third wife. It was impossible for Mr Moor QC, then representing H, to resist

that method of clearing the logjam that H had created, and so I gave directions that led to pronouncement by me of decree nisi the following day, 15 June 2004. I amended the order for maintenance pending suit from the £24,000 pa that had been fixed on 2 February 2004 to the more realistic level of £40,000 pa (given that W was now having to meet all the running costs of the apartment in Portland Place). I also made an order for maintenance pending suit for costs, in accordance with the now established practice in cases such as this: see *A v A (Maintenance Pending Suit: Provision for Legal Fees)* [2001] 1 WLR 605, [2001] 1 FLR 377 and *G v G (Maintenance Pending Suit: Costs)* [2002] EWHC 306 (Fam), [2003] 2 FLR 71. I made orders joining as parties to these proceedings CI as trustees of FT, DM and MM. I made directions for the issue of letters of request directed to Nicholas Morgan and Conrad Whitehead, the nominee directors of the two companies and the managers of FT; and for an inspection appointment directed to Standard Chartered Bank.

[32]   I am satisfied that H realised that the inevitable consequence of the issue of the letters of request would be the revelation of documentation demonstrating, as W was asserting, that H was indeed the true beneficial owner of FT and of the two companies. It is apparent to me that following that hearing on 15 June 2004 H embarked upon a programme of withdrawal from the proceedings in the UK and from the UK itself. Following that hearing (apart from one matter to which I refer below) he ceased to instruct counsel who had been acting for him in the case, Philip Moor QC and Justin Warshaw. He did not attend the FDR on 22 July 2004, where he was represented by his solicitor alone. He dispensed with the services of those solicitors in September 2004. He paid not a penny in respect of the order of maintenance pending suit for costs. In respect of the general maintenance, he paid £3,250 in June 2004: he has paid nothing since. It would also appear that at about the same time he decided that he would no longer actively participate in an arbitration with Rotary Watches Ltd in which (via one of his commercial enterprises) he was involved.

[33]   Before he in effect distanced himself from this investigation in the way that has since become apparent, H gave instructions to Mr Warshaw to settle a notice of appeal against the order for maintenance pending suit that had been made on 15 June. That was lodged on 29 June 2004 and led, in due course, to an oral hearing for permission to appeal (with appeal to follow if granted) on 3 November 2004. Mr Pointer submits, and I accept, that H had no real intention of participating in that appeal (or even of paying under the order were the appeal to be dismissed): but that instead his sole purpose was to cause W to incur considerable extra legal costs in dealing with that appeal.

[34]   It is plain, however, that H has kept abreast and to some extent ahead of the steps that W has been taking to try and discover the truth about his financial affairs. I have little doubt but that he has learned of her attempted pursuit of the funds held by DM at Standard Chartered Bank and, latterly, at EFG Private Bank in Guernsey. The order for letters of request made on 15 June led to the production by Mr Morgan of a bundle of documents pertaining to DM and MM; and the inspection appointment against Standard Chartered Bank revealed (a fact until then unknown to W) the transmission of funds to EFG Bank. That new information led, after the FDR on 22 July 2004, to a broadening of the freezing injunction and to other investigatory directions. Documents very recently produced by EFG Bank show that in September 2004 H was taking steps to shift

funds originating from DM, but by then transferred to Jealott Investments Ltd, from EFG Bank in Guernsey to a new company and a new bank, namely BMM Holdings (which is probably a Dubai limited liability company) at ABN Amro in Dubai.

[35] As has been described, W has been compelled to undertake a tortuous and costly process to try to ascertain as much as she has of the truth of H's financial affairs. By far and away the major and certainly the primary responsibility for this rests with H, whose duty it was to set out his financial circumstances in a full, frank and clear manner; and I conclude from what I have seen that his stance stems from his sense of affront at what he perceives to be the temerity of W in bringing these divorce proceedings and financial claims against him. I find that he continues to be driven by ill will towards W, and is determined to cause her to incur significant legal costs not only in pursuing her claim against him, but in dealing with proceedings that he has set in train against her and (as seems likely) with others which he threatens to foment in a number of jurisdictions and at the suit (in name) of a variety of entities he controls or influences.

[36] First, at the hearing on 14 and 15 June 2004, my attention was drawn to a proposed redevelopment of the Hotel Metropole in Karachi which, it was being suggested by Mr Pointer for W, was being undertaken at H's direction. I was shown a substantial glossy brochure that had been prepared by a firm of developers, incorporating a series of financial projections. The response from Mr Moor (then appearing for H, and no doubt relaying his instructions) was a simulacrum of what appeared soon after in H's textual answers to an outstanding questionnaire, namely:

> 'Karachi Properties [the owner of the hotel] commissioned the report based on a potential investor from Singapore in 1997 or 1998. The plan was scrapped as it was impracticable. There are no other proposals for the development of this site, save as is already stated, demolition and commissioning into a parking lot/marriage hall.'

[37] Nevertheless, on 4 August 2004 a firm of advocates in Karachi were writing to W, through her solicitors, suggesting that the injunctions that had been granted on 16 January 2004 and which have continued throughout this case had precluded the redevelopment of the Metropole Hotel which, the letter stated, was 'in the process of transformation from an hotel to a shopping mall and commercial centre'. It was alleged that the freezing injunction had inhibited the progress of that development, and that the company had suffered a loss of £19m. That letter has been followed with the issue of proceedings by Karachi Properties on 11 October 2004 in the High Court of Sindh. I have been shown the copy of the claim in those proceedings. The claim, astonishingly, relies upon the contents of the self-same brochure which was produced to me on 14/15 June 2004, and which H alleged related to a dead-letter project long since abandoned. The company alleges that that very project (in the statement of claim it is termed the company's 'mega project') had been embarked upon, but had now become frustrated because of the freezing injunction made in these divorce proceedings. The analysis is that because of the freezing injunction Standard Chartered Bank have called in a guarantee of US$223,000, secured (it is said) on certain saving certificates that belong to H. Even assuming (though there is no concrete evidence to demonstrate it) that the guarantee issued by Standard Chartered Bank to support a borrowing

of Karachi Properties may have been called in, I reject the assertion that the freezing injunction granted by this court has in some way impeded the development. The scale of the resources truly available to H personally or through his various service companies is such that he could readily have replaced the guarantee or the security in the sum of US$223,000 (or even the larger figure of US$300,000 that is referred to in the bank's own documentation). Secondly, were it demonstrably the case that the freezing injunction made in this court were in some way inhibiting the progress of the redevelopment of the hotel, application could (and no doubt would) have been made to this court to vary the injunction. But what is significant for present purposes is that the newly launched litigation in Karachi against W is, first, entirely at variance with the presentation that was being made by H in these proceedings in June and July 2004 as to the use to which the Hotel Metropole was going to be put; and, secondly, is, as I find, undoubtedly instigated by H in order to subject W to yet further pressure and expense. She has had to fund representation in Karachi at the so far modest cost of £500 and has been given the (I venture to think optimistic) augury that the case may be ground to a satisfactory conclusion for the expenditure of only a further like sum. The litigation in Sindh is brought in the name of the company. I am satisfied, however, that the proceedings would not have started without not merely the imprimatur of H, but also his impetus and his animus.

[38]　Secondly, as I have already recorded, H ignored that part of the freezing injunction that prohibited him from disposing of his New York apartment. He seeks to place responsibility for the marketing and attempted sale of this property on the Habib Bank in New York which, he says, has security over it for money that it has lent to one of H's businesses, Trade Wind Associates Inc. As recently as 7 September 2004 H has been writing threatening yet further litigation against W. He wrote as follows:

> 'I do intend to make your client fully responsible for my having lost this property to the Bank and will be claiming separately from her the market value of the property and all losses that I have incurred in the USA as a result of the freezing injunction.'

[39]　I recall that on 15 June 2004 there was before the court an application by H to vary the freezing injunction of 2 February 2004 so as to permit the sale by H of the New York flat. I was not satisfied from the exiguous evidence that H had chosen to place before me that the sale of that flat was necessary, nor that the bank was genuinely pressing for its realisation. I did not dismiss the application, but instead adjourned it, giving H the facility to restore the matter before the court, should there indeed be evidence of the nature that his counsel on his behalf was suggesting H would be able to produce. He has chosen not to restore it. I conclude that this threatened further litigation against W is another illustration of his determination to pressurise W, both financially and psychologically.

[40]　It does not stop there. In his latest affidavit H, at paras 3 (headed 'Harassment' – ie of him by her) and 8, threatens to unleash a barrage of litigation against W once these proceedings have been concluded. The tone of his threats can be read if there is any need to remove doubt about the extent of his animosity towards W and the lengths to which it may indeed carry him. The institution already of the Karachi litigation supports the conclusion that from H such threats are real. This aspect of the case will find reflection in my award.

[41] H has not participated in this trial. I am fully satisfied that that results from tactical decision on his part rather than any inhibiting incapacity. On 8 November 2004 I considered an application that H had made in writing for this trial to be adjourned. He protested that his health was not good and that the trial should be adjourned until he might be better. There was no medical evidence in support of that ground for his application. He said, secondly, that he had insufficient funds to pay his lawyers, and that he had a pending application for Legal Aid which he hoped would be successful, and that the trial should be adjourned until the application had been determined. I refused to accede to the application to adjourn.

[42] On the day of the trial H sent by fax to the court a letter dated 22 November 2004. The letter stated that on Saturday 20 November 2004 'a cyst in [his] skull was ruptured' and that he was undergoing essential surgery on 23 November 2004. W cast doubt on the truth of this assertion. She produced a copy of an invitation to a reception, a significant social event that H was hosting at his apartment in Karachi on the evening of Sunday 21 November 2004, the eve of the first day fixed for this hearing. She reported to me that that reception had taken place, and had been attended by H who was in apparent good health. Although W's account had come from someone else, who was present at the party, and is thus only indirect evidence of what occurred, I regard it as more likely accurate than the assertion of ill health coming from H, which, I was satisfied, was merely his latest attempt to derail these proceedings.

[43] On day 2 of the trial, a medical report was faxed to W's solicitors' offices and brought to court. This stated that a sebaceous cyst had been operated upon. It was not materially more informative as to H's health and his ability (even if he had been willing) to attend this trial.

[44] On resuming this hearing on 29 November I was handed faxes sent by H complaining he had had inadequate notice, by post alone, of the relevant hearing dates. I reject his assertions and accept the assurance of W's solicitors that before each relevant letter was posted it was faxed to H's fax machine at the Karachi flat to and from which communication has been satisfactorily conducted hitherto. H's blusters that the progress of these proceedings before me these last 2 weeks violates his rights to a fair trial are just empty wind.

[45] As is already apparent from this judgment thus far, I am far from persuaded that H has made proper disclosure of his financial resources in this case. He has set out at every juncture to obstruct W's investigation of his financial affairs. He has, I find, concealed resources, and has been taking steps throughout the pendency of these proceedings to put them beyond the reach of this court and of any enforcement process that W may be minded to pursue against him, whether in this country or elsewhere. In *J v V (Disclosure: Offshore Corporations)* [2003] EWHC 3110 (Fam), [2004] 1 FLR 1042, to which I referred at the start of this judgment, Coleridge J condemned the all-too frequent practice of attempting to conceal resources behind the screen of off-shore structures and identified the costs consequences that would flow from such litigation conduct. I agree entirely with each of those observations. The suppression of assets is not of course behaviour that of itself enhances an award. But the non-disclosing spouse does make himself vulnerable to adverse inferences being drawn against him, in accordance with the well-established line of authorities recording that principle, of which *Baker v*

Baker [1995] 2 FLR 829 was a useful example. In this case, given the relative modesty of the claim that is advanced by W in the context of the standard of living enjoyed by the parties during the marriage, I readily conclude that H has available to him ample resources with which to satisfy an award at or about that level.

[46] Nevertheless, it is of course appropriate that I should examine (so far as I can despite his lies and obfuscations) what are the actual resources of H in order that the probable scale of his fortune may be understood, against which I can then measure the claim by W and the award that I have in mind to make.

The Fountain Trust

[47] I reject completely the multiple assertions by H that he has no beneficial interest in this trust. There are in the complex and voluminous documentation amassed in the preparation of this case a number of examples of documents (letters, but notably also periodic wealth statements prepared by H) which proclaim that FT is his, and incorporate values for it and the companies in the presentation of his wealth and income. Such assertions are supported rather than belied by the way in which he has operated the assets (including the companies) of this supposed trust with utter disregard for any but his own wishes, decision-making and – in short – total control.

[48] But there is more to it than that, were that not enough. Among the documents produced by Nicholas Morgan pursuant to the letters of request that were issued in June 2004 are two letters of wishes, both signed by H. These bear identical dates of 22 September 1998. However, they incorporate different directions. One provides that during H's lifetime he is to be considered the principal beneficiary of the trust. It provides that in the event of H's death W is to be consulted as to investment matters and as to the distribution of the trust fund; and that in the event of his death one-third of the fund was to belong to W absolutely; that W should be permitted to occupy any property in which she may be resident at the date of H's death; and that the other two thirds of the fund were to pass to H's four sons. The other letter omits any reference to H as the principal beneficiary. It provides that in the event of H's death the whole of the funds within the trust are to go to H's sons. There is no third document indicating that one or other of the two contemporaneous letters of wishes should take priority, or the circumstances in which one rather than the other should (subject always to their discretion, theoretically at least) guide or influence the trustees.

[49] The circumstances in which there came to be two divergent contemporaneous letters of wishes were the subject of inquiry in the second round of letters of request that were issued in July 2004. A set of answers in writing was supplied shortly ahead of the hearing that took place in Jersey on 25 August 2004. The answers comprised (just as if in answer to a questionnaire) a text and accompanying documentation. Behind the documentation was enclosed what was plainly an earlier draft of the textual answers. The draft document [V119] itself showed that it had been transmitted by fax from H's fax number in Karachi. Unsurprisingly W's solicitors asked the solicitors for the trustees to confirm that H was the author of the draft document. The trustees' solicitors refused to answer and demanded the return of the draft, suggesting it was privileged. W's solicitors did not concede the claim of privilege. As is now plain the document was indeed a

communication between H and Mr Morgan, and Mr Pointer contends that no question of litigation privilege can properly be maintained. The point was never pursued. However, the explanation given in the draft text and reproduced in the final text was that the letter of wishes under which W was a beneficiary was merely an initial draft that had been prepared by the trustees and despatched to H for his consideration. The other letter of wishes was said to have been prepared by H in response to the trustees' draft and was sent by him to the trustees: he having decided, it was said, to exclude W on account of her affair. I reject that explanation. There is no material to support the proposition that any draft letter of wishes was ever sent by Mr Morgan to H. There is no evidence of any dialogue between H and Mr Morgan concerning the change in H's plan or his reasons for the exclusion of himself (as principal beneficiary) and W from the 'second' letter. There is no document produced from Mr Morgan's file to demonstrate how or why it was that one letter or the other was to be regarded as having priority. Furthermore, in correspondence passing between W's solicitors in London and the trustees' solicitors in London, it was suggested on behalf of the trustees that while it was true that the draft set of answers had come from H in Karachi, that had been in response to an earlier draft set of answers that had been despatched from Jersey to Karachi for consideration by H. The problem with that explanation is that while this correspondence was being exchanged, Mr Morgan was being examined by Mr Kingscote before the Royal Court in Jersey. The transcript of that examination records Mr Morgan as acknowledging that the set of draft answers had originated from H and not from his firm.

[50] Mr Pointer submits that the only sensible reason to have two inconsistent signed contemporaneous letters of wishes is to enable the dishonest selection of one or other letter to meet the circumstances in which the letter may have to be produced or otherwise relied upon. Thus, in the context of divorce proceedings, H, if obliged to produce a letter, would produce the one that excluded W. For other purposes, he would produce the alternative. In the absence of any overarching letter of stage 1 wishes containing further instructions as to which of the stage 2 letters is effective in what circumstances it is difficult to conceive what other explanation there can be. Mr Morgan accepted that for a trustee to hold on file or in its safe two such letters is, in what seems to be his very extensive experience, unique. I would hope so.

[51] The nature and structure of sophisticated off-shore arrangements such as have been deployed by H is well understood in this Division. No doubt the professional advisers and trustees of wealthy individuals wish honestly to strive to construct a network of interwoven trusts and companies able successfully to withstand the scrutiny of the internal revenue services of the parts of the world relevant to the interested parties. That shelter is dependent upon there being properly constituted corporate and trust structures in place; and there being a level of competence and of formality in the production of minutes of board meetings, powers of attorney and so on. There must also be supporting evidence (if and when questions arise which must be answered) for the proposition that proper consideration has been given by the trustees to the exercise of their discretionary powers. Two divergent letters of wishes do not fit anywhere into such a structure. I do not see how any professional trustee can properly have in his possession two such contemporaneous documents without there being the clearest instructions in writing as to which prevails.

[52] I would have no hesitation in concluding that H should in his lifetime be regarded as the owner of FT. If bounty from the trust reaches other individuals it does so as H's gift or to meet his requirements, rather than as the result of any exercise of trustees' discretion independently exercised. The resources within FT have been and (insofar as they still remain there) remain available to him, at any rate in the sense in which resources are appraised under the Matrimonial Causes Act 1973, s 25(2)(a).

[53] However, Mr Pointer invites me to go further than that. He submits that I should find that FT is a sham. It is, in reality, no more than a piece of paper utilised by H as a fiscal and/or financial screen. In this connection I have been referred to a number of authorities on this topic. Some of the earlier cases, including in particular some observations of Diplock LJ in *Snook v London and West Riding Investments Ltd* [1967] 2 QB 786 suggest that in order for the court to conclude that a document or transaction is a sham, it is necessary that all the parties to it must have a common intention that the 'documents are not intended to create the legal rights and obligations which they give the appearance of creating'. However, in *Midland Bank plc v Wyatt* [1995] 1 FLR 696 at 699 DEM Young QC sitting as a deputy judge of the High Court held, as to that principle:

> '... I do not understand Diplock LJ's observations regarding the requirement that all the parties to a sham must have a common interest to be a necessary requirement in respect of all sham transactions. I consider a sham transaction will still remain a sham transaction even if one of the parties to it merely went along with the shammer not either knowing or caring about what he or she was signing. Such a person would still be a party to the sham and could not rely on any principle of estoppel such as was the case in *Snook*, the defendant there not being a party to the transaction at all.'

[54] Support for that analysis can be gleaned from the judgment of Arden LJ In *Hitch v Stone (Inspector of Taxes)* [2001] EWCA Civ 63, [2001] STC 214 in which she said at 234 'in my judgment, the law does not require that in every situation every party to the actual document should be a party to the sham'. I have also read a lucid and scholarly paper on the topic of sham trusts written in 2004 by Stuart Pryke, a member of the specialist Bar, in which he refers to and analyses what appear to be the most relevant authorities.[1] In that paper he concludes:

> 'In order for a trust to be found to be a sham, both of the parties to the establishment of the trust (that is to say the settlor and the trustees in the usual case) must intend not to act on the terms of the trust deed. Alternatively in the case where one party intends not to act on the terms of the trust deed, the other party must at least be prepared to go along with the intentions of the shammer neither knowing or caring about what they are signing or the transactions they are carrying out.'

[55] That seems to me to by a fair analysis of the current state of the law, and I adopt it.

---

[1] See 'Sham Trusts' at www.11oldsquare.co.uk/articles/docs/sham_trusts.pdf.

[56] What are the factors here that support the proposition that the trust is a front, and that H, at least, had no intention of treating it as such? First, the assets of the trust comprise only the shares in DM and the shares in MM. As to the former, it is clear that H has treated the bank accounts of DM as if they were his own. He has caused to be paid into them the funds to which he was entitled under his various consultancy agreements with Cathay Pacific. He has withdrawn money from those accounts as if it were his own. No formal trading accounts for DM have been drawn up, at least since the execution of the trust deed in 1998. Transfers have been made from DM to MM, without any accounting ever being undertaken between the two companies. Transfers have been made from DM to Jealott Investments Ltd, as if the money were H's own funds to move around as he chose, which is precisely as he has always regarded them, a practice from which the trustees/directors have been unwilling or unable to restrain him. The documents to which I have referred above show that H was planning to wind up DM (because too many people knew about it). Plainly, there would have been no accounting between him and DM, or Jealott and DM, or MM and DM, were DM to have been wound up. MM was a vehicle acquired simply to own his matrimonial home. Expenditure on it was met from the DM account. Again, no trading accounts have ever been drawn up. H's presentation in this case has been that he had a consultancy agreement with DM. No such document has ever been produced. Mr Morgan was never aware that there was one. It is true that at certain stages Mr Morgan took the trouble to draw up powers of attorney in favour of H, in order to permit him to utilise the company's bank accounts. But that was an empty and in any event inconsistent and ineffective formality: window-dressing, it might fairly be called, or going through some of the motions. The last such power of attorney expired in June 2003. That did not prevent H continuing to use the bank accounts as if they were his own: he remained a signatory on those accounts, and the mandate did not change until after the freezing injunction was made in January 2004. In his testimony in Jersey Mr Morgan conceded in answer to questions from Mr Kingscote that DM was in truth H's alter ego; that H had total investment control over that company and, in Mr Morgan's own words, H treated DM as his own 'personal fiefdom' [AA51]. Not only had Mr Morgan never seen any consultancy agreement between H and DM, he had not until this summer seen any of DM's bank accounts, and could not be sure at which banks accounts were operative. He was until shortly before he gave evidence in July wholly ignorant about a series of three agreements between Cathay and DM concluded as long ago as May 2001 under which DM would receive up to a total of US$4,750,000 in one-off fees contingent upon securing certain deals, plus an annual fee income until April 2006 of US$850,000.

[57] I have, therefore, no hesitation in coming to the conclusion that H never had the slightest intention of respecting even the formalities of the trust and corporate structures that had been set up at his direction. His purpose was only to set up a screen to shield his resources from other claims or unwelcome scrutiny and investigation. In most cases where off-shore structures are put in place the primary objective is fiscal, and for all I know such considerations here played their part. But in this case, where H has already been through three divorces, it may well be that he was keen to shield his resources from matrimonial claims as well. Undoubtedly, H's intention always was that the resources were his and would continue to be his.

[58] I conclude also that the trustees were privy to the sham, at least in the sense that they went along with the intentions of H. In this regard I have observed that the trustees were willing to go along with all of H's actions and did not, from what has been shown to me, attempt at any stage to rein him in. There is support for this interpretation from the evidence given by Mr Morgan in Jersey. In the course of that testimony he said that 'I believe he [H] is the protector of the trust – and, as such, he is effectively the client' [AA106]. Mr Morgan also observed that he had regarded H as 'de facto principal beneficiary' [AA114]. When dealing with the letters of wishes Mr Morgan was at pains to emphasise that letters of wishes are precatory only and he said that 'where you have a settlor situation, a letter of wishes is for guidance only and the settlor can verbally or in writing give different wishes at any stage' [AA115]. He went on to say that a letter of wishes 'could be changed yesterday; it could be changed tomorrow' [AA113]. That was troubling evidence. It, of course, provokes the question whether or not what H says in the second letter of wishes had in fact been backdated; and I have given due consideration to that possibility. However, I have rejected the evidence that the 'second' letter of wishes was a refinement of the first draft. And I adhere to the conclusion voiced above that these letters were both deliberately produced at the same time: a time when, according to W's evidence about his reaction to discovery of her affair and her offer to depart the marriage if that was what he required, he seemed anxious that on the contrary the marriage should be saved, which she thought was what they set about achieving. That analysis serves too to confirm me in the view that this was not and was never intended by H to be a properly managed and independent trust; but was instead simply an extension of H himself. I conclude, on the material to which I have referred, that the CI were certainly prepared to go along almost totally passively with the way in which H made plain he intended to manage and was managing this trust.

[59] I should record here that in the latter stages of CI's relationship with H, some suggestion was being made that H and they should part company. The reason for this appears to have been that the regulatory requirements for the management of off-shore companies and trusts in Jersey have become more restrictive; and that Mr Morgan was keen, therefore, to see that proper trading accounts for DM at least were drawn up. He was (for the reasons I have indicated) entirely dependent upon H for the information necessary to have such accounts prepared; and H was not prepared to supply that information to him. Thus it was that Mr Morgan was contemplating an exit strategy for his firm; but in the event that never occurred. This late development in the relationship between H and CI cannot, in my judgment, operate to undermine the conclusion that I have reached on the other material, namely that this trust is a sham. Indeed, it serves to reinforce it.

[60] The result of my findings as to the status of the trust will be that the assets of the trust, namely the shares in DM and in MM, vest in H, as their true and sole owner. It is necessary, therefore, that I should consider what assets remain within those companies and potentially available for the purposes of assessing this ancillary relief claim, and to meet it.

DM Investments SA

[61] Assessing the true value of the assets within this company is a Sisyphean labour. H has never revealed the assets of the company. His presentation has been that he owes the company several hundred thousand pounds, but that it is otherwise nothing to do with him. Nicholas Morgan was required under the letters of request to furnish a schedule of assets, but, notwithstanding that he is on paper a director of the company, he has failed to do so: saying that only H has the necessary information. Whenever W has seemed to be approaching what appear to be funds available to meet her claim, they have in the main been removed elsewhere.

(i)   The combination of the inspection appointment against Standard Chartered Bank in London and the letters of request to Standard Chartered's Jersey offshoot has revealed a series of accounts at that bank which hold in aggregate about £1.15m. However, that sum is vulnerable to reduction on account of three guarantees that Standard Chartered had issued at the request of H, two in connection with the Rotary Watches arbitration amounting to £337,500 and a third in support of an account in Karachi for the benefit of the Hotel Metropole in the sum of US$300,000. The aggregate of £500,000 may, therefore, be called in and reduce that cash of £1.15m to about £650,000.

(ii)   There are the proceeds of the two investment bonds that in February 2004 H was attempting to surrender and to transmit to the EFG Bank in Guernsey. The bonds were surrendered, but, because of the freezing injunction the current net proceeds of about US$800,000 are (subject to a little doubt in the light of some evidence given by Mr Morgan in Jersey on the 19 November 2004) held by Mr Morgan's firm in Jersey. At the present depressed value of the dollar that approximates to only about £420,000.

(iii)   There should also be the sum of US$500,000 that at the time of the breakdown of this marriage H sent from Jersey to EFG Bank in Guernsey. However, it is likely that that is part of the money that has now been sent on by H from Guernsey to Dubai. Properly, that money belongs to DM: but it is doubtful whether it will find its way back to that company.

(iv)   The company technically enjoys the benefit of certain contracts that H has negotiated with Cathay Pacific. Under those contracts DM was due to receive US$4.7m as commissions under a series of transactions that were due to take place between May 2001 and June 2003. I am satisfied that those commissions have been paid, but to what extent they are now represented in the resources I have been describing above, it is difficult to say. In addition, there is a rolling contract under which Cathay is due to pay to DM US$850,000 p a. I have little doubt but that in the context of this divorce H has redirected those payments from Cathay, almost certainly to his new service vehicle, Aviation International Consulting Ltd.

Midfield Management SA and the Portland Place flat

[62]   In this case it has been H's presentation that the Portland Place apartment is not his. In correspondence his solicitors wrote on his instructions that he 'knows nothing about the actions of MM ... it is an entirely independent legal entity in which he has no interest whatsoever'. On 8 September 2004 H wrote to Sheridans (his erstwhile commercial solicitors in London) stating that 'the property ... is not my matrimonial home, it is not my property and I am not the beneficiary of the trust that owns the property. You are, therefore, trying to take a charge over a property in which I have no personal interest'. In answers to questionnaire H even went so far [F204] as to state that, as well as not having anything to do with the

decision-making, he does not know who the directors of MM are. I have already rejected the assertions by H that FT, DM and MM are properly to be regarded as independent legal entities. The conclusion that I have already expressed is supported by H's own presentations both to his bankers and to Mr Morgan. Thus, in a letter dated 27 February 2002 [L96], H wrote to Mr Morgan, saying as follows:

> 'I am enclosing herewith an updated net worth statement of myself as the sole beneficiary of the Trust and as promised also give you a bird's eye view of the last year's activities and income source. Midfield Management was purchased with the sole aim of owning flat no 2, 55 Portland Place and this was completed on 17 October 2001. I have full possession of the property and am in occupation of the same.'

[63] The value of this apartment is agreed on the face of the parties' Forms E at £1.1m. More recently, W has gained sight of a valuation of the property at £1,050,000, obtained for lender security purposes last December, no doubt in connection with H's unsuccessful attempt to raise a further £300,000 to reduce the available equity. I shall take the property to be worth the lower figure as does Mr Pointer's final schedule, because in it he makes no allowance for the notional costs of sale, usually taken as 3% including VAT, which near enough removes the differential. It remains subject to the balance under the original mortgage with Standard Chartered Bank, standing at £300,000. Secondly, it has become subject during the course of these proceedings to a charging order in favour of Sheridans. As is already recorded, they instituted proceedings against H for fees owing to them in the sum of £162,053. H did not defend the claim. Judgment was entered on 2 July 2004 in the sum of £177,953 (a figure that included interest and fixed costs). On 9 August 2004 Sheridans obtained a charging order nisi alleging (entirely in parallel with what W has been saying in this case) that H is the true beneficial owner of the property. Accordingly, if I make an order for transfer of the shares in MM and/or the property itself to W, she will take the property subject to both those charges. For I have, pending delivery of this judgment, made the charging order absolute once those acting for FT, DM and MM had (having considered an earlier draft of this judgment upon the status of the trust) abandoned the stance that H was not the true owner of the apartment.

[64] After recording the principal identifiable assets of H, the task becomes significantly more demanding. W has pointed to a series of assets that she says are the property of H: but he has not co-operated in the investigative process, and, as I have already found, has obstructed the inquiry at every turn.

Hotel Metropole

[65] Historically this was an important building in Karachi. The original hotel was opened by the late Shah of Iran in 1950. It occupies a large site comprising a whole block in the heart of Karachi. The site is owned by Karachi Properties Investment Co Ltd. Until the doubtful letter of resignation at the time these divorce proceedings began, H was the chief executive of this company. Of the 4,900 issued shares at least 2,000 are registered in H's name. W says that she believes that H owns 58% of the company [B5]. I have no particular reason to doubt her evidence. H claims that whatever shares may be registered in his name, they are held in trust for his children. He has produced a form of Pakistani trust deed that he says was drawn up in 1994, and under which he holds the shares in that company on trust for three of his sons, F, J and H. However, the validity of that trust is open to doubt. W has conducted investigations in Pakistan. It transpires that under Pakistani law it is probably necessary for a trust such as this to be formally registered. Inquiries have shown that this trust is not registered. In any case all the documentary material that has been unearthed by W relating to this hotel indicates that H does indeed have a beneficial interest in it of at least 50%. In all the bankers' material, including the statements of net worth to which I refer below, the hotel is treated by H as his. In September 2003 H is recorded as having told Standard Chartered Bank that he was going to sell the hotel for US$10m, of which US$5m would go to him. When H began to divert his banking arrangements to EFG Bank he informed them that he owned the hotel [DD208]. There are two documents in the bundle which give an indication of what may be the value of the site. The first is the development report that I have mentioned above, which puts a value on the site of (the Pakistani rupee equivalent of) £7.5m. The second is a valuation that H produced in the course of his answers to questionnaire, which gave a value of about £7.3m. Of course, the claim that has been brought against W in the High Court in Karachi indicates that the value of the property with its redevelopment potential is very significantly greater, for otherwise a claim for as much as £33m could not have been formulated. I conclude that H is beneficially entitled to not less than 50% of the value of the hotel and that the figure of £7.5m is the absolute minimum for its worth.

EFG Bank

(i)   Funds have been diverted from Standard Chartered to EFG Bank. The benefits of the contracts with Cathay Pacific have been diverted from DM to Jealott Investments and have, I conclude, found their way into the EFG Bank. What remains there has not been ascertained.

(ii) Some of the accounts at EFG Bank are in the name of Jealott Investments and Aviation International Consultants. These accounts are run by and for the benefit of H in the same way that the accounts of DM were.

Aviation Services Ltd

[66]   This company is (it is agreed) the general sales agent for Cathay Pacific. H has claimed in these proceedings that he has no interest in the company. In answer to the direct question what is his association with the company, he answered merely that he is neither a shareholder nor a director. However, W holds 619,150 shares in the company. In her oral evidence to me she explained that she had not realised that shares had been placed in her name; and that it must have been done by H. She tells me that Aviation Services Ltd generates substantial income for H. She tells me that the paper shareholdings disguise the true beneficial ownership of the company. (The majority of the other shares are registered in the name of H's son F.) I am satisfied on the evidence I have seen that on the balance of probabilities H is the true underlying beneficial owner of this company, and that it generates significant income for him from its agency with Cathay Pacific.

Trade Wind Associates Inc

[67] This is the travel agency business that operates in North America, of which H owns 50%. Until recently this generated an income for H of US$250,000 p a. H has claimed, during the course of these proceedings, that the company has fallen on hard times, is losing money and that its bankers are therefore seeking to recover his flat in New York, which is security for the business's borrowings. No up-to-date financial material in respect of Trade Wind Associates has been forthcoming, nor its sister company Trade Wind Associates Canada Inc.

[68] There is a series of other companies that have been identified in the course of the case with which H has some connexion and in most cases, I am satisfied either a partial or the whole beneficial interest, but about which the information is sparse.

[69] Trade Wind Associates (UK) Ltd is said by H to be dormant, but there is no proper material to demonstrate that. Trade Wind Gulf Aviation Ltd is said by H to be closed but that too has not been corroborated. There are sister companies in Pakistan and in Dubai, but H has provided no information about them at all. Rotary Watches (USA) Inc I accept can be regarded as having no value, together with its associated company Import Export Inc, in the light of the unsuccessful arbitration. Alongside Karachi Properties Investment Co Ltd stands Hotel Metropole Ltd, which is said to be the company that manages the hotel from that site. H acknowledges that he has a 35% interest (at least) in this company, but there is no material upon which those shares can be valued. There is a series of companies that bear H's familiar name of Happy. These are Happy Associates Ltd, Happy Development Corporation Ltd and Happy Trading Corporation Ltd. Again, there is no information that allows me to ascribe any proper value to these companies. There are two companies that are apparently concerned with freight: Freight Systems Pakistan LLC and Strategic Freight Systems Ltd (which is said to be a subsidiary of Freight Systems LLC). Again, the material concerning these companies is completely inadequate. There is a property owning company in Pakistan called Properties Services Ltd, in which H has either one-third or a 25% share. Again, it is not possible to assess the value of that interest. There is a relatively new company that has been created by H called Al-Abda Pakistan Ltd. I have no more material about that company. I have recorded above that H has caused the formation of Jealott Investments Ltd and Aviation International Consultancy Ltd as his personal service companies. Given that he has not even revealed the existence of these companies to the court, he has, unsurprisingly, not provided any information as to what assets they contain. The bank documents show that he is the 100% beneficial owner of those two companies. It is also apparent that H has set up a further company called BMM Investments Ltd as an additional service company into which he has transferred money.

[70] I need to address two other factors that may bear upon H's financial circumstances.

Rotary Watches arbitration

[71] H set up a company called Rotary Watches Inc. He has asserted a 75% interest in the company. This company obtained the franchise for distribution of Rotary watches in the USA. The agreement was terminated by the UK parent, Rotary Watches Ltd, in about 1998. The US company made a claim against the UK company for alleged wrongful termination of the distribution agreement. The UK company counterclaimed. A commercial silk was appointed arbitrator. The proceedings took a very long time. Each side incurred substantial legal costs. H's company was required to provide security for costs in the sum of £609,000. Of that sum either £272,500 or £350,000 (the position is unclear) was evidently covered by an insurance policy. The balance of £337,500 was secured by two guarantees given by Standard Chartered Bank. Those London guarantees were themselves secured on cash held by DM in Jersey. It would appear that H agreed to indemnify Sheridans, the London solicitors acting on behalf of Rotary Watches (US) Inc in relation to the costs of the arbitration [E326/J231].

[72] In June 2004, after H had decided to withdraw from all litigation in the UK, he was sued by Sheridans for the balance then owing to them in fees, namely £162,053. The claim was issued on 15 June 2004. Judgment was entered on 2 July 2004. It is suggested that there is a further balance due of £228,611 [E451] but it has also been confirmed that recovery thereof will not be sought against the Portland Place property.

Jersey police

[73] A letter from Jersey police dated 19 May 2004 [E272] records that the police are interested in a series of transactions on the bank account of DM, namely the receipt of sums from Cathay Pacific amounting to US$4.85m in 2002 and 2003, and a number of smaller payments out. H has recently suggested that this interest by the Jersey police was provoked by W securing a freezing injunction [E463]. In fact the Standard Chartered documents show that the initial report was made by CI Law Trustees Ltd. Documentary evidence has been produced to me which demonstrates that the money that was paid to H by Cathay Pacific was being paid pursuant to a legitimate commercial contract. His function under the contract was to negotiate the sale of a number of aircraft to Pakistan International Airways. The material, so far as it goes, that I have read does not suggest that there was anything tainted about those transactions.

[74] Arriving at a precise arithmetical conclusion as to what may be the overall fortune of H is, therefore, a task that has been frustrated by H's dishonest presentation of his financial affairs. Should I then derive guidance from the presentations that H has made to his own bankers? The letter of 22 February 2002 to Mr Morgan to which I have made reference above included with it a statement of net worth. Oddly, when the letter itself was produced by Mr Morgan in July 2004, the net worth statement was not included, and W's solicitors had to press for it. The document purported to summarise H's financial affairs as at 31 December 2001, and gave his total net worth at US$19,580,000. A later net worth statement was elicited from Standard Chartered Bank, dated 31 December 2002. That put H's net fortune at US$24m. The most recent presentations in papers from EFG Bank suggest that he may be worth US$28m. When I consider the financial presentations as at December 2001 and December 2002, I have to bear in

mind that since those dates H has suffered the adverse outcome of the arbitration proceedings concerning Rotary Watches, so that the value ascribed to Rotary Watches USA Inc is to be regarded as lost, along with such legal costs and securities as H has himself been obliged to put up. On the other hand, I remind myself that the litigation was being conducted not in H's personal name, but in the name of the United States Corporation, so that any liability for damages rests with that business and not with H. Moreover, insofar as he has made himself responsible for loans to the company or in respect of arbitration costs, it would be wrong to ignore the fact that he may have recourse as to 25% against the other beneficial shareholder in Rotary.

[75] But as against that, the significant contracts with Cathay Pacific and Rolls-Royce have been generating funds for H since the date of the earliest of the statements of net worth referred to above. There are other indications in the documents produced by EFG Bank that H's fortune may be considerably more. There is a manuscript note which suggests that US$25m is being transmitted from Canada to the Bank of Punjab. There are references in both the EFG papers and in the documents produced by Mr Morgan that indicate that there may be bank accounts in Switzerland either at UBS or at Lloyds TSB or both. In the documents produced by Standard Chartered Bank is evidence that H transferred US$750,000 to a company called Leetonia Properties [O99, O117]. In his evidence in Jersey, Mr Morgan suggested that a company bearing that name had been set up by him just before the purchase of the apartment in Portland Place with the intention that it would be used to hold that property; but that, in the event, the shares in MM were acquired instead, so that the company was no longer used. That appears to be gainsaid by the Standard Chartered documents. It is also suggested in the EFG documents that H is the owner of the site of the Hyatt Regency Hotel in Karachi; and there are queries from W as to whether or not H owns a property in Texas and, maybe, another property in London.

[76] In the absence of supporting evidence I apply the same principle of disbelief to other areas of H's assertions during these proceedings, and, when it has suited him, outside them. I, therefore, conclude that I should make no allowance for the possibility that H might be garaging funds for others in DM. It is all too easy a suggestion to make. It is true that CI became concerned at the regulatory implications of H's assertions to them on this topic and, therefore, sought corroboration and greater detail (without great success). H has produced nothing tangible to support the assertion that some of the funds from time to time sheltered in DM were moneys he had allowed friends, business associates or relatives to park there to accommodate their own personal needs for fiscal, financial or familial invisibility. Yet today H has sent a fax to W's solicitors, commenting in relation to an injunction I authorised on 1 December (designed to preserve the funds in Jersey intact): 'I am passing [the injunction] on to the third parties whose funds have been blocked in the account of DM, so they may send their affidavits directly to the court and to you for the release of their funds, as these assets are neither part of any assets of mine or part of the matrimonial proceedings'. The funds in question have been blocked for months, and, therefore, one wonders why it is at this juncture only, when (as the letter makes clear) H erroneously believes 'the hearings ... are over' that such claims are to be pursued.

[77] Nor do I, without firm evidence, credit H's claim that his business associate and relative Mr Bamboat of Dubai has on the strength of a series of IOUs

promising repayment by the end of the year lent him £73,500 which he has disbursed direct to firms of lawyers. There is no evidence to demonstrate the source of the money Mr Bamboat laid out in these transactions.

[78] In the end, I am driven to conclude that H's fortune must be measured as having a minimum worth of US$25m; and in all probability considerably more.

[79] So far as W is concerned, she has net debts of about £45,000. She has in the course of the hearing ascertained that there are £3,500 of service charge arrears unpaid on Portland Place. (She may have an interest jointly with H in two small funds in the USA which I will transfer to her upon the basis that any value she achieves will be offset against H's total liabilities under my order, but is likely that they will not long be available to her or have any material value when she comes to investigate them.)

Income

[80] H's presentation in this case has been that his total income is a consultancy fee of US$48,000 p a from Cathay Pacific. He has asserted that he retired from his former position at Cathay Pacific in 2002 and that his contract with Cathay Pacific is limited to that consultancy agreement. The documents obtained by W have demonstrated the falsity of that presentation. H has a continuing right under the contract of 1 May 2001 with Cathay Pacific to US$850,000 p a (albeit diverted by him into one of his service companies). The documents from EFG Bank show that he has a rolling contract with Rolls-Royce for the maintenance of aero engines under which the fee to which he is entitled is US$500,000 p a. Through Aviation Services Ltd H has the benefit of the sales agency contracts for Pakistan, Afghanistan and the Central Asian republics. H undoubtedly was able to draw an income from Trade Wind Associates Inc at the rate of US$250,000 p a; and I am sure that that income can and will be restored once this case is over. On that footing, H's income should be taking at a minimum of US$1,650,000 p a. My sense is that he should be regarded as having an income of the order of £1m p a, on which, because of his diversion of that income to his off-shore entities, he pays at most negligible tax. His presentation to his banks of his living expenses puts them no higher than about US$300,000 p a. So the surplus that he generates each year is substantial. On one view, the figures that I have taken for H's income are modest. The documentation produced by his bankers shows that H has been presenting his income to them as ranging from £1.4m to US$4.1m p a in the last 4 years.

[81] For her part, W has an interest in a modest business in Karachi called AM Flowers. This is involved in the importation of flowers from Dubai and from Thailand for sale in Karachi. The business has struggled due to the absence of W in London during the course of these proceedings and also, she says (and I accept), because of pressure that H, in Karachi, has brought to bear upon W's business partner. She tells me that it could generate a small income for her, were she able to go to Karachi and apply herself to it. I am satisfied that, having regard to the history of this relationship, W should not, at her age, be subject to any obligation to generate any income of substance. It was H's desire, if not requirement, during the marriage that she should not work, but be dependent

wholly upon him. Now his assertions that it is a veritable and inexhaustible goldmine for her lack credibility as much as do many of his other uncorroborated utterances.

[82] Inevitably, the focus of this judgment has been upon the financial circumstances of the parties, and H in particular, but it is important that I should not overlook the other criteria that are set out in the Matrimonial Causes Act 1973, s 25.

Needs and obligations

[83] W needs accommodation for herself. She resides at present in the Portland Place apartment and, although she can foresee a time when she may wish to move to another property, she would wish to remain there for the foreseeable future. The remaining lease is not long, and she would like to have the funds to buy an extension to take the lease beyond 2035. I have taken the property to be worth £1,050,000 net of notional sale costs, but the charges upon it (the mortgage of £300,000 and the charging order in favour of Sheridans) reduce its net value to about £570,000. To purchase a lease extension would cost, probably, £460,000 when I make an allowance for associated costs. The resultant value of the property would hopefully be no less than £1.55m to justify the purchase. That will be a matter for her. In order to place W in that position it would be necessary to direct the transfer to her of that apartment, and to require H to pay a lump sum to discharge the indebtedness secured on it as well as to fund the acquisition of the lease extension. In aggregate the sum required amounts to £940,000. Is this an unreasonable aspiration? When I survey the probable true scale of H's resources, and the standard of living that was enjoyed by the parties during the marriage, for W to have about £1.5m for her housing requirement in London does not seem to me to be excessive, though I shall consider it in conjunction with the balance of her claim below. I appreciate that a time may well arrive when W could decide to move somewhere less extensive than this 2,500 square foot flat, at which point she will release free capital (in all likelihood) and may reduce some elements of her expenditure (for instance in relation to service charges). These considerations do not persuade me that it would be unfair for her to have such a degree of flexibility and self-determination after a relationship and marriage such as these parties have had.

[84] In the course of this case, W has had to sell her Mercedes car and some of her jewellery and borrow money from her children and others (some £45,000) in order to maintain herself. She needs, therefore, funds for a replacement car. She seeks the price of a Mercedes C320, which is about £30,000. She needs to pay off the service charge arrears.

[85] H has stated that his intention is to reside in Karachi. He retains a large apartment there, where he is supported by seven staff. He has a continuing obligation to maintain his minor son, HO, who lives in the USA with his mother, D. Having regard to the conclusions to which I have come as to the scale of the husband's resources, I am confident that he is able financially to provide for HO at an appropriate level.

[86] I have recorded above that the standard of living enjoyed by the parties during the marriage was extremely high. H is now 61, and W is 55. The marriage lasted for about 9 years. However, I do not overlook the fact that the parties were in a settled relationship from 1986 and that, from inception, W and her children became financially completely dependent upon H. I observe that H's continuing marriage to D was an obstacle in the way of these parties becoming married very much earlier than they were.

[87] As to health: H is a diabetic. This is a condition that was diagnosed many years ago and is managed satisfactorily. H has concern about the condition of his heart, but there is no current medical evidence to indicate that this is a matter of any serious concern. I discount the recent presentation by H on the eve of the trial as signifying any genuine or genuinely serious health problem.

[88] As to contributions: it is acknowledged that the sole financial contribution has been from H. On the other hand there does not seem to be any dispute but that W played her part as wife and as supporter to H in his business activities throughout their relationship. This is not a case in which there is any basis for differentiation between the spouses in the area of their respective contributions.

[89] The aspiration of W in the case is for owned accommodation (to include the capacity to acquire an extended lease if she so chooses) and for an investment fund that will on accepted *Duxbury* principles generate an income for her at the level of the budget she has advanced. Her budgeted figure was £90,000 p a. That budget was tested in the course of W's oral testimony, and I am satisfied that (as it then stood) it is not excessive. Since she gave her evidence it has emerged that it was understated to the tune of £11,750 p a while she remains at Portland Place, the current scale of the ground rent and service charges. For however long that particular element in her budget remains payable, however, I doubt whether annual expenditure at the level of £101,750 net would in fact permit her to maintain in London (where she anticipates continuing to make her home whether at Portland Place or elsewhere, and where her two children are established) the same standard of living that she enjoyed during the marriage. The total sought is to be measured against H's own annual budget for himself (not that which he produced for forensic purposes in the sum of £46,000 but rather his living expenses figure given to his bankers) in the sum of US$300,000.

[90] W's corrected budget of £101,750 translates (as the *Capitalise* computer programme shows) into a *Duxbury* fund requirement of £2,100,000. I remind myself that H, upon the available evidence, has a number of high-earning years ahead of him, whereas any income W may generate will (in my judgment) be very modest by comparison. He, therefore, has the prospect of increasing his capital base: her income-producing fund will, if she applies the *Duxbury* rationale and methodology, diminish to projected extinction over the 32-year balance of her life-span upon which the computation is based.

[91] If I aggregate the *Duxbury* fund requirement with the housing aspiration and the price of a new car and debt repayment for W, the total provision sought by her under those heads comes to £3.685m.

[92] W, however, in the particular circumstances of this case, has another identifiable prospective need which, in my judgment, is not so remote that I should

disregard it. I view it as more likely than not, such is his animosity towards W and his determination that she should not receive more than whatever he would choose for her to receive, that H will carry out his threat of pattern-bombing W with litigation brought by him and his creatures. The cost of meeting those assaults should not deplete the other aspects of her award or invade what, in my view, is her fair entitlement. She will, moreover, most likely sustain some significant irrecoverable costs in seeking to enforce the order so as to obtain its fruits. Her difficulties will flow entirely from the stance and actions adopted by H in response to her legitimate claim. She should be shielded from what I understand Thorpe LJ, when rejecting his application for permission to appeal my June maintenance pending suit order, described as H's policy of poisoning the water and burning the crops as he retreats to havens fresh. That policy of waste should ricochet to his account, if W is ever so fortunate as to obtain full performance of the obligations which this order will impose on H.

[93]   I propose, in short and without separate analysis of its legal justification, to follow the course adopted by Munby J in *Al-Khatib v Masry* [2001] EWHC 108 (Fam), [2002] 1 FLR 1053. I allocate £500,000 to those purposes, inevitably an estimate, to be designated in this court's order as a separate and additional instalment of the lump sum, payable only once the whole of the balance of the lump sum (and costs) orders I will make have been met, and at that stage subject to variation if H then wishes to demonstrate that £500,000 has proved to be excessive by way of provision for these purposes until that point, and/or to bind himself that there will be no future occasion for her to meet such expenditure. The jurisdiction for such a variation application is founded in s 31(2)(d) of the Matrimonial Causes Act 1973, and that it may have the effect of reducing or extinguishing (as well as rescheduling) the ordered instalment is at present decided by authority such as *Tilley v Tilley* (1980) Fam Law 89 through to *Westbury v Sampson* [2001] EWCA Civ 407, [2002] 1 FLR 166. But any such application might well, as a practical prerequisite, involve H first meeting the orders (including the costs orders) which I shall make. That will, however, be a matter for the judge hearing the application.

[94]   Therefore, the total value of the provision which H should make to W is £4,185,000 (subject to costs). The form of the order will be fixed immediately after this judgment has been handed down.

Fairness

[95]   It is not easy to undertake any evaluation by reference to equality of division, for the totality of the whole is unknown. If I am right that H's resources are a minimum of US$25m, or between £13m and £14m at least, W's claim is for between about 32.2% and 29.9%. I remind myself that although the committed relationship between the parties was a long one, it was a fourth marriage for H, and he has been developing his expertise and building up his fortune in the aviation, hotel and travel services businesses over many years, including before he met W. I do not see, however, that it would be fair to do other than provide fully but still reasonably for what I have assessed to be the reasonable needs of W for her immediate and longer term accommodation and for her revenue requirements. As to £500,000, the award contingently meets a need which H is entirely responsible for creating. I am confident that he has ample resources with which to satisfy the overall award.

[96] Before turning to the structure of the order that I propose to make and the extant matters upon which it is still necessary to hear argument and to rule, it is appropriate that I should make a number of observations on procedural matters that have arisen in the course of this case.

[97] First, the use of letters of request. During this case there has been a series of three letters of request addressed to CI in Jersey. In each case the requests have attracted maximum co-operation from the Jersey courts. They have been dealt with with the utmost courtesy, speed and efficiency. I am given to understand that Deputy Judicial Greffier Matthews, who has had the management in Jersey of this case, has gone out of his way to accommodate the timetable laid down by this court for the progress of the case, and has fitted in hearings so as to enable the information to be produced speedily. I am informed that there is statutory provision in Jersey that, if there be an oral hearing on the letters of request, English counsel have a right of audience, so that they may investigate the matters arising on the letters of request with the respondent to the hearing; and, secondly, that no order as to costs is made by the court. (Although that is not to say that in an appropriate case the witness should not recover the expense, including professional time, incurred in meeting the request: in this case and understandably CI did not pursue the totality of their potential claim under this head.) This is, therefore, an efficacious and comparatively inexpensive method of extracting necessary information concerning off-shore trusts where the settlor or beneficiary is unwilling to provide relevant information.

[98] It has, however, been courteously drawn to my attention in a letter from Mr Jowitt, the Senior Legal Adviser to the Law Officers' Department in Jersey, that it is important for English courts and lawyers to bear well in mind that such assistance as letters of request can provide must be sought in accordance with the formal requirements of the Hague Convention of 18 March 1970 on the Taking of Evidence Abroad in Civil or Commercial Matters, which in the case of Jersey requires that they be sent to Her Majesty's Attorney General for Jersey, and not direct to residents of the island or to public authorities there.

[99] I repose confidence in the courts of Jersey and of Guernsey that they will do their best, of course always in accordance with their domestic law and procedures, to ensure the speedy and efficient implementation of the orders that I will make to reflect the findings and the award contained in this judgment, so that W receives what is due to her without significant expense and delay.

[100] Next, I have referred above to the existence of the inquiry being undertaken in Jersey by the state's police. The result of the order that I am proposing to make will be that beneficial ownership of DM will pass to W. She will thereupon become entitled as the owner of the company to take whatever steps may be appropriate and necessary to take control of the moneys held within the DM accounts, which are at the moment frozen because of the police investigation there. It would, therefore, seem appropriate for the terms of my order (insofar as they relate to FT and the two companies) to be brought to the attention of the state police, in the hope that they will give urgent consideration to the release of the money in Jersey.

[101] Thirdly, it is evident that funds have been diverted by H from Jersey to EFG Bank in Guernsey. I am concerned to have read, amongst the documentation produced by that bank in response to the letters of request, an internal memorandum which records the bank as saying, at the time when they were given notice of the worldwide freezing injunction, that not only did it not bite upon them because there was no equivalent injunction then made in Guernsey; but also because they held no funds in Guernsey. That latter observation is gainsaid by their own documentary material which shows that there were significant funds on deposit with the bank at that time that were held to the order of H in his own name. I express the hope that EFG Private Bank will henceforth be fully co-operative with W in tracing the funds that were placed with them in the name of DM, but which have since, it would appear, been wrongfully diverted from that company to other companies acting under the direction and control of H.

[102] Fourthly, I have recited above that H has chosen to institute separate proceedings against W in Pakistan, through the vehicle of Karachi Properties Investment Co Ltd, a corporation acting under his direction, in order to inhibit W in the prosecution of her ancillary relief claim. As part of his claim in the High Court in Karachi, H seeks an injunction restraining W from 'disposing of any asset which [W] owns or may acquire by virtue of the matrimonial proceedings'. I express the confident hope that if and when any proceedings involving H or W come before the courts in Karachi, they will recognise that the essential dispute between them arises from this divorce, and that this court has been the one charged with an appraisal of the totality of their financial affairs. I accordingly hope that it would be regarded as unjust to allow this (or other) satellite litigation in Karachi (or elsewhere) to run on or to be used an oppressive tool against W. These comments apply with equal force to the litigation with which H has threatened he and/or others will unleash. My order will contain provisions which seek to deflect back onto him the ultimate liability for any awards which may be made against W in this way.

[103] I have given consideration to the structure of the order that I should make in this case. The total value of the award in favour of W that I will be making is £4,185,000. £570,000 of that is represented by the equity in the Portland Place apartment. Thus cash provision of £3,615,000 is required. Provided that funds are still held by Standard Chartered Bank and that the US$800,000 remains with CI (as I am assured by CI's counsel Miss Shekerdemian is the case), W should be in a position to recover about £1,104,000 in Jersey (at current exchange rates). When, where and at what cost she may recover the balance owing to her is more difficult to predict.

[104] I have considered whether or not I should adjourn the lump sum part of the claim (having made provision for transfers of the shares in the two companies and of the Portland Place apartment to W), so that I can ascertain what recovery is made over the course of the next few months, and then formally quantify the lump sum award when that recovery is known. The alternative is for me to fix the lump sum now, but stay execution of that part of it which seems to equate to the probable recovery from the money held in Jersey. The latter course seems to me to be preferable. Accordingly, there will be an order (and consequential directions to CI as trustee and to the relevant individual nominee directors of the companies) for transfer by H to W of the shares in DM and the shares in MM. There will be an order that the property at Portland Place be transferred into W's sole name as and when she may require such transfer to be effected, subject to the mortgage in favour of Standard Chartered Bank and the charging order absolute obtained by

Sheridans. There will be a lump sum order for £4,185,000. But I will stay execution of £1.1m of that lump sum until further order, my intention being that W should give credit against the total lump sum order for such sums as she recovers from any source (including, if Portland Place is transferred to her, £570,000 to be taken for computation purposes as the value to be ascribed to the net equity in that apartment).

[105] The contents of Portland Place will be transferred to W in their entirety. Pending payment of the full lump sum the maintenance obligation upon H will be £100,000 p a. When and if the lump sum payment and costs are paid in full a clean break will operate between the parties.

[106] I have already granted some injunctive relief designed to enable W to protect her position in relation to assets I have determined are beneficially H's, and anticipate I may be asked to consider more. I will hear submissions on the form of the order and as to costs between H and W. I will give leave for this judgment to be published, and see no reason why anonymity should be preserved in the circumstances of this case.

Order accordingly.

Solicitors: *Mishcon de Reya* for the petitioner
                Isadore Goldman for the second, third and fourth respondents

PHILIPPA JOHNSON
Law Reporter

MUBARAK v MUBARAK

[2001] 1 FLR 673, FD

Family Division

Bodey J

23 October 2000

Financial provision – Company assets – Lifting corporate veil – Concession by spouse that company assets could be treated as his own – Circumstances in which orders could be made against company/company assets

Judgment summons – Impact of European Convention for the Protection of Human Rights and Fundamental Freedoms 1950 – Criminal proceedings – Proof beyond all reasonable doubt – Reliance on husband's own evidence given at judgment summons hearing – Reliance on information as to husband's means given by him for purposes of ancillary relief hearing – Balancing husband's rights in judgment summons proceedings

The husband, a highly successful international jeweller, held his assets through a foreign discretionary trust, of which he was one of the potential beneficiaries. Prior to the main hearing of the wife's application for ancillary relief, the husband had conceded that he could be treated as owning the trust assets, which included two companies, an English company DJL, and a Hong Kong company DIL. Following a finding that the husband had been attempting to mislead the court and to conceal assets, the judge awarded the wife a lump sum of £4,875,000. The wife was concerned that the husband would continue to try to defeat her claims by any means possible, and indeed the husband failed to pay the sum. The only significant assets within the jurisdiction consisted of jewellery owned by DJL and DIL. The wife was granted an order over the jewellery, but the English company, DJL, then went into administration, and the question arose whether the wife could enforce her lump sum order by seizing and selling jewellery owned by DIL, or by DJL if discharged from administration. The companies resisted the wife's applications, arguing that the court could only lift the corporate veil and make orders directly against a company where the company or its assets had been formed or used as a device or sham.

Held – dismissing the wife's applications in respect of the company assets but, in respect of the wife's judgment summons, making a finding to the criminal standard of proof that the husband had made wilful default – even where a spouse conceded that the assets of a company could be treated as his own, the court could only lift the corporate veil and make orders directly or indirectly regarding the company's assets where (i) the spouse was the owner and controller of the company concerned, and (ii) there were no adverse third party interests. Lifting the veil was most likely to be acceptable where the asset concerned was the parties' former matrimonial home, or some other asset owned for purposes other than day-to-day trading. In this case both companies were bona fide trading companies, the husband was a director of one, but not of the other, and there were genuine third party rights and interests, in the form of commercial creditors and directors with fiduciary duties, which ought to be respected. The corporate veil could not be lifted.

Per curiam: it is incumbent on a party making a concession of the type referred to above to state specifically if he does not have the authority to make it from other persons potentially interested in the company or trust, or in the assets thereof. If the concession is intended to be limited merely to computing the extent of the maker's wealth, then it should say so in terms.

Statutory provisions considered
Debtors Act 1869, s 5
Civil Evidence Act 1968
Matrimonial Causes Act 1973, ss 23(1)(c), 24(1), 37
European Convention for the Protection of Human Rights and Fundamental Freedoms 1950, Arts 6(2), (3), 7, as enacted by Human Rights Act 1998, Sch 1

Cases referred to in judgment
Adams and Others v Cape Industries plc and Another [1990] Ch 433, [1990] 2 WLR 657, [1991] 1 All ER 929, CA
Aron Salomon (Pauper) v A. Salomon and Company Limited; A. Salomon and Company Limited v Aron Salomon [1897] AC 22, HL
Crittenden v Crittenden [1990] 2 FLR 361, CA
Dianoor Jewels Ltd, Re (unreported) 23 June 2000, ChD
Director of Public Prosecutions v Humphrys [1977] AC 1, [1976] 2 WLR 857, [1976] 2 All ER 497, HL
Engel and Others v The Netherlands (No 1) (1979) 1 EHRR 647, ECHR
Gilford Motor Company, Limited v Horne [1933] Ch 935, CA
Green v Green [1993] 1 FLR 326, FD
H (Minors) (Sexual Abuse: Standard of Proof), Re [1996] AC 563, [1996] 2 WLR 8, [1996] 1 All ER 1, sub nom H and R (Child Sexual Abuse: Standard of Proof), Re [1996] 1 FLR 80, HL
Jones and Another v Lipman and Another [1962] 1 WLR 832, [1962] 1 All ER 442, ChD
Macaura v Northern Assurance Company, Limited, and Others [1925] AC 619, HL
Mubarak v Mubarak (unreported) 3 April 2000, CA
Nicholas v Nicholas [1984] FLR 285, CA
Ord and Another v Belhaven Pubs Ltd [1998] 2 BCLC 447, CA
Saunders v UK (1996) 23 EHRR 313, ECHR
West Mercia Safetywear Ltd v Dodd [1988] BCLC 250, CA
Wicks v Wicks [1999] Fam 65, [1998] 1 FLR 470, CA
Woodley v Woodley [1992] 2 FLR 417, CA
Woodley v Woodley (No 2) [1993] 2 FLR 477, [1994] 1 WLR 1167, [1993] 4 All ER 1010, CA

Martin Pointer QC and *Justin Warshaw* for the petitioner (Mrs Mubarak)
Charles Howard QC and *Richard Harrison* for the first respondent (Mr Mubarak)
Ian Hunter QC and *Vernon Flynn* for the third respondent (DIL)
Susan Prevezer QC for the fourth respondent (DJL)
The intervenor did not appear and was not represented.

BODEY J:

This unhappy case now comes back before the court for the resolution of further issues. For convenience I shall refer to the parties as 'husband' and 'wife'.

The first issue is as to whether the wife should now be able to take jewellery belonging to a company which I shall call DIL in part satisfaction of a lump sum owing to her by the husband.

The second issue is as to whether the husband should be ordered to bring back into this jurisdiction certain jewellery belonging to DIL or (which comes to much the same thing) whether his removal of that jewellery in the months before the main hearing of this matter in December 1999 should be set aside. The total value of the jewellery involved in the first and second issues is many millions of pounds.

The third matter is a judgment summons brought by the wife against the husband.

A   Summary of background

The background appears from the various previous judgments, but can be quite shortly stated here. In December 1999 I heard ancillary relief proceedings by the wife against the husband in which I determined, amongst other things, that the husband should pay the wife a lump sum of £4,875,000. The husband, a highly successful international jeweller, had in 1997 placed the assets of his businesses into a discretionary Jersey trust ('the trust') of which he and the wife and the four children of the family were the original beneficiaries. Later, when the marriage was in difficulties, the husband caused the wife to be removed as a beneficiary of the trust. The professional trustees of the trust owned and own all the shares in a Bermudan company, which in turn owned and owns all the shares in a Jersey holding company, which in turn owned and owns all the shares in a Hong Kong company DIL and in an English company DJL. Both are trading companies employing a number of staff and holding their own stock and other assets. The husband is a director of DJL but not of DIL, although he was so prior to 1997. There are various other companies in the group and other companies in which the husband has interests, but they are not directly involved in these applications.

Prior to the main hearing the husband had made a concession, which I will set out in more detail below, that he could be treated as owning the assets of the trust.

Within the first 2 or 3 days of the start of the main hearing (having been caught out in a serious lie involving a forged document purporting to minimise his ownership of his businesses), the husband chose to absent himself from the remainder of the hearing. In my judgment dated 10 December 1999, I made a number of critical findings about him, including that he had manifested a determination to impede and to minimise the wife's financial claims; had put various forms of pressure on her to accede to his grossly inadequate proposals; had misled the court (which by then he had admitted) and had failed in his duty fully to disclose his financial resources, having substantial undisclosed assets.

At the conclusion of the hearing on 10 December 1999, the wife's lawyers expressed her considerable anxieties that the husband would continue to do everything possible to defeat her claims, there being little of value in the jurisdiction apart from the valuable jewellery stock of the companies then held at DJL's retail shop in the West End of London. Her particular fear was that he would immediately remove such stock from the jurisdiction and that, given the small size and high value of the individual items, it would be impossible to police any contrary injunction.

No dialogue being possible in the husband's self-imposed absence as to how these anxieties could be met in an orderly manner, I was asked to and did make a draconian order [para 15] requiring him almost forthwith to deliver up jewellery and artefacts in the UK belonging to one or other company in the group, such that (should the lump sum not be met) those items would be available for sale on behalf of the wife, subject to further directions from the court. Paragraph 19 of the order gave the husband permission to apply to vary or discharge that provision.

The husband duly applied for a stay on para 15 and shortly before Christmas 1999 I acceded to his application, backing it with various quite complicated provisions as to security pending a further hearing in January 2000.

At that hearing junior counsel appeared on behalf of DJL and DIL, seeking leave for those two companies to intervene and be heard against the enforcement of para 15. I gave a judgment in which I set out my reasons for refusing that application, stating that the companies could always re-apply for joinder in the light of any changed circumstances. In particular I then noted that the husband himself, through his leading counsel, submitted that there was no justification for the companies intervening, even though it could be seen that the husband had himself signed the resolution (he being a director) authorising DJL to instruct solicitors to make the application to intervene.

I further noted that the husband in his notice of appeal to the Court of Appeal was not attacking the legitimacy of para 15 (ie was not asserting that there had been no power to make it) but was merely mounting a challenge to the quantum of the lump sum order.

Given the husband's obstructive attitude and his earlier concession upon which the proceedings had been based (that the assets of the trust could be treated as his) it appeared to me at the time that this application by the companies was a ploy often seen in cases of this type, to impede the wife obtaining her award by wearing her down and depleting her resources. I was particularly concerned at the likely increase of costs if the companies were joined, with pockets deep enough to cope with the costs, but leaving the wife reliant on her lawyers being prepared to continue to act for her on credit.

I therefore refused the companies permission to intervene, having considered in the process three particular Family Division cases to which I was referred: *Nicholas v Nicholas* [1984] FLR 285, *Crittenden v Crittenden* [1990] 2 FLR 361 and *Green v Green* [1993] 1 FLR 326. I concluded on the state of things as it then was, that an order against the companies' assets was justified, provided that caution was exercised about creating a 'preference' or causing other prejudice to third parties. As to the then financial health of the companies, I made the point that the husband had never condescended to explain or dissent from a Barclays Bank record of November 1999 that:

'... he had been depressing the banking picture as the court views the [bank] statements. The [financial] settlement is due to be agreed in a month's time after which business and banking will return to "normal". I understand there are large sums owing from wealthy overseas clients.'

I then considered the husband's substantive application for a further stay of para 15 and allowed it on various terms, including that the husband should pay £3,200,000 by 31 May 2000 (which he has not done) and £1,675,000 by 30 November 2000. In view of my finding that the husband had undisclosed assets (which finding he was not challenging in his then pending appeal to the Court of Appeal) I pointed out that it was not actually necessary for company assets to be put at risk: it was a matter for the husband's choice.

Thereafter, many further applications were heard during the spring and summer of 2000 by Cazalet J. During this period of time, both companies were joined in these proceedings – DIL on an application made by the wife herself. Interposed amongst these applications, on 3 April 2000, the Court of Appeal heard the husband's application for permission to appeal the substantive order for ancillary relief. No appeal was advanced by the husband against para 15 of the order (entitling the wife to take company assets) nor did either of the companies seek permission to appeal the order refusing them leave to intervene.

The husband's stance before the Court of Appeal was to accept that there should be a lump sum award of £3m, although paid over time (a far cry from his position prior to the main hearing that the right lump sum was £180,000 comprising the transfer to the wife of a flat in Bombay). Thorpe LJ, who gave the judgment of the Court of Appeal, referred to the husband's determined and dishonest strategy designed to diminish the wife's judicial award and to divert the court from its proper adjudication. The husband's application for permission to appeal was refused together, inferentially, with the application in his skeleton argument that the award should be payable by instalments.

On 12 June 2000, after a full hearing (and after the husband had failed in his earlier assurances to Cazalet J that he would pay the wife £400,000 from the proceeds of certain auctions of company jewellery in May 2000), Cazalet J determined that the husband should be given no further time to pay the lump sum and he released the stay on para 15. However, he was persuaded to grant the husband a day or two's grace, on the basis that the husband said he wanted personally to supervise the packing arrangements.

Late that afternoon, however, DJL applied ex parte to Blackburne J in the Chancery Division and obtained an order that it be put into administration.

Subsequently, on application by the wife to set aside that administration order and following a fully argued hearing, Blackburne J gave a judgment dated 23 June 2000 (*Re Dianoor Jewels Ltd* (unreported) 23 June 2000). He was very clear on the r 2.2 report then placed before him that DJL was insolvent and therefore declined to set aside the administration order. He said in his judgment (transcript, p 14):

'The fact that in ancillary relief proceedings no-one has made a distinction between the husband, on the one hand, and the assets belonging to the various companies ... on the other, does not, of course, enable the court when considering the interests of DJL's creditors to disregard the corporate structure through which the businesses have been conducted. It is not suggested that DJL is a sham. It is plainly operated as a separate trading entity. Its creditors can only look to DJL and ultimately, through a liquidation, to DJL's assets for satisfaction of their claim. The fact that there are other companies in the group and that the husband regards them all as one and their assets as his to deal with, and the fact that the husband, the controlling shareholder, is a man of great wealth, is irrelevant so far as the claims of DJL's creditors are concerned.'

Thereafter, several further applications came before Cazalet J, particularly on or about 25 July 2000 when he directed that the surviving issues as regards DIL's jewellery stock should be heard by me in October 2000, at the same time as the judgment summons which had by then been taken out by the wife against the husband. I decided to hear the company issues first and thereafter the judgment summons, so that the company lawyers could leave, thus saving some costs in a case where the costs have now become enormous.

B   Can the wife enforce her order against the company assets?

Against that brief background and having now heard the companies' cases argued in full, I have to determine whether the wife can seize and sell company assets by way of enforcement of her lump sum award. This raises the question whether on the facts of this case the court can ignore the company/trust structure through which the jewellery stock is owned, ie 'lift the corporate veil'.

The test propounded by Mr Pointer QC for the wife is that the court can lift the corporate veil and make an order directly against a company's assets binding on the company when it can be shown that the husband (as I shall assume) controls the company and when any minority interests can properly be disregarded, for example as being mere nominees of the husband.

Mr Hunter QC, for DIL, supported by Miss Prevezer QC, for DJL, and by Mr Howard QC, for the husband, all challenge this proposition head-on and take issue with the basis of the Family Division's assuming this power directly or indirectly against company assets. They assert that the 'veil of incorporation' can only be lifted in circumstances where a company has been formed or used as a device or sham: in other words where corporate status has been or is being abused, and not merely where the spouse in question has full ownership and control.

In this respect there are two strands of authority – those decided in the company/commercial sphere and those decided in the family sphere. As counsel has said, there does not seem to be any decided case in which the authorities in the family sphere have been considered in the company sphere; nor do the authoritative textbooks of *Palmer's Company Law* (Loose-Leaf, Sweet & Maxwell) and *Gore-Browne on Companies* (Loose-Leaf, Jordans) mention those family cases where the lifting of the veil has been discussed. Only in one of the family cases (*Green v Green* [1993] 1 FLR 326) were any of the company authorities noted as having been referred to, and then only two of them.

The company law approach

Looking first at the authorities in the company/commercial sphere, the starting point is recognition of and respect for the juridical concept of the company as a separate legal entity. Upon this premise company law and practice is founded: *Aron Salomon (Pauper) v A. Salomon and Company Limited; A. Salomon and Company Limited v Aron Salomon* [1897] AC 22. It is as an incident of a company's separate legal persona that:

> '... no shareholder has any right to any item of property owned by the company, for he has no legal or equitable interest therein. He is entitled to a share in the profits while the company continues to carry on business and a share in the distribution of the surplus assets when the company is wound up.' (*Macaura v Northern Assurance Company, Limited, and Others* [1925] AC 619, 626–627, per Lord Buckmaster).

In *Ord and Another v Belhaven Pubs Ltd* [1998] 2 BCLC 447, Hobhouse LJ (as he then was) stated at 457:

> 'The approach of the judge in the present case was simply to look at the economic unit, to disregard the distinction between the legal entities that were involved and then to say: since the company cannot pay, the shareholders who are the people financially interested should be made to pay instead. That of course is radically at odds with the whole concept of corporate personality and limited liability and the decision of the House of Lords in *Salomon* ...'

The parent company in organising the group had there been entitled '... to expect that the court should apply the principles of *Salomon* ... in the ordinary way' (458). Hobhouse LJ further noted that in *Adams and Others v Cape Industries plc and Another* [1990] Ch 433, the Court of Appeal had considered both the 'single economic unit' and the 'piercing the corporate veil' arguments for lifting the veil and had '... clearly recognised that the concepts were extremely limited indeed' (457).

Whilst there are circumstances in company law when the court will go behind a company's separate legal personality, *Gore-Browne on Companies* states:

> '... It is not possible to formulate any single principle as the basis for these decisions, nor are all the decisions as to when the separate legal entity of the company must be respected or when it may be disregarded entirely consistent with one another.'

The principle of most general application in company law for doing so is that a company will not be allowed to be used as a device or sham to evade obligations nor for the purposes of fraud: *Gilford Motor Company, Limited v Horne* [1933] Ch 935 (company used to avoid individual's personal covenant in restraint of trade) and *Jones and Another v Lipman and Another* [1962] 1 WLR 832 (company formed to avoid vendor's personal obligation to complete contract). Hobhouse LJ specifically noted in *Ord and Another v Belhaven Pubs Ltd* [1998] 2 BCLC 447, 456, that: 'The companies were operating at material times as trading companies and they were not being interposed as shams or for some ulterior motive'.

Mr Hunter and Miss Prevezer rely here on the fact that there is no suggestion of a sham and that DIL and DJL have as such been run perfectly properly for their own legitimate trading purposes. They submit strongly, relying on *Adams and Others v Cape Industries plc and Another* [1990] Ch 433, that no principle exists whereby, if reliance on the strict technicalities would produce injustice, then the veil of incorporation can, without more, be lifted.

One can well see that, at least conceptually, the willingness of those who deal commercially with companies large or small, could well be compromised if the general principle were that the former wife of the owner and alter ego of the company might be able, with an ancillary relief order in her favour, to make off with company assets.

The family law approach

Turning to the authorities in the family sphere, in *Nicholas v Nicholas* [1984] FLR 285, the Court of Appeal held that the court could not there pierce the veil of incorporation regarding a company's ownership of the matrimonial home because minority interests in the company were owned by the husband's business associates. Cumming-Bruce LJ said at 287E:

> '... a question arises whether, having regard to the shareholdings in the two relevant companies ... it is proper for the court to pierce the corporate veil with the effect that though the company is the legal owner of the realty the court would disregarded the corporate ownership and make an order which, in effect, is an order against the husband, an individual shareholder. Of course it is quite clear, and there is abundant authority, that where the shareholding is such that the minority interests can for practical purposes be disregarded, the court does and will pierce the corporate veil and make an order which has the same effect as an order that would be made if the property was vested in the majority shareholder.'

He continued (at 287–288):

> '... it is not open to the court to supplement the express powers specified in s. 23(1)(c) and s. 24(1) [of the Matrimonial Causes Act 1973] in such a way as to exercise an inherent power, the effect of which will be to force a third party, to wit the company, to sell property vested in the company by way of sale to the petitioner. The difficulty, I feel, is that Parliament has in s. 24(1)(a) specifically limited the property that shall be the subject of a property adjustment order and has limited it to property which is property to which the first-mentioned party is entitled in possession or reversion.'

At 292–293 Dillon LJ said:

> '... If the company was a one-man company and the *alter ego* of the husband, I would have no difficulty in holding that there was power to order a transfer of the property, but that is not this case. The evidence shows that the husband only has a 71% interest in this company. The remaining 29% is held by individuals who, on the evidence available to this court, are not

nominees but business associates of the husband ... I find it quite impossible, therefore, to disregard the corporate entity of [the company] ...'

In *Crittenden v Crittenden* [1990] 2 FLR 361, Dillon LJ, citing s 24A of the Matrimonial Causes Act 1973 (court's power to order sale of property in which or in the proceeds of sale of which either or both of the parties has or have a beneficial interest either in possession or reversion) said (at 364):

'That wording can relate to the shares in the company ... which are owned in their own right by Mr or Mrs Crittenden, but it cannot relate to the assets of [the company].'

For the same reason s 37 (which refers to 'any property') was held not to apply to dealings with property belonging to the company concerned.

In *Green v Green* [1993] 1 FLR 326, simplifying the facts, the case had been conducted throughout on the basis that the husband had complete control over a company, the assets of which included some land. The husband then took the point that the court's only jurisdiction was over his shares as distinct from over the land itself, being property of the company. Connell J stated at 337:

'... it would, it seems to me on the face of it, be an irony if the court was precluded from ordering a sale of the land which was very much central to the litigation, simply because a party has only a 100% interest in the shares in the company which owns the land, rather than the actual title to the land himself.'

Having considered both *Nicholas v Nicholas* [1984] FLR 285 and *Crittenden v Crittenden* [1990] 2 FLR 361, Connell J said, at 340, he unhesitatingly preferred the judgments in *Nicholas* since they '... accord with the practice in this Division which, if I may refer to my own experience, is a practice which has been followed for some time'. Accordingly, he made the necessary orders to achieve sales of parts of the company's land.

Green v Green [1993] 1 FLR 326 represents first instance authority applying the approach referred to in *Nicholas v Nicholas* [1984] FLR 285 (although that approach was not actually applied in *Nicholas* on its particular facts).

Green was itself considered in *Wicks v Wicks* [1999] Fam 65, [1998] 1 FLR 470 and overruled to the extent that it had permitted an interim lump sum payment. Gibson LJ alone considered the rationale of *Green* from the point of view of its having lifted the corporate veil to deal directly with company assets. He said at 89 and 490:

'... I find it difficult to see how the application for ancillary relief in *Green* ... could have been said to relate to land when the husband merely owned shares in two companies which owned land. I can well understand Connell J.'s desire to find a solution so that the petitioner and her child could be provided with a home, but I do not think that the court had power in that case to order a sale of the land.'

Duckworth's *Matrimonial Property and Finance* (Family Law, 6th edn, 2000) describes lifting the veil in the Family Division as 'a somewhat ill- defined exception' and this whole area as 'highly contentious'.

Drawing all these authorities together, the precise extent of the Family Division's power to go directly against the property of a company owned or controlled by one of the spouses appears less than clear. In both the Court of Appeal decisions disowning the power (*Crittenden v Crittenden* [1990] 2 FLR 361 and *Wicks v Wicks* [1999] Fam 65, [1998] 1 FLR 470) no reference was seemingly made to *Nicholas v Nicholas* [1984] FLR 285, which contained strong Court of Appeal observations that the power exists when the circumstances there specified pertain. The one reported case to which I have been referred where the veil was actually lifted (*Green v Green* [1993] 1 FLR 326) has been disapproved by one of the judgments of the Court of Appeal in *Wicks v Wicks* [1999] Fam 65, [1998] 1 FLR 470, but that disapproval was not the ratio of the decision: neither were *Crittenden v Crittenden* [1990] 2 FLR 361 nor *Nicholas v Nicholas* [1984] FLR 285 seemingly cited to the Court of Appeal in *Wicks*.

Further, it is quite certain that company law does not recognise any exception to the separate entity principle based simply on a spouse's having sole ownership and control.

Rationalisation of approach

Ideally the Family Division and the Chancery Division should plainly apply a common approach. However, the fact remains that different considerations do frequently pertain: the company approach, on the one hand, being predominantly concerned with parties at arm's length in a contractual or similar relationship; the family approach, on the other hand, being concerned with the distributive powers of the court as between husband and wife applying discretionary considerations to what will often be a mainly, if not entirely, family situation.

I would echo the experience referred to by both Cumming-Bruce LJ and Connell J (above) as regards lifting the veil in the Family Division when it is just and necessary. In practice, especially in 'big money' cases, the husband (as I will assume) will often make a concession that company/trust assets can be treated as his, whereafter the case proceeds conveniently on that basis. It is pragmatic, saves expense and usually works. Problems such as have arisen in this case are rare and anyway can be avoided where there are other assets against which the lump sum order can be enforced.

The difficulty remains in defining those situations when lifting the veil is appropriate by way of enforcement following such a concession in ancillary relief proceedings. I would suggest that the Family Division can make orders directly or indirectly regarding a company's assets where (a) the husband (as I am assuming) is the owner and controller of the company concerned and (b) where there are no adverse third parties whose position or interests would be likely to be prejudiced by such an order being made. I include as third parties those with real minority interests in the company and (where relevant on the facts) creditors and directors. The reason for my including the latter two categories will become apparent later in this judgment.

I adopt the rationalisation of this offered by Mr Hunter, that it would amount merely to a short-circuiting of the full company law route, namely the declaration of a dividend to the husband comprising the company asset concerned (eg the matrimonial home) enabling him and/or the court then to transfer it onwards to the wife. It would amount to his property for the purposes of s 24 in the same sense that the law may look on that as done as ought to be done; whilst the mechanics of the order would be along the lines adopted by Connell J in *Green v Green* [1993] 1 FLR 326 at 341G: '... the respondent do sell, or cause G Ltd to sell, four plots of the blue land to ...'.

I would add that lifting the veil is most likely to be acceptable where the asset concerned (being the property of an effectively one-man company) is the parties' former matrimonial home, or other such asset owned by the company other than for day-to-day trading purposes.

The evidence

Before moving on to apply this suggested approach here, I must say a little about the evidence. It is clear that the husband made a concession of the very type just discussed, namely by his solicitor's letter dated 31 July 1998 that:

'... For the purposes of these proceedings the husband accepts that the assets of the trust will be treated as being his, subject to ...'

[It was there suggested that the husband had only shared ownership with the intervener, his adopted brother, a suggestion which I rejected at the substantive hearing: the intervener was also incidentally caught out in the lie surrounding the forged document referred to at the outset of this judgment, and he too abandoned the hearing, in his case never to return.]

What is the effect of this concession and can it bind the companies? It is said on the husband's behalf that this was only a concession relating to his ownership of the shares in the companies concerned and not relating to the companies' assets, viz the jewellery. On a strict reading of the concession alone that may be right; but the tone of the case was set not only by that concession, but also by the report of the husband's highly respected forensic accountants which stated:

'... We are instructed that the husband acknowledges his beneficial entitlement to 55% of all the business assets described above [I rejected this 55% argument] *and of any assets derived from them* ...' [emphasis added]

The tone was also set by the husband's financial presentations at the start of the hearing, namely by way of intermingling in one schedule both his own and the company's debts and assets as if all were his.

Whilst I have little doubt that the overall impression was to give the wife a false sense of security and to deter her from eg applying to vary the trust as a post nuptial settlement and/or from joining the companies, there is a valid distinction between (1) a husband accepting that he will be treated as the ultimate owner of resources for the purposes of computing his wealth and (2) his accepting, with the necessary authority, that any such award can be satisfied out of and directly enforced against a particular fund of assets not juridically within his immediate legal control.

Accordingly, in my judgment, it is incumbent on a party making a concession of this type to state specifically if he does not have the authority (ie to make the concession) from other persons potentially interested in the company or trust or in the assets thereof. If the concession is intended to be limited merely to computing the extent of the maker's wealth, then it should say so in terms.

Looking at the totality of the husband's presentation, it was, in my view, sufficient to amount to a concession that he was to be treated for the purpose of the proceedings as the ultimate owner, not only of the company shares but also of the assets belonging to the companies. However, that concession cannot, in my view, be binding on the companies: he was not a director of DIL at the material time and did not, on the evidence, have the authority to bind either Board of Directors in saying that company assets could be seized and used for the satisfaction of his personal liabilities towards the wife.   There are company law concepts involved here as to the day-to-day management and control of a company's assets for so long as it remains a going concern; and these are quite distinct from the right of the company's ultimate owner to assert (accurately) that he controls and owns the company, ie in the sense that he has the right through orderly procedures to have the company wound up and its affairs resolved so as to have paid to him any surplus resources (*Macaura v Northern Assurance Company, Limited, and Others* [1925] AC 619).

The fact that the husband purported and appeared to be able during the various 'stay' hearings to use and control company assets as if his own and the fact that the directors may in practice not have objected to that course whilst a stay was in place or in the offing, does not prove that in the last analysis he was able to establish and enforce against the companies the right in law to do so.

So although the earlier findings based on the husband's concession that he was the owner of the companies are res judicata against him, they are not binding on the companies and nothing in the way of evidence or argument which I have heard at this hearing has served to change this.

Turning now to the oral evidence at this hearing, I heard briefly from the wife and from Mr Aiyer (a chartered accountant, Group Financial Director and a director of DIL). The wife told me in short that the husband was quite simply the boss and the controlling force of everything. I do not doubt that this was her perception, nor that the various staff of the companies took instructions from the husband who is, after all (by his own concession) the ultimate owner.

Mr Aiyer has been described on behalf of the wife as a mere cipher of the husband, the implication being that he is masterminding the companies' intervention and opposition to the seizure of its jewellery simply to assist the husband in avoiding his proper obligations to the wife. However, having seen Mr Aiyer, albeit briefly (and whilst I do not doubt he has discussed with the husband the tactical advantages of the companies fighting to retain the stock and that he is acting in line with the husband's wishes) I conclude that, nonetheless, he is also genuinely concerned with his duty as a director to safeguard company assets.

I did not get the impression from him that the board's resistance to the order is driven purely by instructions from the husband, nor purely by the board's wish to help the husband in resisting payment of the lump sum order. In any event, provided that a director is acting in part for the interests of the company, I am not at all sure that any such ulterior or secondary motivation would be relevant.

I also found Mr Aiyer to be genuinely concerned as to his own position in view of the financial state of DIL. That financial state is set out in the various accounts and management accounts exhibited by Mr Aiyer in bundle Z and I need not repeat them here. Suffice it to say that, with one major caveat, DIL appears as presented to be in a worrying financial position. On the latest draft accounts, it has net assets of less than the full amount of the lump sum which the wife seeks to enforce against its assets (although that is allowing provision for £3m due to it from DJL, which may well not in the event turn out to be a necessary provision). If the various notes on the accounts by Mr Aiyer in bundle Z are factored in, including an apparent downturn in property values, there appears on paper (again with one major caveat) to be an insolvency or near insolvency situation.

In particular it is to be noted that DIL has creditors of some £5m including inter-group liabilities, amongst which is a loan owing to BNP Hong Kong of approximately £1.5m, as security for which BNP holds a floating charge by way of a debenture over all DIL's assets, including jewellery stock.

The caveat just mentioned is that the Bermudan parent company owes the husband personally a sum in the region of £20m (money which the Bermudan company has lent on to DIL) with the result that for so long as those loans are left outstanding, the net position of DIL is very healthy. However, I do not think that when the court is looking at the propriety of lifting the veil to seize DIL's jewellery, it is acceptable to assume that the husband will leave this loan outstanding. Admittedly he has given undertakings to BNP and to the auditors not to call in the loan until the company is 'financially capable of paying'; but that is a very ill-defined concept and I see little, if anything, to stop him calling on the ultimate parent company to repay him the money which it owes him. (That is one of ways in which, notionally, the paperwork could have been dealt with if the sales of jewellery in auction earlier this year had in fact produced cash for the wife).

If the husband were to call in his loan, the ultimate holding company (which has lent a similar amount of money to DIL) would have to call in its loan from DIL in spite of its undertaking to BNP not to do so. BNP would then rely on its security, which would leave DIL in what again appears to be an insolvency situation, placing the directors, including Mr Aiyer, in an exposed position regarding their fiduciary duties towards the company, ie by that stage towards the company's creditors (*West Mercia Safetywear Ltd v Dodd* [1988] BCLC 250).

I am fortified by the need for the court to be alive to the position of creditors (and consequentially of the position at least of oppositional directors) by an observation in *Crittenden v Crittenden* [1990] 2 FLR 361 when Dillon LJ said at 366–367:

'It may be that something else can be resurrected ... a proposal to which Mr Crittenden will agree, while at the same time satisfactorily protecting the creditors of the company whose interests in a company's parlous position cannot be overlooked.'

In similar vein Blackburne J in his judgment above (*Re Dianoor Jewels Ltd* (unreported) 23 June 2000) said (transcript, pp 12–13):

'There is, I venture to suggest, nothing in this [protecting the interests of creditors] which is inconsistent with the law and practice of the Family Division in ancillary relief matters. In *Nicholas* ... it is clear that the minority interests in a company, unless for some reason it is possible to disregard them, must be safeguarded before the assets of the company can be applied in satisfaction of a lump sum payment obligation owed by the controlling shareholder to his spouse. The position of creditors seems to me to be a fortiori ...'

Conclusion on lifting the veil

At the end of the day, both companies are bona fide trading companies incorporated well before the matrimonial difficulties of the husband and wife. DIL is indeed incorporated outside this jurisdiction and the husband is not a director. It is not suggested that they are as such being used as a sham or device, albeit that their existence is very convenient to the husband. In my judgment, there do exist genuine third party rights and interests which ought to be respected, namely the interests of bona fide commercial creditors (one of them secured on the jewellery) and the position of directors who have fiduciary duties and who oppose the seizure of stock in trade. The facts of this case are far away from those of *Green v Green* [1993] 1 FLR 326 which Mr Pointer asks me to follow.

Applying the above proposed approach as regards lifting the corporate veil to the evidence now before me and having heard full legal argument, I come to the conclusion that this case does not fall within the necessarily circumscribed circumstances in which lifting the veil would be acceptable. However much the court may wish to assist a wife and children where a lump sum has not been paid, I am satisfied that doing so here, whensoever it may be permissible, would be a step too far in all the circumstances. This is a conclusion strengthened by Art 1 of the first protocol that every natural and legal person is to be entitled, subject to the specified exceptions, to the peaceful possession of their possessions.

It was agreed by all parties that if I decided the veil of incorporation point in the way that I have, then the wife could not succeed on her summonses seeking to achieve the return to this jurisdiction of company jewellery earlier removed and so I say no more about that.

C The judgment summons

The gravamen of the judgment summons is the wife's assertion that the husband has wilfully failed to pay the lump sum or any part of it, although having had the means so to do. The Debtors Act 1869, s 5 provides that the court:

'... may commit to prison for a term not exceeding six weeks ... any person who makes default in payment of any debt or instalment of any debt due from him in pursuance of any order or judgment ...'

Such jurisdiction may only be exercised where it is:

'... proved to the satisfaction of the court that the person making default either has or has had since the date of the order or judgment the means to pay the sum in respect of which he has made default ...

Proof of the means of the person making default may be given 'in such manner as the court thinks just;'

Various points have been raised on the husband's behalf under the Human Rights Act 1998, which I have kept in mind throughout. The particular Article of relevance is Art 6 of the European Convention for the Protection of Human Rights and Fundamental Freedoms 1950:

'(2)   Everyone charged with a criminal offence shall be presumed innocent until proved guilty according to law.
(3)   Everyone charged with a criminal offence has the following minimum rights:
    (a)   to be informed promptly, in a language which he understands and in detail, of the nature and cause of the accusation against him;
    (b)   to have adequate time and facilities for the preparation of his defence;
    ...
    (d)   to examine or have examined witnesses against him ...'

Preliminary points taken on behalf of the husband

Preliminary points were taken by Mr Howard that I should strike out the judgment summons without hearing it at all (in limine) as being an abuse of the process. If I were against him on that, he submitted that he should be granted an adjournment. I ruled against those submissions at the outset of the judgment summons part of the hearing, saying that I would give my reasons later, which I now do.

Mr Howard's first argument on dismissing the judgment summons without hearing it at all was that a previous judgment summons was issued on behalf of the wife during the currency of a stay of the lump sum order. He submitted that this was just a device to justify retention of the husband's passport and that it renders this whole enforcement process abusive. I cannot accept that argument. I am satisfied that the wife's primary objective has been to enforce her order rightfully obtained. To complain of the husband having had enforcement processes hanging over him for a long time seems to ignore the position of the wife who has had no option but to take these expensive and stressful steps (at the same time as trying to care for four children); for the husband has paid nothing under the lump sum order except the modest amount of some £170,000 that she has been able to wring out of him by execution on his few assets within the jurisdiction.

In any event, the second judgment summons (the one now before me) was properly issued after the stay in question had been removed by Cazalet J and I see no reason to hold that it is tainted by any criticisms relating back to the earlier judgment summons, even if I found such criticisms justifiable, which I do not.

Mr Howard's second argument for a dismissal without any hearing and/or for an adjournment was based on his assertion that the wife has not got her tackle in order in spite of many opportunities to do so. He submitted that her failure to give the husband sufficient notice of her case constituted an infringement of his right to a fair trial under Art 6(3)(a) (above).

The relevant sequence in this respect can be summarised as follows. On 27 June 2000 the wife was ordered to file and serve any evidence on which she wished to rely regarding her judgment summons by 11 July 2000. In response, the wife's solicitors wrote that they were not going to file any evidence. On 25 July 2000 the wife was ordered to file an affidavit setting out the matters she relied on regarding the judgment summons.

On 15 August 2000 the wife swore an affidavit saying she would be relying on all the evidence adduced at the trial of her claim for ancillary relief, also on the judgments and on the husband's affirmations. On 17 August and 8 September 2000 the husband's solicitors wrote to say that this was not good enough, and alerting the wife to the Human Rights Act 1998 implications. On 3 October 2000 the wife was ordered to set out any oral evidence of fact she proposed to call, any documents she sought to rely on, any expert evidence she proposed to adduce and a concise summary of her case regarding the husband's failure to pay the lump sum.

On 5 October 2000 a notice was filed on the wife's behalf that she did not intend to call any witnesses, that the documents relied on would comprise the judgments and all the sworn or affirmed evidence since the ancillary relief hearing (thus narrowing the ambit of her case) and that it was not proposed to adduce expert evidence. By way of concise summary of the wife's case, the notice stated that the husband had failed to pay the lump sum ordered to be paid on 10 December 1999 having at all times had the means to pay it.

Having regard to this sequence, I considered at the outset of this part of the hearing whether this degree of forc-knowledge of the wife's case would be sufficient for the husband, or whether it would or might compromise the fairness of the proceedings from his point of view and/or mean that he should have an adjournment, bearing in mind that his liberty was and is at stake. Having done so, my conclusion was and is that the husband could have a fair hearing, knowing as he clearly has done the gravamen of the wife's case, namely (subject to argument as to the appropriateness of this course) her reliance (1) on my judgments, which contain clear findings (a) as to the extent of his admitted resources and (b) of his having substantial undisclosed assets; together with reliance (2) on the material in the affirmations since the main hearing, and reliance (3) on cross-examination of the husband at this hearing (if in these latter two respects that stage were reached).

Accordingly, I did not accede to the husband's submissions that the judgment summons should be dismissed without any hearing, nor that it should be adjourned; nor, later in the hearing, did I accede to his subsequent submission of 'no case to answer' (as to which I will not repeat the reasons I gave) nor his renewed application for an adjournment to call further evidence.

The substance of the judgment summons

Mr Pointer relies on the two findings in my judgments just mentioned. Mr Howard responds by reference to the Art 6 provisions mentioned above, asserting that such reliance by the wife cannot facilitate a fair hearing because this judgment summons proceeding constitutes an assertion of a 'criminal offence'.

Therefore he relies on the presumption of innocence and the right of silence whereby he says the husband can sit back and say 'prove it', putting the wife to proof beyond all reasonable doubt that he has or has had the means to pay some or all of the lump sum and that he has wilfully refused to do so. Mr Howard further says that the husband is entitled to examine or have examined witnesses against him, which could not occur if any reliance is placed on the previous judgments.

It has not been submitted that the Debtors Act 1869 is incompatible with the Convention for the Protection of Human Rights and Fundamental Freedoms 1950, and I accept that the former has to be read so as to be compatible with the latter, although I would suggest not in such a way that the former is rendered pointless. I further accept that a judgment summons is to be classed as asserting a 'criminal offence' (*Engel and Others v The Netherlands (No 1)* (1979) 1 EHRR 647), and that the husband must be accorded the minimum rights set out in Art 6(2) and (3).

Looking realistically at the overall nature of the process here, however, including through the eyes of the European jurisprudence, it must be said that there is something of a hybrid flavour to it. Certainly a 'quasi criminal' element was acknowledged in the domestic case of *Woodley v Woodley* [1992] 2 FLR 417; and Mr Howard himself relied at this hearing on the Civil [sic] Evidence Act 1968 in persuading me to admit certain evidence of jewellery expertise by way of letters.

Whilst a fair hearing is clearly essential, the overall circumstances are not, in my view, wholly analogous with a purely criminal proceeding where the State sets out to prove a citizen's guilt of some offence, in circumstances where there is no litigation background between the parties. By contrast, there is, ex hypothesi, on a judgment summons such an earlier background: namely that the parties are looking to the legal system and its procedures both for ending their relationship in law and for resolving financial issues between them.

The relevant procedure, although varying as between different States, will surely have as its starting point the ascertainment of the nature and extent of each party's resources, so as to facilitate what is certainly in this jurisdiction an exercise of discretion. Therefore, under defined checks and balances the parties supply information as to their respective means followed by a hearing, with both sides having rights of representation, of discovery, of cross-examination, of appeal with leave and so on. It may be, as here, difficult, time-consuming and expensive.

If the conclusion of this procedure comprises a financial award which is unmet, then enforcement will be necessary, sometimes by judgment summons. That is as a part of what is properly to be regarded, in my view, as a continuum of proceedings between the parties with the objective, where possible, of achieving their financial independence. This is not the same as a case starting off with a completely clean sheet between the parties, as criminal proceedings do, where it is simply up to the State to prove its case against an otherwise innocent citizen. I am not assisted by cases such as *Director of Public Prosecutions v Humphrys* [1977] AC 1 to which I have been referred, which do not seem to me to be on all fours.

Whilst I accept the presumption of innocence and other Art 6 rights to which the husband is entitled, I must (if I am to take any, albeit secondary, account of the wife's reasonable expectation that meaningful procedures will exist to assist her in legitimately enforcing her award) also have some regard to the fact that a full hearing took place previously. The husband chose to absent himself from the process but he had the right to attend the hearing and to be heard at all times.

At that hearing (where the husband clearly started with a presumption of innocence as regards the wife's assertion of the existence of the undisclosed assets) findings were made on the balance of probabilities, particularly as to the amount which he could reasonably and should pay to the wife as a lump sum. This was based on his likely assets, as I held them to be on the balance of probabilities, directing myself by reference to *Re H (Minors) (Sexual Abuse: Standard of Proof)* [1996] AC 563, 584, sub nom *Re H and R (Child Sexual Abuse: Standard of Proof)* [1996] 1 FLR 80, 96, that the 'more serious the allegation the more cogent is the evidence required ... to prove it.' (Lord Nicholls of Birkenhead, approving Ungoed-Thomas J's formulation in *Re Dellow's Will Trusts, Lloyds Bank v Institute of Cancer Research* [1964] 1 WLR 451, 455).

The particular allegation in question was the serious one of fraud, by way of non-disclosure of assets, and I was satisfied by the quality of the evidence on the *H* test that such allegation had been made out. That must be the starting point on the judgment summons, although not the be all and end all, by reason of the higher standard of proof for committal. As the Court of Appeal said in *Woodley v Woodley* [1992] 2 FLR 417, 422:

> '... the fact is that the standard of proof is the criminal standard and, as Johnson J [who tried the original ancillary relief hearing] had specifically made his findings on the balance of probability, it was not sufficient for Judge Owen [who tried the Judgment Summons] to say that the finding of Johnson J was binding and that the husband had the ability to meet [the order].
>
> The judge should have reminded himself, having regard to the findings of Johnson J, that the case needed to be decided beyond all reasonable doubt. There probably was material before him on which he could have been so satisfied, but he did not consider that aspect and this matter, on its own, would be sufficient, in my judgment, to justify allowing the appeal.'

So is there sufficient evidence now before me to be satisfied to the criminal standard that the husband has undisclosed assets?

Undisclosed assets?

First I accept Mr Howard's submission that it would not be fair to 'upgrade' my view of the cogency of the evidence by reference to a later observation of mine at a stay hearing that the evidence of undisclosed assets was 'overwhelming'. I do not propose to do so, nor let that influence my decision.

Second, I have now heard evidence from the Bank Manager regarding the above-mentioned note in the bank records about the husband suppressing the turnover of the businesses pending the main hearing, by holding back payments. The bank manager said that the information on which his note had been based had not come directly from the husband, but from two members of his (the husband's) staff. Although the husband told me that those two members of staff are reliable and trustworthy, it would not be satisfactory on the criminal standard of proof to regard that particular evidence as indicative of undisclosed resources.

Third, I have now heard the husband give evidence and I am bound to express the view that it contained a number of features which I found very unsatisfactory:

(a)   Asked whether he presently has any income to pay the substantial rent and periodical payments which he is in fact paying the wife, the husband replied 'not really' – or words to that effect. He explained he was able to make these payments by way of borrowings. He referred to one or two relatives as being the lenders, but the amounts which he mentioned of their loans bore no relation to the sum of £14,000 odd per month which he is having to find for the wife, the children and their rental payments.

(b)   He admitted when asked that he is effectively employing a chauffeur/ assistant, someone whom he took on about 2 months ago. This was at a time when the English company was in administration and when he was and is deeply in debt to the wife under the order in these proceedings. I do not know how he is paying for this convenience or why.

(c)   He admitted forgery of the 1996 supposed Joint Venture Agreement, which forgery had previously only been a matter of inference. It meant that he had arranged for an Indian lawyer and two other witnesses to give false evidence, and it now appears from his evidence that (just as the wife was alleging at the original hearing) the 1996 purported Agreement was in fact prepared much later than its stated date, even after the husband had filed his 'Form E'.

(d)   The husband has at no stage explained why he stayed away from the main hearing which must I think, unless and until explained, be regarded as having been tactical (ie to avoid full investigation of his means).

(e)   He was casual about the value of an Australian property development company in which he has an interest, saying that 'off the top of his head' he could not say whether it presently has any assets. Previously he valued his interest in or contribution to it at around $500,000.

(f)   He gave evidence which was unacceptable about his inability to get money (viz the potential net proceeds of sale of a flat in Bombay) out of India. In fact, and on his own case to explain so-called 'Parties 1–11', he has huge experience and acumen in handling other people's money through his Swiss bank account, by way of assisting them as regards exchange control regulations.

(g)   He fenced with Mr Pointer as to whether he it was who arranged for the Indian lawyer (above) to swear false evidence, which he eventually accepted; and as regards whether the trustees of the Jersey trust do actually exercise any real independent discretion (he suggesting that they do so, when their removal of the wife as beneficiary at his behest shows that they do not).

(h)   When asked whether he has been paying so-called 'Creditors A–D' pursuant to a repayment schedule relied on by him at the outset of the original hearing, the husband said he was unsure. This was a quite unsatisfactory answer because the sums due, if being paid, are substantial and one could hardly be in a state of uncertainty about them.

(i)   He says in his recent affirmation that in his original presentation he omitted to mention a BVI company, saying it is dormant; but he produces no documents whatsoever to support this.

(j)   He further says in that recent affirmation that, when he gave Barclays Bank information about his financial circumstances in 1998, he omitted to mention his creditors (said by him to have been, first, of £10m and, secondly, of one half of all his net assets). Accepting for the sake of argument the husband's case as to this ie his presenting a rosy picture to the bank (which is anyway contrary to my findings at the main hearing) it would clearly demonstrate his willingness and ability to make inaccurate and self-serving statements convincingly.

I accept that the husband's recent affirmation does appear to give a prima facie explanation for many of the 'signposts' referred to in the original judgment as pointing towards undisclosed assets, and I repeat the point about the bank manager's notes mentioned above. However, when I say 'prima facie' I do stress that caveat, for the way in which the cross-examination of the husband took place at this hearing was necessarily shortened by the time available for what was intended merely as an enforcement proceeding; it was not possible for Mr Pointer to go into the sort of depth regarding the husband's complex affairs as would have been possible at the original hearing if the husband had not chosen to absent himself.

I have to decide whether the totality of all this is sufficient for me to be able to say beyond all reasonable doubt that the husband has undisclosed assets from which he could make the lump sum payment. On the evidence now before me I have to say that applying the criminal standard I am satisfied I can do so. As in *Woodley v Woodley (No 2)* [1993] 2 FLR 477 it is inadequately explained how the husband has been paying the £14,000 a month to the wife since the administration of DJL, and it does not make sense that he employs a chauffeur having 'no real income'. Nor is it credible that he does not know if he has been paying substantial sums to his alleged creditors. In the several ways which I have indicated above, he has shown himself to be economical with the truth and I am sure he is in receipt of funding from somewhere which has not been uncovered.

Ability to have paid out of disclosed assets?

The matter does not end there. By way of preparation for the ancillary relief hearing the husband made the concession referred to above that, put shortly, the assets of the trust could be treated as being his. This was adopted and restated in the presentations of his highly respected accountant and leading counsel referred to above and further recorded in my judgment, which in turn set out (taking all the issues as to the value of the company's jewellery stock in the husband's favour and if everything were sold at auction) that the husband's net asset position was £8m [judgment, p 8].

That did not, and would not now, involve any question of standard of proof, because it was taking the husband's own case at its lowest and accepting it at face value. If the jewellery were to have been taken at its book value of £22m, instead of its agreed market (ie auction) value of £8m, then his net asset position would of course have been very greatly higher.

I acknowledge that the net asset value of DJL should be extracted from the husband's presentation of his net asset value of about £8m because it is now in administration, and I note from its accounts that at the material times its net assets have been around £400,000. So that has to be notionally taken out of the husband's net worth figure of £8m. Likewise it must be taken off the costs of sales of stock and/or indeed of liquidation. But the court has to take a pragmatic, although cautious, view of such costs in the circumstances of a case such as this. Before finding in the wife's favour on the judgment summons, I would have to be sure that the husband's disclosed net asset value is on any reasonable view of such contingencies sufficient to meet the outstanding lump sum order.

In spite of the burden of proving her case being on the wife, she is, in my view, entitled to proceed on the basis that the figures formally put forward by the husband as part of his presentation pertain, unless and until there is evidence produced by him on the judgment summons by way of a full overview of his financial position, which shows something different.

Now, the above information regarding the husband's case as to his net asset value was of course based upon his own affirmations and upon instructions he had given. Mr Howard submits that one cannot look at those affirmations and presentations to get to that net asset figure, because to do so would offend the husband's privilege against self-incrimination by analogy with *Saunders v UK* (1996) 23 EHRR 313. I cannot accept that submission. In *Saunders v UK*, the issue as to the use of the defendant's earlier answers given to the DTI under a duty to give them arose as part of a free-standing issue between himself and the State, not as part of a continuum of private litigation for resolving the financial affairs of a formerly married couple.

The husband's affirmations here, albeit given under his duty to give full and frank disclosure, were merely a concomitant of the court being able to undertake the necessary task of dealing equitably with the resources of the parties, with the wife owing reciprocal duties. They were made under the full protection of court overview in the event of issues arising and they would not be used against him per se in criminal proceedings, unless he were to default on meeting his established liability to his wife and a judgment summons were to issue.

Further, the husband was not actually under any legal obligation to put in concessions, nor presentations by his accountants and/or leading counsel; but chose to do so for the better presentation of his case.

I therefore reject Mr Howard's submission that the court cannot during a judgment summons hearing look at the husband's own earlier disclosure of his means, more particularly if recorded in the earlier judgment, and take that disclosure as its starting point. Were it otherwise, the husband's presumption of innocence and his claimed right not now to be bound to give any information to the wife or to court as to his means by reason of the asserted right of silence, could effectively emasculate the judgment summons procedure.

I now turn to the submission that the husband was not prepared for the case against him that he could pay the lump sum through, and by virtue of, his conceded ownership of the trust assets and that the wife should have spelled this out better under the above orders and/or in the light of Art 6, so that therefore the husband needs an adjournment to meet this case.

I cannot accept that submission. The husband made the above concessions via quality professional advisers as to his ownership of the trust assets, which concessions were as plain as a pikestaff. They were intended to be and were acted upon in the proceedings. It is also as plain as a pikestaff that the husband in fact controlled the trust, both from the documentation when he set it up (placing into it for fiscal advantage his business assets) and from the fact that at the time of the marriage breakdown, he simply instructed the professional trustees to remove the wife as beneficiary and created his father protector.

Making such a concession prior to the original hearing, as the husband did, is a potent power in the maker's hands and, as this case shows, is capable of abuse. It is quite clear that the wife was grievously misled by it, believing that the husband was accepting he owned and controlled the pyramid of his business assets and that therefore the case could be dealt with pragmatically and without resort to legal technicality.

Unfortunately, that was a forlorn hope. Technical points have in fact been taken by both the husband and 'his companies' (as the companies were described by Mr Howard to Cazalet J on 9 June 2000, before Mr Howard's going on to make the point that the companies are separate legal entities). Such technical points have been taken, for example, by way of the submission that the concession did not extend down to the jewellery stock of the companies – a submission to which I felt bound to accede (above) at the instance of the companies, by reason of their separate legal personae and the position of their creditors and directors.

Had the wife known this sort of thing was going to happen, she would, as mentioned above, clearly have availed herself of the more cumbersome route of applying to vary the discretionary trust as a post-nuptial settlement, or would have sought a transfer to her of so much of the husband's director's loan account in the Bermudan company as would have been equivalent to her lump sum award and/or would have sought to join the companies at the outset.

So I am unconvinced that the husband is justified in saying he was unready to face the assertion that he has/has had access to the substantial assets represented by the pyramid of his business resources.

I reiterate that I am referring to his own case, both as to ownership and value. There are plainly a variety of options for raising cash from or by the medium of substantial business assets, whether by asset sales, share sales, liquidation, borrowings, or permutations of these. The details of how all this can best be handled are peculiarly a matter for the businessman husband and for his commercial preference. It is trite law that it is not for a wife, even if she had the detail to do so, to propose and/or demonstrate the specific ways by which such could be achieved, particularly not to a successful international businessman well used to the world of high finance.

The fact that the court may not be able or willing, as I have ruled above, directly to seize company assets in the day-to-day management and control of oppositional directors and where there are genuine creditors, is not the same as saying that the husband himself cannot in practice use his ultimate ownership of the business structure to raise cash by accessing the underlying resources.

In any event, the husband has already demonstrated his ability in practice, and without reference apparently to Mr Aiyer, to place into auction company assets of considerable value with a view (as he proposed both to the wife and to the court) to paying the net proceeds to her in partial satisfaction of the lump sum. If those net proceeds had in fact made their way to the husband, as they appear not to have done, if would have been a simple and commonplace matter for a sum equivalent to those net proceeds of sale to have been debited against his director's loan account in the Bermudan company, with any necessary inter-company paperwork being done administratively.

As I said during argument, this case has gone past the stage of making an assessment of a lump sum for the wife calculated so as not to make life too difficult for the husband, as would be the court's usual target. The issue at this hearing is one of pure enforcement of a lump sum order in respect of which the husband's application for permission to appeal to the Court of Appeal has been dismissed and which remains extant and unmet.

I must now mention an important issue over timing. Mr Howard makes the point that the lump sum order was stayed between 20 January 2000 and 12 June 2000, and he relies on *Woodley v Woodley (No 2)* [1993] 2 FLR 477 in support of his proposition that, particularly bearing in mind Art 7 of the Convention, this effectively gave the husband a moratorium (or impression he had a moratorium) as regards paying the money.

(There is a subsidiary issue as to whether the order of 20 January 2000 actually stayed the lump sum, or whether it only stayed enforcement of it by way of execution on the company's assets. But I find as a matter of construction of the order, and on balance, that the lump sum itself was stayed).

Again, however, I feel unable to accede to the husband's submission. The husband's obligation to pay continued throughout. It was merely enforcement which was put on hold, specifically on the basis of his paying instalments, the first of which he failed even partially to meet. The case is therefore factually different from *Woodley v Woodley (No 2)* [1993] 2 FLR 477, where the only period during which the husband could be shown to have had the funds to pay the lump sum ordered had been during the currency of a stay of the order pending his appeal.

Throughout the breathing-space which the husband here was given by the stay, he could and should have been making the necessary arrangements to raise this money; yet he told me that he had not even taken the first step towards formally calling in that part of the £20m or so outstanding to him from the Bermudan company as would facilitate his paying some cash on to the wife. I am (as already mentioned) unimpressed with any suggestion that he could not do so because of undertakings to the auditors or to the BNP in Hong Kong.

Other steps which the husband has not even attempted to take to raise cash towards the wife's award include the sale of his debentures in a country club in Hong Kong worth some £20,000–£30,000; the sale of his watches and jewellery said by him to be worth some £35,000; the sale of his Range Rover worth, net of HP, about £25,000 (although I understand that this was in fact seised under a writ of fi fa last week); and the sale of the flat in Bombay which he owns with his sister, his half share of which is worth roughly £90,000. I have already mentioned my view of his telling me that in practice the proceeds would not be transferable out of India.

Mr Howard submitted that he had not had any notice that a realisation of this flat in Bombay was going to be alleged as a way by which the husband could have paid something off the sum due. However, I cannot accept that a judgment debtor needs notice, even given all his rights to a fair hearing, that it will be said he should have converted into cash assets in which he has an interest so as to use that cash in partial satisfaction of his liability. Nor, as I have said, has the husband on his own evidence made any attempt to ascertain the present state of the Australian company, Design Development Pty, in which his investment was apparently some $500,000.

It is not for the husband to take the view that sums of money like this are too small compared to the award to be worth his taking steps to obtain by selling the underlying assets; and I imagine that the wife, who is deeply in debt as to costs and has a Mareva injunction against her by her former solicitors, would have been glad of such sums in partial satisfaction of the lump sum.

Conclusion on judgment summons

In conclusion, I am satisfied beyond reasonable doubt that the husband has had the ability either to call on undisclosed assets or else to access his disclosed business resources so as to meet the original order, or at least that part of it which should have been met by 31 May 2000, even bearing in mind that doing so would involve various professional and other costs.

His failure alone to realise the more modest assets just mentioned and pay the proceeds to the wife renders him liable to sanction at this hearing, bearing in mind that judgment summons proceedings are both penal as well as coercive, (*Woodley v Woodley (No 2)* [1993] 2 FLR 477). The fact that he has not done so, nor paid any part of the order (except about £170,000 under court compulsion through a charging order) seems to be part and parcel of his determination not to pay the wife's legitimate award if he can help it.

I do pay regard (merely in parenthesis) to the way in which he messed the wife about over his promises to pay her £400,000 from the Geneva sales in May 2000. Accepting for present purposes that he has a genuine explanation, the simple fact is that it was for him to sort out the arrangements for the £400,000 to come to the wife, as he proposed more than once to the wife and to the court. This he signally failed to do. As Cazalet J said on 25 July 2000:

> '... He time and again made clear that the proceeds of sale of the May sale would go to the wife at the end of June ...'

The court obviously looks to proportionality before subjecting a respondent to committal and it may be described as a remedy of last resort. There being no other accessible funds which have actually been located whether in this jurisdiction or elsewhere, I shall now hear counsel, as I said I would, as to the appropriate form of disposal of this application.

Applications in relation to company assets dismissed, but husband found to have wilfully failed to pay lump sum previously ordered and suspended committal order made.

Solicitors: *Sears Tooth* for the petitioner (Aaliya Mubarak)
            Bates Wells & Braithwaite for the first respondent (Iqbal Mubarak)
            Taylor Joynson Garrett for the third respondent (DIL)
            Clifford Chance for the fourth respondent (DJL)
            The intervener did not appear and was not represented.

PHILIPPA JOHNSON
Barrister

MUBARAK v MUBARAK

[2001] 1 FLR 698, CA

Court of Appeal

Thorpe and Brooke LJJ and Jacob J

14 December 2000

Enforcement – Judgment summons – Human rights – Whether judgment summons Human Rights Act 1998 compliant – Procedure to be used

The husband was a highly successful international jeweller. At a hearing in which it became clear that the husband had submitted fraudulent evidence the judge awarded the wife a lump sum of £4,875,000. On the husband's failure to pay the first instalment of £3,200,000 the wife issued a judgment summons. The summons was in conventional form, supported by an affidavit deposing to the default, in compliance with Family Proceedings Rules 1991, r 7.4, paras (3), (5). No evidence was filed in support, although as a result of judicial intervention the wife added a sworn affidavit in which she stated that she would be relying on findings made in previous hearings. The husband corresponded with the wife's solicitors, complaining that the information provided was insufficient in the light of the Human Rights Act 1998, and the judge ordered the wife to serve on the husband a document setting out the evidence on which she intended to rely, together with a concise summary of her case. The wife's concise summary stated simply that the husband had not paid the money which he had been ordered to pay. In a judgment which also considered the court's inability to enforce the lump sum order against the husband's companies, the judge made an order on the judgment summons, committing the husband to prison for 6 weeks, not to be put into force if the husband paid. The husband appealed the committal order, arguing that the judgment summons procedure was not Human Rights Act 1998 compliant.

Held – allowing the appeal – although a judgment summons application might originate in family proceedings, it was clearly a procedure subjecting the respondent to the risk of the criminal sanction of imprisonment, and was therefore a criminal proceeding. The difficulties of adapting the judgment summons procedure, under the Debtors Act 1869 to the requirements of the European Convention for the Protection of Human Rights and Fundamental Freedoms 1950 were considerable, as the judgment summons procedure made no reference to the criminal standard of proof, required individuals to incriminate themselves, placed the burden of proof on the person facing committal, and muddled up the two processes of the means enquiry and the subsequent proceedings which might lead to committal. *Practice Direction: Committal Proceedings* (28 May 1999), which was intended to ensure that proceedings for civil committal would be conducted in a fashion that complied with the Human Rights Act 1998, applied in the Family Division as in other divisions, and extended to applications under the Debtors Act 1869, s 5, although this was not crystal clear from the text of the *Practice Direction*. The wide application of the *Practice Direction* was of great importance and needed to be recognised immediately by all family practitioners. The practical effect was likely to be that the Debtors Act 1869 would become a largely obsolete means of enforcement, as use of the Act in such a way as to comply with the Human Rights Act 1998 would require the court to reconsider all the issues raised in the original ancillary relief action, with the application of a much higher standard of proof. Issuing a judgment summons would be more or less useless in cases involving fraudulent husbands seeking to conceal assets difficult or impossible to identify specifically.

Per Jacob J: since the Debtors Act 1869 many more remedies have been devised which enable creditors (including those entitled to payments under Family Division court orders) to obtain their money. A freezing order with all the disclosure that can be obtained is an extremely powerful weapon. The remedies available extend to constructive trusts (even those situated abroad) and the obtaining of information by bankers. Other remedies, for example, orders for the production of documents, have been designed to enable creditors to get at the property.

Per Thorpe LJ: it was to be hoped that the family justice system's long-awaited reforms would be tackled swiftly, and that any decisions taken would fully recognise the particular and often very special needs of the family justice system, which were very different from the needs of the civil justice system.

Per Brooke LJ: it would be very helpful if the President of the Family Division could issue a new *Practice Direction*, to make clear the procedure which was to apply to judgment summonses in the High Court and in the county court.

Statutory provisions considered
Debtors Act 1869, s 5
Administration of Justice Act 1970, s 11, Sch 4
County Courts Act 1984, s 92
Human Rights Act 1998
Rules of the Supreme Court 1965 (SI 1965/1766), Ord 52, r 1(1)
Family Proceedings Rules 1991 (SI 1991/1247), r 7.4, Part 7, ch 2
Civil Procedure Rules 1998 (SI 1998/3132)
County Court Rules 1981 (SI 1981/1687), Ord 28, 29
European Convention for the Protection of Human Rights and Fundamental Freedoms 1950

Cases referred to in judgment
Bankers Trust Co v Shapira and Others [1980] 1 WLR 1274, [1980] 3 All ER 353, CA
Engel and Others v The Netherlands (No 1) (1979) 1 EHRR 647, ECHR
James Edgecombe, Re, Ex Parte James Edgecombe [1902] 2 KB 403, CA
Newman v Modern Bookbinders Ltd [2000] 1 WLR 2559, [2000] 2 All ER 814, CA
Practice Direction: Committal Proceedings (28 May 1999) (referred to in Scott et al *The White Book Service 2000* (Sweet & Maxwell, Autumn edn, 2000), p 1192)

Charles Howard QC and *Richard Harrison* for the applicant
Jeremy Russell for the respondent

THORPE LJ:

[1] In July 1998, Mrs Mubarak initiated ancillary relief proceedings against her husband, as I will call him for convenience. At the very outset, leading counsel on her behalf applied to Bracewell J and obtained an order in very wide terms, freezing his assets as defined in subparas (i) and (ii) of para 1. Paragraph 2 of the order required almost the impossible, namely that he should disclose his assets in writing within 72 hours, and by affidavit of means within 7 days. However, Messrs Withers, on his behalf, more or less performed the impossible, since on 31 July they wrote a letter to the solicitors then representing Mrs Mubarak, in which they said, on the second page:

> 'Mr Marks (of counsel) indicated to the court on Wednesday, without prejudice and without instructions, that Mr Mubarak *may* have assets of about £15,000,000. On hearing this Mr Mubarak said it was a misleading figure. For our part we cannot give any indication, however broad-brush, of what our client is worth until Arthur Anderson has completed a worldwide audit.
>
> Mr Mubarak is one of the beneficiaries of the IMK Family Trust ... based in Jersey. The other potential beneficiaries are the children, Mrs Mubarak was recently removed as a potential beneficiary. For the purpose of these proceedings our client accepts that the assets of the trust will be treated as being his, subject as your client knows, to 45% of the business interests being held beneficially for Mr Mubarak's brother in law Mohamed Hussain Wani. The intention in creating the trust was to hold all of the business interests. Some of the businesses are now held within the umbrella (as appears below), others have not yet been transferred.'

[2] The letter proceeded to give details by way of schedule of the business affiliates. In very broad terms, Mr Mubarak is a trader in very expensive items of jewellery. He has companies that retail such very expensive jewellery items, at the sort of centres worldwide where very rich people congregate.

[3] The case proceeded to a fully-contested hearing before Bodey J in December 1999. By then the husband was represented by Manches & Co, instructing Mr Dyer and Miss Florence Baron QC. On the third day, evidence emerged that demonstrated that the husband and Mr Wani, who at that stage was an intervener represented by counsel, had submitted fraudulent evidence, particularly as to the creation of the asserted partnership. Not surprisingly, since that was not only a betrayal of the judge but also a betrayal of the litigation team, Miss Baron, Mr Dyer and Manches & Co withdrew from the case. That, of course, left Mr Mubarak with a number of options. The one for which he elected was to walk out of the proceedings, together with Mr Wani.

[4] The judge went on to do what he could to perform his statutory duty without any assistance from the husband. He made a number of very damaging findings against the husband, both as to his integrity and as to the quality of his disclosure. In the end, he ordered a lump sum of £4,875,000 which, amongst other things, was enforceable against company assets. However, that last provision was independently the subject of a stay until 12 June 2000. On the day that the stay was lifted, the trading company within the jurisdiction, Dianoor Jewels Ltd, was

put into administration by Blackburne J in the Chancery Division. The wife swiftly applied for that order to be set aside, but Blackburne J refused her application. In consequence, both Dianoor Jewels Ltd and Dianoor International Ltd were joined in the proceedings. They sought the discharge of the paragraph of the order of 10 December 1999 that made the lump sum enforceable against company assets, and they succeeded at the hearing before Bodey J on 23 October 2000, the hearing which gives rise to the present appeal.

[5] The husband, having perhaps regretted his boycott of the principal hearing, appeared in person early in the New Year, seeking time to pay the lump sum. On 19 January 2000 Bodey J said that he should pay £3,200,000 by 31 May 2000 and the balance by 30 November 2000. The husband made an application for further time to Cazalet J on 12 June 2000, but that application was rejected. Meanwhile, the wife issued her first judgment summons on 9 June 2000, relying on the husband's default in paying the first instalment which had, of course, become due on 31 May 2000. That application was procedurally defective, since at its date of issue the stay on the enforcement against company assets was still in being. Accordingly, the wife issued the second judgment summons, which is the summons at the root of this appeal.

[6] The summons was dated 15 June 2000. It is in conventional form. It recites in its first paragraph that the wife, as the judgment creditor, obtained an order for the payment of £4,875,000 on 10 December 2000. The second recital refers to the default, and then there follows:

> 'You are hereby summoned to appear personally before [blank] on the 4 day of July 2000 at or after 10.30 o'clock, to be examined on oath touching the means you have or have had since the date of the said Order to pay the said sum in payment of which you have made default and also to show cause why you should not be committed to prison for such default.'

[7] The judgment summons was supported by what might be described as a conventional affidavit. The affidavit was sworn by a partner in the firm of Sears Tooth, then representing Mrs Mubarak. She simply deposed to the default and then deposed to the fact that there had been a modest collection, of approximately £161,000, since judgment, as a consequence of the forced sale of one of the husband's properties. That summons and affidavit in support were in compliance with the provisions of r 7.1 of the Family Proceedings Rules 1991. Paragraphs (3) and (5) of that rule provide:

> '(3) The application shall be made by filing a request in Form M 16 together with the affidavit required by rule 7.1(1), and except where the application is made to the registry or divorce county court in which the order was made, a copy of the order should be exhibited to the affidavit. ...

> (5) Every judgment summons shall be in Form M 17 and shall be served on the debtor personally not less than 10 days before the hearing and at the time of service there shall be paid or tendered to the debtor a sum reasonably sufficient to cover his expenses in travelling to and from the court at which he is summoned to appear.'

[8]   So the summons served on the husband was in Form M 17 and the affidavit in support complied with r 7.1.

[9]   The first order on this summons was made by Cazalet J on 27 June 2000, when he sagaciously directed that it should stand over to be tried by Bodey J on 3 days commencing on 9 October 2000. He said that the wife should file evidence in support of her application by 11 July 2000. The wife's response took the form of a letter from Sears Tooth dated 11 July 2000, which simply says:

'I am writing to confirm that (given the volume of evidence already filed) my client does not propose to file any further affidavit evidence in respect of the judgment summons proceedings.'

[10]   Accordingly the matter returned before Cazalet J on 25 July 2000, when he heard submissions from junior counsel for the husband, pressing his client's entitlement, in view of the impending commencement of the Human Rights Act 1998, to see a proper statement of the case that he was being asked to meet. Although, for somewhat obscure reasons, no order was drawn, it is accepted that Cazalet J ordered the wife to file a succinct statement of her case.

[11]   In compliance with that order, on 15 August 2000 the wife swore an affidavit, in which she told the reader little that was not already stated in the previous evidence. The nearest thing to a supplement is para 5, the final paragraph, in which she said:

'In support of my judgment summons, I rely on the following:

(a)   The evidence adduced at the trial of my claim for ancillary relief;
(b)   The judgments given and findings made by Bodey J on 10 December 1999 and 19 January 2000;
(c)   The judgments given and findings made by Cazalet J on 10 February 2000 and 12 June 2000;
(d)   The judgment [of] the Court of Appeal on 4 April 2000;
(e)   The affirmations made by the [husband] on 22 December 1999, 1 February 2000, 23 May 2000 and 8 June 2000.'

[12]   I interpolate that the husband had sought permission to appeal the order of 10 December 1999. His application for permission was rejected by a two-judge constitution after an oral hearing on 4 April 2000.

[13]   The husband's advisers were, not surprisingly, dissatisfied with the range of the wife's affidavit of 15 August 2000, and accordingly initiated a correspondence with Sears Tooth. That commenced with a letter of 17 August 2000, which acknowledged receipt of the affidavit and made plain that its contents had been discussed with leading counsel. Complaint was then made of its sufficiency.

[14]   The response of 21 August 2000 included these sentences:

'On this side of the case, we do feel that there does appear to be some confusion, with respect, on your side of the case, between evidence on the one hand, and the standard of proof to be applied to that evidence on the other.'

[15] Then they said:

'A judge has already looked at some of that evidence, and has made a finding on it on a balance of probability. The judge will now be looking at the same evidence, together with new evidence about subsequent events, this time applying a different burden of proof. I fail to understand why that could possibly be said to cause any confusion or difficulty.'

[16] That attracted a three-page letter, which carefully set out why it was that the husband and his advisers regarded the wife's presentation of her application for a judgment summons as quite inadequate. The letter included these paragraphs:

'Furthermore, we reject your suggestion that, in effect, Bodey J can read his previous judgment and then recall the evidence which was before him at that time and having considered the said evidence (without further probing or cross-examination) apply a different standard of proof in relation to the new application before him.

If the hearing is to be conducted in a manner which is not only fair but also seen to be fair, then Bodey J must hear evidence afresh which is relevant to the issue in question. Having considered such evidence he must apply the criminal standard of proof before reaching his decision.'

[17] Later it was said:

'Your client's failure to set out clearly the facts on which her application for a judgment summons is based raises the suspicion that she is using the application as a means of keeping my client in this country. As you are aware, he has been without a passport and therefore unable to travel freely for 9 months. This is a particular hardship given that he is not a citizen of this country and has been unable to be with his family and conduct business overseas for that period.

I wish to make it clear that both leading counsel and I consider that the points raised in this letter are of a substantial nature and not merely technical. I do not wish to labour the point, but the forthcoming hearing is extremely important so far as my client's welfare is concerned and I must insist that the correct evidential and procedural requirements are complied with by your client and that my client's rights under the Human Rights Act 1998 are not infringed. In that respect, I wish to make it clear that you do not have authority to rely on hearsay evidence and unless I notify you to the contrary we shall object to the production of any such evidence.'

[18] The correspondence continued, the wife's solicitors seeking time in which to consult counsel. It concluded with a letter from the husband's solicitors of 14 September 2000, in which it was said:

'I made it clear in my letter why my client is unable to file an affirmation or prepare his case at present, namely, because your client's case is vague and imprecise. Her recent affidavit should have been used to narrow the issues which it conspicuously failed to do. Until she does so, it is extremely difficult for my client to make much progress in preparing his defence.'

[19] The letter went unanswered. Nevertheless, on 29 September 2000 the husband filed his affidavit, which is a substantial document running to some 21 pages with the exhibited correspondence from which I have already read excerpts.

[20] The dispute was extended to a directions hearing before Bodey J on 3 October 2000. Of course, that was the day after the commencement of the Human Rights Act 1998. During the course of submissions, Mr Pointer QC, for the wife, said, in relation to Debtors Act 1869 applications:

'The procedure is different. The respondent to the judgment summons is obliged to attend court and be examined as to his means. Your Lordship will remember those happy days of appearing in courts 51 and 52 on judgment summonses and going before Judge Callman, or someone like that, and the counsel for the wife would stand up and say: "There is a debt of so and so, it is admitted the money has not been", and the judge would say, "Well, Mr Smith had better go in the witness-box and explain why he has not paid it". That is the procedure that obtained, and obtains, and rightly obtains on a judgment summons, because the procedure is that the husband is obliged to attend court and obliged to give evidence about his means and give excuse, if he can, as to why he has not paid. It is not the same as a committal summons.

My learned friend may want to argue on another occasion in front of a different court that that cannot now withstand the Human Rights Act. That is a different question. At the moment that is the procedure.'

[21] It seems to me that that submission aptly encapsulates the stance that had been taken by the wife's advisers ever since the first reliance on the Human Rights Act 1998 and the first request for a new procedural approach advanced by the husband's advisors.

[22] Bodey J was clearly not with Mr Pointer in his submission. The order that he gave on 3 October 2000 included a paragraph – the first paragraph, in fact – which is in these terms:

'[The wife] do serve on [the husband] by ... 5 October 2000 a document setting out:

(a) What oral evidence of fact she proposes to call at the judgment summons hearing, including the names and addresses of her witnesses, the witness order and where the substance of their oral evidence is to be found;
(b) Upon what documents she seeks to rely at the said hearing;
(c) What expert evidence she proposes to adduce at the said hearing; and
(d) A concise summary of how she puts her case in relation to [the husband's] failure to pay her the lump sum ordered herein by Mr Justice Bodey on 10 December 1999.'

[23] Mr Howard QC for the husband today accepted that that order sufficiently recognised the procedural requirements as a consequence of the commencement of the Human Rights Act 1998, given the fact that the direction went at such a late stage, only 7 days before the commencement of the trial.

[24]   The wife's response was as unhelpful as had been her earlier contributions. She simply said that she did not intend to call any witnesses, but that if the amount in dispute was not conceded, she would be tendered for cross-examination; the documents she relied upon were the judgments and 'all sworn or affirmed evidence filed since the ancillary relief hearing'; and she did not propose to call experts. The concise summary of her case was:

> 'H[usband] has failed to pay W[ife] the lump sum which was ordered to be paid under paragraph 1 of the order of Bodey J dated 10 December 1999
>
> AND H[usband] has, and has had at all times, the means to pay the lump sum.'

[25]   It can be seen that the document added nothing to anybody's knowledge of what to expect at the trial.

[26]   The hearing was relatively complex, in that the judge disposed not only of the judgment summons but also of the applications of the intervening companies, where he was obliged to rule on the submissions of Mr Pointer to the effect that, in all the circumstances, the judge was justified in piercing the corporate veil between the husband and the intervening companies. That submission the judge rejected. But he was with Mr Pointer on the judgment summons, and he made an order committing the husband to prison for 6 weeks, that order not to be put into force if the husband paid £3,200,000 on or before 4 December 2000, plus the net proceeds of the sale of personal jewellery and some debentures in a golf club by 4 December 2000, and proceeds of sale of a flat by 23 April 2001.

[27]   In arriving at that order, the judge heard evidence from the husband and from the husband's bank manager, who had been subpoenaed by the wife. The judge clearly concluded that the husband was not a witness upon whose evidence he could rely, and he equally clearly concluded that the husband was still not complying with his duty of full and frank disclosure.

[28]   The husband issued his notice of appeal on 13 November 2000. Arrangements were made for an expedited hearing and for an additional stay to carry the suspension of the committal order on the determination of his appeal.

[29]   Mr Howard for the husband has prepared for this appeal with conscientious care. He has put before the court five bundles of documents and an extensive skeleton argument. But, essentially, he says that the old Court 51 procedure is manifestly not Human Rights Act 1998 compliant. He said that this development was flagged up by himself and his instructing solicitors throughout all the interlocutory stages, the wife's solicitors stubbornly refused to accept the validity of all that was asserted, and the judge, although making partial recognition of the impact of the statute, did not fully or sufficiently reflect its effect in his conduct of the proceedings before him and in the judgment which he delivered. He submits that the judge did not sufficiently appreciate that in terms of Convention law, an application under the Debtors Act 1869 constituted a criminal proceeding. The judge went no further than to label it as a 'hybrid' proceeding. Mr Howard particularly relies on the decision in the case of *Engel and Others v The Netherlands (No 1)* (1979) 1 EHRR 647, which at 677, paras 80 and 81 very

clearly classifies proceedings such as applications under the Debtors Act 1869 as criminal proceedings for Convention purposes.

[30] Mr Howard says that, accordingly, any respondent to a Debtors Act 1869 summons has, as his minimum rights, first the right to a presumption of innocence throughout; secondly, the right to precise articulation of the charge that he meets; thirdly, adequate time to prepare this defence; and, fourthly, a right to examine any evidence adduced in support of the summons. He particularly points to lapses in the language of the judgment of Bodey J. He cites the paragraph of the judgment where the judge said:

'Having regard to this sequence, I considered at the outset of this part of the hearing whether this degree of fore-knowledge of the wife's case would be sufficient for the husband, or whether it would or might compromise the fairness of the proceedings from his point of view and/or mean that he should have an adjournment, bearing in mind that his liberty was and is at stake. Having done so, my conclusion was and is that the husband could have a fair hearing, knowing as he clearly has done the gravamen of the wife's case, namely (subject to argument as to the appropriateness of this course) her reliance (1) on my judgments, which contain clear findings (a) as to the extent of his admitted resources and (b) of his having substantial undisclosed assets; together with reliance (2) on the material in the affirmation since the main hearing, and reliance (3) on cross-examination of the husband at this hearing (if in these latter two respects that stage were reached).'

[31] He also criticises the passage where the judge said:

'I accept that the husband's recent affirmation does appear to give a prima facie explanation for many of the "signposts" referred to in the original judgment as pointing towards undisclosed assets, and I repeat the point about the bank manager's notes mentioned above. However, when I say "prima facie" I do stress that caveat, for the way in which the cross-examination of the husband took place at this hearing was necessarily shortened by the time available for what was intended merely as an enforcement proceeding; it was not possible for Mr Pointer to go into the sort of depth regarding the husband's complex affairs as would have been possible at the original hearing if the husband had not chosen to absent himself.'

[32] Mr Howard also submits that, at various stages during the proceedings, he pointed out to the judge that matters were being put to his client either for the first time or without any prior warning, and that he wished the opportunity to call evidence in response or rebuttal, and needed time in which to do so.

[33] All in all, says Mr Howard, the judge failed to recognise that, upon the hearing of a judgment summons, it was his obligation to apply a different test from that which he had applied at the principal hearing, and he had to apply that different test to a different time, namely the time intervening between the two hearings, and particularly to the facts and circumstances as they were at the hearing in October 2000. Above all, he says that, effectively, the burdens and presumptions were simply reversed. There was nowhere any recognition of the

presumption of innocence, and there was nowhere a recognition of the fact that the burden was upon the wife to prove his default, and not upon the husband to prove that he had not had the ability to comply.

[34] Mr Russell, for the wife, is in a particularly difficult position in responding to Mr Howard's submissions. For since the hearing in front of the judge the wife has changed her solicitors and, either because Mr Pointer is not available or for whatever other reason, Mr Russell has come into the case to put the wife's response to the appeal. He therefore has to seek to justify a litigation campaign in which he has had no part and to which he has made no contribution. He has done his best by stressing all the merit points in favour of his client. He has said that, plainly, the submission advanced by Mr Howard at the close of the wife's case, to the effect that she had demonstrated no case to answer, failed because the judge, in the position of a reasonable jury properly directed, inevitably concluded that this husband, who had himself admitted to a net worth of £8,000,000, an admission that was particularised by expert evidence from accountants and valuers, could not credibly escape having to explain why, during the course of the intervening 10 months, he had done nothing to satisfy his obligations. Mr Russell says that the husband then, having chosen to go into the witness-box, gave half-answers and throughout was sparing with information as to his own affairs, when he well knew that he was there for the precise purpose of informing the court as to the realities. He says that the judge was fully entitled to conclude that the husband had not been frank, and that it was a case not of inability but of unwillingness. The judge was entitled to weigh up the evidence and decide whether the husband had the ability to pay as though he were a reasonable jury, of course on the application of the criminal standard. Mr Russell even goes so far as to submit that the Human Rights Act 1998 has not made any substantial difference to the procedural conduct of applications under the Debtors Act 1869.

[35] The Debtors Act 1869 confers a limited jurisdiction on the court to imprison for a maximum period of 6 weeks. The Act was introduced to restrict the imprisonment of debtors for non-payment of ordinary debts, and the scope of s 5 of the statute was further curtailed by s 11 of the Administration of Justice Act 1970, which limited its application to maintenance orders and orders for the payment of certain taxes, contributions and other liabilities specified in Sch 4 to the Act.

[36] However an application under the Act may originate in family proceedings, it is clearly a procedure subjecting the respondent to the risk of the criminal sanction of imprisonment, and it seems to me manifest that Mr Howard is correct in his submissions as to its proper classification in terms of Convention law. The difficulties of adapting the age-old Court 51 procedure to the arrival of the European Convention for the Protection of Human Rights and Fundamental Freedoms 1950 are, it seems to me, considerable. As my Lord has pointed out during the course of argument, the procedure under the Debtors Act 1869 essentially combines in one what might be said to be two distinct exercises, namely the examination of means, for which the husband respondent may well be a compellable witness; and the determination of whether he is in default and whether or not the sanction should be applied, as to which the husband is certainly not a compellable witness.

[37]   The researches which Brooke LJ has conducted over the adjournment have demonstrated that the *Practice Direction*, which is headed *Practice Direction: Committal Proceedings* (28 May 1999) (referred to in Scott et al *The White Book Service 2000* (Sweet & Maxwell, Autumn edn, 2000), p 1192) and which was issued at the beginning of this term to ensure that proceedings for civil committal should be conducted in a fashion that would comply with the Human Rights Act 1998, actually extends to applications under the Debtors Act 1869. He has further demonstrated that that was the case when Bodey J sat on 9 October 2000. Unfortunately, it seems that this development – then, of course, extremely fresh – was not recognised by the court and was not specifically drawn to the court's attention by counsel. It seems to me that the fact that the *Practice Direction* is of equal application in the Family Division as it applies to committal proceedings in other divisions, and the further fact that the *Practice Direction* extends to applications under the Debtors Act 1869 as well as to any other application for civil contempt, is something of great importance that needs to be recognised immediately by all family practitioners. If that recognition follows, and if the *Practice Direction* is strictly adhered to in any future applications under the Debtors Act 1869, then the objections which Mr Howard has raised on this appeal should not be open in future cases. The *Practice Direction* should be sufficient to make the procedures under Family Proceedings Rules 1991, r 7.4 compliant with the Convention.

[38]   It seems to me, in short, that Mr Howard has triumphantly vindicated, during the hearing of this appeal, the stance that he and his team have adopted ever since the initiation of the Debtors Act 1869 application. I also conclude that he has convincingly demonstrated that the stance taken by the wife's litigation team was plainly wrong, in that it insufficiently reflected the impact of the Human Rights Act 1998 in this relatively obscure corner of family proceedings. I have great sympathy with Bodey J, who conducted a difficult inquiry with conspicuous care and endeavoured to afford the husband his newly-arrived rights. He obviously and inevitably was influenced by the sense of professional frustration that any judge feels where a respondent has abused the litigation process to the extent to which this husband has, and I hazard that if I were the trial judge I would no doubt have made an order very similar to that made by Bodey J. But the fact is that it has been demonstrated by Mr Howard to be quite unsupportable. In my judgment the appeal must be allowed and the order must be set aside.

[39]   But, before concluding, I would like to draw attention to a number of facts. The first is that we have been provided with schedules of costs incurred to date by the parties to the proceedings; that is to say, the petitioner and the respondent. The petitioner's costs to date amount to just over £930,000. The respondent's costs to date amount to £778,000. There have at different times been three interveners. We have no idea how much was incurred in costs on the account of the intervener, Mr Wani. One of the companies has been represented by Messrs Clifford Chance, instructing Miss Prevezer QC. Another intervener has been represented by Taylor Joynson Garrett, instructing Mr Ian Hunter QC and a junior. We have no idea what costs have been incurred by those two interveners, but it would be quite naive not to see that the total money spent on this absolutely fruitless litigation now exceeds £2,000,000, and it is little short of tragic folly that seemingly intelligent and civilised people should think that that is a responsible way to make use of the family justice system in this jurisdiction.

[40] The second point that I would wish to make is that, in a sense, the impact of the Human Rights Act 1998 on this particular enforcement remedy could be said to be a licence for the rogue. First of all, he manipulates the first instance trial, by either a fraudulent or an irresponsible performance of his obligation to make full and frank disclosure. Then, when an effort is made to enforce the resultant judgment by reliance on an enforcement remedy with a criminal sanction, he says, 'You have to start all over again and this time you have to down me on the application of a much higher standard of proof.' Bodey J made some reference to this in the course of the hearing, when he said:

> 'We cannot in this judgment summons procedure have a rerun of the original ancillary relief hearing, can we? It seems to me to be wholly impracticable and it would be expensive and it would be a disproportionate use of court time.'

[41] I suspect that the consequence of the re-evaluation of the utility of the Debtors Act 1869 procedure in the light of the advent of the Human Rights Act 1998 will be that it will become a largely obsolete means of enforcement. I doubt whether experienced specialist practitioners will think that it has sufficient value for money to be worth its initiation. Certainly it seems to me that it will be more or less useless in cases involving fraudulent husbands seeking to conceal assets difficult or impossible to identify specifically.

[42] Finally, I would like to draw attention to the fact that a sub-committee of the Lord Chancellor's Ancillary Relief Working Group submitted a report to the Lord Chancellor on the modernisation of all enforcement remedies in family proceedings over 2 years ago. It seems that the Lord Chancellor has taken no decisions on the sub-committee's report, and it seems that a policy decision has been taken to subjugate the reform of enforcement remedies in family proceedings to a wider review of enforcement proceedings in civil justice. I have two hopes. One is that the family justice system's long awaited reforms will be tackled swiftly; and, two, that any decisions taken will fully recognise the particular and often very special needs of the family justice system, which are very different from the needs of the civil justice system.

[43] Those are the only additional observations that I would wish to make.

BROOKE LJ:

[44] I agree. I am adding a few words of my own, because this appeal raises some points of general importance in relation to enforcement proceedings in a civil or family context which may lead to the loss of the liberty of the subject.

[45] The Human Rights Act 1998 has now been in force for just over 2 months, and it is already clear that the introduction of a code setting out modern international standards of fairness is doing work of considerable value in shining light into some of the dustier corners of our law. The experience of this case shows, at any rate to my satisfaction, that corners do not get much dustier than those inhabited by s 5 of the Debtors Act 1869 and the prescribed procedures under that Act.

[46] In *Newman v Modern Bookbinders Ltd* [2000] 1 WLR 2559, judgment was given in this court on 20 January 2000 in a case which was concerned with the statutory offence of rescuing goods seized in execution pursuant to s 92 of the County Courts Act 1984. In paras 20–29 of the judgment of a division of this court of which I was a member, Sedley LJ set out principles of general application to all cases of civil contempt which were going to be caught by Art 6 of the European Convention for the Protection of Human Rights and Fundamental Freedoms 1950 when that Article, in effect, became part of our law on 2 October 2000. Although the facts of that case are very far removed from the present, Sedley LJ spelt out the requirement for clarity of procedure and also the requirement that a person who faces what is now to be regarded as a criminal charge under Art 6 of the Convention should understand in detail the true nature and cause of the accusation against him. In para 26 of his judgment, Sedley LJ pointed out that this was one of the rights known longest to the law of England, 'since, at least, the moment 350 years ago when John Lilburne demanded and finally obtained the sight of the indictment on which he was to be tried'.

[47] I accept Mr Russell's submission that, so far as the charge was concerned, Mr Mubarak had ample notice of what was complained of under s 5 of the Debtors Act 1869. But, in relation to the matters to be relied on in support of that charge, for the reasons given by Thorpe LJ, the strategy adopted by those formerly advising Mrs Mubarak fell very far short of what modern international standards of fairness require.

[48] A *Practice Direction* was promulgated, as Thorpe LJ has said, in response to the judgment of this court in *Newman v Modern Bookbinders Ltd* [2000] 1 WLR 2559, to spell out what was already well-recognised as proper practice by those with experience of committal proceedings in the Queen's Bench and Chancery Divisions. Proper practice was set out clearly in writing because the power to commit people to custody in civil or family proceedings now extends to many more courts than those which were accustomed to exercise this jurisdiction in days gone by.

[49] The new *Practice Direction* simply describes, in clear terms, what is required on the making of an application for an order for committal of a person to prison for contempt of court. Paragraph 1.4 of the *Practice Direction* reads:

> 'In all cases the Convention rights of those involved should particularly be borne in mind. It should be noted that the burden of proof, having regard to the possibility that a person may be sent to prison, is that the allegation be proved beyond reasonable doubt.'

[50] Order 52 of the Rules of the Supreme Court 1965 (which is now in a Schedule to the Civil Procedure Rules 1998) provides by r 1(1) that the 'power of the High Court or Court of Appeal to punish for contempt of court may be exercised by an order of committal.' To a very great extent, the procedure to be followed on judgment summonses in the High Court has been subsumed into ch 2 of Part 7 of the Family Proceedings Rules 1991, and in the county court into Ord 28 of the County Court Rules 1981. However, the fact that these are contempt proceedings is clear from the judgment of Vaughan Williams LJ in *Re James Edgecome, Ex Parte James Edgecombe* [1902] 2 KB 403, 410, when he said, in relation to the powers of the court, pursuant to s 5 of the Debtors Act 1869, to commit a debtor to prison for non-payment of a judgment debt:

> '... when one looks at the conditions under which such an order is allowed to be made, it is perfectly plain that they can only be made when there is a contumacious debtor who has the means, or has had the means, to pay the debt, and his conduct is in the nature of contempt.'

[51] The fact that Ord 52, 'Civil committal for contempt' covers proceedings of this kind is clear from p 1177 of Vol 1 (*Civil Procedure*) of the current edition of *The White Book Service 2000* (Sweet & Maxwell, 2000), which refers to 'disobedience to a judgment order for the payment of money within a time specified subject to the provisions of the Debtors Act 1869'.

[52] Those who framed this *Practice Direction*, however, did not make it crystal clear that it applied to proceedings by way of judgment summons, for which most of the relevant rules are set out in the Family Proceedings Rules 1991 and, as I have said, in Ord 28 of the County Court Rules 1981. So far as the county court is concerned, the *Practice Direction* is said to apply to Ord 29, which contains the general rules about committal, and not to Ord 28, which contains the rules relating to judgment summonses. Despite this anomaly I, for my part, am completely satisfied that the practice set out in this *Practice Direction* is the practice which must be applied, both in civil courts and in family courts, in proceedings in which committal to prison may be in issue.

[53] I would add that it would be very helpful if the President of the Family Division could make it clear, by a new *Practice Direction*, that this *Practice Direction* does indeed apply to judgment summonses both in the High Court and in the county court. The wording might perhaps be adapted so that it applies the requirements of Art 6 of the Convention unmistakably to the procedure to be followed under the Debtors Act 1869.

[54] I return to the problems created by s 5 of the Debtors Act 1869 and the procedure prescribed for judgment summonses. Section 5 of the 1869 Act, which preserves the right of committal to prison for a term not exceeding 6 weeks in certain limited circumstances, contains, as proviso (2), the rule:

> 'That such jurisdiction shall only be exercised where it is proved to the satisfaction of the court that the person making default either has or has had since the date of the order or judgment the means to pay the sum in respect of which he has made default, and has refused or neglected, or refuses or neglects, to pay the same.'

[55] In other words, it is putting the onus correctly on the judgment creditor to prove those matters to the satisfaction of the court, and modern case law shows that they have to be proved to the criminal standard of proof.

[56] What follows in s 5 is a procedure for a means inquiry. It reads:

'Proof of the means of the person making default may be given in such manner as the court thinks just; and for the purposes of such proof the debtor and any witnesses may be summoned and examined on oath, according to the prescribed rules.'

[57] As Thorpe LJ has said, this postulates a requirement that a person who is facing what is now to be regarded as a criminal charge is to be cross-examined on oath as part of the same proceedings as part of the process of gathering evidence for the charge against him. That procedure cannot remain in place under the European Convention for the Protection of Human Rights and Fundamental Freedoms 1950: nobody is obliged to incriminate themselves.

[58] To make matters worse, under the Family Proceedings Rules 1991, r 7.4(5) provides that:

'Every judgment summons shall be in Form M 17 ...'

[59] When one looks at Form M 17, it provides that it is addressed to the judgment debtor and it reads:

'You are hereby summoned to appear personally before one of the judges sitting in this Division at the Royal Courts of Justice, Strand, London [and then the date and time is mentioned] to be examined on oath touching the means you have or have had since the date of the said order to pay the said sum in payment of which you have made default and also to show cause why you should not be committed to prison for such default.'

[60] This involves putting the burden of proof upside down, so far as the requirements of Art 6 of the European Convention for the Protection of Human Rights and Fundamental Freedoms 1950 are concerned.

[61] In the context of the more modern codes for enforcing orders in the magistrates' court, the means inquiry is separated from the subsequent proceedings which may lead to committal. Under the Debtors Act 1869 and the rules and the prescribed form made under it, on the other hand, these two processes are muddled up, and muddled up impermissibly so far as the requirements of the European Convention are concerned.

[62] I have mentioned the requirements of the Convention. So far as they are relevant for current purposes, Art 6(1) requires 'a fair and public hearing'. Article 6(2) requires that 'Everyone charged with a criminal offence shall be presumed innocent until proved guilty according to law' – and Mr Howard rightly submitted that the presumption of innocence appeared to be being turned upside down by the procedure adopted by Mrs Mubarak's advisors. Article 6(3) provides that:

'Everyone charged with a criminal offence has the following minimum rights:

(a)   to be informed promptly, in a language which he understands and in detail, of the nature and cause of the accusation against him; ...
(d)   to examine or have examined witnesses against him ...'

[63] Both these requirements seem to have been completely overlooked by Mrs Mubarak's former advisors when preparing their case in these proceedings.

[64] In my judgment, it is essential for family law practitioners who are concerned with proceedings which may lead to committal to be fully acquainted with the requirements of Art 6 of the Convention before they embark on any similar process in future.

[65] For the reasons which my Lord has given, with which I agree, I agree that this appeal should be allowed.

JACOB J:

[66] I also agree. I doubt whether s 5 of the Debtors Act 1869 was ever intended for this kind of substantial case. The side note reads 'Saving of power of committal for small debts'. I am not sure that I go as far as saying it can never be used for such cases but if it is to be used, the *Practice Direction* must be complied with. It has been said that the power of committal is very much a power of last resort, and that would seem to me to be right. Since the Debtors Act 1869, a Victorian Act, many more remedies have been devised which enable creditors – that would include people entitled to payments under orders made in the Family Division – to obtain their money in one way or another. A freezing order, with all the disclosure that can be obtained, is an extremely powerful weapon. The remedies available extend to constructive trusts and the obtaining of information from bankers.

[67] In this case the freezing order granted does not in fact require disclosure of documents. We know from the answer given by the solicitors on behalf of the husband that he has a substantial interest under a trust. What that is precisely we do not know, nor do we know the details of the trust; but almost certainly all those details are extractable, if necessary by court orders. There is no reason, as far as I can see, why some sort of remedy against the husband's interest in that trust is not directly obtainable. The fact that the trust is abroad, the fact that many of the assets of the trust are also abroad, is neither here nor there. He is here and any order made will be in personam and enforceable against him. Other remedies which have been designed over the years to enable people to get at property – orders for the production of documents (eg orders of the kind approved in *Bankers Trust Co v Shapira and Others* [1980] 1 WLR 12/4) – all make the Victorian remedy probably of less use than it was, save as to the small cases which I suspect was all the Victorian legislators had in mind.

Application allowed and committal order set aside. No order for costs in court below. Applicant to have costs of appeal but order is not to be enforced independently and is to be set off against liabilities for petitioner's costs in earlier proceedings and against debts.

Solicitors: *Bates Wells & Braithwaite* for the applicant
                Pullig & Co for the respondent

PHILIPPA JOHNSON
Barrister

MUBARAK v MUBARAK

[2002] EWHC 2171 (Fam), [2003] 2 FLR 553, FD

Family Division

Hughes J

4 October 2002

Financial provision – Enforcement – Oral examination – Power to adjourn – Power to order production of documents – Meaning of 'in the possession of' – Issue estoppel – Whether order to produce documents amounted to finding that documents in possession of judgment debtor

The husband, a successful international retailer of jewellery, had been ordered to pay the wife a lump sum of over £4.8 million. Three years after the making of the order he had paid only £260,000, leaving over £4.6 million as the unsatisfied judgment debt. The husband's corporate identity was founded on a Jersey-based family discretionary trust, of which the husband and the children were sole beneficiaries. The trust held all the shares in a Bermudan holding company, whose main liability was a debt of £20 million owed to the husband and whose assets included the former matrimonial home, a retail shop and business in Paris, and a subsidiary holding company which, in turn, owned three trading companies, two in Hong Kong and one in England. There had been a finding in previous proceedings that the companies were not merely the alter ego of the husband. The husband had made a number of assertions which had been shown to be untruthful, and had abused the litigation process in a number of ways in order to avoid his obligations to the wife, including putting the English trading company into administration to prevent sale of its stock. The wife applied for the husband to undergo oral examination as to his means, an application governed, in family proceedings, by RSC Ord 48. On the second day of the examination the district judge ordered the husband to produce a number of documents, including credit card statements and company accounts, and adjourned the case for a number of days. When the hearing resumed the husband produced a number of documents, but not all those contained in the wife's schedule of documents. The district judge adjourned the examination for a further 3 months and made orders requiring the husband to produce further documents at or before the adjourned hearing. The husband appealed this second order. The documents at issue were credit card statements relating to a credit card account held in the name of one of the Hong Kong trading companies and that company's statement of accounts. The husband claimed that the judge had no power to adjourn the oral examination and make orders for production, that the two categories of document were not in the possession of the husband for the purpose of Ord 48, that the documents were not relevant to the wife's attempted enforcement, and that there had been excessive use by the wife of processes of examination of the husband. The wife claimed that the husband was prevented from contesting the judge's second order by issue estoppel, in that the first order of the court encompassed the disputed documents.

Held – allowing the appeal and quashing the order for production of the documents –

(1) There was no issue estoppel, as the first of the district judge's orders required the husband to provide such of the documents in the wife's schedule as were in his possession, and did not amount to a ruling that all the documents in the schedule were in the husband's possession and must be produced.

(2) Although Ord 48 did not authorise a freestanding process of specific discovery, the rules did permit the examination to be adjourned from time to time, if necessary, and permitted the making of orders for the production of documents relevant to the question of debts owed to the judgment debtor and to his property or other means of paying what he owed from time to time, specific as well as general.

(3) The oral examination was conducted by the district judge. It was for him to say what questions needed answering and when the process was over. Moreover, counsel for the judgment creditor had only concluded his questions subject to sight of the outstanding documents. Accordingly the examination had not been concluded and the adjournment was proper.

(4) The expression 'in the possession of' in Ord 48 extended to documents not physically held by the judgment debtor but to sight of which he had a clear and enforceable right in his personal capacity, not merely qua director or agent.

(5) The documents in question were in the possession of the company, not the husband, and the husband did not have an enforceable right to sight of the documents. In relation to the accounts it was simply not accurate to say that a creditor of a holding company was in possession of the accounts of the subsidiary company. In relation to the credit card statements, other people held cards upon the same credit card account therefore the husband did not have an enforceable right to inspect the credit card statement for the account, which would contain details concerning the expenditure of others, and the court had no power to direct that a document be created showing only the husband's expenditure.

Statutory provisions considered
Rules of the Supreme Court 1965 (SI 1965/1766), Ords 24, 48
County Court Rules 1981 (SI 1981/1687)
Civil Procedure Rules 1998 (SI 1998/3132), r 31.8, Part 71

Cases referred to in judgment
B v B (Matrimonial Proceedings: Discovery) [1978] 3 WLR 624, [1979] 1 All ER 801, FD
Dubai Bank Ltd v Galadari and Others [1990] Ch 98, [1989] 3 All ER 769, CA
Lonrho Ltd and Another v Shell Petroleum Co Ltd and Another [1980] QB 358, CA
Republic of Costa Rica v Strousberg (1880) 16 ChD 8, CA

Charles Howard QC *and* Richard Harrison *for the appellant*
Khawar Qureshi *and* Giles Richardson *for the respondent*

HUGHES J:

As long ago as 10 December 1999, in ancillary relief proceedings, the husband in the present case, Mr Iqbal Mubarak, was ordered by Bodey J to pay his wife a lump sum of over £4.8 million. His application for leave to appeal the quantum of the order failed. Nearly 3 years and a good deal of expensive legal manoeuvring later, he has paid only £260,000-odd, and that under execution, which leaves more than £4.6 million as the unsatisfied judgment debt. Unlike other judgment debts, which may sometimes be incurred far beyond the means of the debtor, this one is a debt which the judge has not only ordered the husband to pay but which he has determined, as a matter of fact, the husband has the means to pay.

Amongst other steps taken by the wife to attempt to enforce this order, she applied on 15 March 2001 for the husband to undergo oral examination as to his means. The examination took place before the district judge on 12 and 13 September 2001 and on 2 November 2001. On the last-mentioned date the district judge adjourned the examination for a further 3 months and made orders requiring the husband to produce at or before the adjourned hearing a number of documents. That last order the husband has appealed, and this has been the hearing of his appeal.

Since the issues on the present appeal are comparatively narrow, it is not necessary to set out the history of the marriage or of the litigation, except quite briefly. A more detailed history is readily available in the judgments of Bodey J given on 10 December 1999 (unreported) and 23 October 2000.[1] For present purposes, what follows suffices.

The husband is a successful international retailer of jewellery, and has been in business as such since about 1980. He has established retail businesses selling prestigious jewellery in Kuwait, Hong Kong, Paris and London. He and the wife were married in 1983, lived together until 1998, and have four children who live with the wife, the youngest of whom is still only 4. By the time of the separation the corporate structure of the husband was, and substantially it still remains, this. There is a family discretionary trust established in Jersey, of which he and the wife were the settlors. A Jersey limited company is the trustee. That trust holds all the shares in a holding company incorporated in Bermuda called 21st Century Holdings Ltd. That holding company owns a house in Hong Kong, which was at one time the matrimonial home, and a retail shop and business in Paris. It also wholly owns a subsidiary holding company called Dianoor Jewels International Ltd, incorporated in Jersey (DJIL). In its turn, DJIL wholly owns three trading companies:

(1)   Dianoor International Ltd (DIL), incorporated in Hong Kong, and trading principally, but perhaps not wholly, there;
(2)   Dianoor Jewel Craft Ltd, also incorporated and trading in Hong Kong, though it seems probably now not very actively; and
(3)   Dianoor Jewels Ltd (DJL), incorporated in England and trading principally through a prominent West End outlet.

The beneficiaries under the discretionary trust were originally the husband, wife and children. Very shortly after the separation the husband had the wife removed

---

[1]   Editor's note: see *Mubarak v Mubarak* [2001] 1 FLR 673.

as a beneficiary. He and the children remain. The head holding company, 21st Century Holdings, owes to the husband on a loan account approximately £20 million. This money is due to the husband, albeit it represents part of the working capital of the group. The husband asserts an undertaking given by him not to require repayment unless and until the group is in a position to make it.

In the ancillary relief proceedings the husband expressly accepted, through experienced solicitors, leading counsel and highly qualified forensic accountants, that the assets of the trust and of the group of companies could be treated as owned by and available to him, although he made what turned out to be an untruthful assertion that a close relative of his, Mr Wani, owned 45% and himself only 55% of those assets. That assertion was supported by forged documents and suborned perjured evidence.

That exposed untruthfulness apart, it is sad to have to record that the husband has now been found on a number of occasions to have behaved very badly in many ways in relation to his obligations to his ex-wife. In the Court of Appeal at one stage Thorpe LJ referred to the extent to which he had abused the litigation process. The concession that a pragmatic and cost-saving approach could be taken to the assets without reliance on the technicalities of ownership has not been maintained. The wife, having relied upon it, and, in consequence, probably not having sought other forms of primary ancillary relief which might have been open to her, has been confronted by reliance upon the technicalities of ownership ever since, including in the course of the present proceedings. Although in the Court of Appeal the husband accepted that a lump sum of approximately £3 million was appropriate, albeit payable over a period, the payments actually made have been the very small ones that I have recited.

It has been necessary to characterise the husband's evidence on occasion as evasive, and he has been found, as I have indicated, to be untruthful. An indication to Cazalet J in the course of successive applications for stays of payment, to the effect that some £400,000 would be paid to the wife from the proceeds of sale of some jewellery, was not honoured, although the property was sold. When the last stay application failed and the prospect was faced of Bodey J's order being enforced through the sale of some of the stock of one or more of the companies, the husband applied that day for the London trading company to be put into administration, and there it remains, it being, by then at least, within the legal definition of insolvency.

With that history, it is wholly unsurprising that the wife should wish to press to their limits such steps as she can take to try to redress her position, nor is it to be wondered at that any judge should be ready, where he properly can, to afford her such relief as is legitimately available to her. It is, however, necessary in the light of this history to remind myself that the husband's behaviour, however disgraceful, is not a reason to justify going beyond what can legitimately be achieved in the particular process before the court.

It is the husband's submission, through Mr Howard QC, that, insofar as the district judge ordered production of two classes of document, amongst a great many others, this is what has occurred.

Rules of the Supreme Court 1965, Ord 48

This application for oral examination is governed by the old Ord 48 of the RSC. It was made before that rule was superseded by the new CPR, Sch 1, Ord 71, which apply to applications made from 25 March 2002 onwards, but, in any event, family proceedings, which these are, continue to be governed by Ord 48. Order 48 provides as follows:

'1(1)   Where a person has obtained a judgment or order for the payment by some other person (hereinafter referred to as "the judgment debtor") of money, the Court may, on an application made ex parte by the person entitled to enforce the judgment or order, order the judgment debtor ...'

And I omit irrelevant words:

'... to attend before such Master, district judge or nominated officer as the Court may appoint and be orally examined on the questions—

(a)   whether any and, if so, what debts are owing to the judgment debtor, and

(b)   whether the judgment debtor has any and, if so, what other property or means of satisfying the judgment or order;

and the Court may also order the judgment debtor ...'

Again I omit irrelevant words:

'... to produce any books or documents in the possession of the judgment debtor relevant to the questions aforesaid at the time and place appointed for the examination.'

The district judge's order

After the first 2 days of the oral examination, the district judge adjourned it to 2 November 2001, and he made an order. That was on 13 September 2001. The order included the following, in para 2:

'The respondent is to provide the documents in his possession as contained in the documents as amended by the court dated 13 September 2001 and placed on the court file by 2 November, save for item 12.'

The reference to documents amended by the court was a reference to a very substantial schedule which accompanied the order. It ran to 23 categories of document, many of them multiples, and thus referred potentially to a very large number of individual documents. What happened was that the husband did provide a substantial body of those documents contained, I am told, in two lever-arch files. He did not, however, provide everything which the wife sought.

When the hearing was resumed on 2 November 2001 the district judge heard argument as to the production of outstanding documents. He gave a judgment and he ordered a further adjournment of the oral examination. Next, he ordered the husband to produce the following:

(1)   all credit card statements relating to the American Express credit card in the name of DIL Hong Kong;
(2)   DIL statements of account from 1998 to the present;
(3)   DJL statements of account for two specific years; and
(4)   any existing up-to-date valuation of the assets of DJL (that is, the London company).

Lastly, the district judge ordered the husband to use all necessary endeavours to produce a further series of documents consisting, very broadly, of trust accounts.

There was no appeal against the first order of 13 September 2001. The present appeal is against the second order, that of 2 November 2001. Before me, the wife has, without conceding that the orders were wrongly made, elected not to seek to uphold the order for the production of items (3) and (4) just mentioned, nor does she seek to uphold the order that the husband use all necessary endeavours to produce the further series of trust accounts. That means that what is left in issue here is the order to produce items (1) and (2), the credit card statements and DIL accounts. Item (2), the accounts of DIL, speak for their own description.

Item (1) relates to an American Express credit card. DIL has a credit card account with American Express. It appears that a number of people may hold cards enabling them to use that account. One of them is in the hands of the husband. The husband gave evidence before the district judge that he used the card frequently to maintain his ordinary lifestyle, which appears to be not inconsiderable.

The husband's evidence before the district judge was that the company had been reluctant to permit him to have the use of the card, but that he had been enabled to have it through the generosity of Mr Wani, that same Mr Wani earlier referred to. Mr Wani, he told the district judge, had agreed with DIL to underwrite the husband's expenditure on the card and pay the appropriate amounts to DIL, apparently by means of offset against a loan which he was owed by that company.

Issues

The following issues arise.

(1)   Is the husband prevented by issue estoppel from contesting the order of 2 November 2001?
(2)   Did the district judge have power to adjourn the oral examination and to make orders for production?
(3)   Were the two categories of document in question in the possession of the husband for the purpose of Ord 48?
(4)   Was the district judge plainly wrong to order the production of these documents because they were of no or no sufficient relevance to the wife's

attempted enforcement of her award or because there had been by then an excessive use by the wife of processes of examination of the husband?

1   Issue estoppel

For the wife, Mr Qureshi contends that the issue of the production of these documents had been determined as between the parties by the district judge's first order on 13 September 2001. I have already set out the relevant terms of that order. The schedule attached to it contained, inter alia, the following entry:

'3   All charge/credit and debit card statements since May 1998.'

The schedule did not contain an explicit reference to the accounts of DIL, referring instead to 'Dianoor Jewels International Ltd, Hong Kong', which does not exist, as well as to 'Dianoor Jewels International Ltd, Jersey', which certainly does. This must have been a typographical error. The wife had, in anticipation of the oral examination, served a list of proposed topics for questioning, which specifically foreshadowed a request for sight of the DIL accounts. If this order of 13 September amounted to a ruling that the DIL credit card statements and (subject to the typographical error) the DIL accounts were in the possession of the husband and were to be produced, then the issue estoppel contended for might arise. It is, however, clear that that is not what the district judge did order. On the contrary, what he was ordering was that the husband should provide such of the documents on the schedule as were in his possession. That is plain as a matter of construction. If the district judge had meant otherwise there would have been no occasion for the words 'in his possession' to appear in the order; it would simply have said 'shall produce the documents on the schedule'.

In addition to that, perusal of the transcript of proceedings on those first 2 days in September more than amply confirms that construction. The district judge did not in September rule on the question of whether the documents were in the husband's possession. The husband was attended, perhaps a little unusually for an oral examination, but certainly assiduously, by leading counsel, who, as the district judge went through the wife's request for documents, submitted from time to time that a particular category was not in the husband's possession. The district judge explicitly responded that, if that was so, the husband had only to say so by way of response to the order. Moreover, if the district judge had determined this issue in September there would have been no occasion for the reasoned judgment on the point which he gave in November, when there were submissions on the question and a ruling was given.

I hold that the district judge did not in the 13 September order determine the issue of whether the documents were in possession of the husband. No issue estoppel arises, and it is open to the husband to challenge the November ruling by the present appeal.

2   Propriety of adjournment and order to produce

I accept the submission of Mr Howard, for the husband, that Ord 48 does not authorise a freestanding process of specific discovery. The oral examination is, however, a process of considerable potential utility to a judgment creditor in a case where the judgment debtor is deliberately evading his obligation to pay. Whilst the obligation on the judgment debtor to produce books or documents is necessarily ancillary to the process of examination and not independent of it, that does not mean that it is anything other than an important and often vital part of the process. It is a significant tool in the enforcement of the court's order in relation to which, ex hypothesi, the judgment debtor is in default.

I do not accept Mr Howard's further submission that the only time when the court can order production of documents is on first ordering attendance for oral examination, nor that that order can only be a generalised one in the terms of Ord 48, that is to say, to produce anything relevant to any debts owing or other assets. It is no doubt the case that the great majority of Ord 48 oral examinations are quite brief and the documents relating to them comparatively few. The rules permit the examinations to be conducted by non-judicial court officers, and straightforward ones conventionally are so conducted. No doubt a salaried householder who has contracted a consumer debt which remains unpaid can be examined very concisely and will have little by way of documents to produce, other than evidence of salary, committed outgoings and bank or building society balances. That, however, is not to say that the process is not available in and adaptable to the very complex case, such as the present, where the debt and the assets are counted in millions and the potential relevant documents require a trolley rather than an envelope to bring them to court. Indeed, it may be all the more important a process in a case of that kind.

I am quite satisfied that the rules permit the examination to be adjourned from time to time, if that is necessary, and that orders for the production of relevant documents may also be made from time to time. Such orders may be specific as well as general, providing of course that what is specified for production is relevant to the two questions to which the examination is directed, that is to say, debts owing to the judgment debtor and his property or other means of paying what he owes. If it were not so, a judgment debtor in a complex case such as the husband here, and even if benefiting from skilled advice, which is often not the case, would be faced with real doubt about what documents to bring. At the very least, the court has the power to explain by way of specific order which documents are relevant and thus covered by the generalised order for production which Mr Howard contends goes with the original summons. But there is no need for such analysis; the power to order production may be exercised from time to time.

There is nothing inconsistent with this in the terms of the order made by Bodey J on 12 June 2001, when he dealt with what was in effect a preliminary hearing of the application for oral examination and considered the husband's request that the examination should take place before himself. In directing that the examination should be before the district judge, Bodey J expressed as a recital to his order, not itself a direction, that the husband would have at the initial hearing such documents as may be reasonably necessary to support his answers to certain revised written questions of which the wife proposed to give advance notice. The recital to the judge's order went on to add:

> '... but that he is not under an obligation without more to bring all other documents touching upon his means.'

That was a sensible recital of the position since the wife had indicated that she would give advance notice of some of the questions to be asked. It did not fetter the ability of the district judge to allow other questions, providing of course that the husband had a proper opportunity to deal with them fairly; nor did it fetter the jurisdiction of the district judge to order the production of further documents. Indeed, the words 'without more' clearly contemplated such a possibility.

Mr Howard submits that what has happened in this case is that the oral examination was over by the time of the order of 2 November 2001, and that the adjournment was artificially devised to enable the district judge to order production of documents. I do not find that to be so. It is certainly correct that Mr Qureshi had completed the questions which he had, subject to sight of the documents which he sought, including the present. Mr Qureshi had, however, punctuated his cross-examination by indicating that he sought sight of this document or that.

It is also correct that the learned district judge was clearly well aware that production could be ordered only as an ancillary to the oral examination and that, accordingly, the examination was not over until the documents had been seen. It may have turned out to be the case that if the documents had been produced there would have been no further questions. That that might have been the situation does not mean that production of them was not ancillary to the process of oral examination. It is perfectly clear that there might well have been further questions arising out of sight of the documents. A simple example is that if DIL's accounts had been in the husband's possession and had been produced, questions might very well have arisen about the assets shown in the balance sheet, about the basis of valuation of them in the books, about their saleability, or about the viability of the business if some repayment up the chain of holding companies were made such as to release funds for the repayment of part of the husband's loan to 21st Century, thus in turn opening the door to enforcement by the wife against those funds.

Although in the present case the examination was carried out by counsel for the judgment creditor, and the district judge no doubt exercised a proper judicial restraint himself, the oral examination is conducted by the district judge. It is for him to say what questions need answering and for him to say when it is over. The process is intended to be a severe and testing one. As long ago as 1880, James LJ observed, in *Republic of Costa Rica v Strousberg* (1880) 16 ChD 8 at 12, that the examination is:

> '... not only intended to be an examination but to be a cross-examination, and that of the severest kind.'

It is an examination which is necessary only because there has been default, and, in an ancillary relief case, necessarily by a judgment debtor who has been held to have the means to pay.

3 Possession

The next question is what is the ambit of the expression 'in the possession of', as used in Ord 48. In particular, does it or does it not extend to documents not physically held by the judgment debtor but to sight of which he has a clear and enforceable right. Mr Howard submits not. He contrasts Ord 48, with its references to documents in the possession of the judgment debtor, with Ord 24 of the same RSC, which contained the rules for discovery of documents in advance of trial. That rule or its equivalent has, ever since 1975, applied the duty of discovery of documents to those currently or previously in the 'possession or power' of a party, and from 1965 onwards has added the words 'or custody'. Custody has, in this context, been held to refer to documents which are in the physical holding of a party but not in his personal capacity, rather qua company director/agent or similarly: see *B v B (Matrimonial Proceedings: Discovery)* [1978] 3 WLR 624. 'Power' has been held to mean documents which the debtor has an enforceable right to obtain into his possession or control or to inspect, again in his personal capacity rather than qua officer of a company: see *Lonrho Ltd and Another v Shell Petroleum Co Ltd and Another* [1980] QB 358, and *B v B*. Both those authorities indicate also that if the case arises in which a company is so much a one-man company that it is merely the alter ego of the party, then documents which are in his custody or power qua director may be considered to be in his possession personally. To that possibility I will return later.

Whilst in some cases a difference in wording between one statutory provision and another in the same or a comparable enactment may be a valuable aid to construction, this will not always be so. I am not satisfied that the present two Rules provide such an example. Although from 1965 to 1999 they co-existed in the RSC, it is not at all clear that they were framed by the same hand or in contemplation of one another. It is conceded by Mr Howard that possession for the purposes of Ord 48 must clearly encompass something more than actual physical holding. For example, if a judgment debtor had lodged documents which are unquestionably his with a bank, or with a friend, or otherwise well away from his own person, such, it is agreed, would remain in his possession.

It is of course true that the range of documents which are relevant to oral examination under Ord 48 will often be narrower than the range of documents relevant to pre-trial discovery, for the former must be relevant to enforcement and to the ability to pay. But within the appropriate area of relevance there are powerful reasons of policy for construing the word 'possession' widely rather than narrowly in Ord 48. In particular, if a document is within the power of the judgment debtor in the sense defined by the House of Lords in *Lonrho Ltd and Another v Shell Petroleum Co Ltd and Another* [1980] QB 358, and by Dunn J in *B v B (Matrimonial Proceedings: Discovery)* [1978] 3 WLR 624, that he has a presently enforceable legal right to obtain inspection of it wherever it is, there is every reason, in the interests of justice, why he should be required to produce it on oral examination in order to see if it sheds light on his ability to satisfy the judgment. Such documents are, it seems to me, in his possession, just as documents with which he has parted are in his possession. The common feature of the two categories is that he has a right to them; they are in his power.

I am reinforced in the view that that is the correct construction of possession by the long-standing Queen's Bench practice form for an order under Ord 48. Practice Form 99 provides, so far as relevant, as follows:

'It is ordered that the judgment debtor attend ... [etc.] and that the said judgment debtor produce any books or documents in his possession or power relating to the same.'

Form N37, provided by the equivalent CCR, similarly refers to documents in the possession or power of the debtor. The new rule in CPR Part 71, albeit not at present applicable to family proceedings, is also consistent with this conclusion. It requires a judgment debtor to produce documents 'in his control'. Rule 31.8, which deals with discovery, defines control as including the right to inspect.

What is, however, clear is that to be in the possession or power of a judgment debtor the document must be one which he has the necessary enforceable right to call for, and in his personal capacity not merely qua director or agent. This is further consistent with the actual decision in *B v B*, where Dunn J held that, absent the case of a one-man company, which is the alter ego of the party, a party who has the physical holding of documents or a right to inspect them simply as a director, will, although obliged to disclose their existence at the discovery stage, not be ordered to produce them for inspection.

The credit card statements which have been ordered to be produced in this case are statements of an account held with American Express by DIL, a limited company. The accounts ordered to be produced are the accounts of that same company.

When the original lump sum order was made, Bodey J, relying on the husband's concession that the trust assets could be treated as available to him, ordered him to make some of the stock in trade of one or other of the companies, DIL and DJL, available to supply the lump sum. However, on subsequent application by the companies, and after a further substantial hearing, the same judge was compelled to come to the conclusions: (a) that the husband's original concession could not bind the companies; (b) that DIL had an interest independent of the husband and was not merely his alter ego; (c) that DJL, now in administration, necessarily had such an independent interest; and thus (d) that the order for direct provision of assets to meet the lump sum must be set aside. The wife's application for permission to appeal that conclusion was refused, with the observation that the judge was plainly right.

It follows that the issue of whether DIL is merely the alter ego of the husband has been investigated at a substantial hearing, and the conclusion is that it is not, however influential the husband may be in its affairs. Documents in the possession of DIL cannot therefore be held, on that ground, to be in the possession of the husband, nor would it be sufficient if the husband were a director of DIL, for the reasons already explained, although in fact he is not and has not been since well before any proceedings.

Mr Qureshi submits that the husband has a present enforceable right to obtain the DIL accounts. He does not suggest that he has such a right against DIL itself. He says that the husband's loan account with 21st Century, together with the alleged undertaking not to call for repayment until the company is in a position to part with the money, carries with it the entitlement as against 21st Century to inspect that company's accounts and papers. Then, in turn, he says that since 21st Century's ability to pay depends upon the profitability of the subsidiary company, DJIL, and, through that company, of the trading companies, which include DIL, therefore the husband has a right to insist that 21st Century obtain DIL's accounts and pass them on to him.

I regret to say that that argument is unsustainable. It is not the law that a holding company necessarily has a presently enforceable right to see the accounts of its subsidiaries. That is a question of fact in every case, as was decided in *Lonrho Ltd and Another v Shell Petroleum Co Ltd and Another* [1980] QB 358. Even allowing for the ability of the court to draw proper inferences from the evidence, and remembering, as I do, that I am not obliged to accept the evidence of the husband as either complete or accurate – indeed there is good reason not to do so – I am nevertheless quite unable to say that DIL's accounts are in his possession or his power. It may very well be that he would in fact be afforded access to them by consent of one or other of the companies if he asked, but that, it is clear, is not good enough. If he has any right to them it would require a chain of claims of right from him to 21st Century, from 21st Century to DJIL, and from DJIL to DIL. None of those links in that chain is clearly established. To say that a creditor of a holding company is in possession of the accounts of the subsidiary company is simply not accurate.

I accept the formulation of the learned district judge that this is a man who has a 'very big interest' in the trading companies in the ordinary, but not the legal, sense. That, however, cannot, without more, be equated with possession of the trading companies' documents. In effect, to hold that he had possession of these accounts would mean treating the group as if it were a one-man company and the alter ego of the husband. Tempting as that conclusion may be, it has been found not to be justified. This, in other words, is a case in which the husband appears to have great influence over the companies, and indeed an apparent ability in many ways to manipulate their affairs to his advantage, and with a view to avoiding his obligations. But there is not that complete merger of interests or unfettered control which enables the court to treat the companies as his alter ego.

The credit card statements are the property of DIL, which holds the account. I am prepared to accept that in order to give business efficacy to the arrangement which the husband described, and in particular to protect DIL against ultra vires expenditure, it is necessary to imply into the agreement between DIL and the husband a term that if Mr Wani were unable or unwilling to indemnify the company in respect of the liabilities created by the husband's use of the card, the husband himself would do so. Indeed, as a matter of the balance of probabilities, I find that that was the understanding in fact, without the need for implication of law.

It does not, however, follow that the husband has a presently enforceable right to inspect the credit card statements. Other people hold cards upon the same account. Their expenditure and that of the company generally is unconnected with the husband's use of the card, but it would be revealed by the statements. This difficulty was recognised at the hearing before the district judge. The district judge expressed the view that he would be very sympathetic to that consideration, but that the answer was for the statements to be edited to show only the husband's expenditure. That, however, unfortunately reveals the flaw in the argument. The question is not whether the husband, if in possession of the document, would be required to disclose it in an edited form, the question is whether he has a presently enforceable right to inspect the document, that is to say, the unedited document.

He has not. What he no doubt has is a right to information from DIL about his own expenditure. The only way to achieve the object which is sought here by the wife would be to direct that a new document be brought into existence, that is to say, a list of the husband's expenditure. That would certainly be a useful power, if available to the court, but it is not the power given by Ord 48. Order 48 enables the court to order the husband to produce an existing document which is in his possession.

I should perhaps add in passing that, for the same reason, there is clear authority, not as I understand it put before the district judge, that there is no power to order the husband to use all necessary endeavours to obtain possession of documents which are not in his possession: see *Dubai Bank Ltd v Galadari and Others* [1990] Ch 98.

It follows that I am unable to support the order for production of either of the two remaining documents in issue in this appeal.

4   Relevance and discretion

That last conclusion means that this question does not arise. I should, I think, say that if I had held that these documents were in the possession of the husband, I should not have been persuaded that I ought to interfere with the district judge's conclusion on grounds that he was plainly wrong. He was in a better position than I am to assess relevance because he dealt with a large range of documents relating to the husband's affairs generally, whereas my attention has been focused on two only. I have, in any event, not the slightest doubt that the DIL accounts are relevant to the possibility of enforcement against the loan account with the head holding company.

Credit card statements are more difficult. Their relevance can only be marginal. The husband is paying the periodical payments ordered. It is the lump sum with respect to which he is in default. To show that he is living well at the expense of someone else, and to have grave suspicion about the nature of the financial relationship with that someone else, may perhaps endorse the previous conclusion that the husband is deliberately evading his solemn obligations, and that he cares little either for the order of the court or for his duty to his wife. But the extent of his spending is of extremely limited value in assisting the wife to enforcement of her lump sum. The wife should also bear in mind that the court must, in exercising its discretion as to what order to make in the course of an oral examination, in this case bear in mind that there has already been a substantial cross-examination before Bodey J in judgment summons proceedings. Those proceedings may have been abortive so far as an order for committal went on legal grounds, but there was nevertheless the extended opportunity, fully taken, for cross-examination of the husband. Now there have been a further 2 days of examination and substantial production of documents. Absent some significant further development, it may very well be that that part of the process is likely to be regarded as concluded by any court which has to consider the question.

For all these reasons, the order must be that the appeal is allowed, the order for production of the credit card statements and the DIL account is quashed, and, no resistance being offered by the wife, also quashed must be the other orders for production made on 2 November 2001.

I will hear submissions from the parties as to the order for adjournment, but, unless I have overlooked some consideration, it appears that must go also, since there are now no fresh documents upon which the husband can be further cross-examined, and it appears that the questions to him had, subject to any further documents, been concluded.

Appeal allowed; order for production quashed.

Solicitors: *Hughes Fowler Carruthers* for the appellant
               Pullig & Co for the respondent

PHILIPPA JOHNSON
Law Reporter

MUBARAK v MUBARIK

[2004] EWHC 1158 (Fam), [2004] 2 FLR 932, FD

Family Division

Ryder J

14 May 2004

Financial provision – Enforcement – Application to vary periodical payments –
Applicant in contempt for failure to pay lump sum – Whether court entitled to refuse
to hear contemnor subject to conditions – Whether refusal infringed right of access
to court

At the end of the ancillary relief proceedings the judge ordered the husband to
pay the wife a lump sum of £4,875,000, to deliver up jewellery as security for that
sum, and until that sum was paid, to make periodical payments of £12,900 pcm
(later increased to £14,733 pcm), those payments to be credited against the interest
accruing on the lump sum. The judge's findings included failure by the husband to
make full and frank disclosure, and that the husband was the beneficial owner of,
and in full control, of two substantial companies. Refusing the husband
permission to appeal, the Court of Appeal described the husband's conduct as
dishonest litigation strategy. Apart from £266,195, obtained from the husband by
means of charging orders, the lump sum remained unpaid. A committal order on
a judgment summons brought by the wife was set aside, on the basis that the
committal process had been unfair, and was not compliant with the European
Convention for the Protection of Human Rights and Fundamental
Freedoms 1950 (the European Convention). The wife then brought enforcement
proceedings in respect of the periodical payments orders. In response, the husband
sought to vary the periodical payments order. At the hearing of the variation
application, the wife made a preliminary application, arguing, in reliance on
Hadkinson v Hadkinson, that the court should refuse to hear the husband's
variation application, or, in the alternative, should impose conditions as to its
continuance, on the basis that a court might refuse to hear a party to a cause who
was in contempt.

Held – imposing conditions as to the continuance of the husband's variation
application –

(1) *Hadkinson v Hadkinson* remained good law, was European Convention
compliant, and in an appropriate case provided an important discretionary power
for the court, albeit for use as a last resort. Refusing to hear an application unless
certain conditions were fulfilled was not an infringement of the husband's right of
access to the court and thereby a breach of Art 6 of the European Convention.
Provided the conditions imposed were proportionate and in pursuit of a legitimate
aim, *Hadkinson* conditions did not impair the very essence of the right to a fair
trial. The right of access to a court was not unfettered for all purposes. The
legitimate aim being pursued was that of clearing an impediment to the course of
justice arising from wilful and continuing disobedience which was making it more

difficult for the court to ascertain the truth or enforce its orders, and there being no other method of securing compliance with the court's orders (see paras [48], [51], [57]).

(2) A *Hadkinson* application remained available in the context of family proceedings generally, and within a *Corbett* variation application specifically. There was no necessary inconsistency with the purposes described in *Corbett v Corbett*, or with the court's statutory duty, to consider a variation application (see para [58]).

(3) When considering whether to make a *Hadkinson* order, the following questions had to be answered: (a) was the husband in contempt; (b) was there an impediment to the course of justice; (c) was there any other effective means of securing compliance with the court's orders; (d) should the court exercise its discretion to impose conditions having regard to the question; (e) was the contempt wilful (ie contumacious and continuing); (f) if so, what conditions would be proportionate? Simple disobedience of an order was sufficient to find the contempt, and although the existence of wilful conduct was a component which the court must consider, it was relevant to the exercise of the discretion, not whether the discretion existed on the facts of the instant case (see para [59]).

Per curiam: the variation application was a free-standing process; it was not actually or necessarily interlinked with any subsequent committal. The grounds for the committal had to be proved again to the criminal standard, and any European Convention Art 6 objection based on self-incrimination could be taken within the committal process. A husband who accepted the result of a *Corbett* inquiry would likely satisfy the elements of good will and motivation, thereby causing the Debtors Act 1869 process to fall away (see paras [45], [46]).

Statutory provisions considered
Debtors Act 1869
Matrimonial Causes Act 1973, ss 31, 37
European Convention for the Protection of Human Rights and Fundamental
    Freedoms 1950, Art 6

Cases referred to in judgment
Arrow Nominees Inc v Blackledge [2000] 2 BCLC 167, (2000) *The Times* July 7, CA
Ashingdane v United Kingdom (Application No 8225/78) (1985) 7 EHRR 528,
    ECHR
Baker v Baker (No 2) [1997] 1 FLR 148, CA
Corbett v Corbett [2003] EWCA Civ 559, [2003] 2 FLR 385, CA
Golder v United Kingdom (Application No 4451/70) (1979–80) 1 EHRR 524,
    ECHR
Grupo Torras SA v Sheikh Fahad Mohammed al Sahah and Others (1999) *The
    Independent* February 25, CA
Hadkinson v Hadkinson [1952] P 285, (1952) FLR Rep 287, [1952] 2 All ER
    567, CA
Leavis v Leavis [1921] P 299, PDAD
Motorola Credit Corporation v Uzan & Others [2003] EWCA Civ 752, [2004]
    1 WLR 113, CA
Mubarak v Mubarak [2001] 1 FLR 673, FD

Mubarak v Mubarak [2001] 1 FLR 698, CA
N v N (Jurisdiction: Pre-Nuptial Agreement) [1999] 2 FLR 745, FD
Roman Polanski v Conde Nast Publications Ltd [2003] EWCA Civ 1573, [2004]
    1 All ER 1220, CA
Saunders v United Kingdom (1997) 23 EHRR 313, ECHR
Swaptronics Ltd, Re (1998) *The Times* July 31, [1998] All ER (D) 407, [1998]
    36 LS Gaz R 33, ChD
X Ltd v Morgan-Grampian (Publishers) Ltd and Others [1991] 1 AC 1, [1990]
    2 WLR 1000, [1990] 2 All ER 1, HL

Michael Horowitz QC *and* Gavin Smith *for the wife*
Charles Howard QC *and* Richard Harrison *for the husband*

Cur adv vult

RYDER J:

Background

[1]   This is the well-known case of Mubarak.

[2]   The applicant is Aaliya Mubarak. She is 44 and comes from a prominent Kashmiri political family. Both her father and uncle have served as Chief Minister for Jammu and Kashmir. She is a highly educated woman with a Masters degree from Srinagar University. She is represented by Mr Michael Horowitz QC and Mr Gavin Smith.

[3]   The respondent is Iqbal Mubarik. He is 45 and is also a Kashmiri Indian by origin. He comes from a highly successful family of jewellers. He is represented by Mr Charles Howard QC and Mr Richard Harrison.

[4]   The parties married in Kashmir on 21 August 1983 and moved to London from their then home in Hong Kong on 29 August 1997. They finally separated on 20 April 1998. The decree absolute of divorce was pronounced in this jurisdiction on 10 December 1999. I shall for convenience refer to them in this judgment as husband and wife.

[5]   They have four children: A who was born on 10 July 1984 and is now 19 rising 20; B who was born on 23 July 1988 and is now nearly 16; C who was born on 19 October 1991 and is now 12½; and D who was born on 11 December 1997 and is now 6½. The children live with their mother and have contact with their father. They are all in full-time education.

[6]   On 10 December 1999 Bodey J made an order at the end of an ancillary relief hearing between the husband and the wife. The order was varied to increase the amount of the wife's periodical payments on 20 January 2000. In summary the order provided as follows:

•   The husband to pay the wife a lump sum of £4,875,000.
•   Unless the husband paid the lump sum or provided security for it, the husband was to deliver up jewellery and artefacts to be sold in satisfaction of the lump sum, interest and costs.

- Until payment of the lump sum the husband was to pay to the wife periodical payments at the rate of £12,900 pcm (subsequently increased to £14,733 pcm).
- The periodical payments made to the wife during any period of non-payment of the lump sum were to be credited against the interest accruing upon the lump sum.
- From payment of the lump sum the husband was to pay periodical payments for the children at the rate of £60,000 p a.
- The husband to pay indemnity costs.

[7]   The basis for the calculation of the wife's lump sum and periodical payments sums can be seen from the December 1999 judgment of Bodey J at p 58:

> 'Taking the wife's income requirement for herself at £100,000 p a ... (which would require a *Duxbury* lump sum of about £2,440,000), I propose to allow £2,250,000 for the wife's income-producing fund. I shall further award £25,000 to enable her to ... purchase an alternative car. The aggregate of (the) three funds (home, *Duxbury* and car) is £4,875,000.'

[8]   The lump sum order remains unpaid save as to the sum of £266,195 which was not a voluntary payment made by the husband but as the result of charging orders obtained by the wife.

[9]   From the outset, the focus of the ancillary relief proceedings has been the companies with which the family are concerned, known as the Dianoor Group. At Appendix 1 to this judgment there is a simplified diagram of the structure of the Dianoor Group. On 23 June 2000, in a judgment concerning the administration of the UK company, Dianoor Jewels Ltd (DJL), Blackburne J[1] described the structure as follows:

> 'DJL was incorporated in this country in September 1993. Its principal business is the manufacturing, wholesaling and retailing of jewellery. It trades from retail premises in New Bond Street in the West End of London. It is the wholly owned subsidiary of Dianoor Jewels International Ltd., which is an overseas company, which in turn is wholly owned by a company called 21st Century Holding Ltd., another overseas company, which in its turn is owned by an offshore trust called IMK Trust. DIL [Dianoor International Ltd], the associated company, was incorporated in, and I understand operates out of, Hong Kong.'

[10]   The husband and wife were the settlors of the IMK Trust. The wife was removed as a beneficiary of the trust shortly before the petition was issued.

[11]   The assets of the Dianoor Group comprise substantial stocks of jewellery owned either by DJL or DIL. As Blackburne J found: a substantial proportion of the jewellery available for sale by DJL (and which was to be delivered up in the absence of the payment of the lump sum or the provision of security by the husband in accordance with Bodey J's order) was stock which belongs to DIL and which is available for sale by DJL on a sale-or-return basis.

---

[1]   Editor's note: see *Dianoor Jewels Ltd, Re* [2001] BPIR 234, at 236.

[12] In the event, as history records, although the husband was found to have intermingled his description of company and personal assets, no effective enforcement of the lump sum order has been made against the Dianoor Group.

[13] It should also be noted that there has been almost constant litigation between the parties since their separation in relation to financial and children issues. Both parties have been the subjects of adverse judicial criticism. I am told that the overall costs bill for the litigation in this jurisdiction alone now exceeds £2.25m.

The applications

[14] The substantive application before the court is that of the husband, by notice in Form A dated 24 April 2003, to vary the periodical payments order made by Bodey J in favour of the wife. The application was made in consequence upon a hearing of the wife's enforcement proceedings in the West London Magistrates' Court (WLMC).

[15] The varied periodical payments order of £14,733 pcm made on 20 January 2000 had been registered by the wife at the WLMC by an application issued on 20 November 2002. On 23 April 2003, after the husband had fallen into arrears, he was summoned before that court. The husband indicated to the WLMC that in accordance with the Court of Appeal's decision in *Corbett v Corbett* [2003] EWCA Civ 559, [2003] 2 FLR 385 he would be seeking a variation of the periodical payments order. He promptly made his variation application the following day.

[16] There are various subsidiary applications concerned with reserved costs and Mr Horowitz has intimated an intention to pursue an application under s 37 of the Matrimonial Causes Act 1973 to put the wife back in the position she was as a beneficiary of the trust. Mr Howard takes strong objection to that intimation and asks for an adjournment if it is pursued, on the basis that the husband is prejudiced by the lack of formal notice and opportunity to prepare his materials or case in response.

[17] The hearing that has taken place before me this week has not been concerned with the husband's substantive application (save as to the basis and outline of the same) or with the subsidiary applications but with a preliminary application made on behalf of the wife. Mr Horowitz submits in reliance upon *Hadkinson v Hadkinson* [1952] P 285, (1952) FLR Rep 287 that the court should refuse to hear the husband's variation application or in the alternative should impose conditions as to its continuance on the basis that a court may refuse to hear a party to a cause who is in contempt. The preliminary application has been strenuously opposed and because of that and the importance of the preliminary issue to the parties, I shall set out their arguments and my conclusions in some detail.

The findings

[18] In order to consider the parties' submissions on the *Hadkinson* application it has been necessary for this court to consider the detail of the findings made on and after 10 October 1999. In doing so I do not pre-judge Mr Howard's submissions that are yet to be developed in the variation application on the question of issue estoppel. It is necessary for me to consider the findings because the parties do not agree the construction of the clear words used by Bodey J in his judgments of 10 December 1999 and 23 October 2000. Those findings underpin the order which the husband seeks to vary and will need to be compared with the positions of the parties, in particular the husband, if the *Hadkinson* application is not to be dismissed out of hand by this court. No similar objection is taken to the findings of Blackburne J in his judgment of 23 June 2000 in the proceedings concerning the administration of DJL, but inferentially where the latter are based upon the former, I must presume that issue is taken.

[19]   In the interests of brevity I am not going to set out all of the relevant findings seriatim in this judgment: they are clear for all to read on the face of the three judgments, but the following summary is helpful and I am again indebted to Blackburne J for his industry in setting out the same:

'(Bodey J) found that the husband had sought to mislead the court, told lies, grossly understated his assets and over-stated his liabilities, and had been prepared to go to great lengths in an attempt to thwart the wife's just claims. Indeed, after the first few days of the contested hearing the husband's legal advisors found themselves unable to continue acting further for him. The husband himself had been absent from the hearing, I think from the third day, and on the withdrawal of his legal team, indicated through them that he did not intend to take any further part in the hearing. Nor did he ...

(Bodey J) took the view that the husband was, for all practical purposes, to be regarded as the beneficial owner and in full control of both DJL and DIL, with the result that in accordance with well established authority concerned with the court's exercise of its jurisdiction in ancillary relief claims, it was open to the court, where a person was found, like the husband here, to be beneficial owner and in control of the company, to treat that person as if he were the owner of the company's underlying assets ...

I should add that another of DJL's directors, namely Mr Wani, had intervened in the ancillary relief proceedings at an earlier stage to claim a 45% interest in, among other matters, the assets of the Dianoor Group. That intervention came to nothing when it emerged that the joint venture agreement upon which he and the husband relied had been falsely created and that his and the husband's evidence about the circumstances in which it has come to be made could be shown to be entirely false ...

I accept that a number of propositions concerning the husband's behaviour are justified, namely: (1) that he conspired with Mr Wani and others to present to the court a fraudulent account of his affairs in order to minimise his exposure to his wife and thus to pervert the course of justice; (2) that in order to go about this dishonest litigation strategy he had been willing to incur over £800,000 in legal costs; (3) that he was a man of great fortune with undisclosed resources running to many millions; (4) that he is the creator, controller and sole beneficiary of the IMK Family Trust; (5) that he wholly controls all of the Dianoor companies; (6) that Mr Wani and Mr Aiyer act under his direction and control and that I should, therefore, exercise great caution before accepting anything they or any of them say; (7) that between September 1999 and 29 November 1999, he and Mr Wani caused jewellery having an auction value of £3.5 million to be removed from the UK, and that he has consistently refused to bring any of that jewellery back into this country, thereby, it is said, demonstrating his preparedness to engage in tactics with a view to frustrating his wife's claims ...

... the court should readily accept that the husband's underlying purpose continues to be, by one means or another, to frustrate the orders made against him in the wife's favour in the course of the ancillary relief proceedings.'

[20] Mr Wani it should be recalled is the husband's adopted brother. It should also be noted that the husband had made a concession prior to the main hearing that he, the husband, could be treated as owning the assets of the trust (by his solicitor's letter of 31 July 1998) and his only caveat to that concession was that that ownership was subject to the interest of Mr Wani: a contention rejected by Bodey J (see *Mubarak v Mubarak* [2001] 1 FLR 673, at 676). It is not surprising then that both Bodey and Blackburne JJ were able to be so clear as to the husband's ownership and control of the Dianoor Group, an issue upon which I find myself in complete agreement.

[21] On 3 April 2000, the Court of Appeal[2] (Otton and Thorpe LJJ) refused permission for the husband to appeal (an appeal directed primarily against the quantum of the lump sum order). Thorpe LJ records at para [3] of his judgment that the asserted partnership document between the husband and Mr Wani was nothing more or less than a fraud. At paras [4] and [5], he described the husband's conduct as dishonest litigation strategy and records Bodey J's finding that the husband had failed to make full and frank disclosure. At para [29] he held that Bodey J was not to be criticised for the consequential judicial inference about the husband's undisclosed assets and the necessary lack of precision in quantifying the same.

[22] Thorpe LJ's final comment is, if I may say so, worthy of repetition in full:

'If a respondent husband, faced with an ancillary relief claim by a wife who has given the major part of her life to the marriage and to the birth of four children and who proposes to give the ensuing part of her life to the nurturing of those children, responds with a determined and dishonest strategy designed to diminish her judicial award and to divert the judge from his proper adjudication and if he on exposure boycotts the proceedings, he is not to be heard in this court on an application for appellate review unless it can be demonstrated that the judge in the court of trial has manifestly departed from principle, or has overreacted in his sense of condemnation of such undesirable litigation practices. I can detect no sign of anything of that sort in what reads like a dispassionate and objective judgment from a very experienced judge in the field of ancillary relief.'

[23] On 23 October 2000 Bodey J considered a judgment summons brought by the wife against the husband. There is no question but that Bodey J came to the

---

[2] Editor's note: *Mubarak v Mubarak* (unreported) 3 April 2000.

conclusion that it was unacceptable to lift the corporate veil on the facts of this case and to that extent he revised his judgment on the ability and/or willingness of the court to seize the company assets. But he equally made it abundantly clear that that is not the same as saying that the husband cannot in practice use his underlying ownership of the business structure to raise cash by accessing the underlying resources (see *Mubarak v Mubarak* [2001] 1 FLR 673, at 694).

[24] It is submitted to me by Mr Howard for the husband that Bodey J resiled from or diluted his 1999 finding that there were undisclosed assets or that in re-expressing that finding in October 2000 (as he did to the criminal standard in what was subsequently held to be a flawed committal process) there is no effective finding of undisclosed assets upon which I should place reliance.

[25] I do not accept that on a proper reading of the October 2000 judgment, Bodey J has in any real sense resiled from or weakened his essential finding of undisclosed assets. It is correct to say that he re-analyses the evidence of Barclays Bank documentation, having regard to new evidence from a bank manager (with at least some advantageous consequences for the husband), and that he finds answers to a number of the 'signposts' he expressed in 1999 as being indicative of the adverse view he took of the husband and his undisclosed assets, but the summary relied upon by Mr Howard at 692B–D ([2001] 1 FLR 673) must be read in the context of the findings against the husband expressed between 690H and 692B. They remain adverse to the husband and specifically reiterate the court's view that the husband has undisclosed assets: a finding based upon the evidence considered at both hearings and with a logical continuity of finding between the two.

[26] Accordingly I reject the husband's contention that the totality of Bodey J's reconsideration of the evidential material then available to him in October 2000 undermined the fundamental finding that the husband had undisclosed assets.

[27] In the alternative Mr Howard submits that I should not rely upon any findings made or re-expressed against the husband in the October 2000 hearing because the process was subsequently held to be fundamentally flawed. On 14 December 2000 the Court of Appeal (Thorpe and Brooke LJJ and Jacob J) set aside Bodey J's committal order against the husband in their well-known redefinition of European Convention for the Protection of Human Rights and Fundamental Freedoms 1950 (the European Convention) compliance and fair process in enforcement procedure (see *Mubarak v Mubarak* [2001] 1 FLR 698).

[28] I find no suggestion in that judgment that any of Bodey J's findings made to the civil standard are vitiated by the flawed committal process.

[29] Indeed, in his affirmation of 19 May 2003 the husband concedes that Bodey J had the opportunity to consider matters in some detail at the October 2000 hearing that he describes as 'lengthy' and when detailed evidence was given by the husband and his witnesses.

[30] It ill behoves a party in the husband's situation to accept those findings made in the 'flawed process' that are advantageous to him but to reject those that are not simply because there has been a flawed process.

The husband's position

[31] In these proceedings the husband asserts, as he has done repeatedly in submissions and in evidence (see, for example, his affirmations of 29 September 2000, 13 December 2000, 8 May 2001 and 5 June 2003) that: (a) he does not have any undisclosed assets; (b) although he accepts that the document he relied upon to prove Mr Wani's 45% interest was a fraud (not to mention the witnesses who were procured to support the same), the essential fact of Mr Wani's 45% interest is true; and (c) he does not effectively own and control the Dianoor Group. It is an important and critical element of the husband's variation application before me that he both wishes and needs to prove that the court was wrong, i e he needs to fundamentally undermine the factual basis for the lump sum award in order to succeed on his variation application before this court.

[32] Mr Howard for the husband submitted and conceded (a) that he would not get far with his client's variation application unless he could show that there were 'no undisclosed assets in millions', i e not that they had existed but no longer did so, but rather that they never existed and (b) that he had to persuade the court to go behind the finding of undisclosed assets in order to get anywhere: he said 'I accept that if the court finds that the husband has undisclosed assets of the nature and extent to pay periodical payments, he will not succeed'. It must follow that the husband's case is that he could never afford to make the periodical payments ordered and indeed the husband says that he has made payments up until April 1993 by relying upon loans from his family and friends (and I note by way of example his solicitor's 'proposal' letter dated 27 February 2001 which flagged up his alleged dependence upon loans to make the maintenance payments ordered).

[33] The only caveat to the concession made by Mr Howard was that if the wife's needs have reduced (and the husband asserts they have) there may be an alternative, though relatively marginal, prospect of variation on that basis alone.

[34] If one considers carefully the factors relied upon by the husband in his skeleton argument (No 1) at p 29 from para 98 that are asserted to be sufficient to establish a change of circumstances, one can readily see why it is so important to the husband to go behind the original findings. In other words, the concession of Mr Howard was rightly made (postscript: on handing down this judgment I am told that the concession was intended to be retracted on the basis that a variation application is justified in the light of the parties' changed circumstances – that does not change my view).

[35] The husband also relies upon the submission that he cannot get money out of the group structure to pay the lump sum and by implication the periodical payments because, he says, it is on the verge of insolvency. There are two aspects to this submission: his lack of absolute control (no longer relied upon as relevant to his ability to obtain monies but still asserted) and the existence of an undertaking by the husband not to remove his loan account of over £21m with the Bermudan holding company (21st Century Holdings). Having regard to the findings of Bodey and Blackburne JJ set out above, it is apparent that this limb of the husband's variation application is also a fundamental attack on the factual basis for the lump sum order.

[36]   The husband says, and I record in fairness to him, the undoubted fact that the wife has been involved in repeated and misconceived litigation strategies and misconduct for which she has been criticised by the court and penalised in costs in her attempts to enforce the payment of that which is due to her from the husband. In addition, she has been strongly condemned by Singer J in her conduct of the proceedings concerning the children. But none of that (inexcusable though it is) in any way dilutes or deflects the gravamen of the issues already determined against the husband.

The husband's procedural objection

[37]   I set out the husband's substantive response to the wife's *Hadkinson* application later in this judgment but the husband begins with a procedural objection. He says that the wife should be barred from bringing this application for late non-compliance with the court's orders. I disagree. It is correct that the wife has, while in person, characterised her application to dismiss the husband's variation application as being res judicata and that the court has not determined that as a preliminary issue, standing the matter over to this hearing in part at the wife's request (per Bodey J on 7 July 2003 and per Coleridge J on 16 February 2004). It is also the case that having instructed her present solicitors in readiness for this hearing, they wrote to the husband's solicitors on 31 March 2004 indicating that in the absence of a reasonable offer their client would ask the court to debar the husband from making any further applications.

[38]   Furthermore, on 28 April 2003 (only 4 days after the husband's variation application was issued and while she was still acting in person) the wife applied in writing to dismiss the variation application expressly because the lump sum was unpaid, asserting that that was a contempt of this court (see the preamble to, the postscript of and paras 2 and 9 of her document at A2–A4 of the core bundle). That application was included at para 1 of the wife's consolidated notice of application dated 10 October 2003 (A5–A6). The consolidated application was filed in response to paras [13] and [14] of the directions order of Bodey J of 15 September 2003 which contained a debarring clause. I hold that the wife made a reasonable attempt to comply with the directions orders and that the subsequent recasting of her application in *Hadkinson* form is not a sufficiently new event to be caught by the debarring order.

[39]   In any event, having listened with great care to the careful and well-prepared material presented on the husband's behalf in response to the *Hadkinson* application, I have come to the clear conclusion that the husband has not been prejudiced by any later recasting of the wife's intentions in the form of the preliminary application that has been pursued before me.

The Hadkinson application

[40]   The wife relies upon the dictum of Denning LJ (as he then was) in *Hadkinson v Hadkinson* [1952] P 285, (1952) FLR Rep 287 as subsequently applied and approved in a line of authorities. Mr Horowitz submits that the court should not entertain the husband's application where he is in contempt and where his only response is to assert that his disobedience is because the findings upon which the orders were based were unjustified (even more so in the context of the husband's failed application for permission to appeal the same). That assertion, and the consequential attempt to undermine the fundamental basis of the orders, is, he says, both wilful and an impediment to the course of justice, for example, in the manner in which it has rendered enforcement impossible.

[41] Mr Horowitz goes further and submits that the husband's frank and continuing reliance upon matters that have been firmly determined against him necessarily means that the court will either not be able to ascertain the truth of the facts asserted to underpin his variation application or will have great difficulty in doing so and that frustrates a fair hearing before this court.

[42] On behalf of the husband Mr Howard submits that *Hadkinson v Hadkinson* [1952] P 285, (1952) FLR Rep 287 is bad law, it is not European Convention compliant and is inconsistent with the *Corbett* process. Alternatively, he says that if it can survive rigorous examination to modern Art 6 standards, I should take the view that a fair trial of this cause is still possible despite the existence of any contempt (which is not admitted). He submits that the alleged contempt is, in any event, not wilful as it is predicated on the essential factual fallacy that the husband now seeks to rectify, ie there is no fault or blameworthiness in the husband's position. He submits that the wilful element is one which I must be satisfied of before I can exercise any discretion to make a *Hadkinson* order (whereas Mr Horowitz submits that wilfulness is an element in discretion).

[43] Mr Howard submits that the court has a statutory duty to inquire having regard to s 31 of the Matrimonial Causes Act 1973 and that a clear distinction can be drawn between a voluntary or appellate process commenced by an applicant in contempt and a process which is a prerequisite to a party's ability to defend subsequent committal proceedings which he regards as being inextricably linked.

The law

[44] By way of introduction, and because there was debate before me about the nature and extent of the decision of the Court of Appeal in *Corbett v Corbett* [2003] EWCA Civ 559, [2003] 2 FLR 385, I reiterate what Thorpe LJ said at paras [24], [29] and [30]: Thorpe LJ placed express reliance upon the earlier decision of *Mubarak* (*Mubarak v Mubarak* [2001] 1 FLR 673) and provided a pragmatic resolution of the need to ensure that there is a fair and European Convention compliant committal process with the desirability to case manage a full investigation of means, motivation and good faith.

[45] A husband who accepts the result of a *Corbett* inquiry will likely satisfy the elements of good faith and motivation causing the Debtors Act 1869 process to fall away. A husband who does not is at risk of the separate committal process. For the avoidance of doubt, I do not agree with Mr Howard that there is an inevitability of committal following upon an unsuccessful variation application or that *Corbett v Corbett* may itself have to be reconsidered on a close reading of *Saunders v United Kingdom* (1997) 23 EHRR 313 so as to protect the husband's privilege against self-incrimination (in that in a *Corbett* application the party seeking to vary has a duty of full and frank disclosure which may place him at risk of incrimination in any subsequent committal process).

[46] The latter point was not fully argued before me and I express no concluded view save to repeat what Thorpe LJ said at para [29]: the variation application is a free-standing process, it is not actually or necessarily interlinked with any subsequent committal. For my part I add that the grounds for the committal have to be proved again to the criminal standard and any Art 6 objection including as to self-incrimination can be taken within the committal process. It is not right to say that by bringing a *Hadkinson* application the wife has an unfair advantage should committal be pursued, if advantage it be. She would have had it, in any event, as a result of full and frank disclosure to which she *and the court* are entitled in a variation application.

[47] The modern restatement of the law begins with the dictum of Denning LJ in *Hadkinson v Hadkinson* [1952] P 285, (1952) FLR Rep 287, at 298 and 574H–575C respectively:

> 'Those cases seem to me to point the way to the modern rule. It is a strong thing for a court to refuse to hear a party to a cause and it is only to be justified by grave considerations of public policy. It is a step which a court will only take when the contempt itself impedes the course of justice and there is no other effective means of securing his compliance. In this regard I would like to refer to what Sir George Jessel, MR, said (46 LJ Ch 383) in a similar connection in *Re Clements and Costa Rica Republic v Erlanger* (14):
>
> > "I have myself had on many occasions to consider this jurisdiction, and I have always thought that necessary though it be, it is necessary only in the sense in which extreme measures are sometimes necessary to preserve men's rights, that is, if no other pertinent remedy can be found. Probably that will be discovered after consideration to be the true measure of the exercise of the jurisdiction."
>
> Applying this principle, I am of opinion that the fact that a party to a cause has disobeyed an order of the court is not of itself a bar to his being heard, but if his disobedience is such that, so long as it continues, it impedes the course of justice in the cause, by making it more difficult for the court to ascertain the truth or to enforce the orders which it may make, then the court may in its discretion refuse to hear him until the impediment is removed or good reason is shown why it should not be removed.'

[48] The emphasis is on the impediment to the course of justice, the wilful and continuing nature of the disobedience that makes it more difficult for the court to ascertain the truth or enforce its orders and there being no other method of securing compliance with the court's orders.

[49] These principles were followed in *Baker v Baker (No 2)* [1997] 1 FLR 148 at 151, a case on the facts that is almost on all fours with the position presented to this court by the husband, ie an application for a variation in periodical payments in the context of the refusal to pay the lump sum to the wife. The passages in the judgment of Sir John Balcombe at 150F–H and 151B–F set out the essential conclusions of the court:

> 'I should say that the way the matter came before Cazalet J was with affidavit evidence on behalf of the husband filed in support of his

application for a reduction of the amount of periodical payments which set out in some detail what he said were his present assets and his present income and his present commitments including his position with his new wife and their children. But at no stage did the husband accept the criticisms made about him by Ward J in the Court of Appeal that he had withheld from the court relevant information as to his assets. Nor did he say that there had been previous assets but that, by the time of his application, those assets had been spent so that, although Ward J's order might have been justified at the time it was made, nevertheless he was no longer in a position to comply with it.

That was not the attitude taken by the husband before Cazalet J. His attitude was that on what he said were his present resources and capital income and present commitments he could not afford to keep up the periodical payments at the rate ordered and he asked for a reduction.

In support of that submission, counsel for the wife relied upon the case of *Hadkinson v Hadkinson* [1952] P 285 and, in particular, on a passage from the judgment of Denning LJ at 298. Although Denning LJ was giving, in effect a minority judgment, all the judges came to the same conclusion. Denning LJ's reasons were slightly different to those of the other two members of the court, Somerville and Romer LJJ. Nevertheless, it is Denning LJ's judgment which now represents the modern practice as appears from the speeches of Lord Bridge of Harwich and Lord Oliver of Aylmerton in *X Ltd v Morgan-Grampian (Publishers) Ltd and Others* [1991] 1 AC 1, the references being at 46 and 47 in the speech of Lord Bridge of Harwich and 50 and 51 in the speech of Lord Oliver of Aylmerton. It is to the judgment of Denning LJ that I turn in particular to the passage at 298.'

[50] Importantly, the court in *Baker v Baker (No 2)* [1997] 1 FLR 148 considered whether the disobedience to an order is contempt in itself and whether the wilful element of the *Hadkinson* test was an element of discretion (rather than an integral component of the existence of the contempt). Sir John Balcombe at 152E approves Hill J in *Leavis v Leavis* [1921] P 299 as follows:

'In the case of *Leavis v Leavis* [1921] P 299 the headnote reads as follows:

"Non-compliance with orders of the Divorce Division for the payment of costs and alimony is still a contempt of court, although since the Debtors Act, 1869, the orders cannot be enforced by attachment."

What Hill J said [at 301] was:

"Though the contempt constituted by disobedience to these orders cannot be enforced by attachment, it is nonetheless a contempt, and does not cease to be a contempt because the statute has taken away attachment as a remedy."

A little later:

> "I have come to the conclusion that it is a matter of discretion for the Court to consider, upon all the circumstances of the case, whether the summons of the respondent should be heard and that it is matter material to the exercise of that discretion to consider whether those circumstances are due to the fault or to the misfortune of the respondent."

> In other words, what Hill J was saying was that the non-payment of the sums ordered was, in itself, a contempt and that the question of whether that non-payment was contumelious was relevant to the exercise of the discretion.'

[51] Nothing in the analysis presented to me by Mr Howard about those two elements convinces me that *Baker v Baker (No 2)* [1997] 1 FLR 148 is in that regard wrongly decided, is not a statement of the modern law or has been authoritatively reconsidered. In particular, it is not correct to say that a *Hadkinson* order is an infringement of the husband's right of access to a court and accordingly a breach of Art 6 (applying *Golder v United Kingdom* (1979–80) 1 EHRR 524). I do not believe that *Hadkinson* conditions impair the very essence of the right to a fair trial provided the conditions imposed are proportionate and in pursuit of a legitimate aim (following *Ashingdane v United Kingdom* (1985) 7 EHRR 528, at para 57). The right of access to a court is not unfettered for all purposes.

[52] No one suggests in the context of the above that *Hadkinson* conditions are otherwise than the pursuit of a legitimate aim.

[53] Accordingly, I agree with Mr Horowitz that simple disobedience with an order is sufficient to find the contempt and that although the existence of wilful conduct is a component that the court must consider, it is relevant to the exercise of discretion, not whether the discretion exists on the facts of the instant case.

[54] Finally, as regards the application of *Baker v Baker (No 2)* [1997] 1 FLR 148 on the facts before me, the observations that Sir John Balcombe makes in conclusion at 154B–F are all highly pertinent to the circumstances of Mr Mubarik.

[55] More recently Wall J (as he then was) affirmed the continuing existence of the *Hadkinson* power in *N v N (Jurisdiction: Pre-Nuptial Agreement)* [1999] 2 FLR 745.

[56] In the course of submissions, I have been taken through an exhaustive collection of modern authorities that confirm that the restatement of the law in *Hadkinson v Hadkinson* [1952] P 285, (1952) FLR Rep 287 and *Baker v Baker (No 2)* [1997] 1 FLR 148 is still regarded as correct. I do not propose to do other than highlight the references that confirm me in that view:

(a)	*X Ltd v Morgan-Grampian (Publishers) Ltd and Others* [1991] 1 AC 1 and in particular the speeches of Lord Bridge of Harwich at 46B–H and Lord Oliver of Aylmerton at 50D–51D;

(b)	*Re Swaptronics Ltd* (1998) *The Times* July 31, full transcript at paras [15]–[21] and in particular para [20] (but subject to the caveat at para [38] of *Roman Polanski v Conde Nast Publications Ltd* [2003] EWCA Civ 1573, [2004] 1 All ER 1220 below that Laddie J may go too far);

(c)   *Grupo Torras SA v Sheikh Fahad Mohammed al Sahah and Others* (1999) *The Independent* February 25, full transcript at pp 8–11, 22, 24;

(d)   *Arrow Nominees Inc v Blackledge* [2000] 2 BCLC 167, (2000) *The Times* July 7 full transcript at paras [32], [33], [54];

(e)   *Motorola Credit Corporation v Uzan & Others* [2003] EWCA Civ 752, [2004] 1 WLR 113 at paras [44], [45], [47], [48], [51]–[55], [58];

(f)   *Roman Polanski v Conde Nast Publications Ltd* [2003] EWCA Civ 1573, [2004] 1 All ER 1220 at paras [38]–[40], [44], [46], [48].

[57]   I have, therefore, concluded that *Hadkinson* remains good law, is European Convention compliant and, in an appropriate case, provides an important discretionary power in the court, albeit for use as a last resort.

[58]   A *Hadkinson* application remains available in the context of family proceedings generally and within a *Corbett* variation application specifically. There is no necessary inconsistency with the purposes described in *Corbett v Corbett* [2003] EWCA Civ 559, [2003] 2 FLR 385, or with the court's statutory duty to consider a variation application, for the same reasons that I have described the application as being, in my view, European Convention compliant.

The principles

[59]   Without detracting from the careful language used in the authorities cited above, which I have continued to bear in mind, it seems to me that the following questions should be answered:

(a)   Is the husband in contempt?

(b)   Is there an impediment to the course of justice?

(c)   Is there any other effective means of securing compliance with the court's orders?

(d)   Should the court exercise its discretion to impose conditions having regard to the question;

(e)   Is the contempt wilful (ie is it contumacious and continuing)?

(f)   If so, what conditions would be proportionate?

[60]   No party has suggested to me that the standard of proof I should apply, in being satisfied as to any element of the *Hadkinson* test, is the criminal standard of proof. I raised the issue in opening and it has not been pursued.

Conclusion

[61]   I am satisfied that Mr Mubarik is in contempt by his continuing refusal to pay to Mrs Mubarak the lump sum ordered by Bodey J.

[62]   I am satisfied that the non-payment is a serious impediment to the course of justice. The essential link between the lump sum order and the means to pay is such that it is impossible to ascertain the truth while the husband remains in contempt and continues to deny the findings of the court. The court is faced (as it always will be in cases where a party's conduct leads to necessarily inchoate

findings of undisclosed assets) with an impossible exercise. There will not be a fair trial. The position would be different were Mr Mubarik to accept the court's findings (although I specifically do not say that he has as yet demonstrated the merits of his application).

[63] There is no other effective means of securing the husband's compliance with the order of this court. The voluminous enforcement papers are more than sufficient testimony of that. Furthermore, compliance is impossible unless and until the husband changes his stance, so that the essential truth can be ascertained by this court.

[64] I am of the firm view, in the absence of hearing oral evidence from the husband, that his contempt is wilful, ie contumacious and continuing. He is the controlling force behind the Dianoor Group and he refuses to acknowledge the truth or effect of that. In light of the existing findings I do not accept that the husband is impecunious or that he needs to go cap-in-hand to the Dianoor Group companies to obtain a consultancy for a modest fee. That contention is predicated upon the assertion that there are no assets available to him, an assertion that is itself based upon his rejection of the finding that there are undisclosed assets (which would satisfy any and all of the loans that he asserts he has had to enter into). The matters I set out at paras [19]–[21] of this judgment have continuing validity and, with respect, I find myself in complete agreement.

[65] This is a strong set of circumstances. I am not persuaded that there are other discretionary factors that outweigh the facts I set out above. I have, therefore, decided to accede to Mr Horowitz's preliminary application. I emphasise that I do not do so to penalise the husband: my aim is to secure a fair trial of this and any subsequent applications including enforcement. Mr Mubarik asks me not just to exercise a discretion in his favour but to go behind binding authority: that is something I cannot do.

[66] What conditions would be proportionate? I shall invite further submissions at the conclusion of this judgment as to the proposals made by Mr Horowitz as follows:

(a)   That the husband must notify the trustees that he irrevocably accepts that he is bound by the findings of Bodey J is respect of the issue of Mr Wani's interest, ie that Mr Wani has no interest or sub-interest in the trust and that he, the husband, requests the trust to act accordingly.
(b)   The husband shall not oppose an order of this court (if necessary under s 37 of the Matrimonial Causes Act 1973) that the act of excluding the wife from the trust be set aside forthwith.
(c)   That the husband shall not oppose an order of this court varying the order of Wall J of 2 November 2002 which restrained the wife from beginning proceedings in Jersey against the husband so that the wife is not thereby incidentally restrained from enforcing any rights she may have as a beneficiary under the trust.

[67] I have more than once indicated to Mr Howard that I would hear Mr Mubarik on the issue of whether he had been wilful, ie a limited inquiry into means, good faith and motivation as questions relevant to both the *Hadkinson* test and *Corbett v Corbett* [2003] EWCA Civ 559, [2003] 2 FLR 385 (see

paras [27]–[30] of Thorpe LJ's judgment). Mr Howard firmly opposed such a course on the basis that it was inappropriate. I reiterate my view that that is the appropriate course before the court imposes *Hadkinson* conditions. If Mr Mubarik chooses to decline my invitation, he cannot complain.

Appendix 1

Simplified diagram of the structure of the Dianoor Group

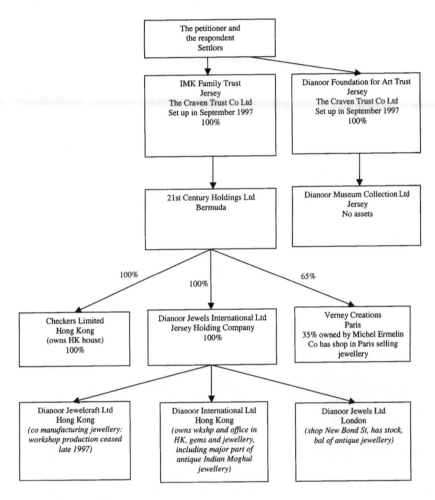

Order accordingly.

Solicitors: *Dean and Dean* for the wife
                Hughes, Fowler, Carruthers for the husband

PHILIPPA JOHNSON
Law Reporter

INDEX

References are to paragraph numbers.